America
Past and Present

BRIEF SEVENTH EDITION

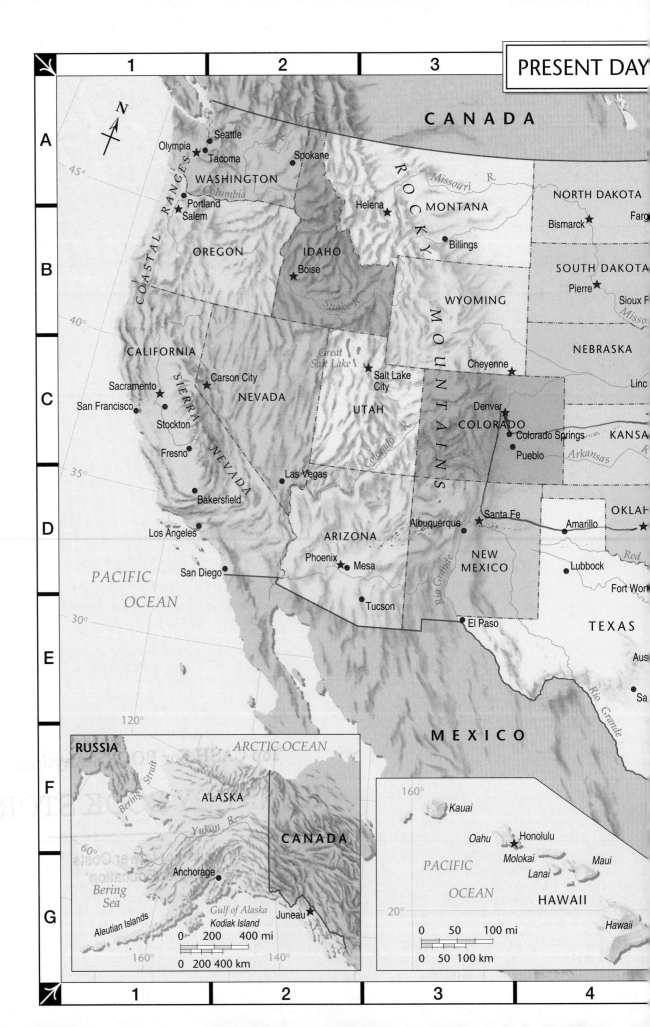

1 2 3

A

CANADA

Seattle
Olympia
Tacoma
Spokane
WASHINGTON
Columbia
Portland
Salem
ROCKY
Missouri R.
MONTANA
Helena
NORTH DAKOTA
Bismarck
Farg

OREGON
IDAHO
Billings

B

Boise
Snake R.
WYOMING
SOUTH DAKOTA
Pierre
Sioux F
Misso

CALIFORNIA
Great Salt Lake
NEBRASKA
Cheyenne
Linc

Sacramento
Carson City
Salt Lake City
Denver
COLORADO
KANSA

C

San Francisco
SIERRA
NEVADA
UTAH
Colorado Springs
Arkansas R.

Stockton
Colorado R.
Pueblo

Fresno

Las Vegas
Santa Fe
Amarillo
OKLAH

D

Bakersfield
Albuquerque
Lubbock

Los Angeles
ARIZONA
NEW MEXICO
Fort Wor

San Diego
Phoenix
Mesa
Rio Grande
Red

PACIFIC
El Paso
TEXAS

OCEAN
Tucson

E

Aus

Sa
Rio Grande

MEXICO

120°

RUSSIA
ARCTIC OCEAN

F

160°
Kauai

ALASKA
Oahu
Honolulu

Bering Strait
Yukon R.
CANADA
Molokai
Maui
PACIFIC
Lanai

Anchorage
OCEAN
HAWAII

Bering Sea

G

Juneau
Gulf of Alaska
Kodiak Island
20°

Aleutian Islands
0 50 100 mi

0 200 400 mi
Hawaii

0 200 400 km
0 50 100 km

1 2 3 4

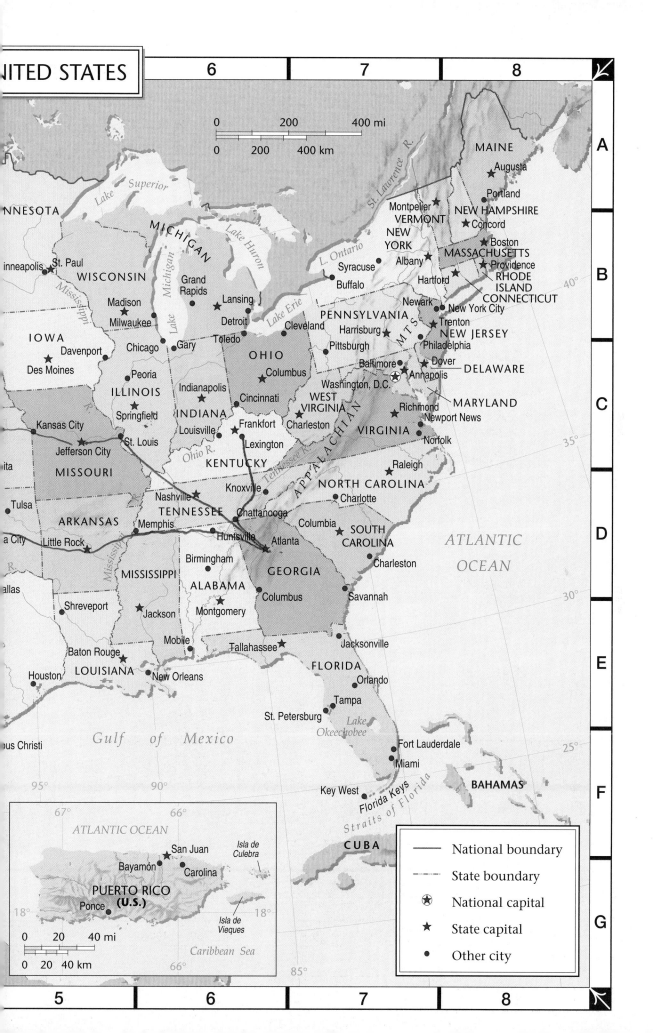

America
Past and Present

BRIEF SEVENTH EDITION
VOLUME II: SINCE 1865

ROBERT A. DIVINE
University of Texas

T. H. BREEN
Northwestern University

GEORGE M. FREDRICKSON
Stanford University

R. HAL WILLIAMS
Southern Methodist University

ARIELA J. GROSS
University of Southern California

H. W. BRANDS
University of Texas

RANDY ROBERTS
Purdue University

PEARSON
Longman

New York   San Francisco   Boston
London   Toronto   Sydney   Tokyo   Singapore   Madrid
Mexico City   Munich   Paris   Cape Town   Hong Kong   Montreal

Executive Editor: Michael Boezi
Development Editor: Karen Helfrich
Executive Marketing Manager: Sue Westmoreland
Supplements Editor: Brian Belardi
Production Manager: Ellen MacElree
Project Coordination, Text Design, and Electronic Page Makeup: Elm Street Publishing Services, Inc.
Senior Cover Design Manager: Nancy Danahy
Cover Designer: Susan Koski Zucker
Cover and Frontispiece Images: Cover Inset: © Rykoff Collection/CORBIS. All Rights Reserved. Large Photo:
     Jupiterimages.com/PictureQuest. Frontispiece Photo: The Granger Collection.
Art Studio: Maps.com and Burmar Technical Corporation
Photo Research: Julie Tesser
Senior Manufacturing Buyer: Dennis J. Para
Printer and Binder: Quebecor World/Dubuque
Cover Printer: Phoenix Color Corps.

For permission to use copyrighted material, grateful acknowledgment is made to the following copyright holders
and to those on pp. C-1–C-2, which are hereby made part of this copyright page.

Text credits: p. 362, Arthur Miller, *The Price.* New York, New York: Viking Penguin, 1968.

Library of Congress Cataloging-in-Publication Data

America past and present / Robert A. Divine . . . [et al.].—Brief 7th ed.
        p. cm.
     Includes bibliographical references and index.
     ISBN 0-321-42180-9
       1. United States—History—Textbooks.   I. Divine, Robert A.

E178.1.A4894 2008
973—dc22

                                                                              2006050944

ISBN 0-321-42180-9 (Complete Brief Edition)
ISBN 0-321-42181-7 (Volume I)
ISBN 0-321-42182-5 (Volume II)

2 3 4 5 6 7 8 9 10—QWV—09 08 07

Contents

CHAPTER 20

Political Realignments in the 1890s   388

Hardship and Heartache   388

CHAPTER 21

Toward Empire   405

Roosevelt and the Rough Riders   405

CHAPTER 22

The Progressive Era   423

Muckrakers Call for Reform   423

CHAPTER 23

From Roosevelt to Wilson in the Age of Progressivism   439

The Republicans Split   439

CHAPTER 24

The Nation at War   461

The Sinking of the Lusitania   *461*

CHAPTER 25

Transition to Modern America   483

Wheels for the Millions   483

CHAPTER 26

Franklin D. Roosevelt and the New Deal   500

The Struggle Against Despair   500

CHAPTER 27

America and the World, 1921–1945   519

A Pact Without Power   519

Maps, Charts, Figures, Tables, and Features

Preface

*A*merica *Past and Present*, Brief Seventh Edition, is derived from the full-length *America Past and Present*, Eighth Edition. The Brief Seventh Edition shares the goal of its parent text: to present a clear, relevant, and balanced history of the United States as an unfolding story of national development, from the days of the earliest inhabitants to the present. The goal of the abridgement is to produce a condensation true to the original in all its dimensions—a miniaturized replica or *bonsai,* as it were—retaining the style and tone, and the interpretations, with their nuances and subtleties intact. This Brief Seventh Edition contains about two-thirds of the text of the full-length book, more than one-half of the maps, charts, and figures, and a commensurate proportion of the illustration program.

Presenting American history as the story of a nation in flux, *America Past and Present,* Brief Seventh Edition, goes beyond recounting the major events that have helped to shape the nation—the wars fought, the presidents elected, the treaties signed. The impact of change on human lives adds a vital dimension to the understanding of history. How did the American Revolution affect the lives of ordinary citizens? What was it like for both blacks and whites to live in a plantation society? How did the shift from an agrarian to an industrial economy affect men and women alike? What impact did technology, in the form of the automobile and the computer, have on patterns of life in the twentieth century? As the narrative explores answers to these and other questions, it blends the excitement and drama of the American experience with insights about the social, political, economic, and cultural issues that underlie it.

America Past and Present, Brief Seventh Edition, espouses no particular ideology or point of view; instead the text encourages readers to explore the American past and reach their own conclusions about its significance in their lives. And yet the text does not avoid examining controversial issues but seeks to offer balanced and reasoned judgments on such morally charged subjects as the nature of slavery and the use of nuclear weapons. Although history may rarely repeat itself, the story of the American past is relevant to the problems and dilemmas facing the American nation and the American people today.

TEXT REVISIONS

The principal revisions in *America Past and Present,* Brief Seventh Edition, have been undertaken with the goals of clarifying the prose and sharpening the analysis, taking account of new scholarship, and offering new perspectives. As in previous editions, the roles that women and minority groups have played in the nation's development merit particular attention. These people appear not as passive witnesses to the historical narrative but as active participants in its evolution. New and expanded material throughout the chapters includes the following:

- Chapter 3, expanded discussion of mercantilism and free markets in the seventeenth century.

- Chapter 5, new opening vignette highlighting the personal sacrifices of one family in the Revolutionary fight for liberty.

- Chapter 7, new discussion of George Washington's mastery of symbolic political power and bringing the new government to the people.

- Chapter 9, expanded discussion of Native American societies before the Indian Removal, emphasizing the cultural transformation of Southeastern Indians under pressure of contact from white settlers.

- Chapter 11, augmented discussion of paternalism and racial theories used as justification for slavery.

- Chapter 12, expanded discussions of marriage in the American middle class and experiences of childhood across class and ethnic lines in the mid-nineteenth century.

- Chapters 31 through 33 have been revised, restructured, and condensed into two chapters: Chapter 31, "To a New Conservatism, 1969–1988," and Chapter 32, "To the Twenty-first Century, 1989–2006." Although some material in the previous edition's final three chapters has been carefully trimmed to make these chapters more manageable, we have also updated content and added new sections. These enhancements include discussions of the new environmentalism of the oil shock 1970s and challenges of the new century, including the continued war in Iraq, renewed culture wars, immigration issues, and concerns about

American quality of life, particularly employment and health care. Chapter 32 begins with a new opening vignette about George H. W. Bush, the first Persian Gulf War, and the initiation of a new foreign policy in the post–Cold War era.

STRUCTURE AND FEATURES

The structure and features of *America Past and Present,* Brief Seventh Edition, are intended to stimulate student interest and to reinforce learning. Each chapter begins with a vignette that introduces the chapter themes and previews topics to be discussed. The chapter chronology includes key events covered in the chapter. The recommended readings and suggested Web sites at the end of each chapter are sources students can consult for further information on many topics. Key terms, highlighted in boldface type in the chapter text, are defined in context and in a running glossary in the text margins.

Eight essays entitled "We Americans" appear in the text, each focusing on some aspect of diversity or multiculturalism in America. Some of the "We Americans" essays explore the roles different ethnic groups have played in shaping the nation; others examine change and constancy in the American population and national ethos. The eight "We Americans" essays are:

- "Learning to Live with Diversity in the Eighteenth Century: What Is an American?" (Chapter 4)
- "Counting the People: The Federal Census of 1790" (Chapter 7)
- "Women of Southern Households" (Chapter 11)
- "The Irish in Boston, 1845–1865" (Chapter 13)
- "Hispanic America After 1848: A Case Study in Majority Rule" (Chapter 14)
- "Blacks in Blue: The Buffalo Soldiers in the West" (Chapter 17)
- "Ellis Island: Isle of Hope, Isle of Tears" (Chapter 19)
- "Unintended Consequences: The Second Great Migration" (Chapter 30)

Each "We Americans" essay now includes new "Questions for Discussion" to spark class discussion or to prompt writing assignments.

A second feature in *America Past and Present,* Brief Seventh Edition, is "A Look at the Past." These representations of material culture artifacts show students some of the variety of materials that historians use to learn about and interpret the past. Captions with the photographs include critical thinking questions that encourage students to reflect on the historical purpose and significance of the object pictured.

A new feature in this edition is "Past and Present." Each of these eight brief essays explores connections between a past event, phenomenon, or trend and a similar or related event or phenomenon in a later period. These features explore contrasts as well as similarities. The "Past and Present" essays are:

- "Politics of Fear: From the Wars of Empire to the Cold War" (Chapter 4)
- "Revolutionary Communication" (Chapter 5)
- "Evangelical Religion in Politics" (Chapter 12)
- "Anti-Immigrant Movements" (Chapter 14)
- "Connecting the World: From the Transcontinental Railroad to the World Wide Web" (Chapter 18)
- "From John D. Rockefeller to Bill Gates: Philanthropy in American Life" (Chapter 23)
- "Challenging Social Security" (Chapter 26)
- "War Strategy: Korea and Iraq" (Chapter 28)

SUPPLEMENTS FOR QUALIFIED COLLEGE ADOPTERS

Instructor Supplements

MyHistoryLab

MyHistoryLab provides students with an online package complete with the entire comprehensive electronic textbook and numerous study aids. With several hundred primary sources, many of which are assignable and  link to a gradebook, pre- and post-tests that result in an individualized study plan, and map activities with gradable quizzes, the site offers students a unique, interactive experience that brings history to life. The comprehensive site also includes original videos, images and audio clips, as well as a History Bookshelf with fifty of the most commonly assigned history books and a History Toolkit with tutorials and helpful links.

Delivered in CourseCompass™, BlackBoard™, or WebCT™, as well as in a non-course-management Web site version, MyHistoryLab is easy to use and flexible. MyHistoryLab is organized according to the table of contents of this textbook. With the course management version, instructors can create a further customized product by adding their own syllabus, content, and assignments, or they can use the materials as presented and download our comprehensive test bank.

Please see www.myhistorylab.com to learn more, or to see a demo.

Instructor's Resource Manual

Created for the full version of *America Past and Present,* this resource manual is appropriate for the Brief Seventh Edition as well. Prepared by James Walsh of Central Connecticut State University, each chapter of this resource manual contains chapter outlines, interpretive essays, anecdotes and references to biographical or primary sources, and a comprehensive summary of the text. ISBN: 0-321-48540-8.

Test Bank

This test bank contains notations indicating questions that are particularly relevant to the Brief Seventh Edition. Prepared by Denise Wright of the University of Georgia, the test bank contains more than 1200 multiple-choice, true/false, matching, and completion questions. ISBN: 0-321-21721-7.

TestGen-EQ Computerized Testing System

This flexible, easy-to-master computerized test bank on a dual-platform CD includes all of the items in the printed test bank and allows instructors to select specific questions, edit existing questions, and add their own items to create exams. Tests can be printed in several different fonts and formats and can include figures such as graphs and tables. ISBN: 0-321-48675-7.

History Digital Media Archive CD-ROM

The Digital Media Archive CD-ROM contains electronic images and interactive and static maps, along with media elements such as video. These media assets are fully customizable and ready for classroom presentation or easy downloading into your PowerPoint™ presentations or any other presentation software. ISBN: 0-321-14976-9.

Digital Media Archive, Updated Second Edition

Now on two CD-ROMs and with added content, this Digital Media Archive is an encyclopedic collection that contains dozens of narrated vignettes and videos as well as hundreds of photos and illustrations ready for use in your own PowerPoint™ presentations, course Web sites, or on-line courses. Available to qualified college adopters when bundled. ISBN 0-321-18694-X.

The American History Study Site

Students can take advantage of this online resource that supports the American history survey course. The site includes practice tests, Web links, and flash cards that cover the scope of topics covered in a typical world history classroom. Available for no additional cost at www.longmanamericanhistory.com.

PowerPoint™ Presentations

These presentations contain an average of fifteen PowerPoint™ slides for each chapter. These slides may include key points and terms for a lecture on the chapter as well as four-color slides of all maps, graphs, and charts within a particular chapter. The presentations are available for download at www.ablongman.com/irc.

Comprehensive American History Transparency Set

This collection includes more than 200 four-color American history map transparencies on subjects ranging from the first Native Americans to the end of the Cold War, covering wars, social trends, elections, immigration, and demographics. The transparencies are available for download at www.ablongman.com/irc.

Text-specific Transparency Set

Created for the full version of *America Past and Present,* this transparency set is appropriate for the Brief Seventh Edition as well. The transparencies are available for download at www.ablongman.com/irc.

For Students

MyHistoryLab

MyHistoryLab provides students with an online package complete with the entire comprehensive electronic textbook, numerous study aids, primary sources, and chapter exams. With several hundred primary sources, maps, images, videos, and audio clips, many of which link to a gradebook, and pre- and post-tests that result in an individualized study plan, the site offers students a unique, interactive experience that brings history to life. The comprehensive site also includes a History Bookshelf with fifty of the most commonly assigned history books and a History Toolkit with tutorials and helpful links. Available for purchase at www.myhistorylab.com, or packaged with your textbook.

Study Guide and Practice Tests

Prepared by Thomas F. Jorsch of Ferris State University, each volume of the study guide begins with an introductory essay, "Skills for Studying and Learning History." Each chapter contains a summary; learning objectives; identification list; map exercises; glossary; multiple-choice, completion, and essay questions; and critical thinking exercises involving primary sources. Volume One: ISBN: 0-205-52177-0; Volume Two: ISBN: 0-205-52178-9.

VangoNotes

Study on the go with Vango Notes. Just download chapter reviews from your text and listen to them on any mp3 player. Now wherever you are—whatever you're doing—you can study by listening to the following for each chapter of your textbook:

- **Big Ideas:** Your "need to know" for each chapter
- **Practice Test:** A gut check for the Big Ideas—tells you if you need to keep studying
- **Key Terms:** Audio "flashcards" to help you review key concepts and terms
- **Rapid Review:** A quick drill session—use it right before your test.

VangoNotes are flexible; download all the material directly to your mp3 player, or only the chapters you need. And they're efficient. Use them in your car, at the gym, walking to class, wherever. So get yours today. And get studying. Find out more, or download a chapter at www.VangoNotes.com.

Longman American History Atlas

A four-color reference tool and visual guide to American history that includes almost one hundred maps and covers the full scope of history. This Atlas is $3.00 when bundled with college adoptions. ISBN: 0-321-00486-8.

Mapping American History, **Third Edition**

This two-volume workbook, written by Sharon Bollinger of El Paso Community College, presents the basic geography of the United States and helps students place the history of the United States into spatial perspective. Available at no additional cost to qualified college adopters when bundled. Volume I: ISBN: 0-321-47559-3; Volume II: ISBN: 0-321-47560-7.

Research Navigator Guide

This guidebook includes exercises and tips on how to use the Internet to further your study of American history. It also includes an access code for Research Navigator™—the easiest way for students to start a research assignment or research paper. Research Navigator™ is composed of three exclusive databases of credible and reliable source material including EBSCO's ContentSelect™ Academic Journal Database, New York Times Search by Subject Archive, and "Best of the Web" Link Library. This comprehensive site also includes a detailed help section. ISBN: 0-205-40838-9.

A Short Guide to Writing About History, **Sixth Edition**

Richard Marius, Harvard University; Melvin E. Page, Eastern Tennessee University. This engaging and practical text helps students get beyond merely compiling dates and facts; it teaches them how to incorporate their own ideas into their papers and to tell a story about history that interests them and their peers. Covering both brief essays and the documented resource paper, the text explores the writing and researching processes, different modes of historical writing including argument, and concludes with guidelines for improving style. ISBN: 0-321-43536-2.

Study Card for American History

Colorful, affordable, and packed with useful information, Longman's Study Cards make studying easier, more efficient, and more enjoyable. Course information is distilled down to the basics, helping you quickly master the fundamentals, review a subject for understanding, or prepare for an exam. Because they're laminated for durability, you can keep these Study Cards for years to come and pull them out whenever you need a quick review. ISBN: 0-321-29232-4.

Additional Readers

Longman offers a variety of options for reading beyond the textbook, from primary and secondary sources to biographies and Penguin titles. All of these options can be packaged with the textbook at a discount to students. Here are a few Longman titles. For a complete listing of Longman readers, please go to www.ablongman.com/history.

Voices of **America Past and Present**

This two-volume collection of primary sources includes both classic and lesser-known documents describing the rich mosaic of American life from the pre-contact era to the present day. The sources, both public and private documents—ranging from letters, diary excerpts, stories, and novels, to speeches, court cases, and government reports—tell the story of American history in the words of those who lived it. Available at no additional cost to qualified college adopters when bundled. Volume I: 0-321-41161-7; Volume II: 0-321-39601-4.

Library of American Biography Series

Each of these interpretive biographies focuses on a figure whose actions and ideas significantly influenced the course of American history and national life. At the same time, each biography relates the life of its subjects to the broader theme and developments of the times. Brief and inexpensive, they are ideal for any U.S. history course. Volumes include Edmund S. Morgan, *The Puritan Dilemma: The Story of John Winthrop;* Charles W. Akers, *Abigail Adams: A Revolutionary*

American Woman; Harold C. Livesay, *Andrew Carnegie and the Rise of Big Business;* Randolph B. Campbell, *Sam Houston and the American Southwest;* Walter L. Hixson, *Charles Lindbergh: Lone Eagle;* Jack N. Rakove, *James Madison and the Creation of the American Republic;* Sam W. Haynes, *James K. Polk and the Expansionist Impulse;* and J. William T. Youngs, *Eleanor Roosevelt: A Personal and Public Life.* New additions to the series include Allan M. Winkler, *Franklin D. Roosevelt and the Making of Modern America,* Dan La Botz, *César Chávez and* la Causa, and Jules Tygiel, *Ronald Reagan and the Triumph of American Conservatism,* Second Edition.

Please see www.ablongman.com/html/lab for a complete listing.

Penguin Books

The partnership between Penguin USA and Longman Publishers offers your students a discount on many Penguin titles when they are bundled with any Longman survey text. Please see www.ablongman.com/penguin for a complete listing of titles. Available titles include the following:

Horatio Alger, Jr., *Ragged Dick*

Horatio Alger, Jr., *Struggling Upward*

Louis Auchincloss, *Woodrow Wilson*

Edward Bellamy, *Looking Backward*

Roy Blount, Jr., *Robert E. Lee*

Clayborne Carson (Editor), *Eyes on the Prize Civil Rights Reader*

Willa Cather, *My Antonia*

Willa Cather, *O Pioneers!*

Ina Chang, *A Separate Battle*

Abraham Chapman (Editor), *Black Voices*

Charles W. Chesnutt, *The Marrow of Tradition*

George Dawson, *Life Is So Good*

Alexis De Tocqueville, *Democracy in America*

Frederick Douglass, *My Bondage and My Freedom*

Frederick Douglass, *Narrative of the Life of Frederick Douglass*

W. E. B. DuBois, *Souls of Black Folk*

William Fletcher, *Rebel Private: Front and Rear*

Benjamin Franklin, *Ben Franklin: The Autobiography and Other Writings*

Nelson George, *The Death of Rhythm and Blues*

William Golding, *Lord of the Flies*

Al Gore, *Earth in the Balance*

Woody Guthrie, *Bound for Glory*

Joel Chandler Harris (Editor), *Nights with Uncle Remus*

Nathanial Hawthorne, *The Scarlet Letter*

Gordon Hunter (Editor), *Immigrant Voices*

Harriet Jacobs, *Incidents in the Life of a Slave Girl*

Thomas Jefferson, *Notes on the State of Virginia*

James Weldon Johnson, *The Autobiography of an Ex-Colored Man*

Alvin M. Josephy, *The Patriot Chiefs*

Jack Kerouac, *On the Road*

Ralph Ketcham, *The Anti-Federalist Papers and the Constitutional Convention Debates*

Martin Luther King, Jr., *Why We Can't Wait*

Julius Lester, *From Slave Ship to Freedom Road*

Ellen Levine, *Freedom's Children*

David Lewis, *The Portable Harlem Renaissance Reader*

Sinclair Lewis, *Babbitt*

Brian Macarthur, *The Penguin Book of Twentieth-Century Speeches*

James McBride, *The Color of Water*

Joe McGinniss, *The Selling of the President*

Herman Melville, *Moby-Dick*

John Stuart Mill, *On Liberty*

Arthur Miller, *Death of A Salesman*

Toni Morrison, *The Bluest Eye*

George Orwell, *1984*

George Orwell, *Animal Farm*

Samuel K. Padover, *Jefferson*

Thomas Paine, *Common Sense*

Dorothy Parker, *The Portable Dorothy Parker*

Rosa Parks, *Rosa Parks: My Story*

William L. Riordan, *Plunkitt of Tammany Hall*

Randall Robinson, *The Debt*

Upton Sinclair, *The Jungle*

John Steinbeck, *The Grapes of Wrath*

John Steinbeck, *Of Mice & Men*

John Steinbeck, *The Pear*

Harriet Beecher Stowe, *Uncle Tom's Cabin*

Sojourner Truth, *The Narrative of Sojourner Truth*

Mark Twain, *The Adventures of Huckleberry Finn*

Various, *Against Slavery*

Various, *The Classic Slave Narratives*

Various, *Colonial American Travel Narratives*

Various, *The Federalist Papers*

Rebecca Walker, *Black, White, and Jewish: Autobiography of a Shifting Self*

Booker T. Washington, *Up From Slavery*

Phyllis Wheatley, *Complete Writings*

August Wilson, *Fences*

August Wilson, *Joe Turner's Come & Gone*

Hamet L. Wilson, *Our Nig*

Acknowledgments

We extend special thanks to Professor Jeanne Whitney of Salisbury State University for her contribution in selecting images for several of the "Look at the Past" illustrations in a previous edition and writing the informative and thought-provoking captions to accompany them. We also express our gratitude to the following reviewers who gave generously of their time and knowledge to provide thoughtful evaluations and suggestions for revision of the full-length edition:

Samantha Barbas, *Chapman University*
James Baumgardner, *Carson-Newman College*
Joseph E. Bisson, *San Joaquin Delta College*
Cynthia Carter, *Florida Community College at Jacksonville*
Katherine Chavigny, *Sweet Briar College*
Cole Dawson, *Warner Pacific College*
James Denham, *Florida Southern College*
Kathleen Feely, *University of Redlands*
Jennifer Fry, *King's College*
Paul B. Hatley, *Rogers State University*
Sarah Heat, *Texas A&M University–Corpus Christi*
Ben Johnson, *Southern Arkansas University*
Carol Keller, *San Antonio College*
Elizabeth Kuebler-Wolf, *Indiana University-Purdue University, Fort Wayne*
Rick Murray, *College of the Canyons*
Carrie Pritchett, *Northeast Texas Community College*
Thomas S. Reid, *Valencia Community College*
Mark Schmellor, *Binghamton University*
C. Edward Skeen, *University of Memphis*
Ronald Spiller, *Edinboro University of Pennsylvania*
Pat Thompson, *University of Texas, San Antonio*
Stephen Tootle, *University of Northern Colorado*
Stephen Warren, *Augustana College*
Stephen Webre, *Louisiana Tech University*

We also acknowledge with gratitude the contributions of reviewers of previous editions of this text. Their suggestions, too, have helped shape this book.

Gisela R. Ables, *Houston Community College*
James Barringer, *Hillsborough Community College*
Albert Berger, *University of North Dakota*
Vincent F. Bonelli, *Bronx Community College*
John P. Boubel, *Bethany Lutheran College*
John Braeman, *University of Nebraska*
Susan Meyer Butler, *Cerritos College*
William R. Cario, *Concordia University*
Simon Cordery, *Monmouth College*
Sandra McGee Deutsch, *University of Texas, El Paso*
Alan L. Golden, *Lock Haven University*
Gregory L. Goodwin, *Bakersfield College*
James Graham, *Carl Sandburg College*
Robert Hilderbrand, *University of South Dakota*
Howard Jablon, *Purdue University, North Central*
Chana Kai, *Indiana University*
Ted Kallman, *San Joaquin Delta College*
Lawrence F. Kohl, *University of Alabama*
Armand S. LaPotin, *State University College*
Margaret Lowe, *Bridgewater State College*
Jonathan Lurie, *Rutgers University*
James E. McMillan, *New Mexico State University*
Manuel F. Medrano, *University of Texas, Brownsville*
Douglas C. Oliver, *Skyline College*
Marguerite Renner, *Glendale Community College*
John Ricks, *Middle Georgia College*
Rob Schorman, *Miami University–Middletown*
Megan Seaholm, *University of Texas*
Charles J. Shindo, *Louisiana State University*
William P. Short, Jr., *Cecil Community College*
Sheila Skemp, *University of Mississippi*
Grant W. Smart, *Salt Lake Community College*
Kay C. Starnes, *University of North Carolina, Charlotte*
Roger Tate, *Somerset Community College*
Jason Tetzloff, *Defiance College*
Kenneth Townsend, *Coastal Carolina University*
Dean Wolfe, *Kingwood College*

THE AUTHORS

About the Authors

ROBERT A. DIVINE

Robert A. Divine, George W. Littlefield Professor Emeritus in American History at the University of Texas at Austin, received his Ph.D. from Yale University in 1954. A specialist in American diplomatic history, he taught from 1954 to 1996 at the University of Texas, where he was honored by both the student association and the graduate school for teaching excellence. His extensive published work includes *The Illusion of Neutrality* (1962); *Second Chance: The Triumph of Internationalism in America During World War II* (1967); and *Blowing on the Wind* (1978). His most recent work is *Perpetual War for Perpetual Peace* (2000), a comparative analysis of twentieth-century American wars. He is also the author of *Eisenhower and the Cold War* (1981) and editor of three volumes of essays on the presidency of Lyndon Johnson. His book *The Sputnik Challenge* (1993) won the Eugene E. Emme Astronautical Literature Award for 1993. He has been a fellow at the Center for Advanced Study in the Behavioral Sciences and has given the Albert Shaw Lectures in Diplomatic History at Johns Hopkins University.

T. H. BREEN

T. H. Breen, William Smith Mason Professor of American History at Northwestern University, received his Ph.D. from Yale University in 1968. He has taught at Northwestern since 1970. Breen's major books include *The Character of the Good Ruler: A Study of Puritan Political Ideas in New England* (1974); *Puritans and Adventurers: Change and Persistence in Early America* (1980); *Tobacco Culture: The Mentality of the Great Tidewater Planters on the Eve of Revolution* (1985); and, with Stephen Innes of the University of Virginia, *"Myne Owne Ground": Race and Freedom on Virginia's Eastern Shore* (1980). His *Imagining the Past* (1989) won the 1990 Historic Preservation Book Award. His most recent book is *Marketplace of Revolution: How Consumer Politics Shaped American Independence* (2004). In addition to receiving several awards for outstanding teaching at Northwestern, Breen has been the recipient of research grants from the American Council of Learned Societies, the Guggenheim Foundation, the Institute for Advanced Study (Princeton), the National Humanities Center, and the Huntington Library. He has served as the Fowler Hamilton Fellow at Christ Church, Oxford University (1987–1988), the Pitt Professor of American History and Institutions, Cambridge University (1990–1991), and the Harmsworth Professor of American History at Oxford University (2000–2001), and was a recipient of the Humboldt Prize (Germany). He is currently completing a book tentatively entitled, *America's Insurgency: The People's Revolution, 1774–1776.*

GEORGE M. FREDRICKSON

George M. Fredrickson is Edgar E. Robinson Professor Emeritus of United States History at Stanford University. He is the author or editor of several books, including *The Inner Civil War* (1965), *The Black Image in the White Mind* (1971), and *White Supremacy: A Comparative Study in American and South African History* (1981), which won both the Ralph Waldo Emerson Award from Phi Beta Kappa and the Merle Curti Award from the Organization of American Historians. His most recent books are *Black Liberation: A Comparative History of Black Ideologies in the United States and South Africa* (1995), *The Comparative Imagination: Racism, Nationalism, and Social Movements* (1997), and *Racism: A Short History* (2002). He received his A.B. and Ph.D. from Harvard and has been the recipient of a Guggenheim Fellowship, two National Endowment for the Humanities senior fellowships, and a fellowship from the Center for Advanced Studies in the Behavioral Sciences. Before coming to Stanford in 1984, he taught at Northwestern. He has also served as Fulbright lecturer in American History at Moscow University and as the Harmsworth Professor of American History at Oxford. He served as president of the Organization of American Historians in 1997–1998.

R. HAL WILLIAMS

R. Hal Williams is professor of history at Southern Methodist University. He received his A.B. from Princeton University in 1963 and his Ph.D. from Yale University in 1968. His books include *The Democratic Party and California Politics, 1880–1896* (1973), *Years of*  *Decision: American Politics in the 1890s* (1978), and *The Manhattan Project: A Documentary Introduction to the Atomic Age* (1990). A specialist in American political history, he taught at Yale University from 1968 to 1975 and came to SMU in 1975 as chair of the Department of History. From 1980 to 1988, he served as dean of Dedman College, the school of humanities and sciences, at SMU, where he is currently dean of Research and Graduate Studies. In 1980, he was a visiting professor at University College, Oxford University. Williams has received grants from the American Philosophical Society and the National Endowment for the Humanities, and has served on the Texas Committee for the Humanities. He is currently working on a study of the presidential election of 1896 and a biography of James G. Blaine, the late-nineteenth-century speaker of the House, secretary of state, and Republican presidential candidate.

H. W. BRANDS

H. W. Brands is the Dickson Allen Anderson Centennial Professor of History at the University of Texas at Austin. He is the author of numerous works of history and international affairs, including *The Devil We Knew: Americans and the Cold War* (1993), *Into the Labyrinth: The United*  *States and the Middle East* (1994), *The Reckless Decade: America in the 1890s* (1995), *TR: The Last Romantic* (a biography of Theodore Roosevelt) (1997), *What America Owes the World: The Struggle for the Soul of Foreign Policy* (1998), *The First American: The Life and Times of Benjamin Franklin* (2000), *The Strange Death of American Liberalism* (2001), *The Age of Gold: The California Gold Rush and the New American Dream* (2002), *Woodrow Wilson* (2003), and *Andrew Jackson* (2005). His writing has received critical and popular acclaim; *The First American* was a finalist for the Pulitzer Prize and a national best-seller. He lectures frequently across North America and in Europe. His essays and reviews have appeared in the *New York Times,* the *Wall Street Journal,* the *Washington Post,* the *Los Angeles Times,* and *Atlantic Monthly.* He is a regular guest on radio and television, and has participated in several historical documentary films.

ARIELA J. GROSS

Ariela J. Gross is professor of law and history at the University of Southern California. She received her B.A. from Harvard University, her J.D. from Stanford Law School, and her Ph.D. from Stanford University. She is the author of *Double*  *Character: Slavery and Mastery in the Antebellum Southern Courtroom* (2000) and numerous law review articles and book chapters, including "'Caucasian Cloak': Mexican Americans and the Politics of Whiteness in the Twentieth-Century Southwest" in *Georgetown Law Journal* (2006). Her current work in progress, *What Blood Won't Tell: Racial Identity on Trial in America,* to be published by Farrar, Straus & Giroux, is supported by fellowships from the Guggenheim Foundation, the National Endowment for the Humanities, and the American Council for Learned Societies.

RANDY ROBERTS

Randy Roberts earned his Ph.D. from Louisiana State University. His areas of special interest include modern U.S. history and the history of sports and films in America. He is a faculty member at Purdue University where he  has won the Murphy Award for outstanding teaching, the Teacher of the Year Award, and the Society of Professional Journalists Teacher of the Year Award. The books he has authored or co-authored include *Jack Dempsey: The Manassa Mauler* (1979, expanded ed., 1984), *Papa Jack: Jack Johnson and the Era of White Hopes* (1983), *Heavy Justice: The State of Indiana vs. Michael G. Tyson* (1994), *My Lai: A Brief History with Documents* (1998), *John Wayne: American* (1995), *Where the Domino Fell: America in Vietnam, 1945–1990* (1990, rev. ed., 1996), *Winning Is the Only Thing: Sports in America Since 1945* (1989), *Pittsburg Sports: Stories from the Steel City* (2000), and *A Line in the Sand: The Alamo in Blood and Memory* (2001). He edited *The Rock, The Curse, and The Hub: A Random History of Boston Sports* (2005). Roberts serves as co-editor of the Sports and Society series, University of Illinois Press, and is on the editorial board of the *Journal of Sports History.*

Chapter 16

The Agony of Reconstruction

Robert Smalls and Black Politicians During Reconstruction

During the Reconstruction period immediately following the Civil War, African Americans struggled to become equal citizens of a democratic republic. They produced a number of remarkable leaders who showed that blacks were as capable as other Americans of voting, holding office, and legislating for a complex and rapidly changing society. Among these leaders was Robert Smalls of South Carolina. Although virtually forgotten by the time of his death in 1915, Smalls was perhaps the most famous and most widely respected southern black leader of the Civil War and Reconstruction era. His career reveals some of the main features of the African American experience during that crucial period.

Born a slave in 1839, Smalls had a white father whose identity has never been clearly established. But his white ancestry apparently gained him some advantages, and as a young man he was allowed to live and work independently, hiring his own time from a master who may have been his half-brother. Smalls worked as a sailor and trained himself to be a pilot in Charleston harbor. When the Union Navy blockaded Charleston in 1862, Smalls, who was then working on a Confederate steamship called the *Planter,* saw a chance to win his freedom in a particularly dramatic way. At three o'clock in the morning on May 13, 1862, when the white officers of the *Planter* were ashore, he took command of the vessel and its slave crew, sailed it out of the heavily fortified harbor, and surrendered it to the Union Navy. Smalls immediately became a hero to those antislavery Northerners who were seeking evidence that the slaves were willing and able to serve the Union. The *Planter* was turned into a Union transport, and Smalls was made its captain after being commissioned as an officer in the armed forces of the United States. During the remainder of the war, he rendered conspicuous and gallant service as captain and pilot of Union vessels off the coast of South Carolina.

Like a number of other African Americans who had fought valiantly for the Union, Smalls went on to a distinguished political career during Reconstruction, serving in the South Carolina constitutional convention, the state legislature, and several terms in the U.S. Congress. He was also a shrewd businessman and became the owner of extensive properties in Beaufort, South Carolina, and its vicinity. (His first purchase was the house of his former master, where he had spent his early years as a slave.) As the leading citizen of Beaufort during Reconstruction and for some years thereafter, he acted like many successful white Americans, acquiring both wealth and political power. The electoral organization he established resembled in some ways the well-oiled political machines being established in northern towns and cities. His was so effective that Smalls was able to control local government and

309

get himself elected to Congress even after the election of 1876 had placed the state under the control of white conservatives bent on depriving blacks of political power. Organized mob violence defeated him in 1878, but he bounced back to win a contested congressional election in 1880 by decision of Congress. He did not leave the House of Representatives for good until 1886, when he lost another contested election that had to be decided by Congress. It revealed the changing mood of the country that his white challenger was seated despite evidence of violence and intimidation against black voters.

In their efforts to defeat him, Smalls's white opponents frequently charged that he had a hand in the corruption that was allegedly rampant in South Carolina during Reconstruction. But careful historical investigation shows that he was, by the standards of the time, an honest and responsible public servant. In the South Carolina convention of 1868 and later in the state legislature, he was a conspicuous champion of free and compulsory public education. In Congress, he fought for the enactment and enforcement of federal civil rights laws. Not especially radical on social questions, he sometimes bent over backward to accommodate what he regarded as the legitimate interests and sensibilities of South Carolina whites. Like other middle-class black political leaders in Reconstruction-era South Carolina, he can perhaps be faulted in hindsight for not doing more to help poor blacks gain access to land of their own. But in 1875, he sponsored congressional legislation that opened for purchase at low prices the land in his own district that had been confiscated by the federal government during the war. As a result, blacks were able to buy most of it, and they soon owned three-fourths of the land in Beaufort and its vicinity.

Smalls spent the later years of his life as U.S. collector of customs for the port of Beaufort, a beneficiary of the patronage that the Republican party continued to provide for a few loyal southern blacks. But the loss of real political clout for Smalls and men like him was one of the tragic consequences of the failure of Reconstruction.

For a brief period of years, black politicians such as Robert Smalls exercised more power in the South than they would for another century. A series of political developments on the national and regional stage made Reconstruction "an unfinished revolution," promising but not delivering true equality for newly freed African Americans. National party politics, shifting priorities among Northern Republicans, and white Southerners' commitment to white supremacy, which was backed by legal restrictions as well as massive extra-legal violence against blacks, all combined to stifle the promise of Reconstruction. Yet the Reconstruction era also saw major transformations in American society in the wake of the Civil War—new ways of organizing labor and family life, new institutions within and outside of the government, and new ideologies regarding the role of institutions and government in social and economic life. Many of the changes begun during Reconstruction laid the groundwork for later revolutions in American life.

THE PRESIDENT VERSUS CONGRESS

The problem of how to reconstruct the Union in the wake of the South's military defeat was one of the most difficult challenges ever faced by American policymakers. The Constitution provided no firm guidelines, and once emancipation became a northern war aim, the problem was compounded by a new issue: How far should the federal government go to secure freedom and civil rights for four million former slaves?

The debate that evolved led to a major political crisis. Advocates of a minimal Reconstruction policy favored quick restoration of the Union with no protection for the freed slaves beyond the prohibition of slavery. Proponents of a more radical policy wanted readmission of the southern states to be dependent on guarantees that "loyal" men would replace the Confederate elite and that blacks would acquire some of the basic rights of American citizenship. The White House favored the minimal approach, while Congress came to endorse the more radical policy. The resulting struggle between Congress and the chief executive was the most serious clash between two branches of government in the nation's history.

Wartime Reconstruction

Tension between the president and Congress over how to reconstruct the Union began during the war. Although Lincoln did not set forth a final and comprehensive plan, he did indicate that he favored a lenient and conciliatory policy toward Southerners who would give up the struggle and repudiate slavery. In December 1863, he offered a full pardon to all Southerners (with the exception of certain classes of Confederate leaders) who would take an oath of allegiance to the Union and acknowledge the legality of emancipation. This **Ten Percent Plan** provided that once 10 percent or more of the voting population of any occupied state had taken the oath, they were authorized to set up a loyal government. By 1864, Louisiana and Arkansas had established fully functioning Unionist governments.

Lincoln's policy was meant to shorten the war by offering a moderate peace plan. It was also intended to further his emancipation policy by insisting that the new governments abolish slavery. When constitutional conventions operating under the 10 percent plan in Louisiana and Arkansas dutifully abolished slavery in 1864, emancipation came closer to being irreversible.

But Congress was unhappy with the president's reconstruction experiments and in 1864 refused to seat the Unionists elected to the House and Senate from Louisiana and Arkansas. A minority of congressional Republicans—the fiercely antislavery **Radical Republicans**—favored strong protection for black civil rights and provision for their franchisement as a precondition for the readmission of southern states. A larger group of moderates also opposed Lincoln's plan, but they did so primarily because they did not trust the repentant Confederates who would play a major role in the new governments.

Also disturbing Congress was a sense that the president was exceeding his authority by using executive powers to restore the Union. Lincoln operated on the theory that secession, being illegal, did not place the Confederate states outside the Union in a constitutional sense. Since individuals and not states had defied federal authority, the president could use his pardoning power to certify a loyal electorate, which could then function as the legitimate state government. The dominant view in Congress, however, was that the southern states had forfeited their place in the Union and that it was up to Congress to decide when and how they would be readmitted.

After refusing to recognize Lincoln's 10 percent governments, Congress passed a Reconstruction bill of its own in July 1864. Known as the **Wade-Davis Bill,** the legislation required that 50 percent of the voters take an oath of future loyalty before the restoration process could begin. Once this had occurred, those who could swear that they had never willingly supported the Confederacy could vote in an election for delegates to a constitutional convention. Lincoln exercised a pocket veto by refusing to sign the bill before Congress adjourned, angering many congressmen.

Congress and the president remained stalemated on the Reconstruction issue for the rest of the war. During his last months in office, however, Lincoln showed a willingness to compromise. But he died without clarifying his intentions, leaving historians to speculate on whether his quarrel with Congress would have escalated or been resolved. Given Lincoln's record of political flexibility, the best bet is that he would have come to terms with the majority of his party.

Ten Percent Plan
Reconstruction plan proposed by President Lincoln as a quick way to readmit the former Confederate states. It called for full pardon of all Southerners except Confederate leaders and readmission to the Union for any state after 10 percent of its voters in the 1860 election signed a loyalty oath and the state abolished slavery.

Radical Republicans The Radical Republicans in Congress, headed by Thaddeus Stevens and Charles Sumner, insisted on black suffrage and federal protection of civil rights of African Americans. They gained control of Reconstruction in 1867 and required the ratification of the Fourteenth Amendment as a condition of readmission for former Confederate states.

Wade-Davis Bill In 1864, Congress passed the Wade-Davis bill to counter Lincoln's Ten Percent Plan for Reconstruction. The bill required that a majority of a former Confederate state's white male population take a loyalty oath and guarantee equality for African Americans. President Lincoln pocket-vetoed the bill.

Andrew Johnson at the Helm

Andrew Johnson, the man suddenly made president by an assassin's bullet, attempted to put the Union back together on his own authority in 1865. But his policies eventually put him at odds with Congress and the Republican party and provoked a serious crisis in the system of checks and balances among the branches of the federal government.

Johnson's approach to Reconstruction was shaped by his background. Born in dire poverty in North Carolina, he migrated as a young man to eastern Tennessee, where he made his living as a tailor. Although poorly educated (he did not learn to write until adulthood), Johnson was an effective stump speaker who railed against the planter aristocracy. Entering politics as a Jacksonian Democrat, he became the political spokesman for Tennessee's nonslaveholding whites. He advanced from state legislator to congressman to governor and in 1857 was elected to the U.S. Senate.

When Tennessee seceded in 1861, Johnson was the only senator from a Confederate state who remained loyal to the Union and continued to serve in Washington. But his Unionism did not include antislavery sentiments or friendship for blacks. He wished that "every head of family in the United States had one slave to take the drudgery and menial service off his family."

During the war, while acting as military governor of Tennessee, Johnson implemented Lincoln's emancipation policy as a means of destroying the power of the hated planter class rather than as a recognition of black humanity. He was chosen as Lincoln's running mate in 1864 in order to strengthen the ticket. No one expected that this southern Democrat and fervent white supremacist would ever become president.

Some Radical Republicans initially welcomed Johnson's ascent to the nation's highest office. Like the Radicals themselves, he was loyal to the Union and believed that ex-Confederates should be treated severely. He seemed more likely than Lincoln to punish southern "traitors" and prevent them from regaining political influence. Only gradually did Johnson and the Republican majority in Congress drift apart.

The Reconstruction policy that Johnson initiated on May 29, 1865, created some uneasiness among the Radicals, but most other Republicans were willing to give it a chance. Johnson placed North Carolina and eventually other states under appointed provisional governors mainly chosen from among prominent southern politicians who had opposed the secession movement and had rendered no conspicuous service to the Confederacy. They were then responsible for calling constitutional conventions to elect "loyal" officeholders. Johnson's plan was specially designed to prevent his longtime adversaries, the planter class, from participating in the reconstruction of southern state governments.

Thirteenth Amendment
Ratified in 1865, this amendment to the U.S. Constitution prohibited slavery and involuntary servitude.

Johnson urged the conventions to declare the ordinances of secession illegal, repudiate the Confederate debt, and ratify the **Thirteenth Amendment** abolishing slavery. After governments had been reestablished under constitutions meeting these conditions, the president assumed that the process of Reconstruction would be complete and that the ex-Confederate states would regain their full rights under the Constitution.

Many congressional Republicans were troubled by the work of the southern conventions, which balked at fully implementing Johnson's recommendations. Furthermore, in no state was even limited black suffrage approved. Johnson, however, seemed eager to give southern white majorities a free hand in determining the civil and political status of freed slaves.

Black Codes Laws passed by Southern states immediately after the Civil War in an effort to maintain the prewar social order. The codes attempted to tie freedmen to field work and prevent them from becoming equal to white Southerners.

Republican uneasiness turned to disillusionment and anger when the state legislatures elected under the new constitutions proceeded to pass **Black Codes** subjecting the former slaves to a variety of special regulations and restrictions on their freedom. Especially troubling were vagrancy and apprenticeship laws that forced blacks to work and denied them a choice of employers. To Radicals, the Black Codes looked suspiciously like slavery under a new guise.

The growing rift between the president and Congress came into the open in December when the House and Senate refused to seat the recently elected southern delegation. Instead of endorsing Johnson's work and recognizing the state governments he had called into being, Congress established a joint committee, chaired by William Pitt Fessenden of Maine, to review Reconstruction policy and set further conditions for readmission of the seceded states.

Congress Takes the Initiative

The struggle over how to reconstruct the Union ended with Congress doing the job all over again. The clash between Johnson and Congress was a matter of principle and could not be reconciled. Johnson's stubborn and prideful nature did not help his political cause. But the root of the problem was that he disagreed with the majority of Congress on what Reconstruction was supposed to accomplish. An heir of the Democratic states' rights tradition, he wanted to restore the prewar federal system as quickly as possible, except for the prohibition on slavery and secession.

■ *In this cartoon, President Andrew Johnson (left) and Thaddeus Stevens, the Radical Republican congressman from Pennsylvania, are depicted as train engineers in a deadlock on the tracks. Indeed, neither Johnson nor Stevens would give way on his plans for Reconstruction.* ■

Most Republicans wanted firm guarantees that the old southern ruling class would not regain regional power and national influence by devising new ways to subjugate blacks. They favored a Reconstruction policy that would give the federal government authority to limit the political role of ex-Confederates and provide some protection for black citizenship.

Except for a few extreme Radicals, Republican leaders were not convinced that blacks were inherently equal to whites. They were certain, however, that all citizens should have the same basic rights and opportunities. Principle coincided easily with political expediency; southern blacks were likely to be loyal to the Republican party that had emancipated them and thus increase that party's political power in the South.

The disagreement between the president and Congress became irreconcilable in early 1866 when Johnson vetoed two bills that had passed with overwhelming Republican support. The first bill extended the life of the **Freedmen's Bureau**—a temporary agency charged with providing former slaves with relief, legal help, and educational and employment assistance. The second, a civil rights bill, was intended to nullify the detested Black Codes and guarantee "equal benefit of all laws."

The vetoes shocked moderate Republicans, who had expected Johnson to accept the relatively modest measures. Congress promptly passed the Civil Rights Act over Johnson's veto, signifying that the president was now hopelessly at odds with most of the congressmen from what was supposed to be his own party.

Johnson soon revealed that he intended to abandon the Republicans and place himself at the head of a new conservative party uniting the small minority of Republicans who supported him with a reviving Democratic party that was rallying behind his Reconstruction policy. As the elections of 1866 neared, Johnson stepped up his criticism of Congress.

Freedman's Bureau Agency established by Congress in March 1865 to provide freedmen with shelter, food, and medical aid and to help them establish schools and find employment.

Fourteenth Amendment
Ratified in 1868, this amendment provided citizenship to the ex-slaves after the Civil War and constitutionally protected equal rights under the law for all citizens. Its provisions were used by Radical Republicans to enact a congressionally controlled Reconstruction policy in the former Confederate states.

Meanwhile, the Republican majority on Capitol Hill passed the **Fourteenth Amendment.** This, the most important of the constitutional amendments, gave the federal government responsibility for guaranteeing equal rights under the law to all Americans. The major section defined national citizenship for the first time as extending to "all persons born or naturalized in the United States." The states were prohibited from abridging the rights of American citizens and could neither "deprive any person of life, liberty, or property, without due process of law; nor deny to any person . . . equal protection of the laws." The amendment was sent to the states with an implied understanding that Southerners would be readmitted to Congress only if their states ratified it.

The congressional elections of 1866 served as a referendum on the Fourteenth Amendment. With the support of Johnson, all the southern states except Tennessee rejected the amendment. But bloody race riots in Memphis and New Orleans and maltreatment of blacks throughout the South made it painfully clear that southern state governments were failing abysmally to protect the "life, liberty, or property" of the ex-slaves.

Johnson further weakened his cause by taking the stump on behalf of candidates who supported his policies. His undignified speeches and his inflexibility enraged northern voters. The Republican majority in Congress increased to a solid two-thirds in both houses, and the radical wing of the party gained strength at the expense of moderates and conservatives.

Congressional Reconstruction Plan Enacted

Radical Reconstruction The Reconstruction Acts of 1867 divided the South into five military districts. They required the states to guarantee black male suffrage and to ratify the Fourteenth Amendment as a condition of their readmission to the Union.

Congress was now in a position to implement its own plan for Reconstruction. In 1867 and 1868, it passed a series of acts that reorganized the South on a new basis. Generally referred to as **Radical Reconstruction,** these measures actually repre-

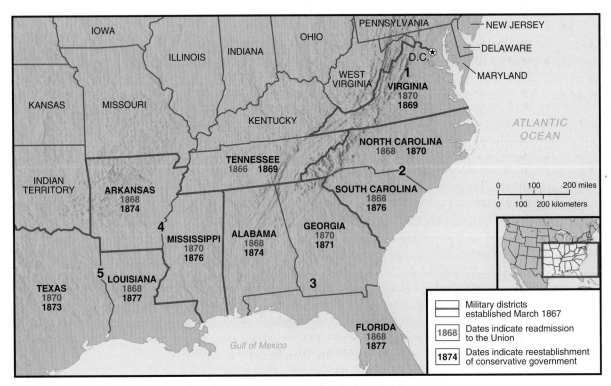

RECONSTRUCTION   *During the Reconstruction era, the southern state governments passed through three phases: control by white ex-Confederates; domination by Republican legislators, both black and white; and, finally, the regain of control by conservative white Democrats.* ∎

RECONSTRUCTION AMENDMENTS, 1865–1870

Amendment	Main Provisions	Congressional Passage (2/3 majority in each house required)	Ratification Process (3/4 of all states required, including ex-Confederate states)
13	Slavery prohibited in United States	January 1865	December 1865 (27 states, including 8 southern states)
14	National citizenship; State representation in Congress reduced proportionally to number of voters disfranchised; Former Confederates denied right to hold office; Confederate debt repudiated	June 1866	Rejected by 12 southern and border states, February 1867; Radicals make readmission of southern states hinge on ratification; ratified July 1868
15	Denial of franchise because of race, color, or past servitude explicitly prohibited	February 1869	Ratification required for readmission of Virginia, Texas, Mississippi, Georgia; ratified March 1870

sented a compromise between genuine Radicals and the more moderate elements within the party.

Consistent Radicals, such as Charles Sumner of Massachusetts and Thaddeus Stevens of Pennsylvania, wanted to reshape southern society before readmitting ex-Confederates to the Union. Their program required an extended period of military rule, confiscation and redistribution of large landholdings among freedmen, and federal aid for schools that would educate blacks for citizenship. But the majority of Republican congressmen found such a program unacceptable because it broke with American traditions of federalism and regard for property rights.

The First Reconstruction Act, passed over Johnson's veto on March 2, 1867, did place the South under military rule—but only for a short period. The act opened the way for the readmission of any state that framed and ratified a new constitution providing for black suffrage. Since blacks (but not ex-Confederates) were allowed to participate in this process, Republicans thought they had found a way to ensure that "loyal men" would dominate the new governments.

Radical Reconstruction was based on the dubious assumption that once blacks had the vote, they would have the power to protect themselves against the efforts of white supremacists to deny them their rights. The Reconstruction Acts thus signaled a retreat from the true Radical position that a sustained use of federal authority was needed to complete the transition from slavery to freedom and prevent the resurgence of the South's old ruling class.

Even so, congressional Reconstruction did have a radical aspect. It strongly endorsed black suffrage. The principle that even the poorest and most underprivileged should have access to the ballot box was bold and innovative. The problem was how to enforce it under conditions then existing in the postwar South.

The Impeachment Crisis

President Johnson was unalterably opposed to the congressional Reconstruction program, and he did everything within his power to prevent its full implementation. Congress responded by passing laws designed to limit presidential authority over Reconstruction matters. One of the measures was the Tenure of Office Act, requiring Senate approval for the removal of cabinet officers and other officials whose appointment had needed the consent of the Senate. Another measure sought to limit Johnson's authority to issue military orders.

Johnson objected vigorously to the restrictions on the grounds that they violated the constitutional doctrine of the separation of powers. Faced with Johnson's opposition, some congressmen began to call for his impeachment. When Johnson tried to discharge Secretary of War Edwin Stanton—the only Radical in his cabinet—the proimpeachment forces grew.

In January 1868, Johnson ordered General Grant to take over Stanton's job as head of the War Department. But Grant had his eye on the Republican presidential nomination and refused to defy Congress. Johnson then appointed General Lorenzo Thomas. Vexed by this apparent violation of the Tenure of Office Act, the House of Representatives voted overwhelmingly to impeach the president, and he was placed on trial before the Senate.

Johnson narrowly avoided conviction and removal from office when the impeachment effort fell one vote short of the necessary two-thirds. This outcome resulted in part from a skillful defense. Responding to the charge that Johnson had deliberately violated the Tenure of Office Act, the defense contended that the law did not apply to the removal of Stanton because he had been appointed by Lincoln.

The prosecution was more concerned that Johnson had abused the powers of his office in an effort to sabotage the congressional Reconstruction policy. Obstructing the will of the legislative branch, they claimed, was sufficient grounds for conviction. The Republicans who broke ranks to vote for acquittal feared that removal of a president for essentially political reasons would threaten the constitutional balance of powers and open the way to legislative supremacy over the executive. In addition, more conservative Republicans opposed the man who, as president pro tem of the Senate, would have succeeded Johnson, Ohio Senator Benjamin Wade.

The impeachment episode helped create an impression in the public mind that the Radicals were ready to turn the Constitution to their own use to gain their objectives. But the evidence of congressional ruthlessness and illegality is not as strong as most historians used to think. Modern legal scholars have found merit in the Radicals' claim that their actions did not violate the Constitution.

The failed conviction effort was an embarrassment to congressional Republicans, but the episode did ensure that Reconstruction in the South would proceed as the majority in Congress intended. During the trial, Johnson helped influence the verdict by pledging to enforce the Reconstruction Acts, and he held to this promise during his remaining months in office.

RECONSTRUCTING SOUTHERN SOCIETY

The Civil War left the South devastated, demoralized, and destitute. Slavery was dead, but what this meant for future relationships between whites and blacks was still in doubt. Most whites were determined to restrict the freedmen's rights, and many blacks were just as set on achieving real independence. For blacks, the acquisition of land, education, and the vote seemed the best means of achieving their goal. The thousands of Northerners who went south after the war for economic or humanitarian reasons hoped to extend Yankee "civilization" to what they viewed as a barbarous region. For most of them, this reformation required the aid of the freedmen.

The struggle of these groups to achieve their conflicting goals bred chaos, violence, and instability. It was not the ideal setting for an experiment in interracial democracy. When the federal government's support of reform faltered, the forces of reaction and white supremacy were unleashed.

Reorganizing Land and Labor

The Civil War scarred the southern landscape and wrecked its economy. Many plantations were ruined, and several major cities, including Atlanta and Richmond, were gutted by fire. Most factories were dismantled or destroyed, and long stretches of railroad were torn up.

Nor was there adequate investment capital for rebuilding. The substantial wealth represented by Confederate currency and bonds had melted away, and emancipation of the slaves had divested the propertied classes of their most valuable and productive assets. According to some estimates, the South's per capita wealth in 1865 was only about half what it had been in 1860.

Recovery could not even begin until a new labor system replaced slavery. The lack of capital hindered the rebuilding of plantations, and most Americans assumed that southern prosperity would depend on plantation-grown cotton. In addition, southern whites believed that blacks would work only under compulsion, and freedmen resisted labor conditions that recalled slavery.

Blacks strongly preferred to be small independent farmers rather than plantation laborers. For a time, they had reason to hope that the federal government would support their ambitions. Some 40-acre land grants were given by federal authorities to freedmen. By July 1865, forty thousand black farmers were at work on 300,000 acres of what they thought would be their own land.

But for most of them, the dream of "40 acres and a mule" was not to be realized. Neither President Johnson nor most congressmen favored a program of land confiscation and redistribution. Consequently, the vast majority of blacks in physical possession of small farms failed to acquire title and were left with little or no prospect of becoming landowners.

Despite their poverty and landlessness, ex-slaves were reluctant to settle down and commit themselves to wage labor for their former masters. Many took to the road, hoping to find something better. Some were still expecting grants of land, but others were simply trying to increase their bargaining power. As the end of 1865 drew nearer, many freedmen had still not signed up for the coming season; anxious planters feared that they were plotting to seize the land by force. Within a few weeks, however, most of the holdouts signed for the best terms they could get. The most common form of agricultural employment in 1866 was contract labor. Under this system, workers committed themselves for a year in return for fixed wages. Although blacks occasionally received help from the Freedmen's Bureau, more often than not they were worked hard and paid little, and the contracts normally protected the employers more than the employees.

Growing up alongside the contract system and eventually displacing it was the alternative capital-labor relationship of **sharecropping**—the right to work a small piece of land independently in return for a fixed share of the crop produced on it, usually one-half. A shortage of labor gave the freedmen enough leverage to force this arrangement on planters who were unwilling, but many landowners found it advantageous because it did not require much capital and forced the tenant to share the risks of crop failure or a fall in cotton prices.

Blacks initially viewed sharecropping as a step up from wage labor in the direction of landownership. But during the 1870s, this form of tenancy evolved into a new kind of servitude. Croppers had to live on credit until their cotton was sold, and planters or merchants seized the chance to "provision" them at high prices and exorbitant rates of interest. Soon croppers discovered that debts multiplied faster than profits. Furthermore, various methods were eventually devised to bind indebted tenants to a single landlord for extended periods, although some economic historians argue that considerable movement was still possible.

sharecropping After the Civil War, the southern states adopted a sharecropping system as a compromise between former slaves, who wanted land of their own, and former slave owners, who needed labor. The landowners provided land, tools, and seed to a farming family, who in turn provided labor. The resulting crop was divided between them, with the farmers receiving a "share" of one-third to one-half of the crop.

Black Codes: A New Name for Slavery?

While landless African Americans in the countryside were being reduced to economic dependence, those in towns and cities found themselves living in an increasingly segregated society. The Black Codes of 1865 attempted to require separation of the races in public places and facilities; when most of the codes were overturned by federal authorities as violations of the Civil Rights Act of 1866, the same end was

The Civil War brought emancipation to slaves, but the sharecropping system kept many of them economically bound to their employers. At the end of a year the sharecropper tenants might owe most—or all—of what they had made to their landlord. Here, a sharecropping family poses in front of their cabin. Ex-slaves often built their living quarters near woods in order to have a ready supply of fuel for heating and cooking. The cabin's chimney lists away from the house so that it can be easily pushed away from the living quarters should it catch fire.

often achieved through private initiative and community pressure. Blacks found it almost impossible to gain admittance to most hotels, restaurants, and other privately owned establishments catering to whites. Although separate black, or "Jim Crow," cars were not yet the rule on railroads, African Americans were often denied first-class accommodations. After 1868, black-supported Republican governments passed civil rights acts requiring equal access to public facilities, but little effort was made to enforce the legislation.

The Black Codes had other onerous provisions meant to control African Americans and return them to quasi-slavery. Most codes even made black unemployment a crime, which meant blacks had to make long-term contracts with white employers or be arrested for vagrancy. Others limited the rights of African Americans to own property or engage in occupations other than those of servant or laborer. The codes were set aside by the actions of Congress, the military, and the Freedmen's Bureau, but vagrancy laws remained in force across the South.

Furthermore, private violence and discrimination against blacks continued on a massive scale unchecked by state authorities. Hundreds, perhaps thousands, of blacks were murdered by whites in 1865–1866, and few of the perpetrators were brought to justice. The imposition of military rule in 1867 was designed in part to protect former slaves from such violence and intimidation, but the task was beyond the capacity of the few thousand troops stationed in the South. When new constitutions were approved and states readmitted to the Union under the congressional plan in 1868, the problem became more severe. White opponents of Radical Reconstruction adopted systematic terrorism and organized mob violence to keep blacks away from the polls.

The freed slaves tried to defend themselves by organizing their own militia groups for protection and to assert their political rights. However, the militia groups were not powerful enough to overcome the growing power of the anti-Republican forces. As the military presence was progressively reduced, the new Republican regimes were left to fight a losing battle against armed white supremacists.

Republican Rule in the South

Hastily organized in 1867, the southern Republican party dominated the constitution-making of 1868 and the regimes that came out of it. The party was an attempted coalition of three social groups: businessmen seeking aid for economic development, poor white farmers, and blacks. Although all three groups had different goals, their opposition to the old planter ruling class appeared to give them a basis for unity.

To be sure, the coalition faced difficulties even within its own ranks. Small farmers of the yeoman class had a bred-in-the-bone resistance to black equality. Conservative businessmen questioned costly measures for the elevation or relief of the lower classes of either race. In some states, astute Democratic politicians exploited the divisions by appealing to disaffected white Republicans.

But during the relatively brief period when they were in power in the South, the Republicans chalked up some notable achievements. They established (on paper at least) the South's first adequate system of public education, democratized state and local government, and appropriated funds for an enormous expansion of public services and welfare responsibilities.

Important though it was, social and political reform took second place to the major effort that Republicans made to foster economic development and restore southern prosperity by subsidizing the construction of railroads and other internal improvements. Although it addressed the region's real economic needs and was initially very popular, the policy of aiding railroads turned out disastrously. Extravagance, corruption, and the determination of routes based on political rather than sound economic considerations meant an increasing burden of public debt and taxation; the policy did not produce the promised payoff of reliable, cheap transportation. Subsidized railroads frequently went bankrupt, leaving the taxpayers holding the bag. When the Panic of 1873 brought many southern state governments to the verge of bankruptcy and railroad building came to an end, it was clear that the Republicans' "gospel of prosperity" through state aid to private enterprise had failed miserably. Their political opponents, most of whom had originally favored these policies, now saw an opportunity to make gains by charging that Republicans had ruined the southern economy.

These activities were often accompanied by inefficiency, waste, and corruption. State debts and tax burdens rose enormously, mainly because governments had undertaken heavy new responsibilities but partly as a result of waste and graft. In short, the Radical regimes brought needed reforms to the South, but they were not always model governments.

Southern corruption, however, was not exceptional, nor was it a special result of the extension of suffrage to uneducated blacks, as critics of Radical Reconstruction have claimed. It was part of a national pattern during an era when private interests considered buying government favors a part of the cost of doing business, and many politicians expected to profit by obliging them.

Blacks bore only a limited responsibility for the dishonesty of the Radical governments because they never controlled a state government and held few major offices. The biggest grafters were opportunistic whites; some of the most notorious were **carpetbaggers**—recent arrivals from the North—but others were native Southerners. Some black legislators went with the tide and accepted "loans" from those railroad lobbyists who would pay most for their votes, but the same men could usually be depended on to vote the will of their constituents on civil rights or educational issues. Although blacks who served or supported corrupt and wasteful regimes did so because they had no viable alternative, opponents of Radical Reconstruction were able to capitalize on racial prejudice and persuade many Americans that "good government" was synonymous with white supremacy. Contrary to myth, the small number of blacks elected to state or national office during Reconstruction demonstrated on the average more integrity and competence than their white counterparts. Most were fairly well educated, having been free Negroes or unusually privileged slaves before the war. Many battled tirelessly to promote the interests of their race.

carpetbaggers This term was applied to Northerners who moved to the South after the Civil War in order to aid in the reconstruction of the South or to invest in the southern economy. It derives from the claim that these Northerners carried everything they owned in one bag.

Claiming Public and Private Rights

As important as party politics to the changing political culture of the Reconstruction South were the ways that freed slaves claimed rights for themselves. They did so not only in negotiations with employers and in public meetings and convention halls, but also through the institutions they created, and perhaps most important, the households they formed.

On either side of Frederick Douglass on this poster are two African American heroes of the Reconstruction era. Senator Blanche K. Bruce of Mississippi, on the left, was the first African American to be elected to a full term in the U.S. Senate. Senator Hiram R. Revels, also representing Mississippi, was elected to the Senate in 1870 to fill the seat previously occupied by Confederate President Jefferson Davis.

As one black corporal in the Union Army told an audience of ex-slaves, "The Marriage covenant is at the foundation of all our rights. In slavery we could not have *legalized* marriage: *now* we have it . . . and we shall be established as a people." Through marriage, African Americans claimed citizenship. Freedmen hoped that marriage would allow them to take on not only political rights, but the right to control the labor of wives and children.

While they were in effect in 1865–1866, many states' Black Codes included apprenticeship provisions, providing for freed children to be apprenticed by courts to some white person (with preference given to former masters) if their parents were paupers, unemployed, of "bad character," or even simply if it were found to be "better for the habits and comfort of a child." Ex-slaves struggled to win their children back from what often amounted to re-enslavement for arbitrary reasons. Freed people challenged the apprenticeship system in county courts, and through the Freedmen's Bureau.

While many former slaves lined up eagerly to formalize their marriages, many also retained their own definitions of marriage. Perhaps as many as 50 percent of ex-slaves chose not to marry legally, and whites criticized them heavily for it. African American leaders worried about this refusal to follow white norms. Yet many poor blacks continued to recognize as husband and wife people who cared for and supported one another without benefit of legal sanction. The new legal system punished couples who deviated from the legal norm through laws against bastardy, adultery, and fornication. Furthermore, the Freedmen's Bureau made the marriage of freedpeople a priority so that husbands, rather than the federal government, would be legally responsible for families' support.

Some ex-slaves used the courts to assert rights against white people as well as other blacks, suing over domestic violence, child support, assault, and debt. Freedwomen sued their husbands for desertion and alimony, in order to enlist the

Freedman's Bureau to help them claim property from men. Other ex-slaves mobilized kin networks and other community resources to make claims on property and family.

Immediately after the war, freed people flocked to create institutions that had been denied to them under slavery: churches, fraternal and benevolent associations, political organizations, and schools. Many joined all-black denominations such as the African Methodist Episcopal church, which provided freedom from white dominance and a more congenial style of worship. Black women formed all-black chapters of organizations such as the Women's Christian Temperance Union, and their own women's clubs to oppose lynching and work for "uplift" in the black community.

A top priority for most ex-slaves was the opportunity to educate their children; the first schools for freed people were all-black institutions established by the Freedmen's Bureau and various northern missionary societies. At the time, having been denied all education during the antebellum period, most blacks viewed separate schooling as an opportunity rather than as a form of discrimination. However, these schools were precursors to the segregated public school systems first instituted by Republican governments. Only in city schools of New Orleans and at the University of South Carolina were there serious attempts during Reconstruction to bring white and black students together in the same classrooms.

In a variety of ways, African American men and women during Reconstruction claimed freedom in the "private" realm as well as the public sphere, by claiming rights to their own families and building their own institutions. They did so in the face of the vigorous efforts of their former masters as well as the new government agencies to control their private lives and shape their new identities as husbands, wives, and citizens.

RETREAT FROM RECONSTRUCTION

The era of Reconstruction began coming to an end almost before it started. Although it was only a scant three years from the end of the Civil War, the impeachment crisis of 1868 represented the high point of popular interest in Reconstruction issues. That year, Ulysses S. Grant was elected president. Many historians blame Grant for the corruption of his administration and for the inconsistency and failure of his southern policy. He had neither the vision nor the sense of duty to tackle the difficult challenges the nation faced. From 1868 on, political issues other than southern Reconstruction moved to the forefront of national politics, and the plight of African Americans in the South receded in white consciousness.

Rise of the Money Question

In the years immediately following the Civil War, the question of how to manage the nation's currency and, more specifically, what to do about "greenbacks"—paper money issued during the war—competed with Reconstruction and corruption issues for public attention. Defenders of "sound" money, mostly financial interests in the East, wanted the greenbacks withdrawn from circulation and Civil War debts redeemed in specie payments (silver and gold). Opponents of this hard-money policy and the resulting deflation of the currency were mainly credit-hungry Westerners and expansionist-minded manufacturers, known as **greenbackers,** who wanted to keep greenbacks in circulation. Both political parties had hard- and easy-money factions, preventing the money question from becoming a heated presidential election issue in 1868 and 1872.

But the Panic of 1873, which brought much of the economy to its knees, led to agitation to inflate the currency by issuing more paper money. Debt-ridden farmers, who would be the backbone of the greenback movement for years to come, now

greenbackers Members of the National Greenback Party, founded in 1874, who wanted to keep wartime paper money (greenbacks) in circulation. They believed that a floating currency, not tied to either gold or silver, would provide relief to debtors and impoverished farmers by increasing the money supply.

joined the easy-money clamor for the first time. Responding to the money and credit crunch, Congress moved in 1874 to authorize a modest issue of new greenbacks, but Grant vetoed the bill. In 1875, Congress enacted the Specie Resumption Act, which provided for a gradual reduction of greenbacks leading to full resumption of specie payment by 1879. The act was interpreted as deflationary, and farmers and workers, who were already suffering from deflation, reacted with dismay and anger.

The Democratic party could not capitalize adequately on these sentiments because of the influence of its own hard-money faction, and in 1876, an independent Greenback party entered the national political arena. Greenbackers kept the money issue alive through the next decade.

Final Efforts of Reconstruction

Fifteenth Amendment Ratified in 1870, this amendment prohibited the denial or abridgment of the right to vote by the federal government or state governments on the basis of race, color, or prior condition as a slave. It was intended to guarantee African Americans the right to vote in the South.

The Republican effort to make equal rights for blacks the law of the land culminated in the **Fifteenth Amendment,** ratified in 1870, which prohibited any state from denying a male citizen the right to vote because of race, color, or previous condition of servitude. Much to the displeasure of advocates of women's rights, however, the amendment made no provision for woman suffrage. And states could still limit male suffrage by imposing literacy tests, property qualifications, or poll taxes allegedly applying to all racial groups; such devices would eventually be used to strip southern blacks of the right to vote. But the makers of the amendment did not foresee this result.

The Grant administration was charged with enforcing the amendment and protecting black voting rights in the reconstructed states. Since survival of the Republican regimes depended on black support, political partisanship dictated federal action, even though the North's emotional and ideological commitment to black citizenship was waning.

Ku Klux Klan A secret terrorist society first organized in Tennessee in 1866. The original Klan's goals were to disfranchise African Americans, stop Reconstruction, and restore the prewar social order of the South. The Ku Klux Klan reformed after World War II to promote white supremacy in the wake of the "Second Reconstruction."

Between 1868 and 1872, the main threat to southern Republican regimes came from the **Ku Klux Klan** and other secret societies bent on restoring white supremacy by intimidating blacks who sought to exercise their political rights. A grassroots vigilante movement rather than a centralized conspiracy, the Klan thrived on local initiative and gained support from whites of all social classes. Its secrecy, decentralization, popular support, and utter ruthlessness made it very difficult to suppress. Blacks who voted ran the risk of being verbally intimidated, whipped, or even murdered.

The methods were first used effectively in the presidential election of 1868. Terrorism by white supremacists cost Grant the electoral votes of Louisiana and Georgia. In Louisiana, political violence claimed hundreds of lives, and in Arkansas, more than two hundred Republicans were assassinated. Thereafter, Klan terrorism was directed mainly at Republican state governments. Insurrections broke out in Arkansas, Tennessee, North Carolina, and parts of South Carolina. In Tennessee, North Carolina, and Georgia, Klan activities helped undermine Republican control, thus allowing the Democrats to come to power in all those states by 1870.

Force Acts Congress attacked the Ku Klux Klan with three Enforcement or "Force" Acts in 1870–1871. Designed to protect black voters in the South, these laws placed state elections under federal jurisdiction and imposed fines and imprisonment on those guilty of interfering with any citizen exercising his right to vote.

Faced with the violent overthrow of the southern Republican party, Congress and the Grant administration were forced to act. A series of laws passed in 1870 and 1871 sought to enforce the Fifteenth Amendment by providing federal protection for black suffrage and authorizing use of the army against the Klan. Although the **Force Acts,** also known as the Ku Klux Klan Acts, did not totally destroy the Klan, the enforcement effort was vigorous enough to put a damper on hooded terrorism and ensure relatively fair and peaceful elections in 1872.

A heavy black turnout in the elections enabled the Republicans to hold on to power in most states of the Deep South, despite efforts of the Democratic-Conservative opposition to woo Republicans by taking moderate positions on racial and economic issues. This setback prompted the Democratic-Conservatives

A Look at the Past

Cartoon "Worse Than Slavery"

Political cartoonist Thomas Nast offered his commentary on and critique of contemporary events through his cartoons in *Harper's Weekly,* a popular magazine that had a circulation of more than 100,000 readers. This Nast cartoon, "Worse Than Slavery," appeared in the magazine on October 24, 1874. Carefully examine the individuals and items depicted in the cartoon. Note that the phrase near the top of the drawing, "This is a white man's government," is a quotation from the 1868 Democratic Party platform. ✱ According to the cartoon, what conditions or events are "worse than slavery"? What view of Reconstruction policy does the cartoonist appear to be expressing?

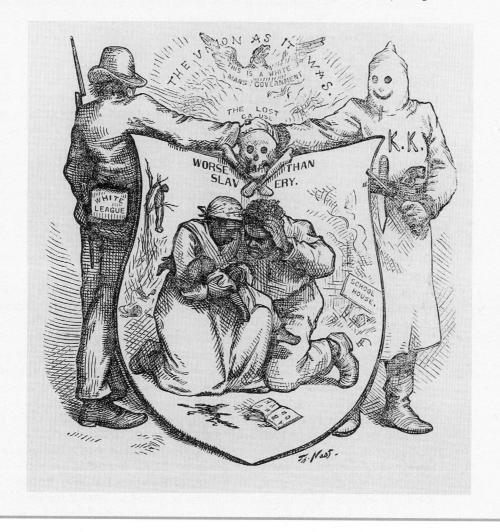

to make a significant change in their strategy and ideology. No longer did they try to take votes away from the Republicans by proclaiming support for black suffrage and government aid to business. Instead, they began to appeal openly to white supremacy and to the traditional Democratic agrarian hostility to governmental promotion of economic development. Consequently, they were able to bring back to the polls a portion of the white electorate, mostly small farmers, who had not been turning out because they were alienated by the leadership's apparent concessions to Yankee ideas.

The new and more effective electoral strategy dovetailed with a resurgence of violence meant to reduce Republican—especially black Republican—voting. The new reign of terror differed from the previous Klan episode; its agents no longer wore masks but acted quite openly. They were effective because the northern public was increasingly disenchanted with federal intervention on behalf of what were widely viewed as corrupt and tottering Republican regimes. Grant used force in the South for the last time in 1874. When an unofficial militia in Mississippi instigated a series of bloody race riots prior to the state elections in 1875, Grant refused the governor's request for federal troops. As a result, intimidation kept black voters away from the polls.

By 1876, Republicans held on to only three southern states—South Carolina, Louisiana, and Florida. Partly because of Grant's hesitant and inconsistent use of presidential power but mainly because the northern electorate would no longer tolerate military action to sustain Republican governments and black voting rights, Radical Reconstruction was falling into total eclipse.

Spoilsmen versus Reformers

One reason Grant found it increasingly difficult to take strong action to protect southern Republicans was the charge by reformers that his administration was propping up bad governments in the South for personal and partisan advantage. In some cases, the charges held a measure of truth.

The Republican party in the Grant era was rapidly losing the idealism and high purpose associated with the crusade against slavery. By the beginning of the 1870s, men who had been the conscience of the party had been replaced by a new breed of Republicans, such as Senator Roscoe Conkling of New York, whom historians have dubbed "spoilsmen" or "politicos." More often than not, Grant sided with the spoilsmen of his party.

During Grant's first administration, an aura of scandal surrounded the White House but did not directly implicate the president. In 1869, the financial buccaneer Jay Gould enlisted the aid of a brother-in-law of Grant's to further a fantastic scheme to corner the gold market. Gould failed in the attempt, but he did manage to come away with a huge profit.

Grant's first-term vice president, Schuyler Colfax of Indiana, was directly involved in the notorious Crédit Mobilier scandal. Crédit Mobilier was a construction company that actually served as a fraudulent device for siphoning off profits that should have gone to the stockholders of the Union Pacific Railroad, which was the beneficiary of massive federal land grants. To forestall government inquiry into this arrangement, Crédit Mobilier stock was distributed to influential congressmen. The whole business came to light just before the campaign of 1872.

Republicans who could not tolerate such corruption or had other grievances against the administration broke with Grant in 1872 and formed a third party committed to "honest government" and "reconciliation" between the North and the South. The Liberal Republicans, led initially by such high-minded reformers as Senator Carl Schurz of Missouri, endorsed reform of the civil service to curb the corruption-breeding patronage system and advocated strict laissez-faire economic policies, which meant low tariffs, an end to government subsidies for railroads, and hard money.

The Liberal Republicans' national convention nominated Horace Greeley, editor of the respected *New York Tribune* newspaper. This was a curious and divisive choice, seeing that Greeley was at odds with the founder of the movement on the tariff question and indifferent to civil service reform. The Democrats also endorsed Greeley, mainly because he vowed to end Radical Reconstruction. Greeley, however, did not attract support and was soundly defeated by Grant.

Grant's second administration bore out the reformers' worst suspicions about corruption in high places. In 1875, the public learned that federal revenue officials had conspired with distillers to defraud the government of millions of dollars in liquor taxes. Grant's private secretary, Orville E. Babcock, was indicted as a member of the "Whiskey Ring" and was saved from conviction only by the president's personal intercession. The next year, Grant's secretary of war, William W. Belknap, was impeached by the House after an investigation revealed that he had taken bribes for the sale of Indian trading posts. He avoided a Senate conviction by leaving office before the trial.

There is no evidence that Grant profited personally from any of the misdeeds of his subordinates. Yet he is not entirely without blame for the corruption of his administration. He failed to take action against the malefactors, and even after their guilt had been clearly established, he tried to shield them from justice. Ulysses S. Grant was the only president between Jackson and Wilson to serve two full and consecutive terms. But unlike other chief executives so favored by the electorate, Grant is commonly regarded as a failure. Although the problems he faced would have challenged any president, the shame of Grant's administration was that he made loyalty to old friends a higher priority than civil rights or sound economic principles.

REUNION AND THE NEW SOUTH

The end of Radical Reconstruction in 1877 opened the way to a reconciliation of North and South. But the costs of reunion were high for less privileged groups in the South. The civil and political rights of blacks, left unprotected, were stripped away by white supremacist regimes. Lower-class whites saw their interests sacrificed to those of capitalists and landlords. Despite the rhetoric hailing a prosperous "New South," the region remained poor and open to exploitation by northern business interests.

The Compromise of 1877

The election of 1876 pitted Rutherford B. Hayes of Ohio, an honest Republican governor, against Governor Samuel J. Tilden of New York, a Democratic reformer. Honest government was apparently the electorate's highest priority. When the returns came in, Tilden had clearly won the popular vote and seemed likely to win a narrow victory in the electoral college. But the result was placed in doubt when the returns from the three southern states still controlled by the Republicans were contested. If Hayes were to be awarded these three states, plus one contested electoral vote in Oregon, Republican strategists realized, he would triumph in the electoral college by a single vote.

The outcome of the election remained undecided for months. To resolve the impasse, Congress appointed a special electoral commission of fifteen members to determine who would receive the votes of the disputed states. The commission split along party lines and voted 8 to 7 to award Hayes the disputed states. But this decision still had to be ratified, and in the House there was strong Democratic opposition.

To ensure Hayes's election, Republican leaders negotiated secretly with conservative southern Democrats, some of whom seemed willing to abandon their opposition if the last troops were withdrawn and "home rule" was restored to the South. Vague pledges of federal support for southern railroads and internal improvements were made, and Hayes assured southern negotiators that he had every intention of ending Reconstruction. Eventually, an informal bargain, dubbed the **Compromise of 1877,** was struck. Precisely what was agreed to and by whom remains a matter of dispute, but one thing at least was understood by both sides: Hayes would be president, and southern Republicans would be abandoned to their fate.

Compromise of 1877 The Compromise of 1877 was struck during the contested presidential election of 1876. In the compromise, Democrats accepted the election of Rutherford B. Hayes (Republican) in exchange for the withdrawal of federal troops from the South and the ending of Reconstruction.

With southern Democratic acquiescence, the main opposition was overcome, and Hayes took the oath of office. He immediately ordered the army not to resist a Democratic takeover in South Carolina and Louisiana. Thus fell the last of the Radical governments.

"Redeeming" a New South

Redeemers Redeemers were a loose coalition of prewar Democrats, Confederate Army veterans, and Southern Whigs who took over southern state governments in the 1870s, supposedly "redeeming" them from the corruption of Reconstruction. They shared a commitment to white supremacy and laissez-faire economics.

The men who came to power after the ending of Radical Reconstruction in one southern state after another are usually referred to as the **Redeemers.** They had differing backgrounds and previous loyalties. Some were members of the Old South's ruling planter class who had warmly supported secession and now sought to reestablish the old order with as few changes as possible. Others, of middle-class origin or outlook, favored commercial and industrial interests over agrarian groups and called for a New South, committed to diversified economic development. A third group consisted of professional politicians bending with the prevailing winds.

Rather than supporters of any single ideology or program, these leaders can perhaps best be understood as power brokers mediating among the dominant interest groups of the South in ways that served their own political advantage. In many ways, the "rings" that they established on the state and county levels were analogous to the political machines developing at the same time in northern cities.

They did, however, agree on and endorse two basic principles: laissez-faire and white supremacy. Laissez-faire, the notion that government should be limited and neutral in its economic activities, could unite planters, frustrated at seeing direct state support going to businessmen, and capitalist promoters, who had come to realize that low taxes and freedom from government regulation were even more advantageous than state subsidies. It soon became clear that the Redeemers responded only to privileged and entrenched interest groups, especially landlords, merchants, and industrialists, and offered little or nothing to tenants, small farmers, and working people. As industrialization began to gather steam in the 1880s, Democratic regimes became increasingly accommodating to manufacturing interests and hospitable to agents of northern capital who were gaining control of the South's transportation system and its extractive industries.

White supremacy was the principal rallying cry that brought the Redeemers to power in the first place. Once in office, they found that they could stay there by charging that opponents of ruling Democratic cliques were trying to divide the "white man's party" and open the way for a return to "black domination." Appeals to racism could also deflect attention away from the economic grievances of groups without political clout.

The new governments were more economical than those of Reconstruction, mainly because they cut back drastically on appropriations for schools and other needed public services. But they were scarcely more honest. Embezzlement of public funds and bribery of public officials continued to an alarming extent.

The Redeemer regimes of the late 1870s and 1880s badly neglected the interests of small white farmers.

■ *Perhaps no event better expresses the cruel and barbaric nature of the racism and white supremacy that swept the South after Reconstruction than lynching. Although lynchings were not confined to the South, most occurred there, and African American men were the most frequent victims. Here, two men lean out of a barn window above a black man who is about to be hanged. Others below prepare to set on fire the pile of hay at the victim's feet. Lynchings were often public events, drawing huge crowds to watch the victim's agonizing death.* ■

SUPREME COURT DECISIONS AFFECTING BLACK CIVIL RIGHTS, 1875–1900

Case	Effects of Court's Decisions
Hall v. *DeCuir* (1878)	Struck down Louisiana law prohibiting racial discrimination by "common carriers" (railroads, steamboats, buses). Declared the law a "burden" on interstate commerce, over which states had no authority.
United States v. *Harris* (1882)	Declared federal laws to punish crimes such as murder and assault unconstitutional. Declared such crimes to be the sole concern of local government. Ignored the frequent racial motivation behind such crimes in the South.
Civil Rights Cases (1883)	Struck down Civil Rights Act of 1875. Declared that Congress may not legislate on civil rights unless a state passes a discriminatory law. Declared the Fourteenth Amendment silent on racial discrimination by private citizens.
Plessy v. *Ferguson* (1896)	Upheld Louisiana statute requiring "separate but equal" accommodations on railroads. Declared that segregation is *not* necessarily discrimination.
Williams v. *Mississippi* (1898)	Upheld state law requiring a literacy test to qualify for voting. Refused to find any implication of racial discrimination in the law, although it permitted illiterate whites to vote if they "understood" the Constitution. Using such laws, southern states rapidly disfranchised blacks.

Whites, as well as blacks, were suffering from the notorious crop lien system, which gave the local merchants who advanced credit at high rates of interest during the growing season the right to take possession of the harvested crop on terms that buried farmers deeper and deeper in debt. As a result, increasing numbers of whites lost title to their homesteads and were reduced to tenancy.

The Rise of Jim Crow

African Americans bore the greatest hardships imposed by the new order. From 1876 through the first decade of the twentieth century, Southern states imposed a series of restrictions on black civil rights known as **Jim Crow laws.** While segregation and disfranchisement began as informal arrangements, they culminated in a legal regime of separation and exclusion that took firm hold in the 1890s.

Jim Crow laws Laws enacted by states to segregate the population. They became widespread in the South after Reconstruction.

The rise of Jim Crow in the political arena was especially bitter for Southern blacks who realized that only political power could ensure other rights. The Redeemers had promised, as part of the understanding that led to the end of federal intervention in 1877, to respect the rights of blacks as set forth in the Fourteenth and Fifteenth Amendments. But when blacks tried to vote Republican in the "redeemed" states, they encountered renewed violence and intimidation. Blacks who withstood the threat of losing their jobs or being evicted from tenant farms if they voted for Republicans were visited at night and literally whipped into line. The message was clear: Vote Democratic, or vote not at all.

Furthermore, white Democrats now controlled the electoral machinery and were able to manipulate the black vote by stuffing ballot boxes, discarding unwanted votes, or reporting fraudulent totals. Some states also imposed complicated new voting requirements to discourage black participation. Full-scale disfranchisement did not occur until literacy tests and other legalized obstacles to voting were imposed in the period from 1890 to 1910, but by that time, less formal and comprehensive methods had already made a mockery of the Fifteenth Amendment.

Nevertheless, blacks continued to vote freely in some localities until the 1890s; a few districts, like the one Robert Smalls represented, even elected black Republicans to Congress during the immediate post-Reconstruction period. The last of these, Representative George H. White of North Carolina, served until 1901.

The dark night of racism that fell on the South after Reconstruction seemed to unleash all the baser impulses of human nature. Between 1889 and 1899, an average of 187 blacks were lynched every year for alleged offenses against white supremacy.

Chronology

1863	Lincoln sets forth his 10 percent Reconstruction plan
1864	Wade-Davis Bill passes Congress, is pocket-vetoed by Lincoln
1865	Johnson moves to reconstruct the South on his own initiative ▪ Congress refuses to seat representatives and senators elected from states reestablished under the presidential plan
1866	Congress passes the Fourteenth Amendment ▪ Republicans increase their congressional majority in the fall elections
1867	First Reconstruction Act is passed over Johnson's veto
1868	Johnson is impeached, avoids conviction by one vote ▪ Grant wins the presidential election, defeating Horatio Seymour
1869	Congress passes the Fifteenth Amendment, granting blacks the right to vote
1870–1871	Congress passes the Force Acts to protect black voting rights in the South
1872	Grant is re-elected president, defeating Horace Greeley, candidate of the Liberal Republicans and Democrats
1873	Financial panic plunges the nation into a depression
1875	Congress passes the Specie Resumption Act ▪ "Whiskey Ring" scandal is exposed
1876–1877	Disputed presidential election is resolved in favor of Republican Hayes over Democrat Tilden
1877	"Compromise of 1877" results in an end to military intervention in the South and the fall of the last Radical governments

Those convicted of petty crimes against property were often little better off; many were condemned to be leased out to private contractors whose brutality rivaled that of the most sadistic slaveholders. The convict-lease system enabled entrepreneurs, such as mine owners and extractors of forest products, to rent prisoners from the state and treat them as they saw fit. Unlike slaveowners, they suffered no loss when a forced laborer died from overwork. Finally, the dignity of blacks was cruelly affronted by the wave of segregation laws passed around the turn of the century, to some extent a white reaction to the refusal of many blacks to submit to voluntary segregation of railroads, streetcars, and other public facilities.

The North and the federal government did little or nothing to stem the tide of racial oppression in the South. A series of Supreme Court decisions between 1878 and 1898 gutted the Reconstruction amendments and the legislation passed to enforce them, leaving blacks virtually defenseless against political and social discrimination.

CONCLUSION: THE "UNFINISHED REVOLUTION"

By the late 1880s, the wounds of the Civil War were healing, and white Americans were seized by the spirit of sectional reconciliation. "Reunion" was becoming a cultural as well as political reality. But whites could come back together only because Northerners had tacitly agreed to give Southerners a free hand in their efforts to reduce blacks to a new form of servitude. The "outraged, heart-broken, bruised, and bleeding" African Americans of the South paid the heaviest price for sectional reunion. Reconstruction remained, in the words of historian Eric Foner, an "unfinished revolution." It would be another century before African Americans rose up once more to demand full civil and political rights.

KEY TERMS

Ten Percent Plan, p. 311	Fourteenth Amendment, p. 314	Ku Klux Klan, p. 322
Radical Republicans, p. 311	Radical Reconstruction, p. 314	Force Acts, p. 322
Wade-Davis Bill, p. 311	sharecropping, p. 317	Compromise of 1877, p. 325
Thirteenth Amendment, p. 312	carpetbaggers, p. 319	Redeemers, p. 326
Black Codes, p. 312	greenbackers, p. 321	Jim Crow laws, p. 327
Freedman's Bureau, p. 313	Fifteenth Amendment, p. 322	

RECOMMENDED READING

The best one-volume account of Reconstruction is Eric Foner, *Reconstruction: America's Unfinished Revolution* (1988). Two excellent short surveys are Kenneth M. Stampp, *The Era of Reconstruction, 1865–1877* (1965), and John Hope Franklin, *Reconstruction: After the Civil War* (1961). Both were early efforts to synthesize modern "revisionist" interpretations. W. E. B. DuBois, *Black Reconstruction in America, 1860–1880* (1935), remains brilliant and provocative. On the politics of Reconstruction, see Stephen David Kantrowitz, *Ben Tillman and the Reconstruction of White Supremacy* (2001), Laura F. Edwards, *Gendered Strife and Confusion: The Political Culture of Reconstruction* (1997), J. Morgan Kousser and James M. McPherson, eds., *Region, Race, and Reconstruction: Essays in Honor of C. Vann Woodward* (1982), and Eric Foner, *Nothing But Freedom: Emancipation and Its Legacy* (1983).

Leon F. Litwack, *Been in the Storm So Long: The Aftermath of Slavery* (1979), provides a moving portrayal of the black experience of emancipation. On changing society and family life during Reconstruction, see Noralee Frankel, *Freedom's Women: Black Women and Families in Reconstruction Era Mississippi* (1999), Dylan Penningroth, *Claiming Kin and Property: African American Life Before and After Emancipation* (2003), and Amy Dru Stanley, *From Bondage to Contract: Wage Labor, Marriage, and the Market in the Age of Slave Emancipation* (1998). On what freedom meant in economic terms, see Gerald David Jaynes, *Branches Without Roots: Genesis of the Black Working Class in the American South, 1862–1882* (1986). A work that focuses on ex-slaves' attempts to create their own economic order is Julie Saville, *The Work of Reconstruction: Free Slave to Wage Laborer in South Carolina, 1860–1870* (1994). The best overview of the postwar southern economy is Gavin Wright, *Old South, New South* (1986). On the end of Reconstruction, see David W. Blight, *Race and Reunion: The Civil War in American Memory* (2000). On the character of the post-Reconstruction South, see the classic work by C. Vann Woodward, *Origins of the New South, 1877–1913* (1951) and Edward Ayers, *The Promise of the New South* (1992).

SUGGESTED WEB SITES

Diary and Letters of Rutherford B. Hayes
www.ohiohistory.org/onlinedoc/hayes/index.cfm
The Rutherford B. Hayes Presidential Center in Fremont, Ohio, maintains this searchable database of Hayes's writings.

Images of African Americans from the Nineteenth Century
digital.nypl.org/schomburg/images_aa19/
The New York Public Library–Schomburg Center for Research in Black Culture site contains numerous visuals.

Freedmen and Southern Society Project (University of Maryland, College Park)
www.inform.umd.edu/ARHU/Depts/History/Freedman/home.html
This site contains a chronology and sample documents from several print collections or primary sources about emancipation and freedom in the 1860s.

Andrew Johnson
www.whitehouse.gov/WH/glimpse/presidents/html/aj17.html
White House history of Johnson.

Ulysses S. Grant
www.whitehouse.gov/WH/glimpse/presidents/html/ug18.html
White House history of Grant.

History of the Suffrage Movement
www.rochester.edu/SBA
This site includes a chronology, important texts relating to woman suffrage, and biographical information about Susan B. Anthony and Elizabeth Cady Stanton.

Chapter *17*

The West: Exploiting an Empire

Lean Bear's Changing West

In 1863, federal Indian agents took a delegation of Cheyenne, Arapaho, Comanche, Kiowa, and Plains Apache to visit the eastern United States, hoping to impress them with the power of the white man. The visitors were, in fact, impressed. In New York City, they stared at the tall buildings and crowded streets, so different from the wide-open plains with which they were accustomed. They visited the museum of the great showman Phineas T. Barnum, who in turn put them on display; they even saw a hippopotamus.

In Washington, they met with President Abraham Lincoln. Lean Bear, a Cheyenne chief, assured Lincoln that Indians wanted peace but worried about the numbers of white people who were pouring into their country. Lincoln swore friendship, said the Indians would be better off if they began to farm, and promised he would do his best to keep the peace. But, he said, smiling at Lean Bear, "You know it is not always possible for any father to have his children do precisely as he wishes them to do."

Lean Bear, who had children of his own, had understood what Lincoln had said in Washington, at least in a way. Just a year later, back on his own lands, he watched as federal troops, Lincoln's "children," approached his camp. Wearing a peace medal that Lincoln had given him, Lean Bear rode slowly toward the troops to once again offer his friendship. When he was twenty yards away, they opened fire, then rode closer, and fired again and again into his fallen body.

As Lean Bear had feared, in the last decades of the nineteenth century, a flood of settlers ventured into America's newest and last West. Prospectors searched for "pay dirt," railroads crisscrossed the continent, eastern and foreign capitalists invested in cattle and land bonanzas, and farmers took up the promise of free western lands. In the rhetoric of the day, the West was a land of hope and abundance.

With the end of the Civil War, white Americans again claimed a special destiny to expand across the continent. In the process, they crushed the culture of the American Indians and ignored the special contributions of other nationalities, such as the Chinese miners and laborers and the Mexican herdsmen. As millions moved west, new states were carved out of the vast lands beyond the Mississippi. By 1900, there were forty-five states in the Union; only Arizona, New Mexico, and Oklahoma remained territories.

The West became a great colonial empire, harnessed to eastern capital and tied increasingly to national and international markets. Western economies depended to an unusual degree on the federal government, which subsidized their railroads, distributed their land, and spent millions of dollars for the upkeep of soldiers and Indians.

By the 1890s, the West of the buffalo and Indian was gone, replaced by cities, health resorts, and the latest magazines. The beginnings of irrigated agriculture pointed toward the future of the West. Ghost towns, abandoned farms, and scarred earth left behind by miners and farmers reflected the less favorable side of settlement. The West, the mythic land of cowboys and quick fortunes, was also a place of conquest and exploitation.

BEYOND THE FRONTIER

The line of white settlement had reached the edge of the timber country of Missouri by 1840. Beyond lay an enormous land of rolling prairies, parched deserts, and rugged, majestic mountains. Emerging from the timber country, travelers first encountered the Great Plains. The Prairie Plains, the eastern part of the region, enjoyed rich soil and good rainfall. To the west were the High Plains, rough and semiarid, rising gently to the foothills of the Rocky Mountains.

Running from Alaska to central New Mexico, the Rockies presented a formidable barrier. Although the passes were rich in beaver and gold, most travelers hurried through them, emerging in the desolate basin of present-day southern Idaho and Utah. Indians lived there, scrabbling out a bare subsistence by digging for roots, seeds, and berries. To the west, the lofty Coast ranges—the Cascades and the Sierra Nevada—held back rainfall; beyond were the temperate lands of the Pacific Coast.

Early explorers and mapmakers thought the country beyond the Mississippi uninhabitable. Between 1815 and 1860, American maps showed this land as the "Great American Desert." Settlement paused on the edge of the Plains, which daunted settlers dashing across them for California and Oregon.

Few rivers cut through the Plains. Those that did flooded in spring and trickled in summer. The land lacked rainfall for crops and lumber for homes and fences; the cast-iron plow and ax—the tools of eastern settlement—were virtually useless on the tough and treeless Plains soil.

Hot winds seared the Plains in summer, and blizzards and hailstorms froze them in winter. Despite these extremes, wildlife roamed in profusion—antelope, wolves, coyote, jackrabbits, and prairie dogs. The American bison, better known as the buffalo, grazed in enormous herds from Mexico to Canada. In 1865, perhaps 15 million buffalo lived on the Plains.

CRUSHING THE NATIVE AMERICANS

In 1867, when Horace Greeley, editor of the *New York Tribune,* urged New York City's unemployed to head West, where "you will crowd nobody, starve nobody," he, like most of his countrymen, ignored the fact that large numbers of people already lived there. In 1865, nearly a quarter of a million Indians lived in the western half of the country. The Cherokee and other tribes were resettled there after being forced out of their eastern lands by advancing white settlement. Other tribes, such as the Hopi, Zuni, Navajo, Apache, Chinook, and Shasta, were native to the region. By the 1870s, most of these tribes had been destroyed or beaten into submission. The powerful Ute, crushed in 1855, ceded most of their Utah lands to the United States and settled on a small reservation near the Great Salt Lake. The Navajo and Apache fought back desperately, but between 1865 and 1873, they too were confined to reservations. California Indians succumbed to the contagious diseases carried by whites during the Gold Rush of 1849. By 1880, fewer than twenty thousand Indians remained in all of California.

Life of the Plains Indians

Nearly two-thirds of the Indians west of the Mississippi lived on the Great Plains. The Plains tribes included the Sioux, Blackfoot, Cheyenne, Crow, Arapaho, Pawnee, Kiowa, Apache, and Comanche. Nomadic and warlike, the Plains Indians depended on the buffalo—and later the horse as well—for their existence. Skilled horsemen and warriors, the Plains Indians were the superior adversaries in conflicts with white settlers and cavalry. Even the introduction of the new Colt six-shooters during the 1850s did not entirely offset the Indians' advantage.

Migratory by culture, the Plains Indians formed tribes of several thousand people but lived in smaller "bands" of three hundred to five hundred. Each band was governed by a chief and a council, and each acted independently, which caused difficulties for the United States government. The bands followed and lived off the buffalo, using every part of the animal to provide food, clothing, shelter, and even fuel.

Warfare between tribes usually took the form of brief raids and skirmishes. Plains Indians fought few prolonged wars and rarely coveted territory. Most conflicts involved only a few warriors intent on stealing horses or "counting coups"—touching an enemy's body with the hand or a special stick. Certain tribes did, however, develop a fierce warrior class.

The Plains tribes divided labor by gender. Men hunted, traded, supervised ceremonial activities, and cleared ground for planting. Women were responsible for child rearing and artistic creativity. They also performed the camp work, grew vegetables, prepared buffalo meat and hides, and gathered roots and berries. Men were respected for their prowess in hunting and war, women for their skill with quill and paint.

"As Long as Waters Run": Searching for an Indian Policy

Before the mid-nineteenth century, Americans used the land west of the Mississippi as "one big reservation." The government named the area Indian Country, moved eastern tribes there with firm treaty guarantees, and in 1834 passed the Indian Intercourse Act, which prohibited any white person from entering Indian Country without a license.

The situation changed in the 1850s. Americans pushed toward the goldfields and the rich farmland of the West Coast. To clear the way for settlement, the federal government in 1851 abandoned "one big reservation" in favor of a new policy of "concentration." For the first time, it assigned boundaries to each tribe. The land was given to the tribes for "as long as waters run and the grass shall grow."

The concentration policy lasted only a few years. Accustomed to hunting widely for buffalo, many Indians refused to stay within their assigned areas. White settlers poured into Indian lands, then called on the government to protect them. In the 1850s, Indians were pushed out of Kansas and Nebraska; in 1859, gold miners moved into the Pikes Peak country, touching off warfare with the Cheyenne and Arapaho. Although the two tribes fought hard, they were no match for the federal government. In 1864, they asked for peace. Certain that the war was over, Chief Black Kettle led his seven hundred followers to camp on Sand Creek in southeastern Colorado. Early on the morning of November 29, 1864, a Colorado militia led by Colonel John M. Chivington attacked the sleeping Indians, clubbing, stabbing, and scalping Indian men, women, and children. The Chivington massacre set off angry protests in Colorado and the East. The government condemned the "gross and wanton outrages." Still, the two tribes were forced to surrender their Sand Creek reservation in exchange for lands elsewhere.

Before long, the powerful Sioux were on the warpath in the great Sioux War of 1865–1867. An invasion of gold miners in Montana touched off the war, which flared even more intensely when the federal government announced plans to con-

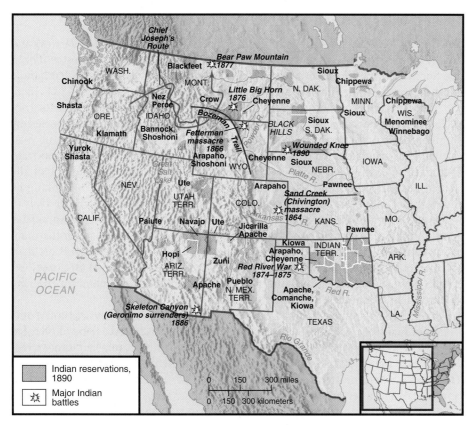

NATIVE AMERICANS IN THE WEST: MAJOR BATTLES AND RESERVATIONS
"They made us many promises, more than I remember, but they never kept but one; they promised to take our land, and they took it." So said Red Cloud of the Oglala Sioux, summarizing Native American–white relations in the 1870s. ■

nect the various mining towns by building the Bozeman Trail through the heart of the Sioux hunting grounds. Red Cloud, the Sioux chief, was determined to stop the trail. In December 1866, pursued by a U.S. army column under Captain William J. Fetterman, he lured the incautious Fetterman deep into the wilderness, ambushed him, and wiped out all eighty-two soldiers in his command.

The Fetterman massacre, coming so soon after the Chivington massacre, sparked a public debate over the nation's Indian policy. The debate reflected differing white views of the Indians. In the East, some humanitarian and church groups wanted a humane peace policy, directed toward educating and "civilizing" the tribes. Many people, in the East and the West, questioned this approach, convinced that Indians were savages unfit for civilization. Westerners in general favored firm control over the Indians, including swift punishment of any who rebelled.

In 1867, the peace advocates won the debate. Halting construction on the Bozeman Trail, Congress created a peace commission to end the Sioux War. After studying the situation, the peace commission agreed that only one policy offered a permanent solution: a policy of "small reservations" to isolate the Indians on distant lands, teach them to farm, and gradually "civilize" them.

The commission chose two areas to hold all the Plains Indians. The 54,000 Indians on the northern Plains would be moved north of the Black Hills in Dakota Territory. On the southern Plains, the 86,000 Indians would be moved into present-day Oklahoma. Both regions were considered unattractive to whites. In both areas, tribes would be assigned to specific reservations where government agents could supervise them.

Final Battles on the Plains

Few Indians settled peacefully into life on the new reservations. Young warriors and minor chiefs denounced the treaties and drifted back to the open countryside. In the Southwest, the Kiowa and Comanche rampaged through the Texas Panhandle until the army crushed them into submission in the Red River War of 1874–1875.

On the northern Plains, fighting resulted from the Black Hills Gold Rush of 1875. As prospectors tramped across Indian hunting grounds, the Sioux—led by Rain-in-the-Face, the great war chief Crazy Horse, and the famous medicine man Sitting Bull—gathered to stop them. One army column, under flamboyant Lieutenant Colonel George A. Custer, pushed recklessly ahead in pursuit of the Indians, eager to claim the victory. On the morning of June 25, 1876, thinking he had a small band of Indians surrounded on the banks of the Little Bighorn River in Montana, Custer divided his column and took 265 men toward the Indian village. Instead of fighting a small band, he discovered that he had stumbled on the main Sioux camp of 2500 warriors. By midafternoon, it was over: Custer and his men were dead. Custer was largely responsible for the loss, but "Custer's Last Stand," set in blazing headlines across the country, signaled a nationwide demand for revenge. Within a few months, the Sioux were surrounded and subdued.

The Sioux War ended the major Indian warfare in the West, but occasional outbreaks occurred for several years thereafter. In 1877, the Nez Percé tribe of Oregon, a people who had warmly welcomed Lewis and Clark in 1805, rebelled under Chief Joseph but were defeated and sent to barren lands in the Indian Country of Oklahoma, where most of them died from disease. In 1890, the Teton Sioux of South Dakota, bitter and starving, became restless. Many of them turned to the **Ghost Dances,** a set of dances and rites designed to bring back Indian lands and cause the whites to disappear.

The army intervened to stop the dancing, touching off violence that killed Sitting Bull and a number of other warriors. Frightened Indians fled southwest to join other Ghost Dancers under the aging chief Big Foot. Moving quickly, troops caught up with Big Foot's band, who agreed to come to the army camp on Wounded Knee Creek in South Dakota. An Indian, it is thought, fired the first shot, which was returned by the army's new machine guns. Firing a shell a second, they shredded tepees and people. In the infamous **Wounded Knee Massacre,** about two hundred men, women, and children were killed in the snow.

The End of Tribal Life

The final step in Indian policy came in the 1870s and 1880s. Some reformers had long argued against segregating the Indians on reservations, urging instead that the nation assimilate them individually into white culture. These "assimilationists" wanted to use education, land policy, and federal law to eradicate tribal society.

Congress began to adopt the policy in 1871 when it ended the practice of treaty making with Indian tribes. Because tribes were no longer separate nations, they lost many of their political and judicial functions, and the power of the chiefs was weakened. Increasingly, Indians became answerable in regular courts for certain crimes.

While Congress worked to break down the tribes, educators trained young Indians to adjust to white culture. Schools such as the Carlisle Indian School in Carlisle, Pennsylvania, taught students to fix machines and farm. They also forced them to trim their long hair, speak English, dress like "civilized" whites, and discontinue tribal ceremonies and dances. "Kill the Indian and save the man," said the founder of the Carlisle School.

Land ownership was the final and most important link in the new policy. Indians who owned land, it was thought, would become responsible, self-reliant cit-

Ghost Dances A religious movement that arose in the late nineteenth century under the prophet Wavoka, a Paiute Indian. It involved a set of dances and rites that its followers believed would cause white men to disappear and restore lands to the Native Americans.

Wounded Knee Massacre In December 1890, troopers of the Seventh Cavalry, under orders to stop the Ghost Dance religion among the Sioux, took Chief Big Foot and his followers to a camp on Wounded Knee Creek in South Dakota. Violence ensued and about two hundred Native Americans were killed.

■ *This pictogram by Oglala Sioux Amos Bad Heart Bull is a Native American version of the Battle of Little Bighorn, also known as Custer's Last Stand.* ■

izens. Deciding to give each Indian a farm, Congress in 1887 passed the **Dawes Severalty Act,** the most important legal development in Indian-white relations in more than three centuries.

Aiming to end tribal life, the Dawes Act divided tribal lands into small plots for distribution among members of the tribe. Each family head received 160 acres, single adults 80 acres, and children 40 acres. To keep the Indians' land from falling into the hands of speculators, the federal government held it in trust for twenty-five years. In addition, American citizenship was granted to Indians who accepted their land, lived apart from the tribe, and "adopted the habits of civilized life."

Through the Dawes Act, 47 million acres of land were distributed to Indians and their families. There were another 90 million acres in the reservations, and these lands, often the most fertile, were sold to white settlers. To evade the twenty-five year rule, speculators leased rather than purchased the land from the Indians. Many Indians knew little about farming. Their tools were rudimentary, and in the culture of the Plains Indians, farming was women's work. In 1934, the government returned to the idea of tribal land ownership, but by then, 138 million acres of Indian land had shrunk to 48 million acres, half of which was barren.

The final blow to tribal life came with the virtual extermination of the buffalo, the Plains Indians' chief resource and the basis for their unique way of life. The slaughter began in the 1860s as the transcontinental railroads pushed west and accelerated after 1871 when a Pennsylvania tannery discovered that buffalo hides made valuable leather. Professional hunters such as William F. "Buffalo Bill" Cody swarmed across the Plains, killing millions of the helpless beasts—three million a year between 1872 and 1874. A good hunter killed a hundred buffalo a day; skinners took off the hides, removed the tongue, hump, and tallow, and left the rest. The

Dawes Severalty Act
Legislation passed by Congress in 1887 that aimed at breaking up traditional Indian life by promoting individual land ownership. It divided tribal lands into small plots that were distributed among members of each tribe, with provisions for Indian education and eventual citizenship.

waste was incredible, and by 1883, the buffalo were almost gone. When the government later set out to produce the famous "Buffalo nickel," the designer had to go to the Bronx Zoo in New York City to find a living specimen.

By 1900, there were only 200,000 Indians in the country, most of them on reservations. Poverty, alcoholism, and unemployment were growing problems. Indians, no longer able to live off the buffalo, became wards of the state. Once possessors of the entire continent, they had been crowded into smaller and smaller areas, overwhelmed by the demand to become settled, literate, and English-speaking, like the white man.

Even as the Indians lost their identity, they entered the romantic folklore of the West. Dime novels told exciting tales of Indians fighting on the Plains. Buffalo Bill Cody turned it all into a profitable business. Beginning in 1883, Cody's Wild West Show ran for more than three decades, playing to viewers in the United States and Europe. Perhaps the end of an era was most fittingly symbolized in 1885 when Sitting Bull himself, victor over Custer at the battle of Little Big Horn, performed in the show.

SETTLEMENT OF THE WEST

Between 1870 and 1900, white—and some black—Americans settled the enormous total of 430 million acres west of the Mississippi; they occupied more land than in all the years before 1870. People moved west for many reasons. Some sought adventure; others wanted to escape the drab routine of the factory or city life. Many moved to California for their health. The Mormons settled Utah to escape religious persecution.

Whatever the specific reason, most people moved west to better their lot. On the whole, their timing was good, for as the nation's population grew, so did demand for the livestock and the agricultural, mineral, and lumber products of the expanding West. Contrary to older historical views, the West did not act as a major "safety valve," an outlet for social and economic tensions. The poor and unemployed did not have the means to move there and establish farms; most people moved west in periods of expanding demand, when the prospects for making money from this new land looked brightest.

Men and Women on the Overland Trail

Overland Trail The route taken by thousands of travelers from the Mississippi Valley to the Pacific Coast in the last half of the nineteenth century. It was extremely difficult, often taking six months or more to complete.

The first movement west aimed not for the nearby Plains but for California and Oregon. Between 1848 and 1878, perhaps half a million individuals made the long journey over the **Overland Trail** leading west. Some walked; others rode horses alone or in small groups. About half joined great caravans that inched across the 2000 miles between the Missouri River and the Pacific Coast.

More often than not, men made the decision to make the crossing; wives either went along or faced being left behind. Four out of five men on the Overland Trail had moved before. Most had little cash, but they needed only strong legs, a few staples, and a willingness to tighten the belt when game was scarce. The majority of people traveled in family groups, including in-laws, grandchildren, aunts, and uncles, meaning that their "quest for something new would take place in the context of the very familiar."

Individuals and wagon trains set out from various points along the Missouri River. Leaving in the spring and traveling through the summer, they hoped to reach their destination before the first snowfall. During April, travelers gradually assembled in spring camp. There they carefully packed their wagons, elected the train's leaders, and decided on the rules that they would observe during their trip west.

Setting out in early May, travelers divided the enormous route into manageable portions. From a distance, the white-topped wagons seemed driven by a common force, but in fact, internal discipline was a constant problem. Arguments erupted over the pace of the march, the choice of campsites, whether to rest or push on. Elected leaders quit; new ones were chosen.

Men, women, and children had different tasks on the trail. Men concerned themselves almost entirely with hunting, guard duty, and transportation. The women prepared the food, and the children kindled the fire, brought water to camp, and searched for wood and other fuel. Rising before the sun and walking 15 miles a day, in searing heat and mountain cold, travelers were weary by late afternoon.

For women, the trail was lonely, and they worked to exhaustion. Before long, they adjusted their clothing to the harsh conditions, adopting the new bloomer pants or shortening their skirts. Like men, they carried firearms in case of Indian attacks. Most emigrants, however, saw few Indians en route.

What they did often see was trash, miles of it, for the overland travelers dumped garbage, tin cans, furniture, tools, and clothing willy-nilly on their way west. They abandoned wagons, deserted dying animals, and stirred up dust to such an extent that drivers wore goggles to see.

■ *The migration westward on the Overland Trail was long and difficult. In this photograph from the 1870s, a caravan of covered wagons attempts to cross a river.* ■

The first stage of the journey was deceptively easy, and travelers usually reached Fort Kearney, in the Nebraska Territory, by late May. From there the trip became more demanding. Summer heat baked the route to Fort Laramie, on the eastern edge of the Wyoming Territory. Anxious to beat the early snowfalls, travelers rested a day or two at the fort, then hurried on to South Pass, the best route through the forbidding Rockies. Although still summer, the mountain nights were so cold that ice formed atop the water buckets.

Beyond South Pass, migrants went in different directions; some headed south through Utah, others toward Fort Hall in Idaho and then on to California. Months of hard traveling were still before them. They had to cross deserts and the towering Sierra Nevada. Not until September or October would they reach the verdant Sacramento Valley.

Under the best of conditions, the trip took almost six months—hard, grueling labor, sixteen hours a day, dawn to dusk. Journeying halfway across the continent was a never-to-be-forgotten experience for those who did it. The wagon trains, carrying the dreams of thousands of individuals, reproduced society in small focus: individualistic, hopeful, mobile, divided by age and gender roles, apprehensive, yet willing to strike out for the distant and the new.

Land for the Taking

As railroads pushed west in the 1870s and 1880s, locomotive trains replaced wagon trains, but the shift was gradual. Like many Americans, thousands of Europeans traveled by rail to designated outfitting places and then continued their trek in wagons drawn by oxen. Traffic flowed in both directions; eager settlers heading west passed defeated ones returning east. Immigrants from Asia and Mexico joined the flow by moving to the American West from the east and south.

Why did they come? In a word, land. The federal government had promised to give land to the head of each family that settled in the new territories. A popular camp song reflected this motive:

Come along, come along—don't be alarmed.
Uncle Sam is rich enough to give us all a farm.

Homestead Act of 1862
Legislation granting 160 acres of land to anyone who paid a $10 fee and pledged to live on and cultivate the land for five years. The act encouraged a large migration to the West.

Uncle Sam owned about 1 billion acres of land in the 1860s, much of it mountain and desert land unsuited for agriculture. By 1890, the government had distributed 48 million acres under the **Homestead Act of 1862.** But far more acres were sold—to private citizens, to corporations, and to the states. Huge tracts were granted to railroad companies to tempt them to build across the unsettled West.

The Homestead Act of 1862, a law of great significance, gave 160 acres of land to anyone who would pay a $10 registration and pledge to live on it and cultivate it for five years. The offer set off a mass migration of land-hungry Europeans dazzled by a country that gave its land away. Americans also seized on the act's provisions, and between 1862 and 1900, nearly 600,000 families claimed free homesteads under it.

Yet the Homestead Act did not work as Congress had hoped. Tailored to the timber and water conditions of the East, the act was not suited to the semiarid West. Without irrigation, a 160-acre farm was simply not large enough to be self-supporting on the Great Plains.

The Timber Culture Act of 1873 attempted to adjust the Homestead Act to western conditions. It allowed homesteaders to claim an additional 160 acres if they planted trees on a quarter of it within four years. A moderately successful act, it encouraged forestation and expanded farms to a workable size. By contrast, the Desert Land Act of 1877, which allowed individuals to obtain 640 acres in the arid states for $1.25 an acre, provided that they irrigated part of it within three years, invited wholesale fraud; irrigation was sometimes interpreted by ranchers as a bucket of water dumped on the ground.

The Timber and Stone Act of 1878 permitted anyone in California, Nevada, Oregon, and Washington to buy up to 160 acres of forestland, deemed "unfit for cultivation," for $2.50 an acre. As the ranchers had, timber companies used employees to file false claims and other fraudulent practices to acquire more land than the law allowed.

Speculators made ingenious use of the land laws. Sending agents in advance of settlement, they moved along choice river bottoms or irrigable areas, accumulating large holdings to be held for high prices. In the arid West, where control of water meant control of the surrounding land, shrewd ranchers plotted their holdings accordingly. In Colorado, one cattleman, John F. Iliff, owned only 105 small parcels of land, but by placing them around the few waterholes, he effectively dominated an empire stretching over 6,000 square miles.

Half a billion acres of western land were given or sold to speculators and corporations. At the same time, only 600,000 homestead patents were issued, covering 80 million acres. Thus only one acre in every nine initially went to individual pioneers, the intended beneficiaries of the nation's largesse.

Water, in fact, became the dominant western issue, since much of the trans-Mississippi West was arid, receiving less than 20 inches of rainfall annually. People speculated in water as if it were gold and planned great irrigation systems to "make the desert bloom." The federal government helped fuel their dreams. The 1902 **National Reclamation Act (Newlands Act)** set aside most of the proceeds from the sale of public lands in sixteen western states to finance irrigation projects. Over the next decades, dams, canals, and irrigation systems channeled water into dry areas, creating a "hydraulic" society where control of water often brought enormous power.

National Reclamation Act (Newlands Act) Passed in 1902, legislation that set aside the majority of the proceeds from the sale of public land in sixteen Western states to fund irrigation projects in the arid states.

As beneficiaries of the government's policy of land grants for railway construction, the railroad companies were the West's largest landowners. Eager to have immigrants settle on the land they owned and also to boost their freight and passenger business, the companies sent attractive sales brochures to the East and Europe, touting life in the West. Union Pacific's advertisement described the rocky Platte Valley in Nebraska as "a flowery meadow clothed in nutritious grasses."

As new areas of the West opened, they were organized as territories under the control of Congress and the president. The president appointed the governor and judges in each territory; Congress detailed their duties, set their budgets, and oversaw their activities. Territorial officials had almost absolute power over the territories.

The Spanish-Speaking Southwest

In the nineteenth century, almost all Spanish-speaking people in the United States lived in California, Arizona, New Mexico, Texas, and Colorado. Their numbers were small, but the influence of their culture and institutions was large. In some respects, the southwestern frontier was more Hispanic American than Anglo-American.

Pushing northward from Mexico, the Spanish brought to the Southwest irrigation, stock raising, weaving, and mining. Both the Spanish and, later, the Mexicans created the legal framework for distributing land and water. They gave large grants of land to communities for grazing, to individuals as rewards for service, and to the various Indian pueblos (villages).

The Californios, descendants of the original colonizers of California, began to lose their once vast landholdings to drought and mortgages after the 1860s. Some turned to banditry; others lived in poverty and remembered better days. But as the Californios died out, Mexican Americans continued the Spanish Mexican influence. In 1880, one-quarter of the residents of Los Angeles County were Spanish-speaking.

In New Mexico, Hispanic culture dominated the territory. The movement of Anglo ranchers onto contested Spanish land grants met with resistance by hooded nightriders in the 1880s. Spanish-speaking citizens remained the majority ethnic group in New Mexico until the 1940s.

Throughout the Southwest, the Spanish Mexican heritage gave a distinctive shape to society. Men headed the family and dominated economic life. Women had substantial economic rights (though few political ones), and they enjoyed a status their English American counterparts did not have. Wives kept full control of property acquired before marriage; they also held half-title to all property in a marriage, which later caused many southwestern states to pass community property laws.

In addition, the Spanish Mexican heritage fostered a modified economic caste system, a strong Roman Catholic influence, and the primary use of the Spanish language. Continuous immigration from Mexico kept language and cultural ties strong. Spanish names and customs spread, even among Anglos. Confronted by Sheriff Pat Garrett in a darkened room, New Mexico's famous outlaw, Billy the Kid, died asking, "*Quién es? Quién es?*" ("Who is it? Who is it?")

THE BONANZA WEST

Between 1850 and 1900, wave after wave of newcomers swept over the trans-Mississippi West. There were riches for the taking, hidden in gold-washed streams, spread lushly over grass-covered prairies, or available in the gullible minds of greedy newcomers. The nineteenth-century West took shape in the search for mining, cattle, and land bonanzas that drew eager settlers from the East and around the world.

As with all bonanzas, the consequences in the West were uneven growth, boom-and-bust economic cycles, and wasted resources. As a society, it seemed constantly in the making. People moved here and there, following river bottoms, gold strikes, railroad tracks, and other opportunities. "Instant cities" such as San Francisco, Salt

Lake City, and Denver arose, and cow towns and mining camps sprang up seemingly overnight. San Francisco grew to a third of a million people in a little more than two decades; Boston took more than two centuries to do the same.

The Mining Bonanza

Mining was the first important magnet to attract people to the West. Many came to "strike it rich" in gold and silver, but at least half the newcomers had no intention of working in the mines. Instead, they provided food, clothing, and services to the thousands of miners. For example, Leland Stanford and Collis P. Huntington, who later built the Central Pacific Railroad, set up a general store in Sacramento where they sold shovels and supplies.

The California **Gold Rush of 1849** began the mining boom and set the pattern for subsequent experience. Individual prospectors made the first strikes, discovering pockets of gold along streams flowing westward from the Sierra Nevada. Practicing a simple process called **placer mining,** they needed only a shovel, a washing pan, and a good claim. As the placers gave out, a great deal of gold remained, but it was locked in quartz or buried deep in the earth. Mining became an expensive business, far beyond the reach of the average miner.

Large corporations moved in to dig the deep shafts and finance costly equipment. Eastern and European financiers assumed control, labor became unionized, and mining towns took on some of the characteristics of industrial cities. Individual prospectors, meanwhile, dashed on to the next find. Unlike other frontiers, the mining frontier moved from west to east as the original California miners hurried eastward in search of the big strike.

In 1859, fresh strikes were made near Pikes Peak in Colorado and in the Carson River Valley of Nevada. News of both discoveries set off wild migrations, and the gold near Pikes Peak quickly played out. But the Nevada find uncovered a thick, bluish black ore that was almost pure silver and gold. A quick-witted drifter named Henry T. P. Comstock talked his way into partnership in the claim, and word of the **Comstock Lode** flashed over the mountains.

Thousands of miners climbed the Sierra Nevada that summer of 1859. But the biggest strike was yet to come. In 1873, John W. Mackay and three partners formed a company to dig deep into the mountain, and at 1167 feet they hit the Big Bonanza, a seam of gold and silver more than 54 feet wide. It was the richest discovery in the history of mining. Although most of the profits went to financiers and corporations, Mackay himself became the richest person in the world.

In the 1860s and 1870s, important strikes were made in Washington, Idaho, Nevada, Colorado, Montana, Arizona, and the Dakota Territory. Miners flocked from strike to strike, and new camps and mining towns sprang up overnight. The miners were extremely mobile, usually moving on when the pay dirt played out.

The final fling came in the Black Hills rush of 1874–1876. The army had tried to keep miners out of the area, the heart of the Sioux hunting grounds, and even sent a scientific party under Colonel George A. Custer to disprove the rumors of gold. Instead, Custer found gold all over the hills, and the rush was on. Miners, gamblers, desperadoes, and prostitutes flocked to Deadwood, the most lawless of all the mining camps.

Towns such as Deadwood, in the Dakota Territory; Virginia City, Nevada; Leadville, Colorado; and Tombstone, Arizona, began a new process in the frontier experience. Unlike the rural setting of the farming frontier, the mining camp became the germ of a city, and theaters, the latest fashions, schools, and lending libraries came quickly to them, providing civilized refinements not available on other frontiers. But urbanization also created the need for municipal government, sanitation, and law enforcement.

Gold Rush of 1849 Individual prospectors made the first gold strikes along the Sierra Nevada Mountains in 1849, touching off the mining boom that helped shape the development of the West and set the pattern for subsequent strikes in other regions.

placer mining A form of mining that required little technology or skill, placer mining techniques included using a shovel and a washing pan to separate gold from the ore in streams and riverbeds.

Comstock Lode Discovered in 1859 near Virginia City, Nevada, this ore deposit was the richest discovery in the history of mining. Between 1859 and 1879, it produced silver and gold worth more than $306 million.

Mining camps were governed by a simple democracy. Soon after a strike, the miners in the area met to organize a mining "district" and adopted rules governing behavior in it. Rules regulated the size and boundaries of claims, established procedures for settling disputes, and set penalties for crimes. Petty criminals were banished from the district; serious offenders were hanged. Early visitors to the mining country were struck by the way miners, solitary and competitive, joined together, founded a camp, and created a society.

The camps were mostly male, made up of "men who can rough it" and a few women of "spirit and energy." Prostitutes followed the camps around the West, and "respectable" women were objects of curiosity. Some women worked claims, but more often they took jobs as cooks, housekeepers, and seamstresses—for wages considerably higher than in the East.

The lure of gold drew large numbers of Chinese, Chileans, Peruvians, Mexicans, English, French, and Germans to the mining camps. The Latin Americans brought valuable mining techniques, and the painstaking Chinese profitably worked claims others had abandoned. In the 1860s, almost one-third of the miners in the West were Chinese.

Hostility often surfaced against foreign miners, particularly the French, Latin Americans, and Chinese. In California, special taxes were levied to drive away foreign competition. Finally, after several riots and intense political pressure, Congress passed the Chinese Exclusion Act of 1882, which suspended immigration of Chinese laborers for ten years.

By the 1890s, the early mining bonanza was over. All told, the western mines contributed billions of dollars to the economy. They helped finance the Civil War and provided needed capital for industrialization. The vast boost in silver production thanks to the Comstock Lode changed the relative value of gold and silver, the bases of American currency. Bitter disputes over the currency affected politics and led to the famous "battle of the standards" during the presidential election of 1896 (see Chapter 20).

The mining frontier populated portions of the West and sped its political organization. Nevada, Idaho, and Montana were granted early statehood because of mining. Merchants, editors, lawyers, and ministers flocked to the frontier and established permanent settlements. But the industry also left behind painful scars in the form of ravaged Indian reservations, pitted hills, and lonely ghost towns.

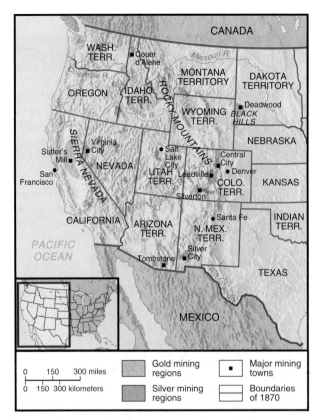

MINING REGIONS OF THE WEST *Gold and silver mines dotted the West, drawing settlers and encouraging political organization in many areas.* ∎

Gold from the Roots Up: The Cattle Bonanza

"There's gold from the grass roots down," said California Joe, a guide in the gold districts of the Dakota Territory in the 1870s, "but there's more gold from the grass roots up." Ranchers began to recognize the potential of the vast grasslands of the West. The Plains were covered with buffalo or grama grass, a wiry variety with short, hard stems. Cattle thrived on it.

For twenty years after 1865, cattle ranching dominated the "open range," a vast, fenceless area extending from the Texas Panhandle north into Canada. Such techniques of the business as branding, roundups, and roping came from Mexico. The

A Look at the Past

Cowboy Clothing

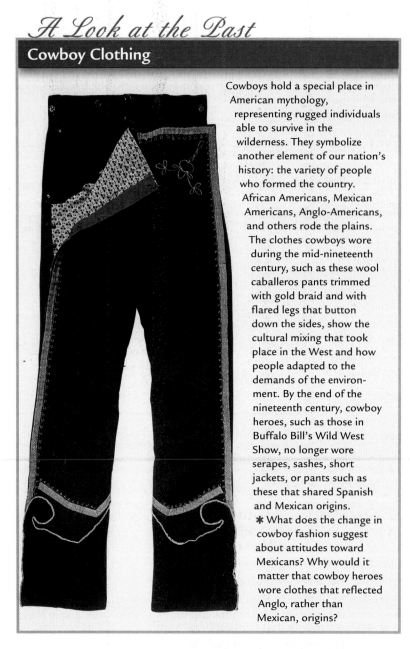

Cowboys hold a special place in American mythology, representing rugged individuals able to survive in the wilderness. They symbolize another element of our nation's history: the variety of people who formed the country. African Americans, Mexican Americans, Anglo-Americans, and others rode the plains. The clothes cowboys wore during the mid-nineteenth century, such as these wool caballeros pants trimmed with gold braid and with flared legs that button down the sides, show the cultural mixing that took place in the West and how people adapted to the demands of the environment. By the end of the nineteenth century, cowboy heroes, such as those in Buffalo Bill's Wild West Show, no longer wore serapes, sashes, short jackets, or pants such as these that shared Spanish and Mexican origins.

✱ What does the change in cowboy fashion suggest about attitudes toward Mexicans? Why would it matter that cowboy heroes wore clothes that reflected Anglo, rather than Mexican, origins?

cattle themselves, the famous Texas longhorns, also came from Mexico. Although their meat was coarse and stringy, they fed a nation hungry for beef at the end of the Civil War.

The problem was to get the beef to eastern markets, and Joseph G. McCoy, a livestock shipper from Illinois, solved it. Looking for a way to market Texas beef, McCoy conceived the idea of taking the cattle on "long drives" to railheads in Kansas. After several rebuffs, the persistent McCoy signed a contract in 1867 with the Hannibal and St. Joseph Railroad. Searching for an appropriate rail junction, he settled on the sleepy Kansas town of Abilene.

In September 1867, McCoy shipped the first train of twenty cars of longhorn cattle. By the end of the year, a thousand carloads had followed, all headed for Chicago markets. In 1871, some 700,000 head of Texas cattle reached Abilene. The profits were enormous; drivers bought cheap Texas steers for $7 a head and sold them for $60 or $70 each at a northern railhead.

Cowboys pushed steers northward on the Chisholm and other trails in herds of two to three thousand. Novels and films have portrayed the mounted herdsmen as white, but at least one-quarter of them were black and possibly another quarter were Mexicans. A typical crew on the trail north might have eight men, half of them black or Mexican. Most of the trail bosses were white; they earned about $125 a month.

Like miners, cattlemen lived beyond the formal reach of the law and so established their own. A cowboy who shot another was hanged on the spot. Ranchers adopted rules for cattle ownership, branding, roundups, and drives, and they formed associations to enforce them. The Wyoming Stock Growers' Association, the largest and most formidable, was often "the law" in Wyoming and extended its reach well into Colorado, Nebraska, Montana, and the Dakota Territory.

Hollywood to the contrary, there was little violence in the booming cow towns. Doc Holliday and William B. (Bat) Masterson never killed anyone, and the number of homicides in a year never topped five in any cattle town. In fact, famous western sheriffs such as Wild Bill Hickok and Wyatt Earp repaired streets and sidewalks far more frequently than they used their guns.

By 1880, more than six million head of cattle had been driven to northern markets. But the era of the great cattle drive was ending. Farmers were planting wheat on the old buffalo ranges; barbed wire, a recent invention, cut across the trails and divided up the big ranches. Mechanical improvements in slaughtering, refrigerated

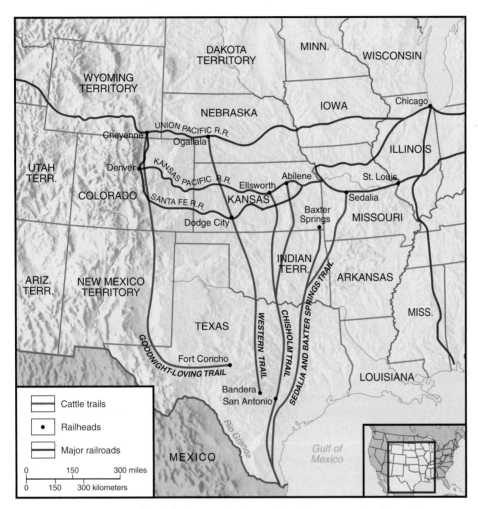

CATTLE TRAILS   *Cattle raised in Texas were driven along the cattle trails to the northern railheads, and trains carried them to market.* ■

transportation, and cold storage modernized the industry. Ranchers bred the Texas longhorns with heavier Hereford and Angus bulls, and as the new breeds proved profitable, more and more ranches opened on the northern ranges. By the mid-1880s, large investments had transformed ranching into big business, often controlled by absentee owners.

By 1885, the northern ranges were becoming dangerously overcrowded. To make matters worse, the winter of 1885–1886 was cold, and the following summer was one of the hottest on record. Waterholes dried up; the grass turned brown. Beef prices fell. The winter of 1886–1887 was one of the worst in western history. Temperatures dropped to 45 degrees below zero, and cattle that once would have saved themselves by drifting ahead of the storms perished when they came up against the new barbed wire fences. When the snows thawed, ranchers found tens of thousands of carcasses stacked up against fences.

The cattle business recovered, but it took different directions. Outside capital, so plentiful in the boom years, dried up. Ranchers began fencing their lands, reducing the size of their herds, and growing hay for winter food. To the dismay of cowboys, mowing machines and hay rakes became as important as chuck wagons and branding irons. The last roundup on the northern ranges took place in 1905. Ranches grew smaller, and some ranchers switched to raising sheep. Homesteaders, armed with barbed wire and new strains of wheat, pushed onto the Plains, and the day of the open range was over.

Sodbusters on the Plains: The Farming Bonanza

Like miners and cattlemen, millions of farmers moved west in the decades after 1870 to seek crop bonanzas and new ways of life. Some realized their dreams; many fought just to survive.

Between 1870 and 1900, farmers cultivated more land than ever before in American history. They peopled the Plains from the Dakota Territory to Texas, pushed the Indians out of their last sanctuary in Oklahoma, and poured into the basins and foothills of the Rockies. By 1900, the western half of the nation contained almost 30 percent of the population, compared to less than 1 percent just a half-century earlier.

Unlike mining, farm settlement often followed predictable patterns, taking population from states east of the frontier line and moving gradually westward. The movement slumped during the depression of the 1870s, but after several years of above-average rainfall on the Great Plains, a new wave of optimism carried thousands more west. Between 1870 and 1900, the population on the Plains tripled.

In some areas, the newcomers were blacks who had fled the South, fed up with beatings and murders, crop liens, and the Black Codes that institutionalized their subordinate status. In 1879, about six thousand African Americans known as the **Exodusters** left their homes in Louisiana, Mississippi, and Texas to establish new and freer lives in Kansas, the home of John Brown and the Free-Soil campaigns of the 1850s. Once there, they farmed or worked as laborers; women worked in the fields alongside the men or cleaned houses and took in washing to make ends meet. All told, the Exodusters homesteaded 20,000 acres of land, and though they met prejudice, it was not as extreme as they had known at home.

Other African Americans moved to Oklahoma, thinking they might establish the first African American state. Whether headed for Oklahoma or Kansas, they picked up and moved in sizable groups that were based on family units; they took with them the customs they had known, and in their new homes they were able, for the first time, to have some measure of self-government.

For blacks and whites alike, farming on the Plains presented new problems. There was little surface water, and wells ranged between 50 and 500 feet deep. Lumber for homes and fences was also scarce. Water could be brought to the surface by windmills and lumber could be imported, but both solutions required more money than most farmers had.

Unable to afford wood, farmers often started out in dreary sod houses. Cut into 3-foot sections, the thick prairie sod was laid like brick. Since glass was scarce, cloth hung over the windows; a blanket was hung from the ceiling to make two rooms. A sod house provided little light or air but cost only $2.78 to build.

Outside, the Plains environment sorely tested the men and women who moved there. Neighbors were distant; the land stretched on as far as the eye could see. Always the wind blew. A sense of loneliness and desolation pervaded prairie life.

In winter, savage storms swept the open grasslands. Summertime temperatures stayed near 110 degrees for weeks at a time. Fearsome rainstorms, building in the summer's heat, beat down the young corn and wheat. The summers also brought grasshoppers, flying in swarms so huge they shut out the sun. The grasshoppers ate everything in sight: crops, clothing, mosquito netting, tree bark, even plow handles.

New Farming Methods

Farmers embraced new technology to meet conditions on the Plains. Cheap and effective fencing material became available with the invention of barbed wire by an Illinois farmer, Joseph Glidden, in 1874. Other inventions, similarly designed to meet the new conditions, included James Oliver's patented chilled-iron plow with a smooth-surface mold board that did not clog in the thick prairie soils.

Exodusters A group of about six thousand African Americans who left their homes in Louisiana, Mississippi, and Texas in 1879, seeking freer lives in Kansas, where they worked as farmers or laborers.

Farming techniques also adapted to the new environment. **Dry farming** helped compensate for the lack of rainfall. By plowing furrows 12 to 14 inches deep and creating a dust mulch to fill the furrows, farmers loosened the soil and slowed evaporation. New milling methods were developed in the 1870s to process the hard-kerneled imported varieties of wheat. Scientific agriculture advanced with new discoveries linking soil minerals and plant growth. The Hatch Act, passed in 1887, established a network of agricultural experiment stations that provided information about the new discoveries to farmers.

In the late 1870s, huge **bonanza farms** arose, run by the new machinery and financed with outside capital. Oliver Dalrymple, the most famous of the bonanza farmers, hired armies of workers, bought machinery by the carload, and planted on a scale that dazzled the West. Using 200 pairs of harrows, 155 binders, and 16 threshers, Dalrymple produced 600,000 bushels of wheat in 1881. He and other bonanza managers profited from the economics of scale, buying materials at wholesale prices and receiving rebates from the railroads.

Then a period of drought began. Rainfall dropped between 1885 and 1890, and the large-scale growers found it hard to compete with smaller farmers who diversified their crops and cultivated more intensively. Many of the large bonanzas slowly disintegrated, and Dalrymple himself went bankrupt in 1896.

Discontent on the Farm

Struck by the drabness of rural life, Oliver H. Kelley, a clerk in the Department of Agriculture, in 1867 founded the **National Grange of the Patrons of Husbandry,** known simply as the Grange. The Grange provided social, cultural, and educational activities for its members. Its constitution banned involvement in politics, but Grangers often ignored it and supported railroad regulation and other measures.

The Grange grew rapidly during the depression of the 1870s, and by 1875, it had more than 800,000 members. Local Granges set up cooperative stores, grain elevators, warehouses, insurance companies, and farm machinery factories. Many failed, but in the meantime the organization made its mark. Discontent grew, spilling over into the turbulent Populist movement of the 1890s. (See Chapter 20 for a more detailed discussion.)

Like the cattle boom, the farming boom ended sharply after 1887. A severe drought that year cut harvests, and other droughts followed in 1889 and 1894. Thousands of new farmers were wiped out on the western Plains. Between 1888 and 1892, more than half the population of western Kansas left.

Farmers grew angry and restless. They complained about declining crop prices, rising railroad rates, and heavy mortgages. In the wheat-growing Plains, the economic problems were persistent. Returning home to Iowa in 1889, the author Hamlin Garland found his farming friends caught up "in a sullen rebellion against government and against God."

Although many farmers were unhappy, the peopling of the West in those years transformed American agriculture. The states beyond the Mississippi became the

A Look at the Past

Barbed Wire

Barbed wire forever altered land use in the West. Perfected in 1874, barbed wire made effective, economical fencing. Reflecting its importance to western farmers, barbed wire soon came in hundreds of varieties, including decorative versions. Most variations performed equally well, however, making so many designs unnecessary. ✱ Why do you think so many types existed?

dry farming A farming technique developed to allow farming in the more arid parts of the West. Furrows were plowed a foot or so deep and filled with a dust mulch to loosen soil and slow evaporation.

bonanza farms Huge farms covering thousands of acres on the Great Plains. In relying on large size and new machinery, they represented a development in agriculture similar to that taking place in industry.

National Grange of the Patrons of Husbandry Founded by Oliver H. Kelly in 1867, the Grange sought to relieve the drabness of farm life by providing a social, educational, and cultural outlet for its members. It also set up grain elevators, cooperative stores, warehouses, insurance companies, and farm machinery factories.

Chronology

1849	Gold draws prospectors to California
1859	More gold discoveries are made in Colorado and Nevada
1862	Congress passes the Homestead Act, encouraging western settlement
1864	Nevada is admitted to the Union ■ Colonel John Chivington leads a massacre of Indians at Sand Creek, Colorado
1865–1867	Sioux fight white miners and the U.S. Army in the Great Sioux War
1866	"Long drive" of cattle touches off cattle bonanzas
1867	Horace Greeley urges Easterners to go west ■ National Grange of the Patrons of Husbandry is founded to enrich farmers' lives
1867–1868	Policy of "small reservations" for Indians is adopted
1873	Congress passes the Timber Culture Act ■ Big Bonanza is discovered on the Comstock Lode in Nevada
1874	Joseph F. Glidden invents barbed wire ■ Discovery of gold in Dakota Territory sets off Black Hills Gold Rush
1876	Colorado is admitted to the Union ■ Custer and his men are defeated and killed by the Sioux at Little Bighorn
1883	Museum expedition discovers fewer than two hundred buffalo in the West ■ Buffalo Bill Cody organizes and begins touring with his Wild West Show
1886–1887	Severe drought and winter damage cattle and farming bonanzas
1887	Congress passes the Dawes Severalty Act, making Indians individual landowners ■ Hatch Act provides funds for the establishment of agricultural experiment stations
1889	Washington, Montana, and the Dakotas are admitted to the Union ■ Oklahoma Territory is opened to settlement
1890	Idaho and Wyoming are admitted to Union ■ Teton Sioux are massacred at Wounded Knee, South Dakota
1893	Young historian Frederick Jackson Turner analyzes the closing of the frontier

garden land of the nation. California sent fruit, wine, and wheat to eastern markets. Under the Mormons, Utah flourished with irrigation. Texas beef stocked the country's tables, and vast wheat fields, stretching to the horizon, covered Minnesota, the Dakotas, Montana, and eastern Colorado. All produced more than Americans could consume. By 1890, American farmers were exporting large amounts of wheat and other crops.

Farmers became more commercial and scientific. They needed to know more and work harder. Mail-order houses and rural free delivery diminished their isolation and tied them ever closer to the national future. "This is a new age to the farmer," said a statistician in the Department of Agriculture in 1889. "He is now, more than ever before, a citizen of the world."

The Final Fling

As the West filled in with people, pressure mounted on the federal government to open the last Indian territory, Oklahoma, to settlers. Congress and the president responded, forcing the Creek and Seminole to surrender their rights. President

Benjamin Harrison announced the opening of the Oklahoma District as of noon, April 22, 1889.

Preparation was feverish all along the frontier. On the morning of April 22, nearly 100,000 people lined the Oklahoma borders. At noon, the starting flag dropped, and horses and wagons loaded with people and hopes moved into the "last" territory. By sunset that day, settlers had claimed twelve thousand homesteads, and the 1,920,000 acres of the Oklahoma District were officially settled. Reflecting the speed of western settlement, a character in Edna Ferber's novel *Cimarron* declared: "Creation! Hell! That took six days. This was done in one."

CONCLUSION: THE MEANING OF THE WEST

Between the Civil War and 1900, the West witnessed one of the greatest migrations in history. With the Indians driven into smaller and smaller areas, farms, ranches, mines, and cities rose up on the vast lands from the Mississippi to the Pacific. The 1890 census noted that for the first time in the country's history, "there can hardly be said to be a frontier line."

Picking up the theme, historian Frederick Jackson Turner, in an influential 1893 paper, claimed that the existence of the frontier and of free land explained American development. It shaped customs and character; gave rise to independence, self-confidence, and individualism; and fostered invention and adaptation. Historians have substantially modified **Turner's thesis** by pointing to frontier conservatism and imitativeness, the influence of various ethnic groups, and the persistence of European ideas and institutions. Most recently, they have shown that family and community loomed just as large as individualism on the frontier.

Rejecting Turner almost completely, a group of "new Western historians" has advanced a different and complex view of the West. They emphasize the region's racial and ethnic diversity, show a concern for the environmental consequences of the westward migration, detail the role of women, and trace the struggles between economic interests. White English-speaking Americans, they suggest, could be said to have conquered the West rather than settled it.

The West, in this view, was not settled by a wave of white migrants moving across the continent but by a set of waves—Anglo, Mexican American, African American, Asian American, and others—moving from different directions and interacting with one another and with Native Americans. These movements and clashes created the modern West, a process that continues today.

But of one thing there can be no doubt: the West as an image and an economic reality exerted a powerful influence in the nineteenth and twentieth centuries. Immigrants were drawn there, and natural resources were hauled from there. The West was the first American empire, and it had a profound impact on the American mind and imagination.

Turner's thesis Put forth by historian Frederick Jackson Turner in an 1893 paper, this thesis asserted that the existence of a frontier and its settlement had shaped American character; given rise to individualism, independence, and self-confidence; and fostered the American spirit of invention and adaptation.

KEY TERMS

RECOMMENDED READING

The best traditional account of the movement west is Ray Allen Billington, *Westward Expansion* (1967), which also has a first-rate bibliography. Walter Prescott Webb, *The Great Plains* (1931) offers a fascinating analysis of development on the Plains.

For examples of the work of "new Western historians," see Donald Worster, *Rivers of Empire* (1985), a powerful study of the "hydraulic" society, and his *Under Western Skies: Nature and History in the American West* (1992); William Cronon, *Nature's Metropolis: Chicago and the Great West* (1991), a provocative analysis of the relationship of Chicago and the West; Patricia Nelson Limerick, *The Legacy of Conquest* (1987); and Richard White, *"It's Your Misfortune and None of My Own": A History of the American West* (1991).

More recent authors have taken fresh and stimulating looks at older or ignored questions. Robert R. Dykstra, *The Cattle Towns* (1968), examines five Kansas cattle towns, with interesting results. Elliott West discusses the Plains in *The Contested Plains: Indians, Goldseekers, and the Rush to Colorado* (1998). Gregory Nobles, *American Frontiers: Cultural Encounters and Continental Conquest* (1997), Eugene P. Moehring, *Urbanism and Empire in the Far West, 1840–1890* (2004), and David M. Wrobel, *Promised Lands: Promotion, Memory, and the Creation of the American West* (2002), offer engaging interpretations of frontier history. Martha A. Sandweis, *Print the Legend: Photography and the American West* (2002), is superb on the subject.

There are a number of insightful recent studies of the environment, including Andrew C. Isenberg, *The Destruction of the Bison: An Environmental History, 1750–1920* (2000), Shepard Krech III, *The Ecological Indian: Myth and History* (1999), Karl Jacoby, *Crimes Against Nature: Squatters, Poachers, Thieves, and the Hidden History of American Conservation* (2001), and Dan L. Flores, *The Natural West: Environmental History in the Great Plains and Rocky Mountains* (2001). Susan Lee Johnson, *Roaring Camp: The Social World of the California Gold Rush* (2000), is a fascinating examination of the gold camps.

On the Native Americans, there are a number of valuable works, including Colin G. Calloway, *One Vast Winter Count: The Native American West before Lewis and Clark* (2003), Steven Conn, *History's Shadow: Native Americans and Historical Consciousness in the Nineteenth Century* (2004), R. Douglas Hurt's excellent *Indian Agriculture in America* (1987), Janet A. McDonnell, *The Dispossession of the American Indian, 1887–1934* (1991), Robert A. Trennert, Jr., *The Phoenix Indian School* (1988), Scott Riney, *The Rapid City Indian School, 1898–1933* (1999), Paul H. Carlson, *The Plains Indians* (1998), and John William Sayer, *Ghost Dancing the Law: The Wounded Knee Trials* (1997).

Nell Irvin Painter, *Exodusters: Black Migration to Kansas After Reconstruction* (1976), tells the story of the Exodusters, as Monroe Lee Billington does for New Mexico's *Buffalo Soldiers, 1866–1900* (1991). Also see Frank N. Schubert, *Buffalo Soldiers, Braves, and the Brass* (1993), William A. Dobak and Thomas D. Phillips, *The Black Regulars, 1866–1898* (2001), and James N. Leiker, *Racial Borders: Black Soldiers along the Rio Grande* (2002).

Julie Roy Jeffrey, *Frontier Women: The Trans-Mississippi West* (1979), Virginia Scharff, *Twenty Thousand Roads: Women, Movement, and the West* (2003), Quitard Taylor and Shirley Ann Wilson Moore, *African American Women Confront the West, 1600–2000* (2003), Joanna L. Stratton, *Pioneer Women: Voices from the Kansas Frontier* (1981), and Deena J. González, *Refusing the Favor: The Spanish-Mexican Women of Santa Fe, 1820–1880* (1999), are perceptive works on a neglected topic. John Mack Faragher, *Women and Men on the Overland Trail* (1979), and John Phillip Reid, *Law for the Elephant* (1980), examine relationships on the trails west.

SUGGESTED WEB SITES

Indian Affairs: Laws and Treaties, compiled and edited by Charles J. Kappler (1904)
digital.library.okstate.edu/kappler
This digitized text at Oklahoma State University includes preremoval treaties with the Five Civilized Tribes and other tribes.

Native American Documents Project
www.csusm.edu/projects/nadp/nadp.htm
California State University at San Marcos has several digital documents relating to Native Americans on this site.

Geronimo
odur.let.rug.nl/~usa/B/geronimo/geronixx.htm
This site contains biographical and autobiographical information about this famous Native American who resisted European American domination.

National Museum of the American Indian
www.nmai.si.edu/
The Smithsonian Institution maintains this site, providing information about the museum. The museum is dedicated to everything about Native Americans.

The Northern Great Plains, 1880–1920: Photographs from the Fred Hultstrand and F. A. Pazandak Photograph Collections
memory.loc.gov/ammem/award97/ndfahtml/ngphome.html
This American Memory site from the Library of Congress contains collections from the Institute for Regional Studies at North Dakota State University, including 900 photographs of rural and small town life at the turn of the century.

On the Trail in Kansas

www.Kancoll.org/galtrl.htm

This Kansas collection site holds several good primary sources with images concerning the Oregon Trail and America's early movement westward.

"California as I Saw It": First-Person Narratives of California's Early Years, 1849–1900

memory.loc.gov/ammem/cbhtml/cbhome.html

This site is a part of the American Memory series and contains "full texts and illustrations of 190 works documenting the formative era of California's history through eyewitness accounts." It covers the Gold Rush, the interaction of various groups, and the settling of the region.

Home on the Range/Cowboy Heritage

www.vlib.us/old_west/cowboy.html

This site tells this history of the cattle trails and towns such as Dodge City with useful text, links, documents, and maps.

The Evolution of the Conservation Movement, 1850–1920

memory.loc.gov/ammem/amrvhtml/conshome.html

This American Memory site brings together scores of primary sources and photographs about "the historical formation and cultural foundations of the movement to conserve and protect America's natural heritage."

Heroes and Villains in Kansas

www.Kancoll.org/galhero.htm

The Kansas Collection Gallery of both famous and little known people who made up the history of the state.

Blacks in Blue
The Buffalo Soldiers in the West

On Saturday afternoons, youngsters used to sit in darkened movie theaters and cheer the victories of the U.S. Cavalry over the Indians. Typically, the Indians were about to capture a wagon train when army bugles suddenly sounded. Then the blue-coated cavalry charged over the hill. Few in the theaters cheered for the Indians; fewer still noticed the absence of black faces among the on-charging cavalry. But, in fact, more than two thousand African American cavalrymen served on the western frontier between 1867 and 1890. Known as the "buffalo soldiers," they made up one-fifth of the U.S. Cavalry.

Black troops were first used on a large scale during the Civil War. Organized in segregated units, with white officers, they fought with distinction. Nearly 180,000 blacks served in the Union army; 34,000 of them died. When the war ended in 1865, Congress for the first time authorized black troops to serve in the regular peacetime army. In addition to infantry, it created two cavalry regiments—the Ninth and Tenth, which became known as the famous buffalo soldiers.

Like other black regiments, the Ninth and Tenth Cavalry had white officers who took special examinations before they could serve. The chaplains were assigned not only to preach but to teach reading, writing, and arithmetic. The food was poor; racism was widespread. The army stocked the first black units with worn-out horses, a serious matter to men whose lives depended on the speed and stamina of their mounts. "Since our first mount in 1867 this regiment has received nothing but broken down horses and repaired equipment," an officer said in 1870.

Many white officers refused to serve with black troops. George A. Custer, the handsome "boy general," turned down a position in the Ninth and joined the new Seventh Cavalry, headed for disaster at Little Bighorn. The *Army and Navy Journal* carried ads that told a similar story:

**A FIRST LIEUTENANT
OF INFANTRY**
(white)
Stationed at a
very desirable post
in the Department of the South
desires a transfer with
an officer of the same grade
on equal terms
if in a white regiment
but if in a colored regiment
a reasonable bonus
would be expected.

There was no shortage of black troops for the officers to lead. Blacks enlisted because the army offered some advancement in a closed society. It also paid $13 a month, plus room and board.

In 1867, the Ninth and Tenth Cavalry were posted to the West, where they remained for two decades. Under Colonel Benjamin H. Grierson, a Civil War hero, the Tenth went to Fort Riley, Kansas; the regiment arrived in the midst of a great Indian war. The Kiowa, Comanche, Cheyenne, Arapaho, and Sioux were on the warpath. Troopers of the Tenth defended farms, stages, trains, and work crews building railroad tracks to the West. Cornered by a band of Cheyenne, they beat back the attack and won a new name. They had been known as the "brunettes" or "Africans," but the Cheyenne now called them the buffalo soldiers, a name that soon ap-

plied to all African American soldiers in the West.

From 1868 to 1874, the Tenth served on the Kansas frontier. The dull winter days were filled with drills and scouting parties outside the post. In spring and summer, the good weather brought forth new forays. Indian bands raided farms and ranches and stampeded cattle herds on the way north from Texas. They struck and then melted back into the reservations.

The Ninth Cavalry also had a difficult job. Commanded by Colonel Edward Hatch, who had served with Grierson in the Civil War, it was stationed in West Texas and along the Rio Grande. The summers were so hot that men collapsed with sunstroke, the winters so cold that water froze in canteens. Native Americans from outside the area frequently raided it. From the north, Kiowa and Comanche warriors rode down the Great Comanche War Trail; Kickapoo crossed the Rio Grande from Mexico. Gangs of Mexican bandits and restless Civil War veterans roamed and plundered at will.

In 1874–1875, the Ninth fought in the great Red River War, in which the Kiowa and Comanche, fed up with conditions on the reservations, revolted against Grant's peace policy. Marching, fighting, then marching again, the soldiers harried and wore out the Indians, who finally surrendered in the spring of 1875. Herded into a new and desolate reservation, the Mescalero Apache of New Mexico took to the warpath in 1877 and again in 1879. Each time, it took a year of grueling warfare to effect their surrender. In 1886, black cavalrymen surrounded and captured the famous Apache chief Geronimo. In that and

■ Although they were not, in fact, treated as well as the white soldiers in their regiments, many African American cavalrymen such as those pictured here were probably drawn into service by hard-sell recruitment posters promising them equal pay and rations and entitlement to any horses or goods taken from the Indians. ■

other campaigns, several buffalo soldiers won the Congressional Medal of Honor.

Black troops hunted Big Foot and his band before the slaughter at Wounded Knee in 1890, and they served in many of the West's most famous Indian battles. While one-third of all army recruits deserted between 1865 and 1890, the Ninth and Tenth Cavalry had few desertions. In 1880, the Tenth had the fewest desertions of any regiment in the country.

It was ironic that in the West, black men fought red men to benefit white men. Once the Indian wars ended, the buffalo soldiers worked to keep illegal settlers out of Indian or government land; much of this land was later opened to settlement. Both regiments saw action in the Spanish-American War, the Ninth at San Juan Hill, the Tenth in the fighting around Santiago. Unlike white veterans of the same campaigns, the old buffalo soldiers were forgotten in retirement, although some of them had the satisfaction of settling on the western lands they had done so much to pacify.

Questions for Discussion

✳ Why do you think the Indians named the black cavalrymen the "buffalo soldiers"?

✳ Why did many African American men join the military during this period? What larger social factors may have shaped their decision?

✳ Why did so few buffalo soldiers desert, at a time when many others did?

✳ How do the experiences of the buffalo soldiers compare to the experiences of African Americans in the military today? What has changed? Why?

Chapter 18

The Industrial Society

A Machine Culture

In 1876, Americans celebrated a century of independence. Survivors of a recent civil war, they observed the centenary proudly and rather self-consciously in song and speech and in a grand Centennial Exposition, held in Philadelphia, Pennsylvania.

Spread over hundreds of acres, the exposition occupied 180 buildings and attracted nine million visitors, about one-fifth of the country's population at the time. It focused more on the present than the past, featuring machines, inventions, and new products. Fairgoers saw linoleum, a new, easy-to-clean floor covering. For the first time, they tasted root beer and the exotic banana, wrapped in foil and selling for a dime. They saw their first bicycle, an awkward, high-wheeled contraption with solid tires.

Machinery was the focus of the exposition, and Machinery Hall was the most popular building. Here were the products of an ever-improving civilization. Long lines of the curious waited to see Alexander Graham Bell's new device, the telephone. Thomas A. Edison displayed several recent inventions. The typewriter, the elevator, and the Westinghouse railroad air brake similarly amazed the fairgoers.

But the exhibit drawing the largest crowds was the mighty Corliss engine, the focal point of the exposition. A giant steam engine, it dwarfed everything in Machinery Hall. Alone it supplied power for the eight thousand other machines on the exposition grounds. The Corliss captured the nation's imagination, symbolizing America's swift movement toward an industrial and urban society.

At the start of the Civil War, the United States lagged well behind industrializing nations such as Great Britain, France, and Germany. By 1900, it had vaulted far into the lead, with a manufacturing output that exceeded the *combined* output of its three European rivals. During the same years, cities grew, technology advanced, and farm production rose. Developments in manufacturing, mining, agriculture, transportation, and communication transformed American society.

INDUSTRIAL DEVELOPMENT

American industry owed its remarkable growth to several considerations. It fed on an abundance of natural resources: coal, iron, timber, petroleum, waterpower. Labor was also abundant, drawn from established farm families and the hosts of European immigrants who flocked to America. Nearly eight million immigrants arrived in the 1870s and 1880s; another fifteen million came between 1890 and 1914.

The burgeoning population led to expanded markets, which new devices such as the telegraph and telephone helped exploit. Swiftly growing urban populations devoured goods, and the railroads linked cities and opened a national market. Within its boundaries, the United States had the largest free trade market in the world, while tariff barriers partially protected its producers from outside competition.

Expansive market and labor conditions buoyed the confidence of European and American investors who provided large amounts of capital. Technological progress and invention increased productivity in many important industries and also helped foster a firm agricultural base, on which industrialization depended.

Eager to promote economic growth, government at all levels—federal, state, and local—gave manufacturers money, land, and other resources. The American system of government itself was a boon to industry, thanks to its stability, its commitment to the concept of private property, and its reluctance to regulate industrial activity.

In this atmosphere, entrepreneurs flourished. Taking steps crucial for industrialization, they organized, managed, and assumed the financial risks of the new enterprises. Admirers called them "captains of industry"; foes labeled them "robber barons." To some degree, they were both—creative *and* acquisitive. If sometimes they seemed larger than life, it was because they dealt in concepts, distances, and quantities often unknown to earlier generations.

■ *The Corliss engine, a "mechanical marvel" at the Centennial Exposition, was a prime example of the giantism so admired by the public.* ■

Industrial growth, it must be remembered, was neither steady nor inevitable. Growth varied from industry to industry and from year to year. It was concentrated in the North and East. The more sparsely settled West provided raw materials, while the South had to rebuild after wartime devastation.

Still, industrial development proceeded at an extraordinary pace. Between 1865 and 1914, the real gross national product (GNP)—the total monetary value of all goods and services produced in a year, with prices held stable—grew at an average rate of more than 4 percent a year. As one economic historian noted, "Never before had such rapid growth continued for so long."

AN EMPIRE ON RAILS

A revolution in transportation and communication occurred in the nineteenth century. The steamship sliced in half the time it took to cross the Atlantic. The telegraph, flashing messages almost instantaneously along miles of wire, transformed communications, as did the telephone a little later. But the railroad wrought the largest changes of all. Along with Bessemer steel, it was the most significant technical innovation of the century.

More than most innovations, the railroad dramatically affected economic and social life. It contributed advantages that canals and other inland waterways could not match. Those advantages included more direct routes, greater speed, greater safety and comfort than other modes of land travel, more dependable schedules, a larger volume of traffic, and year-round service. A day's land travel on stagecoach or horseback might cover 50 miles. The railroad covered 50 miles in little more than an hour. It went where canals and rivers did not go—directly to the loading platforms of great factories or across the arid West.

Linking widely separated cities and villages, the railroad ended the relative isolation and self-sufficiency of the country's "island communities." It tied people together, brought in outside products, fostered greater interdependence, and encouraged economic specialization. The railroad forged a national market and in so doing pointed the way toward mass production and mass consumption, two of the hallmarks of twentieth-century society.

It also pointed the way toward a new kind of business development. Railroads were America's first big business, stretching over thousands of miles, employing thousands of people, dealing with countless consumers, and requiring a scale of organization and decision making unknown in earlier business. Year by year, railroad companies consumed great quantities of iron, steel, coal, lumber, and glass; such purchases stimulated growth and employment in numerous industries.

No wonder, then, that the railroad captured the country's imagination so completely. Walt Whitman, the poet, chanted the locomotive's praises: "Emblem of motion and power—pulse of the continent. . . . Fierce-throated beauty!" For nearly a hundred years, children gathered at depots, paused in fields to wave as the express flashed by, listened at night to far-off whistles, and wondered what lay down the tracks. They lived in a world grown smaller.

Building the Empire

When the Civil War ended, the country already had 35,000 miles of track, and much of the railroad system east of the Mississippi River was in place. Farther west, the rail network stood poised on the edge of settlement. Although America already had nearly as much railroad track as the rest of the world, rail construction increased spectacularly after 1865. Trackage peaked at 254,037 miles in 1916, just before the industry began its long decline into the mid-twentieth century.

To build such an empire took vast amounts of capital. American and European investors provided some of the money; government supplied the rest. Altogether, local and state governments gave railroad companies about $525 million. In addition, the federal government donated millions of acres of public land to the railroad companies. Federal land grants helped build 18,738 miles of track, less than 8 percent of the rail system. The companies sometimes sold the land to raise cash but more often used it as security for bonds or loans.

Beyond doubt, the grants of cash and land promoted waste and corruption. The companies built fast and wastefully, eager to collect the subsidies that went with each mile of track. The corruption involved in the Crédit Mobilier is but one example of the excesses of the railroad companies.

Yet on balance, the grants probably worked more benefits than evils. As Congress had hoped, the grants were the lure for railroad building across the rugged, unsettled West, where it would be years before the revenues would repay construction. The grants seemed necessary in a nation that, unlike Europe, expected private enterprise to build the railroads. In return for aid, Congress required the railroads to carry government freight, troops, and mail at substantially reduced rates.

Linking the Nation via Trunk Lines

The early railroads may seem to have linked different regions, but in fact they did not. Built with little regard for through traffic, they were designed more to protect local interests than to tap outside markets. To avoid cooperating with other lines, they adopted conflicting schedules, built separate depots, and used tracks of varying widths.

The Civil War showed the value of fast, long-distance transportation, and after 1865, railroad managers worked to provide it. In a burst of consolidation, the large swallowed the small; integrated rail networks became a reality. Railroads also adopted standard schedules, signals, equipment, and finally, in 1866, the standard track width (or gauge) of 4 feet, 8½ inches.

In the Northeast, four great **trunk lines** took shape, all intended to link eastern seaports with the rich traffic of the Great Lakes and western rivers. Like a massive river system, trunk lines drew traffic from dozens of tributaries (feeder lines) and carried it to major markets. The Baltimore and Ohio Railroad was one. The Erie Railroad, running from New York City to Chicago, ran parallel to the New York Central Railroad built by Cornelius Vanderbilt. The fourth line, the Pennsylvania Railroad, initially ran from Philadelphia to Pittsburgh, but it was expanded to unite Cincinnati, Indianapolis, St. Louis, Chicago, New York City, Baltimore, and Washington. In the war-damaged South, consolidation took longer. But by 1900, just four decades after secession, the South had five major systems that tied into a national transportation network.

Over the rail system, passengers and freight moved in relative speed, comfort, and safety. Automatic couplers (1868), air brakes (1869), refrigerated cars (1867), dining cars, heated cars, Pullman sleeping cars, and stronger locomotives transformed railroad service. Passenger miles per year increased from 5 billion in 1870 to 16 billion in 1900. The railroads even changed time, establishing a standard system of time zones for the country.

Rails Across the Continent

The dream of a transcontinental railroad stretched back many years but had always succumbed to sectional quarrels over the route. In 1862 and 1864, with the South out of the picture, Congress passed legislation to build the first transcontinental line. The act incorporated the Union Pacific Railroad Company to build westward from Nebraska to meet the Central Pacific Railroad Company, building eastward from the Pacific Coast. The federal government directly subsidized construction with grants of land and cash loans.

Construction began simultaneously at Omaha and Sacramento in 1863, lagged during the war, and moved vigorously ahead in 1865. It became a race, each company vying for land, loans, and potential markets. Along the way, construction crews for both companies confronted dangerous and difficult obstacles. Workers of the Union Pacific encountered frequent Indian attacks but had the advantage of building over flat prairie. Central Pacific crews faced more trying conditions in the high Sierra Nevada along

trunk lines Four major railroad networks designed to connect the eastern seaports to the Great Lakes and western rivers emerged after the Civil War. They reflected the growing integration of transportation across the country that helped spur large-scale industrialization.

Cornelius, the "Commodore," Vanderbilt, in this cartoon of the "Modern Colossus of (Rail) Roads," is shown towering over his rail empire and pulling the strings to control its operations. In addition to the New York Central, Vanderbilt gained control of the Hudson River Railroad, the Lake Shore and Michigan Southern Railway, and the Canadian Southern Railway.

California's eastern border. Under the most difficult conditions, Central Pacific workers, most of them Chinese, dug, blasted, and pushed their way slowly east.

On May 10, 1869, the two lines met at Promontory, Utah, near the northern tip of the Great Salt Lake. The Union Pacific and Central Pacific presidents hammered in a golden spike (both missed it on the first try), and the dreamed-of connection was made.

The transcontinental railroad symbolized American unity and progress. Along with the Suez Canal, completed the same year, it helped knit the world together. Bret Harte, the exuberant poet of the West, wrote of the coupling at Promontory:

> What was it the Engines said,
> Pilots touching,—head to head
> Facing on the single track,
> Half a world behind each back?

In the next twenty-five years, four more railroads reached the coast. By the 1890s, business leaders talked comfortably of railroad systems stretching deep into South America and across the Bering Strait to Asia, Europe, and Africa. In an age of progress, anything seemed possible.

Problems of Growth

Overbuilding during the 1870s and 1880s caused serious problems for the railroads. Lines paralleled each other, and where they did not, speculators such as Jay Gould often laid one down to force a rival line to buy the new one out at inflated prices. Speculators like Gould bought and sold railroads like toys and watered their stock—distributed it in excess of the real value of the assets—in the process.

Competition was severe, and managers fought desperately for traffic. They offered special rates and favors: free passes for large shippers; low rates on bulk freight, carload lots, and long hauls; and rebates—secret, privately negotiated reductions below published rates. Soon fierce rate wars convinced managers that ruthless competition helped no one.

At first, managers tried to control competition by sharing traffic, but intense competitive pressures killed every agreement. Customers grew adept at bargaining for rebates and other privileges, and railroads rarely felt able to refuse them.

Failing to cooperate, railroad owners next tried to consolidate. Through purchase, lease, and merger, they gobbled up competitors and built "self-sustaining systems" that dominated entire regions. But many of these systems, expensive and unwieldy, collapsed in the Panic of 1893.

Needing money, railroads turned naturally to bankers, who finally imposed order on the industry. J. Pierpont Morgan, head of the New York investment house of J. P. Morgan and Company, took the lead. The most powerful figure in American finance, Morgan liked efficiency, combination, and order. He disliked "wasteful" competition. In 1885, during a bruising rate war between the New York Central and the Pennsylvania, Morgan invited the combatants to a conference aboard his palatial steam yacht. There he arranged a traffic-sharing agreement and collected a $1 million fee. Bringing peace to an industry could be profitable. It also satisfied Morgan's passion for stability.

After 1893, Morgan and a few other bankers refinanced ailing railroads and in so doing took control of the industry. Their methods were direct: fixed costs and debt were ruthlessly cut, new stock was issued to provide capital, rates were stabilized, rebates and competition were eliminated, and control was vested in a "voting trust" of handpicked trustees. By 1900, Morgan and his methods dominated American railroading.

Past and Present

Connecting the World: From the Transcontinental Railroad to the World Wide Web

The dream to travel farther and faster and to communicate better has long been with us. Evidenced in the modern world in inventions such as the telephone and television, the everyday use of jet airplanes, and our exploration of space, the dream was realized in a dramatic way during the nineteenth century with the arrival of the transcontinental railroad, a network of tracks that linked the east and west coasts of the United States. A century later, virtual travel and instant communication became possible through a new kind of network: the World Wide Web.

Railroads took several decades to develop after the improvement of the steam engine in the 1760s. By 1869, the completion of the transcontinental railroad across the United States signaled their triumph, shrinking the world and allowing goods, news, and people to go places and at speeds they had not been able to go before. Inspired, some entrepreneurs soon turned to designing global transportation systems that would literally circle the world. After 1900, E. H. Harriman, a railroad magnate and "a man with a passion for thinking in continents," as someone once said, tried to put together a line of steamships and railroads to span the globe. Developments in global transportation have since continued to reach farther and faster than Harriman could have ever imagined.

But as fast as physical travel became, some people sought other more efficient ways to link people, information, and goods across continents. In the 1970s and 1980s, scientists and computer professionals worked to expand and refine a decentralized communications network through computers, a system that had its roots in government and university research. This system became known in 1982 as the Internet. Tim Berners-Lee developed a software program that not only would store things hierarchically, as computers already did, but would allow them to call up random associations from their enormous memories. From that insight came the idea of links, hypertext, and the World Wide Web.

The idea spread quickly, far more so than the railroad, which required considerable material resources and human labor to construct. As more businesses and individuals purchased personal computers, and as scientists and engineers made navigating the Internet easier for the average person, the newest communications revolution was well under way. The development of electronic commerce was not far behind, as retailers discovered they had a huge market among Internet users. Chat rooms, instant messaging, and blogs soon made the Web increasingly interactive.

The Web has forever changed the way we communicate and do business. It has enabled people to work, "talk" to friends across town and across the ocean, and buy goods from on-line retailers without leaving their houses. It has also made some criminal enterprises and unethical behavior easier to do and harder to trace—for example, people can distribute child pornography, scam unwitting people out of large sums of money, buy school term papers, and learn how to build an atomic bomb.

Spreading with remarkable rapidity, the Web symbolized the pace of change in modern life—and its great unevenness. At the end of 1994, there were about 10,000 Web servers in the world; five years later, the number approached 10 million and was still growing fast. In 1995, fewer than one in seven Americans were online; today, two out of three are. Although there are now about 146 million people connected to the Internet, the circle is far from complete. Most users are in the United States and Europe, leaving about five billion people around the world without access to this revolutionary link to people and ideas in distant places. The World Wide Web, in short, is not yet worldwide.

As the new century began, the railroads had pioneered the pattern followed by most other industries. Seven giant systems controlled nearly two-thirds of the mileage, and they in turn answered to a few investment banking firms like the house of Morgan. For good and ill, a national transportation network, centralized and relatively efficient, was now in place.

AN INDUSTRIAL EMPIRE

Along with railroads, the new industrial empire was based on a number of dramatic innovations, including steel, oil, and inventions of all kinds that transformed ordinary life. Harder and more durable than other kinds of iron, steel wrought changes in manufacturing, agriculture, transportation, and architecture. It permitted longer bridges, taller buildings, stronger railroad track, better plows, heavier machinery, and faster ships. From the 1870s onward, steel output became the worldwide accepted measure of industrial progress.

■ *The machinery dwarfs the workers in this colored engraving of steel making using the Bessemer process at Andrew Carnegie's Pittsburgh steel works. Men worked twelve hours a day in the blazing heat and deafening roar of the machines.* ■

vertical integration A form of business organization in which a single firm owns and controls the entire process of production, from the procurement of raw materials to the manufacture and sale of the finished product.

The Bessemer process, developed in the 1850s by Henry Bessemer in England and independently by William Kelly in the United States, made it possible. Both men discovered that a blast of air through molten iron burned off carbon and other impurities, resulting in steel of a more uniform and durable quality. The discovery transformed the industry. Earlier methods had produced amounts a person could lift; a Bessemer converter dealt with 5 tons of molten metal at a time. The mass production of steel was now possible.

Carnegie and Steel

Bessemer plants demanded extensive capital investment, abundant raw material, sophisticated production techniques, and modern research departments. Costly to build, they limited entry into the industry to the handful who could afford them.

Great steel districts arose in Ohio, Alabama, and Pennsylvania—especially near Pittsburgh, which became the center of the industry. Output shot up; by 1890, the United States took the world lead in production.

Iron ore abounded in the fabulous deposits near Lake Superior, the greatest deposits in the world. Through a series of intricate steps involving large and complex machines, such as giant steam shovels, the raw ore was transported to the steel mills.

Like the railroads, steel companies grew larger and larger. As operations expanded, managers needed greater skills. Product development, marketing, and consumer preferences became important. Competition was fierce, and steel companies, like the railroads, tried secret agreements, pools, and consolidation. During the 1880s and 1890s, they moved toward **vertical integration,** a type of organization in which a single company owns and controls the entire process, from unearthing of the raw materials to the manufacture and sale of the finished product.

Andrew Carnegie emerged as the undisputed master of the industry. Born in Scotland, he came to the United States in 1848 at the age of 12. Settling near Pittsburgh, he went to work as a bobbin boy in a cotton mill, earning $1.20 a week. In 1852, his hard work and skill in a telegraph office caught the eye of Thomas A. Scott of the Pennsylvania Railroad. By 1859, Carnegie had become a divisional superintendent with the company. He was 24.

Soon rich from shrewd investments, Carnegie plunged into the steel industry in 1872. On the Monongahela River south of Pittsburgh he built the giant J. Edgar Thomson Steel Works. With his warmth and salesmanship, he attracted able subordinates whom he drove hard and paid well. Carnegie kept the wages of the laborers in his mills low, disliked unions, and crushed a violent strike at his Homestead works near Pittsburgh in 1892.

In 1878, Carnegie won the steel contract for the Brooklyn Bridge. As city building boomed during the 1880s, he converted the huge Homestead works to the manufacture of structural beams and angles, which went into the first skyscrapers. Carnegie profits mounted: from $2 million in 1888 to $40 million in 1900. Employing twenty thousand people, it was the largest industrial company in the world.

In 1901, Carnegie sold out. Believing that wealth brought social obligations, he wanted to devote his full time to philanthropy. J. Pierpont Morgan, who in the late 1890s had put together several rival steel companies, paid Carnegie almost half a billion dollars for Carnegie Steel.

Drawing other companies into the combination, Morgan on March 3, 1901, announced the creation of the United States Steel Corporation. The first billion-dollar company, it employed 168,000 people, produced nine million tons of iron and steel a year, and controlled three-fifths of the country's steel business. Soon there were other giants, and as the nineteenth century ended, steel products—rare just thirty years before—had altered the landscape. Huge firms, investment bankers, and professional managers dominated the industry.

Rockefeller and Oil

Petroleum worked comparable changes in the economic and social landscape, although mostly after 1900. Distilled into oil, it lubricated the machinery of the industrial age. Kerosene, another major distillate of petroleum, brought inexpensive illumination into almost every home. Since tallow candles and whale oil were expensive to burn, many people went to bed at nightfall. Kerosene lamps opened the evenings to activity, which altered the patterns of life.

Like other changes in these years, the oil boom happened with surprising speed. In the mid-1850s, petroleum was a bothersome, smelly fluid that occasionally rose to the surface of springs and streams. But in 1859, Edwin L. Drake drilled the first oil well near Titusville in northwest Pennsylvania, and "black gold" fever struck. Chemists soon discovered ways to turn petroleum into lubricating oil, grease, paint, wax, varnish, naphtha, and paraffin. In just a few years, there was a world market for oil.

At first, growth of the oil industry was chaotic. Early drillers and refiners produced for local markets, and since drilling wells and even erecting refineries cost little, competition flourished. Output fluctuated dramatically; prices rose and fell with devastating effect.

A young merchant from Cleveland named John D. Rockefeller imposed order on the industry. Beginning in 1863, at the age of 24, he built a titan of corporate business, the Standard Oil Company. Like Morgan, Rockefeller considered competition wasteful, small-scale enterprise inefficient, and consolidation the path of the future. Methodically, Rockefeller absorbed or destroyed competitors in Cleveland and elsewhere. As ruthless in his methods as Carnegie, he lacked the steel master's spontaneous charm. Like Carnegie, he demanded efficiency, relentless cost cutting, and the latest technology. He was a man of great vision, and he attracted exceptional lieutenants.

Paying careful attention to detail, Rockefeller realized that in large-scale production, even small reductions meant huge savings. In one famous incident, he reduced the number of drops of solder on kerosene cans from forty to thirty-nine. In the end, Rockefeller triumphed over his competitors by marketing products of

■ *John D. Rockefeller, satirized in a 1901* Puck *cartoon, is enthroned on oil, the base of his empire; his crown is girded by other holdings.* ■

high quality at the lowest unit cost. But he employed other, less savory methods as well. He threatened rivals and bribed politicians, exploited railroad rebates, and employed spies to harass the customers of competing refiners. By 1879, he controlled 90 percent of the country's oil-refining capacity.

Vertically integrated, Standard Oil owned wells, timberlands, barrel and chemical plants, refineries, warehouses, pipelines, and fleets of tankers and oil cars. Its marketing organization served as a model for the industry, and it exported oil throughout the world.

To manage it all, the company developed a new plan of business organization, the **trust,** which had profound significance for American business. In 1882, Samuel C. T. Dodd, Standard's attorney, set up the Standard Oil Trust, with a board of nine trustees empowered "to hold, control, and manage" all of Standard's properties. As Dodd intended, the trust immediately centralized control of Standard's far-flung empire.

Competition almost disappeared; profits soared. A trust movement swept the country, as industries with similar problems—whiskey, lead, and sugar, among others—followed Standard's example. The word *trust* became synonymous with monopoly, amid vehement public protests. *Antitrust* became a watchword for a generation of reformers from the 1880s through 1920. But Rockefeller's purpose had been *management* of a monopoly, not monopoly itself, which he had already achieved.

During the 1890s, Rockefeller helped pioneer another form of industrial consolidation, the holding company. Taking advantage of an 1889 New Jersey law that allowed one company to purchase another, he moved Standard Oil to New Jersey and bought up his own subsidiaries to form a holding company. The trust, he had learned, was cumbersome, and it was under attack in Congress and the courts. Holding companies offered the next step in industrial development. They were simply large-scale mergers in which a central corporate organization purchased the stock of the member companies and established direct, formal control. Soon other companies followed Rockefeller's example, and by 1900, a mere 1 percent of the nation's companies controlled more than one-third of its industrial production.

Rockefeller retired in 1897 with a fortune of nearly $900 million, but for Standard Oil and petroleum in general, the most expansive period was yet to come. The great oil pools of Texas and Oklahoma had not yet been discovered. There were only four usable automobiles in the country, and the day of the gasoline engine lay just ahead.

The Business of Invention

During the last third of the nineteenth century, an extraordinary group of American inventors added to the world's knowledge. Some inventions gave rise to new industries; a few actually changed the quality of life. The number of patents issued to inventors reflected the trend. Between 1790 and 1860, the U.S. Patent Office issued just 36,000 patents; in the decade of the 1890s alone, it issued more than 200,000.

Some of the inventions transformed communications. In 1866, Cyrus W. Field improved the transatlantic cable linking the telegraph networks of Europe and the United States. By 1900, land and submarine cables reached around the world. Diplomats and business leaders could now "talk" to their counterparts in Berlin or Hong Kong. Even before the telephone, the cables quickened the pace of diplomacy, revolutionized journalism, and allowed businesses to expand and centralize.

The typewriter (1867), stock ticker (1867), cash register (1879), and adding machine (1888) helped business transactions. High-speed looms and sewing machines transformed the clothing industry, which for the first time in history turned out ready-made clothes for the masses.

Other innovations improved the diet. There were new processes for flour, canned meat, vegetables, condensed milk, and even beer. Refrigerated railroad cars, ice-cooled, brought fresh fruit from Florida and California to all parts of the coun-

---

trust A business management device designed to centralize and make more efficient the management of diverse and far-flung business operations. It allowed stockholders to exchange their stock certificates for trust certificates, on which dividends were paid.

try. In the 1870s, Gustavus F. Swift, a Chicago meatpacker, hit on the idea of using the cars to distribute meat nationwide. Setting up "dissembly" factories to butcher meat (Henry Ford later copied them for his famous "assembly" lines), he started what a newspaper called an "era for cheap beef."

No innovation, however, rivaled in importance the telephone and the use of electricity for light and power. The telephone was the work of Alexander Graham Bell, a teacher of the deaf. Bell experimented with ways to transmit speech electrically, and he developed electrified metal disks that converted sound waves to electrical impulses and back again. On March 10, 1876, he transmitted the first sentence over a telephone: "Mr. Watson, come here; I want you." By 1905, there were ten million telephones in the country—one for almost every ten people.

Thomas Alva Edison invented an array of processes and products of incalculable significance. Born in 1847, Edison had little formal education, although he was an avid reader. After earning a reputation for his work in telegraphy, Edison built and organized the first modern research laboratory at Menlo Park, New Jersey.

In 1877, Edison invented a "telephone repeater," which became the phonograph. Those unable to afford a phone, he thought, could record their voices for replay from a central telephone station. Using tin foil wrapped around a grooved, rotating cylinder, he shouted the verses of "Mary Had a Little Lamb" and then listened in awe as the machine played them back. Within a generation, Edison's invention had evolved into the phonograph record. For the first time in history, people could listen again and again to a favorite piece of music. The phonograph made human experiences repeatable in a way never before possible.

In 1879 came an even larger triumph, the incandescent lamp. In tackling this idea, Edison set out to do nothing less than change light. A trial-and-error inventor, he tested sixteen hundred materials before producing the carbon filament he wanted. With the financial backing of J. Pierpont Morgan, he organized the Edison Illuminating Company and built the Pearl Street power station in New York City. Power stations soon opened in Boston, Philadelphia, and Chicago. In a nation alive with light, the habits of centuries changed. A flick of the switch lit homes and factories at any hour of the day or night.

In a rare blunder, Edison based his system on low-voltage direct current, which could be transmitted only about 2 miles. George Westinghouse demonstrated the advantages of high-voltage alternating current, transmitted over great distances. With the inventor Nikola Tesla, Westinghouse developed an alternating-current motor that could convert electricity into mechanical power. Electricity could light a lamp or illuminate a skyscraper, pull a streetcar or drive an entire railroad, run a sewing machine or power a mammoth assembly line. Buried under pavement or strung from pole to pole, wires of every description—trolley, telephone, and power—soon distinguished the modern city.

The Sellers

The increased output of the industrial age was one thing, but the products still had to be sold, and that gave rise to the new "science" of marketing. Some business leaders built extensive marketing organizations of their own. Others relied on retailers, merchandising techniques, and advertising, developing a host of methods to convince consumers to buy.

In 1867, businesses spent about $50 million on advertising; in 1900, they spent more than $500 million, and the figure was increasing rapidly. The rotary press (1875) churned out newspapers and, with rotogravure illustrations, began a new era in newspaper advertising. Brand names became popular; already Kellogg was promising cornflake eaters "Genuine Joy, Genuine Appetite, Genuine Health and therefore Genuine Complexion."

Bringing producer and consumer together, nationwide advertising was the final link in the national market. From roadside signs to newspaper ads, it pervaded

American life. In a candid address, the owner of the *Ladies' Home Journal* told an audience of manufacturers that he published his magazine not for the benefit of American women but for them, the people who manufactured products, to sell to American women.

R. H. Macy in New York, John Wanamaker in Philadelphia, and Marshall Field in Chicago turned the department store into a national institution. There people could browse (a relatively new concept) and buy. Innovations in pricing, display, and advertising helped customers develop wants they did not know they had. In 1870, Wanamaker took out the first full-page newspaper ad.

The "chain store"—an American term—spread across the country. The Atlantic & Pacific Tea Company opened its first grocery store in 1859, and by 1915, there were a thousand A&Ps. In 1880, F. W. Woolworth opened the first "five and ten cent store"; twenty years later, he had fifty-nine of them. Sears, Roebuck and Company and Montgomery Ward sold to rural customers through mail-order catalogs—a means of selling that depended on effective transportation and a high level of customer literacy. By the early 1900s, Sears was distributing six million catalogs annually.

Advertising, brand names, chain stores, and mail-order houses brought Americans of all varieties into a national market. Even as the country grew, a certain homogeneity of goods bound it together. There was a common language of consumption. The market, some contemporaries thought, bridged regional, class, and even ethnic differences.

The theory had limits; ethnic and racial differences remained deep in the society. But Americans *had* become a community of consumers, surrounded by goods unavailable just a few decades before and able to purchase them. They had learned to make, want, and buy. As Arthur Miller, a twentieth-century playwright, said in *The Price:* "Years ago a person, he was unhappy, didn't know what to do with himself—he'd go to church, start a revolution—*something.* Today you're unhappy? Can't figure it out? What is the salvation? Go shopping."

THE WAGE EARNERS

Although entrepreneurs were important, it was the labor of millions of men and women that built the new industrial society. Their individual stories, nearly all unrecorded, reflected the achievement, drama, and pain of these years. In a number of respects, their lot improved during the last quarter of the nineteenth century. Real wages rose, working conditions got better, and the workers' influence in national affairs increased. Like others, workers also benefited from expanding health and educational services.

Working Men, Working Women, Working Children

Still, life for workers was not easy. Before 1900, most wage earners worked ten hours a day, six days a week. If skilled, they earned around 20 cents an hour; if unskilled, about half that. Most earned between $400 and $500 a year, at a time when it took about $600 to live decently. Construction workers, machinists, government employees, printers, clerical workers, and western miners made more than the average. Eastern coal miners, agricultural workers, garment workers, and unskilled factory hands made considerably less.

There were few holidays or vacations and little respite from the grueling routine. Work was not only exhausting but also often dangerous. Safety standards were low, and accidents were common. On the railroads, one in every 26 workers was injured and one in every 399 killed each year. Thousands suffered from chronic illness, unknowing victims of dust, chemicals, and other pollutants.

The breadwinner might be a woman or a child; both worked in increasing numbers. Between 1870 and 1900, the number of working children rose nearly 130 percent, and the percentage of women who worked rose from 15 to 20 percent. Most working women were young and single. Many began work at age 16 or 17, worked five or six years, married, and quit. As clerical work expanded, women learned new skills such as typing and stenography. Moving into formerly male occupations, they became secretaries, bookkeepers, typists, telephone operators, and clerks in the new department stores. The number of women gainfully employed rose from 2.6 million in 1880 to 5.3 million in 1900.

A very few women became ministers, lawyers, and doctors, but change was slow, and in the 1880s, some law schools were still refusing to admit women because they "had not the mentality to study law." Among women entering the professions, the overwhelming majority became nurses, schoolteachers, and librarians. Consequently, those fields underwent a process of *feminization:* as women became the majority of the workers, a small number of men took the management roles, and most men left for other jobs, lowering the profession's status.

In most jobs, status and pay were allotted unequally between men and women. Many people of both sexes thought a woman's place was in the home. When employed in factories, women tended to occupy jobs that were viewed as natural extensions of household activities. They made clothes and textiles, processed food, and made cigars, tobacco, and shoes.

In general, adults earned more than children, the skilled more than the unskilled, native-born more than foreign-born, Protestants more than Catholics or Jews, and whites more than blacks or Asians. On average, women made a little more than half as much as men. These economic realities reflected bias based on race, creed, and gender. In the industrial society white, native-born Protestants—the bulk of the population, though by 1900 no longer the bulk of the workforce—reaped the greatest rewards.

Blacks labored on the fringes, usually in menial occupations. They earned less than other workers at almost every level of skill. On the Pacific Coast, the Chinese—and later the Japanese—lived in enclaves and suffered periodic attacks of discrimination. At times, immigration of both Chinese and Japanese was prohibited through legislation such as the **Chinese Exclusion Act.** Passed by Congress in 1882, the act banned the entry of Chinese workers for ten years.

Culture of Work

Among almost all groups, industrialization shattered age-old patterns, including work habits and the culture of work. It made people adapt "older work routines to new necessities and strained those wedded to premodern patterns of labor." Men and women fresh from farms were not accustomed to the factory's discipline. Now they worked indoors rather than out, paced themselves to the clock rather than the movements of the sun, and followed the needs of the market rather than the natural rhythms of the seasons. They had foremen and hierarchies and strict rules. Piecework determined wages, and always there was the relentless clock.

As industries grew larger, work became more impersonal. Machines displaced skilled artisans, and the unskilled tended them for employers they never saw. Workers picked up and left their jobs with startling frequency, and factories drew on a churning, highly mobile labor supply. Many workers were seemingly rootless, moving wherever new opportunities beckoned.

Substantial economic and social mobility accompanied the geographic mobility. The rags-to-riches stories of Horatio Alger had always said so, and careers such as Andrew Carnegie's seemed to confirm it. The actual record was considerably more limited. Most business leaders in the period came from well-to-do or middle-class families of old American stock. Still, many workers made major progress during their lifetimes. Movement from the working class to the middle class was not an uncommon occurrence.

Chinese Exclusion Act
Legislation passed in 1882 that excluded Chinese immigrant workers for ten years and denied U.S. citizenship to Chinese nationals living in the United States. It was the first U.S. exclusionary law that was aimed at a specific racial group.

The chance for advancement played a vital role in American industrial development. It gave workers hope, wedded them to the system, and tempered their response to the appeal of labor unions and working-class agitation. Very few workers rose from rags to riches, but a great many rose to better jobs and higher status.

Labor Unions

Weak throughout the nineteenth century, labor unions never attracted more than 2 percent of the total labor force or more than 10 percent of industrial workers. To many workers, unions seemed "foreign," radical, out of step with the American tradition of individual advancement. Craft, ethnic, and other differences fragmented the labor force, and its extraordinary mobility made organization difficult. Employers strongly opposed unions. Said one U.S. Steel executive, "If a worker sticks up his head, hit it." As the national economy emerged, however, national labor unions gradually took shape. The early unions often represented skilled workers in local areas, but in 1866, William H. Sylvis united several unions into a single national organization, the National Labor Union. Sylvis sought long-range humanitarian reforms rather than specific, bread-and-butter goals. A talented propagandist, he won over many members, but when he died in 1869, the organization did not long survive him.

The year Sylvis died, Uriah S. Stephens and a group of Philadelphia garment workers formed a far more successful organization, the Noble and Holy Order of the Knights of Labor, known simply as the **Knights of Labor.** A secret fraternal order, it grew slowly through the 1870s until Terence V. Powderly ended the secrecy and embarked on an aggressive program. The Knights welcomed all laborers, regardless of skill, creed, gender, or color.

Harking back to the Jacksonians, the Knights set the "producers" against monopoly and special privilege. As members they excluded only "nonproducers"—bankers, lawyers, liquor dealers, and gamblers. Since employers were "producers," they could join; and since workers and employers had common interests, workers should not strike. The order's program included the eight-hour workday and the abolition of child labor, but more often it focused on uplifting, utopian reform, such as ending drunkenness and establishing worker-run factories, railroads, and mines.

Membership grew steadily—from 42,000 in 1882 to a peak of 725,000 in 1886. But neither Powderly nor the union's loose structure could handle the growth, and when Jay Gould crushed their strike on the Texas and Pacific Railroad, the Knights crumbled. In 1886, the Haymarket Riot (to be discussed shortly) turned public sympathy against unions such as the Knights. By 1890, the order had shrunk to 100,000 members. A few years later, it was virtually defunct.

As the Knights waxed and waned, another organization emerged that was to endure. Founded in 1886, the **American Federation of Labor (AFL)** was a loose alliance of national craft unions. Unlike the Knights, it organized only skilled workers along craft lines, avoided politics, and worked for specific practical objectives. Samuel Gompers, the founder and longtime president, was determined to better the material lives of the workers. He accepted capitalism, and for labor he wanted simply a recognized place within the system and a greater share of the rewards.

Unlike Powderly, Gompers and the AFL assumed that most workers would remain workers throughout their lives. The task, then, lay in improving lives in "practical" ways: higher wages, shorter hours, and better working conditions. The AFL offered some attractive assurances to employers. As trade unionists, they would use the strike and boycott, but only to achieve limited gains, and if treated fairly, they would provide a stable labor force.

By the 1890s, the AFL was the most important labor group in the country. By 1901, the organization had more than a million members, or almost one-third of the country's skilled workers, and by 1914, it had more than two million. The great

Knights of Labor Also known as the Noble and Holy Order of the Knights of Labor. Founded in 1869, this labor organization pursued broad-gauged reforms as much as practical issues such as wages and hours.

American Federation of Labor (AFL) Founded by Samuel Gompers in 1886, the AFL was a loose alliance of national craft unions that organized skilled workers by craft and worked for specific practical objectives such as higher wages, shorter hours, and better working conditions.

majority of workers, skilled and unskilled, remained unorganized, but Gompers and the AFL had become a significant force in national life.

Although two of the AFL's national affiliates accepted women as members, others prohibited them outright, and Gompers himself often complained that women workers undercut the pay scales for men. Conditions improved after 1900, but unions remained largely a man's world. The AFL did not expressly forbid black workers from joining, but member unions used high initiation fees, technical examinations, and other means to discourage black membership.

Labor Unrest

Workers used various means to adjust to the factory age. To the dismay of managers and "efficiency" experts, they often dictated the pace and quality of their work, and they set the tone of the workplace. Friends and relatives of newly arrived immigrants obtained jobs for them, taught them how to deal with factory conditions, and humanized the workplace.

Many employers believed in an "iron law of wages" in which supply and demand, not the welfare of their workers, dictated pay. Wanting a docile labor force, employers fired workers who joined unions, hired scabs to replace strikers, and used a powerful new weapon, the court injunction, to quell strikes. The injunction, which forbade workers to interfere with their employers' business, was used to break the great Pullman strike of 1894, and the Supreme Court upheld use of the injunction in *In re Debs* (1895).

As employers' attitudes hardened, strikes and violence broke out. Between 1880 and 1900, there were more than 23,000 strikes involving 6.6 million workers. The railroad strike of 1877 paralyzed railroads from West Virginia to California, resulted in the deaths of more than one hundred workers, and required federal troops to suppress it. In another year, 1886, more than 600,000 workers were off the job because of strikes and lockouts.

The worst incident took place in Chicago. In early May 1886, police, intervening in a strike at the McCormick harvester works, shot and killed two workers. The next evening, May 4, labor leaders called a protest meeting at Haymarket Square, near downtown Chicago. The meeting was peaceful, but police ordered the crowd to disperse. Someone threw a dynamite bomb, instantly killing one policeman and fatally wounding six others. Police fired into the crowd, killing four.

No one ever discovered who threw the bomb, but many Americans immediately labeled the incident the **Haymarket Riot** and demanded action against labor "radicalism." Cities strengthened their police forces and armories. Chicago police rounded up eight anarchists who were found guilty of murder on the basis of incendiary opinions. Although there was no evidence of their complicity in the bomb-throwing incident, four were hanged, one committed suicide, and three were jailed.

A Look at the Past

Typewriter

By the end of the nineteenth century, typewriters became increasingly common in offices. The earliest typewriters worked in a variety of ways and did not even have similar keyboards. By the 1890s, however, the keyboard known today had become standard. The standardized keyboard made it easier for people to learn to type, and also made it possible to type more quickly. The awkward arrangement on the keyboard intentionally slowed typists to prevent keys from jamming as a result of rapid typing. Even though typewriters did not work as quickly as typists could, they offered numerous advantages over pen and ink. ✽ What do typewriters suggest about business practices? How did they affect the amount of paper used in offices How could typed and printed forms alter the pace of business?

Haymarket Riot On May 4, 1886, a demonstration in Chicago's Haymarket Square to protest the slayings of two workers during a strike turned into a violent riot after a bomb explosion killed seven policemen.

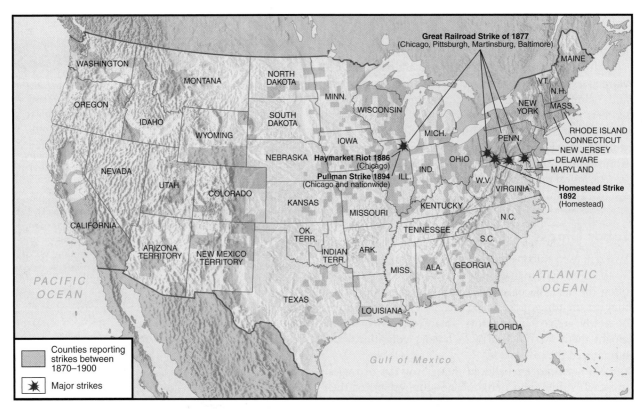

LABOR STRIKES, 1870–1890 *More than 14,000 strikes occurred in the 1880s and early 1890s, involving millions of workers. Labor violence brought public clamor against labor unions. Four violent strikes in particular weakened the labor movement: the Great Railroad strike of 1877, the Haymarket Riot of 1886, the Homestead Strike of 1892, and the Pullman Strike of 1894.* ■

Homestead Strike In July 1892, wage-cutting at Andrew Carnegie's Homestead Steel plant in Pittsburgh provoked this violent strike. Using ruthless force and strikebreakers, company officials effectively broke the strike and destroyed the union.

Violence again broke out in the unsettled conditions of the 1890s. In 1892, Carnegie and Henry Clay Frick, his partner and manager, lowered wages nearly 20 percent at the Homestead steel plant. The Amalgamated Iron and Steel Workers, an AFL affiliate, struck, and Frick responded by locking the workers out of the plants. The workers surrounded it, and Frick, furious, hired a small private army of Pinkerton detectives to drive them off. Before the battle ended, the detectives were forced to surrender, and thirteen people were killed.

A few days later, the Pennsylvania governor ordered the state militia to impose peace at Homestead. On July 23, an anarchist named Alexander Berkman, who was not one of the strikers, walked into Frick's office and shot and stabbed him. Incredibly, Frick survived, watched the police take Berkman away, called in a doctor to bandage his wounds, and stayed in the office until closing time. The Homestead works reopened under military guard in late July; in November, the strikers gave up.

Events like the **Homestead Strike** troubled many Americans, who wondered whether industrialization, for all its benefits, might carry a heavy price in social upheaval, class tensions, and even outright warfare. Most workers did not share in the immense profits of the industrial age, and as the nineteenth century came to a close, some felt the need to rebel against the inequity.

CONCLUSION: INDUSTRIALIZATION'S BENEFITS AND COSTS

In the half century after the Civil War, the United States became the leading industrial nation in the world. On the one hand, industrialization meant "progress,"

Chronology

1859	First oil well is drilled near Titusville, Pennsylvania
1866	William Sylvis establishes the National Labor Union
1869	Transcontinental railroad is completed at Promontory, Utah ▪ Knights of Labor is organized
1876	Alexander Graham Bell invents the telephone ▪ Centennial Exposition is held in Philadelphia
1877	Railroads cut workers' wages, provoking a bloody and violent strike
1879	Thomas A. Edison invents the incandescent lamp
1881	Samuel Gompers founds the American Federation of Labor (AFL)
1882	Rockefeller's Standard Oil Company becomes the nation's first trust ▪ Edison opens the first electricity generating station in New York
1886	Labor protest erupts in violence in the Haymarket Riot in Chicago ▪ Railroads adopt a standard gauge
1892	Workers strike at the Homestead steel plant in Pennsylvania
1901	J. P. Morgan announces the formation of U.S. Steel Corporation, the nation's first billion-dollar company

growth, world power, and fulfillment of the American promise of abundance. For the bulk of the population, the standard of living—a particularly American concept—rose. But on the other hand, industrialization also meant rapid change, social instability, exploitation of labor, and growing disparity in income between rich and poor. Industry flourished, but control rested in fewer and fewer hands. Maturing quickly, the young system embarked on a new corporate capitalism: giant businesses, interlocking in ownership, managed by a new professional class, and selling an expanding variety of goods in an increasingly controlled market. As goods spread through American society, so did a sharpened and aggressive materialism. Workers felt the strains of the shift to a new social order.

In 1902, a well-to-do New Yorker named Bessie Van Vorst decided to see what it was like to work for a living in a factory. Disguising herself in worn, inexpensive clothes, she went to Pittsburgh and got a job in a canning factory. She worked ten hours a day, six days a week, including four hours on Saturday afternoons when she and the other women, on hands and knees, scrubbed the tables, the stands, and the entire factory floor. She worked until her body ached and her hands blistered, until the noise of the machines and monotony of the labor made her dazed and weary. She earned $4.20 a week, $3 of which went for food alone. Van Vorst was lucky; she could return to her comfortable life in New York. The working men and women around her were not so fortunate. They stayed on the factory floor and, by the dint of their labor, created a new industrial society.

KEY TERMS

trunk lines, p. 355

vertical integration, p. 358

trust, p. 360

Chinese Exclusion Act, p. 363

Knights of Labor, p. 364

American Federation of Labor (AFL), p. 364

Haymarket Riot, p. 365

Homestead Strike, p. 366

RECOMMENDED READING

Samuel P. Hays, *The Response to Industrialism: 1885–1914* (1957), is an influential interpretation of the period. Douglass C. North, *Growth and Welfare in the American Past: A New Economic History* (1966), is stimulating. David Montgomery, *The Fall of the House of Labor* (1987), is an outstanding study of labor in the period. Richard Franklin Bensel, *The Political Economy of American Industrialization, 1877–1900* (2000), and Charles Perrow, *Organizing America: Wealth, Power, and the Origins of Corporate Capitalism* (2002), trace the underlying ideas of the new industrialization.

Alfred D. Chandler, *The Visible Hand: The Managerial Revolution in American Business* (1978), Olivier Zunz, *Making America Corporate, 1870–1920* (1990), and JoAnne Yates, *Control Through Communication: The Rise of System in American Management* (1989), are perceptive. The railroad empire is treated in John R. Stilgoe, *Metropolitan Corridor: Railroads and the American Scene* (1983), Claire Strom, *Profiting from the Plains: The Great Northern Railway and Corporate Development of the American West* (2003), John Hoyt Williams, *A Great and Shining Road: The Epic Story of the Transcontinental Railroad* (1988), and John F. Stover, *American Railroads* (1961); its legal implications in James W. Ely, Jr., *Railroads and American Law* (2001) and Barbara Young Welke, *Recasting American Liberty: Gender, Race, Law,* and the Railroad Revolution, 1865–1920 (2001). On the steel industry, see Peter Temin, *Iron and Steel in Nineteenth-Century America* (1964).

Two superb books by Sam Bass Warner, Jr., *Streetcar Suburbs: The Process of Growth in Boston, 1870–1900* (1962), and *The Urban Wilderness: A History of the American City* (1973), examine technology and city development. The wage earner is examined in Herbert G. Gutman, *Work, Culture, and Society in Industrializing America* (1976), and Joshua L. Rosenbloom, *Looking for Work, Searching for Workers: American Labor Markets during Industrialization* (2002). Two books by Stephan Thernstrom, *Poverty and Progress: Social Mobility in the Nineteenth-Century City* (1964) and *The Other Bostonians: Poverty and Progress in the American Metropolis, 1880–1970* (1973), examine mobility. Walter A. Friedman, *Birth of a Salesman: The Transformation of Selling in America* (2004), looks at the growing importance of advertising. Philip S. Foner, *Women and the American Labor Movement,* 2 vols. (1979), Susan E. Kennedy, *If All We Did Was to Weep at Home* (1979), Barbara Mayer Wertheimer, *We Were There: The Story of Working Women in America* (1977), and Alice Kessler-Harris, *Out to Work: A History of Wage-Earning Women in the United States* (1982), are excellent on the subject of women in the workplace.

SUGGESTED WEB SITES

Alexander Graham Bell Family Papers at the Library of Congress

memory.loc.gov/ammem/bellhtml/bellhome.html

This site contains papers from 1862 to 1939, but includes a chronology, images, selected documents, and interpretive essays about Bell.

The Richest Man in the World: Andrew Carnegie

www.pbs.org/wgbh/amex/carnegie/

This American Experience/PBS site provides images and text about Carnegie's life and activities.

The Anarchy Archives at Pitzer University

dwardmac.pitzer.edu/Anarchist_Archives/archivehome.html

This archive includes classic anarchist texts, especially information and graphics about the Haymarket Riot.

John D. Rockefeller and the Standard Oil Company

www.micheloud.com/FXM/SO/

This study with accompanying images by François Micheloud tells of the rise of Rockefeller and his mammoth company.

National Refinery Company

www.enarco.com/

This positive history of the company reflects the industrial changes of late-nineteenth-century America.

American Labor History

www.geocities.com/CollegePark/Quad/6460/AmLabHist/index.html

This site takes a general look at the history of labor in America.

Labor-Management Conflict in American History

history.osu.edu/projects/laborconflict/

This site at Ohio State University includes primary accounts of some of the major events in the history of labor-management conflict in the late nineteenth and early twentieth centuries.

Samuel Gompers Papers at the University of Maryland

www.inform.umd.edu/HIST/Gompers/web1.html

This site includes information about the papers project but also has a photo gallery, selected documents, and a brief history of the first president of the American Federation of Labor.

Chapter 19

Toward an Urban Society, 1877–1900

The Overcrowded City

One day around 1900, Harriet Vittum, a settlement house worker in Chicago, went to the aid of a young Polish girl who lived in a nearby slum. The girl, aged 15, had discovered she was pregnant and had taken poison. An ambulance was on the way, and Vittum, told of the poisoning, rushed over to do what she could.

When Vittum arrived at the girl's squalid three-room apartment, she found the rooms crammed with at least fourteen boarders and young children, some sleeping on the floor. Glancing out the window, Vittum saw the wall of another building so close she could reach out and touch it. She was struck by the girl's life in the crowded tenement, with its lack of light and air. Did she have the right, Vittum asked herself, to bring the girl back "to the misery and hopelessness of the life she was living in that awful place?"

The young girl died, and in later years, Vittum often told her story. It was easy to see why. The girl's life in the slum reflected the experience of millions of other people in the late nineteenth century. The glitter and excitement of the cities attracted people from rural America, Europe, South America, and Asia. Between 1860 and 1910, the number of people living in American cities increased sevenfold. They were lured by the prospects of greater economic opportunities, but their lives were often bleak and painful.

Two major forces reshaped American society between 1870 and 1920: industrialization and urbanization. In these years, cities grew upward and outward, attracting millions of newcomers and influencing politics, education, entertainment, and family life. By 1920, they had become the center of American economic, social, and cultural life.

THE LURE OF THE CITY

Between 1870 and 1900, the city—like the factory—became a symbol of a new America. Drawn from farms, small towns, and foreign lands, newcomers swelled the population of older cities and created new ones almost overnight. At the beginning of the Civil War, only one-sixth of the American people lived in communities of eight thousand people or more. By 1900, one-third did; by 1920, one-half.

The movement to urban life brought explosive growth. Thousands of years of history had produced only a handful of cities in which more than half a million people lived. In 1900, the United States had six such cities, including three—New York, Chicago, and Philadelphia—with populations more than a million.

Skyscrapers and Suburbs

Beginning in the 1800s, a revolution in technology transformed American cities. The age of steel and glass produced the skyscraper; the streetcar produced the suburbs and new residential patterns.

On the eve of the change, American cities were a crowded jumble of small buildings. Buildings were usually made of masonry, and since the massive walls had to support their own weight, they could be no taller than a dozen or so stories. Steel frames and girders ended that limitation and allowed buildings to soar higher and higher. "Curtain walls," which concealed the steel framework, were no longer load-bearing; they were pierced by many windows that let in fresh air and light.

To a group of talented Chicago architects, the new trends served as a springboard for innovative forms. The leaders of the movement were John Root and Louis H. Sullivan, both of whom were attracted by the chance to rebuild Chicago after the great fire of 1871. Root noted that the fire had fed on fancy exterior ornamentation, and he developed a plain stripped-down style, bold in mass and form—the keynotes of modern architecture. He also expounded on his belief that in an age of business, the office tower, more than the church or the government building, symbolized society, and he designed buildings that followed his code of simplicity, stability, breadth, and dignity. Sullivan, who had studied at MIT and in Paris before settling in Chicago, had his great inspiration in 1866, at the age of 30, when he conceived of the skyscraper. Sullivan's skyscrapers changed the urban skyline.

Architects must discard "books, rules, precedents," Sullivan announced; responding to the new, they should design for a building's function. "Form follows function," Sullivan believed, and he passed the idea on to a talented disciple, Frank Lloyd Wright. The modern city should stretch to the sky, "rising in sheer exaltation."

Electric elevators carried passengers upward in the new skyscrapers. During the same years, streetcars carried them outward to expanded boundaries that transformed urban life. Urban centers were no longer "walking cities," confined to a radius of 2 or 3 miles, a distance an individual might walk. Streetcar systems extended the radius and changed the urban map. Cable lines, electric surface lines, and elevated rapid transit brought shoppers and workers into central business districts and sped them home again. Cheap to ride, the mass transit systems fostered commuting; widely separated business and residential districts sprang up. The middle class moved farther and farther out to the leafy greenness of the suburbs.

As the middle class moved out of the cities, the immigrants and working class poured in. They took over the older brownstones, row houses, and workers' cottages, turning them under the sheer weight of numbers into the slums of the central city. In the cities of the past, classes and occupations had been thrown together. The streetcar city, sprawling and specialized, became a more fragmented and stratified society with middle-class residential rings surrounding a business and working-class core.

Tenements and the Problems of Overcrowding

In the shadows of the skyscrapers, grimy rows of tenements filled the central city. As Jacob Riis illustrated in words and pictures in *How the Other Half Lives* (1890), it was a world of dark halls, poor ventilation, and squalid conditions.

Tenement houses on small city lots crowded people into cramped apartments. In 1890, nearly half the dwellings in New York City were tenements. That year, more than 1.4 million people lived on Manhattan Island, one ward of which had a population density of 334,000 people per square mile. Many people lived in alleys and basements so dark they could not be photographed until flashlight photography was invented in 1887.

Everywhere was the smell of poverty and neglect. In the 1870s and 1880s, cities stank. One problem was horse manure, hundreds of tons of it a day in every city. Another was the privy, "a single one of which," said a leading authority on public health, "may render life in a whole neighborhood almost unendurable in the summer."

Cities dumped their wastes into the nearest body of water, then drew drinking water from the same site. Many built modern, purified waterworks but could not keep pace with spiraling growth. Factories, the pride of the era, polluted the urban air. At night, Pittsburgh looked and sounded like "Hell with the lid off," according to contemporary observers. Smoke poured from hundreds of glass factories, iron and steel mills, and oil refineries.

Crime was another growing problem. The nation's homicide rate nearly tripled in the 1880s, much of the increase coming in the cities. Slum youths formed street gangs and committed crimes. In San Francisco, the gangs gave rise to the new word *hoodlums,* described by a disgusted English traveler as "young embryo criminals" who robbed and murdered at night.

After remaining constant for many decades, the suicide rate rose steadily between 1870 and 1900. Alcoholism was also on the rise, especially among men. A 1905 survey of Chicago counted as many drinking establishments as grocery stores, meat markets, and dry goods stores combined.

Strangers in a New Land

Some of the new city dwellers had moved from farms and small towns; many others arrived from abroad. Most of those came from Europe, where unemployment, food shortages, and increasing threats of war sent millions fleeing across the Atlantic to make a fresh start in the United States. Italians first came in large numbers to escape an 1887 cholera epidemic in southern Italy; tens of thousands of Jews sought refuge from the pogroms (anti-Jewish massacres) that swept Russia and Poland after 1880. The immigration was so great that by 1890, about 15 percent of the U.S. population was foreign-born.

Most newcomers were job seekers. Nearly two-thirds were men; most were between the ages of 15 and 40 and unskilled. They tended to crowd into northern seaboard cities, settling in areas where others of their nationality or region had settled.

They were often dazzled by what they saw. They stared at electric lights, indoor plumbing, streetcars, ice cream, lemons, and bananas. America's teeming markets, department stores, and Woolworth's new five-and-dime stores offered goods unknown in the homeland.

Cities had increasingly large foreign-born populations. In 1900, three-fourths of Chicago's population was foreign-born or of foreign-born parentage, two-thirds of Boston's, and one-half of Philadelphia's. In New York City, where most immigrants entered the country and many stayed, four out of five residents in 1890 were of foreign birth or foreign parentage.

Beginning in the 1880s, the sources of immigration shifted dramatically away from northern and western Europe, the chief source of immigration for more than two centuries. More and more immigrants came from southern and eastern Europe: Italy, Greece, Austria-Hungary, Poland, and Russia. The **new immigrants** tended to be Catholics or Jews rather than Protestants, and they often spoke "strange" languages. Most were poor and uneducated; sticking together in communities, they clung to their native tongues, customs, and religions.

More than any previous group, the new immigrants troubled the mainstream society. Could they be assimilated? Did they share "American" values? Sneering epithets became part of the national vocabulary: *wop* and *dago* for Italians; *bohunk* for Bohemians, Hungarians, and other Slavs; *grease-ball* for Greeks; and *kike* for Jews. Anti-Catholicism and anti-Semitism led to shameful treatment of the immigrants. In 1889, the head of the Fresh Air Fund, a program that sent New York City children on vacations to the suburbs, noted that "no one asked for Italian children." By the end of the 1890s, a number of organizations worked to restrict or end immigration.

new immigrants Starting in the 1880s, immigration into the United States began to shift from northern and western Europe, its source for most of the nation's history, to southern and eastern Europe. These "new" immigrants tended to be poor, non-Protestant, and unskilled; they tended to stay in close-knit communities and retain their languages, customs, and religions.

■ In a Puck cartoon titled "Looking Backward," the shadows of their immigrant origins loom over the rich and powerful who want to deny the "new" immigrants from central and southern Europe admission to the United States. The caption on the cartoon reads, "They would close to the newcomer the bridge that had carried them and their fathers over." ■

Immigrants and the City

Industrial capitalism—the world of factories and machines—tested the immigrants and placed an enormous strain on their families. Many immigrants came from peasant societies where life proceeded according to outdoor routine and age-old tradition. In their new city homes, they found both new freedoms and a novel set of customs and expectations. Historians have only recently begun to discover the remarkable ways in which they learned to adjust.

Like native-born families, most immigrant families were nuclear in structure, consisting of two parents and their children. Generally, the men were wage earners; the women, household managers and mothers. The father normally played a minor role in child rearing or managing the family finances. "His to earn and hers to spend" was the standard of domestic virtue.

Although patterns varied between ethnic groups and between economic classes within ethnic groups, immigrants tended to marry within the group more than did the native-born. Immigrants also tended to marry at a later age than natives, and they tended to have more children, a fact that worried nativists opposed to immigration.

Most immigrants tried to retain their traditional culture for themselves and their children while at the same time adapting to life in their new country. To do this, they spoke their native language, practiced their religious faith, read their own newspapers, established their own schools, and formed a myriad of social organizations to maintain ties between members of the group.

Immigrant associations offered fellowship in a strange land. They helped newcomers find jobs and homes; they provided important services such as unemployment and health insurance. Some groups were no larger than a neighborhood; others spread nationwide. Many women belonged to and participated in the work of the immigrant associations; in addition, there were groups exclusively for women. Such associations as the Polish National Alliance served to maintain Old World traditions while helping members become accustomed to American life.

Church, school, and fraternal societies shaped the way in which immigrants adjusted to life in America. Eastern European Jews established synagogues and religious schools wherever they settled to preserve their ancient heritage. Among groups such as the Irish and the Poles, the Roman Catholic Church provided spiritual and educational guidance. In the parish schools, Polish priests and nuns taught

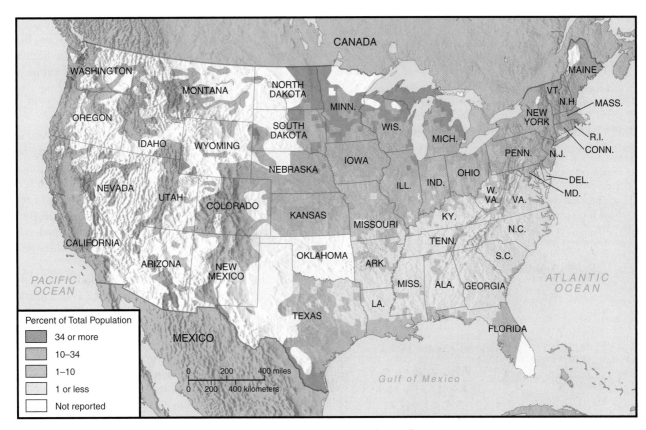

FOREIGN-BORN POPULATION, 1890 *Many immigrants settled in the rapidly growing cities of the northeast, where factory jobs were more plentiful than in the South. Immigrants looking for land to farm made their way west to the grain belt of the Midwest.* ■

Polish American children in the Polish language about Polish as well as American culture. By preserving language, religion, and heritage, they shaped the city—and the country—as much as it shaped them.

The House that Tweed Built

Closely connected with explosive urban growth was the emergence of the powerful city political machine. As cities grew, lines of responsibility in city governments became hopelessly confused, increasing the opportunity for corruption and greed. Burgeoning populations required streets, buildings, and public services; immigrants needed even more services. In this situation, party machines played an important role.

The machines traded services for votes. Loosely knit, they were headed by a strong, influential leader—the "boss"—who tied together a network of ward and precinct captains, each of whom looked after his local constituents. During the second half of the nineteenth century, such cities as New York, Chicago, Philadelphia, and San Francisco developed powerful political machines.

William M. Tweed, head of the famed Tweed Ring in New York, provided the model for them all. Nearly 6 feet tall, weighing almost 300 pounds, Tweed rose through the ranks of the New York Democratic machine known as Tammany Hall. A man of culture and warmth, he moved easily between the rough back alleys of New York and the parlors and clubs of the city's elite. Behind the scenes, he headed a ring that plundered New York for tens of millions of dollars.

A Look at the Past

Toy Bank

Political boss William Tweed of Tammany Hall pockets money as a mechanical bank. This bank was first patented in the 1870s, after Tweed's fall from power in 1872, and it became a very popular model. While charming children with his moving hand and head that nodded thanks upon the deposit of a coin, the bank also satirized the political machines, graft, and corruption. ✱ What does such a satirical toy suggest about attitudes toward politicians and political corruption at the time? Why do you think the bank was so popular?

The New York County Courthouse was his masterpiece. The three-story "House that Tweed Built" was designed to cost $250,000, but the bill ran a bit higher. Furniture, carpets, and window shades alone came to more than $5.5 million. In the end, the building cost more than $13 million—and in 1872, when Tweed fell, it was still not finished.

Some bosses were plainly corrupt; others believed in "honest graft," a term Tammany's George Washington Plunkitt coined to describe "legitimate" profits made from advance knowledge of city projects. Why did voters keep them in power? The answers are complex, but for the most part, the bosses stayed in power because they paid attention to the needs of the least privileged city voters. They offered valued services in an era when neither government nor business lent a hand.

If an immigrant, tired and bewildered after the long crossing, came looking for a job, bosses like Tweed found him one in city offices or local business. If a family's breadwinner died or was injured, the bosses donated food and clothing and saw to it that the family made it through the crisis. They contributed to hospitals, orphanages, and dozens of worthy neighborhood causes.

Most bosses became wealthy; they looked after their own needs first. Reformers occasionally ousted them. But reformers rarely stayed in power long. Drawn mainly from the middle and upper classes, they had little understanding of the needs of the poor. Before long, they returned to private concerns, and the bosses cheerily took power again.

SOCIAL AND CULTURAL CHANGE, 1877–1900

From 1877 to the 1890s, the nation underwent sweeping changes that affected economic, political, and social life. Technology changed mores; bright lights and new careers drew young men and women to the cities; family ties loosened. Cities, suburbs, and factories took new forms. While many people worked harder and harder, others had increased leisure time. Thanks to advancing technology, news flashed quickly across the oceans, and for the first time in history, people shook open their evening newspapers to read of that day's events in distant lands.

Old issues—questions of racial, social, and economic justice and of federal-state relations—were not settled, but people wanted new directions. Politics lost the sharp focus of the Civil War and its aftermath. With the end of Reconstruction, concern over the Union and slavery faded into the past.

In 1877, the country had 47 million people; a little more than a decade later, there were nearly 63 million. Nine-tenths of the population was white; just under one-tenth was black. The bulk of the white population, most of whom were Protestant, came from the so-called Anglo-Saxon countries of northern Europe. WASPS—white Anglo-Saxon Protestants—dominated American society.

Most people still lived on farms or in small towns. Their lives revolved around the farm, the church, and the general store. In 1880, nearly 75 percent of the population lived in communities of fewer than 2500 people. In 1900, in the midst of city growth, 60 percent still did. The average family in 1880 had three children, and life expectancy was about forty-three years. By 1900, it had risen to forty-seven years, the result of improved health care. For blacks and other minorities, often living in unsanitary rural areas, life expectancy was substantially lower: thirty-three years in 1900.

Meals tended to be heavy, and so did people. Even breakfast had several courses and could include steak, eggs, fish, potatoes, toast, and coffee. Food prices were low. Toward the end of the century, eating habits changed. New packaged breakfast cereals became popular, fresh fruit and vegetables came in on fast trains from Florida and California, and commercially canned food processing became safer and cheaper. The newfangled ice box, cooled by blocks of ice, kept food fresher.

Medical science was in the midst of a major revolution. Louis Pasteur's recent discovery that germs cause infection and disease created the new science of microbiology and led the way to the development of vaccines and other preventive measures. But tuberculosis, typhoid, diphtheria, and pneumonia—all then curable—were still the leading causes of death. Many families knew the wrenching pain of a child's death. Infant mortality declined between 1877 and 1900, but the great drop did not come until after 1920.

There were few hospitals and no hospital insurance. Most patients stayed at home, although medical practice expanded rapidly. In the field of surgery, anesthetics—ether and chloroform—eliminated pain, and antiseptic practices helped prevent postoperative infections. An earlier discovery—nitrous oxide, called laughing gas—eased the discomfort of dentistry. The new science of psychology began to explore the mind, hitherto uncharted. William James, a leading American psychologist and philosopher, stressed the importance of the environment on human development.

Manners and Mores

The code of Victorian morality set the tone for the era. The code prescribed stern standards of dress, manners, and sexual behavior. It was both obeyed and disobeyed, and it reflected the tensions of a generation that was undergoing a change in moral standards.

In 1877, children were to be seen and not heard. They spoke when spoken to, listened rather than chattered—at least that was the ideal. Older boys and girls were often chaperoned, although they could always find moments alone. They played kissing games such as post office and spin the bottle; they puffed cigarettes behind the barn. Counterbalancing such youthful exuberance was strong pride in virtue and self-control. "Thank heaven I am absolutely pure," Theodore Roosevelt wrote in 1880 after proposing to Alice Lee. "I can tell Alice everything I have ever done."

Gentlemen of the middle class dressed in heavy black suits, derby hats, and white shirts with paper collars. Women wore tight corsets, long dark dresses, and black shoes reaching well above the ankles. As with so many things, styles changed dramatically toward the end of the century, spurred in part by new sporting fads such as golf, tennis, and bicycling, which required looser clothing. Middle-class women adopted tailored suits and "shirtwaist" blouses modeled after men's shirts.

Religious and patriotic values were strong. A center of community life, the church often set the tenor for family and social relationships. In the 1880s, eight out of ten church members were Protestants; most of the rest were Roman Catholics. Evangelists such as Dwight L. Moody conducted successful mass revival meetings across the country.

Mugwumps Drawing their members mainly from the educated and upper class, these reformers crusaded for lower tariffs, limited federal government, and civil service reform to end political corruption.

Women's Christian Temperance Union (WCTU) Founded by Francis E. Willard, this organization campaigned to end drunkenness and the social ills that accompanied it.

With slavery abolished, reformers turned their attention to new moral and political issues. One group, known as the **Mugwumps,** worked to end corruption in politics. Drawn mostly from the educated and upper class, they included important newspaper and magazine editors. Other zealous reformers campaigned for prohibition of the sale of intoxicating liquors, hoping to end the social evils that stemmed from drunkenness. In 1874, the **Women's Christian Temperance Union (WCTU)** was formed to combat the consumption of alcohol. By 1898, the WCTU had ten thousand branches and half a million members.

In New York City, Anthony Comstock formed the Society for the Suppression of Vice, which supervised public morality. At his behest, Congress passed the Comstock Law (1873) prohibiting the mailing or transporting of "obscene, lewd or lascivious" articles. The law was not successful, and Comstock reported frequent violations of the act.

Leisure and Entertainment

In the 1870s, people tended to rise early. After dressing and eating, they went off to work and school; housewives marketed daily. In the evenings, families gathered in the "second parlor" or living room, where the children did their lessons, played games, sang around the piano, and listened to the day's verse from the Bible.

Indoor popular games included cards, dominoes, backgammon, chess, and checkers. Many of them were instructional as well as entertaining. The newest outdoor game was croquet, so popular that candles were mounted on the wickets to allow play at night. It was the first outdoor game designed for play by both sexes, and it frequently served as a setting for courtship.

New York's Broadway was the center of the theater, but road shows took popular plays to many cities and towns. American taste in the theater ran to intrigue, swordplay, melodrama, and grandiloquent language. Most plays were imported from Europe; the United States had few serious playwrights.

Sentimental ballads remained the most popular musical form, but the insistent syncopated rhythms of ragtime were being heard. By the time the strains of Scott Joplin's "Maple Leaf Rag" (1899) popularized ragtime, critics complained that "a wave of vulgar, filthy and suggestive music has inundated the land." Critics of ragtime took more comfort from the growth of classical music, which flourished during these years.

In the hamlets and small towns of America, traveling circuses were enormously popular. The larger circuses, run by entrepreneurs such as P. T. Barnum and James A. Bailey, played the cities, but every town attracted its own smaller versions. When the circus left town, Buffalo Bill's Wild West Show arrived, reenacting Indian field battles and displaying frontier marksmanship.

Football and baseball contests attracted avid fans. The years between 1870 and 1900 saw the rise of organized spectator sports, a trend reflecting the new uses of leisure. Baseball's first professional team, the Cincinnati Red Stockings, appeared in 1869, and baseball soon became the preeminent national sport. In 1869, Princeton and Rutgers played the first intercollegiate football game. Soon other schools picked up the sport, and by the early 1890s, crowds of fifty thousand or more attended the most popular contests. Boxing, though outlawed in most states, also gained a large following. John L. Sullivan, the era's most popular champion, won the last bare-knuckle heavyweight championship fight when he defeated Jake Kilrain in 1889 in a brutal seventy-five-round contest.

As gas and electric lights brightened the night and streetcars crisscrossed city streets, leisure habits changed. With so many things to do, people stayed home less often. New York City's first electric sign appeared in 1881, and people filled the streets on their way to the theater, vaudeville shows, or dance halls or just out for an evening stroll.

Changes in Family Life

Industrialization and urbanization changed family relationships. On the farm, parents and children worked more or less together, and the family was a producing unit. In factories, family members rarely worked together. In working-class families, mothers, fathers, and children separated at dawn and returned, ready for sleep, at dark. Middle-class fathers began to move their families out of the city to the suburbs; they commuted to work on the new streetcars, leaving wives and children at home and school.

Increasingly, middle-class wives and children became isolated from the world of work. Unlike the rural or urban working class—where mothers and children as well as fathers labored to support the family economy—middle-class families turned inward. Older children spent more time in adolescence, and periods of formal schooling were lengthier. Fewer wives participated directly in their husbands' work. As a result, they and their children occupied what contemporaries called a "separate sphere of domesticity," a place apart from the crass materialism of the outside world.

As the middle-class family's economic function declined, it took on increased emotional significance. "In the old days," said a woman in 1907, "a married woman was supposed to be a frump and a bore and a physical wreck. Now you are supposed to keep up intellectually, to look young and well and be fresh and bright and entertaining." Nonetheless, while society's leaders spoke fondly of the value of homemaking, the status of housewives declined under the factory system, which emphasized money rewards and devalued household labor.

Underlying all the changes was one of the modern world's most important trends, a major decline in fertility rates that lasted from 1800 to 1939. Although blacks, immigrants, and rural dwellers continued to have more children than white U.S.-born city dwellers, the trend affected all races and classes. Late marriages accounted for part of the decline, but a more important factor was the conscious decision by women and men to postpone or limit families. Women decided in some cases to devote greater attention to a smaller number of children and in other cases to pursue their own careers. In large part, the decline in fertility stemmed from people's responses to the social and economic forces around them, the rise of cities and industry. As a result, they reshaped some of the fundamental attitudes and institutions of American society.

■ Victorian fashion ideals for women emphasized elaborate, confining dress styles with tiny waistlines and full skirts that reached to the floor. Throughout the 1890s, as women began to participate in some of the new sports or go to work in factories, stores, or business offices, styles gradually became less restrictive. This 1900 cover of Ladies' Home Journal shows women wearing tailored jackets and simple pleated skirts hemmed above the ankle playing golf with men. ■

Changing Views: A Growing Assertiveness Among Women

In and out of the family, there was a growing recognition of the self-sufficient working women who were entering the workforce in increasing numbers. Most were single and worked because of economic necessity. For many Americans, this "new woman" was regarded as a threat, a corruption of the ideal woman of men's imaginations, innocent, helpless, and good.

Views changed, albeit slowly. One important change occurred in the legal codes pertaining to women, particularly in the common-law doctrine of *femme couverte*. Under that doctrine, wives were chattel of their husbands; they could not legally control their own earnings, property, or children unless they had drawn up a specific contract before marriage. By 1890, many states had substantially revised the doctrine to allow wives control of their own earnings and inherited property. In cases of divorce, which rose sharply in the last third of the century, the new laws also recognized women's rights to custody or joint custody of their children.

In the 1870s and 1880s, a growing number of women were asserting their humanness and seeking self-fulfillment. Increasing interest in medical and psychological studies led women such as Charlotte Perkins Gilman, author of *Women and Economics* (1898), to argue that what men called womanly "innocence" was really ignorance; they began approaching old taboos—menstruation, sexual intercourse, childbirth—as natural functions and appropriate subjects of open inquiry.

More and more women were willing to voice their opinions about public policy, too, espousing causes with new fervor. They fought for the vote, lobbied for equal pay, and protested against price gouging by merchants, sometimes taking to the streets in organized demonstrations. Susan B. Anthony, fined $100 (which she refused to pay) when she tried to vote in the presidential election of 1872, helped form the **National American Woman Suffrage Association** in 1890 to work for female franchisement.

National American Woman Suffrage Association Founded by Susan B. Anthony in 1890, this organization worked to secure women the right to vote through careful organization and peaceful lobbying.

Educating the Masses

Continuing a trend that stretched back a hundred years, childhood was becoming a distinct time of life. There was still only a vague concept of adolescence, but the role of children was changing. Children were no longer perceived as "little adults," valued for the additional financial gain they might bring into the family. Now children were to grow and learn and be nurtured rather than rushed into adulthood.

As a result, schooling became more important, and American educators came closer than ever before to universal education. More states and territories made school attendance compulsory, more public schools were constructed, and more money was spent on education. Between 1870 and 1900, illiteracy declined from 20 percent to just over 10 percent of the population. Still, even as late as 1900, the average adult had only five years of schooling.

Most schools stressed a highly structured curriculum, focused on discipline and routine in a rigid environment. School began early; boys attended all day, but girls often stayed home after lunch, since it was thought they needed less in the way of learning. On the teacher's command, students stood and recited from *Webster's Spellers* and *McGuffey's Eclectic Readers*, the period's two most popular textbooks, which taught ethics, values, and religion as well as reading. In the *Readers*, boys grew up to be heroes, girls grew up to be mothers, and hard work always meant success.

The South lagged far behind in education. Family size was about twice as large as in the North, and a greater proportion of the population lived in isolated rural areas. Many southern states refused to adopt compulsory education laws. Most important, Southerners insisted on maintaining separate school systems to segregate the races. Supported by the 1896 U.S. Supreme Court decision in *Plessy v. Ferguson*, which upheld the constitutionality of "separate but equal" facilities, segregated schooling added a devastating financial burden to education in the South.

Plessy v. *Ferguson* A Supreme Court case in 1896 that established the doctrine of "separate but equal" and upheld a Louisiana law requiring that blacks and whites occupy separate rail cars.

North Carolina and Alabama mandated segregated schools in 1876, South Carolina and Louisiana in 1877, Mississippi in 1878, and Virginia in 1882. The laws often implied that the schools would be "separate but equal," but they rarely were. In 1890, only 35 percent of black children attended school in the South; 55 percent of white children did. At that time, nearly two-thirds of the country's black population was illiterate.

Educational techniques changed after the 1870s. Educators paid more attention to early elementary education. The kindergarten movement, started in St. Louis in

1873, spread across the country. In kindergartens, 4- to 6-year-olds learned by playing, not by rigid discipline. For older children, social reformers advocated "practical" courses in manual training and homemaking. For the first time, education became a field of university study. Teacher training became increasingly professional. By 1900, there were 345 normal schools (teacher-training institutions) throughout the United States.

Higher Education

Nearly 150 new colleges and universities opened in the twenty years between 1880 and 1900. The Morrill Land Grant Act of 1862 gave large grants of land to the states for the establishment of colleges to teach "agriculture and the mechanical arts." The act fostered sixty-nine "land-grant" institutions. Private philanthropy, born of the large fortunes of the industrial age, also spurred growth in higher education. Leland Stanford gave $24 million to endow Stanford University, and John D. Rockefeller gave $34 million to found the University of Chicago.

As universities increased, their function changed, and their curriculum broadened. No longer did they exist primarily to train young men for the ministry. They moved away from the classical curriculum of rhetoric, mathematics, Latin, and Greek toward "reality and practicality." The Massachusetts Institute of Technology (MIT), founded in 1861, focused on science and engineering.

Influenced by the new German universities, which emphasized specialized research, Johns Hopkins University in Baltimore opened the nation's first separate graduate school in 1876. By 1900, more than nine thousand Americans had studied in Germany, and some of them returned home to become presidents of institutions such as Harvard, Yale, Columbia, the University of Chicago, and Johns Hopkins.

One of them, Charles W. Eliot, who became president of Harvard in 1869 at the age of 35, set up an elective system in which students chose their own courses rather than following a rigidly prescribed curriculum. Lectures and discussions replaced rote recitation, and courses in the natural and social sciences, fine arts, and modern languages multiplied.

Educational opportunities also increased for women. A number of women's colleges opened, including Vassar (1865), Wellesley (1875), Smith (1875), and Radcliffe (1893). The land-grant colleges of the Midwest, open to women from the outset, spurred a nationwide trend toward coeducation. By 1900, women made up about 40 percent of college students.

Fewer opportunities existed for African Americans and other minorities. Most colleges did not accept minorities, and few applied. W. E. B. Du Bois, the brilliant black sociologist and civil rights leader, attended Harvard in the late 1880s but found the society of Harvard Yard closed against him. Black students turned to black colleges such as Hampton Normal and Industrial Institute in Virginia, which were often supported by whites who favored manual training for blacks. At the Tuskegee Institute in Alabama, which opened in 1881, Booker T. Washington, an ex-slave, put his educational ideals into practice. By 1900, Tuskegee was a model industrial and agricultural training school. It offered instruction in thirty trades to fourteen hundred students.

Washington stressed patience, manual training, and hard work. Rather than fighting for equal rights, blacks should acquire property and show they were worthy of their rights. Outlined most forcefully in Washington's speech in Atlanta, the philosophy became known as the Atlanta Compromise; many whites and some blacks welcomed it. Acknowledging white domination, it called for slow progress through self-improvement, not through lawsuits or agitation. But Washington did believe in black equality. Often secretive in his methods, he worked behind the scenes to organize black voters and lobby against harmful laws. In his own way, he

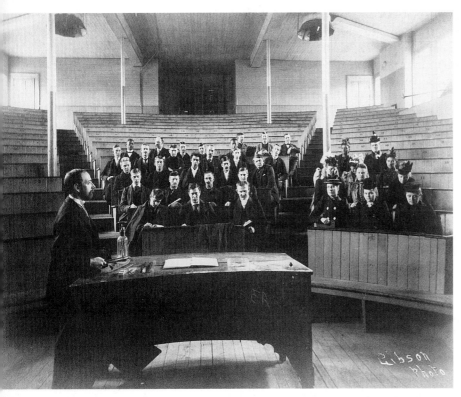

■ *A physics lecture at the University of Michigan in the late 1880s or early 1890s. The land-grant university admitted women, but seating in the lecture hall was segregated by gender—although not by race. Notice that both whites and African Americans are seated in the back rows of the men's section.* ■

bespoke a racial pride that contributed to the rise of black nationalism in the twentieth century.

Du Bois wanted a more aggressive strategy. Born in 1868, the son of poor parents, he studied at Fisk University in Tennessee and the University of Berlin before he went to Harvard. Unable to find a teaching job in a white college, he took a low-paying research position at the University of Pennsylvania. He had no office but did not need one. Du Bois used the new discipline of sociology, which emphasized factual observation in the field, to study the condition of blacks.

Notebook in hand, he set out to examine crime in Philadelphia's black Seventh Ward. He interviewed five thousand people, mapped and classified neighborhoods, and produced *The Philadelphia Negro* (1898), a book of nearly a thousand pages. The first study of the effect of urban life on blacks, it cited a wealth of statistics, all suggesting that crime in the ward stemmed not from inborn degeneracy but from the environment in which blacks lived. Change the environment, and people would change, too; education was a good way to go about it. Calling for integrated schools with equal opportunity for all, Du Bois also urged blacks to educate their "talented tenth," a highly trained intellectual elite, to lead them.

Throughout higher education, there was increased emphasis on professional training, particularly in medicine, dentistry, and law. Enrollments swelled, even as standards of admissions of the early twentieth century tightened. Doctors, lawyers, and others became part of a growing middle class that shaped the concerns of the Progressive Era.

Although fewer than 5 percent of the college-age population attended college between 1877 and 1890, the new trends had great impact. A generation of men and women encountered new ideas that changed their views of themselves and society. Many students emerged from American colleges with a heightened sense of the social problems facing the nation and the belief that they could help cure society's ills.

THE STIRRINGS OF REFORM

Intellectual beliefs of the period emphasized the slow process of evolution rather than radical reform. This stress on the slow pace of change reflected the doctrine of **social Darwinism,** based on the evolutionary theories of Charles Darwin and the writings of English social philosopher Herbert Spencer. In several influential books, Spencer applied Darwinian principles of natural selection to society, combining biology and sociology in a theory of "social selection" that explained human progress. Like animals, society evolved, slowly, by adapting to the environment. The "survival of the fittest"—an expression that Spencer, not Darwin, invented—preserved the strong and weeded out the weak.

social Darwinism Adaptation of Charles Darwin's theory of evolution, this theory held that the "laws" of evolution applied to human life, that change or reform therefore took centuries, and that the "fittest" would succeed in business and social relationships. It promoted the ideas of competition and individualism; it saw as futile any intervention of government into human affairs; and it was used by influential members of the economic and social elite to oppose reform.

Social Darwinism had a number of influential followers in the United States, including William Graham Sumner, a prominent professor at Yale University who was also a forceful writer. He argued that government action on behalf of the poor or weak interfered with evolution and sapped the species. Reform tampered with the laws of nature and was ultimately harmful to society as a whole.

The influence of social Darwinism on American thinking has been exaggerated, but in the powerful hands of Sumner and others, it did influence some journalists, ministers, and policymakers. Between 1877 and the 1890s, however, it came under increasing attack. In fields such as religion, economics, politics, literature, and law, thoughtful people raised questions about established conditions and suggested the need for reform.

New Currents in Social Thought

Henry George's nationwide best-seller *Progress and Poverty* (1879) led the way to a more critical appraisal of American society in the 1880s and beyond. The book jolted traditional thought by questioning the assumptions of social Darwinism.

"The present century," George wrote, "has been marked by a prodigious increase in wealth-producing power. . . . It was natural to expect, and it was expected, that . . . real poverty [would become] a thing of the past." Such, however, was not the case. Instead, he argued, "the wealthy class is becoming more wealthy; but the poorer class is becoming more dependent."

George proposed a simple solution. Land formed the basis for wealth; a "single tax" on it, replacing all other taxes, would equalize wealth and raise revenue to help the poor. "Single-tax" clubs sprang up around the country, but George's solution, simplistic and unappealing, had much less impact than his analysis of the problem itself. He raised questions a generation of readers set out to answer.

George's emphasis on deprivation in the environment excited a young country lawyer in Ashtabula, Ohio, named Clarence Darrow. Unlike the social Darwinists, Darrow was sure that criminals were made and not born. They grew out of "the unjust condition of human life." In the mid-1880s, he left for Chicago and a forty-year career working to convince people that poverty lay at the root of crime.

As Darrow rejected the implications of social Darwinism, in similar fashion did Richard T. Ely and a group of young economists poke holes in traditional economic thought. Ely attacked classical economics for its dogmatism, simple faith in laissez-faire, and reliance on self-interest as a guide for human conduct. He refused to "acknowledge laissez-faire as an excuse for doing nothing while people starve."

In 1885, Ely led a small band of rebels in founding the American Economic Association, which linked economics to social problems and urged government intervention in economic affairs. Social critic Thorstein Veblen saw economic laws as a mask for human greed. In *The Theory of the Leisure Class* (1899), Veblen analyzed the "predatory wealth" and "conspicuous consumption" of the business class.

Lawyer Edward Bellamy dreamed of a cooperative society where poverty, greed, and crime no longer existed. Bellamy published *Looking Backward, 2000–1887* in 1887 and became a national reform figure virtually overnight. The novel's protagonist, Julian West, falls asleep in 1887 and awakes in the year 2000. He finds himself in a socialist utopia where cooperation, rather than competition, is the watchword. The vision captured the imagination of many Americans, who responded by calling for the nationalization of public utilities and a wider distribution of wealth.

Walter Rauschenbusch, a young Baptist minister, read widely from the writings of Bellamy, George, and other social reformers. When he took his first church post in Hell's Kitchen, a blighted area of New York City, he soon discovered the weight of the slum environment. In the 1890s, Rauschenbusch became a professor at the Rochester Theological Seminary, and he began to expound on the responsibility of organized religion to advance social justice.

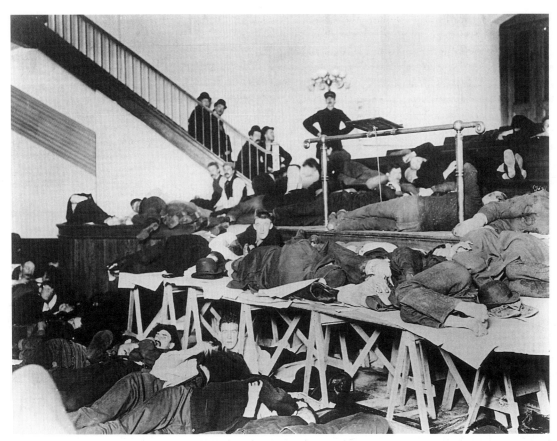

■ *Men sleeping in crowded conditions at the Salvation Army headquarters in New York City, 1897. The Salvation Army's missions for the homeless tended to the material and spiritual needs of the poor, unemployed, and outcast in the city's slums.* ■

Social Gospel Preached by a number of urban Protestant ministers, this doctrine focused as much on improving the conditions of life on earth as on saving souls for the hereafter. Its adherents worked for child-labor laws and measures to alleviate poverty.

Some Protestant sects stressed individual salvation and a better life in the next world, not in this one. Poverty was evidence of sinfulness; the poor had only themselves to blame. Wealth and destitution, suburbs and slums—all formed part of God's plan.

Challenging those traditional doctrines, a number of churches in the 1880s began establishing missions in the city slums. Living among the poor and the homeless, the urban missionaries grew impatient with religious doctrines that endorsed the status quo. Instead, many of them supported the emerging religious philosophy known as the **Social Gospel,** which focused on improving living conditions as well as saving souls. Churches became centers for social uplift as well as religious activity.

The most active Social Gospel leader was Washington Gladden, a Congregational minister and prolific writer. Linking Christianity to the social and economic environment, Gladden spent a lifetime working for "social salvation." Emphasizing a fellowship of love, he denounced competition, urged an "industrial partnership" between employers and employees, and called for efforts to help the poor.

The Settlement Houses

A growing number of social workers, living in the urban slums, shared Gladden's concern. Like Tweed and Plunkitt, they appreciated the dependence of the poor; unlike them, they wanted to eradicate the conditions that underlaid it.

Youthful, idealistic, and mostly middle-class, these social workers established **settlement houses** to help the poor. The first such house was opened in New York City in 1886; by 1910, there were more than four hundred of them. Reformers such as Jane Addams, who established the famous Hull House in Chicago (1889), wanted to bridge the socioeconomic gap between rich and poor and to bring education, culture, and hope to the slums. They sought to create in the heart of the city the values and sense of community of small-town America.

Many of the settlement workers were women, some of them college graduates who found that society had little use for their talents and energy. When Jane Addams opened Hull House, she was 29 years old. Endowed with a forceful and winning personality, she intended "to share the lives of the poor" and humanize the industrial city. Her staff stressed education, offering classes in elementary English and Shakespeare, lectures on ethics and the history of art, and courses in cooking, sewing, and manual skills.

Like settlement workers in other cities, Addams and her colleagues studied the immigrants in nearby tenements. Finding people of eighteen different nationalities living within one square mile of Hull House, they taught them American history and the English language yet also encouraged them, through folk festivals and arts, to preserve their heritage. Other settlement workers—among them Robert Woods in Boston and Lillian Wald in New York City—concentrated on such social and human problems as hunger, school dropouts, exploitive child labor, and health care for the poor.

settlement houses Located in poor districts of major cities, these were community centers that tried to soften the impact of urban life for immigrant and other families. Often run by young, educated women, they provided social services and a political voice for their neighborhoods.

A Crisis in Social Welfare

When the depression of 1893 struck, it jarred the young settlement workers, many of whom had just begun their work. In cities and towns across the country, traditional methods of helping the needy foundered in the crisis. Gradually, a new class of professional social workers arose to fill the need. Unlike the church and charity volunteers, these social workers wanted not only to feed the poor but also to study their condition and alleviate it. Revealingly, they called themselves "case workers" and daily collected data on the income, housing, jobs, health, and habits of the poor. Prowling tenement districts, they gathered information about the number of rooms, number of occupants, ventilation, and sanitation, putting together a fund of useful data.

Studies of the poor popped up everywhere. Walter Wyckoff embarked in 1891 on what he called "an experiment in reality." For eighteen months, he worked as an unskilled laborer in jobs from Connecticut to California. Wyckoff summarized his findings in *The Workers* (1897), a book immediately hailed as a major contribution to sociology. Following Wyckoff's lead, other investigators examined the lives of domestic servants, miners, lumberjacks, and factory laborers. Calls for reform of urban life grew louder, spawning numerous task forces and civic organizations committed to that purpose.

CONCLUSION: THE PLURALISTIC SOCIETY

"The United States was born in the country and moved to the city," historian Richard Hofstadter said. Much of that movement occurred during the nineteenth century when the United States was the most rapidly urbanizing nation in the Western world. American cities bustled with energy; they absorbed millions of migrants from Europe and other parts of the world. The migration, and the urban growth that accompanied it, reshaped American politics and culture.

Chronology

1862	Morrill Land Grant gives land to states for establishment of colleges
1869	Rutgers and Princeton play in the nation's first intercollegiate football game ▪ Cincinnati Red Stockings, baseball's first professional team, is organized
1873	Comstock Law bans obscene articles from the U.S. mail ▪ Nation's first kindergarten opens in St. Louis, Missouri
1874	Women's Christian Temperance Union formed to crusade against evils of liquor
1876	Johns Hopkins University opens the first separate graduate school
1879	Henry George analyzes problems of urbanizing in *Progress and Poverty* ▪ Salvation Army arrives in the United States
1881	Booker T. Washington opens the Tuskegee Institute in Alabama
1883	Metropolitan Opera opens in New York
1885	Home Insurance Building, the country's first metal-frame structure, is erected in Chicago
1887	Edward Bellamy promotes the idea of a socialist utopia in *Looking Backward, 2000–1887*
1889	Jane Addams opens Hull House in Chicago
1890	National American Woman Suffrage Association is formed to work for women's right to vote
1894	Immigration Restriction League is formed to limit immigration from southern and eastern Europe
1896	Supreme Court decision in *Plessy* v. *Ferguson* establishes the constitutionality of "separate but equal" facilities for blacks and whites ▪ John Dewey's Laboratory School for testing and practice of new educational theory opens at the University of Chicago

The 1920 census showed that, for the first time, most Americans lived in cities. It also revealed that about half the population was descended from people who arrived after the American Revolution. As European, African, and Asian cultures met in the American city, a culturally pluralistic society emerged. The residents of the United States proudly declared their hybrid cultural identities as Polish Americans, African Americans, Irish Americans, and so on. The metaphor of the melting pot reflected a new national image as, in the decades after the 1870s, a jumble of ethnic and racial groups responded to the challenges of industrialization and urbanization.

KEY TERMS

new immigrants, p. 371

Mugwumps, p. 376

Women's Christian Temperance Union (WCTU), p. 376

National American Woman Suffrage Association, p. 378

Plessy v. *Ferguson*, p. 378

social Darwinism, p. 380

Social Gospel, p. 382

settlement houses, p. 383

RECOMMENDED READING

On urban America, see Sam Bass Warner, Jr., *Streetcar Suburbs* (1962) and *The Urban Wilderness* (1972). William R. Taylor, *In Pursuit of Gotham: Culture and Commerce in New York* (1992), Eric H. Monkkonen, *America Becomes Urban* (1988), John Jakle, *City Lights: Illuminating the American Night* (2003), Jon A. Peterson, *The Birth of City Planning in the United States, 1840–1917* (2003), John Henry Hepp IV, *The Middle-Class City: Transforming Space and Time in Philadelphia, 1876–1926* (2003), Sven Beckert, *The Monied Metropolis: New York City and the Consolidation of the American Bourgeoisie, 1850–1896* (2001), and David Schuyler, *The New Urban Landscape* (1986), are also valuable. See also two books by Jon C. Teaford: *The Unheralded Triumph: City Government in America, 1870–1900* (1984) and *City and Suburb: The Political Fragmentation of Metropolitan America, 1850–1970* (1979).

For family life, see Joseph Kett, *Rites of Passage: Adolescence in America* (1977), Elaine Tyler May, *Great Expectations: Marriage and Divorce in Post-Victorian America* (1980), Steven Mintz, *A Prison of Expectations: The Family in Victorian Culture* (1983), Helen Lefkowitz Horowitz, *Rereading Sex: Battles over Sexual Knowledge and Suppression in Nineteenth-Century America* (2002), Maureen A. Flanagan, *Seeing With Their Hearts: Chicago Women and the Vision of the Good City, 1871–1933* (2002), Stephen M. Frank, *Life With Father: Parenthood and Masculinity in the Nineteenth-Century American North* (1998), and Norma Basch, *In the Eyes of the Law: Women, Marriage, and Property in Nineteenth-Century New York* (1982). Karen Lystra, *Searching the Heart: Women, Men, and Romantic Love in Nineteenth-Century America* (1989), is valuable, as is Jean V. Matthews, *The Rise of the New Woman: The Women's Movement in America, 1875–1930* (2003).

Urban reform is examined in Judith Ann Trolander, *Professionalism and Social Change: From the Settlement House Movement to Neighborhood Centers, 1886 to the Present* (1987), Shannon Jackson, *Lines of Activity: Performance, Historiography, Hull-House Domesticity* (2001), Allen F. Davis, *Spearheads for Reform: The Social Settlements and the Progressive Movement, 1890–1914* (1967), and *American Heroine: The Life and Legend of Jane Addams* (1973). Also, the more recent Victoria Bissell Brown, *The Education of Jane Addams* (2004).

SUGGESTED WEB SITES

The American Experience: America 1900
www.pbs.org/wgbh/amex/1900/
This site is the companion site to the PBS documentary. It includes audio clips of respected historians on the economics, politics, and culture of 1900, a primary source database, a timeline of the year, downloadable software to compile a personal family tree, and other materials.

Touring Turn-of-the-Century America: Photographs from the Detroit Publishing Company, 1880–1920
memory.loc.gov/ammem/detroit/dethome.html
This Library of Congress collection has thousands of photographs from turn-of-the-century America.

World's Columbian Exposition:
Idea, Experience, Aftermath
xroads.virginia.edu/~MA96/WCE/title.html
This site has a virtual tour of the fair, along with contemporary reactions and modern analysis.

United States History: The Gilded Age (1890) to World War I
www.emayzine.com/lectures/Gilded~1.htm
This site consists of a good overview essay of the era.

Chapter Three: American Socialists and Reformers
www.vineyard.net/vineyard/history/pdgech3.htm
This site includes a fine essay about Edward Bellamy and some of the movements and ideas he inspired.

Jane Addams Hull-House Museum
www.uic.edu/jaddams/hull/hull_house.html
This site offers information on Addams, her settlement house programs, and the neighborhoods they served.

African American Perspectives:
Pamphlets from the Daniel A. P. Murray
Collection, 1818–1907
memory.loc.gov/ammem/aap/aaphome.html
This collection includes writings of famous African Americans including Frederick Douglass, Booker T. Washington, Ida B. Wells-Barnett, Benjamin W. Arnett, Alexander Crummel, and Emanuel Love.

Ellis Island
Isle of Hope, Isle of Tears

Ten years after he left Selo, his small Bulgarian village, for the United States, Michael Gurkin returned to tell of the wonders he had seen, including "buildings that scratched the sky," rooms in them that moved up and down, buttons that, when pushed, lit a house or a street. Stoyan Christowe, 13, listened intently, caught up in the "Americamania," as he called it, that swept through his village. Soon he was on his way to the new land, his pockets stuffed with walnuts, because he was too young to drink the farewell toast.

Unknowingly, he had joined a flood of people who were making their way to the United States. Between 1880 and 1920, a period of just forty years, a remarkable total of 23.5 million immigrants arrived in the country. They came from around the world, though mostly from Europe, driven from their homelands by economic, religious, or other troubles, lured across the ocean by the chance for a better life. They entered the country through several ports, but by far the most—about seven out of every ten—landed in the city of New York.

Until 1892, they landed at a depot known as Castle Garden, a sprawling building on the tip of Manhattan Island. When it could no longer handle the flow, the entry site was moved to Ellis Island, close to the Statue of Liberty. Contractors erected a wooden structure, which opened in 1892 and burned down five years later. They then put up the current edifice, an imposing red brick building with triple-arch entrances and corner steeples. A small city, it had dormitories, a hospital, a post office, and showers that could bathe eight thousand people a day. It opened in 1900.

The change to Ellis Island represented more than just a shift in site.

Entrance at Castle Garden had been fairly informal, since control over immigration still rested largely in the hands of the states. Officials merely registered newcomers, a process that took about thirty seconds.

In 1891, worried about the growing numbers of people who wanted in, Congress acted to bring immigration under federal control. Ellis Island was given tasks Castle Garden had never had, including mandates to keep out people some Americans considered undesirable. It became, one observer said, "the nearest earthly likeness to the Final Day of Judgement, when we have to prove our fitness to enter Heaven."

Many of those who sailed into the harbor, it should be remembered, never passed through the island at all. Arriving in first or second class, they had a fast on-board examination and went ashore, monied enough, it was assumed, not to become wards of the state. But those in third class—"steerage" as it was known—had a very different experience, and they faced it full of fear that they would fail some test and be sent back home.

The day they docked, Christowe and others washed thoroughly, hoping to look clean enough to pass inspection. Crowding the ship's rails, they gazed in wonder at the statue in the harbor, its arm lifted in the air. It was a saint, some guessed; Christopher Columbus, others said. It was a monument to freedom, Christowe was told, with Emma Lazarus's inviting poem at its base, "Give me your tired, your poor, Your huddled masses yearning to breathe free."

Once on the island, those huddled masses were under scrutiny from the moment they landed. Officials watched them climb the stairs, looking

for heart problems or lameness. Physicians administered the "six-second exam," checking quickly for disabilities or contagious diseases. If anything seemed out of sort, they put a chalk mark on the immigrant's coat calling for closer examination.

The next exam was the most feared: a doctor using a tailor's buttonhook to pull back eyelids to look for signs of diseases such as trachoma, a highly contagious bacterial eye infection that could lead to blindness. Most immigrants had never heard of trachoma, nor even knew they had the disease, but it alone could strand them in the island's hospital or put them on a boat back home.

No one who went through the exam ever forgot it, as an immigrant poet wrote:

> A stranger receives us
> Harshly and asks: "And your
>   health?"
> He examines us. His look
> Assesses us like dogs.
> He studies in depth
> Eyes and mouth. No doubt
> That if he'd probed our hearts
> He would have seen the wound.

Immigrants with chalk marks were herded to the left, while most went to the right, filing by a matron who searched the faces of women for evidence of "loose character." With so many languages among the arrivals, there were few written signs, and officials used metal barricades to guide people along, "like puppets on conveyor-belts," Christowe later recalled.

Last there were the inspectors, seated behind desks, asking name, age, occupation, among dozens of other questions. On a busy day, the inspectors had two minutes to decide the fate of a newcomer. Those who "failed" went before a feared Board of Special Inquiry for final decision. For most immigrants the whole process took less than five hours; many others, held for proof of funds or further examination, spent days in the dormitories or hospital. Despite the harsh rumors, no more than 3 percent in a given year were turned away.

Still, it was becoming harder to get in. People who feared the effect of immigrants on the nation clamored to keep them out. Some worried about the numbers of people who were arriving; others about disease or "radical" political views. Some did not like the shift in immigration after 1890 from largely Protestant northern and western Europe to Catholics, Jews, and others from southern and eastern Europe.

Reflecting such concerns, Congress passed laws to keep certain types of people out. In 1875, it prohibited the entrance of criminals and prostitutes. In 1882, it barred convicts and lunatics and excluded laborers from China, the first measure aimed directly at a racial group. In 1885, it banned the entry of laborers under contract, imported by industries to work at low wages; in 1891, polygamists and people with "loathsome" diseases; in 1903, anarchists. In 1917, it passed, over Woodrow Wilson's veto, a literacy test that required immigrants to read a passage in their native tongue.

The great burst of immigration, halted during World War I, ended with the adoption of restrictive legislation in the 1920s. Ellis Island became a detention center for "radicals" and other people awaiting deportation. Once the gateway to the United

■ A view of the landing station at Ellis Island in 1905, where millions of immigrants entered the country. ■

States, the famous island had become an exit.

Ellis Island closed in 1954; in 1965, recognizing its historic importance, the government made it a national monument. It reopened in 1990 as a museum of American immigration, attracting more than two million tourists a year; many retrace the footsteps of their ancestors who landed there. Stoyan Christowe's name is in the records. Starting with a miserable job in a railroad yard in St. Louis, he went to college, served in military intelligence during World War II, wrote several books, and became a member of the Vermont legislature.

His experience on Ellis Island blended into the nation's experience. More than 100 million Americans—about four in every ten—trace their ancestry to those who found a new home through its gates.

Questions for Discussion

* Do you think it was fair for prospective immigrants at Ellis Island to have to undergo multiple tests and rigorous physical examinations in order to get into the United States? Why or why not?

* What were some of the arguments that Americans in the early 1900s used to justify limiting immigration? What do you think of these arguments? How are they similar to or different from the arguments about immigration today?

Chapter 20

Political Realignments in the 1890s

Hardship and Heartache

In June 1894, Susan Orcutt, a young farm woman from western Kansas, wrote the governor of her state a letter. She was desperate. The nation was in the midst of a devastating economic depression, and like thousands of other people, she had no money and nothing to eat. "I take my pen in hand to let you know that we are starving to death," she wrote. There appeared to be no hope. Her husband had been to ten counties and could not find work, and her family had run out of food.

As bad as conditions were on the farms, they were no better in the cities. Thousands of homeless, starving men wandered in the streets, and charity societies and churches could not help the huge numbers of people who were in need. The records of the Massachusetts state medical examiner told a grim story of despondency and suicide. Rather than face more hunger and humiliation, men and women took their own lives.

Lasting until 1897, the depression was the decisive event of the decade. At its height, three million people were unemployed—20 percent of the workforce. The human costs were enormous, even among the well-to-do. "They were for me years of simple Hell," shattering "my whole scheme of life," said Charles Francis Adams, descendant of two American presidents.

The depression of the 1890s had profound and lasting effects. Bringing to a head many of the tensions that had been building in society, it increased rural hostility toward the cities, brought about a bitter fight over the currency, and changed people's thinking about government, unemployment, and reform. There were outbreaks of warfare between capital and labor, farmers demanded a fairer share of economic and social benefits, and the "new" immigrants came under fresh attack.

Under the cruel impact of the depression, ideas changed in many areas, including a stronger impulse toward reform, a larger role for the presidency, and a call for help from many farmers and laborers. One of the most important of these areas was politics. A realignment of the American political system, in process since the end of Reconstruction, finally reached fruition in the 1890s, establishing new patterns that gave rise to the Progressive Era and lasted well into the twentieth century.

POLITICS OF STALEMATE

Politics was a major fascination of the Gilded Age, as both mass entertainment and sport. Millions of Americans read party newspapers, listened to three-hour speeches by party leaders, and turned out in enormous numbers to vote. In the six presidential elections between 1876 and 1896, an average of almost 80 percent of the electorate voted.

White males made up the bulk of the electorate; until after the turn of the century, women could vote in national elections in only four western states. In 1875, the Supreme Court, in *Minor* v. *Happersett,* upheld the power of the states to deny the right to women, and Congress continued to refuse to pass a constitutional amendment for woman suffrage. In addition, black men were increasingly kept from the polls by various methods. In 1877, Georgia adopted the poll tax, which forced voters to pay an annual tax for the right to vote. It was a tax few blacks could afford to pay. In 1898, Louisiana adopted the famous "grandfather clause," demanding a literacy test for all voters except the sons and grandsons of those who had voted in the state before 1867—a time, of course, when no blacks could vote. The number of registered black voters in Louisiana decreased from 130,334 in 1896 to 1342 in 1904.

The Party Deadlock

The 1870s and 1880s were still dominated by the Civil War generation, the unusual group of people who rose to power in the turbulent 1850s. Five of the six presidents elected between 1865 and 1900 had served in the war, as had many civic, business, and religious leaders.

Party loyalties—rooted in Civil War traditions, ethnic and religious differences, and perhaps class distinctions—were remarkably strong. Although linked to the defeated Confederacy, the Democrats revived quickly after the war. In 1874, they gained control of the House of Representatives, which they maintained for all but four of the next twenty years. While identification with civil rights and military rule cut Republican strength in the South, the Democratic party's principles of states' rights, decentralization, and limited government won supporters everywhere.

The Republicans pursued policies in which local interests merged into nationwide patterns, and government became an instrument to promote moral well-being and material wealth. The Republicans passed the Homestead Act (1862), granted subsidies to the transcontinental railroads, and pushed other measures to encourage economic growth. They also enacted legislation to protect civil rights and advocated a high protective tariff as a tool of economic policy.

In national elections, sixteen states, mostly in New England and the North, consistently voted Republican; fourteen states, mostly in the South, consistently voted Democratic. Elections therefore depended on a handful of "doubtful" states—New York, New Jersey, Connecticut, Ohio, Indiana, and Illinois—which received special attention at election time. Presidential candidates usually came from these states. From 1868 to 1912, eight of the nine Republican presidential candidates and six of the seven Democratic candidates came from these states, especially New York and Ohio.

The two parties were evenly matched, and elections were closely fought. In three of the five presidential

A Look at the Past

Ballot Box

Until the 1890s, political parties printed their own ballots, which voters requested in order to cast a ballot. Voters revealed their political decisions simply by obtaining a ballot. Glass ballot boxes such as this one made it possible for others to witness that the voter actually cast the ballot. While today voters make their decisions and cast their votes privately, before 1890 voting was a visible, public act, and political intimidation could and did occur. ✷ Why would Americans use such a system? Why did they change to secret balloting at the end of the nineteenth century?

elections between 1876 and 1892, the victor won by less than 1 percent of the vote; in 1876 and 1888, the losing candidates actually received more popular votes than the winners but lost in the electoral college. Knowing that small mistakes could lose elections, politicians became extremely cautious. It was difficult to govern. Only twice during these years did one party control both the presidency and the two houses of Congress.

Historians once believed that politicians accomplished little between 1877 and 1900, but they were wrong. After the impeachment of Andrew Johnson, the authority of the presidency dwindled in relation to congressional strength. For the first time in many years, power rested in Congress and, even more significant, in state and local governments.

Experiments in the States

Across the country, state bureaus and commissions were established to regulate the new industrial society. Commodities shippers, especially farmers and merchants, in protest against the railroads' policies of rate discrimination and other corrupt practices, turned to the states for government action. By 1900, twenty-eight states had established commissions to oversee the railroads. These early commissions served as models for later policy at the federal level.

Illinois had one of the most thoroughgoing provisions. Responding to local merchants who were upset with existing railroad rate policies, the Illinois state constitution of 1870 declared railroads to be public highways and authorized the state legislature to pass laws establishing maximum rates and preventing rate discrimination. In the important case of *Munn* v. *Illinois* (1877), the Supreme Court upheld the Illinois legislation.

But the Court soon weakened that judgment. In the *Wabash* case of 1886 (*Wabash, St. Louis & Pacific Railway Co.* v. *Illinois*), it narrowed the *Munn* rule and held that states could not regulate commerce extending beyond their borders. Only Congress could do that. The *Wabash* decision spurred Congress to pass the Interstate Commerce Act (1887), which created the **Interstate Commerce Commission (ICC)** to investigate and oversee railroad activities and outlawed rebates and pooling agreements. The ICC became the prototype of the federal commissions that today regulate many parts of the economy.

Interstate Commerce Commission (ICC) The first federal regulatory agency, created by Congress in 1887 to investigate and oversee railroad activities.

Reestablishing Presidential Power

Johnson's impeachment, the scandals of the Grant years, and the controversy surrounding the 1876 election (see Chapter 16) weakened the presidency. During the last two decades of the nineteenth century, presidents fought to reassert their authority, and by 1900, they had largely succeeded. The late 1890s, in fact, mark the birth of the modern powerful presidency.

Rutherford B. Hayes entered the White House with his title clouded by the disputed election of 1876. Although opponents called him "His Fraudulency," he worked to reassert the authority of the presidency. Hayes worked for reform in the civil service, placed well-known reformers in high offices, and by ordering the last troops out of South Carolina and Louisiana, ended military Reconstruction. Committed to the gold standard, in 1878 he vetoed a bill that called for the partial coinage of silver, but Congress passed this **Bland-Allison Silver Purchase Act** over his veto.

Bland-Allison Silver Purchase Act This 1878 act, a compromise between groups favoring the coinage of silver and those opposed to it, called for the partial coinage of silver.

James A. Garfield, a Union army hero and longtime member of Congress, succeeded Hayes. Ambitious and eloquent, Garfield planned to reunite the Republican party, lower the tariff to reduce surplus revenues, and assert American economic and strategic interests in Latin America. But he was soon besieged by office seekers. Each one wanted a government job, and each one thought nothing of cornering the president on every occasion. On July 2, 1881, Charles J. Guiteau, a deranged lawyer and disappointed office seeker, shot Garfield. Suffering through the summer, Garfield died on September 19, and Vice President Chester A. Arthur became president.

Arthur was a better president than many had expected. He modernized the navy and worked to lower the tariff; in 1883, with his backing, Congress passed the **Pendleton Act** to reform the civil service. In part a reaction against Garfield's assassination, the act created a bipartisan Civil Service Commission to administer competitive examinations and appoint officeholders on the basis of merit.

In the election of 1884, Grover Cleveland, the Democratic governor of New York, narrowly defeated Republican nominee James G. Blaine. The first Democratic president since the outbreak of the Civil War, Cleveland was known for his honesty, stubbornness, and hard work. His first term in the White House (1885–1889) reflected the Democratic party's desire to curtail federal activities. Cleveland vetoed more bills than all his predecessors combined. Late in 1887, he committed himself and the Democratic party to lower the tariff. The Republicans accused him of undermining American industries, and in 1888, they nominated for the presidency Benjamin Harrison, a defender of the tariff. Although Cleveland garnered ninety thousand more popular votes, Harrison won in the electoral college.

Pendleton Act Passed by Congress in 1883, this act sought to lessen the involvement of politicians in the running of the government. It created a bipartisan commission to administer competitive exams to candidates for civil service jobs and to appoint officeholders based on merit. It also outlawed forcing political contributions from appointed officials.

REPUBLICANS IN POWER: THE BILLION-DOLLAR CONGRESS

Despite Harrison's narrow margin, the election of 1888 was the most sweeping victory for either party in almost twenty years; it gave the Republicans the presidency and control of both houses of Congress. Eager to block Republican-sponsored laws, the Democrats in Congress used minority tactics, especially the "disappearing quorum" rule, which let members of the House of Representatives join in debate but then refuse to answer the roll call to determine if a quorum was present.

After two months of such tactics, the Republicans had had enough. On January 29, 1890, they fell two votes short of a quorum, and Speaker of the House Thomas B. Reed made congressional history. "The Chair," he said, "directs the Clerk to record the following names of members present and refusing to vote." Tumult continued for days, but in mid-February, the Republicans adopted the Reed rules and proceeded to enact the party's program.

Law after law poured out of the 1890 Republican Congress; Democrats labeled it the "Billion-Dollar Congress" for spending that much in appropriations and grants. The Republicans passed the McKinley Tariff Act, which raised tariff duties about 4 percent, higher than ever before. In addition, the act used duties to promote new industries.

■ *A toy scale pitting the presidential candidates of 1888 (Harrison and Cleveland) against each other invites participation in determining the election outcome. More than a plaything, the scale symbolized the high level of voter participation during the late nineteenth century when elections hung in balance until the last vote was counted.* ■

Sherman Antitrust Act Passed by Congress in 1890, this act was the first federal antitrust legislation. Penalties for violations were strict, ranging from fines to imprisonment and even the dissolution of guilty trusts.

The Republicans also passed the **Sherman Antitrust Act,** the first federal attempt to regulate big business. As the initial attempt to deal with the problem of trusts and industrial growth, the act shaped all later antitrust policy. It declared illegal "every contract, combination in the form of trust or otherwise, or conspiracy, in restraint of trade or commerce." Penalties for violation were stiff, including fines and imprisonment and the dissolution of guilty trusts.

One of the most important laws Congress has enacted, the Sherman Antitrust Act made the United States virtually the only industrial nation to regulate business combinations. It tried to restore competition in the marketplace to appease small businessmen. But the Supreme Court crippled the act in *United States* v. *E. C. Knight Co.* (1895) by ruling that it applied only to commerce and not to manufacturing. Not until after the turn of the century did the antitrust law gain fresh power.

Sherman Silver Purchase Act An 1890 act that attempted to resolve the controversy over silver coinage. Under it, the U.S. Treasury would purchase 4.5 million ounces of silver each month and issue legal tender (in the form of Treasury notes) for it.

Another measure, the **Sherman Silver Purchase Act,** was intended to end the troublesome problem of silver as part of the nation's currency. Support for silver coinage was especially strong in the South and West, where people thought it might inflate the currency, raise wages and crop prices, and challenge the hated power of the gold-oriented Northeast. Eager to avert the free coinage of silver, which would require the coinage of all silver presented at U.S. mints, President Harrison and other Republican leaders pressed for a compromise that took shape in the Sherman Silver Purchase Act of 1890.

The act directed the Treasury to purchase 4.5 million ounces of silver a month and to issue legal tender in the form of Treasury notes in payment for it. The act was a compromise; it satisfied both sides. Opponents of silver were pleased that it did not include free coinage. Silverites were delighted that the monthly purchases would buy up most of the country's silver production and move the country toward a bimetallic system based on silver and gold.

As a final measure, Republicans in the House passed a federal elections bill to protect the voting rights of blacks in the South. It set off a storm of denunciation among the Democrats, who called it a "force bill" that would station army troops in the South. Defeated in the Senate, it was the last major effort until the 1950s to enforce the Fifteenth Amendment to the Constitution.

The 1890 elections crushed the Republicans, who lost seventy-eight seats in the House, an extraordinary reversal. Political veterans went down to defeat, and new leaders vaulted to sudden prominence. In the Midwest state elections, as well as the national elections, Democrats made substantial gains.

THE RISE OF THE POPULIST MOVEMENT

The elections of 1890 drew attention to a fast-growing movement among farmers that soon came to be known as populism. The movement had begun rather quietly, and for a time it went almost unnoticed in the press. But during the summer of 1890, thousands of hard-pressed farmers from the South and West made their problems known. At campgrounds, they picnicked, talked, and listened to recruiters from an organization called the **National Farmers' Alliance and Industrial Union,** which promised unified action to solve agricultural problems.

National Farmers' Alliance and Industrial Union One of the largest reform movements in American history, the Farmers' Alliance sought to organize farmers in the South and West to fight for reforms, including measures to overcome low crop prices, burdensome mortgages, and high railroad rates. The alliance ultimately organized a political party, the People's (Populist) party.

The Farm Problem

Farm discontent was a worldwide phenomenon between 1870 and 1900. With the new means of transportation and communication, farmers everywhere were caught up in a complex international market that they neither controlled nor entirely understood.

American farmers complained bitterly about declining prices for their products, rising railroad rates for shipping them, and burdensome mortgages. Some of the grievances were valid. Farm profits were certainly low, and the prices of farm commodities fell between 1865 and 1890. But they did not fall as low as other commodity prices. Farmers received less for their crops, but their purchasing power in fact increased.

Neither was the farmers' griping about rising railroad rates entirely justified. Rates actually fell during these years, benefiting shippers of all products. Farm mortgages, while certainly burdensome, were common because many farmers mortgaged their property to expand their holdings or buy new farm machinery. Most mortgages were short, and the new machinery enabled farmers to triple their output and increase their income.

The actual situation varied from area to area and year to year. Still, many farmers were convinced that their condition had declined, and this perception sparked growing anger. In an age excited about factories, farmers were seen as "hayseeds," to use a word that first appeared in 1889. A literature of rural disillusionment emerged, most notably Hamlin Garland's writings, which described the grimness of farm life.

The Fast-Growing Farmers' Alliance

By the end of the 1880s, farmers had formed two major organizations: the National Farmers' Alliance, located on the Plains west of the Mississippi and known as the Northwestern Alliance, and the Farmers' Alliance and Industrial Union, based in the South and known as the Southern Alliance.

The Southern Alliance began in Texas in 1875 but did not assume major proportions until Dr. Charles W. Macune took over the leadership in 1886. Its agents spread across the South, where farmers were fed up with crop liens, depleted lands, and sharecropping. By 1890, the Southern Alliance claimed more than a million members. Like the Grange, the Alliance distributed educational materials, and it also established cooperative grain elevators, marketing associations, and retail stores.

Loosely affiliated with the Southern Alliance, the separate Colored Farmers' National Alliance and Cooperative Union enlisted black farmers in the South. Claiming more than a million members, it probably had closer to 250,000. Blacks organized at considerable peril. In 1891, when black cotton pickers struck for higher wages near Memphis, the strike was violently put down; fifteen strikers were lynched. The abortive strike ended the Colored Farmers' Alliance.

On the Plains, the Northwestern Alliance, a smaller organization, was formed in 1880. But it lacked the centralized organization of the Southern Alliance. In 1889, the Southern Alliance changed its name to the National Farmers' Alliance and Industrial Union and persuaded the three strongest state alliances on the Plains to join. Thereafter, the new organization dominated the Alliance movement.

The Alliance turned early to politics. In the West, its leaders rejected both the Republicans and the Democrats and organized their own party. The Southern Alliance resisted the idea of a new party for fear it might divide the white vote, thus undercutting white supremacy. Instead, the Southerners wanted to capture control of the dominant Democratic party. But regardless of their political positions, such figures as Leonidas Polk, president of the National Farmers' Alliance; Jeremiah Simpson of Kansas; and Mary E. Lease provided the movement with forceful leadership.

Meeting in Ocala, Florida, in 1890, the Alliance adopted the **Ocala Demands,** the platform it pushed for as long as it existed. First and foremost, the demands called for the creation of a "subtreasury system," which would allow farmers to store their crops in government warehouses. In return, they could claim Treasury notes for up to 80 percent of the local market value of the crop, a loan to be repaid when the crops were sold. Farmers could thus hold their crops for the best price. The Ocala Demands also urged the free coinage of silver, an end to protective tariffs and

■ *Populist Mary E. Lease advised farmers to "raise less corn and more hell." She also said, "If one man has not enough to eat three times a day and another man has $25 million, that last man has something that belongs to the first."* ■

Ocala Demands Adopted by the Farmers' Alliance at an 1890 meeting in Ocala, Florida, these demands became the organization's main platform. They called for the creation of a system to allow farmers to store their crops until they could get the best price, the free coinage of silver, an end to protective tariffs and national banks, a federal income tax, the direct election of senators by voters, and tighter regulation of railroads.

national banks, a federal income tax, the direct election of senators, and stricter regulation of the railroad companies.

The Alliance strategy worked well in the elections of 1890. Alliance leaders claimed thirty-eight Alliance supporters elected to Congress, with at least a dozen more pledged to Alliance principles.

The People's Party

People's (or Populist) party
This political party was organized in 1892 by farm, labor, and reform leaders, mainly from the Farmers' Alliance. It offered a broad-based reform platform reflecting the Ocala Demands. After 1896, it became identified as a one-issue party focused on free silver and gradually died away.

After the 1890 elections, Northern Alliance leaders urged the formation of a national third party to promote reform. In July 1892, a convention in Omaha, Nebraska, established the new **People's (or Populist) party.** Disillusioned with the response of the Democrats to agrarian difficulties, Southern Alliance leaders joined the new party. In the South, party members, known as Populists, worked with some success to unite black and white farmers under the same party banner.

The delegates at the Omaha convention nominated James B. Weaver of Iowa to run for president in 1892. As its platform, the People's party adopted many of the Ocala Demands. Weaver won 1,039,000 votes, the first third-party presidential candidate ever to attract more than a million votes, and he carried several western states for a total of twenty-two electoral votes. The Populists elected governors in Kansas and North Dakota, ten congressmen, five senators, and about fifteen hundred members of state legislatures.

Despite the Populists' victories, the election brought disappointment. Using fraud and manipulation, Southern Democrats deflected the Populists' efforts; Weaver was held to less than a quarter of the vote in almost every Southern state. He lost heavily in most urban areas and failed to win over most farmers in the settled Midwest. In no midwestern state except Kansas and North Dakota did he win as much as 5 percent of the vote. Although the Populists did run candidates in the next three presidential elections, their heyday was over.

While it lived, the People's party was one of the most powerful protest movements in American history. Catalyzing the feelings of hundreds of thousands of farmers, it attempted to solve specific economic problems while advancing a larger vision of harmony and community, in which people who cared about one another were rewarded for what they produced.

THE CRISIS OF THE DEPRESSION

Building on the Democratic party's sweeping triumph in the midterm elections of 1890, Grover Cleveland decisively defeated incumbent President Benjamin Harrison in 1892. For the first time since the 1850s, the Democrats controlled the White House and both branches of Congress.

Unfortunately for Cleveland, the Panic of 1893 struck almost as he took office. The economy had expanded too rapidly in the 1870s and 1880s. The mood changed early in 1893. Business confidence sagged, and investors became timid and uneasy. Panic hit the stock market. During 1893, fifteen thousand businesses and more than six hundred banks closed.

The year 1894 was even worse. By midyear, the number of unemployed stood at three million. One out of every five workers was unemployed, and unprecedented numbers of needy people taxed the ability of churches and charities to help. In the summer, a heat wave and drought struck the farm belt west of the Mississippi River. Corn withered in the fields. In the South, the price of cotton fell below 5 cents a pound, far under the break-even point.

People became restless and angry. There was even talk of revolution and bloodshed. "Everyone scolds," Henry Adams, the historian, wrote a British friend. "Everyone also knows what ought to be done. Everyone reviles everyone who does not agree with him, and everyone differs, or agrees only in contempt for everyone else. As far as I can see, everyone is right."

Coxey's Army and the Pullman Strike

Some of the unemployed wandered across the country—singly, in small groups, and in small armies. During 1894, there were some fourteen hundred strikes involving more than a half million workers. On Easter Sunday 1894, an unusual "army" of perhaps three hundred people left Massillon, Ohio. At its head rode "General" Jacob S. Coxey, a middle-aged businessman who wanted Congress to print $500 million to finance a massive road-building program that would put the nation's jobless to work.

Other armies sprang up around the country, and all headed for Washington armed with other demands and hopes. Coxey himself reached Washington on May 1, 1894, after a difficult, tiring march. Police were everywhere. Coxey made it to the foot of the Capitol steps, but before he could do anything, the police were on him. He was clubbed, arrested for trespassing, and sentenced to twenty days in jail.

The armies melted away, but discontent did not. The great **Pullman Strike**—one of the largest strikes in the country's history—began just a few days after Coxey's arrest when the employees of the Pullman Palace Car Company struck to protest wage cuts, continuing high rents for company-owned housing, and layoffs. On July 26, 1894, the American Railway Union (ARU) under Eugene V. Debs joined the strike by refusing to handle trains that carried Pullman sleeping cars.

Within hours, the strike paralyzed the western half of the nation. Grain and livestock could not reach markets. Factories shut down for lack of coal. The strike renewed talk of class warfare. In Washington, President Cleveland decided to break it because it obstructed delivery of the mail.

On July 2, he secured a court injunction against the ARU and ordered troops to Chicago. When they arrived on Independence Day, violence broke out, and mobs composed mostly of nonstrikers overturned freight cars, looted, and burned. Restoring order, the army occupied railroad yards in Illinois, California, and other points. By late July, the strike was over; Debs was jailed for violating the injunction.

The Pullman strike had far-reaching consequences for the development of the labor movement. Upholding Debs's sentence in *In re Debs* (1895), the Supreme Court endorsed the use of the injunction in labor disputes, thus giving business and government an effective antilabor weapon that hindered union growth in the 1890s. The strike also catapulted Debs into prominence. Working people resented Cleveland's actions in the strike.

Pullman Strike Beginning in May 1894, this strike of employees at the Pullman Palace Car Company near Chicago was one of the largest strikes in American history. Extending into twenty-seven states and territories, it effectively paralyzed the western half of the nation. President Grover Cleveland secured an injunction to break the strike on the grounds that it obstructed the mail and sent federal troops to enforce it.

The Miners of the Midwest

The plight of miners in the Illinois, Indiana, and Ohio coalfields illustrated the personal and social impact of the depression. Even in the best of times, mining was a dirty and dangerous business. Mines often closed for as long as six months, and wages fell with the depression.

Mining was often a family occupation, passed down from father to son. It demanded delicate judgments about when to blast, where to follow a seam, and how to avoid rockfalls. Until 1890, English and Irish immigrants dominated the business, moving from mine to mine. They were poorly paid and usually lived in flimsy shacks that were owned by the mining company. After 1890, immigrants from southern and eastern Europe came to the mines to find work.

As the depression deepened, tensions grew between miners and their employers and between the "old" miners and the "new." The new miners, who usually spoke no English and lacked many skills, were often blamed for accidents, but they were willing to work longer hours for less pay.

In April 1894, a wave of wage reductions sparked an explosion of labor unrest in the mines. The United Mine Workers, a struggling union formed just four years earlier, called for a strike of bituminous coal miners, and on April 21, virtually all midwestern and Pennsylvania miners quit working. The flow of coal slackened; cities faced blackouts; factories closed.

The violence that soon broke out followed a significant pattern. The new miners were much more prone than the old miners to violent action to win a strike. The depression hit them especially hard. In many areas, anger and frustration turned the 1894 strikes into outright war.

For nearly two weeks in June 1894, fighting rocked the coalfields. Mobs ignited mine shafts, dynamited coal trains, and defied the state militias. Although miners of all backgrounds participated in the violence, the new miners led the most radical and destructive assaults.

Shocked by the violence, public opinion shifted against the strikers. The strike ended in a matter of weeks, but its effects lingered. English and Irish miners moved out into other jobs or up into supervisory positions. Jokes and songs poked cruel fun at the new immigrants. The United Mine Workers, dominated by the older miners, began in 1896 to persuade Congress to stop the "demoralizing effects" of immigration.

The Pullman strike, which occurred at the same time, pulled attention away from the crisis in the coalfields, even though the miners' strike involved three times as many workers and provided a revealing glimpse of the tensions within American

■ *A United Mine Workers certificate of membership illustrates some of the work undertaken by the brother members. The United Mine Workers of America was formed in 1890 in Columbus, Ohio, and sought to provide its members with a safe workplace and fair wages and benefits. Although the union pledged to seek ways to maintain peace between miners and their employers and to make strikes unnecessary, such means as arbitration and conciliation often failed and strikes did occur, many of them violent and destructive.* ■

society. The miners of the Midwest were the first large group of skilled workers seriously affected by the flood of immigrants from southern and eastern Europe. Buffeted by depression, they reflected the social and economic discord that permeated every industry.

A Beleaguered President

President Cleveland was sure that he knew the cause of the depression. The Sherman Silver Purchase Act of 1890, he believed, had damaged business confidence, exhausted the Treasury's gold reserve, and caused the panic. The solution to the depression was equally simple: repeal the act.

In June 1893, Cleveland summoned Congress into special session. Rejecting the silverites' pleas for a compromise, Cleveland pushed the repeal bill through Congress, and on November 1, 1893, he signed it into law. Ever sure of himself, he had staked everything on a single measure.

Repeal of the Sherman Silver Purchase Act was probably a necessary action. It responded to the realities of international finance, reduced the flight of gold out of the country, and over the long run boosted business confidence. Unfortunately, it contracted the currency at a time when inflation might have helped. It also failed to bring economic revival. The stock market remained listless, businesses continued to close, unemployment spread, and farm prices dropped.

The repeal battle of 1893 discredited the conservative Democrats who had dominated the party since the 1860s. Reshaping the politics of the country, it confined the Democratic party largely to the South, helped the Republicans become the majority party in 1894, and strengthened the position of the silver Democrats in their bid for the presidency in 1896. By 1896, most Americans believed that Cleveland's economic policies had not benefited the country.

Breaking the Party Deadlock

In 1894, Cleveland and the Democrats tried to fulfill their long-standing promise to reduce the tariff. The Wilson-Gorman Tariff Act, passed by Congress that year, contained only modest reductions in duties. It also imposed a small income tax, a provision the Supreme Court overturned in 1895. Discouraged, Cleveland let the bill become law without his signature.

The Democrats were buried in the elections of 1894, suffering the greatest defeat in congressional history. Wooing labor and the unemployed, the Populists made striking inroads in parts of the South and West, yet these didn't go quite far enough. Across the country, the discontented tended to vote for the Republicans, not the Populists.

For millions of people, Grover Cleveland became a scapegoat for the country's economic ills. The Democratic party split, and southern and western Democrats deserted him in droves. At Democratic conventions, Cleveland's name evoked jeers.

The elections of 1894 marked the end of the party deadlock that had existed since the 1870s. The Democrats lost, the Populists gained somewhat, and the Republicans became the majority party in the country. The Republican doctrines of activism and national authority, repudiated in the elections of 1890, became more attractive in the midst of depression.

CHANGING ATTITUDES

Across the country, people were rethinking older ideas about government, the economy, and society. The depression, brutal and far-reaching, undermined traditional views. As men and women concluded that established ideas had failed to deal with the depression, they looked for new ones.

⊠ *Meager earnings such as those from young children peddling newspapers were desperately needed during the depression of the 1890s.* ⊠

In prosperous times, Americans had thought of unemployment as the result of personal failure, affecting primarily the lazy and the immoral. Now, in the midst of depression, everyone knew people who were both worthy *and* unemployed. People began to debate issues they had long taken for granted. New discussion clubs, women's clubs, reform societies, university extension centers, church groups, and farmers' societies all gave people a place to discuss alternatives to the existing order. Pressures for reform increased, and demand grew for government intervention to help the poor and the unemployed.

"Everybody Works But Father"

As husbands and fathers lost their jobs, more and more women and children went to work. Even as late as 1901, well after the depression had ended, a study of working-class families showed that more than half the principal breadwinners were out of work. So many women and children worked that in 1905 the song "Everybody Works but Father" became a popular hit.

During the 1890s, the number of working women rose from 4 million to 5.3 million. Trying to make ends meet, they took in boarders and found jobs as laundresses, cleaners, or domestics. Where possible, they worked in offices and factories. Far more black urban women than white worked to supplement their husbands' meager earnings. Women worked as telegraph and telephone operators, as clerks in the new five-and-tens and department stores, and as nurses, typists, and teachers.

The depression also caused an increasing number of children to work. During the 1890s, boys and girls under 16 years of age made up nearly a third of the labor force of the southern textile mills. In most cases, children worked not in factories but in farming and city street trades such as peddling and shoe shining. In 1900, the South had more than half the child laborers in the nation.

Concerned about child labor, middle-class women in 1896 formed the League for Protection of the Family, which called for compulsory education to get children out of factories and into classrooms. Soon other organizations were started to fight for reforms in the fields of child welfare, education, and sanitation.

Changing Themes in Literature

The depression also gave impetus to a growing movement in literature toward realism and naturalism. In the years after the Civil War, literature often reflected the mood of romanticism—sentimental and unrealistic. But after the 1870s, a number of talented authors rejected romanticism in favor of realism. Determined to portray life as it was, they studied local dialects, wrote regional stories, and emphasized the "true" relationships between people. In doing so, they reflected broader trends in the society: industrialism; evolutionary theory, which emphasized the effects of environment on humans; and the new philosophy of pragmatism, which stressed the relativity of values. (See Chapter 23 for a more detailed discussion of pragmatism.)

A regionalist author who soon outgrew that genre, Mark Twain went on to become the country's most outstanding realist writer. Growing up along the Mississippi River in Hannibal County, Missouri, the young Samuel Langhorne Clemens observed life around him with a humorous and skeptical eye. Adopting a pen name from the river term *mark twain* ("two fathoms"), he drew on his own experiences. In such books as *The Adventures of Huckleberry Finn* (1884), Twain used dialect and common speech instead of literary language, touching off a major change in American prose style.

William Dean Howells came more slowly to the realistic approach. Writing initially about the happier side of life, he grew worried about the impact of industrialization. In his more powerful works, he portrayed an urban society that produced great riches—at a terrible price. In the poem "Society" (1895), he compared society to a splendid ball at which men and women danced on flowers covering the bodies of the poor.

Other writers became impatient even with realism. Pushing Darwinian theory to its limits, they wrote of a world in which a cruel and merciless environment determined human fate. Often focusing on economic hardship, naturalist writers scrutinized the poor, the lower classes, and the criminal mind; they brought to their writing the social worker's passion for direct and honest experience.

Stephen Crane spent a night in a 7-cent lodging house on the Bowery and in "An Experiment in Misery" captured the smells and sounds of the poor. He also depicted the carnage of war in *The Red Badge of Courage* (1895). Frank Norris assailed the power of big business in two dramatic novels, *The Octopus* (1901) and *The Pit* (1903), both emphasizing individual futility in the face of the heartless corporations. Jack London traced the power of nature over civilized society in novels such as *The Call of the Wild* (1903) and *The Sea Wolf* (1904).

Theodore Dreiser, the foremost naturalist writer, grimly portrayed a dark world in which human beings were tossed about by forces beyond their understanding or control. In his great novel *Sister Carrie* (1901), he followed a young farm girl who took a job in a Chicago shoe factory. Like other naturalists, Dreiser focused on environment and character. He thought writers should tell the truth about human affairs, not fabricate romance.

THE PRESIDENTIAL ELECTION OF 1896

The election of 1896 was known as the "battle of the standards" because it involved the gold and silver standards of value in the monetary system of the nation. New voting patterns replaced old, the new majority party confirmed its control of the country, and national policy shifted to suit the new realities.

The Mystique of Silver

People wanted quick solutions to the economic crisis. During 1896, unemployment shot up, and farm income and prices fell to their lowest point of the decade. The silverites offered a solution, simple but compelling: the free and independent coinage of silver at the ratio of sixteen to one. Free coinage meant that the U.S. mints would coin all the silver offered to them. Independent coinage meant that the country would coin silver regardless of the policies of other nations, nearly all of which were on the gold standard.

Above all, the silverites believed in a quantity theory of money: The amount of money in circulation determined the level of activity in the economy. A shortage of money meant declining activity and depression. Silver meant more money and thus prosperity. Added to the currency, it would increase the money supply and stir new economic activity.

By 1896, silver was a symbol. It had moral and patriotic dimensions and stood for a wide range of popular grievances. For many Americans, it reflected rural values rather than urban ones, suggested a shift of power away from the Northeast, and spoke for the downtrodden instead of the well-to-do.

Silver was a social movement, one of the largest in American history, but its life span turned out to be brief. As a mass phenomenon, it flourished between 1894 and 1896, then succumbed to electoral defeat, the return to prosperity, and the onset of fresh concerns. But in its time, it bespoke a national mood and won millions of followers.

The Campaign and Election

Scenting victory over the discredited Democrats, numerous Republicans fought for the party's presidential nomination. In the end, William McKinley, an able, calm Civil War veteran, won the nomination. As a congressman, he had been the chief sponsor of the tariff act named for him. In the months before the 1896 national convention, Marcus A. Hanna, his campaign manager and trusted friend, raised $16 million and built up a powerful national organization that proved successful. McKinley's platform favored the gold standard.

Despite President Cleveland's opposition, more than twenty Democratic states' platforms came out for free silver in 1894. Power in the party shifted to the South, where it remained for decades. The party's base narrowed; its outlook increasingly reflected southern views on silver, race, and other issues. In effect, the Democrats became a sectional—no longer a national—party.

The anti-Cleveland Democrats had their issue, but they lacked a leader. Out in Nebraska, William Jennings Bryan saw the opportunity. He was barely 36 years old and had relatively little political experience. But he had spent months wooing support, and he was a captivating public speaker.

From the outset of the 1896 Democratic convention, the silver Democrats were in charge, and they put together a platform that stunned the Cleveland wing of the party. It demanded the free coinage of silver, attacked Cleveland's actions in the Pullman strike, and censured his 1895 and 1896 gold bond sales. On July 9, as delegates debated the platform, Bryan's moment came. Striding to the stage, he stood for an instant, a hand raised for silence, waiting for the applause to die down.

He spoke with confidence, captivating the delegates. The country, he said, praised businessmen but forgot that laborers, miners, and farmers were businessmen, too. He defended silver and in his famous closing said, "Having behind us the producing masses of this nation and the world . . . we will answer their demand for a gold standard by saying to them: 'You shall not press down upon the brow of labor this crown of thorns, you shall not crucify mankind upon a cross of gold.'" He ended with his arms outstretched as on a cross. Suddenly there was pandemonium. When the tumult subsided, the delegates adopted the anti-Cleveland platform, and the next day, Bryan won the presidential nomination.

The Democratic convention presented the Populists with a dilemma. The People's party had staked everything on the assumption that neither major party would endorse silver. Now it faced a painful

■ *The religious symbolism in Bryan's "Cross of Gold" speech is satirized in this cartoon, but his stirring rhetoric captivated his audience and won him the Democratic presidential nomination for the election of 1896.* ■

choice: nominate an independent ticket and risk splitting the silverite forces, or nominate Bryan and give up its separate identity as a party.

The choice was unpleasant, and it shattered the People's party. Meeting late in July, the party's national convention nominated Bryan, but the Populists' endorsement probably hurt Bryan as much as it helped. It won him relatively few votes, since many Populists would have voted for him anyway. It identified him as a Populist, which he was not, and allowed the Republicans to accuse him of heading a ragtag army of malcontents.

In August 1896, Bryan set off on a campaign that became an American legend. Much of the conservative eastern press had deserted him, and he took his campaign directly to the voters, the first presidential candidate to do so in a systematic way. By his own count, Bryan traveled 18,009 miles, visited twenty-seven states, and spoke six hundred times to a total of three million people. He built skillfully on a new "merchandising" style of campaign in which he worked to educate and persuade voters.

Bryan summoned voters to an older America, a land where farms were as important as factories, where the virtues of rural and religious life outweighed the doubtful lure of the city, where common people still ruled and opportunity existed. He drew on the Jeffersonian tradition of rural virtue, distrust of central authority, and abiding faith in the powers of human reason.

McKinley let voters come to him. Railroads brought them by the thousands into his hometown of Canton, Ohio, and he spoke to them from his front porch. Never had a party spent so much money on a campaign. Through use of the press, he reached fully as many people as Bryan's more strenuous effort. Appealing to labor, immigrants, wealthy farmers, businessmen, and the middle class, McKinley defended economic nationalism and the advancing urban-industrial society.

On election day, voter turnout was extraordinarily high, a measure of the intense interest, but McKinley won a clear victory, capturing 50 percent of the vote to Bryan's 46 percent. The election struck down the Populists, whose totals sagged nearly everywhere. Although many Populist proposals were later adopted—the graduated income tax, crop loans to farmers, and the secret ballot, for example— the party never again could win a majority of the voters. It vanished after 1896.

THE MCKINLEY ADMINISTRATION

The election of 1896 cemented the voter realignment of 1894 and initiated a generation of Republican rule. For more than three decades after 1896, with only a brief Democratic resurgence under Woodrow Wilson, the Republicans remained the country's majority party.

McKinley took office in 1897 under favorable circumstances. To everyone's relief, the economy had begun to revive. The stock market rose, factories once again churned out goods, and farmers prospered. Discoveries of gold in Australia and Alaska and new extraction techniques enlarged the world's gold supply, decreased its price, and inflated the currency as the silverites had hoped.

McKinley and the Republicans basked in the glow. They became the party of progress and prosperity, an image that helped them win victories until the 1930s. McKinley's popularity soared. An activist president, he set the policies of the administration. He maintained close ties with Congress and worked hard to educate the public on national choices and priorities. McKinley struck new relations with the press and traveled far more than previous presidents. In some ways, he began the modern presidency.

In July 1897, with his support, Congress passed the Dingley Tariff, which raised average tariff duties to a record level. As the final burst of nineteenth-century protectionism, it caused trouble for the Republican party. By the end of the 1890s,

■ *Gold triumphs over silver in this* Puck *cartoon referring to the Gold Standard Act of 1900.* ■

however, even some Republicans themselves had begun to conclude that the tariff had outlived its usefulness in the maturing American economy.

From the 1860s to the 1890s, the Republicans had built their party on a pledge to *promote* economic growth through the use of state and national power. By 1900, with the industrial system firmly in place, the focus had shifted. The need to *regulate,* to control the effects of industrialism, became a central public concern of the new century.

McKinley prodded his party to move toward regulation, but he died before his plans matured. One problem was the government's need for revenue. Tariff duties were one of the few taxes the public would support. The Spanish-American War of 1898 persuaded people to accept greater federal power and, with it, new forms of taxation. By the end of the nineteenth century, McKinley realized that economic nationalism, the creed on which he was raised, was a dying concept.

In 1898 and 1899, the McKinley administration focused on the war with Spain, the peace treaty that followed, and the dawning realization that the war had thrust the United States into a position of world power. In March 1900, Congress passed the **Gold Standard Act,** which declared gold the standard of currency and ended the silver controversy that had dominated the 1890s.

The presidential campaign of 1900 was a replay of the McKinley-Bryan fight of 1896. McKinley's running mate was Theodore Roosevelt, hero of the Spanish-American War (see Chapter 21) and former governor of New York, who was nominated for vice president to capitalize on his popularity and, his enemies hoped, to sidetrack his political career into oblivion. McKinley won in a landslide. But on September 6, 1901, mere months after his second inauguration, McKinley was shot while standing in a receiving line at the Pan-American Exposition in Buffalo, New York. His assailant was Leon Czolgosz, a 28-year-old unemployed laborer and anar-

Gold Standard Act Passed by Congress in 1900, this law declared gold the nation's standard of currency—meaning that all currency in circulation had to be redeemable in gold. The United States remained on the gold standard until 1933.

Chronology

1876	Mark Twain publishes *The Adventures of Tom Sawyer,* setting off a major change in American literary style
1877	Disputed election of 1876 results in the awarding of the presidency to Republican Rutherford B. Hayes
1880	Republican James A. Garfield is elected president
1881	Garfield is assassinated; Vice President Chester A. Arthur becomes president
1884	Democrat Grover Cleveland is elected president, defeating Republican James G. Blaine
1887	Cleveland calls for a lowering of tariff duties
1888	Republican Benjamin Harrison wins the presidential election
1889	National Farmers' Alliance and Industrial Union is formed to address the problems of farmers
1890	Republican-dominated Congress enacts the McKinley Tariff Act, the Sherman Antitrust Act, and the Sherman Silver Purchase Act ■ Farmers' Alliance adopts the Ocala Demands
1892	Democrat Cleveland defeats Republican Harrison for the presidency ■ People's party is formed
1893	Financial panic touches off a depression that lasts until 1897 ■ Sherman Silver Purchase Act is repealed
1894	Coxey's Army marches on Washington ■ Employees of Pullman Palace Car Company strike
1896	Republican McKinley defeats William Jennings Bryan, Democratic and Populist candidate
1897	Gold is discovered in Alaska ■ Dingley Tariff Act raises tariff duties
1900	McKinley is re-elected, again defeating Bryan ■ Gold Standard Act establishes gold as the standard of currency
1901	McKinley is assassinated; Vice President Theodore Roosevelt assumes the presidency ■ Naturalist writer Theodore Dreiser publishes *Sister Carrie*

chist. On September 14, McKinley died, and Vice President Theodore Roosevelt became president. The new century had begun in earnest.

CONCLUSION: A DECADE'S DRAMATIC CHANGES

As the funeral train carried McKinley's body back to Ohio, Mark Hanna, McKinley's old friend and ally, sat slumped in his parlor car. "I told William McKinley it was a mistake to nominate that wild man at Philadelphia," he mourned. "I asked him if he realized what would happen if he should die. Now look, that damned cowboy is president of the United States!"

The nation had changed—not so much because "that damned cowboy" was suddenly president, but because events of the 1890s had had powerful effects. In the course of that decade, political patterns shifted, the presidency acquired fresh power, and massive unrest prompted social change. The war with Spain brought a new empire and worldwide responsibilities. Economic hardship posed difficult questions about industrialization, urbanization, and the quality of American life.

Worried, people embraced new ideas and causes. Reform movements begun in the 1890s flowered in the Progressive Era after 1900.

Technology continued to alter the way Americans lived. In 1896, Henry Ford produced a two-cylinder, four-horsepower car. At Kitty Hawk, North Carolina, Wilbur and Orville Wright, two bicycle manufacturers, neared the birth of powered flight. The pace of the world was quickening.

The realignments that reached their peak in the 1890s shaped nearly everything that came after them. In character and influence, the 1890s were as much a part of the twentieth century as of the nineteenth and continue to have repercussions into the twenty-first century.

KEY TERMS

Interstate Commerce Commission (ICC), p. 390

Bland-Allison Silver Purchase Act, p. 390

Pendleton Act, p. 391

Sherman Antitrust Act, p. 392

Sherman Silver Purchase Act, p. 392

National Farmers' Alliance and Industrial Union, p. 392

Ocala Demands, p. 393

People's (or Populist) Party, p. 394

Pullman Strike, p. 395

Gold Standard Act, p. 402

RECOMMENDED READING

The best study of the 1890s depression is Charles Hoffman, *The Depression of the Nineties: An Economic History* (1970). H. Wayne Morgan, *From Hayes to McKinley: National Party Politics, 1877–1896* (1969), Michael E. McGerr, *The Decline of Popular Politics: The American North, 1865–1928* (1986), Mark Lawrence Kornbluh, *Why America Stopped Voting: The Decline of Participatory Democracy and the Emergence of Modern American Politics* (2000), and Richard J. Jensen, *The Winning of the Midwest* (1971) are good on politics. David P. Thelen, *The New Citizenship: Origins of Progressivism in Wisconsin, 1885–1900* (1972), Carl Smith, *Urban Disorder and the Shape of Belief: The Great Chicago Fire, the Haymarket Bomb, and the Model Town of Pullman* (1995), Susan Eleanor Hirsch, *After the Strike: A Century of Labor Struggle at Pullman* (2003), and Douglas W. Steeples and David O. Whitten, *Democracy in Desperation: The Depression*

of 1893 (1998), stress the impact of the depression on ideas and attitudes. C. Vann Woodward examines the South in *Origins of the New South, 1877–1913* (1951). Also, Michael Perman, *Struggle for Mastery: Disfranchisement in the South, 1888–1908* (2001), and Thomas Adams Upchurch, *Legislating Racism: The Billion Dollar Congress and the Birth of Jim Crow* (2004).

On Populism, see John D. Hicks, *The Populist Revolt* (1931), Lawrence Goodwyn, *Democratic Promise: The Populist Moment in America* (1976), James L. Hunt, *Marian Butler and American Populism* (2003), Steven Hahn, *The Roots of Southern Populism* (1983), and Elizabeth Sanders, *Roots of Reform: Farmers, Workers, and the American State, 1877–1917* (1999). Steven W. Usselman, *Regulating Railroad Innovation: Business, Technology, and Politics in America, 1840–1920* (2002), looks at regulatory reform.

SUGGESTED WEB SITES

World's Columbian Exposition: Idea, Experience, Aftermath
xroads.virginia.edu/~MA96/WCE/title.html
This site has a virtual tour of the fair, along with contemporary reactions and modern analysis.

Pullman Links on the Web—Historic Pullman Foundation
www.pullmanil.org/links.htm
This page offers several links to sites with Pullman-related information, including a section of sites on the Pullman strike and labor history.

Election of 1896
jefferson.village.virginia.edu/seminar/unit8/home.htm
This University of Virginia site contains biographical information, images, cartoons, and related links about the pivotal 1896 election.

The Era of William McKinley
history.osu.edu/projects/Mckinley/default.cfm
This site contains numerous images from various stages of William McKinley's career along with a brief biographical essay. This Ohio State University site also has a section with an excellent collection of cartoons from the era.

Chapter 21

Toward Empire

Roosevelt and the Rough Riders

When war with Spain began in April 1898, many Americans regretted it, but others welcomed it. Many people believed that nations must fight every now and then to prove their power and test the national spirit.

Theodore Roosevelt, the 39-year-old assistant secretary of the navy, was one of them. For months, Roosevelt had argued strenuously for war with Spain, first on grounds of freeing Cuba and expelling Spain from the hemisphere; second, to take Americans' minds off material gain; and third, because the army and navy needed the practice.

When the war finally came, Roosevelt resigned his navy post and joined the army. In those days, officers supplied their own uniforms, and Roosevelt, the son of well-to-do parents, wanted his to be stylish. He ordered it from Brooks Brothers, the expensive New York clothier. He also chose to enlist his own regiment, and after a few telephone calls to friends and telegrams to several western governors asking for "good shots and good riders," he had more than enough men. The First United States Volunteer Cavalry was an intriguing mix of Ivy League athletes and western frontiersmen that became known as the Rough Riders.

Eager for war, the men trained hard and played harder. Discipline was lax, and officers and enlisted men got along well together. Everyone howled with joy when orders came to join the invasion army for Cuba, and the Rough Riders set sail on June 14, 1898. Lieutenant Colonel Roosevelt performed a war dance for the troops the night before.

Roosevelt believed the war would establish the United States as a world power, whose commerce and influence would extend around the globe, particularly in Latin America and Asia. As he hoped, the nation in the 1890s underwent dramatic expansion, building on the foreign policy approaches of administrations from Abraham Lincoln to William McKinley. Policymakers fostered business interests abroad, strengthened the navy, and extended American influence into Latin America and the Pacific. Differences over Cuba resulted in a war with Spain that brought new colonies and colonial subjects, establishing for the first time an American overseas empire.

AMERICA LOOKS OUTWARD

The overseas expansion of the 1890s differed in several important respects from earlier expansionist moves of the United States. The American republic had always pursued growth, but as settlers pushed westward, most of the lands they moved into

405

were contiguous to existing territories of the United States and were earmarked for settlement.

The expansion of the 1890s involved the acquisition of island possessions, most of them already thickly populated. The new territories were intended less for settlement than for their usefulness as naval bases, trading outposts, or commercial centers on major trade routes. They were viewed primarily as colonies, not as states in the making—a natural outgrowth of a century of expansionist tendencies in thought and foreign policy.

Catching the Spirit of Empire

Most people in most times in history tend to look at domestic concerns, and Americans in the years following the Civil War were no exception. They focused on Reconstruction, the movement westward, and the growing industrial system. Throughout the nineteenth century, Americans enjoyed "free security" without fully appreciating it. Sheltered by two oceans and the British navy, they could enunciate bold policies such as the Monroe Doctrine while remaining virtually impervious to foreign attack.

isolationism A belief that the United States should stay out of entanglements with other nations. It was widespread after the Spanish-American War in the late 1890s and influenced later U.S. foreign policy.

In those circumstances, a sense of **isolationism** spread, a desire to stay out of foreign entanglements. Some people even urged the abolition of the foreign service, considering it an unnecessary expenditure, a dangerous profession that might lead to involvement in the struggles of the world's great powers. But such voices lost much of their force by the 1870s, when Americans began taking an increased interest in events abroad. The growing sense of internationalism stemmed in part from the telegraphs, telephones, and undersea cables that kept people better informed about political and economic developments in distant lands. And despite minimal interest in American **imperialism,** most Americans continued to be enthusiastic about the expansion of the country's borders.

imperialism The policy of extending a nation's power through military conquest, economic domination, or annexation.

Several developments combined to shift attention outward across the seas. The end of the frontier, announced officially in the census report of 1890, sparked fears about diminishing opportunities at home. Further growth, it seemed, must take place abroad.

Factories and farms multiplied, producing more goods than the domestic market could consume. Both farmers and industrialists looked for new overseas markets, and the growing volume of exports changed the nature of U.S. trade relations. American exports of merchandise amounted to $393 million in 1870, $858 million in 1890, and $1.4 billion in 1900.

Political leaders began to argue for the vital importance of foreign markets to continue economic growth. Some of them—James G. Blaine, secretary of state under Garfield and Harrison, for one—were caught up in the exhilaration of a worldwide scramble for empire. Like the European powers, they coveted the markets of Latin America, Asia, and Africa. The idea of imperialistic expansion was in the air, and great powers measured their greatness by the colonies they acquired. Inevitably, some Americans succumbed to the spirit and wanted to enter the international hunt for territory.

Intellectual currents that supported expansion drew on Charles Darwin's theories of evolution. Applied to human and social development, Darwin's biological concepts seemed to call for the triumph of the fit and the elimination of the unfit. Theodore Roosevelt, and many like-minded people, lauded virile and adventurous qualities and regarded them as a sign of America's greatness.

The "biogenetic law," formulated by German biologist Ernst Haeckel, suggested that the development of the race paralleled the development of the individual. Primitive peoples were thus in the arrested stages of childhood or adolescence; they needed supervision and protective treatment. In a similar vein, John Fiske, a popular writer and lecturer, argued for Anglo-Saxon racial superiority, a result of the process of natural selection. The English and Americans, Fiske said, would occupy every land on the globe that was not already "civilized," bringing the advances of commerce and democratic institutions.

Such views were widespread among the lettered and unlettered alike. The career of Josiah Strong, a Congregational minister and fervent expansionist, suggested the strength of the developing ideas. A champion of overseas missionary work, in 1885 he published a book titled *Our Country: Its Possible Future and Its Present Crisis.* An immediate best-seller, the book called on foreign missions to civilize the world under the Anglo-Saxon races. Strong also believed that American commerce should follow the missionary. The result, he maintained, would be good for everyone involved.

Taken together, these developments in social, political, and economic thought prepared Americans for a larger role in the world. The change was gradual, but by the 1890s, Americans found themselves ready to reach out into the world in a more determined and deliberate fashion than ever before. For almost the first time, they felt the need for an outward direction in foreign policy.

Foreign Policy Approaches, 1867–1900

Rarely consistent, American foreign policy in the last third of the nineteenth century took different approaches to different areas of the world. In relation to Europe, where the dominant world powers were, policymakers promoted trade and tried to avoid diplomatic entanglements. In North and South America, they based policy on the Monroe Doctrine, a recurrent dream of annexing Canada or Mexico, a hope for extensive trade, and pan-American unity against the nations of the Old World. In the Pacific, they coveted Hawaii and other outposts on the sea lanes to China.

Secretary of State William Henry Seward, who served from 1861 to 1869, aggressively pushed an expansive foreign policy. He developed a vision of an American empire stretching south into Latin America and west to the shores of Asia. His vision included Canada and Mexico, islands in the Caribbean as strategic bases to protect a canal across Central America, and Hawaii and other islands as stepping-stones to Asia.

Seward tried unsuccessfully to negotiate a commercial treaty with the kingdom of Hawaii in 1867, the same year he annexed the Midway Islands. Also in 1867, he concluded a treaty with Russia for the purchase of Alaska (promptly labeled "Seward's Folly"), part of a plan to sandwich western Canada between American territory as a prelude to its annexation. In all this, Seward's target remained the Asian market, which he and many others considered a virtually bottomless outlet for farm and manufactured goods. As the American empire spread, he thought, Mexico City would become its capital.

Hamilton Fish followed Seward as secretary of state, serving under President Ulysses S. Grant. An avid expansionist, Grant wanted to extend American influence

A Look at the Past

Trade Card

Trade cards—postcard-sized advertisements—provided manufacturers with attractive, richly colored attention-grabbers. As firms entered national and even international markets, advertising became increasingly important as a way to promote brand identification and loyalty. The Singer Sewing Machine Company commissioned a set of trade cards in the 1890s, including the one shown here, that showed its products being used around the world. This card, made in 1892, reveals U.S. interest in the Philippines before the Spanish-American War. ✱ Why would Singer depict sewing machines used in foreign lands as a way to attract U.S. consumers? How are Filipinos depicted on this card? How does it seem Americans viewed Filipinos and other Asians?

in the Caribbean and the Pacific; Fish often had to restrain him. They moved first to repair relations with Great Britain, which had become strained during the Civil War. Negotiating patiently, Fish signed the Treaty of Washington in 1871, providing for arbitration of the *Alabama* claims issue—U.S. demands that Britain pay for damages caused by the Confederate vessel *Alabama,* which had been built and outfitted in British shipyards—and other nettlesome controversies. The treaty, one of the landmarks in the peaceful settlement of international disputes, marked a significant step in cementing Anglo-American relations.

Grant and Fish looked most eagerly to Latin America. In 1870, Grant became the first president to proclaim the nontransfer principle—"hereafter no territory on this continent shall be regarded as subject to transfer to a European power." Fish also promoted the independence of Cuba, restive under Spanish rule.

James G. Blaine's first stint as secretary of state lasted only six months, until Garfield's assassination, but he laid extensive plans to establish closer commercial relations with Latin America. When he returned to the State Department in 1889 under President Benjamin Harrison, he moved to expand markets in Latin America. He envisaged a hemisphere system of peaceful intercourse, arbitration of disputes, and expanded trade. He also wanted to annex Hawaii.

In general, Harrison and Blaine focused on pan-Americanism and tariff reciprocity. Blaine presided over the first Inter-American Conference in Washington on October 2, 1889, which Blaine hoped would unite Latin America and the United States in a customs union and create a way to settle conflicts. Although the nineteen countries that were represented refused to accept Blaine's full program, the conference was a major step in hemisphere relations and led to later meetings promoting trade and other agreements. It created an international bureau that later became the Pan-American Union for the exchange of political, scientific, and cultural information.

Reciprocity, Harrison and Blaine hoped, would divert Latin American trade from Europe to the United States. Working hard to sell the idea in Congress, Blaine lobbied for a reciprocity provision in the McKinley Tariff Act of 1890 (see Chapter 20). Once that was enacted, he negotiated important reciprocity treaties with most Latin American nations, resulting in greater American exports of flour, grain, meat, iron, and machinery. But the Wilson-Gorman Tariff Act (1894) ended reciprocity.

Grover Cleveland, Harrison's successor, pursued an aggressive policy toward Latin America. In 1895, he brought the United States precariously close to war with Great Britain over a boundary dispute between Venezuela and British Guiana. Cleveland sympathized with Venezuela, and he and Secretary of State Richard Olney urged Britain to arbitrate the dispute. When Britain failed to act, Olney drafted a stiff diplomatic note affirming the Monroe Doctrine and denying European nations the right to meddle in Western Hemisphere affairs.

Lord Salisbury, the British foreign secretary, rejected Olney's arguments, whereupon Cleveland asked Congress for authority to appoint a commission to decide the boundary and enforce its decision. This veiled threat of war, coupled with British diplomatic problems in Africa and Europe, forced Britain to change its position, and the dispute was peacefully arbitrated.

The Venezuelan incident demonstrated growing American power of persuasion in the Western Hemisphere. Cleveland and Olney had forced Great Britain to recognize United States dominance, and they had sharpened American influence in Latin America. The Monroe Doctrine assumed new importance.

The Lure of Hawaii and Samoa

The islands of Hawaii offered a tempting way station to Asian markets. In the early 1800s, they were already called the "Crossroads of the Pacific," and trading ships of many nations stopped there. In 1820, the first American missionaries arrived to convert the islanders to Christianity. Like missionaries elsewhere, they advertised

Hawaii's economic and other benefits and attracted new settlers, whose children later came to dominate Hawaiian political life and play an important role in annexation.

After the Civil War, the United States tightened its connections with the islands. The reciprocity treaty of 1875 allowed Hawaiian sugar to enter the United States free of duty and increased Hawaiian economic dependence on the United States. In addition, its political clauses effectively made Hawaii an American protectorate.

Following the 1875 treaty, white Hawaiians became more and more influential in the islands' political life. The McKinley Tariff Act of 1890 ended the special status given Hawaiian sugar and in addition awarded American producers a bounty of 2 cents a pound. Hawaiian sugar production dropped dramatically, unemployment rose, and property values fell. Soon thereafter, Queen Liliuokalani, a strong-willed nationalist, retaliated by decreeing a new constitution that gave greater power to native Hawaiians.

Unhappy, the American residents revolted in early 1893 and called on the United States for help. John L. Stevens, the American minister in Honolulu, sent 150 marines ashore, and within three days, the bloodless revolution was over. On February 14, 1893, Harrison's secretary of state, John W. Foster, and delegates of the new government signed a treaty annexing Hawaii to the United States. But only two weeks remained in Harrison's term, and the Senate refused to ratify the treaty. The new president, Cleveland, who disapproved of the American-instigated rebellion, withdrew the treaty and demanded that the queen be restored to her throne. However, the provisional government in Hawaii politely refused and instead proclaimed Hawaii a republic.

The debate over Hawaiian annexation continued through the 1890s. Those in favor of annexation pointed to Hawaii's strategic location, argued that Japan or other powers might seize the islands if the United States did not do so, and suggested that Americans had a responsibility to civilize and Christianize the native Hawaiians. Opponents warned that annexation might lead to a colonial army and colonial problems, the inclusion of a "mongrel" population in the United States, and rule over an area not destined for statehood.

Annexation came swiftly in July 1898 in the midst of excitement over victories in the Spanish-American War. Even before the war, President William McKinley had called for annexation, but opposition was still strong. The outbreak of war caused annexationists to redouble their efforts. McKinley and congressional leaders sought a joint resolution for annexation, which required only a majority of both houses. The annexation measure moved quickly through Congress, and McKinley signed it on July 7, 1898. His signature, giving the United States a naval and commercial base in the mid-Pacific, realized a goal of policymakers since the 1860s.

Hawaii represented a step toward China; the Samoan Islands, 3000 miles to the south, sat astride the sea-lanes of the South Pacific. In 1878, the United States acquired the use of Pago Pago, a harbor on the island of Tutuila. Great Britain and Germany also secured treaty rights in Samoa, and thereafter the three nations jockeyed for position.

The situation grew tense in 1889 when warships from all three countries gathered in a Samoan harbor. But a sudden typhoon destroyed the fleets, and tensions eased. A month later, delegates from the three countries met in Berlin to negotiate the problem. For a time, the indigenous population was granted some degree of authority, but in 1899, the United States and Germany divided Samoa and compensated Britain with lands elsewhere in the Pacific.

The New Navy

Large navies were vital in the scramble for colonies, but in the 1870s, the United States had almost no navy. One of the most powerful fleets in the world during the Civil War, the American navy had fallen into rapid decline. Ships rotted, and many officers left the service.

Conditions changed during the 1880s. A group of rising young officers, steeped in a new naval philosophy, argued for an expanded navy equipped with fast, aggressive ships capable of fighting battles across the seas. Big-navy proponents pointed to the growing navies of Great Britain, France, and Germany, arguing that the United States needed greater fleet strength to protect its interests in the Caribbean and the Pacific.

In 1883, Congress authorized construction of four steel ships, marking the beginning of the new navy. The initial building program focused on lightly armored, fast cruisers for raiding enemy merchant ships and protecting American shores, but after 1890, the program shifted to the construction of a seagoing, offensive battleship navy capable of challenging the strongest fleets of Europe.

Alfred Thayer Mahan and Benjamin F. Tracy were major influences behind the new navy. Austere and scholarly, Mahan was the era's most influential naval strategist. He devoted a lifetime to studying the role of sea power in history, summarizing his beliefs in major books: *The Influence of Sea Power upon History, 1660–1783* (1890) and *The Interest of America in Sea Power* (1897).

Mahan's reasoning was simple and persuasive. Industrialism, he argued, produced vast surpluses of agricultural and manufactured goods, for which markets had to be found. Markets involved distant ports; reaching them required a large merchant marine and a powerful navy to protect it. Navies, in turn, needed coaling stations and repair yards. Coaling stations meant colonies, and colonies became strategic bases, the foundation of a nation's wealth and power. The bases might serve as markets themselves, but they were more important as stepping-stones to other objectives, the markets of Latin America and Asia.

Mahan called attention to the worldwide race for power, a race, he warned, the United States could not afford to lose. To compete in the struggle, the United States needed strategic bases; a powerful, oceangoing navy; a canal across the isthmus connecting North and South America, to link the East Coast with the Pacific; and Hawaii as a way station on the route to Asia.

One of the many men Mahan impressed was Benjamin F. Tracy, who became Harrison's secretary of the navy in 1889. Tracy joined with big-navy advocates in Congress to push for a far-ranging battleship fleet that would be capable of attacking distant enemies. He actually wanted two fleets: eight battleships in the Pacific and twelve in the Atlantic. He got four first-class battleships.

In 1889, when Tracy entered office, the United States ranked twelfth among world navies; in 1893, when he left, it ranked seventh and was climbing rapidly. By the end of the decade, the navy had seventeen steel battleships and six armored cruisers, and it ranked third in the world.

WAR WITH SPAIN

The war with Spain in 1898 built a mood of national confidence; altered older, more insular patterns of thought; and reshaped the way Americans saw themselves and the world. When the war ended, American possessions stretched into the Caribbean and deep into the Pacific. The Spanish-American War established the United States as a world power for the twentieth century. It brought colonies and millions of colonial subjects and confirmed the long-standing belief in the superiority of the New World over the Old. Americans felt more certain than ever that they were touched with a special destiny.

A War for Principle

By the 1890s, Cuba and the nearby island of Puerto Rico comprised nearly all that remained of Spain's once vast empire in the New World. Cuban insurgents had rebelled against Spanish rule several times, but they had failed to free their country.

The depression of 1893 damaged the Cuban economy, and the Wilson-Gorman Tariff of 1894 prostrated it. Duties on sugar, Cuba's lifeblood, were raised 40 percent. With the island's sugar market in ruins, discontent with Spanish rule heightened, and in late February 1895, revolt again broke out.

Cuban insurgents established a junta in New York City to raise money, purchase weapons, and wage a propaganda war to sway American public opinion. Conditions in Cuba were grim. The insurgents engaged in a hit-and-run, scorched-earth policy to force the Spanish to leave while the Spanish commander tried to corner the rebels in the eastern end of the island and destroy them.

After initial failures, Spain in January 1896 sent General Valeriano Weyler y Nicolau to Cuba. Relentless and brutal, Weyler gave the rebels ten days to lay down their arms. He then put into effect a "reconcentration" policy designed to move the native population into camps and liquidate the rebels' popular base. Herded into fortified areas, Cubans died by the thousands, victims of unsanitary conditions, overcrowding, and disease.

There ensued a wave of compassion for the insurgents, stimulated by the newspapers. The so-called yellow press, a group of circulation-hungry New York City newspapers led by Joseph Pulitzer's *New York World* and William Randolph Hearst's *New York Journal,* printed lurid stories of Spanish atrocities.

But **yellow journalism** did not cause the war. It stemmed from larger conflicts in policies and perceptions between Spain and the United States. Throughout his presidency, Grover Cleveland counseled neutrality, and initially President McKinley, who came into office in March 1897, did the same. But McKinley tilted more toward the insurgents. Before the end of 1897, the new president was criticizing Spain's "uncivilized and inhuman" conduct. The United States, he made clear, did not contest Spain's right to fight the rebellion but insisted it be done within humane limits.

Late in 1897, a change in government in Madrid brought a temporary lull in the crisis. The new government recalled Weyler and agreed to offer the Cubans some form of autonomy. The new initiatives pleased McKinley, though he again warned Spain that it must find a humane end to the rebellion. Then, in January 1898, Spanish army officers led riots in Havana against the new autonomy policy and shook the president's confidence in Madrid's control over conditions in Cuba.

McKinley ordered the battleship *Maine* to Havana to "show the flag" and to evacuate American citizens if necessary. On February 9, 1898, the *New York Journal* published a private letter stolen from Enrique Dupuy de Lôme, the Spanish ambassador in Washington. In the letter, de Lôme called McKinley "weak" and "a would-be politician." Many Americans were angered by the insult; McKinley himself was more worried about other sections of the letter, which revealed Spanish insincerity in the negotiations. De Lôme immediately resigned and went home, but the damage was done.

A few days later, on February 15, an explosion tore through the hull of the *Maine,* sinking the ship and killing 266 sailors. McKinley cautioned patience, but Americans cried out for war. Soon they were chanting a new slogan: "Remember the *Maine* and to Hell with Spain!"

Recent studies of the *Maine* incident blame the sinking on an accidental internal explosion, but in 1898, Americans suspected Spain, especially after the report of an investigating board attributed the sinking to an external (and thus presumably Spanish) explosion.

In early March 1898, McKinley asked Congress for $50 million in emergency defense appropriations, a request Congress promptly approved. On March 27, McKinley cabled Spain his final terms. He asked Spain to declare an armistice, end the reconcentration policy, and—implicitly—move toward Cuban independence. The Spanish answer conceded some things, but not, in McKinley's judgment, the

yellow journalism In order to sell newspapers to the public before and during the Spanish-American War, publishers William Randolph Hearst and Joseph Pulitzer engaged in blatant sensationalizing of the news, which became known as "yellow journalism." It helped turn U.S. public opinion against Spain's actions in Cuba.

■ *Lithograph commemorating the sinking of the Maine in Havana harbor on February 15, 1898, killing 266 men. Coverage of the incident in the "yellow" press encouraged readers to believe that Spanish bombs or torpedoes had sunk the ship.* ■

Teller Amendment In this amendment, sponsored by Senator Henry M. Teller of Colorado, the United States pledged that it did not intend to annex Cuba and that it would recognize Cuban independence from Spain after the Spanish-American War.

important ones. It made no mention of a true armistice, McKinley's offer to mediate, or Cuba's independence.

Reluctantly, McKinley prepared his war message, which Congress heard on April 11, 1898. Eight days later, Congress passed a joint resolution declaring Cuba independent and authorizing the president to use the army and navy to expel the Spanish from the island. The **Teller Amendment,** offered by Colorado Senator Henry M. Teller, pledged that the United States had no intention of annexing Cuba. On April 25, Congress passed a declaration of war, and late that afternoon McKinley signed it.

Some historians have suggested that McKinley was weak and indecisive in confronting the war hysteria in the country; others have called him a wily manipulator for war and imperial gains. In truth he was neither. Throughout the Spanish crisis, McKinley pursued a moderate middle course that sought to protect American interests, promote Cuba's independence, and allow Spain time to adjust to the loss of the remnant of empire. He also wanted peace, but in the end, the conflicting national interests of the two countries brought them to war.

"A Splendid Little War"

Ten weeks after the declaration of war, the fighting was over. For Americans, they were ten glorious, dizzying weeks, with victories to fill every headline and slogans to suit every taste. Relatively few Americans died, and the quick victory seemed to verify burgeoning American power. John Hay, soon to be McKinley's secretary of state, called it "a splendid little war."

At the outset, the United States was militarily unprepared. Like the navy, the army had shrunk drastically since the end of the Civil War. In 1898, the regular army consisted of only 28,000 officers and men, most of them more experienced in quelling Indian uprisings than fighting large-scale battles.

When McKinley called for 125,000 volunteers, as many as one million young Americans responded. Men clamored to join the newly formed National Guard units. The secretary of war feared "there is going to be more trouble to satisfy those who are not going than to find those who are willing to go."

Problems of equipment and supply quickly appeared. Some units went into battle carrying Civil War Springfield rifles whose cartridges gave off a puff of smoke when fired, neatly marking the troops' position. Food was also a problem, as was sickness. Tainted food and tropical diseases felled more American troops than enemy bullets did.

Americans then believed that "a foreign war should be fought by the hometown military unit acting as an extension of their community." Soldiers identified with their hometowns and thought of themselves as members of a town unit in a national army. Not surprisingly, then, National Guard units mirrored the social patterns of their communities. Since everyone knew each other, there was an easygoing familiarity. Enlisted men resented officers who grabbed too much authority and expected officers and men to call each other by their first names.

Each community thought of the hometown unit as *its* unit, an extension of itself. There was little government-imposed censorship in the war with Spain, and fresh news arrived with each letter home. Small-town newspapers printed news of the men, and towns sent food, clothing, and occasionally even local doctors to the front.

"Smoked Yankees"

When the invasion force sailed for Cuba, nearly one-fourth of it was black. In 1898, the regular army included four regiments of black soldiers, the Twenty-Fourth and Twenty-Fifth Infantry and the Ninth and Tenth Cavalry. Black regiments had served with distinction in campaigns against the Indians in the West. Most black troops were posted in the West; no eastern community would accept them. When McKinley called for volunteers, more than ten thousand black troops volunteered for the National Guard.

Orders quickly went out to the four black regular-army regiments in the West to move to camps in the South to prepare for the invasion of Cuba. Crowds and cheers followed the troop trains across the Plains, but as they crossed into Kentucky and Tennessee, the cheering stopped. Station restaurants refused to serve the troops; all waiting rooms were segregated.

Many soldiers were not prepared to put up with the shameful treatment. Those stationed near Chickamauga Park, Tennessee, shot at some whites who insulted them and desegregated the railroad cars on the line in Chattanooga. Similar incidents broke out elsewhere in the South. Just before the army's departure for Cuba, the tensions in Tampa, Florida, erupted in a night of rioting during which three white and twenty-seven black soldiers were wounded. Such events demonstrated the irony of black American soldiers committed to fight for Cuban independence. As one black wondered, "Is America any better than Spain?"

Segregation continued on some of the troop ships. But the confusion of war often ended the problem, if only temporarily. Blacks took command as white officers died, and Spanish troops soon came to fear the "smoked Yankees," as they called them. Black soldiers played a major role in the Cuban campaign and probably staved off defeat for the Rough Riders at San Juan Hill. In Cuba, they won twenty-six Certificates of Merit and five Congressional Medals of Honor.

The Course of the War

Mahan's Naval War College had begun studying strategy for a war with Spain in 1895. By 1898, it had a detailed plan for operations in the Caribbean and the Pacific. Naval strategy was simple: destroy the Spanish fleet, damage Spain's merchant marine, and harry the colonies or the coast of Spain. The army's task was

■ *The twenty-fourth and twenty-fifth Colored Infantry regiments served with exceptional gallantry in the Spanish-American War. Charles Young, an 1889 graduate of West Point, was the only African American officer in the army during the Spanish-American War except for a few chaplains.* ■

more difficult. It must defend the United States, invade Cuba and probably Puerto Rico, and undertake possible action in far-flung places such as the Philippines or Spain.

At first, McKinley moved cautiously. On the afternoon of April 20, 1898, he summoned the strategists to the White House and, to the dismay of those who wanted a more aggressive policy, decided on the limited strategy of blockading Cuba, sending arms to the insurgents, and annoying the Spanish with small thrusts by the army.

Victories soon changed the strategy. In the case of war, long-standing naval plans had called for a holding action against the Spanish base in the Philippines. On May 1, 1898, with the war barely a week old, Commodore George Dewey, commander of the Asiatic Squadron located at Hong Kong, crushed the Spanish fleet in Manila Bay. Suddenly, Manila and the Philippines lay within American grasp. Dewey had no troops to attack the Spanish army in Manila, but the War Department, stunned by the speed and size of the victory, quickly raised an expeditionary force. On August 13, 1898, the troops accepted the surrender of Manila and with it the Philippines.

McKinley and his aides were worried about Admiral Pascual Cervera's main Spanish fleet, thought to be headed across the Atlantic for an attack on Florida. In mid-May, Cervera slipped secretly into the harbor of Santiago de Cuba, a city on the island's southern coast. But a spy in the Havana telegraph office alerted the Americans, and on May 28 a superior American force under Admiral William T. Sampson bottled Cervera up.

On June 14, an invasion force of about seventeen thousand men set sail from Tampa. Seven days later, they landed at Daiquiri on Cuba's southeastern coast. All was confusion, but the Spanish offered no resistance. Immediately, the Americans pushed west toward Santiago, which they hoped to surround and capture. At first, the advance was peaceful through the lush tropical countryside.

The first battle broke out at Las Guasimas, a crossroads on the Santiago road. After a sharp fight, the Spanish fell back. On July 1, the Rough Riders, troops from the four black regiments, and the other regulars reached the strong fortifications at El Caney and San Juan Hill. Black soldiers of the Twenty-Fifth Infantry charged the El Caney blockhouses. For the better part of a day, the defenders fought stubbornly and held back the army's elite corps. In the confusion of battle, Roosevelt rallied an assortment of infantry and cavalry to take Kettle Hill, adjacent to San Juan Hill.

They charged directly into the Spanish guns, Roosevelt at their head. Losses were heavy. Dense foliage concealed the enemy; smokeless powder gave no clue to their position. At nightfall, the surviving Spanish defenders withdrew, and the Americans prepared for the counterattack. The worst, many soldiers feared, was yet to come.

American troops now occupied the ridges overlooking Santiago. They were weakened by sickness, a fact unknown to the Spanish, who decided the city was lost. The Spanish command in Havana ordered Cervera to run for the open sea, although he knew the attempt would be hopeless. On the morning of July 3, his squadron steamed down the bay and out through the harbor's narrow channel, but the waiting American fleet closed in, and in a few hours, every Spanish vessel was destroyed. Two weeks later, Santiago surrendered.

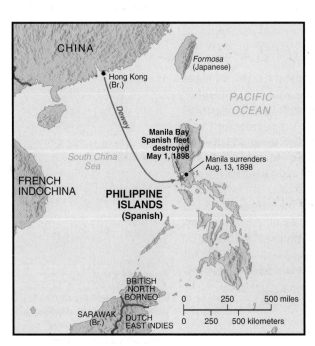

SPANISH-AMERICAN WAR: PACIFIC THEATER
Commodore Dewey, promoted to admiral immediately after the naval victory at Manila Bay, was the first hero of the war. ◼

Soon thereafter, army troops, meeting little resistance, occupied Puerto Rico. Cervera had commanded Spain's only battle fleet, and when it sank, Spain was helpless against attacks on the colonies or even its own shores. The war was over. Lasting 113 days, it took relatively few lives, most of them the result of accident, yellow fever, malaria, and typhoid in Cuba. Of the 5500 Americans who died in the war, only 379 were killed in battle. The navy lost one man in the battle at Santiago Bay, and one sailor died of heat prostration in the stunning victory in Manila Bay.

ACQUISITION OF EMPIRE

The United States emerged from the war with an expansion of its territory and an even larger expansion of its responsibilities. According to the preliminary peace agreement, Spain granted independence to Cuba, ceded Puerto Rico and the Pacific island of Guam to the United States, and allowed Americans to occupy Manila until the two countries reached final agreement on the Philippines. To McKinley, the Philippines were the problem. Unlike Puerto Rico, which was close to the U.S. mainland, and Guam, which was small and unknown, the Philippines were a large, sprawling archipelago thousands of miles from America.

McKinley weighed a number of alternatives for the Philippines, but he liked none of them. He did not want to give the islands back to Spain; public opinion would not allow it. Nor did he want to turn them over to another world power. Germany, Japan, Great Britain, and Russia had all expressed interest in them. He considered independence for the islands but was soon talked out of it. Nearly everyone who had been there believed that the people were not ready for independence. Sifting the choices, McKinley decided that there was only one practical policy: annex the Philippines with an eye to future independence after a period of tutelage.

At first hesitant, American opinion was swinging to the same conclusion. Religious and missionary organizations appealed to McKinley to hold on to the Philippines in order to "Christianize them." Some merchants and industrialists saw them as the key to the China market and the wealth of Asia. Many Americans simply regarded them as the legitimate fruits of war.

In October 1898, representatives of the United States and Spain met in Paris to discuss a peace treaty. Spain agreed to recognize Cuba's independence, to assume the Cuban debt, and to cede Puerto Rico and Guam to the United States. Acting on instructions from McKinley, the American representatives demanded the cession of the Philippines. In return, the United States offered a payment of $20 million. Spain resisted but had little choice, and on December 10, 1898, the American and Spanish representatives signed the **Treaty of Paris.**

Submitted to the Senate for ratification, the treaty set off a storm of debate throughout the country. Such prominent Americans as Andrew Carnegie, Jane Addams, William Jennings Bryan, and Mark Twain argued forcefully against annexation of the Philippines. While some anti-imperialists feared the importation of

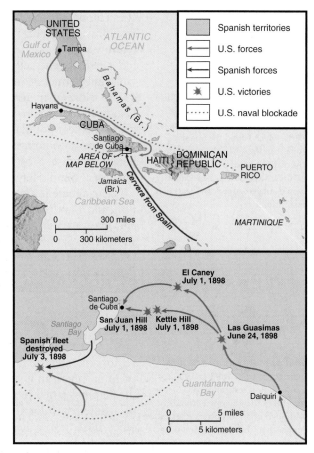

SPANISH-AMERICAN WAR: CARIBBEAN THEATER   *President McKinley set up a war room in the White House, following the action on giant war maps with red and white marking pins.* ∎

Treaty of Paris Signed by the United States and Spain in December 1898, this treaty ended the Spanish-American War. Under its terms, Spain recognized Cuba's independence and assumed the Cuban debt; it also ceded Puerto Rico, Guam, and the Philippines to the United States.

cheap labor from new Pacific colonies and others argued against assimilation of different races, most anti-imperialists focused on a different argument: the exercise of tyranny abroad, they argued, would result in tyranny at home; the very principles of independence and self-determination on which the country was founded would be violated by annexation.

In November 1898, opponents of expansion formed the **Anti-Imperialist League** to fight against the peace treaty. Membership centered in New England; the cause was less popular in the West and South. It enlisted more Democrats than Republicans, though never a majority of either. The anti-imperialists lacked a coherent program. Most simply wished that Dewey had sailed away after beating the Spanish at Manila Bay.

The debate in the Senate lasted a month. McKinley pressed hard for ratification, and Bryan, though opposed to annexation, supported ratification simply to end the war. Still, on the final weekend before the vote, the treaty was two votes short. That Saturday night, news reached Washington that fighting had broken out between American troops and Filipino insurgents who demanded immediate independence. The news increased pressure to ratify the treaty, which the Senate did on February 6, 1899. The United States had a colonial empire.

Anti-Imperialist League This organization formed in November 1898 to fight against the Treaty of Paris, which ended the Spanish-American War. Members opposed the acquisition of overseas colonies by the United States, believing it would subvert American ideals and institutions.

Guerrilla Warfare in the Philippines

Historians rarely write of the **Philippine-American War,** but it was an important event in American history. The war with Spain was over in a few months; war with the Filipinos lasted more than three years. For the first time, Americans fought men of a different color in an Asian guerrilla war. The Philippine-American War of 1899–1902 took a heavy toll: 4300 Americans and perhaps as many as 57,000 Filipinos.

Philippine-American War A war fought from 1899 to 1903 to quell Filipino resistance to U.S. control of the Philippine Islands. Although often forgotten, it lasted longer than the Spanish-American War itself and resulted in more casualties.

Emilio Aguinaldo, the Filipino leader, had welcomed the Spanish-American War. Certain that the United States would grant independence, he had worked for an American victory. On June 12, 1898, the insurgents proclaimed their independence from Spain. Then, cooperating with the Americans, they drove the Spanish out of many areas of the islands. In the liberated regions, Aguinaldo established local governments. He waited impatiently for American recognition, but McKinley and others doubted that the Filipinos were ready. Shortly thereafter, fighting broke out between Filipinos and Americans.

Although by late 1899 the American army had defeated and dispersed the organized Filipino army, Aguinaldo and his followers continued to wage a guerrilla war. The Americans used Weyler-like tactics. After any attack on an American patrol, they burned all the houses in the nearest district. They established protected "zones" and herded Filipinos into them. Seizing or destroying all food outside the zones, they starved many guerrillas into submission.

Bryan tried to turn the election of 1900 into a debate over imperialism, but his attempt failed. For one thing, he himself refused to give up the silver issue, which cost him support among anti-imperialists in the Northeast, who were for gold. McKinley, moreover, was able to take advantage of the surging economy, and he could defend expansion as an accomplished fact. Riding a wave of patriotism and prosperity, McKinley won the election handily.

In 1900, McKinley sent a special Philippine commission under William Howard Taft to establish a civil government. The following year, Aguinaldo was captured. Back in Manila, he signed a proclamation urging his people to end the fighting. On July 4, 1901, authority was transferred from the army to Taft, who was named the civilian governor of the islands, and his civil commission.

Given broad powers, the Taft Commission introduced many changes. The Americans built new schools, roads, and bridges. They reformed the judiciary, re-

A Look at the Past

Cartoon "School Begins"

Uncle Sam teaches a diverse group of students about civilization in this *Puck* cartoon. In the first row, receiving special attention are recent U.S. acquisitions: Cuba, Puerto Rico, Hawaii, and the Philippines. Carefully examine all the individuals in the cartoon. ✳ Who stands outside the classroom and why? How do the students in the first row compare to others in the classroom? Read the message on the chalkboard and consider its meaning. According to this cartoon, how do Americans regard other races and ethnicities? How would Americans define civilization?

constructed the tax system, and introduced sanitation and vaccination programs. Taft also encouraged Filipino participation in government. Slowly, the Filipinos moved toward independence, which came on July 4, 1946, nearly fifty years after Aguinaldo proclaimed it.

Governing the Empire

Ruling the colonies raised new and perplexing questions. How could—and how should—the distant dependencies be governed? Did their inhabitants have the rights of American citizens? Did "the Constitution follow the flag"?

In a series of cases between 1901 and 1904, the Supreme Court asserted the principle that the Constitution did not automatically and immediately apply to the people of an annexed territory and did not confer on them all the privileges of United States citizenship. Instead, Congress could specifically extend such constitutional provisions as it saw fit.

Four dependencies—Hawaii, Alaska, Guam, and Puerto Rico—were organized quickly. In 1900, Congress granted territorial status to Hawaii and gave American citizenship to all citizens of the Hawaiian republic. A similar maneuver made Alaska a territory in 1912. Guam and the Samoan island of Tutuila were simply placed under the control of naval officers.

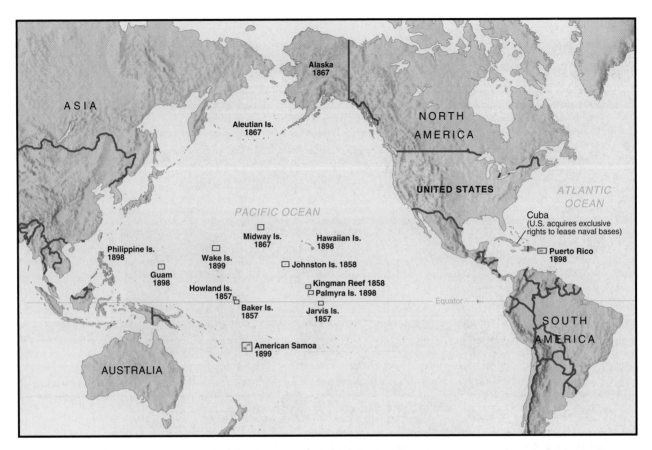

AMERICAN EMPIRE, 1900   *With the Treaty of Paris, the United States gained an expanded colonial empire stretching from the Caribbean to the far Pacific. It embraced Puerto Rico, Alaska, Hawaii, part of Samoa, Guam, the Philippines, and a chain of Pacific islands. The dates on the map refer to the date of U.S. acquisition.* ■

Foraker Act This act established Puerto Rico as an unorganized U.S. territory. Puerto Ricans were not given U.S. citizenship, but the U.S. president appointed the island's governor and governing council.

Puerto Ricans readily accepted the war's outcome, and in 1900, the **Foraker Act** established civil government in Puerto Rico. It organized the island as a territory. In 1917, United States citizenship was extended to the residents of the island.

Cuba proved a trickier matter. McKinley asserted the authority of the United States over conquered territory and promised to govern the island until the Cubans had established a firm and stable government of their own. To oversee this process, McKinley sent General Leonard Wood to Cuba. Wood moved quickly to bring order to the country. Early in 1900, he conducted municipal elections and arranged for the election of delegates to a constitutional convention. The convention adopted a constitution modeled on the U.S. Constitution and, at Woods's prodding, included provisions for future relations with the United States. Known as the **Platt Amendment,** the provisions stipulated that Cuba should make no treaties that might impair its independence and acquire no debts that it could not pay; most important, it empowered the United States to intervene in Cuba to maintain orderly government.

Platt Amendment This amendment to the new Cuban constitution authorized U.S. intervention in Cuba to protect its interests. Cuba pledged not to make treaties with other countries that might compromise its independence, and it granted naval bases to the United States.

Between 1898 and 1902, the American military government worked hard for the economic and political revival of the island. It repaired the damage of the civil war, built roads and schools, and established order in rural areas. A public health campaign headed by Dr. Walter Reed, an army surgeon, wiped out yellow fever. When the last troops left in May 1902, the Cubans at last had their independence, although they were firmly under the domination of their neighbor to the north.

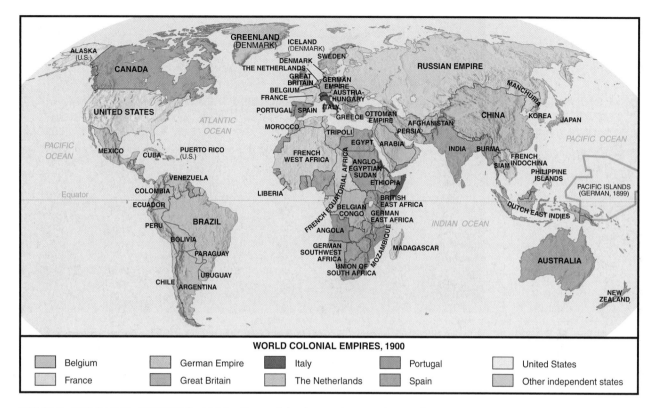

WORLD COLONIAL EMPIRES, 1900   *Events of the nineteenth century increased European hegemony over the world. By 1900, most independent African nations had disappeared, and the major European nations had divided the continent among themselves. In the East, the European powers and Japan took advantage of China's internal weakness to gain both trading ports and economic concessions.* ■

The Open Door

Poised in the Philippines, the United States had become an Asian power on the doorstep of China. Weakened by years of warfare, China in 1898 and 1899 was unable to resist foreign influence. Japan, England, France, Germany, and Russia eyed it covetously, dividing the country into "spheres of influence." They forced China to grant "concessions" that allowed them exclusive rights to develop particular areas and threatened American hopes for extensive trade with the country.

McKinley first outlined a new China policy in September 1898. He wanted Asian trade to be conducted on the analogy of an "open door," meaning that all countries would have an equal opportunity to compete for the Asian markets. In September 1899, Secretary of State Hay addressed identical diplomatic notes to England, Germany, and Russia, and later to France, Japan, and Italy, asking them to join the United States in establishing the **Open Door policy.** This policy urged three agreements: nations possessing a sphere of influence would respect the rights and privileges of other nations in that sphere, the Chinese government would continue to collect tariff duties in all spheres, and nations would not discriminate against other nations in levying port dues and railroad rates within their respective spheres of influence.

Under the Open Door policy, the United States could retain many commercial advantages that were endangered by the partition of China into spheres of influence. McKinley and Hay also attempted to preserve for the Chinese some semblance of national authority. None of the countries fully accepted the Open Door policy, but Hay turned the situation to American advantage by boldly announcing in March 1900 that all the powers had agreed to it.

Open Door policy Established in a series of notes by Secretary of State John Hay in 1900, this policy established free trade between the United States and China and attempted to enlist major European and Asian nations in recognizing the territorial integrity of China. It marked a departure from the American tradition of isolationism and signaled the country's growing involvement in the world.

■ *In this 1899* Puck *cartoon, "Putting His Foot Down," the nations of Europe are getting ready to cut up China to expand their spheres of influence, but Uncle Sam stands firm on American commitments to preserve China's sovereignty.* ■

The policy's first test came just three months later with the outbreak of the Boxer Rebellion in Peking (Beijing). In June 1900, a secret and intensely nationalistic Chinese society called the Boxers tried to oust all foreigners from the country. Overrunning Peking, they drove foreigners into their legations and penned them up for nearly two months. In the end, the United States joined Britain, Germany, and other powers in sending troops to lift the siege.

Fearing that the rebellion gave some nations, especially Germany and Russia, an excuse to expand their spheres of influence, Hay took quick action to emphasize American policy. In July, he sent off another round of Open Door notes affirming the U.S. commitment to equal commercial opportunity and respect for China's independence. Whereas the first Open Door notes had implied recognition of China's continued independence, the second notes explicitly stated the need to preserve it. The two notes set the policy that would guide American diplomacy in the Far East.

CONCLUSION: OUTCOME OF THE WAR WITH SPAIN

The war was over. Roosevelt, now famous, was elected governor of New York. He would soon become McKinley's vice president and then president of the United States. For other Americans, heroism was not so profitable. Bravery in Cuba and the Philippines won some recognition for black soldiers, but the war itself set back the cause of civil rights. It spurred talk about "inferior" races, at home and abroad, and forged new bonds between whites in the North and South. A fresh outburst of segregation and lynching occurred during the decade after the war.

In a little more than a century, the United States had grown from thirteen small states strung along a thin strip of Atlantic coastline into a world power that stretched from the Atlantic and the Caribbean to the far side of the Pacific. As Seward and others had hoped, the nation now dominated its own hemisphere, dealt with European powers on equal terms, and exerted great influence in Asia.

Chronology

1867	United States purchases Alaska from Russia ▪ Midway Islands are annexed
1871	Treaty of Washington between the United States and Great Britain sets a precedent for the peaceful settlement of international disputes
1875	Reciprocity treaty with Hawaii binds Hawaii economically and politically to the United States
1878	United States acquires a naval base in Samoa
1883	Congress approves funds for construction of the first modern steel ships; beginning of the modern navy
1887	New treaty with Hawaii gives United States exclusive use of Pearl Harbor
1889	First Inter-American Conference meets in Washington, D.C.
1893	American settlers in Hawaii overthrow Queen Liliuokalani; provisional government is established
1895	Cuban insurgents rebel against Spanish rule
1898	Battleship *Maine* explodes in Havana harbor (February) ▪ Congress declares war against Spain (April) ▪ Commodore Dewey defeats the Spanish fleet at Manila Bay (May) ▪ United States annexes Hawaii (July) ▪ Americans defeat the Spanish at El Caney, San Juan Hill (actually Kettle Hill), and Santiago (July) ▪ Spain sues for peace (August) ▪ Treaty of Paris ends the Spanish-American War (December)
1899	Congress ratifies the Treaty of Paris ▪ United States sends Open Door notes to Britain, Germany, France, Russia, Japan, and Italy ▪ Philippine-American War erupts
1900	Foraker Act establishes civil government in Puerto Rico ▪ Boxer Rebellion in China occurs
1901	Platt Amendment authorizes American intervention in Cuba
1902	Philippine-American War ends with an American victory

KEY TERMS

isolationism, p. 406

imperialism, p. 406

yellow journalism, p. 411

Teller Amendment, p. 412

Treaty of Paris, p. 415

Anti-Imperialist League, p. 416

Philippine-American War, p. 416

Foraker Act, p. 418

Platt Amendment, p. 418

Open Door policy, p. 419

RECOMMENDED READING

The best general account of the development of American foreign policy during the last part of the nineteenth century is Walter LaFeber, *The New Empire: An Interpretation of American Expansion, 1860–1898* (1963). William Appleman Williams, *The Tragedy of American Diplomacy* (1959), examines the economic motives for expansion. See also Paul Wolman, *Most Favored Nation: The Republican Revisionists and U.S. Tariff Policy, 1897–1912* (1992), Thomas Schoonover, *Uncle Sam's War of 1898 and the Origins of Globalization* (2003), Eric T. L. Lowe, *Race over Empire: Racism and U.S.*

Imperialism, 1865–1900 (2004), and Laura Wexler, *Tender Violence: Domestic Visions in an Age of U.S. Imperialism* (2000). Lewis L. Gould persuasively reassesses McKinley's diplomacy and wartime leadership in *The Presidency of William McKinley* (1980).

Also helpful are Michael H. Hunt, *Ideology and Foreign Policy* (1987), Tom E. Terrill, *The Tariff, Politics, and American Foreign Policy, 1874–1901* (1973), and Matthew Frye Jacobson, *Barbarian Virtues: The United States Encounters Foreign Peoples at Home and Abroad, 1876–1917* (2000).

Graham A. Cosmas presents a detailed account of military organization and strategy in *An Army for Empire: The United States Army in the Spanish-American War* (1971); Willard B. Gatewood, Jr., offers a fascinating glimpse of the thoughts of some black soldiers in the war in *"Smoked Yankees" and the Struggle for Empire: Letters from Negro Soldiers, 1898–1902* (1971). Also, Vincent H. Cirillo, *Bullets and Bacilli: The Spanish-American War and Military Medicine* (2004). Ivan Musicant, *Empire by Default: The Spanish-American War and the Dawn of the American Century* (1998), Kristin L. Hoganson, *Fighting for American Manhood: How Gender Politics Provoked the Spanish-American and Philippine-American Wars* (1998), and John L. Offner, *An Unwanted War: The Diplomacy of the United States and Spain over Cuba, 1895–1898* (1992), trace the background to the war with Spain. Brian McAllister Linn, *The Philippine War, 1899–1902* (2000), examines the often forgotten war against the Filipinos. Gerald F. Linderman relates the war to the home front in *The Mirror of War: American Society and the Spanish-American War* (1974).

SUGGESTED WEB SITES

William McKinley and the Spanish-American War

www.history.osu.edu/Projects/Mckinley/SpanAmWar.cfm

Part of Ohio State University's site about William McKinley, this part highlights the Spanish-American War with an essay and photos.

The Spanish-American War in Motion Pictures

memory.loc.gov/ammem/sawhtml/sawhome.html

This Library of Congress Web presentation features sixty-eight films of the Spanish-American War, the first war to be documented in motion pictures.

The World of 1898: The Spanish-American War

www.loc.gov/rr/hispanic/1898/

This Library of Congress site offers resources and documents about the Spanish-American War and the people who participated in or commented about it.

Sentenaryo/Centennial: The Philippine Revolution and Philippine-American War

www.boondocksnet.com/centennial/index.html

Jim Zwick organizes primary documents, images, and essays focusing on the Philippines and American involvement.

Anti-Imperialism in the United States, 1898–1935

www.boondocksnet.com/ail98-35.html

Jim Zwick edits this extensive site, collating a large number of primary documents about anti-imperialism in America.

The Age of Imperialism

www.smplanet.com/imperialism/toc.html

Focusing on the period around the turn of the century, this site puts much information about American imperialism in one place.

Images from the Philippine-United States War

www.historicaltextarchive.com/USA/twenty/filipino.html

This site includes several images from the Philippine-American War, one of the least discussed military engagements in American history.

Theodore Roosevelt Association

www.theodoreroosevelt.org/

This site contains much biographical and research information about this famous American.

Chapter 22

The Progressive Era

Muckrakers Call for Reform

In 1902, Samuel S. McClure, the shrewd owner of *McClure's Magazine,* sensed something astir in the country that his reporters were not covering. Like *Life,* the *Ladies' Home Journal,* and *Cosmopolitan, McClure's* was reaching more and more people—more than a quarter of a million readers a month. Americans were snapping up the new popular magazines filled with eye-catching illustrations and up-to-date fiction.

McClure was always chasing new ideas and readers, and in 1902, certain that something was happening in the public mood, he told one of his staff editors, 36-year-old Lincoln Steffens, "Get out of here, travel, go—somewhere. . . . " Following McClure's suggestion, Steffens boarded a train and headed west, determined to understand the temper of the nation. In St. Louis, he came across a young district attorney named Joseph W. Folk who had found a trail of corruption linking politics and some of the city's respected business leaders. "It is good business men," Folk stressed, "that are corrupting our bad politicians." Steffens's story, "Tweed Days in St. Louis," appeared in the October 1902 issue of *McClure's.*

The November *McClure's* carried the first installment of Ida Tarbell's scathing "History of the Standard Oil Company," and in January 1903, Steffens was back with "The Shame of Minneapolis," another tale of corrupt partnership between business and politics. McClure had what he wanted. In an editorial in the January issue, he deplored the corruption in American life, "capitalists, working men, politicians, citizens—all breaking the law, or letting it be broken."

Readers were enthralled, and articles and books by other **muckrakers**— Theodore Roosevelt coined the muckraking term in 1906 to describe the practice of exposing the corruption of public and prominent figures—spread swiftly. Muckraking flourished from 1903 to 1909, and while it did, good writers and bad investigated almost every corner of American life: government, labor unions, big business, Wall Street, health care, the food industry, child labor, women's rights, prostitution, ghetto living, and life insurance.

As McClure had hoped, Steffens *had* found something astir in the country, something so important and pervasive that it altered the course of American history. The muckrakers were a journalistic voice of this larger movement in American society. Called **progressivism,** it lasted from the mid-1890s through World War I. Like muckraking itself, it reflected concern with the state of society and a conviction that human compassion and scientific investigation could bring problems to light and solve them. Progressivism took on the character of Theodore Roosevelt and Woodrow Wilson, two important national spokesmen, but it affected large numbers of people and expressed at many levels the excitement of progress and change.

muckrakers Unflattering term coined by Theodore Roosevelt to describe the writers who made a practice of exposing the wrongdoings of public figures. Muckraking flourished from 1903 to 1909 in magazines such as *McClure's* and *Collier's,* exposing social and political problems and sparking reform.

progressivism Movement for social change between the late 1890s and World War I. Its origins lay in a fear of big business and corrupt government and a desire to improve the lives of countless Americans. Progressives set out to cure the social ills brought about by industrialization and urbanization, social disorder, and political corruption.

Outline

HISTORY OF STANDARD OIL BY Ida M. Tarbell

McCLURE'S MAGAZINE
NOVEMBER

PUBLISHED MONTHLY BY THE S. S. McCLURE CO., 141-155 E. 25th ST., NEW YORK CITY

■ *At the beginning of the twentieth century,* McClure's Magazine *was at the forefront of the journalistic crusade for reform, which took the form of muckraking articles by such writers as Ida Tarbell. The November 1902 issue of* McClure's *featured the first installment of Tarbell's two-year series on Standard Oil that exposed the corrupt practices and deals that had helped create the company.* ■

THE CHANGING FACE OF INDUSTRIALISM

Significant changes occurred in the industrial system during the years between the 1890s and World War I. The rapid growth of businesses gave rise to the widely feared trust-forming movement and the progressives' desire to regulate it. Both progressives and business leaders drew on similar visions of the country: complex, expansive, hopeful, managerially minded, and oriented toward results and efficiency. In working for reform, the progressives drew on the managerial methods of a business world they sought to regulate.

Businesses got large in the three decades after the Civil War, but in the years between 1895 and 1915 they became mammoth, employing thousands of workers and equipped with assembly lines to turn out huge numbers of the company's product. Inevitably, management attitudes changed, as did business organization and worker roles.

The Innovative Model T

Mass production of automobiles began in the first years of the century. Using an assembly-line system that foreshadowed later techniques, Ransom E. Olds turned out five thousand Olds runabouts in 1904. And just a year earlier, Henry Ford and a small group of associates had founded the Ford Motor Company, the firm that transformed the business.

Ford was 40 years old. At first, like many others in the newborn automobile industry, he concentrated on building luxury and racing cars. He even raced his own cars; in 1904, he set the world's land speed record—more than 90 miles per hour. However, his expensive cars found few buyers.

In 1907, he lowered the price, and sales picked up. Ford learned an important lesson of the modern economy: a smaller unit profit on a large number of sales could generate enormous revenues. Early in 1908, he introduced the Model T, a stripped-down, four-cylinder, 20-horsepower "Tin Lizzie," costing $850 and available only in black. Eleven thousand were sold the first year.

"I am going to democratize the automobile," Ford proclaimed. The key was mass production, and after many experiments, Ford copied the techniques of meatpackers, who moved animal carcasses along overhead trolleys from station to station. Adapting the process to automobile assembly, Ford in 1913 set up moving assembly lines in his plant in Highland Park, Michigan, that dramatically reduced the time and cost of producing cars. In 1914, he sold 248,000 Model Ts. That year it took ninety-three minutes to assemble a car. By 1925, the Ford plant was turning out a new car every ten seconds of the working day.

While Ford was putting more and more cars on the road, the 1916 Federal Aid Roads Act set the framework for road building in the twentieth century. Removing control from county governments, it required every state desiring federal funds to establish a highway department to plan routes, oversee construction, and maintain roads. Providing for a planned highway system, the act produced a national network of two-lane, all-weather intercity roads.

The Burgeoning Trusts

As businesses like Ford's grew, capital and organization became increasingly important, and the result was the formation of a growing number of trusts. Standard Oil started the trend in 1882, but the greatest momentum came between 1898 and 1903. A series of mergers and consolidations swept the economy. Many smaller firms disappeared, swallowed up by giant commercial enterprises. By 1904, large corporations of one form or another controlled nearly two-fifths of the capital in U.S. manufacturing.

The result was not monopoly but *oligopoly*—control of a commodity or service by a small number of large, powerful companies. Six great financial groups dominated the railroad industry; a handful of holding companies controlled utilities and steel. Rockefeller's Standard Oil owned about 85 percent of the oil business. Copper, tobacco, rubber, and other products were likewise held by only a few producers.

By 1909, just 1 percent of the industrial firms were producing nearly half of the manufactured goods. Giant businesses reached abroad for raw materials and new markets. United Fruit, an empire of plantations and steamships in the Caribbean, exploited opportunities created by victory in the war with Spain. U.S. Steel worked with overseas companies to fix the price of steel rails, an unattainable dream just a few years before.

Though the trend has been overstated, finance capitalists such as J. P. Morgan tended to replace the industrial capitalists of an earlier era. Able to finance the mergers and reorganizations, investment bankers played a greater and greater role in the economy. A multibillion-dollar financial house, J. P. Morgan and Company operated a network of control that ran from New York to every industrial and financial center in the nation. Like other investment firms, it held directorships in many corporations, creating "interlocking directorates" that allowed it to control many businesses.

Massive business growth set off a decadelong debate over what government should do about the trusts. Some critics wanted simply to break them up. Others argued that large-scale business was a mark of the times; it produced more goods and better lives. The debate over the trusts influenced politics throughout the Progressive Era.

■ As early as 1886, cartoonist Thomas Nast attacked trusts. Here, the people's welfare is sinking as the Statue of Liberty is defaced. ■

Managing the Machines

Mass production changed the direction of American industry. Size, system, organization, and marketing became increasingly important. Management focused on speed and product, not on workers. Assembly-line technology changed tasks and, to some extent, values. The goal was no longer to make a unique product that would be better than the one before. The goal now was to make each product come off the line exactly alike.

In a development that rivaled assembly lines in importance, businesses established industrial research laboratories where scientists and engineers developed new products. General Electric founded the first one in 1900 in a barn. It proved so successful that Du Pont, Eastman Kodak, and Standard Oil soon established research laboratories of their own. As the source of new ideas and technology, the labs altered life in the twentieth century.

Through all this, business operations became large-scale, mechanized, and managed. By 1920, close to one-half of all industrial workers labored in factories employing more than 250 people. More than a third worked in factories that were part of multiplant companies.

Industries that processed materials—iron and steel, paper, cement, and chemicals—were increasingly automated and operated continuously. In the glass industry, new machines ended the domination of highly skilled and well-paid craft workers. The machines turned out plate glass and ribbons of automobile window glass, and workers tending them could not fall behind. Foremen still managed the laborers on the factory floor, but more and more the rules came down from a central office where trained, professional managers supervised production flow. Workers lost control of the work pace. Employers sped up the conveyor belt to heighten production. In the automobile industry, output per worker-hour multiplied an extraordinary four times between 1909 and 1919.

Folkways of the workplace—workers passing job-related knowledge to each other, setting their own pace, and in effect running the shop—gave way to "scientific" labor management. More than anyone else, Frederick Winslow Taylor, an inventive mechanical engineer, strove to extract maximum efficiency from each worker. Taylor proposed two major reforms. First, management must take responsibility for job-related knowledge and classify it into "rules, laws, and formulae." Second, management should control the workplace "through *enforced* standardization of methods, *enforced* adoption of the best implements and working conditions, and *enforced* cooperation."

Taylor's methods included training workers for particular tasks, time-and-motion studies, and differential pay rates that rewarded those who worked fastest. Armed with stopwatches, his disciples reduced a factory's operations to the simplest tasks, then devised the most efficient way to perform them. The doctrine of scientific management spread throughout American industry.

Workers caught up in the changing industrial system experienced the benefits of efficiency and productivity; in some industries, they earned more. But they suffered important losses as well. Performing repetitive tasks, they seemed part of the machinery, to whose pace and needs they moved. Bored, they might easily have lost pride of workmanship, though many workers, it is clear, did not. Jobs became not only monotonous but also dangerous. Under pressure of speed, boredom or miscalculation could bring disaster. Meat cutters sliced fingers and hands. Forty-six steel workers were killed on the job in just one mill in 1906. Injuries were part of many jobs.

In March 1911, a fire at the Triangle Shirtwaist Company in New York focused attention on unsafe working conditions. Seamstresses were trapped in the building because exit doors had been closed and locked by the company to prevent theft and to shut out union organizers. Many died in the stampede down the narrow stairways or the single fire escape. Others leaped from the building's top floors to escape the flames. One hundred and forty-six people died.

A few days later, eighty thousand people marched silently in the rain in a funeral procession up Fifth Avenue. The protests impelled New York's governor to appoint a state factory investigating commission that recommended laws to shorten the workweek and improve safety conditions in factories and stores.

SOCIETY'S MASSES

National networks of products and consumers helped fuel the mass society, which depended on an enormous increase in the labor force to work in the factories, mines, and forests. Immigration soared, and women, blacks, and Mexican Americans played larger roles.

For many of these people, life was harsh, spent in crowded slums and long hours on the job. Fortunately, the massive unemployment of the 1890s was over, and there was great demand for skilled labor. But the less skilled continued to be the less fortunate. They fought to make a living, and many, too, fought to improve their lot. Their efforts, along with the efforts of the reform-minded people who came to their aid, became another important hallmark of the Progressive Era.

Better Times on the Farm

While people continued to flee the farms—by 1920, fewer than one-third of all Americans lived on farms, and fewer than half lived in rural areas—farmers themselves prospered, the beneficiaries of greater production and expanding urban markets. Rural free delivery (RFD)—delivery of mail to the farmhouse door, begun in 1896—helped diminish the farmers' sense of isolation, opening their lives to urban thinking, national advertising, and political events. In 1911, more than one billion newspapers and magazines were delivered over RFD routes.

Parcel post (1913) permitted the sending of packages through the U.S. mail. Mail-order houses flourished; rural merchants suffered. Within a year, 300 million packages were being mailed annually. Although telephones and electricity did not reach most rural areas for decades, better roads, mail-order catalogs, and other innovations knit farmers into the larger society. Early in the new century, Mary E. Lease—who in her Populist days had urged Kansas farmers to raise less taxes and more hell—moved to Brooklyn.

Farmers still had problems. Land prices rose with crop prices, and farm tenancy increased, especially in the South. In South Carolina, Georgia, Alabama, and Mississippi, nearly two-thirds of the farms were run by tenant farmers. Many southern tenant farmers were African Americans, and they suffered from farm-bred diseases. In 1909, the Rockefeller Sanitary Commission began a sanitation campaign that eventually wiped out the hookworm disease, and in 1912, the U.S. Public Health Service began work on rural malaria.

In the arid West, irrigation transformed the land as the federal government and private landholders joined to import water from mountain watersheds. Dams and canals channeled water into places such as California's Imperial Valley, and as the water streamed in, cotton, cantaloupes, oranges, tomatoes, lettuce, and other crops streamed out to national markets. But as the land blossomed, the division between owners and workers sharpened, and migrant workers and immigrants from Mexico, China, and Japan worked long, backbreaking hours for meager rewards.

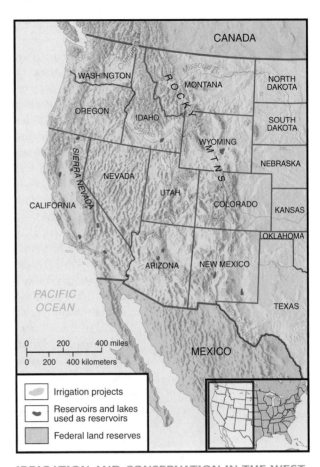

IRRIGATION AND CONSERVATION IN THE WEST TO 1917   *To make the arid lands of the western states productive, the state and federal governments regulated the water supply through irrigation projects and the creation of water reservoirs. The federal government also created land reserves.* ■

Women and Children at Work

Women worked in larger and larger numbers. In 1900, more than five million worked. Of those employed, single women outnumbered married women by seven to one. Most women held service jobs. Only a small number held higher-paying jobs as professionals or managers.

In the 1890s, women made up more than a quarter of medical school graduates. Adopting rigid standards, men gradually squeezed them out. Few women taught in colleges and universities, and those that did were expected to resign if they married. Men believed that once a woman became a "homemaker," she should have no other job.

More women than men graduated from high school, and with professions such as medicine and science largely closed to them, they often turned to the new business schools that offered training in stenography, typing, and bookkeeping. In

1920, more than a quarter of all employed women held clerical jobs. Many others taught school.

In 1907 and 1908, investigators studied 22,000 women workers in Pittsburgh; 60 percent of them earned less than $7 a week, the minimum for "decent living." Fewer than 1 percent held skilled jobs; most tended machines, wrapped and labeled, or did handwork that required no particular skill. Black women had always worked, and in far larger numbers than their white counterparts. The reason was usually economic; an African American man or woman alone could rarely earn enough to support a family. Unlike many white women, black women tended to remain in the labor force after marriage or the start of a family. They also had less opportunity for job advancement, and in 1920, between one-third and one-half of all African American women who were working were restricted to personal and domestic service jobs.

Critics charged that women's employment endangered the home, threatened reproductive functions, and even robbed them of their "special charm." Adding to the fears, the birthrate continued to drop between 1900 and 1920, and the divorce rate soared. By 1916, there was one divorce for every nine marriages, compared to one for every twenty-one in 1880.

Many children also worked. In 1900, about three million children—nearly 20 percent of those between the ages of 5 and 15—held full- or almost full-time jobs. Thousands of children worked in mines and southern cotton mills. The use of child labor shrank as states passed compulsory education and minimum age laws. Families focused greater and greater attention on the children, and child rearing became a central concern of family life.

As the middle-class family changed from an economic to an emotional unit, middle-class women claimed increasing pride in homemaking and motherhood. Mother's Day, as a national holiday, was formally established in 1913. Women who preferred fewer children turned increasingly to birth control, which became a more acceptable practice. Margaret Sanger, a nurse and an outspoken social reformer, led a campaign to give physicians broad discretion in prescribing contraceptives. Her efforts were resisted by the imposition of a ban on interstate transportation of contraceptive devices and information under the federal Comstock Law.

The Niagara Movement and the NAACP

At the turn of the twentieth century, eight of every ten blacks lived in rural areas, mainly in the South. Most were poor sharecroppers. Jim Crow laws segregated many schools, railroad cars, hotels, and hospitals. Poll taxes and other devices disfranchised blacks and many poor whites. Violence was common; between 1900 and 1914, white mobs murdered more than a thousand black people, often mutilating them and burning them alive.

Many blacks labored in the cotton farms, railroad camps, sawmills, and mines of the South under conditions of peonage—trading their lives and labor for food and shelter. Often illiterate, they were forced to sign contracts that tied them to their jobs. Armed guards patrolled the camps and whipped anyone caught trying to escape. Few unions admitted blacks to their ranks, and almost always blacks earned less than whites in the same job. The illiteracy rate among blacks dropped from 45 percent in 1900 to 30 percent in 1910, but nowhere were they given equal school facilities, teachers' salaries, or educational materials.

In 1905, a group of black leaders met near Niagara Falls, New York, and pledged action on behalf of voting, equal access to economic opportunity, integration, and equality before the law. At their head was sociologist W. E. B. Du Bois, professor of history and economics at Atlanta University. Rejecting Booker T. Washington's gradualist approach, the **Niagara Movement** claimed for blacks "every single right that belongs to a freeborn American, political, civil, and social; and until we get

Niagara Movement A movement, led by W. E. B. Du Bois, that focused on equal rights and the education of African American youth. Rejecting the gradualist approach of Booker T. Washington, members kept alive a program of militant action and claimed for African Americans all the rights afforded to other Americans.

these rights we will never cease to protest." It kept alive a program of militant action focusing on equal rights and the education of black youth, and it spawned later civil rights movements. In *The Souls of Black Folk* (1903) and other works, Du Bois eloquently called for justice and equality.

Race riots broke out in Atlanta, Georgia, in 1906 and in Springfield, Illinois, in 1908. White mobs invaded black neighborhoods, burning, looting, and killing. William E. Walling, a wealthy southerner and settlement house worker; Mary Ovington, a white anthropology student; and Oswald Garrison Villard, grandson of the famous abolitionist William Lloyd Garrison, were outraged. Along with other reformers, white and black, they issued a call for the conference that organized the **National Association for the Advancement of Colored People (NAACP)**, which swiftly became the most important civil rights organization in the country. Created in 1909, within five years the NAACP grew to more than six thousand members. The eight top officers included one black—W. E. B. Du Bois, director of publicity and research.

Joined by the National Urban League, founded in 1911, the NAACP pressured employers, labor unions, and the government on behalf of African Americans. It won some victories, but blacks continued to experience disfranchisement, poor job opportunities, and segregation. Little of progressivism's progress came their way.

National Association for the Advancement of Colored People (NAACP) Created in 1909, this organization quickly became one of the most important civil rights organizations in the country. It pressured employers, labor unions, and the government on behalf of African Americans.

"I Hear the Whistle": Immigrants in the Labor Force

Between 1901 and 1920, an extraordinarily high total of 14.5 million immigrants entered the country, more than in any previous twenty-year period. Continuing the trend begun in the 1880s, many came from southern and eastern Europe. Still called the "new" immigrants, they met hostility from older immigrants of northern European stock, who questioned their values and appearance.

Labor agents—called *padroni* among the Italians, Greeks, and Syrians—recruited immigrant workers, found them jobs, and deducted a fee from their wages. Headquartered in Salt Lake City, Leonidas G. Skliris, the "Czar of the Greeks," provided workers for the Utah Copper Company and the Western Pacific Railroad. Agents similarly distributed immigrant workers to major eastern and midwestern cities.

Immigration moved both ways. Fifty percent or more of some groups returned to the "old country." Some migrants—Italian men, in particular—virtually commuted, returning home every slack season. These temporary migrants became known as **birds of passage**. The outbreak of World War I interrupted the practice and "trapped" in the United States hundreds of thousands of Italians and others who had planned to return to Europe.

birds of passage Temporary migrants who came to the United States to work and save money and then returned home to their native countries during the slack season.

Older residents lumped the newcomers together, ignoring geographic, religious, and other differences. Preserving important regional distinctions, Italians tended to settle as Calabreses, Venetians, Abruzzis, and Sicilians. Native-born Americans viewed them all simply as Italians. Henry Ford and other employers tried to erase the differences through English classes and deliberate "Americanization" programs. In similar fashion, the International Harvester Corporation taught Polish laborers to speak English, but it had other lessons to impart as well. Factory Americanization programs were designed to produce good factory workers as well as good American citizens.

Fewer people immigrated from China in these years, deterred in part by anti-Chinese laws and hostility. In the early 1880s, there were about 125,000 Chinese in America, but by 1920, that figure had declined to just over 60,000. And those Chinese who were in America often wanted only to make money and return home. While in America, most lived in communities, dominated by the elderly, where men outnumbered women ten to one. Hard work and communal ties marked their time in the United States.

As the Chinese immigration slowed to a trickle, Japanese and Mexican immigration increased. In 1920, more than 110,000 Japanese immigrants were living in America. At the beginning of the twentieth century, Mexicans for the first time immigrated in large numbers, especially after a revolution in Mexico in 1910 forced many to flee across the border. (The exact number is unknown.) Almost all came from the Mexican lower class, eager to escape peonage and violence in their native land. Labor agents, usually in the employ of either large corporations or ranchers, recruited Mexican workers. After the turn of the century, almost 10 percent of the entire population of Mexico moved to the American Southwest.

The Mexican immigrants helped transform the Southwest. They built highways, dug irrigation ditches, laid railroad track, and picked cotton and vegetables. Yet American society imposed harsh rules on these people. Segregation laws and practices often kept them out of hotels or other public accommodations. Schools either barred them or, ironically, tried to anglicize them in segregated facilities. Yet again, Mexican Americans clung to their culture.

Nativist sentiment, which had accompanied earlier waves of immigration, intensified. Old-stock Americans sneered at the newcomers' dress and language. Racial theories emphasized the superiority of northern Europeans, and the new "science" of eugenics suggested controls over the population growth of "inferior" peoples. Hostility against Catholics and Jews was common but touched other groups as well. In 1902, immigration from China—suspended since 1882—was entirely prohibited.

Congress passed statutes requiring literacy tests designed to curtail immigration from southern and eastern Europe, but they were vetoed by Presidents Taft and Wilson. In 1917, Congress passed such a measure over Wilson's veto. Other bills tried to limit immigration from Mexico and Japan.

CONFLICT IN THE WORKPLACE

Assembly lines, speed-ups, long hours, and low wages produced a dramatic increase in American industrial output and profits after 1900; they also gave rise to numerous strikes and other kinds of labor unrest. Sometimes strikes took place through actions of unions; sometimes workers just decided that they had had enough and walked off the job. Whatever the cause, strikes were frequent.

Strikes and absenteeism increased after 1910; labor productivity dropped 10 percent between 1915 and 1918, the first such decline in memory. Workers changed jobs in droves. Union membership grew. In 1900, only about one million workers belonged to unions; by 1920, five million belonged, about 13 percent of the workforce. But only 1.5 percent of female workers belonged to unions in 1910 due to gender discrimination.

As tensions grew between capital and labor, some middle-class Americans became fearful that unless something was done to improve the workers' situation, there might be violence or even revolution. This fear, along with some genuine desire to improve labor's lot, motivated some of the labor-oriented reforms of the Progressive Era.

Samuel Gompers's American Federation of Labor (AFL), by far the largest union organization, remained devoted to the interests of skilled craftsmen. While striving for better wages and working conditions, it also sought to limit entry into the craft and protect worker prerogatives. Within limits, the AFL found acceptance among giant business corporations eager for conservative policies and labor stability.

Of the 8 million female workers in 1910, only 125,000 belonged to unions. Gompers continued to resist organizing them, saying they were too emotional and, as union organizers, "had a way of making serious mistakes." Margaret Dreier Robins, an organizer of proven skill, scoffed at that.

Robins helped found the **Women's Trade Union League (WTUL)** in 1903. The WTUL led the effort to organize women into trade unions, to lobby for legislation protecting female workers, and to educate the public on the problems and needs of working women. It took in all working women who would join, regardless of skill (though not, at first, African American women), and it won crucial financial support from well-to-do women. Robins's close friend Jane Addams belonged, as did Mary McDowell, the "Angel of the Stockyards," who worked with slaughterhouse workers in Chicago; Julia Lathrop, who tried to improve the lot of wage-earning children; and Dr. Alice Hamilton, a pioneer in American research on the causes of industrial disease. The WTUL never had many members—a few thousand at most—but its influence extended far beyond its membership.

Unlike the AFL, the **Industrial Workers of the World (IWW)** tried to organize the unskilled and foreign-born laborers working in the mass production industries. Founded in Chicago in 1905, it aimed to unite the American working class into a mammoth union to promote labor's interests. The IWW—or Wobblies, as they were known—urged social revolution to create a workers' world.

The IWW led a number of major strikes; two in 1912, in Lawrence, Massachusetts, and Paterson, New Jersey, attracted national attention. Lawrence seized the limelight when the strikers sent their ill-clad and hungry children out of the city to stay with sympathetic families; Paterson did so when they rented New York's Madison Square Garden for a massive labor pageant. They believed that a series of local strikes would intensify capitalists' repression, then bring about a general strike, and eventually usher in a workers' commonwealth.

The IWW fell short of these objectives, but during its lifetime—from 1905 to the mid-1920s—it made major gains among immigrant workers in the Northeast, migrant farm labor on the Plains, and loggers and miners in the South and Far West. In factories such as Ford's, it recruited workers resentful of the speed-ups on the assembly lines.

Women's Trade Union League (WTUL) Founded in 1903, this organization worked to organize women into trade unions. It also lobbied for laws to safeguard female workers and backed several successful strikes, especially in the garment industry.

Industrial Workers of the World (IWW) Founded in 1905, this radical union, also known as the Wobblies, aimed to unite the American working class into one union to promote labor's interests. It worked to organize unskilled and foreign-born laborers, advocated social revolution, and led several major strikes.

■ *Holding signs and banners that proudly display their union allegiance, including a sign with the slogan, "An injury to one is an injury to all," women of the Industrial Workers of the World participate in a strike at the Oliver Iron and Steel Company in Pittsburgh, Pennsylvania, in 1913. The Clayton Act, passed by Congress in 1914, legalized picketing and other union activity.* ■

Concerned about labor unrest, business leaders turned to the new fields of applied psychology and personnel management. A school of industrial psychology emerged. A few businesses established industrial relations departments, hired public relations firms to improve their corporate image, and linked productivity to job safety and happiness. Ivy L. Lee, a pioneer in the field of corporate public relations, advised such corporate clients as Standard Oil and the Pennsylvania Railroad on how to improve relations with labor and the public.

On January 5, 1914, Henry Ford took another significant step: he announced the $5 day. With a single stroke, he doubled the wage rate for common labor, reduced the working day from nine hours to eight, and established a personnel department to place workers in appropriate jobs. As a result, Ford had the pick of the labor force. Turnover declined; absenteeism fell to 0.3 percent; output increased; the IWW at Ford collapsed. At first scornful of the "utopian" plan, business leaders across the country soon copied it.

A New Urban Culture

For many Americans, the quality of life improved significantly between 1900 and 1920. Jobs were relatively plentiful, and in a development of great importance, more and more people were entering the professions as doctors, lawyers, teachers, and engineers. With comfortable incomes, a growing middle class could take advantage of new lifestyles, inventions, and forms of entertainment. Mass consumption, promoted by a mushrooming advertising industry, fueled industry's mass production. Advertisers used sampling techniques, market testing, and research in their effort to sell products.

Mass production swept the clothing industry and dressed more Americans better than any people ever before. Manufacturers developed standard clothing and shoe sizes that fit most bodies. These "off the rack" items resulted in less expensive clothes and blurred the distinctions between rich and poor. By 1900, fully 90 percent of men and boys wore the new ready-to-wear clothes.

The income of people who worked in manufacturing more than tripled from an average of $418 a year in 1900 to $1342 a year in 1920. While the middle class expanded, the rich also grew richer. By 1920, a mere 5 percent of the population received almost one-fourth of all income.

In 1920, the median age of the population was only 25. (It is now 38.) Immigration accounted for part of the youthfulness, as most immigrants were young, and so did death rates. Thanks to medical advances and better living conditions, death rates dropped in the early years of the century, and the average life span increased. Between 1900 and 1920, life expectancy rose dramatically: for white women, from 49 to 56 years; for white men, from 47 to 54 years; for blacks and other minorities, from 33 to 45 years.

Infant mortality remained high. In comparison to today, fewer babies on average survived to adolescence, and fewer people survived beyond middle age. As a result, there were relatively fewer older people—in 1900, only 4 percent of the population was older than 65, compared to 13 percent today. Still, improvements in health care helped people live longer, and as a result, the incidence of cancer and heart disease increased.

Cities grew, and by any earlier standards, they grew on a colossal scale. Downtowns became a central hive of skyscrapers, department stores, warehouses, and hotels. Strips of factories radiated from the center. As street railways spread, cities took on a systematic pattern of socioeconomic segregation, usually in rings. Immigrants lived in the innermost ring, and wealthy suburbs occupied the outermost rings.

The giants were New York, Chicago, and Philadelphia, industrial cities that turned out every kind of product. Smaller cities such as Rochester, New York, or

Cleveland, Ohio, specialized in manufacturing a specific line of goods or processing regional products for the national market. Railroads tied things together.

Step by step, cities took their twentieth-century form. Between 1909 and 1915, Los Angeles passed a series of ordinances that gave rise to modern urban zoning. For the first time, ordinances divided a city into three districts of specified use: a residential area, an industrial area, and a mixed area open to residences and a limited list of industries. Other cities followed suit. New York's zoning law of 1916 was copied across the nation.

Zoning gave order to city development, keeping skyscrapers out of factory districts and factories out of the suburbs. It also had powerful social repercussions. In the South, zoning became a tool to extend racial segregation; in northern cities, it acted against ethnic minorities. Jews in New York, Italians in Boston, Poles in Detroit, blacks in Chicago—zoning laws kept them all at arm's length.

Popular Pastimes

Thanks to changing work rules and mechanization, many Americans benefited from more leisure time. The average workweek for manufacturing laborers fell from sixty hours in 1890 to fifty-one in 1920. White-collar workers often spent even less time at the office. The new leisure time gave more people more opportunity for pleasurable diversions.

People flocked to places of entertainment. Baseball entrenched itself as the national pastime. Attendance at major league games doubled between 1903 and 1910. Football also drew fans, although critics attacked the sport's violence and the use of "tramp athletes," nonstudents whom colleges paid to play. In 1905, the worst year, 18 players were killed and 150 seriously injured. Prodded by Theodore Roosevelt, representatives of the major colleges formed the Intercollegiate Athletic Association to clean up the sport; in 1910, that organization was renamed the National Collegiate Athletic Association.

Movie theaters opened everywhere. By 1910, there were ten thousand of them, drawing a weekly audience of ten million people. Admission was usually 5 cents, and movies stressing laughter and pathos—soundless but accompanied by piano or organ—appealed to a mass market. In 1915, D. W. Griffith, a talented and creative—as well as racist—director, produced the first movie spectacular, *The Birth of a Nation.*

Before 1910, band concerts were the country's most popular entertainment. As many as twenty thousand amateur bands played in parks on summer Sunday afternoons. John Philip Sousa, the famous "March King," led a touring band that profited from the self-confident nationalism that followed the Spanish-American War. Robust, patriotic marches such as "The Stars and Stripes Forever" (1896) earned him wealth and popularity.

A Look at the Past

Sears Catalog

Rural Americans gained access to the same array of consumer goods that urban dwellers had when mail-order companies, such as Sears, Roebuck and Company, offered goods through the mail. Rural Free Delivery, begun in 1896, made shopping by mail easier than visiting the local general store. Sears targeted rural consumers and designed the catalog to appeal to those consumers. Notice the cover decoration depicting goods spilling out in front of the farmstead. ✶ Why do you think the cover includes information about the firm's incorporation and capital? Why are there references from banks? Does the cover suggest that rural Americans were completely comfortable about mail order or that they needed reassurance? Why might some consumers have been nervous about mail order?

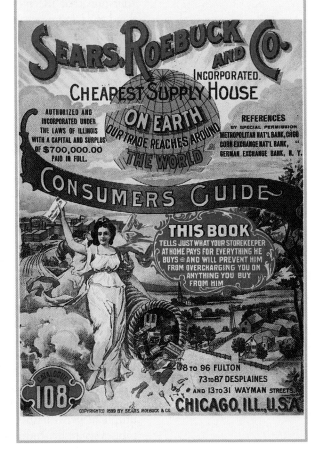

Soon automobiles and phonographs began to lure audiences away from the concerts. Early phonograph records were usually of vaudeville skits; orchestral recordings began in 1906. In 1919, some 2.25 million phonographs were produced; two years later, more than 100 million records were sold. People sang less and listened more.

The faster rhythms of syncopated ragtime became the rage, especially after Irving Berlin, a Russian immigrant, wrote "Alexander's Ragtime Band" in 1911. Ragtime set off a nationwide dance craze. European waltzes and polkas gave way to a host of new American dances, many with animal names: the fox trot, bunny hop, turkey trot, snake, and kangaroo dip. Partners were not allowed to dance too close; bouncers tapped them on the shoulder if they got closer than 9 inches.

Vaudeville, increasingly popular after 1900, reached maturity around 1915. Drawing on the immigrant experience and the rich variety of city life, it included skits, songs, comics, acrobats, and magicians. Dances and jokes expressed an earthiness new to mass audiences. By 1914, stage runways extended into the crowd; female performers had bared their legs, and costumes revealed the midriff as well.

In songs such as "St. Louis Blues" (1914), W. C. Handy took the black southern folk music of the blues to northern cities. Gertrude "Ma" Rainey sang in black vaudeville for nearly thirty-five years, and she discovered the 12-year-old Bessie Smith, who became the "Empress of the Blues." Another musical innovation came from New Orleans. Charles "Buddy" Bolden, Ferdinand "Jelly Roll" Morton, and Louis "Satchmo" Armstrong played an improvisational music that had no formal name. Reaching Chicago, it was finally named "jazz." Jazz jumped, and jazz musicians relied on feeling and mood.

Popular fiction reflected changing interests. Kate Douglas Wiggins's *Rebecca of Sunnybrook Farm* (1903) showed the continuing popularity of rural themes. Westerns also sold well, but readers turned more and more to detective thrillers with hard-bitten city detectives and science fiction tales featuring the latest dream in technology. The Tom Swift series, begun in 1910, looked ahead to spaceships, ray guns, and gravity nullifiers. Edward L. Stratemeyer, the mind behind Tom Swift, brought the techniques of mass production to book writing. He employed a stable of writers to turn out hundreds of Tom Swift, Rover Boys, and Bobbsey Twins stories for young readers.

Experimentation in the Arts

"There is a state of unrest all over the world in art as in all other things," the director of New York's Metropolitan Museum said in 1908. "It is the same in literature, as in music, in painting, and in sculpture." Isadora Duncan and Ruth St. Denis transformed the dance. Departing from traditional ballet steps, both women stressed improvisation, emotion, and the human form. Draped in flowing robes, Duncan told her students to "listen to the music with your soul. . . . Unless your dancing springs from an inner emotion and expresses an idea, it will be meaningless." After a triumphant performance with the New York Symphony in 1908, her ideas and techniques swept the country.

The lofts and apartments of New York's Greenwich Village attracted artists, writers, and poets interested in experimentation and change. To these artists, the city was the focus of national life and the sign of a new culture. Robert Henri and the realist painters—known to their critics as the **Ashcan School**—relished the city's excitement. They wanted "to paint truth and to paint it with strength and fearlessness and individuality." Their paintings depicted street scenes, colorful crowds, and slum children swimming in the river.

In 1913, a show at the New York Armory presented sixteen hundred modernist paintings, prints, and sculptures. The work of Picasso, Cézanne, Matisse, Brancusi,

Ashcan School This school of early twentieth-century realist painters took as their subjects the slums and streets of the nation's cities and the lives of ordinary urban dwellers. They often celebrated life in the city but also advocated political and social reform.

George Bellows, Cliff Dwellers *(1913). Bellows was part of the Ashcan School of painters, so named for their preference for depicting the realities of modern urban life, including its streets and slums, backyards and bars.*

Van Gogh, and Gauguin dazed and dazzled American observers. Critics attacked the show as worthless and depraved, but it was a clear glimpse of the future of art. The postimpressionists changed the direction of twentieth-century art and influenced adventuresome American painters. John Marin, Max Weber, Georgia O'Keeffe, Arthur Dove, and other modernists experimented in ways foreign to Henri's realists. Using bold colors and abstract patterns, they defied convention and worked to capture the energy of urban life.

Poetry experienced an extraordinary outburst. In 1912, Harriet Monroe started the magazine *Poetry* in Chicago; Ezra Pound and Vachel Lindsay, both daring experimenters with ideas and verse, were featured in the first issue. T. S. Eliot published the classic "Love Song of J. Alfred Prufrock" in *Poetry* in 1915. Attacked bitterly by conservative critics, the poem established Eliot's leadership among a group of poets who rejected traditional meter and rhyme as artificial constraints. Eliot, Pound, and Amy Lowell, among others, believed that the poet's task was to capture fleeting images in verse. Others experimenting with new techniques in poetry included Robert Frost, Edgar Lee Masters, and Carl Sandburg. True to the increasingly urban vision of America, Sandburg's poem "Chicago" celebrated the vitality of the city.

Chronology

1898	Mergers and consolidations begin to sweep the business world, leading to fear of trusts
1900	General Electric founds the first industrial research laboratory
1903	Ford Motor Company is formed ■ W. E. B. Du Bois calls for justice and equality for African Americans in *The Souls of Black Folk* ■ Women's Trade Union League is formed to organize women workers
1905	Industrial Workers of the World (IWW) is established ■ African American leaders inaugurate the Niagara Movement, advocating integration and equal opportunity for African Americans
1909	Campaign by Rockefeller Sanitary Commission wipes out hookworm disease
1910	NAACP is founded ■ National Collegiate Athletic Association is formed
1911	Frederick Winslow Taylor publishes *The Principles of Scientific Management* ■ Fire at the Triangle Shirtwaist Company kills 146 people ■ Irving Berlin popularizes the rhythm of ragtime with "Alexander's Ragtime Band" ■ National Urban League is created
1912	IWW leads strikes in Massachusetts and New Jersey ■ Harriet Monroe begins publishing *Poetry* magazine
1913	Ford introduces the moving assembly line at its Highland Park, Michigan, plant ■ Mother's Day becomes a national holiday ■ Show at the New York Armory presents modernist paintings, prints, and sculptures
1915	D. W. Griffith produces the first movie spectacular, *The Birth of a Nation* ■ T. S. Eliot publishes "The Love Song of J. Alfred Prufrock"
1916	Federal Aid Roads Act creates a national road network ■ Margaret Sanger forms the New York Birth Control League
1917	Congress passes a law requiring a literacy test for all immigrants

CONCLUSION: A FERMENT OF DISCOVERY AND REFORM

Manners and morals change slowly, yet in the first two decades of the century, sweeping change was under way: anyone who doubted it could visit a gallery, see a film, listen to music, or read one of the new literary magazines. Garrets and galleries were filled with a breathtaking sense of excitement about new forms of expression.

The ferment of progressivism in the city, state, and nation reshaped the country. In a burst of reform, people built playgrounds, restructured taxes, regulated business, won the vote for women, shortened working hours, altered political systems, opened kindergartens, and improved factory safety. They tried to fulfill the national promise of dignity and liberty.

Across America, there was a mood of excitement, a feeling expressed in the best efforts of artists and politicians. Racism, repression, and labor conflict were present, but there was also talk of hope, progress, and change. In politics, science, journalism, education, and a host of other fields, people believed for a time that they could make a difference, and in trying to do so, they became part of the progressive generation.

KEY TERMS

muckrakers, p. 423

progressivism, p. 423

Niagara Movement, p. 428

National Association for the
Advancement of Colored People
(NAACP), p. 429

birds of passage, p. 429

Women's Trade Union League
(WTUL), p. 431

Industrial Workers of the World
(IWW), p. 431

Ashcan School, p. 434

RECOMMENDED READING

There are several important analyses of the Progressive Era, including Robert H. Wiebe, *The Search for Order, 1877–1920* (1967); Richard Hofstadter, *The Age of Reform* (1955); Michael McGerr, *A Fierce Discontent: The Rise and Fall of the Progressive Movement in America 1870–1920* (2003); Samuel P. Hays, *The Response to Industrialism* (1957); and Gabriel Kolko, *The Triumph of Conservatism* (1963). C. Vann Woodward, *Origins of the New South 1877–1913* (1951), is a superb account of developments in the South, along with William A. Link, *The Paradox of Southern Progressivism, 1880–1930* (1992), and Steven Hahn, *A Nation Under Our Feet: Black Political Struggles in the Rural South from Slavery to the Great Migration* (2003).

George William Shea, *Spoiled Silk: The Red Mayor and the Great Paterson Textile Strike* (2001), Greg Hall, *Harvest Wobblies: The Industrial Workers of the World and Agricultural Laborers in the American West, 1905–1930* (2001), and Elliot J. Gorn, *Mother Jones: The Most Dangerous Woman in America* (2001), look at radical labor movements; David I. Macleod, *The Age of the Child: Children in America, 1890–1920* (1998), at children; Tom Holm, *The Great Confusion in Indian Affairs: Native Americans and Whites in the Progressive Era* (2005), and Alan Trachtenberg, *Shades of*

Hiawatha: Staging Indians, Making Americans, 1880–1930 (2004), at Native Americans; Nancy C. Unger, *Fighting Bob LaFollette: The Righteous Reformer* (2000), Joyce A. Hanson, *Mary McCloud Bethune and Black Women's Political Activism* (2003), and Patricia A. Schechter, *Ida B. Wells-Barnett and American Reform, 1880–1930* (2001), at specific reformers. Gary Scott Smith, *The Search for Social Salvation: Social Christianity and America, 1880–1925* (2000), Clifford Putney, *Muscular Christianity: Manhood and Sports in Protestant America, 1880–1920* (2002), and Thomas Winter, *Making Men, Making Class: The YMCA and Workingmen, 1877–1920* (2002), examine the role of religion. Steven L. Piott, *Giving Voters a Voice: The Origins of the Initiative and Referendum in America* (2003), and Rebecca J. Mead, *How the Vote Was Won: Woman Suffrage in the Western United States, 1868–1914* (2003), look at important political issues.

James T. Kloppenberg, *Uncertain Victory: Social Democracy and Progressivism in European and American Thought, 1870–1920* (1986), examines progressivism at home and abroad. C. Vann Woodward, *The Strange Career of Jim Crow* (1955), traces the civil rights setbacks of the Progressive Era.

SUGGESTED WEB SITES

NAACP Online

www.naacp.org/

The National Association for the Advancement of Colored People official Web site explains its mission and includes a primary document explaining the start of the NAACP.

The Evolution of the Conservation Movement, 1850–1920

memory.loc.gov/ammem/amrvhtml/conshome.html

This American Memory site brings together scores of primary sources and photographs about "the historical formation and cultural foundations of the movement to conserve and protect America's natural heritage."

The Triangle Shirtwaist Factory Fire, March 25, 1911

www.ilr.cornell.edu/trianglefire/

The Kheel Center for Labor-Management Documentation and Archives at Cornell University put together this excellent site composed of oral histories, cartoons, images, and essays.

Labor-Management Conflict in American History

history.osu.edu/projects/laborconflict/

This site at Ohio State University includes primary accounts of some of the major events in the history of labor-management conflict in the late nineteenth and early twentieth centuries.

Inside an American Factory: The Westinghouse Works, 1904

lcweb2.loc.gov/ammem/papr/west/westhome.html

Part of the American Memory Project at the Library of Congress, this site provides a glimpse inside a turn-of-the-century factory.

African American Women Writers of the Nineteenth Century

digital.nypl.org/schomburg/writers_aa19/

The New York Public Library's Schomburg Center for Research in Black Culture maintains this site that contains a large number of digital texts by African American women of the nineteenth century.

Touring Turn-of-the-Century America: Photographs from the Detroit Publishing Company, 1880–1920

memory.loc.gov/ammem/detroit/dethome.html

This Library of Congress collection has thousands of photographs from turn-of-the-century America.

Bill Haywood Trial (1907)

www.law.umkc.edu/faculty/projects/ftrials/haywood/haywood.htm

This site contains images, chronology, court, and official documents maintained by Dr. Doug Linder at University of Missouri-Kansas City Law School.

Margaret Sanger Papers Project

www.nyu.edu/projects/sanger/

This site at New York University contains information about Margaret Sanger and digital versions of several of her works.

Scott Joplin, 1868–1917

www.lsjunction.com/people/joplin.htm

This site offers information on Joplin and ragtime music.

National Arts and Crafts Archives

arts-crafts.com/index.html

This site serves as a guide to materials on the Arts and Crafts movement, which lasted roughly from 1890 to 1929.

Chapter 23

From Roosevelt to Wilson in the Age of Progressivism

The Republicans Split

On a sunny spring morning in 1909, Theodore Roosevelt left New York for an African safari. An ex-president at the age of 50, he had turned over the White House to his chosen successor, William Howard Taft, and now he was off to hunt wild game. Some hoped he would not return. "I trust some lion will do its duty," Wall Street magnate J. P. Morgan said. Though he had built a reputation as an ardent conservationist, Roosevelt shot lions, elephants, hippos, rhinoceroses, and other animals, acquiring nearly three hundred trophies in all.

Afterward, Roosevelt set off on a tour of Europe. He argued with the pope, dined with the king and queen of Italy, and happily spent five hours reviewing troops of the German empire. He also followed events back home, where, in the judgment of many friends, Taft was not working out as president.

Taft was puzzled by his lack of success. Honest and warmhearted, he had intended to continue Roosevelt's policies. But events turned out differently. The conservative and progressive wings of the Republican party split, and Taft often sided with the conservatives. Progressive Republicans urged Roosevelt to take control again of the party and the country.

Roosevelt returned to New York harbor on June 18, 1910, to the sound of naval guns and loud cheers. Greeting Gifford Pinchot, a close friend and one of Taft's leading opponents, with a hearty "Hello, Gifford," Roosevelt slipped away to his home in Oyster Bay, New York, where other friends awaited him.

Taft, who still viewed himself as a disciple of Roosevelt's, invited Teddy to spend a night or two at the White House, but the ex-president declined. Relations between the two friends cooled. "It is hard, very hard," Taft said in 1911, "to see a devoted friendship going to pieces like a rope of sand."

A year later, no hint of friendship remained as Taft and Roosevelt engaged in a desperate fight for the Republican presidential nomination. Taft won the nomination, but Roosevelt, angry and ambitious, bolted and helped form a new party, the Progressive (or Bull Moose) party, to unseat Taft and capture the White House. With Taft, Roosevelt, Woodrow Wilson (the Democratic party's candidate), and Socialist party candidate Eugene V. Debs all in the race, the election of 1912 became one of the most exciting in American history.

It was also one of the most important. The election of 1912 became a forum for Americans' concerns about the social and economic effects of urban-industrial growth. Each candidate offered a different vision for the future, and each expressed an aspect of progressive reform.

Those currents built on a number of important developments, including the rise of a new professional class, reform movements designed to cure problems in the cities and states, and the activist, achievement-oriented administrations of Roosevelt and Wilson. Together they produced the age of Progressivism.

THE SPIRIT OF PROGRESSIVISM

For more than two decades, progressivism dominated American life, and in one way or another, it influenced almost everything that came after it. Politically, it fostered a reform movement that sought solutions for the problems of city, state, and nation. Intellectually, it drew on the expertise of the new social sciences and reflected a shift from older absolutes such as religion to newer schools of thought that emphasized relativism and physiological explanations for behavior and the role of the environment in human development. Culturally, it inspired fresh modes of expression in dance, film, painting, literature, and architecture. Touching individuals in different ways, progressivism became a set of attitudes as well as a definable movement.

Unlike populism, which grew mostly in the rural South and West, progressivism drew support across society. Progressivism appealed to the expanding middle class, prosperous farmers, and skilled laborers; it also attracted significant support in the business community. Leadership came mainly from young, educated men and women. Many of them belonged to the professions—law, medicine, religion, business, teaching, and social work—and they thought they could use their expertise to improve society. They believed in progress and disliked waste. No single issue or concern united them all, but they shared a desire for change. Some wanted to purify municipal politics, others to clean up city streets or to eradicate prostitution. They were Democrats, Republicans, socialists, and independents.

Progressives believed that if people knew the truth, they would act on it. Progress depended on knowledge. The progressives stressed individual morality and collective action, the scientific method, and the value of expert opinion. Like contemporary business leaders, they valued system, planning, management, and predictability. They wanted not only reform but also efficiency.

Historians once viewed progressivism as the triumph of one group in society over another: urban reformers challenged city bosses; farmers took on powerful railroads. Now they stress the way progressivism brought people together rather than driving them apart. Disparate groups united in an effort to improve the well-being of many groups in society.

The Rise of the Professions

Progressivism fed on an organizational impulse that encouraged people to join forces, share information, and solve problems. Between 1890 and 1920, a host of national societies and associations took shape—nearly four hundred of them in just three decades. Groups such as the National Child Labor Committee, which lobbied for legislation to regulate the employment and working conditions of children, were formed to attack specific issues. Other groups reflected one of the most significant developments in American society at the turn of the century—the rise of the professions.

Growing rapidly in these years, the professions—law, medicine, religion, business, teaching, and social work—were the source of much of the leadership of the progressive movement. The professions attracted young, educated men and women, who in turn were part of a larger trend: a dramatic increase in the number of individuals working in administrative and professional jobs. In businesses, these people were managers, architects, technicians, and accountants. In city governments, they were experts in everything from education to sanitation. They organized and ran the urban-industrial society.

Together these professionals formed part of a new middle class whose members did not derive their status from birth or inherited wealth, as had many members of the older middle class. Instead, they moved ahead through education and personal accomplishment. They had worked to become doctors, lawyers, ministers, and teachers. Proud of their skills, they were ambitious and self-confident, and they thought of themselves as experts who could use their knowledge for the benefit of society.

As a way of asserting their status, they formed professional societies to look after their interests and govern entry into their professions. Just a few years before, for example, a doctor had become a doctor simply by stocking up on patent medicines and hanging out a sign. Now, doctors began to insist they were part of a medical profession, and they wanted to set educational requirements and minimum standards for practice. In 1901, they reorganized the American Medical Association (AMA) and made it into a modern national professional society.

Other groups and professions showed the same pattern. Lawyers formed bar associations, created examining boards, and lobbied for regulations restricting entry into the profession. Teachers organized the National Education Association (1905) and pressed for teacher certification and compulsory education laws. Social workers formed the National Federation of Settlements (1911); business leaders created the National Association of Manufacturers (1895) and the U.S. Chamber of Commerce (1912); and farmers joined the National Farm Bureau Federation to spread information about farming and to try to improve their lot.

The Social-Justice Movement

Progressivism began in the cities during the 1890s. It first took hold among settlement workers and others interested in freeing individuals from the crushing impact of the slum and the factory. Ministers, intellectuals, social workers, and lawyers joined in a **social-justice movement** that focused national attention on the need for tenement house laws, more stringent child-labor legislation, and better working conditions for women. They brought pressure on municipal agencies for more and better parks, playgrounds, day nurseries, schools, and community services. Blending private and public action, settlement leaders turned increasingly to government aid.

Social-justice reformers were more interested in societal cures than individual charity. Unlike earlier reformers, they saw problems as endless and interrelated; individuals became part of a city's larger patterns. With that insight, social service casework shifted from a focus on an individual's well-being to a scientific analysis of whole neighborhoods, occupations, and classes.

In 1900, Lawrence Veiller, a young social worker, put together a tenement house exhibition that included more than a thousand photographs, detailed maps of slum districts, statistical tables and charts, and graphic cardboard depictions of tenement blocks. Veiller correlated data on poverty and disease with housing conditions. Stirred by the public outcry, Governor Theodore Roosevelt appointed the New York State Tenement House Commission to do something about the problem.

With Veiller's success as a model, study after study analyzed the condition of the poor. Seeing their common problems, social-justice reformers formed the National Conference of Charities and Corrections, which in 1915 became the National Conference of Social Work. Through it, social workers discovered one another's efforts, shared methodology, and tried to establish themselves as a separate field within the social sciences. They formed professional schools at Harvard, the University of Chicago, and other major universities, and in 1909 they published

social-justice movement
During the 1890s and after, this important movement attracted followers who sought to free people from the often devastating impact of urban life. It focused on the need for tenement house laws, more stringent child-labor regulations, and better working conditions for women. Social-justice reformers also put pressure on municipal agencies for better community services and facilities.

Past and Present

From John D. Rockefeller to Bill Gates: Philanthropy in American Life

Philanthropy, the act of making gifts to improve human welfare, has long been an important aspect of American life. Although separated by a hundred years, John D. Rockefeller of the Standard Oil Company, who created the first large philanthropic foundation, and Bill Gates, the billionaire co-founder of the Microsoft Corporation, provide two examples of the vital role of philanthropy in American life.

Interestingly, both Rockefeller and Gates chose to focus their efforts and resources on fighting disease and used similar methods. "It seems like every new corner we turn," Bill Gates's father, a member of the Gates Foundation, has said, "the Rockefellers are already there. And in some cases, they have been there a long, long time."

Rockefeller foundation administrators functioned in the Progressive Era and, like others in those years, saw themselves as experts able to take the new science of public hygiene into far-off parts of the world. Rockefeller's main philanthropic adviser, who was also a Baptist minister, recalled the times doctors in his congregation lamented their inability to heal their patients. Rockefeller himself was upset when a three-year-old grandson died from scarlet fever, a disease he thought could be cured. In 1901, he founded the Rockefeller Institute for Medical Research.

In 1907, the institute used a serum to stop a meningitis epidemic in New York City. Soon after, it pioneered efforts to freeze blood, discovered the spirochete that caused syphilis, and invented drugs to fight sleeping sickness. In 1909, it began its famed campaign to eliminate the hookworm ravaging the South. The approach again was scientific. Sending experts to teach the importance of sanitation, by 1920 it had largely ended the problem of hookworm in the South.

Though known for his stinginess in business, Rockefeller in all gave about $530 million to philanthropy, nearly 80 percent of it for medical research. His contributions had considerable impact on the development of cures and sanitary practices that affected the health of people around the world.

A century later, the Bill and Melinda Gates Foundation has also focused on global health problems, particularly those affecting the poor in Africa and Asia. Founded in 2000, it quickly became the world's most powerful charity, with an endowment of nearly $29 billion—larger than the gross domestic product of many countries. As a Swiss newspaper put it, "The health of the world depends more on Bill Gates than on the World Health Organization."

The Gates Foundation has targeted diseases such as tuberculosis, HIV, river blindness, measles, and sleeping sickness. "Global health is our lifelong commitment," Gates said. "Until we reduce the burden on the poor so that there is no real gap between us and them, that will always be our priority."

Since 2000, the Gates Foundation has spent $6 billion on health in the Third World. Early in 2005, the Gates Foundation gave $750 million to the United Nations to vaccinate 42 million children against hepatitis B, invest in a new drug for sleeping sickness, and fund a vaccine for pneumonia. Malaria, the most prevalent parasitic disease in the world, kills as many as 3 million people a year, many of them under five, most of them in Africa. "I refuse to accept it," Gates said. His foundation has donated more money to fight malaria than any other charitable organization, a move that has sparked other multinational companies to contribute to research for a malaria vaccine.

The philanthropy of corporate giants such as Rockefeller and Gates shows the way in which so-called captains of industry earning enormous sums of money can also become stewards of a global society, using those earnings to alleviate or even cure various forms of human suffering. As some governments cut back on spending for medical research, philanthropists like Rockefeller and Gates will become ever more vital in funding and finding solutions.

their own magazine, *The Survey.* Instead of piecemeal reforms, they aimed at a comprehensive program of minimum wages, maximum hours, workers' compensation, and widows' pensions.

The Purity Crusade

Working in city neighborhoods, social-justice reformers were often struck by the degree to which alcohol affected the lives of the people they were trying to help. Workers drank away their wages; some men spent more time at the saloon than at home. Drunkenness caused violence, and it angered employers, who did not want intoxicated workers on the job. In countless ways, alcohol wasted human resources, the reformers believed, and along with business leaders, ministers, and others, they launched a crusade to remove the evils of drink from American life.

At the head of the crusade was the Women's Christian Temperance Union (WCTU), which had grown steadily since its founding in the 1870s. By 1911, the WCTU had nearly a quarter of a million members, the largest organization of women in American history to that time. In 1893, it was joined by the Anti-Saloon League, and together the groups pressed to abolish alcohol and the places where it was consumed. In the midst of the moral fervor of World War I, they succeeded, and the Eighteenth Amendment to the Constitution, prohibiting the manufacture, sale, and transportation of intoxicating liquors, took effect in January 1920.

The amendment encountered troubles later in the 1920s as the social atmosphere changed, but at the time it passed, progressives thought prohibition was a major step toward eliminating social instability and moral wrong. In a similar fashion, some progressive reformers also worked to get rid of prostitution, convinced that poverty and ignorance drove women to the trade. By 1915, nearly every state had banned brothels, and in 1910, Congress passed the Mann Act, which prohibited the interstate transportation of women for immoral purposes. Like the campaign against liquor, the campaign against prostitution reflected the era's desire to purify and elevate, often through the instrument of government action.

Woman Suffrage, Women's Rights

Women played an essential role in the social-justice movement. Feminists were particularly active, especially in the political sphere, between 1890 and 1914. Working-class as well as college-educated women pushed for reforms. From 1890 to 1910, the work of a number of national women's organizations, including the National Council of Mothers and the Women's Trade Union League, furthered the aims of the progressive movement. The National Association of Colored Women, the first black-sponsored social service agency in the nation, was founded in 1895.

Organizations such as the General Federation of Women's Clubs transformed literary meetings into social-action gatherings. Drawing attention to women's concern for social reform, Sarah P. Decker, who became president of the federation in 1904, told the members of her organization, "Dante is dead. . . . I think it is time that we dropped the study of his *Inferno* and turned our attention to our own."

Reluctant at first, the federation eventually lent support to woman suffrage, a cause that dated back to 1848. The suffrage movement suffered from disunity, male opposition, disagreement over whether to seek action at the state or national level, resistance from the Catholic Church, and opposition from liquor interests, who linked the cause to prohibition.

Women in the social-justice movement needed to influence elected officials—most of them men—whom women could not reach through the vote. Because politics was an avenue for reform, women activists became involved in the suffrage movement in growing numbers. After years of disagreement, the two major suffrage organizations, the National Woman Suffrage Association and the American Woman Suffrage Association, merged in 1890 to form the National American Woman Suffrage Association. The merger opened a new phase of the suffrage movement, characterized by unity and a tightly controlled national organization.

In 1900, Carrie Chapman Catt became president of the National American Woman Suffrage Association, which by 1920 had nearly two million members. The association believed in peaceful lobbying to win the vote. Members of the Congressional Union, such as Alice Paul, were more militant. They interrupted public meetings, focused on Congress rather than the states, and in 1917 picketed the White House. The issue attracted many progressives, who believed woman suffrage would purify politics. In 1918, the House passed a constitutional amendment stating simply that the right to vote shall not be denied "on account of sex." The Senate and enough states followed, and after three generations of suffragist efforts, the Nineteenth Amendment took effect in 1920.

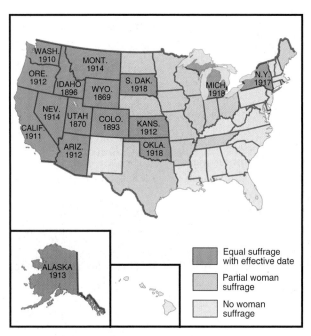

WOMAN SUFFRAGE BEFORE 1920 *State-by-state gains in woman suffrage were limited to the Far West and were agonizingly slow in the early years of the twentieth century.* ■

pragmatism A doctrine that emerged in the early twentieth century, built largely on the ideas of psychologist and philosopher William James. Pragmatists were impatient with theories that held truth to be abstract; they believed that truth should work for the individual. They also believed that people were not only shaped by their environment but also helped to shape it. Ideas that worked, according to pragmatists, became truth.

The social-justice movement had the most success in passing state laws limiting the working hours of women. By 1913, thirty-nine states had set maximum working hours for women or banned the employment of women at night. As early as 1900, twenty-eight states had laws regulating child labor. But the courts often ruled against such laws, and families, needing extra income, sometimes ignored them.

In 1916, President Woodrow Wilson backed a law to limit child labor, the Keating-Owen Act, but the Supreme Court, in *Hammer* v. *Dagenhart* (1918), overturned it as an improper regulation of local labor conditions. In 1919, Congress tried again in the Second Child Labor Act, also struck down by the Court in *Baily* v. *Drexel Furniture Company* (1922). Not until the 1930s did Congress succeed in passing a national child labor law that the Supreme Court allowed to stand.

A Ferment of Ideas: Challenging the Status Quo

A dramatic shift in ideas became one of the most important forces behind progressive reform. Most of the ideas focused on the role of the environment in shaping human behavior. Progressive reformers accepted society's growing complexity and called for a more scientific approach to social problems, allowed room for new theories, and rejected age-encrusted divine or natural "laws" in favor of ideas and actions that worked.

A new doctrine, called **pragmatism,** emerged in this ferment of ideas. It came from William James, the Harvard psychologist who was the key figure in American thought from the 1890s to World War I. A warm, tolerant person, James believed that truth should work for the individual, and it should work best not in abstraction but in action. "True ideas are those we can assimilate, validate, corroborate, and verify. False ideas are those we cannot."

People, James thought, were not only shaped by their environment but gave it shape. In *Pragmatism* (1907), he praised "tough-minded" individuals who could live effectively in a world with no easy answers. The tough-minded accepted change; they knew how to pick manageable problems, gather facts, discard ideas that did not work, and act on those that did. Ideas that worked became truth. "What is the 'cash value' of a thought, idea or belief?" James asked. Does it work? Does it make a difference to the individual who experiences it? "The ultimate test for us of what a truth means," said James, "is the conduct it dictates."

The most influential educator of the Progressive Era, John Dewey, applied pragmatism to educational reform. He introduced an educational revolution, stressing children's needs and capabilities. Dewey argued that thought evolves in relation to the environment and that education is directly related to experience. New ideas in education, he said, are "as much a product of the changed social situation, and as much an effort to meet the needs of the society that is forming, as are changes in modes of industry and commerce." He opposed memorization and dogmatic, authoritarian teaching methods; he emphasized personal growth, free inquiry, creativity, and cooperative learning.

Rejecting the older view of the law as universal and unchanging, lawyers and legal theorists instead interpreted it as a reflection of the environment—an instrument for social change. A movement grew among judges for "sociological jurisprudence" that related the law to social reform. Increasingly, judges and lawyers began

■ *Woman suffrage was a key element in the social-justice movement. Without the right to vote, women working actively for reform had little real power to influence elected officials to support their endeavors.* ■

to consider crime as much the result of problems in society as a reflection of individual weakness.

Louis D. Brandeis's career illustrated the change. A rich corporate lawyer, he changed his mind about social issues during the depression of the 1890s, and as the "people's attorney," he fought corporate abuses and political corruption. In 1908, he accepted an invitation from the National Consumers' League to defend an Oregon law limiting working hours for women to ten hours a day.

Brandeis decided on a new kind of argument. With the help of healthcare reformer Lillian Wald, he compiled masses of medical and sociological data, and in the 104-page brief he submitted to the Court, only two pages were devoted to traditional legal precedents. The rest consisted of reports from factory inspectors, health and hygiene commissioners, and expert commissions, all showing that the ten-hour law was necessary to protect the health, safety, and morals of women in Oregon.

Agreeing, the Supreme Court in *Muller* v. *Oregon* (1908) upheld the Oregon statute, and the famous **Brandeis brief,** based on environmental data rather than legal precedent, influenced lawyers and courts across the country. Like so many other reform efforts during these years, it assumed that changes in the environment could improve the lives of people and produce a better society.

Socialism, a reformist political philosophy, grew dramatically before the First World War. Organized in 1901, the Socialist party of America doubled in membership between 1904 and 1908, then tripled in the four years after that. By 1911, there were Socialist mayors in thirty-two cities. Although its doctrines were aimed at an urban proletariat, the Socialist party also drew support in parts of the rural South and West.

Eugene V. Debs, five times the party's presidential candidate, offset the popular image of the wild-eyed radical. A gentle and reflective man, Debs never developed a cohesive platform, but he was an eloquent, passionate, and visionary leader. He led the American Railway Union into the Pullman strike. Running for president, he garnered 100,000 votes in 1900; 400,000 in 1904; and 900,000 in 1912, the party's peak year.

Muller v. Oregon This 1908 Supreme Court decision established special protections for working women, upholding an Oregon law that limited women working in factories and laundries to a ten-hour work day.

Brandeis brief Filed by attorney Louis D. Brandeis in the 1908 Supreme Court case of *Muller* v. *Oregon,* this brief presented only two pages of legal precedents, but 102 pages of sociological evidence on the negative effects of long workdays on women's health and thus on women as mothers. The brief expanded the definition of legal evidence.

REFORM IN THE CITIES AND STATES

Believing in government as an agent of change, the progressives wanted to curb the influence of "special interests" and make government follow the public will. Once this goal had been achieved, they welcomed government action at whatever level was appropriate. The use of federal power increased, along with the power and prestige of the presidency. Most important, the progressives believed in the ability of experts to solve problems. At every level, thousands of commissions and agencies took form. Staffed by trained experts, they oversaw a multitude of matters, from railroad rates to public health.

Interest Groups and the Decline of Popular Politics

Placing government in the hands of experts was one way to get it out of the clutches of politicians and political parties. The direct primary, which allowed voters rather than parties to choose candidates for office, was another way. Such initiatives were part of a fundamental change in the way Americans viewed their political systems.

One sign of the change was that fewer and fewer people were going to the polls. Voter turnout dropped dramatically after 1900, when the intense partisanship of the decades after the Civil War gave way to media-oriented political campaigns based largely on the personalities of the candidates. From 1876 to 1900, the average turnout in presidential elections was 77 percent. From 1900 to 1916, it was 65 percent, and in the 1920s, it dropped to 52 percent, close to the average today. Turnout was lowest among young people, immigrants, the poor, and, ironically, the newly franchised women.

It was particularly low in the South, where conservative whites used restrictive election laws to keep blacks and others from the polls. Although the decline in the North was less sharp, the reasons for it were more complex. By the 1920s, as many as one-quarter of all eligible northern voters never cast a ballot.

There were numerous causes for the fall-off, but among the most important was the fact that people had found another way to achieve some of the objectives they had once assigned to political parties. They had found the "interest group," a means of action that assumed importance in this era and has been a major feature of politics ever since. Professional societies, trade associations, labor organizations, farm lobbies, and scores of other interest groups worked outside the party system to pressure government for things their members wanted. Social workers, women's clubs, reform groups, and others learned to apply pressure in similar ways, and the result was much of the significant legislation of the Progressive Era.

Reform in the Cities

In the early years of the twentieth century, urban reform movements spread across the nation. In 1894, the National Municipal League was organized, and it became the forum for debate over civic reform, changes in the tax laws, and municipal ownership of public utilities. Within a few years, nearly every city had a variety of clubs and organizations directed at improving the quality of city life.

In the 1880s, reformers would call an evening conference, pass resolutions, and then go home; after 1900, they formed associations, adopted long-range policies, and hired employees to achieve them. In the mid-1890s, only Chicago had an urban reform league with a full-time paid executive; within a decade, there were such leagues in every major city.

In one locale after another, reformers reordered municipal government. They broadened the scope of utility regulation, restricted city franchises, updated tax assessments, and tried to clean up the electoral machinery. Committed to efficiency and, above all, results, they developed a trained civil service to oversee planning and day-to-day operations.

In constructing their model governments, urban reformers often turned to recent advances in business management and organization. They stressed continuity and expertise, a system in which professional experts staffed a government overseen by elected officials. They hired engineers to manage utility and water systems, physicians and nurses to improve public health, and city planners to supervise park and highway development. The growing number of experts and commissions widened the gap between voters and decision makers but dramatically improved the efficiency of government.

As cities exploded in size, they freed themselves from the tight controls of state legislatures and began to experiment with their governments. Galveston, Texas, struggling to recover from a devastating hurricane in 1900, pioneered the commission form of government, with commissions of appointed experts, rather than elected officials, running the city. Other cities simply hired a city manager.

In the race for reform, a number of city mayors won national reputations working to modernize taxes, clean up politics, lower utility rates, and control the awarding of valuable city franchises. In Toledo, Ohio, Mayor Samuel M. ("Golden Rule") Jones labored to improve the quality of life for the people in his city. In Cleveland, Ohio, Mayor Tom L. Johnson also fought to improve city life. He cut down on corruption, cut off special privileges, updated taxes, and gained Cleveland a reputation as the country's best-governed city.

Finding it difficult to regulate powerful city utilities and keep their costs down, Johnson and mayors in other cities turned more and more to public ownership of gas, electricity, water, and transportation. Called "gas and water socialism"—in which cities owned their own gas, electricity, water, and other utilities—the idea spread swiftly. In 1896, fewer than half of American cities owned their own waterworks; by 1915, almost two-thirds did.

Action in the States

Reformers soon discovered, however, that many problems lay beyond a city's boundaries, and they turned for action to the state government. From the 1890s to 1920, they worked to stiffen state laws governing the labor of women and children, create and strengthen commissions to regulate railroads and utilities, impose corporate and inheritance taxes, improve mental and penal institutions, and allocate more funds for state universities, the training ground for the experts and educated citizenry needed for the new society.

Maryland passed the first workers' compensation law in 1902; soon most industrial states had such legislation. Between 1900 and 1920, states also increasingly adopted factory inspection laws, mandated insurance for the victims of factory accidents, and enacted employers' liability laws.

New York was one of the states that led the way. Around 1905, a series of dramatic investigations revealed a systematic and corrupt alliance between politicians and business leaders in the gas, electricity, and insurance industries. Responding immediately, an angry public supported greater state regulation and management by independent expert commissions. In 1905 and 1906, the state established regulatory boards to oversee utilities and insurance; it also outlawed corporate contributions to political campaigns and restricted business lobbying in the state legislature.

To regulate business, virtually every state created regulatory commissions, empowered to examine corporate books and hold public hearings. Building on earlier experience, after 1900 they were given new power to initiate actions, rather than await complaints, and in some cases to set maximum prices and rates. State regulatory commissions pioneered methods later adopted in federal legislation of 1906 and 1910. Some business leaders supported the federal laws, preferring one regulatory agency to dozens of separate state commissions.

Historians have long praised the regulation movement, but the commissions did not always act wisely or even in the public interest. Elective commissions often produced commissioners who had little knowledge of corporate affairs. Appointive commissions sometimes fared better, but they, too, had to oversee extraordinarily complex businesses such as the railroads, shaping everything from wages to train schedules.

Emphasizing people's involvement in politics, progressives, like the populists, backed three measures to make officeholders responsive to popular will: the initiative, which allowed voters to propose new laws; the referendum, which allowed them to accept or reject a law at the ballot box; and the recall, which gave them a way to remove an elected official from office. They also backed the direct election of senators and direct primaries as instruments to expand the role of the electorate.

As attention shifted from the cities to the states, reform governors throughout the country won growing reputations. Robert M. La Follette of Wisconsin—talented, aggressive, and a superb stump speaker—became the most famous of a group that included Hiram Johnson in California, Woodrow Wilson in New Jersey, and Charles Evans Hughes in New York. In 1901, La Follette became governor of Wisconsin. In the following six years, he put together the Wisconsin Idea, one of the most important reform programs in the history of state government. He established an industrial commission to regulate factory safety and sanitation; improved education, workers' compensation, public utility controls, and resource conservation; and lowered railroad rates. In addition, under La Follette, Wisconsin also became the first to adopt a state income tax.

Like other progressives, La Follette drew on expert advice and relied on academic figures such as Richard Ely at the University of Wisconsin to provide facts and figures to support the measures he favored. Theodore Roosevelt called La Follette's Wisconsin "the laboratory of democracy," and the Wisconsin Idea soon spread to many other states.

After 1905, the progressives looked more and more to Washington. For one thing, Theodore Roosevelt was there. But progressives also had a growing sense that many concerns—corporations and conservation, factory safety, child labor—crossed state lines. Federal action seemed desirable; specific reforms fit into a larger plan perhaps best seen from the nation's center. Within a few years, La Follette and Hiram Johnson became senators, and while reform went on back home, the focus of progressivism shifted to Washington.

THE REPUBLICAN ROOSEVELT

When President William McKinley died of gunshot wounds in September 1901 (see Chapter 20), Vice President Theodore Roosevelt succeeded him in the White House. Roosevelt continued some of McKinley's policies, developed others of his own, and brought to them all the particular exuberance of his own personality.

Only 42, Roosevelt was then the youngest president in American history. Open, aggressive, and high-spirited, he worked long hours; a steady procession of politicians, labor leaders, industrialists, poets, artists, and writers paraded through the White House. Most of the people who met Roosevelt were captivated by his charming manner and impressed by the breadth of his knowledge.

If McKinley cut down on presidential isolation, Roosevelt virtually ended it. The presidency, he thought, was the "bully pulpit," a forum of ideas and leadership for the nation. The president was a "steward of the people," and the self-confident Roosevelt enlisted talented associates to help him steer the ship of state.

In 1901, Roosevelt invited Booker T. Washington, the prominent black educator, to lunch at the White House. Many Southerners protested, and they protested again when Roosevelt appointed several blacks to important federal offices in South Carolina and Mississippi. At first, Roosevelt tried to build a biracial, "black and tan" southern Republican party. He also denounced lynching and ordered the Justice Department to act against peonage.

But the president soon retreated to a position consistent with his own belief in black inferiority. He joined others in blaming black soldiers stationed near Brownsville, Texas, after a night of violence there in August 1906. Acting quickly and on little evidence, he discharged without honor three companies of black troops. Six of the soldiers who were discharged held the Congressional Medal of Honor.

Busting the Trusts

Like most people, Roosevelt wavered on the trusts. Large-scale production and industrial growth, he believed, were natural and beneficial; they needed only to be controlled. Still, he questioned the trusts' impact on local enterprise and individual opportunity. Distinguishing between "good" and "bad" trusts, he pledged to protect the former while controlling the latter.

At first, Roosevelt hoped the glare of publicity would be enough to uncover and correct business evils, and in public, he both praised and attacked the trusts. To aid him in this task, he asked Congress in 1903 to create the Department of Commerce and Labor, with a Bureau of Corporations empowered to investigate businesses engaged in interstate commerce. When Congress hesitated, Roosevelt mustered public opinion behind the legislation, which then easily passed.

Roosevelt also undertook more direct legal action. On February 14, 1902, he instructed the Justice Department to bring suit against the Northern Securities Company for violation of the Sherman Antitrust Act. It was a shrewd move. A mammoth holding company, Northern Securities controlled the massive rail networks of the Northern Pacific, the Great Northern, and the Chicago, Burlington and Quincy railroads. Some of the most prominent names in business were behind the giant company, including J. P. Morgan and Company and the Rockefeller interests. Morgan was shocked; he complained that the president had not acted like a "gentleman."

In 1904, the Supreme Court, in a five-to-four decision, upheld the suit against Northern Securities and ordered the company dissolved. Roosevelt was jubilant, and he followed up the victory with several other antitrust suits. Between 1902 and 1907, he moved against the beef trust, the American Tobacco Company, the Du Pont Corporation, and Standard Oil.

But Roosevelt's policies were not always clear, nor were his actions always consistent. He frequently took the advice of important business leaders, and he asked for (and received) business support in his bid for re-election in 1904 (including $150,000 from Morgan). In 1907, he even permitted Morgan's U.S. Steel to absorb the Tennessee Coal and Iron Company, an important competitor.

Roosevelt, in truth, was not a "trust buster," although he was frequently called that. William Howard Taft, his successor in the White House, initiated forty-three antitrust indictments in four years—nearly twice as many as the twenty-five Roosevelt initiated in the seven years of his presidency.

"Square Deal" in the Coalfields

A few months after announcing the Northern Securities suit, Roosevelt intervened in a major labor dispute involving the anthracite coal miners of northeastern Pennsylvania. Led by John Mitchell, a moderate labor leader, the United Mine

A 1909 cartoon illustrates Theodore Roosevelt's promise to break up only those "bad trusts" that were hurtful to the general welfare. Despite his reputation as a trust buster, Roosevelt dissolved relatively few trusts.

Workers demanded wage increases, an eight-hour workday, and company recognition of the union. The coal companies refused, and in May 1902, some 140,000 miners walked off the job. The mines closed.

As months passed and the strike continued, coal prices rose. As winter approached, schools, hospitals, and factories ran short of coal. Public opinion turned against the companies. Morgan and other industrial leaders privately urged them to settle, but George F. Baer, head of one of the largest companies, refused: "The rights and interests of the laboring man," Baer said, "will be protected and cared for—not by the labor agitators, but by the Christian men to whom God in his infinite wisdom has given the control of the property interests of this country."

Roosevelt was furious. Complaining of the companies' arrogance, he invited both sides in the dispute to an October 1902 conference at the White House. There Mitchell took a moderate tone and offered to submit the issues to arbitration, but the companies refused to budge. Roosevelt ordered the army to prepare to seize the mines and then leaked word of his intent to Wall Street leaders.

Alarmed, Morgan and others again urged a settlement, and at last the companies agreed to accept the recommendations of an independent commission to be appointed by the president. In late October, the strikers returned to work, and in March 1903, the commission awarded them a 10 percent wage increase and a cut in working hours. It recommended, however, against union recognition. The coal companies, in turn, were encouraged to raise prices to offset the wage increase.

Roosevelt came increasingly to see the federal government as an honest and impartial broker between powerful elements in society. Rather than leaning toward labor, he pursued a middle path to curb corporate or labor abuses, abolish privilege, and enlarge individual opportunity. Often he backed reforms in part to head off more radical measures.

During the 1904 campaign, Roosevelt called his actions in the coal miners' strike a "square deal" for both labor and capital, a term that stuck to his administration. Roosevelt was not the first president to take a stand for labor, but he was the first to bring opposing sides in a labor dispute to the White House to settle it. He was the first to threaten to seize a major industry, and he was the first to appoint a commission whose decision both sides agreed to accept.

ROOSEVELT PROGRESSIVISM AT ITS HEIGHT

In the election of 1904, the popular Roosevelt soundly drubbed his Democratic opponent, Alton B. Parker of New York, and the Socialist party candidate, Eugene V. Debs of Indiana. In a landslide victory, he received 57 percent of the vote to Parker's 38 percent. Overjoyed, he pledged that "under no circumstances will I be a candidate for or accept another nomination," a statement he later regretted.

Following his election, Roosevelt laid out a reform program that included railroad regulation, employers' liability for federal employees, greater federal control over corporations, and laws regulating child labor, factory inspection, and slum clearance in the District of Columbia. He turned first to railroad regulation. In 1903, he had worked with Congress to pass the moderate Elkins Act to prohibit railroad rebates and increase the powers of the Interstate Commerce Commission (ICC). In 1904 and 1905, he wanted much more, and he urged Congress to empower the ICC to set reasonable and nondiscriminatory rates and prevent inequitable practices.

Widespread demand for railroad regulation strengthened Roosevelt's hand. He maneuvered cannily, skillfully trading congressional support for a strong railroad measure in return for his promise to postpone a reduction of the tariff. The result was the passage of the **Hepburn Act** of 1906, strengthening the rate-making power of the ICC. It made ICC orders binding, pending any court appeals, thus placing the burden of proof on the companies. Delighted, Roosevelt viewed the Hepburn Act as

Hepburn Act A law that strengthened the rate-making power of the Interstate Commerce Commission, reflecting the era's desire to control the power of the railroads. It increased the ICC's membership from five to seven, empowered it to fix reasonable railroad rates, and broadened its jurisdiction. It also made ICC rulings binding pending court appeals.

a major step in his plan for continuous, expert federal control over industry.

President Roosevelt signed two important laws to regulate the food and drug industries. Both laws reflected public outcry over adulterated and poisonous food and drugs. Muckraking articles had touched frequently on filthy conditions in meatpacking houses, and Upton Sinclair's book *The Jungle* (1906) described them in terms graphic enough to send people reeling from the dinner table.

After reading *The Jungle,* Roosevelt ordered an investigation. The result, he said, was "hideous." Meat sales plummeted in the United States and Europe. Alarmed, the meatpackers themselves supported a reform law. The Meat Inspection Act of 1906, stiffer than the packers had wanted, set rules for sanitary meatpacking and government inspection of meat products.

A second measure, the Pure Food and Drug Act, passed more easily. Samuel Hopkins Adams, a reporter for *Collier's* magazine who had once considered a medical career, exposed the dangers of patent medicines. He sent medicine samples to Dr. Harvey W. Wiley, the chief chemist in the Department of Agriculture, for analysis. Wiley and his "poison squad" had previously tested various food preservatives, determined to put an end to adulterated foods. The evidence in hand, Wiley pushed for regulation, Roosevelt joined the fight, and the act passed on June 30, 1906, helped along by the appearance in February of Sinclair's *Jungle.* It represented a pioneering effort, through required labeling information, to ban the manufacture and sale of adulterated, misbranded, or unsanitary food or drugs.

An expert on birds, Roosevelt loved nature and the wilderness, and some of his most enduring accomplishments came in the field of **conservation.** Working closely with Gifford Pinchot, chief of the Forest Service, he established the first comprehensive national conservation policy. He undertook a major reclamation program and strengthened the forest preserve program. Broadening the concept of conservation, he placed power sites, coal lands, and oil reserves as well as national forests in the public domain. To Roosevelt, conservation meant the wise use of natural resources, not locking them away, so those who thought the wilderness should be preserved rather than developed generally opposed his policies.

As 1908 approached, Roosevelt became increasingly strident in his demand for sweeping reforms. He attacked "malefactors of great wealth," urged greater federal regulatory powers, criticized the conservatism of the federal courts, and called for laws protecting factory workers. Many business leaders blamed him for a severe financial panic in the autumn of 1907, and conservatives in Congress stiffened their opposition. Divisions between Republican conservatives and progressives grew.

Immensely popular, Roosevelt prepared in 1908 to turn over the White House to William Howard Taft, his close friend and colleague. He assured Americans that Taft would carry on his policies. As expected, Taft soundly defeated the Democratic

A Look at the Past

Patent Medicine

Patent medicines such as this cough and kidney remedy had long been popular. Note the many ailments it claimed to relieve, the ingredients, and the statement of compliance with the Pure Food and Drug Act. ✳ Based on this information, do you think Reid's Cough and Kidney Remedy was effective? If not, why do you suppose people continued to buy it? What questions does this medicine raise about health, medical care, and the effectiveness of government regulations at the time?

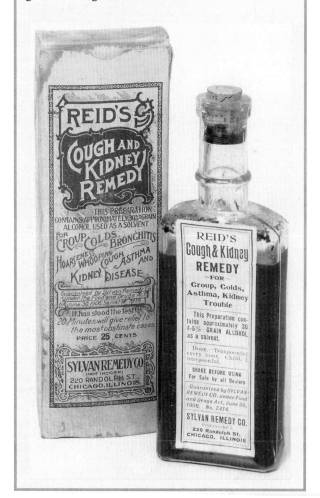

conservation As president, Theodore Roosevelt made this principle one of his administration's top goals. Conservation in his view aimed at protecting the nation's natural resources, but called for the wise use of them rather than locking them away.

standard-bearer, William Jennings Bryan. The Republicans retained control of Congress. Taft prepared to move into the White House, ready and willing to carry on the Roosevelt legacy.

THE ORDEAL OF WILLIAM HOWARD TAFT

The Republican national convention that nominated Taft satisfied neither Roosevelt nor Taft. The conservative Republicans controlled the convention, and the platform reflected conservative views on labor, the courts, and other issues. La Follette and other progressive Republicans were openly disappointed.

Taking office in 1909, Taft felt "just a bit like a fish out of water." A graduate of Yale Law School and a distinguished judge, Taft's public service record was impressive. As the head of the Philippine Commission and later as the first governor general of the Philippines, he had shown a talent for organization. In 1904, Roosevelt appointed him secretary of war, a post that again highlighted Taft's administrative skill. A good-natured man, Taft preferred diplomacy to warfare, and he liked to work behind the scenes rather than in the spotlight.

Weighing close to 300 pounds, Taft enjoyed conversation, golf and bridge, good food, and plenty of rest. He was also honest, kindly, and amiable, and in his own way he knew how to get things done. Next to Roosevelt, however, he seemed lazy and spiritless.

Taft's years as president were not happy. He presided over a Republican party torn with tensions that Roosevelt had either brushed aside or concealed. The tariff, business regulation, and other issues split conservatives and progressives, and Taft often wavered or sided with the conservatives. He never had Roosevelt's faith in the ability of government to impose reform and alter individual behavior, and his ear was attuned more toward business than labor and the unions.

NATIONAL PARKS AND FORESTS   *During the presidency of Theodore Roosevelt, who considered conservation his most important domestic achievement, millions of acres of land were set aside for national parks and forests.* ∎

Party Insurgency

Taft started his term with an attempt to curb the powerful Republican speaker of the House, crusty Joseph "Uncle Joe" Cannon of Illinois. Using the powers of his position, Cannon set House procedures, appointed committees, and virtually dictated legislation. He often opposed reform. In March 1909, thirty Republican congressmen joined Taft's efforts to curb Cannon's power, but Cannon retaliated and, threatening to block all tariff bills, forced a compromise. Taft stopped the anti-Cannon campaign for Cannon's pledge to help with tariff cuts.

The House quickly passed a bill providing for lower rates, but in the Senate, protectionists raised them. Senate leader Nelson A. Aldrich of Rhode Island introduced a revised bill that added more than eight hundred amendments to the House rates. Angry, La Follette and other Republicans attacked the bill as the child of special interests and urged Taft to defeat the high-tariff proposal. Taft wavered but in the end backed Aldrich. The Payne-Aldrich Act, passed in November 1909, called for higher rates than the original House bill, though it lowered them from the Dingley Tariff of 1897. An unpopular law, it helped discredit Taft and revealed the tensions in the Republican party.

Republican progressives and conservatives drifted apart. Taft tried to find middle ground but leaned more and more toward the conservatives. By 1910, progressive Republicans no longer looked to Taft for leadership. To the president's embarrassment, progressive congressmen were able, without presidential support, to curtail Speaker Cannon's authority to dictate committee assignments and schedule debates. In progressive circles, hopes grew of returning Roosevelt to the White House.

The Ballinger-Pinchot Affair

The conservation issue dealt another blow to the relations between Roosevelt and Taft. In 1909, Richard A. Ballinger, Taft's secretary of the interior, offered for sale a million acres of public land that Pinchot, Taft's chief forester, had withdrawn from sale. Pinchot protested. After investigating, Taft supported Ballinger, although he asked Pinchot to remain in office.

Pinchot refused to drop the matter. He secretly provided material for two anti-Ballinger magazine articles, and he wrote a critical public letter that was read to the Senate by Senator Jonathan P. Dolliver of Iowa. Taft fired the insubordinate Pinchot, an appropriate action, but again lost some standing in the process. Newspapers wrongly portrayed the president as an opponent of conservation.

The Ballinger-Pinchot controversy obscured Taft's important contributions to conservation. He won from Congress the power to remove lands from sale, and he used it to conserve more land than Roosevelt did. Still, the controversy tarred Taft; it also upset Roosevelt and widened the gulf between the two men.

Taft Alienates the Progressives

Interested in railroad regulation, Taft backed a bill in 1910 to empower the ICC to fix maximum railroad rates. Although it was hotly debated, the Mann-Elkins Act of 1910 gave something to everyone. It gave the ICC power to set rates, stiffened long- and short-haul regulations, and placed telephone and telegraph companies under ICC jurisdiction. These provisions delighted progressives. The act also created a Commerce Court to hear appeals from ICC decisions, an addition that pleased conservatives. Progressive Republicans wanted to amend the bill to strengthen it, but Taft raised the issue of party loyalty and further alienated the progressives.

Taft attempted to defeat the progressive Republicans in the 1910 elections. He assisted in the establishment of antiprogressive organizations, and he opposed progressive Republican candidates for the Senate, including Hiram Johnson of

California. Progressive Republicans retaliated by organizing a nationwide network of anti-Taft Progressive Republican Clubs.

The 1910 election results were a major setback for Taft and the Republicans, both conservatives and progressives. In party primaries, progressive Republicans overwhelmed most Taft candidates, and in November, the Democrats beat virtually everyone. For the first time since 1894, Republicans lost control of both the House and the Senate.

Despite the defeat, Taft pushed through several important progressive measures before his term ended. With the help of the new Democratic House, he backed laws to regulate safety in mines and on railroads, create a Children's Bureau in the federal government, establish employers' liability for all work done on government contracts, and mandate an eight-hour workday for government workers.

In 1909, Congress initiated a constitutional amendment authorizing an income tax, perhaps the most significant legislative measure of the twentieth century. The Sixteenth Amendment took effect early in 1913. A few months later, another important progressive goal was realized when the direct election of senators was ratified as the Seventeenth Amendment to the Constitution.

An ardent supporter of competition, Taft relentlessly pressed a campaign against trusts. In 1911, the Supreme Court, in cases against Standard Oil and American Tobacco, established the "rule of reason," which allowed the Court to determine whether a business exerted a "reasonable" restraint on trade. Taft thought the decisions gave the Court too much discretion, and he pushed ahead with the antitrust effort.

In October 1911, he sued U.S. Steel for its acquisition of the Tennessee Coal and Iron Company in 1907. Roosevelt had approved the acquisition, and the suit seemed designed to impugn that action. Furious, Roosevelt listened more and more to anti-Taft Republicans who urged him to run for president. In February 1912, he announced: "My hat is in the ring."

Differing Philosophies in the Election of 1912

Delighted Democrats looked on as Taft and Roosevelt fought for the Republican nomination. As the incumbent president, Taft controlled the party machinery, and when the Republican convention met in June 1912, he took the nomination. In early July, the Democrats met in Baltimore and, after a forty-six-ballot struggle, nominated Woodrow Wilson, the reform-minded governor of New Jersey.

A month later, the anti-Taft and progressive Republicans—now calling themselves the **Progressive party**—whooped it up in Chicago. Nominating Roosevelt for president, the Progressive—soon known as the Bull Moose—party convention set the stage for a lively three-cornered presidential contest.

Taft was out of the running before the campaign even began. He stayed at home and made no speeches before the election. Roosevelt campaigned strenuously for his Bull Moose platform, a program he called **New Nationalism.** It demanded a national approach to the country's affairs and a strong president to deal with them. New Nationalism exalted the executive and the expert; urged social-justice reforms to protect workers, women, and children; and accepted "good" trusts. New Nationalism encouraged large concentrations of labor and capital, serving the nation's interests under a forceful federal executive. For the first time in the history of a political party, the Progressive campaign enlisted women in its organization, and New Nationalism gained their widespread support. Some labor and business leaders, seeking relief from destructive competition and labor strife, also got behind the new party.

Wilson, in contrast, set forth a program called the **New Freedom** that emphasized business competition and small government. A states' rights Democrat, he

Progressive party   Also known as the Bull Moose party, this political party was formed by Theodore Roosevelt in an attempt to advance progressive ideas and unseat President William Howard Taft in 1912.

New Nationalism   Theodore Roosevelt's program in his campaign for the presidency in 1912, the New Nationalism called for a national approach to the country's affairs and a strong president to deal with them. It also called for efficiency in government and society; urged protection of children, women, and workers; accepted "good" trusts; and exalted the expert and the executive. Additionally, it encouraged large concentrations of capital and labor.

New Freedom   Woodrow Wilson's program in his campaign for the presidency in 1912, the New Freedom emphasized business competition and small government. It sought to rein in federal authority, release individual energy, and restore competition. It echoed many of the progressive social-justice objectives while pushing for a free rather than a planned economy.

wanted to rein in federal authority, using it only to sweep away special privilege, release individual energies, and restore competition. He echoed the Progressive party's social-justice objectives while continuing to attack Roosevelt's planned state. For Wilson, the vital issue was not a planned economy but a free one.

In New Nationalism and the New Freedom, the election of 1912 offered competing philosophies of government. Both Roosevelt and Wilson saw the central problem of the American nation as the effect of economic growth on individuals and society. Both focused on the government's relation to business, both believed in bureaucratic reform, and both wanted to use government to protect the ordinary citizen. But Roosevelt welcomed federal power, national planning, and business growth; Wilson distrusted them all.

On election day, Wilson won 6.3 million votes to 4.1 million for Roosevelt, 3.5 million for Taft, and 900,000 for Eugene V. Debs, the Socialist party candidate. In the worst defeat ever suffered by an incumbent, Taft garnered only eight electoral votes. The Democrats also won outright control of both houses of Congress.

■ *"I'm feeling like a bull moose!" declared Teddy Roosevelt while campaigning in 1912 as a Progressive and inadvertently renaming the new political party. The patch depicts a strong, independent animal, much like Roosevelt himself. In 1904, he had won re-election by promising to give Americans a "square deal."* ■

WOODROW WILSON'S NEW FREEDOM

If under Roosevelt social reform took on the excitement of a circus, under Wilson, one historian said, "it acquired the dedication of a sunrise service." Born in Virginia in 1856, the son of a Presbyterian minister, Wilson was a moralist; he reached judgments easily that, once reached, were rarely discarded.

After graduating from Princeton University and the University of Virginia Law School, Wilson found that practicing law bored him. Shifting to history and political science, he taught at Princeton from 1890 to 1902, when he became president of the university. Eight years later, he was governor of New Jersey, where he compiled a strong record as a reformer. Although Wilson's rise was rapid and he knew relatively little about national issues and personalities, he learned fast. In some ways, the lack of experience served him well. He had few political debts to repay, and he brought fresh perspectives to older issues.

Wilson loved ideas but was sensitive to criticism and prone to self-righteousness. He often turned differences of opinion into bitter personal quarrels. Like Roosevelt, he believed in strong presidential leadership. He cooperated closely with Democrats in Congress, and his legislative record places him among the most effective presidents. Cold and aloof in individual conversation, Wilson could move crowds with graceful oratory. Unlike Taft, and even more than Roosevelt, he could inspire.

The New Freedom in Action

On the day of his inauguration, Wilson called Congress into special session to lower the tariff. When the session opened on April 8, 1913, Wilson himself was there, the first president since John Adams in 1801 to appear personally before Congress. In forceful language, he urged Congress to reduce tariff rates.

Underwood Tariff Act An early accomplishment of the Wilson administration, this law reduced the tariff rates of the Payne-Aldrich law of 1909 by about 15 percent. It also levied a graduated income tax to make up for the lost revenue.

Federal Reserve Act One of the most important laws in the history of the country, this 1913 act created a central banking system, consisting of twelve regional banks governed by the Federal Reserve Board.

Clayton Antitrust Act An attempt to improve the Sherman Anti-Trust Act of 1890, this law outlawed interlocking directorates (companies in which the same people served as directors), forbade policies that created monopolies, and made corporate officers responsible for antitrust violations. Benefiting labor, it declared that unions were not conspiracies in restraint of trade and outlawed the use of injunctions in labor disputes unless they were necessary to protect property.

Wilson worked hard and skillfully to get the bill through Congress. The result was a triumph for Wilson and the Democratic party. The **Underwood Tariff Act** passed in 1913. It lowered tariff rates about 15 percent and removed duties from sugar, wool, and several other consumer goods. To make up for lost revenue, the act also levied a modest, graduated income tax, authorized under the just-ratified Sixteenth Amendment. Marking a significant shift in the American tax structure, it imposed a 1 percent tax on individuals and corporations earning more than $4000 annually and an additional 1 percent tax on incomes greater than $20,000.

The act reflected the new unity of the Democratic party and the ability of Wilson as a leader. Encouraged by his success, Wilson decided to keep Congress in session through the hot Washington summer. Now he focused on banking reform, and the result in December 1913 was the **Federal Reserve Act,** the most important domestic law of his administration.

Meant to provide the United States with a sound yet flexible currency, the act established the country's first efficient banking system since Andrew Jackson killed the Second Bank of the United States in 1832. It created twelve regional banks, each to serve a district. These banks answered to the Federal Reserve Board, appointed by the president, which governed the nationwide system.

A compromise law, the act blended public and private control of the banking system. Private bankers owned the Federal Reserve banks but answered to the presidentially appointed Federal Reserve Board. The Reserve banks were authorized to issue currency and through the discount rate—the interest rate at which they loaned money to member banks—could raise or lower the amount of money in circulation. Monetary affairs no longer depended solely on the price of gold. Within a year, nearly half the nation's banking resources were in the Federal Reserve System.

The **Clayton Antitrust Act** (1914) completed Wilson's initial legislative program. Motivated in part by the revelations of a congressional committee about the power of interlocking directorates—management and control of competing companies by executives from an interrelated business group—the Clayton Act outlawed such directorates and prohibited unfair trade practices. It forbade pricing policies that created monopoly, and it made corporate officers personally responsible for antitrust violations. Delighting Samuel Gompers and the labor movement, the act declared that unions were not conspiracies in restraint of trade, outlawed the use of injunctions in labor disputes unless necessary to protect property, and approved lawful strikes and picketing.

A related law established the powerful Federal Trade Commission to oversee business methods. The commission could demand special and annual reports, investigate complaints, and order corporate compliance, subject to court review. Although Wilson initially opposed the commission concept, he soon came to see it as the cornerstone of his antitrust plan. To reassure business leaders, he appointed a number of conservatives to the new commission and to the Federal Reserve Board.

In November 1914, Wilson proudly announced the completion of his New Freedom program. Tariff, banking, and antitrust laws promised a brighter future, he said. Many progressives, however, believed the process of reform had only begun.

Wilson Moves Toward the New Nationalism

Distracted by the start of war in Europe, Wilson gave less attention to domestic issues for more than a year. When he returned to concern with reform, he adopted more and more of Roosevelt's New Nationalism and blended it with the New Freedom in ways that set it off from his earlier policies.

One of Wilson's problems was Congress. To his dismay, the Republicans gained substantially in the 1914 elections. At the same time, a recession struck the economy, which had been hurt by the outbreak of the European war in August 1914.

Some business leaders blamed the tariff and other New Freedom enactments. On the defensive, Wilson began to cooperate more with bankers and industrialists. He refused to support a bill providing minimum wages for women workers, sidetracked a child labor bill on the ground that it was unconstitutional, and opposed a bill to establish long-term credits for farmers. He also refused to endorse woman suffrage, arguing that it was a matter for the states to decide.

Wilson's record on race disappointed blacks and many progressives. He had appealed to black voters during the 1912 election but did little to justify their support once in office. A Virginian himself, he appointed many Southerners to high office, and for the first time since the Civil War, southern segregationist views on race dominated the nation's capital.

As the year 1916 began, Wilson again pushed for reform, and the result—a virtual river of reform laws—began the second, national-minded phase of the New Freedom. In part, Wilson was motivated by the approaching presidential election; he was, after all, a minority president. Moreover, many progressives were voicing disappointment with Wilson's limited reforms and his failure to support more advanced reform legislation such as farm credits, child labor, and woman suffrage.

Moving quickly to patch up the problem, Wilson named Louis D. Brandeis to the Supreme Court in January 1916. Popular among progressives, Brandeis was also the first Jew to serve on the Court. In May, Wilson reversed his stand on federally backed farm loans. The Federal Farm Loan Act of 1916 created the Federal Farm Loan Board to give farmers credit in a manner similar to the Federal Reserve's benefits for trade and industry.

Wilson was already popular within the labor movement. He had defended union recognition and collective bargaining. In 1913, he appointed William B. Wilson, a respected leader of the United Mine Workers, as the first head of the Labor Department. In 1914, in Ludlow, Colorado, state militia and mine guards fired machine guns into a tent colony of coal strikers, killing twenty-one men, women, and children. Outraged, Wilson stepped in and used federal troops to end the violence while negotiations to end the strike went on.

In August 1916, a threatened railroad strike again revealed Wilson's sympathies with labor. Like Roosevelt, he invited the two sides to the White House, where he urged the railroad companies to grant an eight-hour workday while asking labor leaders to abandon the demand for overtime pay. Labor leaders accepted the proposal; railroad leaders did not. Soon Wilson signed the Adamson Act (1916), which imposed the eight-hour workday on interstate railways. The act ended the threat of a strike and expanded the federal government's authority to regulate industry.

With Wilson leading the way, the flow of reform legislation continued until the election. The Federal Workmen's Compensation Act established workers' compensation for government employees. The Keating-Owen Act, the first federal child labor law, prohibited the shipment in interstate commerce of products manufactured by children under the age of 14. The Warehouse Act authorized licensed warehouses to issue negotiable receipts for farm products deposited with them. During the campaign, Wilson endorsed the eight-hour workday for all the nation's workers and came out in support of woman suffrage.

The 1916 presidential election was close, but Wilson won it on the issues of peace and progressivism. By the end of 1916, he and the Democratic party had enacted most of the important parts of Roosevelt's Progressive party platform of 1912. To do it, Wilson abandoned portions of the New Freedom and accepted much of New Nationalism, including greater federal power and commissions governing trade and tariffs. In mixing the two programs, he blended some of the competing doctrines of the Progressive Era, established the primacy of the federal government, and foreshadowed the pragmatic outlook of Franklin D. Roosevelt's New Deal of the 1930s.

■ *Miners in Ludlow, Colorado, went on strike in September 1913 for better working conditions and union recognition. Expecting eviction from company housing, they built a tent colony near the company town. The company, John D. Rockefeller's Colorado Fuel and Iron Company, hired guards to break the strike. On Easter Sunday evening, April 20, 1914, state troops and guards sprayed the tents with gunfire, then soaked the tents with kerosene and set the colony afire. Twenty-one of the colonists died, including eleven children.* ■

Conclusion: The Fruits of Progressivism

The election of 1916 showed how deeply progressivism had reached into American society. Candidates were vying for the reform-minded vote, and the future seemed to belong to reform. In retrospect, however, 1916 marked the beginning of progressivism's decline. Many of the problems the progressives addressed they did not solve, and some important ones, like race, they did not even tackle. Yet their regulatory commissions, direct primaries, city improvements, and child labor laws marked an era of important and measured reform.

In 1909, Taft rode to his inauguration in a horse-drawn carriage; in 1913, Wilson rode in an automobile, and change was evident throughout the country. The institution of the presidency expanded. Independent commissions, operating within flexible laws, supplemented executive authority.

These developments owed a great deal to both Roosevelt and Wilson. Wanting to manage a complex society, Roosevelt developed a simple formula: expert advice;

Chronology

1894	National Municipal League is formed to work for reform in cities
1900	Galveston, Texas, is the first city to try the commission form of government
1901	Theodore Roosevelt becomes president ■ Robert M. La Follette is elected reform governor of Wisconsin ■ Doctors reorganize the American Medical Association ■ Socialist party of America is organized
1902	Roosevelt sues the Northern Securities Company for violation of the Sherman Anti-trust Act ■ Coal miners in northeastern Pennsylvania strike ■ Maryland is the first state to pass a workers' compensation law
1903	Department of Commerce and Labor is created
1904	Roosevelt is elected to second term
1906	Hepburn Act strengthens the ICC ■ Upton Sinclair attacks the meatpacking industry in *The Jungle* ■ Congress passes the Meat Inspection Act and the Pure Food and Drug Act
1908	Taft is elected president ■ Supreme Court upholds an Oregon law limiting working hours for women in *Muller* v. *Oregon*
1909	Payne-Aldrich Tariff Act divides the Republican party
1910	Mann-Elkins Act is passed to regulate the railroads ■ Taft fires Gifford Pinchot, head of U.S. Forest Service ■ Democrats sweep midterm elections
1912	Progressive party is formed, nominates Roosevelt for president ■ Woodrow Wilson is elected president
1913	Underwood Tariff Act lowers rates ■ Federal Reserve Act reforms the U.S. banking system ■ Sixteenth Amendment authorizes Congress to collect taxes on incomes
1914	Clayton Antitrust Act strengthens antitrust legislation
1916	Wilson wins re-election
1918	Supreme Court strikes down a federal law limiting child labor in *Hammer* v. *Dagenhart*
1920	Nineteenth Amendment gives women the right to vote

growth-minded policies; a balancing of business, labor, and other interests; the use of publicity to gather support; and stern but often permissive oversight of the economy. He strengthened the executive office and called on young professional, well-educated, public-minded citizens to help him. "I believe in a strong executive," he said. "I believe in power."

Wilson came to office with different ideas, wanting to dismantle much of Roosevelt's governing apparatus. But driven by outside forces and changes in his own thinking, Wilson soon moved in directions similar to those Roosevelt had championed. Starting out to disperse power, he consolidated it, creating governmental agencies to regulate economic forces and correct abuses.

Through such movements, government at all levels accepted responsibility for the welfare of various elements in the social order. A reform-minded and bureaucratic society took shape, one in which men and women, labor and capital, political parties and social classes competed for shares in the expansive framework of twentieth-century life. But there were limits to reform. As both Roosevelt and Wilson found, the new government agencies, understaffed and underfinanced, depended in the end on the responsiveness of the sectors they sought to regulate.

Soon there was a far darker cloud on the horizon. The spirit of progressivism rested on a belief in human potential, peace, and progress. After Napoleon's defeat in 1815, a century of peace began in western Europe, and as the decades passed, war seemed a dying institution. It was not to be. In 1914, the most devastating of wars broke out in Europe, and within three years, Americans were fighting and dying on the battlefields of France.

KEY TERMS

social-justice movement, p. 441

pragmatism, p. 444

Muller v. *Oregon*, p. 445

Brandeis brief, p. 445

Hepburn Act, p. 450

conservation, p. 451

Progressive party, p. 454

New Nationalism, p. 454

New Freedom, p. 454

Underwood Tariff Act, p. 456

Federal Reserve Act, p. 456

Clayton Antitrust Act, p. 456

RECOMMENDED READING

George Mowry, *The Era of Theodore Roosevelt* (1958), and Arthur S. Link, *Woodrow Wilson and the Progressive Era* (1954), trace the social and economic conditions of the period. See also John M. Blum's perceptive and brief *The Republican Roosevelt* (1954), Sarah Watts, *Rough Riders in the White House: Theodore Roosevelt and the Politics of Desire* (2003), and Kathleen Dalton, *Theodore Roosevelt: A Strenuous Life* (2002). The definitive biography of Wilson is Arthur S. Link, *Wilson*, 5 vols. (1947–1965).

Samuel P. Hays offers an influential interpretation of progressivism in *Conservation and the Gospel of Efficiency*

(1959) as does Nancy Cohen, *The Reconstruction of American Liberalism, 1865–1914* (2002), for the broader period. Ambrose Martin, *Enterprise Denied: Origins of the Decline of American Railroads, 1897–1917* (1971), argues persuasively that reformers damaged as well as regulated. Samuel Haber, *The Quest for Authority and Honor in the American Professions, 1750–1900* (1991), examines the changing nature of the professions.

SUGGESTED WEB SITES

Theodore Roosevelt Association
www.theodoreroosevelt.org/
This site contains much biographical and research information about this famous American.

Woodrow Wilson
www.ipl.org/div/potus/wwilson.html
This page contains basic factual data about his election and presidency, speeches, and on-line biographies.

History of the Suffrage Movement
www.rochester.edu/SBA
This site includes a chronology, important texts relating to woman suffrage, and biographical information about Susan B. Anthony and Elizabeth Cady Stanton.

Women and Social Movements in the United States, 1775–2000
womhist.binghamton.edu/
This site offers essays and primary documents on women in social movements.

Chapter 24

The Nation at War

The Sinking of the Lusitania

On the morning of May 1, 1915, the German government printed an important advertisement in the *New York World*. It warned American travelers that a state of war existed in Europe and that waters adjacent to Great Britain were part of the war zone. It emphasized that "travelers sailing in the war zone on ships of Great Britain or her allies do so at their own risk." At 12:30 that afternoon, the British steamship *Lusitania* set sail from New York to Liverpool. The passenger list of 1257 was the largest since the outbreak of war in Europe. Alfred G. Vanderbilt, the millionaire sportsman, was aboard; so were several other famous Americans. Some passengers chose the *Lusitania* for speed; others liked the unmatched comfort of its modern staterooms.

Six days later, the *Lusitania* reached the coast of Ireland. German submarines, known as U-boats, patrolled these dangerous waters. When the war began in 1914, Great Britain imposed a naval blockade of Germany. In return, Germany in February 1915 declared the area around the British Isles a war zone; all enemy vessels, armed or unarmed, were at risk. Germany had only a handful of U-boats, but submarine warfare was new and frightening. On behalf of the United States, President Woodrow Wilson protested the German action, and on February 10, he warned Germany of its "strict accountability" for any American losses resulting from U-boat attacks.

As in peacetime, the *Lusitania* sailed straight ahead, with no zigzag maneuvers to throw off pursuit. But the submarine U-20 was there, and the commander, seeing a large ship, fired a single torpedo. Seconds after it hit, a boiler exploded and blew a hole in the *Lusitania's* side. In eighteen minutes it sank. Nearly 1200 people died, including 128 Americans.

The sinking, the worst since the loss of the *Titanic,* horrified Americans. Most Americans, however, wanted to stay out of war; like Wilson, they hoped negotiations could solve the problem.

In a series of diplomatic notes, Wilson demanded a change in German policy. The first *Lusitania* note (May 13, 1915) called on Germany to abandon unrestricted submarine warfare, disavow the sinking, and compensate for lost American lives. Germany sent an evasive reply, and Wilson drafted a second *Lusitania* note (June 9) insisting on specific pledges. A third note (July 21)—almost an ultimatum— warned Germany that the United States would consider similar sinkings "deliberately unfriendly" acts.

Wilson was unaware that Germany had already ordered U-boat commanders not to sink passenger liners without warning. In August 1915, a U-boat mistakenly torpedoed the British liner *Arabic,* killing two Americans. Wilson protested, and Germany, eager to keep the United States out of war, backed down. In the *Arabic* pledge (September 1), Germany promised to stop and warn liners unless they tried to resist or escape.

Although Wilson's diplomacy had achieved his immediate goal, the *Lusitania* and *Arabic* crises highlighted the elements that led to war. Trade and travel tied the world together, and Americans no longer hid behind safe ocean barriers. New weapons, such as the submarine, strained old rules of international law. But while Americans sifted the conflicting claims of Great Britain and Germany, they hoped for peace. A generation of progressives, inspired with confidence in human progress, did not easily accept war.

Wilson also hated war, but he found himself caught up in a worldwide crisis that demanded the best in American will and diplomacy. In the end, diplomacy failed, and in April 1917, the United States entered a war that changed the nation's history. Building on several major trends in American foreign policy since the 1890s, the years around World War I firmly established the United States as a world power, confirmed the country's dominance in Latin America, and ended with a war with Germany and her allies that had far-reaching results, including establishing the United States as one of the world's foremost economic powers.

A NEW WORLD POWER

As in the late nineteenth century, Americans after 1900 paid little attention to foreign affairs. People focused on what was going on at home. Foreign affairs, they reasoned, was the job of the president, an attitude that suited the interests of Roosevelt, Taft, and Wilson.

American foreign policy from 1901 to 1920 was aggressive and nationalistic. During these years, the United States dominated the Caribbean and intervened in Europe, the Far East, and Latin America.

In 1898, the United States left the peace table possessing the Philippines, Puerto Rico, and Guam. Administering distant lands required a colonial policy and a more outward approach in foreign policy. From the Caribbean to the Pacific, policymakers paid attention to issues and countries they had earlier ignored. Like other nations in these years, the United States built a large navy, protected its colonial empire, and became increasingly involved in international affairs.

The nation also became more and more involved in economic ventures abroad. Turning out goods from textiles to steel, mass production industries sold products overseas, and financiers invested in Asia, Africa, Latin America, and Europe. Though investments and trade never wholly dictated American foreign policy, they fostered greater involvement in foreign lands.

"I Took the Canal Zone"

Convinced the United States should take a more active international role, Theodore Roosevelt spent his presidency preparing the nation for world power. Along with Secretary of War Elihu Root, he modernized the army, established the Army War College, imposed stiff tests for the promotion of officers, and created a general staff to oversee military planning and mobilization. Determined to end dependence on the British fleet, Roosevelt doubled the navy's strength during his term in office.

Stretching his authority to the limit, Roosevelt took steps to consolidate the country's new position in the Caribbean and Central America. European powers, which had long resisted American initiatives there, now accepted American supremacy. Preoccupied with problems elsewhere, Great Britain agreed to U.S. plans for a canal across the isthmus of Central America, withdrawing military forces from the area. Secretary of State John Hay negotiated with Britain the Hay-Pauncefote

Treaty of 1901, which permitted the United States to construct and control an isthmian canal, providing it would be free and open to ships of all nations.

Delighted, Roosevelt set to selecting the course. One route, 50 miles long, wandered through the rough, swampy terrain of the Panama region of Colombia. A French company had recently tried and failed to dig a canal there. Another possible route, through mountainous Nicaragua, was four times as long but followed natural waterways, which would make construction easier. The Isthmian Canal Commission decided in 1899 that the shorter route through Panama was preferable.

Roosevelt backed the idea, and he authorized Hay to negotiate an agreement with the Colombian chargé d'affaires, Thomas Herrán. The Hay-Herrán Convention (1903) gave the United States a ninety-nine-year lease, with option for renewal, on a canal zone 6 miles wide. In exchange, the United States agreed to pay Colombia a onetime fee of $10 million and an annual rental of $250,000.

To Roosevelt's dismay, the Colombian Senate rejected the treaty. Calling the Colombians "contemptible little creatures," Roosevelt considered seizing Panama, then hinted that he would welcome a Panamanian revolt for independence. In November 1903, the Panamanians took the hint, and Roosevelt moved quickly to support them. Sending the cruiser *Nashville* to prevent Colombian troops from putting down the revolt, he promptly recognized the new republic of Panama.

Two weeks later, the **Hay-Bunau-Varilla Treaty** with Panama granted the United States control of a canal zone 10 miles wide across the Isthmus of Panama. In return, the United States guaranteed the independence of Panama and agreed to pay the same fees offered Colombia. On August 15, 1914, the first ocean steamer sailed through the completed canal, which cost $375 million to build.

Roosevelt's actions angered many Latin Americans. Colombian-American relations remained strained until 1921, when the United States agreed to pay Colombia $25 million in cash and give it preferential treatment in using the canal. For his part, however, Roosevelt stoutly defended his actions. "I took the Canal Zone," he said, "and let Congress debate; and while the debate goes on, the Canal does also."

The Roosevelt Corollary

With interests in Puerto Rico, Cuba, and the Canal Zone, the United States developed a Caribbean policy to ensure its dominance in the region. It established protectorates over some countries and subsidized others to keep them dependent. When necessary, it even purchased territories to keep them out of the hands of other powers, as in the case of the Virgin Islands, bought from Denmark in 1917 to prevent Germany from acquiring them.

From 1903 to 1920, the United States intervened often in Latin America to protect the canal, promote regional stability, and exclude foreign influence. One problem worrisome to American policymakers was the scale of Latin American debts to European powers. Many countries in the Western Hemisphere owed money to European governments and banks, yet these same nations were poor, prone to revolution, and unable to pay. The situation invited European intervention. In 1902, Venezuela defaulted on debts; England, Germany, and Italy sent Venezuela an ultimatum and blockaded its ports. American pressure forced a settlement of the issue, but the general problem remained.

In 1904, when the Dominican Republic defaulted on its debts, Roosevelt was ready with a major announcement. Known as the **Roosevelt Corollary** to the Monroe Doctrine, the policy warned Latin American nations to keep their affairs in order or face American intervention. Applying the new policy immediately, the president took charge of the Dominican Republic's revenue system, and within two years, he had also established protectorates in Panama and Cuba. In Cuba, Roosevelt tied the action to the Platt Amendment to the Cuban constitution. Continued by Taft, Wilson, and other presidents, the Roosevelt Corollary guided

Hay-Bunau-Varilla Treaty A 1903 treaty granting the United States control over a canal zone 10 miles wide across the Isthmus of Panama. In return, the United States guaranteed the independence of Panama and agreed to pay Colombia a onetime fee of $10 million and an annual rental of $250,000.

Roosevelt Corollary President Theodore Roosevelt's 1904 foreign policy statement, a corollary to the Monroe Doctrine, asserting that the United States would intervene in Latin American affairs if the countries themselves could not keep their affairs in order. It effectively made the United States the policeman of the Western Hemisphere.

■ *A cartoon from* Judge *titled "The World's Constable." The Roosevelt Corollary claimed the right of the United States to exercise "an international police power," enforced by what many referred to as a "big stick" diplomacy.* ■

American policy in Latin America until the 1930s, when Franklin D. Roosevelt's Good Neighbor policy replaced it.

Ventures in the Far East

The Open Door policy toward China and possession of the Philippine Islands shaped American actions in the Far East. Roosevelt wanted to balance Russian and Japanese power in the area, and he was not unhappy at first when war broke out between them in 1904. As Japan won victory after victory, however, Roosevelt became concerned. He accepted Japan's request to mediate the conflict and in August 1905 convened a peace conference at Portsmouth, New Hampshire. The conference ended the war, but Japan emerged as the dominant force in the Far East. Adjusting policy, Roosevelt sent Secretary of War Taft to Tokyo to negotiate the Taft-Katsura Agreement (1905), which recognized Japan's dominance over Korea in return for its promise not to invade the Philippines. Giving Japan a free hand in Korea violated the Open Door policy, but Roosevelt argued that he had little choice.

In a show of strength, he sent the American fleet around the world, including a safe stop in Tokyo in October 1908. For the moment, Japanese-American relations improved, despite Japan's resentment over the segregation of Asian children in San Francisco's public schools in 1906. In 1908, the two nations signed the comprehensive Root-Takahira Agreement in which they promised to maintain the status quo in the Pacific, uphold the Open Door, and support Chinese independence.

In later years, tensions grew in the Far East. Japan's anger mounted in 1913 when the California legislature prohibited Japanese residents from owning property in the state. By the start of the First World War, Japan longed for an Asian empire and eyed American possessions in the Pacific.

In foreign as well as domestic affairs, President Taft tried to continue Roosevelt's policies. As secretary of state he chose Philander C. Knox, and together they pursued a policy of **dollar diplomacy** to promote American financial and

dollar diplomacy This policy, adopted by President William Howard Taft and Secretary of State Philander C. Knox, sought to promote U.S. financial and business interests abroad and to replace military alliances with economic ties, with the idea of increasing American influence and securing lasting peace.

business interests abroad. The policy had profit-seeking motives, but it also aimed to substitute economic ties for military alliances and bring lasting peace.

In the Far East, Knox worked closely with Willard Straight, an agent of American bankers, who argued that dollar diplomacy was the financial arm of the Open Door. However, Knox's attempt to convince England, Japan, and Russia to join the United States in an international syndicate to loan China money to purchase the Manchurian railroads failed. The outcome was a blow to American policy and prestige in Asia. Instead of cultivating friendship, as Roosevelt had envisioned, Taft started an intense rivalry with Japan for commercial advantage in China.

FOREIGN POLICY UNDER WILSON

When he took office in 1913, Woodrow Wilson knew little about foreign policy. "It would be the irony of fate if my administration had to deal chiefly with foreign affairs," he told a friend. And so it was. During his two terms, Wilson faced crisis after crisis in this area, including the outbreak of World War I.

A supremely self-confident man, Wilson conducted his own diplomacy. He had little respect for the party regulars who received diplomatic posts as patronage plums. He composed important diplomatic notes on his own typewriter, sent personal emissaries abroad, and carried on major negotiations without the knowledge of his secretary of state. The idealistic Wilson believed in a principled, ethical world in which militarism, colonialism, and war were brought under control. Rejecting the policy of dollar diplomacy, Wilson initially chose a course of **moral diplomacy,** designed to bring right to the world, preserve peace, and extend to other people the blessings of democracy.

moral diplomacy Policy adopted by President Woodrow Wilson that rejected the approach of dollar diplomacy. Rather than focusing mainly on economic ties with other nations, Wilson's policy was designed to bring right principles to the world, preserve peace, and extend to other peoples the blessings of democracy.

Conducting Moral Diplomacy

William Jennings Bryan, whom Wilson appointed as secretary of state, was also an amateur in foreign relations. A populist who put his trust in the common people, he was skeptical of experts in the State Department. Bryan was a fervent pacifist, and like Wilson, he believed in the American duty to "help" less favored nations.

In 1913 and 1914, he embarked on an idealistic campaign to negotiate treaties of arbitration throughout the world. Known as "cooling-off" treaties, they provided for submitting all international disputes to permanent commissions of investigation. Neither party could declare war or increase armaments until the investigation ended. The idea drew on the popularity of commissions and a sense that reasonable people could settle disputes without resorting to war. Bryan negotiated cooling-off treaties with thirty nations, but none was ever used.

Wilson and Bryan promised a dramatic new approach in Latin America, concerned not with the "pursuit of material interest" but with "human rights" and "national integrity." Their promise, however, went unfulfilled, and in the end, they continued the Roosevelt-Taft policies. Wilson defended the Monroe Doctrine, gave unspoken support to the Roosevelt Corollary, and intervened in Latin America more than either Roosevelt or Taft had. By 1917, American troops "protected" Nicaragua, Haiti, the Dominican Republic, and Cuba.

Troubles Across the Border

Porfirio Díaz, president of Mexico for thirty-seven years, was overthrown in 1911. Díaz had encouraged foreign investments in Mexican mines, railroads, oil, and land; by 1913, Americans had invested more than $1 billion. His overthrow led to a decade of violence that tested Wilson's policies and brought the United States close to war with Mexico.

A liberal reformer, Francisco I. Madero, followed Díaz as president. But Madero soon lost control of the troubled country. With support from wealthy landowners,

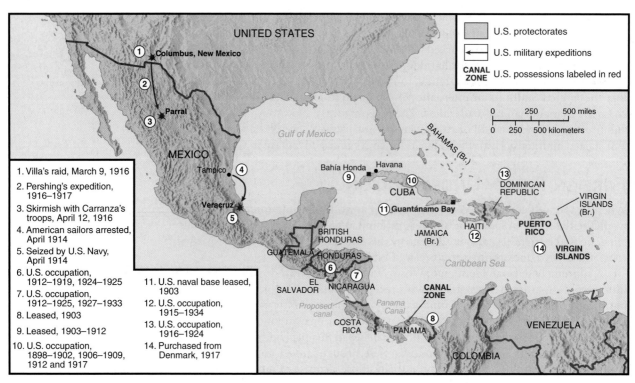

1. Villa's raid, March 9, 1916
2. Pershing's expedition, 1916–1917
3. Skirmish with Carranza's troops, April 12, 1916
4. American sailors arrested, April 1914
5. Seized by U.S. Navy, April 1914
6. U.S. occupation, 1912–1919, 1924–1925
7. U.S. occupation, 1912–1925, 1927–1933
8. Leased, 1903
9. Leased, 1903–1912
10. U.S. occupation, 1898–1902, 1906–1909, 1912 and 1917
11. U.S. naval base leased, 1903
12. U.S. occupation, 1915–1934
13. U.S. occupation, 1916–1924
14. Purchased from Denmark, 1917

ACTIVITIES OF THE UNITED STATES IN THE CARIBBEAN, 1898–1930s　*During the first three decades of the twentieth century, the United States policed the Caribbean, claiming the right to take action when it judged Latin American countries were doing a bad job of running their affairs.* ■

the army, and the Catholic Church, General Victoriano Huerta ousted Madero in 1913, threw him in jail, and arranged his murder. Most European nations immediately recognized Huerta, but Wilson refused to do so. Instead, he announced a new policy toward revolutionary regimes in Latin America. To win American recognition, they must not only exercise power but also reflect "a just government based upon law, not upon arbitrary or irregular force."

On that basis, Wilson withheld recognition from Huerta and maneuvered to oust him. Early in 1914, Wilson stationed naval units off Mexico's ports to cut off arms shipments to the Huerta regime. On April 9, 1914, several American sailors, ashore in Tampico to purchase supplies, were arrested. They were promptly released, but the American admiral demanded an apology and a twenty-one-gun salute to the American flag. Huerta agreed—if the Americans also saluted the Mexican flag.

Shortly after Wilson asked Congress for authority to use military force if needed, he learned that a German ship was landing arms at Veracruz on Mexico's eastern coast. With Wilson's approval, American warships shelled the harbor, and marines took the city. Outraged, Mexicans of all factions denounced the invasion, and for a time, the two countries hovered on the edge of war. Only a hasty diplomatic retreat by Wilson avoided more serious hostilities.

In July 1914, cut off from funds, Huerta resigned. Wilson recognized the new government, headed by Venustiano Carranza. Early in 1916, Francisco ("Pancho") Villa, one of Carranza's generals, revolted. Hoping to goad the United States into an action that would help him seize power, he raided border towns, injuring American civilians. Stepping up his assault, Villa murdered thirty-three Americans in Mexico and the United States.

Stationing militia along the border, Wilson ordered General John J. Pershing on a punitive expedition to seize Villa in Mexico. Pershing led six thousand troops deep into Mexican territory. The expedition was a failure. Carranza protested, Villa eluded Pershing, and Wilson finally ordered his general home.

Wilson's policy had laudable goals: he wanted to help the Mexicans achieve political and agrarian reform. But his motives and methods were condescending. With little forethought, he interfered in the affairs of another country, and in doing so, he revealed the themes—moralism combined with pragmatic self-interest and a desire for peace—that also shaped his policies in Europe.

TOWARD WAR

By May 1914, the mood in Europe was tense. Large armies dominated the Continent. A web of alliances entangled nations, maximizing the risk that a local conflict could trigger a wider war. Germany and its allies Austria-Hungary and Turkey dominated central Europe. Linked in their own alliance, England, France, and Russia agreed to aid each other in case of attack.

On June 28, 1914, a Balkan assassin in the service of Serbia murdered Archduke Franz Ferdinand, heir to the Austro-Hungarian throne. Within weeks, Germany, Turkey, and Austria-Hungary (the Central Powers) were at war with England, France, and Russia (the Allied Powers). Americans were shocked at the events. Wilson immediately proclaimed neutrality and asked Americans to remain "impartial in thought as well as in action." Privately, Wilson was stunned. A lifelong admirer of the British and their government, he said, "Everything I love most in the world is at stake."

The Neutrality Policy

In general, Americans accepted neutrality. They saw no need to enter the conflict, especially after the Allies in September 1914 halted the first German drive toward Paris. Many progressives saw added reason to resist. War violated the very spirit of progressive reform. Why demand safer factories and then kill men by the millions in war? Progressives and others tended to put the blame for war on the greed of "munition manufacturers, stockbrokers, and bond dealers" eager for wartime profits. Above all, progressives were sure that war would end reform. It consumed money and attention; it inflamed emotions. As a result, many progressives—including Jane Addams, Frederick C. Howe, and Lillian Wald—fought to keep the United States out of war.

The war's outbreak also tugged at the emotions of millions of immigrant Americans. Those who came from the British Isles tended to support the Allies; those from Ireland tended to support Germany, hoping that Britain's wartime troubles might free their homeland from British domination. The large population of German Americans often sympathized with the Central Powers.

At the deepest level, a majority in the country, bound by common language and institutions, sympathized with the Allies and blamed Germany for the war. When the war began, Germany invaded Belgium to strike at France, in violation of a

A Look at the Past

Sheet Music Cover

In 1915, the song "I Didn't Raise My Boy to Be a Soldier," written by Alfred Bryan and Al Piantadosi and performed by many different singers, was very popular in the United States. This cover of the song's sheet music includes a photograph of one of the song's performers and an illustration of a mother embracing her son with scenes of battle in their thoughts. ✱ What emotions do you think this image stirred in its audience? What do the song title and cover art suggest about the role women played in the peace movement during World War I? Do the sentiments expressed by this cover help explain why it took years before the United States entered the war?

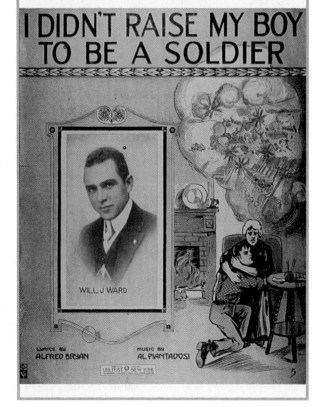

treaty, which the German chancellor called "just a scrap of paper." Many Americans resented this arrogance and were even more aghast when German troops executed Belgian civilians who resisted. Both sides sought to sway American opinion, and fierce propaganda campaigns flourished. But in the end, the propaganda probably made little difference. Ties of heritage and the course of the war decided the American position. But whichever side they cheered for, Americans preferred simply to remain at peace.

Freedom of the Seas

The demands of trade tested American neutrality and confronted Wilson with difficult choices. Under international law, neutral countries were permitted to trade in nonmilitary goods with all belligerent countries. But Great Britain controlled the seas, and it intended to cut off shipments of war materials to the Central Powers.

As soon as war broke out, Britain blockaded German ports and limited the goods Americans could sell to Germany. As time passed, Britain stepped up the economic sanctions by forbidding the shipment to Germany of all foodstuffs and most raw materials. British ships often stopped U.S. ships and confiscated cargoes.

Again and again, Wilson protested such infringements of neutral rights. Sometimes Britain complied, sometimes not, and Wilson often grew angry. But needing American support and supplies, Britain pursued a careful strategy to disrupt German-American trade without disrupting Anglo-American relations. When necessary, it paid (or promised to pay) American businesses for lost trade with Germany.

Other than the German U-boats, there were no constraints on trade with the Allies, and a flood of Allied war orders fueled the American economy. To finance the purchases, the Allies turned to American bankers for loans. By 1917, loans to Allied governments exceeded $2 billion, while loans to Germany came to only $27 million.

Loans and trade drew the United States ever closer to the Allied cause. And even though Wilson often protested British maritime policy, the protests involved American goods and money, whereas Germany's submarine policy threatened American lives.

The U-Boat Threat

A relatively new weapon, the submarine strained the guidelines of international law. Traditional law required a submarine to surface, warn the target to stop, send a boarding party to check papers and cargo, and then allow time for passengers and crew to board lifeboats before sinking the vessel. Flimsy and slow, submarines could ill afford to surface while the prey radioed for help. If they did surface, they might be rammed or blown up by deck guns.

When Germany announced its submarine campaign in February 1915, Wilson protested sharply. The Germans promised not to sink American ships, and thereafter the issue became the right of Americans to sail on the ships of belligerent nations. Bryan urged Wilson to forbid Americans to travel in the war zones, but the president, determined to stand by the principles of international law, refused.

Wilson reacted more harshly in May 1915 when U-boats sank the *Lusitania* and again in August when they attacked the *Arabic.* He demanded that the Germans protect passenger vessels and pay for American losses. Fearing war, Bryan resigned as secretary of state and was replaced by Robert Lansing, a State Department counselor who favored the Allies. He urged strong stands against German violations of American neutrality.

In February 1916, Germany declared unrestricted submarine warfare against all *armed* ships. A month later, a U-boat torpedoed the unarmed French channel steamer *Sussex,* without warning, injuring several Americans. Lansing urged Wilson to break relations with Germany. On April 18, Wilson sent an ultimatum to Germany that unless it immediately called off attacks on cargo and passenger ships, the United States would sever relations. Germany's kaiser, convinced he did not yet have enough submarines to risk war, yielded. In the *Sussex* pledge of May 4, 1916, he agreed to Wilson's demands and promised to shoot on sight only ships of the enemy's navy. He tried to impose the condition that the United States compel the Allies to end their blockade.

The *Sussex* pledge marked the beginning of a short period of friendly relations between Germany and the United States. The agreement applied not just to passenger liners but to *all* merchant ships, belligerent or not. There was one problem: Wilson had taken such a strong position that if Germany renewed submarine warfare on merchant shipping, war with the United States was likely. Nevertheless, most Americans viewed the agreement as a diplomatic stroke for peace by Wilson, and the issues of peace and preparedness dominated the presidential election of 1916.

"He Kept Us Out of War"

The preparedness issue pitted antiwar groups against those who wanted to ready themselves for war. The American Rights Committee and other groups urged stepped-up military measures. In the summer of 1915, they persuaded the War Department to hold a training camp in Plattsburg, New York, in which regular army officers trained civilian volunteers in modern warfare.

Bellicose as always, Teddy Roosevelt led the preparedness campaign. He called Wilson "yellow" for not pressing Germany harder. Defending the military's state of readiness, Wilson refused to be stampeded just because "some amongst us are nervous and excited."

Wilson's position was attacked from both sides: preparedness advocates charged cowardice, while pacifists denounced any attempt at military readiness. The difficulty of his position, plus the growing U-boat crisis, soon changed Wilson's mind. In mid-1915, he asked the War Department to increase military planning, and he quietly notified congressional leaders of a switch in policy. Later that year, Wilson approved large increases in expenditures for the army and navy, a move that upset many peace-minded progressives.

As their standard-bearer in the presidential election of 1916, the Republicans nominated Charles Evans Hughes, a moderate justice of the Supreme Court. Hughes, a dull campaigner, called for a tougher line against Germany. The Democrats nominated Wilson in a convention marked by spontaneous demonstrations for peace. Picking up the antiwar theme, perhaps with reservation, Wilson said in October: "I am not expecting this country to get into war." The campaign slogan, "He kept us out of war," was repeated again and again.

On election night, Hughes had swept most of the East, and Wilson retired at 10 P.M., thinking he had lost. During the night, the results came in from California, New Mexico, and North Dakota; all supported Wilson. Holding the Democratic South, Wilson carried key states in the Midwest and West and won re-election. He took large portions of the labor and progressive vote, and women—who could vote in presidential elections in twelve states—voted heavily for him.

The Final Months of Peace

Just before election day, Great Britain further limited neutral trade, and there were reports from Germany of a renewal of unrestricted submarine warfare. Fresh from his election victory, Wilson redoubled his efforts for peace.

In December 1916, he sent messages to both sides asking them to state their war aims. The Allies refused, although they promised privately to negotiate if the German terms were reasonable. The Germans replied evasively but in January 1917

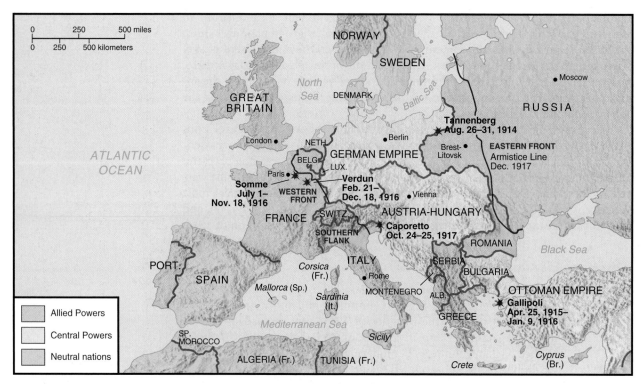

EUROPEAN ALLIANCES AND BATTLEFRONTS, 1914–1917 *Allied forces suffered early defeats on the eastern front (Tannenberg) and in the Dardanelles (Gallipoli). In 1917, the Allies were routed on the southern flank (Caporetto); the western theater then became the critical arena of the war.* ■

revealed their real objectives. Close to forcing Russia out of the war, Germany sensed victory and craved territory—in eastern Europe, Africa, Belgium, and France.

On January 22, in an eloquent speech before the Senate, Wilson called for a "peace without victory." Outlining his own aims, he urged respect for all nations, freedom of the seas, arms limitations, and a league of nations to keep the peace. The speech made a great impression on many Europeans, but it was too late. The Germans had decided a few weeks before to unleash the submarines and gamble on a quick end to the war.

On January 31, the German ambassador in Washington informed Lansing that beginning February 1, U-boats would sink on sight all ships—passenger or merchant, neutral or belligerent, armed or unarmed—in the waters around England and France. German leaders estimated that if their submarine campaign were successful, they could win the war in six months. As he had pledged in 1916, Wilson broke off relations with Germany, although he still hoped for peace.

On February 25, the British government privately gave Wilson a telegram intercepted from Arthur Zimmermann, the German foreign minister, to the German ambassador in Mexico. A day later, Wilson asked Congress for authority to arm merchant ships to deter U-boat attacks. To prevent a filibuster, Wilson divulged the contents of the Zimmermann telegram: it proposed an alliance with Mexico in case of war with the United States, offering financial support and recovery of Mexico's "lost territory" in Texas, New Mexico, and Arizona.

Spurred by a wave of public indignation, the House passed Wilson's measure, but La Follette and others still blocked action in the Senate. On March 9, 1917, Wilson ordered merchant ships armed on his own authority. Between March 12 and March 21, U-boats sank five American ships, and Wilson decided to wait no longer. He called Congress into special session and at 8:30 in the evening on April 2, 1917, asked for a declaration of war. Americans, he said, "shall fight for the things which we have always carried nearest our hearts—for democracy."

OVER THERE

With a burst of patriotism, the United States entered a war its new allies were in danger of losing. That same month, the Germans sank 881,000 tons of Allied shipping, the greatest amount of the war. Mutinies broke out in the French army, and a costly British drive in Flanders stalled. In November, the Bolsheviks seized power in Russia and soon signed a separate peace treaty with Germany, freeing German troops to concentrate on the fight in the west. German and Austrian forces routed the Italian army on their southern flank, and the Allies braced for a spring 1918 offensive.

The United States was not prepared for war. Some Americans hoped that the declaration of war itself might daunt the Germans; others hoped that money and arms, not troops, would be sufficient to produce victory. Bypassing older generals, Wilson named John J. "Black Jack" Pershing to head the American Expeditionary Force (AEF). The army Pershing inherited was small and poorly equipped. Its most recent battle experience had been chasing Pancho Villa unsuccessfully around northern Mexico. And it had no war plans to fight Germany in Europe.

Mobilization

Although some members of Congress preferred a voluntary army of the kind that had fought in the Spanish-American War, Wilson turned to conscription, which he believed was both efficient and democratic. In May 1917, Congress passed the **Selective Service Act,** providing for the registration of all men between the ages of 21 and 30. The act eventually accounted for the induction of about 2.8 million men into the army.

The draft included black men as well as white, and four African American regiments were among the first sent into action. Despite their contributions, however, no black soldiers were allowed to march in the victory celebration that eventually took place in Paris.

Selective Service Act This 1917 law provided for the registration of all American men between the ages of 21 and 30 for a military draft. The age limits were later changed to 18 and 45.

War in the Trenches

The Great War, later referred to as World War I, may have been the most terrible war of all time. After the early offensive, the European armies dug themselves into trenches, in places only hundreds of yards apart. Artillery, poison gas, hand grenades, and a new weapon—rapid-fire machine guns—kept them pinned down. Even in moments of respite, the mud, rats, cold, fear, and disease took a heavy toll. Deafening bombardments shook the earth, and there was a high incidence of the psychological disorder known as "shell shock." From time to time, troops went "over the top" of the embankments in an effort to break through, but the costs were enormous and the gains slight.

The first American soldiers reached France in June 1917. By the war's end, two million men had crossed the Atlantic. No troop ships were sunk, a credit to the British and American navies. After the summer of 1917, a convoy system developed by Admiral William S. Sims that used Allied destroyers to escort merchant vessels across the ocean cut shipping losses in half.

As expected, on March 21, 1918, the Germans launched a massive assault in western Europe. By May, they had driven Allied forces back to the Marne River, just 50 miles from Paris. More than 27,000 Americans saw their first action. They blocked the Germans at the town of Château-Thierry and four weeks later forced them out of Belleau Wood, a crucial strongpoint. On July 15, the Germans threw everything into a last drive for Paris, but in three days they were finished.

With the German drive stalled, the Allies counterattacked along the entire front. On September 12, 1918, half a million Americans and a smaller contingent of French drove the Germans from the St.-Mihiel salient. Two weeks later, 896,000 Americans attacked between the Meuse River and the Argonne Forest. Focusing on the main railroad supply line for the German army in the West, they broke

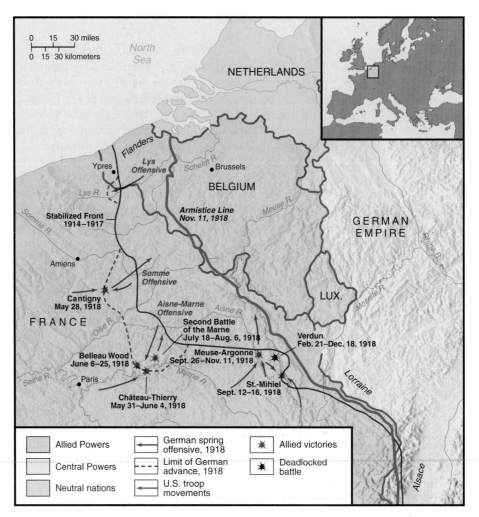

THE WESTERN FRONT: U.S. PARTICIPATION, 1918   *The turning point of the war came in July, when the German advance was halted at the Marne. The "Yanks," now a fighting force, were thrown into the breach. They played a dramatic role in stemming the tide and mounting the counteroffensives that ended the war.* ∎

through in early November, cut the line, and drove the Germans back along the whole front.

The German high command knew that the war was lost. At 4 A.M. on November 11, Germany signed the armistice. The AEF lost 48,909 soldiers, and 230,000 were wounded; losses to disease brought the total dead to more than 112,000. The American contribution was vital, although small in comparison to the enormous costs to European nations, which lost more than three million soldiers. Fresh, enthusiastic American troops raised Allied morale; they helped turn the tide at a crucial point in the war. American soldiers, white and black, distinguished themselves during the last months of the terrible war.

OVER HERE

Victory at the front depended on economic and emotional mobilization at home. Consolidating federal authority, Wilson moved quickly in 1917 and 1918 to organize war production and distribution. An idealist who knew how to sway public

In The Victorious Retreat Back to the Rhine *(1918), American illustrator and painter Frank Schoonover captures the intensity of aerial bombardment supporting the gathering momentum of Allied ground forces to drive back the Germans in the final stages of the war.* ■

opinion, he also recognized the need to enlist American emotions. To him, the war for people's minds, the "conquest of their convictions," was as vital as events on the battlefield.

The Conquest of Convictions

A week after war was declared, Wilson formed the **Committee on Public Information (CPI)** and asked George Creel, an outspoken progressive journalist, to head it. Creel recruited thousands of people in the arts, advertising, and the film industry to publicize the war. He worked out a system of voluntary censorship with the press, plastered walls with colorful posters, and issued more than 75 million pamphlets.

Creel also enlisted 75,000 "four-minute men" to give quick speeches at public gatherings and places of entertainment on the themes "Why We Are Fighting" and "The Meaning of America." By 1918, they were portraying the Germans as bloodthirsty Huns bent on world conquest. Exploiting a new medium, the CPI promoted films such as *The Kaiser: The Beast of Berlin*. Creel secretly subsidized several prowar groups and formed the CPI's Division of Industrial Relations to rally labor to the war.

Helped along by the propaganda campaign, anti-German sentiment spread rapidly. Many schools stopped offering instruction in the German language, sauerkraut was renamed "liberty cabbage," and orchestral works by Bach, Beethoven, and

Committee on Public Information (CPI) Created in 1917 by President Wilson and headed by progressive journalist George Creel, this organization rallied support for American involvement in World War I through art, advertising, and film.

Brahms vanished from some symphonic programs. German Americans and anti-war figures were badgered, beaten, and in some cases killed.

Vigilantism, sparked often by superpatriotism of a ruthless sort, flourished. Frequently, it focused on radical antiwar figures such as Frank Little, an IWW official in Butte, Montana, who was taken from his boardinghouse in August 1917, tied to the rear of an automobile, and dragged through the street until his kneecaps were scraped off. He was then hanged.

Rather than curbing the repression, Wilson encouraged it. At his request, Congress passed the **Espionage Act** of 1917, which authorized sentences of up to twenty years in prison for persons found guilty of aiding the enemy, obstructing the recruitment of soldiers, or encouraging disloyalty. It allowed the postmaster general to remove from the mails materials that incited treason or insurrection.

In 1918, Congress passed the **Sedition Act,** imposing harsh penalties on anyone using "disloyal, profane, scurrilous, or abusive language" about the U.S. government, flag, or uniform. In all, more than fifteen hundred persons were arrested under the new laws, some for such trivial offenses as laughing at rookies drilling at an army camp.

The sedition laws clearly went beyond any clear or present danger. There were German spies in the country, to be sure, but the threat did not warrant a nationwide program of repression. Conservatives seized on the laws to stamp out socialists. In 1918, Eugene V. Debs, the Socialist party leader, delivered a speech denouncing cap-

Espionage Act This law, passed after the United States entered World War I, imposed sentences of up to twenty years on anyone found guilty of aiding the enemy, obstructing recruitment of soldiers, or encouraging disloyalty. It allowed the postmaster general to remove from the mail any materials that incited treason or insurrection.

Sedition Act A wartime law that imposed harsh penalties on anyone using "disloyal, profane, scurrilous, or abusive language" about the U.S. government, flag, or armed forces.

A Look at the Past

Americanization Poster

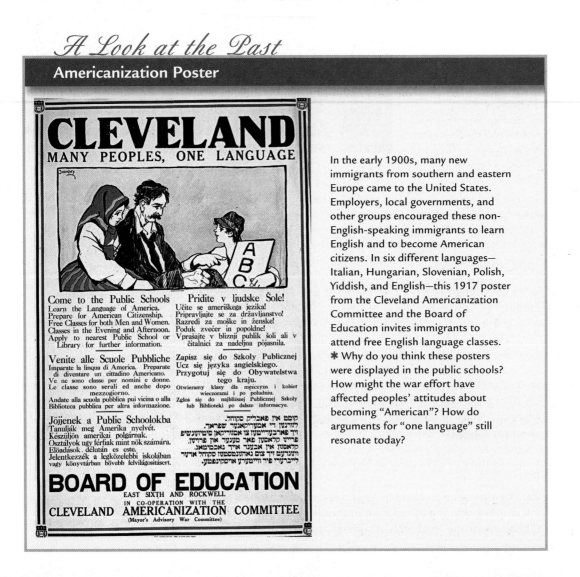

In the early 1900s, many new immigrants from southern and eastern Europe came to the United States. Employers, local governments, and other groups encouraged these non-English-speaking immigrants to learn English and to become American citizens. In six different languages—Italian, Hungarian, Slovenian, Polish, Yiddish, and English—this 1917 poster from the Cleveland Americanization Committee and the Board of Education invites immigrants to attend free English language classes. * Why do you think these posters were displayed in the public schools? How might the war effort have affected peoples' attitudes about becoming "American"? How do arguments for "one language" still resonate today?

italism and the war. He was convicted for violation of the Espionage Act and spent the war in a penitentiary in Atlanta. Nominated as the Socialist party candidate in the presidential election of 1920, Debs—prisoner 9653—won nearly a million votes, but the socialist movement never fully recovered from the repression of the war.

In fostering hostility toward anything that smacked of dissent, the war also gave rise to the great Red Scare that began in 1919. Pleased at first with the Russian Revolution, Americans turned quickly against it after Lenin and the Bolsheviks seized control late in 1917. The Americans feared Lenin's anticapitalist program, and they denounced his decision in early 1918 to make peace with Germany because it freed German troops to fight in France. In the summer of 1918, Wilson even cooperated with the Allied leaders and sent American troops into Russia in an attempt to bring down the fledgling Bolshevik government. Although the plan failed to achieve its goals, Wilson joined in an economic blockade of Russia, sent weapons to anti-Bolshevik insurgents, and refused to recognize Lenin's government. His actions soured Russian-American relations for decades.

A Bureaucratic War

Quick, effective action was needed to win the war. To meet the need, Wilson and Congress set up an array of new federal agencies, nearly five thousand in all. Staffed largely by businessmen, the agencies drew on funds and powers of hitherto unknown scope.

The **War Industries Board (WIB),** one of the most powerful of the agencies, oversaw the production of all American factories. Headed by millionaire Bernard M.

FOOD WILL WIN THE WAR
You came here seeking Freedom
You must now help to preserve it
WHEAT is needed for the allies
Waste nothing
204   UNITED   STATES   FOOD   ADMINISTRATION

◾ *The U.S. Food Administration urged immigrants and newcomers to America to make sacrifices in the cause of freedom.* ◾

Baruch, it determined priorities, allocated raw materials, and fixed prices. It told manufacturers what they could and could not make. Working closely with business, Baruch for a time acted as the dictator of the American economy.

Herbert Hoover, the hero of a campaign to feed starving Belgians, headed a new **Food Administration,** and he set out with customary energy to supply food to the armies overseas. Appealing to the "spirit of self-sacrifice," Hoover convinced people to save food by observing meatless and wheatless days. He fixed prices to boost production, bought and distributed wheat, and encouraged people to plant "victory gardens" at their homes, churches, and schools.

Other agencies rationed fuel and regulated railroads, shipping, and foreign trade. The government intervened in American life as never before: when strikes threatened the telephone and telegraph companies, it simply seized and ran them. The partnership between government and business grew closer. As government expanded, business expanded as well, responding to wartime contracts. Industries such as steel, aluminum, and cigarettes boomed in a war that displayed the triumph of large-scale industrial organization.

Labor in the War

The war also brought organized labor into the partnership with government, although the results were more limited than in the business-government alliance. Samuel Gompers, president of the AFL, served on Wilson's Council of National Defense, an advisory group formed to unify business, labor, and government.

War Industries Board (WIB) A wartime government agency that determined priorities, allocated raw materials, and fixed prices; it told manufacturers what they could and could not produce.

Food Administration A wartime government agency that encouraged Americans to save food in order to supply the armies overseas. It fixed prices to boost production, asked people to observe meatless and wheatless days to conserve food, and promoted the planting of "victory gardens" behind homes, schools, and churches.

Gompers hoped to trade labor peace for labor advances, and he formed the War Committee on Labor to enlist workers' support for the war. With the blessing of the Wilson administration, union membership grew rapidly during the war.

Hoping to encourage production and avoid strikes, Wilson adopted many of the objectives of the social-justice reformers. He supported an eight-hour workday in war-related industries and improved wages and working conditions. The War Labor Board (WLB), headed by Felix Frankfurter, standardized wages and hours, and at Wilson's direction, it protected the right of labor to organize and bargain collectively. Although it did not forbid strikes, it used various tactics to discourage them.

The WLB also ordered that women be paid equal wages for equal work in war industries. Women, blacks, and Mexican Americans filled the labor shortage caused by the draft and the end of large-scale European immigration to America. A million women worked in war industries. Although most held "women's jobs," some were given new opportunities and in some cases higher pay. Working women shared a new sense of confidence and increased expectations.

Looking for more people to fill wartime jobs, corporations found another major source among southern blacks. Beginning in 1916, northern labor agents traveled across the South, promising jobs, high wages, and free transportation. The movement northward became a flood. Between 1916 and 1918, nearly half a million blacks left the Old South for the booming industrial cities of St. Louis, Chicago, Detroit, and Cleveland.

Most of the newcomers were young, unmarried, and semiskilled. The men found jobs in factories, railroad yards, steel mills, packing houses, and coal mines; the women worked in textile factories, department stores, and restaurants. In their new homes, blacks found greater racial freedom but also different living conditions. Northern industrial society struck many blacks as impersonal and lonely, a society ruled by clocks and shop supervisors.

Racial tensions increased, resulting in part from growing competition for housing and jobs. In 1917, a race war in East St. Louis, Illinois, killed nine whites and about forty blacks. In 1919, race riots occurred in Washington, Chicago, New York City, and Omaha. Lynch mobs killed forty-eight blacks in 1917, sixty-three in 1918, and seventy-eight in 1919. Ten of the victims in 1919 were war veterans, several still in uniform.

Blacks were more and more inclined to fight back. Two hundred thousand black soldiers had served in France—42,000 as combat troops. Returning home, they expected better treatment. W. E. B. Du Bois spoke of a "New Negro," proud and more militant: "We return. We return from fighting. We return fighting."

Eager for cheap labor, farmers and ranchers in the Southwest persuaded the federal government to relax immigration restrictions, and between 1917 and 1920, more than 100,000 Mexicans migrated into Texas, New Mexico, Arizona, and California. Tens of thousands of Mexican Americans moved to Chicago, St. Louis, Omaha, and other northern cities to take wartime jobs. Often scorned and insecure, they created urban *barrios,* similar to the Chinatowns and Little Italys around them.

Like most wars, World War I affected patterns at home as much as abroad. Business profits grew, factories expanded, and industries turned out huge amounts of war goods. Government authority swelled, and people came to expect different things of their government. Labor made some gains, as did women and blacks. Society assimilated some of the shifts, but social and economic tensions continued to grow, and when the war ended, they spilled over in the strikes and violence of the Red Scare of 1919 (see Chapter 25).

The United States emerged from the war the strongest economic power in the world. In 1914, it was a debtor nation: American citizens owed foreign investors about $3 billion. Five years later, the United States had become a creditor nation.

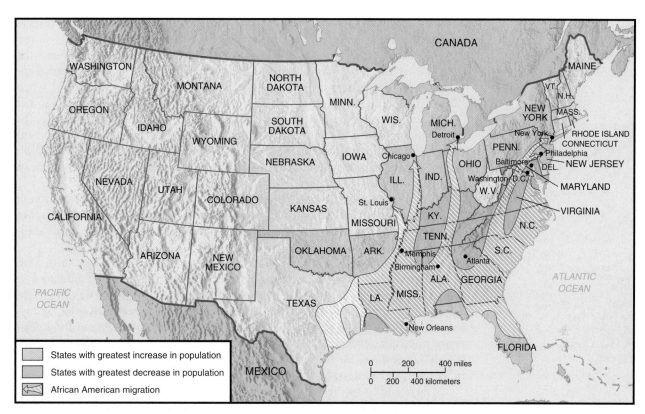

AFRICAN AMERICAN MIGRATION NORTHWARD, 1910–1920   *The massive migration of African Americans from the South to the North during World War I changed the dynamics of race relations in the United States.* ∎

Foreign governments owed more than $10 billion, and foreign citizens owed American investors nearly $3 billion. The war marked a drastic shift in economic power between Europe and America.

THE TREATY OF VERSAILLES

Long before the fighting ended, Wilson began to formulate plans for the peace. On January 8, 1918, appearing before Congress to rebut Bolshevik arguments that the war was merely a struggle among imperialists, the president outlined terms for a far-reaching, nonpunitive settlement. Wilson's **Fourteen Points** were generous and farsighted, but they failed to satisfy wartime emotions.

England and France distrusted Wilsonian idealism as the basis for peace. They wanted Germany disarmed and crippled; they wanted its colonies; and they were skeptical of the principle of self-determination. As the end of the war neared, the Allies, who had made secret commitments with one another, balked at making the Fourteen Points the basis of peace. When Wilson threatened to negotiate a separate treaty with Germany, however, they accepted. Wilson had won an important victory, but difficulties lay ahead.

Fourteen Points In January 1918, President Wilson presented these terms for a far-reaching, non-punitive settlement of World War I. He called for, among other things, removal of barriers to trade, open peace accords, reduction of armaments, and the establishment of a League of Nations. The Fourteen Points were largely rejected by European nations.

A Peace at Paris

Just before the peace conference began, Wilson appealed to voters to elect a Democratic Congress in the 1918 elections. The Democrats lost both the House and Senate, enabling Wilson's opponents to announce that voters had rejected his policies. In fact, the Democratic losses stemmed largely from domestic problems, but they hurt Wilson, who would soon be negotiating with European leaders buoyed by rousing victories at their own polls.

Two weeks after the election, Wilson announced that he would attend the peace conference. This was a dramatic break from tradition, and his personal involvement drew attacks from Republicans. They renewed the criticism when Wilson named no members of the Senate and no prominent Republicans to the delegation to attend the conference. Wilson passed over Henry Cabot Lodge, the powerful Republican senator from Massachusetts who opposed the Fourteen Points and would soon head the Senate Foreign Relations Committee. Wilson wanted a delegation he could control—an advantage at the peace table but not in any battle over the treaty at home.

Upon his arrival in Europe, Wilson received a tumultuous welcome in England, France, and Italy. Overwhelmed, Wilson was sure that people shared his goals, but he was wrong: like their leaders, they hated Germany and wanted victory unmistakably reflected in the peace plan.

Opening in January 1919, the Peace Conference at Paris continued until May. Although twenty-seven nations were represented, the "Big Four" dominated it: Wilson; Georges Clemenceau, the stubborn French premier who was determined to end the German threat forever; David Lloyd George, the crafty British prime minister who had pledged to squeeze Germany "until the pips squeak"; and the Italian prime minister, Vittorio Orlando. A clever negotiator, Wilson traded various "small" concessions for his major goals—national self-determination, a reduction in tensions, and a league of nations to enforce the peace.

Wilson had to surrender some important principles. Instead of peace without victory, the treaty made Germany accept responsibility for the war and demanded enormous reparations. It made no mention of disarmament, free trade, or freedom of the seas, and it violated the goal of self-determination. Instead of an open covenant openly arrived at, the treaty was drafted behind closed doors.

WOODROW WILSON'S FOURTEEN POINTS, 1918:
SUCCESS AND FAILURE IN IMPLEMENTATION

1. Open covenants of peace openly arrived at	Not fulfilled
2. Absolute freedom of navigation on the seas in peace and war	Not fulfilled
3. Removal of all economic barriers to the equality of trade among nations	Not fulfilled
4. Reduction of armaments to the level needed only for domestic safety	Not fulfilled
5. Impartial adjustments of colonial claims	Not fulfilled
6. Evacuation of all Russian territory; Russia to be welcomed into the society of free nations	Not fulfilled
7. Evacuation and restoration of Belgium	**Fulfilled**
8. Evacuation and restoration of all French lands; return of Alsace-Lorraine to France	**Fulfilled**
9. Readjustment of Italy's frontiers along lines of Italian nationality	Compromised
10. Self-determination for the former subjects of the Austro-Hungarian Empire	Compromised
11. Evacuation of Rumania, Serbia, and Montenegro; free access to the sea for Serbia	Compromised
12. Self-determination for the former subjects of the Ottoman Empire; secure sovereignty for Turkish portion	Compromised
13. Establishment of an independent Poland, with free and secure access to the sea	**Fulfilled**
14. Establishment of a League of Nations affording mutual guarantees of independence and territorial integrity	Not fulfilled

Sources: Data from G. M. Gathorne-Hardy, *The Fourteen Points and the Treaty of Versailles* (Oxford Pamphlets on World Affairs, no. 6, 1939), pp. 8–34; Thomas G. Paterson et al., *American Foreign Policy: A History Since 1900,* 2nd ed., vol. 2, pp. 282–293.

But Wilson deflected some of the most extreme Allied demands, and he won his coveted Point 14, the League of Nations, designed "to achieve international peace and security." The League included a general assembly; a smaller council composed of the United States, Great Britain, France, Italy, Japan, and four nations to be elected by the assembly; and a court of international justice. League members pledged to submit every dispute that threatened peace for arbitration and to enjoin military and economic sanctions against nations resorting to war. Article X, for Wilson the heart of the League, obligated members to protect each other's independence and territorial integrity.

Draft treaty in hand, Wilson returned home in February 1919 to discuss it with Congress and the people. Public opinion polls showed that most Americans favored the League, but there was strong congressional opposition to it. Thirty-seven senators, including Lodge, said they would not vote for the treaty without amendment. Should those numbers hold up, Lodge had enough votes to defeat it.

Returning to Paris, Wilson attacked his critics while privately working for changes to improve the chances of Senate approval. The Allies won major concessions in return, but they amended the League draft treaty, agreeing that domestic affairs remained outside the League's jurisdiction, exempting the Monroe Doctrine, and allowing nations to withdraw after two years' notice. On June 28, 1919, they signed the treaty in the Hall of Mirrors at Versailles, and Wilson started home for his most difficult fight.

EUROPE AFTER THE TREATY OF VERSAILLES, 1919 *The treaty changed the map of Europe, creating a number of new and reconstituted nations.* ■

Rejection in the Senate

There were ninety-six senators in 1919, forty-nine of them Republicans. Fourteen Republicans, led by William E. Borah of Idaho, were the "irreconcilables" who opposed the League on any grounds. Frank B. Kellogg of Minnesota led a group of twelve "mild reservationists" who accepted the treaty but wanted to insert several conditions that would not greatly weaken it. Finally, there were the Lodge-led "strong reservationists," twenty-three in all, who wanted major changes that the Allies would have to approve.

With only four Democratic senators opposed to the treaty, the Democrats and compromise-minded Republicans had enough votes to ratify it, once a few reservations were inserted. Playing for time to allow public opposition to grow, Lodge scheduled lengthy hearings on the treaty. Democratic leaders urged Wilson to appeal to the Republican "mild reservationists," but he angrily refused.

Fed up with Lodge's tactics, Wilson set out in early September to take the case directly to the people. In Pueblo, Colorado, toward the end of his tour, he delivered one of the most eloquent speeches of his career. That night, Wilson felt ill. He returned to Washington, and on October 2, his wife found him lying unconscious on the floor of the White House, the victim of a stroke that had paralyzed his left side.

After the stroke, Wilson could not work more than an hour or two at a time, and he saw very few people. He did not meet with the cabinet for seven months. When he learned that Secretary of State Lansing had convened cabinet meetings, Wilson forced the man to resign. Focusing his waning energy on the fight over the

■ *Humanity is the accuser, the U.S. Senate is the assassin, and the Treaty of Versailles is the victim in this commentary on the Senate's rejection of the treaty. Isolationists, who wanted to keep the United States out of European affairs, opposed the treaty because it included the Covenant for the League of Nations.* ■

treaty, Wilson lost touch with other issues, and critics charged that his wife, Edith Bolling Wilson, was running the government.

On November 6, 1919, Lodge finally reported the treaty out of committee, along with "Fourteen Reservations," one for each of Wilson's points. The most important reservation stipulated that implementation of Article X, Wilson's key article, required the action of Congress in each case.

Even though the Democrats could not pass the treaty without reservations, Wilson refused to compromise. When Mrs. Wilson urged her husband to accept the Lodge reservations, he said, "Better a thousand times to go down fighting than to dip your colors to dishonorable compromise."

On November 19, the treaty—with the Lodge reservations—failed, 39 to 55. Following Wilson's instructions, the Democrats voted against it. A motion to approve without the reservations lost 38 to 53, with only one Republican voting in favor. Neither Wilson nor Lodge would compromise. When the treaty with reservations again came up for vote on March 19, 1920, twenty-one Democrats defied Wilson and voted for it. But by a vote of 49 to 35, seven votes short of the necessary two-thirds majority, the treaty was defeated.

To Wilson, one chance remained: the presidential election of 1920. The Democrats nominated Governor James M. Cox of Ohio. Wilson called for "a great and solemn referendum" on the treaty. The Democratic platform endorsed the treaty but agreed to accept reservations to clarify the American role in the League.

On the Republican side, Senator Warren G. Harding of Ohio won the presidential nomination. Harding waffled on the treaty, but it made little difference. Voters wanted a change. Harding won in a landslide. Without a peace treaty, the United States remained technically at war, and it was not until July 1921, almost three years after the last shot was fired, that Congress passed a joint resolution ending the war.

CONCLUSION: POSTWAR DISILLUSIONMENT

After 1919, disillusionment set in. World War I was feared before it started, popular while it lasted, and hated when it ended. To a whole generation that followed, it appeared futile—killing without a cause, sacrifice without benefit. Books, plays, and movies—such as Hemingway's *Farewell to Arms,* John Dos Passos's *Three Soldiers,* and Lawrence Stallings and Maxwell Anderson's *What Price Glory?*—depicted waste, horror, and death.

The war and its aftermath damaged the progressive, humanitarian spirit of the early years of the century. It killed "something precious and perhaps irretrievable in the hearts of thinking men and women." Progressivism survived well into the 1920s and the New Deal, but it no longer had its old conviction or broad popular support. Bruising fights over the war and the League drained people's energy and enthusiasm.

Woodrow Wilson died in Washington in 1924, three years after the new president, Harding, promised "not heroics but healing; not nostrums but normalcy; not revolution but restoration." Nonetheless, the "war to end all wars" and the spirit of Woodrow Wilson left an indelible imprint on the country.

Chronology

1901	Hay-Paunceforte Treaty empowers United States to build an isthmian canal
1904	Theodore Roosevelt introduces his Corollary to the Monroe Doctrine
1904–1905	Russo-Japanese War is fought
1905	Taft-Katsura Agreement recognizes Japanese power in Korea
1908	Root-Takahira Agreement vows to maintain the status quo in the Pacific ■ Roosevelt sends the fleet around the world
1911	Revolution begins in Mexico
1913–1914	Bryan negotiates "cooling-off" treaties to end the war
1914	World War I begins ■ U.S. Marines take Veracruz, Mexico ■ Panama Canal is completed
1915	Japan issues Twenty-One Demands to China (January) ■ Germany declares the waters around the British Isles a war zone (February) ■ *Lusitania* torpedoed (May) ■ Bryan resigns; Robert Lansing becomes secretary of state (June) ■ *Arabic* pledge restricts submarine warfare (September)
1916	Germany issues *Sussex* pledge (March) ■ General John J. Pershing leads a punitive expedition into Mexico to seize Pancho Villa (April) ■ Wilson wins re-election (November)
1917	Wilson calls for "peace without victory" (January) ■ Germany resumes unrestricted U-boat warfare (February) ■ United States enters World War I (April) ■ Congress passes the Selective Service Act (May) ■ First American troops reach France (June) ■ War Industries Board is established (July)
1918	Wilson outlines Fourteen Points for peace (January) ■ Germany asks for peace (October) ■ Armistice ends the war (November)
1919	Peace negotiations begin in Paris (January) ■ Treaty of Versailles is defeated in the Senate
1920	Warren G. Harding is elected president

KEY TERMS

Hay-Bunau-Varilla Treaty, p. 463

Roosevelt Corollary, p. 463

dollar diplomacy, p. 464

moral diplomacy, p. 465

Selective Service Act, p. 471

Committee on Public Information (CPI), p. 473

Espionage Act, p. 474

Sedition Act, p. 474

War Industries Board (WIB), p. 475

Food Administration, p. 475

Fourteen Points, p. 477

RECOMMENDED READING

American foreign policy between 1901 and 1921 has been the subject of considerable study. Richard W. Leopold, *The Growth of American Foreign Policy* (1962), is balanced and informed. Robert E. Osgood, *Ideals and Self-Interest in America's Foreign Relations* (1953), Robert E. Hannigan, *The New World Power: American Foreign Policy, 1898–1917* (2002), and William Appleman Williams, *Roots of the*

Modern American Empire (1969), explore the forces underlying American foreign policy.

For American policy toward Latin America, see Dana G. Munro's detailed account, *Intervention and Dollar Diplomacy in the Caribbean, 1900–1920* (1964); Mary A. Renda, *Taking Haiti: Military Occupation and the Culture of U.S. Imperialism, 1915–1940* (2001); and Emily S. Rosenberg,

Financial Missionaries to the World: The Politics and Culture of Dollar Diplomacy, 1900–1930 (1999). Arthur S. Link examines Wilson's foreign policy in his exceptional five-volume biography, *Wilson* (1947–1965), and in *Woodrow Wilson: Revolution, War, and Peace* (1979).

Studies of events at home during the war include David M. Kennedy, *Over Here* (1980); Alan Dawley, *Changing the World: American Progressives in War and Revolution* (2003); Christopher M. Sterba, *Good Americans: Italian and Jewish Immigrants during the First World War* (2003); Robert D. Cuff, *The War Industries Board* (1973); and Maurine W. Greenwald, *Women, War, and Work* (1980). Susan Zeiger, *In Uncle Sam's Service: Women Workers with the American Expeditionary Force, 1917–1919* (1999), and Kathleen Kennedy, *Disloyal Mothers and Scurrilous Citizens: Women and Subversion During World War I* (1999), look at the role of women; Jennifer D. Keene, *Doughboys, the Great War, and the Remaking of America* (2001), at the war's effects on the soldiers; and Mark Robert Schneider, *"We Return Fighting": The Civil Rights Movement in the Jazz Age* (2001), Mark Ellis, *Race, War, and Surveillance: African Americans and the United States Government during World War I* (2001), and Theodore Kornweibel, Jr., *"Investigate Everything": Federal Efforts to Compel Black Loyalty During World War I* (2002), at its impact on African Americans.

Arthur Walworth, *America's Moment, 1918: American Diplomacy at the End of World War I* (1977), and John Milton Cooper, Jr., *Breaking the Heart of the World: Woodrow Wilson and the Fight for the League of Nations* (2001), examine Wilson's attempt to create a peaceful world order.

SUGGESTED WEB SITES

Woodrow Wilson

www.ipl.org/div/ref/potus/wwilson.html

This page contains basic factual data about his election and presidency, speeches, and on-line biographies.

World War I Document Archive

www.lib.byu.edu/~rdh/wwi/

This archive contains sources about World War I in general, not just America's involvement.

World War One: Trenches on the Web

www.worldwar1.com/index.html

This site provides a mass of data concerning the prosecution of the world's first global war.

The Great Migration in Chicago

lcweb.loc.gov/exhibits/african/afam011.html

This site looks at the black experience in the Great Migration through the lens of one prominent destination.

The American Experience: Influenza

www.pbs.org/wgbh/amex/influenza

This PBS site reveals the impact of the great flu epidemic of 1918.

Chapter *25*

Transition to Modern America

Wheels for the Millions

The moving assembly line that Henry Ford developed in 1913 in Highland Park, Michigan, to manufacture the Model T marked only the first step toward full mass production and the beginning of America's worldwide industrial supremacy. Ford already had a vision of a vast industrial tract where machines, moving through a sequence of carefully arranged manufacturing operations, would transform raw materials into finished cars, trucks, and tractors. By the mid-1920s at River Rouge, his plant southeast of Detroit, his vision had been realized.

Ford expanded his industrial dream in 1919 when he built a blast furnace and foundry to make engine blocks for both the Model T and his tractors. By 1924, more than forty thousand workers were turning out nearly all the metal parts used in making Ford vehicles.

Visitors from all over the world came to marvel at River Rouge. Some were disturbed by the jumble of machines and the apparent congestion on the plant floor, but industrial experts recognized that the arrangement led to incredible productivity because "the work moves and the men stand still." As a whole, the plant was "one huge, perfectly timed, smoothly operating industrial machine."

In 1927, Ford closed the assembly line at Highland Park. For the next six months, his engineers worked on designing a more compact and efficient assembly line at River Rouge for the Model A, which went into production in November. By then, River Rouge had more than justified Ford's vision. For a generation of engineers, wrote historian Geoffrey Perrett, the River Rouge plant was "a monument."

Mass production, born in Highland Park in 1914 and perfected at River Rouge in the 1920s, became a hallmark of American industry. Soon Ford's emphasis on the flow of parts moving past stationary workers became the standard in nearly every American factory. The moving assembly line took away the last vestige of craftsmanship and turned workers into near robots. It also led to amazing efficiency that produced both high profits for manufacturers and low prices for buyers.

Most important, mass production contributed to a consumer goods revolution. American factories turned out a flood of automobiles, electrical appliances, and other items that made life easier and more pleasant for most Americans. The result was the creation of a distinctively modern America, one marked by the material abundance that has characterized American society ever since.

But the abundance came at a price. The 1920s have been portrayed as a decade of escape and frivolity, and for many Americans they were just that. But those years also were an era of transition: a time when the old America of individualistic rural

483

values gave way to a new America of conformist urban values. The transition was often wrenching, and many Americans clung desperately to the old ways. Modernity finally won, but not without a struggle.

THE SECOND INDUSTRIAL REVOLUTION

The first Industrial Revolution in the late nineteenth century had catapulted the United States to the forefront of the world's richest and most highly developed nations. With the advent of the new consumer goods industries, the American people by the 1920s enjoyed the highest standard of living of any nation on earth. From 1922 to 1929, the economy boomed. American industrial output nearly doubled, and the gross national product rose by 40 percent. Most of this explosive growth took place in industries producing goods for consumers. Equally important, the national per capita annual income increased by 30 percent to $681 in 1929. American workers became the highest paid in history. Combined with the expansion of installment credit programs that allowed customers to buy now and pay later, this income growth allowed a purchasing spree unlike anything the nation had ever experienced.

The key to the new affluence was technology. Electric motors replaced steam engines as the basic source of energy in factories, and efficiency experts helped maximize labor's output. Production per worker-hour increased an amazing 75 percent in the 1920s.

The Automobile Industry

The effects of the consumer goods revolution can best be seen in the automobile industry, which became the nation's largest in the 1920s. Rapid growth was its distinguishing feature. In 1920, there were 10 million cars in the nation; by the end of the decade, 26 million were on the road.

Ford continued to lead the way, but General Motors and Chrysler Corporation offered stiff competition. Small manufacturers began to disappear, victims of the huge costs involved in mass production. *Oligopoly,* control of an industry by a few large companies, became the dominant pattern in all the consumer goods industries.

The automobile boom depended on the apparently insatiable American appetite for cars. But soon the market became saturated as more and more of the people who could afford the novel luxury had become car owners. Marketing became as crucial as production. Automobile makers began to rely heavily on advertising and annual model changes, seeking to make customers dissatisfied with their old vehicles and eager to order new ones. Installment buying also helped prolong the boom.

Despite these efforts, sales slumped in 1927 when Ford stopped making the Model T, picked up again the next year with the introduction of the Model A, and began to slide again in 1929. The automobile industry revealed a basic weakness in the consumer goods economy: once people bought an item with a long life, they were out of the market for years.

In the affluent 1920s, few observers recognized the signs of economic instability. They were too enthralled by the stimulating effect the automobile industry had on such industries as steel, rubber, paint, glass, and road construction. Filling stations, tourist cabins (forerunners of the modern motel), and drive-ins of all kinds began to dot the landscape along the major and minor highways. The auto changed the whole pattern of city life, fueling a suburban explosion as real estate developers built houses in ever wider concentric circles around the central cities.

Patterns of Economic Growth

Automobiles were the most conspicuous of the consumer products that flourished in the 1920s but certainly not the only ones. The electrical industry grew nearly as quickly. Two-thirds of all American families had electricity by the end of the decade, and they spent vast sums on washing machines, vacuum cleaners, refrigerators, and ranges. The new appliances eased the burdens of the housewife and ushered in an age of leisure.

Radio broadcasting and motion picture production also boomed in the 1920s. The early success of KDKA in Pittsburgh stimulated the growth of more than eight hundred independent radio stations, and by 1929, NBC had formed the first successful radio network. The film industry thrived in Hollywood, reaching its maturity in the mid-1920s. With the advent of the "talkies" in 1929, average weekly movie attendance climbed to nearly 100 million.

Other industries prospered as well. Production of light metals, chemicals, and synthetics grew into major businesses. Americans found a whole new spectrum of products to buy—cigarette lighters, wristwatches, heat-resistant glass cooking dishes, and rayon stockings were just a few.

The corporation continued to be the dominant business structure in the 1920s. Corporations now had hundreds of thousands of stockholders. The enormous profits the corporations generated provided ample funds to finance growth and expansion, freeing companies from their earlier dependence on investment bankers such as J. P. Morgan. Operating independent of outside restraint, corporate managers were accountable only to other managers.

Another wave of mergers accompanied the growth of corporations during the 1920s. By the end of the decade, the two hundred largest nonfinancial corporations owned almost half of the country's corporate wealth. The greatest abuses took place in public utilities, where promoters such as Samuel Insull built vast paper empires by gaining control of power companies and then draining them of their assets.

The most distinctive feature of the new consumer-oriented economy was the stress on advertising. Skillful practitioners such as Edward Bernays and Bruce Barton sought to control public tastes and consumer spending by identifying the good life with the possession of the latest product of American industry, be it a car, a refrigerator, or a cigarette.

Uniformity and standardization, the characteristics of mass production, now prevailed. Chain stores proliferated at the expense of small retail establishments. Kansas farmers bought the same items as Pennsylvania factory workers. Sectional differences in dress, food, and furniture began to disappear. Radio and films even threatened regional accents by promoting a standard national dialect devoid of any local flavor.

Economic Weaknesses

The New Era, as businessmen labeled the decade, was not as prosperous as it first appeared. The revolution in consumer goods disguised the decline of many traditional industries in the 1920s. Railroads suffered from

A Look at the Past

Radio

Radios became enormously popular during the 1920s and 1930s, giving people access to news and entertainment in their homes on demand. While some radios fit on table tops, other models were large, fine pieces of furniture suitable for covering with doilies and treasured photographs. ✳ What do such expensive, fancy models suggest about the place of radio in the home? Why would radios attain a privileged position in the home?

poor management and from the competition of the growing trucking industry. Coal was being replaced by petroleum and natural gas. Cotton textiles declined with the development of rayon and other synthetic fibers.

Hit hardest of all was agriculture. American farmers had expanded production to meet the demands of World War I. After the war, farm prices and exports fell sharply. Throughout the 1920s, the farmers' share of the national income dropped until by 1929, per capita annual farm income was only $273, compared to the national average of $681.

Urban workers, although better off than farmers, did not share fully in the decade's affluence. The industrial labor force remained remarkably steady for a period of economic growth; the technical innovations meant that the same number of workers could produce far more than before. Most of the new jobs came in the lower-paying service industries. Although wages rose slowly, conditions of life for the worker did improve. Prices remained stable, so workers experienced a gain in real wages.

Organized labor proved unable to advance the interests of workers in the 1920s. Many businessmen used the injunction and "yellow dog" contracts, which forbade employees from joining unions, to establish open shops and deny workers the benefits of collective bargaining. Other employers wooed their workers away from unions using techniques of welfare capitalism, spending money to improve plant conditions and winning employee loyalty with pensions, paid vacations, and company cafeterias. The net result was a decline in union membership from a postwar high of five million to less than three million by 1929.

Black workers remained on the bottom, both economically and socially. Many of the blacks who migrated northward during World War I found jobs only in menial service areas—collecting garbage, washing dishes, sweeping floors. Yet even these jobs offered them a better life than they found on the depressed southern farms, and so the migration continued. The black population in Chicago, New York, and other northern cities more than doubled during the 1920s.

Middle- and upper-class Americans were the groups who thrived in the decade. The rewards of the second Industrial Revolution went to the managers—the engineers, bankers, and executives—who directed the new industrial economy. These were the people who bought the fine new homes in the suburbs and who could afford more than one car. Their conspicuous consumption helped fuel the prosperity of the 1920s, but their disposable income eventually became greater than their material wants. The result was speculation, as men with idle money began to invest heavily in the stock market to reap gains from the industrial growth.

The economic trends of the decade had both positive and negative implications for the future. On the plus side, the growth of new consumer-based industries was solid. Automobiles and appliances were not passing fancies but part of the modern American way of life. The future pattern of American culture—cars and suburbs, shopping centers and skyscrapers—was set by the end of the 1920s.

But at the same time, there were ominous signs of danger. The unequal distribution of wealth, the growth of consumer debt, the saturation of the market for cars and appliances, and the rampant speculation all contributed to economic instability. The boom of the 1920s would end in a great crash; yet the achievements of the decade would survive even that dire experience.

City Life in the Jazz Age

The city replaced the countryside as the center of American life in the 1920s. The 1920 census revealed that for the first time, more than half the population lived in cities, defined broadly to include all places of more than 2,500 people. Between 1920 and 1930, cities with populations of 250,000 or more added some eight million people.

The skyscraper soon became the most visible feature of the city. Constrained by inflated land prices, builders built upward, developing a distinctively American architectural style in the process. By 1929, the United States had 377 buildings more than seventy stories tall. The skyscraper came to symbolize the new mass culture.

In the metropolis, life was different. The old community ties of home, church, and school were loosening, but there were important gains—new ideas, new creativity, new perspectives. Some city-dwellers became lost and lonely without the old institutions; others thrived in the urban environment.

Women and the Family

The urban culture of the 1920s witnessed important changes in the American family, which began to break down under the impact of economic and social change. A new freedom for women and children seemed to be emerging in its wake.

Although World War I accelerated the process by which women left the home for work, the postwar decade witnessed a return to the slower pace of the prewar years. During the 1920s there was no permanent gain in the number of working women. Two million more women were employed in 1930 than in 1920, but this represented an increase of only 1 percent. Most women workers, however, had lower-paying jobs, ranging from stenographers and retail store clerks to maids. For the most part, the professions were reserved for men, with women relegated to such stereotypical fields as teaching and nursing.

Women had won the right to vote in 1920, but the Nineteenth Amendment proved to have less impact than its proponents had hoped. It robbed women of a unifying cause, and the suffrage itself did little to change the prevailing gender roles. Men remained the principal breadwinners in the family; women cooked, cleaned, and reared the children.

The feminist movement, however, still showed signs of vitality. In 1923, the National Woman's party succeeded in having an Equal Rights Amendment (ERA) introduced in Congress. Other women's organizations opposed the amendment on the ground that women needed legal protection, especially laws guaranteeing them at least a minimum wage and limiting the maximum length of the workday. The drive for the ERA failed in the 1920s, but social feminists were more successful in pushing for such humanitarian reforms as the Sheppard-Towner Act of 1921, which provided federal aid to establish state programs for maternal and infant health care.

A generational change had a profound impact on feminism in the 1920s. Instead of crusading for social progress, young women concentrated on individual self-expression by rebelling against Victorian restraints. In the cities, some quickly adopted what critic H. L. Mencken called the "flapper" image. Cutting their hair short, raising their skirts above the knee, and binding their breasts, flappers set out to compete on equal terms with men on the golf course and in the speakeasy.

■ **Sheik with Sheba** *is the title of this John Held, Jr., drawing, which appeared on a 1925 cover of* Judge *magazine. Held's drawings define the image of the "flapper" era—the young woman with rolled-down stockings and rouged knees and the young man with cigarette and pocket flask at the wheel of his car.* ■

Shocking to their elders, the flappers assaulted the traditional double standard in sex, demanding that equality with men should include sexual fulfillment before and during marriage. The new permissiveness led to a sharp rise in the divorce rate.

The sense of women's emancipation was heightened by a drop in the birthrate and the abundance of consumer goods. Yet appearances were deceptive. Many women could not enjoy the new laborsaving devices. The typical childless woman spent between forty-three and fifty hours a week on household duties; for mothers, the average workweek was fifty-six hours, far longer than that of their husbands. And despite the talk of the "new woman," traditional gender roles remained unshaken. As one historian has concluded, "In the 1920s, as in the 1790s, marriage was the only approved state for women."

The family, however, did change. It became smaller as easier access to effective birth control methods enabled couples to limit the number of their offspring. More and more married women took jobs outside the home. Young people, who had once joined the labor force when they entered their teens, now enjoyed adolescence as a stage of life devoted to school and leisure.

This prolonged adolescence led to new strains on the family in the form of youthful revolt. Freed of the traditional burden of earning a living at an early age, youth in the 1920s went on a great spree. Heavy drinking, casual sexual encounters, and a constant search for excitement became the hallmarks of the upper-class youth immortalized by F. Scott Fitzgerald. The theme of rebellion against parental authority, which runs through all aspects of the 1920s, was at the heart of the youth movement.

The Roaring Twenties

Excitement ran high in the cities as crime waves and highly publicized sports events flourished. Prohibition ushered in such distinctive features of the decade as speakeasies, bootleggers, and bathtub gin. Crime rose sharply as middle- and upper-class Americans willingly broke the law to gain access to alcoholic beverages. City streets became the scene of violent shoot-outs between rival bootleggers, and underworld czars such as Al Capone controlled illicit empires.

Sports became a national mania in the 1920s as people gained more leisure time. Golf boomed, with two million men and women playing the sport. Spectator sports attracted even more attention. Millions of Americans found drama in the exploits of boxer Jack Dempsey, footballer Red Grange, and baseball great Babe Ruth. Massive new stadiums had to be built to hold the growing numbers of sports fans.

In what Frederick Lewis Allen called "the ballyhoo years," the popular yearning for excitement led people to seek thrills in all kinds of ways—applauding Charles Lindbergh's solo flight across the Atlantic and flocking to such bizarre events as six-day bicycle races, dance marathons, and flagpole-sittings. Hero worship of sports and entertainment stars became an escape from the drabness of life on the assembly line.

Sex became another focal point in the 1920s as Victorian standards began to crumble. Sophisticated city-dwellers seemed to be intent on exploring a new freedom in sexual expression. Hollywood exploited the obsession with sex by producing movies with such provocative titles as *A Shocking Night* and *Women and Lovers.* Plays and novels focused on adultery, and the new urban tabloids delighted in telling their readers about love nests and kept women. Young people embraced the new permissiveness joyfully, with the automobile providing couples an easy means to escape parental supervision.

There is considerable debate, however, over the extent of the sexual revolution in the 1920s. Actual changes in sexual behavior are beyond the historian's reach, hidden in the privacy of the bedroom, but the old Victorian prudery was a clear casualty of the 1920s. At least in urban areas, sex was no longer a taboo subject; men and women now could and did discuss it openly.

Flowering of the Arts

The greatest cultural advance of the 1920s was the outpouring of literature. The city gave rise to a new class of intellectuals—writers who commented on the new industrial society. Many were bewildered by the rapidly changing social patterns of the 1920s and appalled by the materialism of American culture. Some fled to Europe to live as expatriates. Others stayed at home, observing and condemning the excesses of a business civilization. All shared a sense of disillusionment and wrote pessimistically of the flawed promise of American life. Yet, ironically, their body of writing revealed a profound creativity that suggested that America was coming of age intellectually.

The exiles included the poet T. S. Eliot and the novelist Ernest Hemingway. In *The Waste Land,* (1922), Eliot evoked images of fragmentation and sterility that had a powerful impact on the other disillusioned writers of the decade. Eliot reached the depths of despair in *The Hollow Men* (1925), a biting depiction of the emptiness of modern life. Hemingway sought redemption from the modern plight in the romantic individualism of his heroes. He wrote of men alienated from society who found a sense of identity in their own courage and quest for personal honor. His greatest impact on other writers came from his sparse, direct, clean prose style.

Writers who stayed home were equally critical of contemporary American life. In *The Great Gatsby* (1925), F. Scott Fitzgerald chronicled American high society, emphasizing its emptiness and lack of human concern. Sinclair Lewis became the most popular of the critical novelists. *Main Street* (1920) satirized the values of small-town America as dull, complacent, and narrow-minded, and *Babbitt* (1922) poked fun at the commercialism of the 1920s.

Most savage of all was H. L. Mencken, the Baltimore newspaperman and literary critic who founded *The American Mercury* in 1923. He mocked everything he found distasteful in America, from the Rotary Club to the Ku Klux Klan. A born cynic, he served as a zealous guardian of public integrity in an era of excessive boosterism.

The cultural explosion of the 1920s was surprisingly broad. It included novelists such as Sherwood Anderson and John Dos Passos—who described the way the new machine age undermined such traditional American values as craftsmanship and a sense of community—and playwrights such as Eugene O'Neill and Maxwell Anderson. Women writers were particularly effective in dealing with regional themes. Edith Wharton continued to write penetratingly about eastern aristocrats, and Willa Cather and Ellen Glasgow focused on the plight of women in the Midwest and the South, respectively. The greatest contribution to American music, imbuing it with a new vitality, came from the spread of jazz as blacks migrated northward. The form of jazz known as the blues became an authentic national folk music.

The cultural growth of the 1920s was the work of African Americans as well as whites. W. E. B. Du Bois became the intellectual voice of the African American community developing in New York City's Harlem. Along with James Weldon Johnson, a gifted poet, Du Bois became the leader of the **Harlem Renaissance.** The NAACP moved its headquarters to Harlem, and in 1923, the Urban League began publishing *Opportunity,* a magazine devoted to scholarly studies of racial issues.

Black literature blossomed. In stark images, Claude McKay in *White Shadows* (1922) expressed both his resentment against racial injustice and his pride in blackness. Countee Cullen and Langston Hughes won critical acclaim for the beauty of their poems and the eloquence of their portrayal of the black tragedy.

During Harlem's golden age, "almost everything seemed possible," wrote historian David Lewis. "You could be black and proud, politically assertive and economically independent, creative and disciplined—or so it seemed." Moreover, the mood of the Harlem Renaissance spread to black communities in other cities.

In retrospect, the literary flowering of the 1920s is strikingly paradoxical. Nearly all the writers, black and white, cried out against conformity and materialism. Few took any real interest in politics or in social reform. They retreated instead into individualism, seeking an escape from the prevailing business civilization in their art. Whether they went abroad or stayed home, the writers of the 1920s turned inward to avoid being swept up in the consumer goods revolution. Yet despite their withdrawal—indeed, perhaps because of it—they produced an astonishingly rich and varied body of work. American writing had a greater intensity and depth than in the past; American writers, for the first time, were taken seriously by Europeans.

Harlem Renaissance An African American cultural, literary, and artistic movement centered in Harlem, an area in New York City, in the 1920s. Harlem, the largest black community in the world outside Africa, was considered the cultural capital of African Americans.

THE RURAL COUNTERATTACK

Dominance by the urban centers triggered a response that showed the ugly side of the 1920s, the side where hate and intolerance flourished. For millions of Americans who lived in small towns and on farms, the city came to represent all that was evil in contemporary life. Largely Anglo-Saxon and steeped in traditional Protestantism, these rural folk condemned urban-centered crime, radicalism, and modernism, which they believed were threatening their way of life. Saloons, whorehouses, Little Italys and Little Polands, communist cells, free love, atheism—all were identified with the city. As the urban areas grew in population and influence, the countryside struck back in a deliberate if doomed attempt to restore a lost purity to American life.

Other factors contributed to the intensity of the rural counterattack. The war had unleashed a nationalistic spirit that craved unity and conformity. When the war was over, groups such as the American Legion tried to root out "un-American" behavior and insisted on cultural as well as political conformity. And the prewar progressive reform spirit added to the social tension. Stripped of much of its former idealism, progressivism focused on social problems such as drinking and illiteracy to justify repressive measures such as prohibition and immigration restriction. The result was tragic, for often it pitted rural America against urban America in ugly conflicts.

The Fear of Radicalism

Red Scare A wave of anticommunist, antiforeign, and antilabor hysteria that swept over America at the end of World War I. It resulted in the deportation of many alien residents and the violation of the civil liberties of many of its victims.

The first and most intense outbreak of national alarm, the **Red Scare,** came in 1919. The heightened nationalism of World War I found a new target in bolshevism. The Russian Revolution and the growth of communism in America frightened many Americans. Although the number of American Communists was never great, they were located in the cities, and their influence appeared to be magnified with the outbreak of widespread labor unrest.

A general strike in Seattle, a police strike in Boston, and a violent strike in the iron and steel industry thoroughly alarmed the American people in the spring and summer of 1919. A series of bombings and attempted bombings led to panic. On June 2, a bomb shattered the front of Attorney General A. Mitchell Palmer's home. Although the man who delivered it was blown to pieces, authorities quickly identified him as an Italian anarchist from Philadelphia.

In the public outcry that followed, Attorney General Palmer led the attack on the alien threat. In a series of raids that began on November 7, federal agents seized suspected anarchists and Communists and held them for deportation with no regard for due process of law. In December, 249 aliens were shipped to Russia. Nearly all were innocent of the charges against them. A month later, Palmer rounded up nearly four thousand suspected Communists in a single evening. Aliens rounded up were deported without hearings or trials.

For a time, it seemed that this Red Scare reflected the prevailing views of the American people. Instead of condemning their government's actions, citizens voiced their approval and even urged more drastic steps. In one particularly revolting episode, a group of war veterans in Centralia, Washington, dragged a radical from the town jail, castrated him, and hanged him from a railway bridge. The coroner's report stated that the victim "jumped off with a rope around his neck and then shot himself full of holes."

The very extremism of the Red Scare led to its rapid demise. Courageous government officials and prominent citizens spoke out against the government's violations of constitutional guarantees and the acts of terror. Finally, Palmer himself, with evident presidential ambition, went too far. In April 1920, he warned of a vast revolution to occur on May 1. When no bombings or violence took place on May Day, the public began to react against Palmer's hysteria, trying hard to forget their momentary loss of balance.

Yet the Red Scare exerted a continuing influence on American society in the 1920s. The foreign-born lived with the uneasy realization that they were viewed with hostility and suspicion. Two Italian aliens in Massachusetts, Nicola Sacco and Bartolomeo Vanzetti, were arrested in May 1920 for a payroll robbery and murder. They faced a prosecutor and jury who condemned them more for their ideas than for any evidence of criminal conduct and a judge who referred to them as "those anarchist bastards." Despite a worldwide effort that became the chief liberal cause of the 1920s, the two died in the electric chair on August 23, 1927. Their fate symbolized the bigotry and intolerance that lasted through the 1920s and made this decade one of the least admirable in American history.

Prohibition

In December 1917, Congress passed the Eighteenth Amendment, prohibiting the manufacture and sale of alcoholic beverages, and sent the amendment to the states for ratification. A little more than a year later, in January 1919, Nebraska became the necessary thirty-sixth state to ratify, and **prohibition** became the law of the land.

Effective January 16, 1920, the Volstead Act, which implemented prohibition, banned most commercial production and distribution of beverages containing more than one-half of 1 percent of alcohol by volume. (Exceptions were made for medicinal and religious uses of wine and spirits. Production for one's own private use was also allowed.) Prohibition was the result of both a rural effort of the Anti-Saloon League and the urban progressive concern over the social disease of drunkenness. Although a number of states had already enacted prohibition laws by 1920, the real tragedy resulted from the effort to extend this "noble experiment" to the growing cities, where it was deeply resented by many ethnic groups and nearly totally disregarded by the well-to-do and the sophisticated.

prohibition The ban of the manufacture, sale, and transportation of alcoholic beverages in the United States. The Eighteenth Amendment, ratified in 1919, established prohibition. It was repealed by the Twenty-first Amendment in 1933.

Prohibition did in fact lead to a decline in drinking. The consumption of alcohol dropped sharply in rural areas and among the lower classes, who could not afford the high prices of bootleg liquor. Among the middle class and the wealthy, however, drinking became fashionable. Bootleggers supplied whiskey, which quickly replaced lighter spirits such as wine and beer. Despite the risk of illness or death from drinking the unregulated alcohol, Americans consumed some 150 million quarts of liquor a year in the 1920s as bootleggers took in nearly $2 billion annually, about 2 percent of the gross national product.

Urban resistance to prohibition finally led to its repeal in 1933. But in the intervening years, it damaged American society by breeding a profound disrespect for the law. In city after city, police openly tolerated the traffic in liquor, and judges and prosecutors agreed to let bootleggers pay token fines. The countryside felt vindicated, yet rural and urban America alike suffered from this overzealous attempt to legislate morals.

The Ku Klux Klan

The most ominous expression of rural protest against the city was the rebirth of the Ku Klux Klan. On Thanksgiving night in 1915, on Stone Mountain in Georgia, Colonel William J. Simmons and thirty-four followers founded the modern Klan. Only "native-born, white, gentile Americans" were permitted to join. Membership grew slowly during World War I but mushroomed after 1920. Across the South and the West, the Klan attracted men seeking to relieve their anxiety over a changing society.

The Klan of the 1920s was not just anti-black; the tensions and conflicts in American society, as Klansmen perceived it, came from aliens—Italians and Russians, Jews and Catholics. The Klan punished blacks who did not know their place, women who practiced the new morality, and aliens who refused to conform. Beatings, floggings, burning with acid, even murder were condoned. But they also tried more peaceful methods of coercion, formulating codes of behavior and seeking communitywide support. In addition, the Klan entered politics, showing remarkable strength in Texas, Oklahoma, Oregon, and Indiana.

Its appeal lay in the sanctuary it offered to insecure and anxious people. It gave its members reassurance and an exotic world of titles and practices. Members found a sense of identity in the group activities, whether they were peaceful picnics, ominous parades in white robes, or fiery crosses blazing in the night. By the mid-1920s, the Klan boasted a membership of nearly five million, and it had separate orders for women, boys, and girls.

The Klan fell even more quickly than it rose. Its more violent activities began to offend the nation's conscience. Misuse of funds and sexual scandals among Klan leaders, notably in Indiana, repelled many of the rank and file. Membership declined sharply after 1925; by the end of the decade, the Klan had virtually disappeared. But the spirit lived on, testimony to the recurring demons of nativism and racist hatred that have surfaced periodically throughout the American experience.

Immigration Restriction

The nativism that permeated the Klan found its most successful outlet in the immigration legislation of the 1920s. The sharp increase in immigration in the late nineteenth century had led to a broad-based movement to restrict the flow of people from Europe. In 1917, over Wilson's veto, Congress enacted a literacy test that reduced the number of immigrants, and the war caused an even more drastic decline.

After armistice, however, rumors began to spread of an impending flood of people seeking to escape war-ravaged Europe. Worried members of Congress spoke of a

■ *A 1925 Ku Klux Klan demonstration in Cincinnati, Ohio, attended by nearly thirty thousand robed members and marked by the induction of eight thousand young boys in the Junior Order. Only native-born, white Americans "who believe in the tenets of the Christian religion" were admitted into the Klan. The original Ku Klux Klan, formed during the Reconstruction era to terrorize and intimidate former slaves, disbanded in 1869. The Klan that formed in 1915 declined through the 1920s but did not officially disband until 1944. Two years later, a third Klan emerged, focusing on the civil rights movement and communism as its enemies.* ■

"barbarian horde" that would inundate the United States with "dangerous and deadly enemies of the country." Even though the actual number of immigrants fell below the prewar yearly average, Congress in 1921 passed an emergency immigration act.

The 1921 act failed to satisfy the nativists. It still permitted more than half a million Europeans to come to the United States in 1923, nearly half of them from southern and eastern Europe. The declining percentage of Nordic immigrants alarmed writers such as Madison Grant, who warned the American people that the Anglo-Saxon stock that had founded the nation was about to be overwhelmed by lesser breeds with inferior genes. Psychologists, relying on primitive IQ tests used by the army in World War I, confirmed this judgment.

Responding to such theories, in 1924, Congress adopted the **National Origins Quota Act,** which limited immigration from Europe to 150,000 a year; allocated most of the places to immigrants from Great Britain, Ireland, Germany, and Scandinavia; and banned all Asian immigrants. The measure passed Congress with overwhelming rural support.

The new restrictive legislation marked the most enduring achievement of the rural counterattack. Unlike the Red Scare, prohibition, and the Klan, the quota system would survive until the 1960s. Yet even here, the rural victory was not complete. A growing tide of Mexican laborers, exempt from the quota act, flowed northward across the Rio Grande to fill the continuing need for unskilled workers on farms and in the service trades. The Mexican immigration marked the strengthening of an element in the national ethnic mosaic that would grow in size and influence until it became a major force in modern American society.

National Origins Quota Act
This 1924 act established a quota system to regulate the influx of immigrants to America. The system restricted the "new" immigrants from southern and eastern Europe and Asia. It reduced the annual total of immigrants.

The Fundamentalist Challenge

The most significant—and, as it turned out, longest-lasting—challenge to the new urban culture was rooted in the traditional religious beliefs of millions of Americans who felt alienated from city life, from science, and from much of what modernization entailed. Sometimes this challenge was direct, as when Christian fundamentalists campaigned against the teaching of evolution in the public schools. Their success in Tennessee touched off a court battle, the **Scopes trial,** that drew the attention of the entire country to the small town of Dayton in the summer of 1925. There, William Jennings Bryan engaged in a crusade against the theory of evolution, appearing as a chief witness against John Scopes, a high school biology teacher who had deliberately violated a new Tennessee law that forbade the teaching of Darwin's theory.

In the trial, Bryan testified under oath that he believed Jonah had been swallowed by a big fish and declared, "It is better to trust in the Rock of Ages than in the age of rocks." Chicago defense attorney Clarence Darrow succeeded in making Bryan look ridiculous. The court found Scopes guilty but let him off with a small fine; Bryan, exhausted by his efforts, died a few days later. H. L. Mencken, who covered the trial in person, rejoiced in believing that fundamentalism was dead.

Other aspects of the fundamentalist challenge were more subtle but no less important in countering the modernizing trend. Middle- and upper-class Americans drifted into a genteel Christianity that stressed good works and respectability, but the fervid evangelical denominations continued to hold on to the old faith, and more aggressive fundamentalist sects, such as the Jehovah's Witnesses, grew rapidly.

Many who came to the city in the 1920s brought their religious beliefs with them and found new outlets for their traditional ideas. Thus evangelist Aimee Semple McPherson enjoyed amazing success in Los Angeles with her "Four-Square Gospel." Far from dying out, biblical fundamentalism remained remarkably strong in the cities as well as the country. The rural counterattack, though challenged by the city, did enable some older American values to survive in the midst of the new mass production culture.

POLITICS OF THE 1920S

The tensions between the city and the countryside also shaped the course of politics in the 1920s. On the surface, it was a Republican decade. The GOP controlled the White House from 1921 to 1933 and had majorities in both houses of Congress from 1919 to 1931. The Republicans halted further reform legislation and established a friendly relationship between government and business. Important shifts were taking place, however, in the American electorate. The Democrats, although divided into competing urban and rural wings, were laying the groundwork for the future by winning over millions of new voters, especially among the ethnic groups in the cities. The rising tide of urban voters indicated a fundamental shift away from the Republicans toward a new Democratic majority.

Harding, Coolidge, and Hoover

The Republicans regained the White House in 1920 with the election of Warren G. Harding of Ohio. Handsome and dignified, Harding reflected both the wholesomeness and the narrowness of small-town America. He was basically a genial man who lacked the capacity to govern and who delegated power broadly as president.

He made some good cabinet choices, notably Charles Evans Hughes as secretary of state and Herbert C. Hoover as secretary of commerce, but two corrupt officials sabotaged his administration. Attorney General Harry Daugherty became in-

Scopes trial Also called the "monkey trial," the 1925 Scopes trial was a contest between modern liberalism and religious fundamentalism. John Scopes was on trial for teaching Darwinian evolution in defiance of a Tennessee state law. He was found guilty and fined $100.

volved in a series of questionable deals that led ultimately to his forced resignation, and Secretary of the Interior Albert Fall was the chief figure in the **Teapot Dome scandal.** Two oil promoters gave Fall nearly $400,000 in loans and bribes; in return, he helped them secure leases on naval oil reserves in Elk Hills, California, and Teapot Dome, Wyoming. The scandal came to light after Harding's death from a heart attack in 1923. Fall eventually served a year in jail, and the reputation of the Harding administration never recovered.

Vice President Calvin Coolidge assumed the presidency on Harding's death, and his honesty and integrity quickly reassured the nation. A reserved, reticent man of Yankee stock, Coolidge became famous for his epigrams, which contemporaries mistook for wisdom. "The business of America is business," he proclaimed. Consistent with his philosophy, he believed his duty was simply to preside benignly, not govern the nation. Satisfied with the prosperity of the mid-1920s, the people responded favorably. Coolidge was elected to a full term by a wide margin in 1924.

When Coolidge announced in 1927 that he did not "choose to run" for re-election, Herbert Hoover became the Republican choice to succeed him. By far the ablest GOP leader of the decade, Hoover epitomized the American legend of the self-made man. Orphaned as a boy, he had worked his way through Stanford University and had gained both wealth and fame as a mining engineer. Sober, intelligent, and immensely hardworking, Hoover embodied the nation's faith in individualism and free enterprise.

He used his office to help American manufacturers and exporters expand their overseas trade, and he strongly supported a trade association movement to encourage cooperation rather than cutthroat competition among smaller American companies. He saw business and government as partners, working together to achieve efficiency and affluence for all Americans.

Republican Policies

During the 1920 campaign, Harding had urged a return to "normalcy," a coined word that became the theme for the Republican administrations of the 1920s. Aware that the public was tired of zealous reform-minded presidents, Harding and his successors sought a return to traditional Republican policies. In some areas they were successful, but in others they were forced to adjust to the new realities of a mass production society.

The most obvious attempt to go back to the Republicanism of William McKinley came in tariff and tax policy. Fearful of a flood of postwar European imports, Congress passed an emergency tariff act in 1921 and followed it a year later with the protectionist Fordney-McCumber Tariff Act.

Secretary of the Treasury Andrew Mellon, a wealthy Pittsburgh banker and industrialist, worked hard to achieve a similar return to "normalcy" in taxation. He pressed for repealing excess-profits taxes on corporations and slashing personal rates on the very rich. He also reduced government spending from its wartime peak of $18 billion to just over $3 billion by 1925, creating a slight surplus. Congress cooperated by cutting the highest income tax bracket to a modest 20 percent.

The growing crisis in American farming during the decade forced the Republican administrations to seek new solutions. The end of the war led to a sharp decline in farm prices and a return to the problem of overproduction. Southern and western lawmakers formed a farm bloc in Congress to press for special legislation for American agriculture. Although the farm bloc helped pass several laws, it failed to get at the root problem of overproduction. Farmers then supported more controversial measures designed to raise domestic crop prices by having the government sell the surplus overseas at low world prices. Coolidge

Teapot Dome scandal Scandal in which Secretary of the Interior Albert Fall was convicted of accepting bribes in exchange for leasing government-owned oil lands in Wyoming (Teapot Dome) and California (Elk Hills) to private oil businessmen.

■ *In this 1925 political cartoon, Clifford Berryman depicts Calvin Coolidge and Andrew Mellon in a car racing downhill to tax reductions. The wealthy benefited most from Mellon's tax reduction policies, paying as much as one-third less in 1926 than they had paid in 1921.* ■

vetoed the legislation on grounds that it involved unwarranted government interference in the economy.

Yet the government's role in the economy increased rather than lessened in the 1920s. Republicans widened the scope of federal activity and nearly doubled the ranks of government employees. Hoover led the way in the Commerce Department, establishing new bureaus to help make American industry more efficient in housing, transportation, and mining. Instead of going back to the laissez-faire tradition of the nineteenth century, the Republican administrations of the 1920s were pioneering a close relationship between government and private business.

The Divided Democrats

While the Republicans ruled in the 1920s, the Democrats seemed bent on self-destruction. The pace of the second Industrial Revolution and growing urbanization split the party in two. One faction centered in the rural South and West. Traditional Democrats who had supported Wilson stood for prohibition, fundamentalism, the Klan, and other aspects of the rural counterattack against the city. In contrast, a new breed of Democrat was emerging in the metropolitan areas of the North and Midwest. Immigrants and their descendants began to participate actively in the Democratic party. Primarily Catholics and Jews and strongly opposed to prohibition, they had little in common with their rural counterparts.

The split within the party surfaced dramatically at the national convention in New York in 1924. Held in Madison Square Garden, the convention soon degenerated into what one observer described as a "snarling, cursing, tenuous, suicidal, homicidal roughhouse." Urban and rural factions of the party opposed each other at every turn. The delegates divided between Alfred E. Smith, the governor of New York, and William G. McAdoo of California, Wilson's secretary of the treasury. When it became clear that neither the city nor the rural candidate could win a majority, both men withdrew; on the 103rd ballot, the weary Democrats finally chose John W. Davis as their compromise nominee. Senator Bob La Follette of Wisconsin ran on the independent Progressive party ticket. His campaign was ineffective; so was Davis's. Both were easily defeated by Coolidge.

Yet the Democrats were in far better shape than this setback indicated. Beginning in 1922, the party had made heavy inroads into the GOP majority in Congress. Even in 1924, the Republican vote in the nation's largest cities declined. In 1926, the Democrats came within one vote of controlling the Senate and had picked up more seats in the House. The largest cities were swinging clearly into the Democratic column; all the party needed was a charismatic leader who could fuse the older rural elements with the new urban voters.

The Election of 1928

The selection of Al Smith as the Democratic candidate in 1928 indicated the growing power of the city. Born on the Lower East Side of Manhattan of mixed Irish-German ancestry, Smith was the prototype of the urban Democrat. He was Catholic; he was associated with a big-city machine; he was a "wet" who wanted to end prohibition. Rejected by rural Democrats in 1924, he still had to prove that he could unite the South and West behind his leadership. His lack of education, poor grammar, and distinctive New York accent hurt him, as did his eastern provincialism.

The choice facing the American voter in 1928 seemed unusually clear-cut. Herbert Hoover was a Protestant, a "dry," and an old-stock American who stood for efficiency and individualism. Just as Smith appealed to new voters in the cities, so Hoover won the support of many old-line Democrats who feared the city and the pope.

Yet beneath the surface, as historian Allan J. Lichtman pointed out, there were "striking similarities between Smith and Hoover." Both were self-made men who embodied the American belief in freedom of opportunity and upward mobility. Neither advocated any significant degree of economic change or any redistribution of national wealth or power. Although Smith's religion hurt him the most, his failure to spotlight the growing cracks in prosperity and offer alternative economic policies ensured his defeat.

Chronology

1919	U.S. agents arrest 1700 in Red Scare raids ▪ Eighteenth Amendment (prohibition) ratified
1920	Republican Warren G. Harding is elected president ▪ Nineteenth Amendment is passed, granting women the right to vote
1923	Harding dies; Vice President Calvin Coolidge assumes the presidency ▪ Newspapers expose Ku Klux Klan graft, torture, murder
1924	Coolidge is elected to full term ▪ Senate probes Teapot Dome scandal ▪ National Origins Quota Act restricts immigration from Europe and bans immigration from Asia
1925	John Scopes is convicted of teaching theory of evolution in violation of Tennessee law
1927	Charles Lindbergh completes the first nonstop transatlantic flight from New York to Paris ▪ Coolidge vetoes farm price control bill ▪ Sacco and Vanzetti are executed ▪ The movie *The Jazz Singer* features a soundtrack
1928	Republican Herbert Hoover defeats Democrat Al Smith for the presidency

The 1928 election was a dubious victory for the Republicans. Hoover won easily, but Smith succeeded for the first time in winning a majority of votes for the Democrats in the nation's twelve largest cities. A new Democratic electorate was emerging, consisting of Catholics and Jews, Irish and Italians, Poles and Greeks. Now the task was to unite the traditional Democrats of the South and West with the urban, ethnic populations of the Northeast and Midwest.

CONCLUSION: THE OLD AND THE NEW

The election-night celebrations at Hoover campaign headquarters were muted by prohibition and by the president elect's natural reserve. Had Hoover known what lay just ahead for the country, and for his presidency, no doubt the party would have been even more somber.

During the 1920s, America struggled to enter the modern era. The economics of mass production and the politics of urbanization drove the country forward, but the persistent appeal of individualism and rural-based values held it back. Americans achieved greater prosperity than ever before, but the prosperity was unevenly distributed. Further, as the outbursts of nativism, ethnic and racial bigotry, and intolerance revealed, prosperity hardly guaranteed generosity or unity. Nor, for that matter, did it guarantee continued prosperity, even for those who benefited initially. As much as America changed during the 1920s, in one crucial respect the country remained as before. The American economy, for all its remarkable productive capacity, was astonishingly fragile. This was the message Hoover was soon to learn.

KEY TERMS

Harlem Renaissance, p. 490

Red Scare, p. 490

prohibition, p. 491

National Origins Quota Act, p. 493

Scopes trial, p. 494

Teapot Dome scandal, p. 495

RECOMMENDED READING

William Leuchtenburg provides the best overview of the 1920s in *The Perils of Prosperity, 1914–1932* (1958). He stresses the theme of rural-urban conflict and claims that the achievements of the decade were more significant than its failures. Ellis Hawley, *The Great War and the Search for a Modern Order* (1979), and Donald McCoy, *Coming of Age* (1973), are also valuable as surveys of the period. Frederick Lewis Allen, *Only Yesterday: An Informal History of the 1920s* (1931), is a classic, and still delightfully readable. The changing political alignments of the 1920s are covered in David Burner, *The Politics of Provincialism* (1968). The essays in John Braeman, Robert H. Bremner, and David Brody, eds., *Change and Continuity in Twentieth-Century America: The 1920s* (1968), provide various perspectives on important facets of the period.

Economic developments of the 1920s are the subject of George Soule, *Prosperity Decade* (1947). Helen Lynd and Robert Lynd, *Middletown* (1929), examine the social and cultural trends of the decade. David J. Goldberg, *Discontented America* (1999), finds unhappiness beneath the apparent prosperity.

Edward J. Larson, *Summer for the Gods* (1998), is the most recent and accessible account of the Scopes trial. Lawrence Levine, *Defender of the Faith* (1965), covers the last ten years of William Jennings Bryan's life. The lives of other public figures of the 1920s are traced in David Levering Lewis, *W. E. B. Du Bois*, vol. 2 (2000); Terry Teachout, *The Skeptic* (2002), on H. L. Mencken; Elisabeth Israels Perry, *Belle Moskowitz* (2000); and Robert A. Slayton, *Empire Statesman* (2001), and Christopher M. Finan, *Alfred E. Smith* (2002), both on the leading Democrat of the 1920s.

SUGGESTED WEB SITES

Harlem 1900–1940: An African American Community

www.si.umich.edu/CHICO/Harlem/

The New York Public Library's Schomburg Center for Research in Black Culture hosts this site that includes a database, a timeline, and an exhibit.

William P. Gottlieb—Photographs from the Golden Age of Jazz

memory.loc.gov/ammem/wghtml/wghome.html

The Music Division of the Library of Congress has numerous images, audio, and scanned articles from the 1940s.

The Scopes Trial

www.law.umkc.edu/faculty/projects/ftrials/scopes/scopes.htm

This site provides a detailed discussion of the trial, biographies of the major figures, and excerpts from the trial transcript.

American Temperance and Prohibition

prohibition.history.osu.edu/

This site looks at the temperance movement over time and contains many informative links.

National Arts and Crafts Archives

arts-crafts.com/archive/archive.shtml

This site serves as a guide to materials on the Arts and Crafts movement, which lasted roughly from 1890 to 1929.

The Jazz Age: Flapper Culture and Style

www.geocities.com/flapper_culture

This site contains many links to information about the popular culture of the 1920s with special reference to the flapper.

The Calvin Coolidge Experience

www.geocities.com/CapitolHill/4921/

This site is an unusual look at one of America's less colorful presidents.

Chapter 26

Franklin D. Roosevelt and the New Deal

The Struggle Against Despair

Oscar Heline never forgot the terrible waste of the Great Depression. "Grain was being burned," he told interviewer Studs Terkel. "It was cheaper than coal." Heline lived in Iowa, in the heart of the farm belt. "A county just east of here, they burned corn in their courthouse all winter. . . . You couldn't hardly buy groceries for corn." Farmers, desperate for higher prices, resorted to destruction. As Heline recalled, "People were determined to withhold produce from the market—livestock, cream, butter, eggs, what not. If they would dump the produce, they would force the market to a higher level. The farmers would man the highways, and cream cans were emptied in ditches and eggs dumped out. They burned the trestle bridge, so the trains wouldn't be able to haul grain."

Film critic Pauline Kael recounted a different memory of the 1930s. Kael was a college student in California during the Great Depression, and was struck by the number of students who were missing fathers. "They had wandered off in disgrace because they couldn't support their families. Other fathers had killed themselves, so the family could have the insurance. Families had totally broken down." Kael and many of her classmates struggled to stay in school. "There were kids who didn't have a place to sleep, huddling under bridges on the campus. I had a scholarship, but there were times when I didn't have any food. The meals were often three candy bars."

No American who lived through the Great Depression ever forgot the experience. As the stories of Heline and Kael show, the individual memories were of hard times, but also of determination, adaptation, and survival.

The depression decade had an equally profound effect on American institutions. To cope with the problems of poverty and dislocation, Americans looked to government as never before, and in doing so transformed American politics and public life. The agent of the transformation—the man America turned to in its moment of trial—was Franklin D. Roosevelt. His answer to the country's demands for action was an ambitious program of relief and reform called the **New Deal**.

New Deal President Franklin Roosevelt's program of legislation to combat the Great Depression. The New Deal included measures aimed at relief, reform, and recovery. They achieved some relief and considerable reform but little recovery.

Outline

THE GREAT DEPRESSION

The depression of the 1930s came as a shock to Americans who had grown used to the prosperity of the 1920s. The consumer revolution of that earlier decade had fostered a general confidence that the American way of life would continue to improve. But following the collapse of the stock market in late 1929, factories closed, machines fell silent, and millions of Americans walked the streets looking for jobs that didn't exist.

The Great Crash

The consumer goods revolution contained the seeds of its own demise. The productive capacity of the automobile and appliance industries grew faster than the effective demand. At that point, production began to falter, and in 1927, the nation underwent a mild recession. The sale of durable goods declined, and construction of houses and buildings fell slightly. If corporate leaders had heeded these warning signs, they might have responded by raising wages or lowering prices, both effective ways to stimulate purchasing power and bolster sales. Or if government officials had recognized the danger signs and forced a halt in installment buying and slowed bank loans, the nation might have experienced a sharp but brief depression.

Neither government nor business leaders were so farsighted. The Federal Reserve Board lowered the discount rate, charging banks less for loans in an attempt to stimulate the economy. Much of this additional credit, however, went not into solid investment in factories and machinery but instead into the stock market, touching off a new wave of speculation that obscured the growing economic slowdown and ensured a far greater crash to come.

Individuals with excess cash began to invest heavily in the stock market, and the market moved upward. The strongest surge began in the spring of 1928, when investors ignored the declining production figures in the belief that they could make a living in the market. People bet their savings on speculative stocks. Corporations used their large cash reserves to supply money to brokers, who in turn loaned it to investors on margin.

Investors could now play the market on credit, buying stock listed at $100 a share with $10 down and $90 on margin (the broker's loan for the balance). If the stock advanced to $150, the investor could sell and reap a gain of 400 percent on the $10 investment; in the bull (rising) market climate of the 1920s, everyone was sure that the market would go up.

By 1929, it seemed that the whole nation was engaged in speculation. So great was the public's interest in the stock market that newspapers carried the stock averages on the front pages. Although more people were spectators than speculators, the bull market became a national obsession, assuring everyone that the economy was healthy and preventing any serious analysis of its underlying flaws.

And then things changed, almost overnight. On October 24—later known as Black Thursday—the rise in stock prices faltered, and when it did investors nervously began to sell. Such leading stocks as RCA and Westinghouse plunged, losing nearly half their value in a single day. Speculators panicked as their creditors demanded new collateral, and the panic caused prices to plummet still further. Within weeks the gains of the previous two years had vanished.

The great crash of the stock market soon spilled over into the larger economy. Banks and other financial institutions suffered heavy losses in the market and were forced to curtail lending for consumer purchases. As consumers came up short, factories cut back production, laying off some workers and reducing hours for others. The layoffs and cutbacks lowered purchasing power even further, so fewer people bought cars and appliances. More factory layoffs resulted, and plants closed entirely, leading to even less money for the purchase of consumer goods.

The downward economic spiral continued for four years. By 1932, unemployment had swelled to 25 percent of the workforce. Steel production was down to 12 percent of capacity, and the gross national product fell to two-thirds of the 1929 level. The bright promise of mass production had ended in a nightmare.

The basic explanation for the Great Depression lies in the fact that U.S. factories produced more goods than the American people could consume. There were

UNEMPLOYMENT, 1929–1942

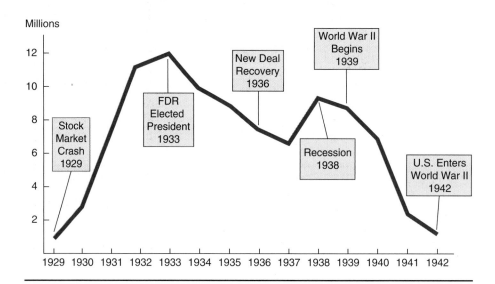

other contributing causes—unstable economic conditions in Europe, the agricultural decline since 1919, corporate mismanagement, and excessive speculation—but at bottom people simply did not have enough money to buy the consumer products coming off the assembly lines.

The failure of the new economic system to distribute wealth more broadly was the chief difficulty. Too much money had gone into profits, dividends, and industrial expansion and not enough into the hands of the workers, who were also consumers. Factory productivity had increased 43 percent during the decade, but the wages of industrial workers had gone up only 11 percent. If the billions that went into stock market speculation had been used instead to increase wages—which would then have increased consumer purchasing power—production and consumption could have been brought into balance. Unfortunately for the prophets and pioneers of the New Era, it took the bitter experience of the Great Depression to teach them the true dynamics of the consumer goods economy.

Effect of the Depression

It is difficult to measure the human cost of the Great Depression. The material hardships were bad enough. Families lived in lean-tos made of scrap wood and metal and went without meat and fresh vegetables for months, existing on soup and beans. The psychological burden was even greater: Americans suffered through years of grinding poverty with no letup in sight. The unemployed stood in line for hours waiting for a relief check; veterans sold apples or pencils on street corners, their image as heroes and family providers now in question. In the country, crops rotted in the fields because prices were too low to make harvesting worthwhile.

Few Americans escaped the suffering. Blacks were often the first to lose their jobs. Mexican Americans were deported in droves, now that citizens were willing to labor in the fields and lay track on the railroads. The poor of all hues survived because they knew better than most Americans how to exist in poverty. They stayed in bed in cold weather, both to keep warm and to avoid unnecessary burning of calories. They patched their shoes with rubber from old tires, heated only their kitchens, and ate scraps of food others would reject.

The middle class, which had always lived with high expectations, was hit hard. Many professional and white-collar workers refused to ask for charity even as their families went without food. People who fell behind on their mortgage payments lost their homes, and health care declined as middle-class families stopped going regularly to doctors and dentists, unable to make the required cash payments in advance.

Even the well-to-do were affected, weighed down with guilt as they watched former friends and business associates join the ranks of the impoverished. "My father lost everything" became an all-too-familiar refrain among young people who dropped out of college.

Many Americans sought new vistas. Men and boys, and some women, rode the rails in search of jobs, hopping freight trains to move south in the winter or west in the summer. Those who became tramps had to keep on the move to avoid arrest for vagrancy, but they did find a sense of community in the "hobo jungles" that sprang up along the major railroad routes. Here the homeless could find a place to eat and sleep and people with whom to share their misery.

FIGHTING THE DEPRESSION

The Great Depression presented an enormous challenge for American political leadership. The inability of the Republicans to overcome the economic catastrophe provided the Democrats with the chance to regain power. Although they failed to achieve full economic recovery before the outbreak of World War II, the Democrats did succeed in alleviating the suffering and establishing their political dominance.

Hoover and Voluntarism

Herbert Hoover was the Great Depression's most prominent victim. Expressing complete faith in the American economic system, he relied primarily on voluntary cooperation with business to halt the slide. He called the leaders of industry to the White House and secured their agreement to maintain prices and wages at high levels. Yet within a few months, employers were reducing wages and cutting prices in a desperate effort to survive.

Hoover also believed in voluntary efforts to relieve the human suffering brought about by the depression. He called on private charities and local governments to help feed and clothe those in need. But when these resources were exhausted, he rejected all requests for direct federal relief, asserting that such handouts would undermine the character of proud American citizens.

As the depression deepened, Hoover reluctantly began to move beyond voluntarism to undertake more sweeping governmental measures. The new Federal Farm Board loaned money to aid cooperatives and bought up surplus crops in the open market in a vain effort to raise farm prices. At Hoover's request, Congress cut taxes and adopted a few federal public works projects. To help imperiled banks and insurance companies, Hoover proposed and Congress established the Reconstruction Finance Corporation. The RFC loaned money to financial institutions to save them from bankruptcy. Hoover's critics, however, pointed out that while he favored aid to business, he still opposed measures such as direct relief and massive public works that would help the millions of unemployed.

By 1932, Hoover's efforts to overcome the depression had clearly failed. His public image suffered its sharpest blow in the summer of 1932 when he ordered General Douglas MacArthur to clear out the **bonus army.** This group of ragged World War I veterans had marched on Washington in a vain effort to get a bill granting them bonuses passed in Congress. Mounted troops drove the bonus marchers out of their shanties in Anacostia Flats along the Potomac River, blinding the veterans with tear gas and burning their shacks.

bonus army In June 1932, a group of unemployed World War I veterans marched on Washington, D.C., to demand immediate payment of their war pensions. Congress rejected their demands, and President Hoover had them forcibly removed from their encampment.

Meanwhile, the nation's banking structure approached collapse. Bank customers responded to rumors of bankruptcy by rushing in to withdraw their deposits, thereby causing bank failures to rise steadily. Everywhere, Americans longed for a new president.

The Emergence of Roosevelt

The man who came forward to meet this national need was Franklin D. Roosevelt, a distant cousin of the Republican Teddy. Born into a wealthy New York family, he enjoyed a privileged life of private tutors and trips to Europe. Well educated and supremely secure, he had served in a number of elected and appointed offices. In 1921, he suffered an attack of polio. Refusing to give in, he fought back bravely, and though he never again walked unaided, he was elected governor of New York in 1928.

Roosevelt's dominant trait was his ability to persuade and convince other people. He possessed a marvelous voice, deep and rich; a winning smile; and a buoyant confidence that was contagious. His bout with polio gave him both an understanding of human suffering and broad political appeal as a man who had faced heavy odds and overcome them. A master politician with an agile mind, he had little patience with philosophical nuances. He dealt with the appearance of issues, not their deepest substance, and he displayed a flexibility toward political principles that often dismayed even his warmest admirers.

Roosevelt took advantage of the political opportunity offered by the Great Depression. With the Republicans discredited, he united the Democratic party. After winning the party's nomination in 1932, he broke with tradition by flying to Chicago and accepting in person, telling the cheering delegates, "I pledge myself to a new deal for the American people."

In the fall, he defeated Herbert Hoover in a near landslide for the Democrats. Roosevelt not only met the challenge of the depression but also solidified the shift to the Democratic party that would dominate American politics for a half century.

The Hundred Days

When Franklin Roosevelt took the oath of office on March 4, 1933, the nation's economy was on the brink of collapse. Unemployment stood at nearly thirteen million—one-fourth the labor force—and banks were closed in thirty-eight states. Speaking from the steps of the capitol, FDR declared boldly, "First of all, let me assert my firm belief that the only thing we have to fear is fear itself—nameless, unreasoning, unjustified terror." Then he announced that he would call Congress into special session and request "broad executive power to wage a war against the emergency, as great as the power that would be given to me if we were in fact invaded by a foreign foe."

Within the next ten days, Roosevelt won his first great New Deal victory by saving the nation's banks. First he closed all the banks; then he presented new banking legislation to Congress, which it promptly passed. The measure provided for government supervision and aid to the banks. Strong ones would be reopened with federal support, weak ones closed, and those in difficulty bolstered by government loans.

On March 12, FDR addressed the nation by radio in the first of his "fireside chats." In conversational tones, he told the public what he had done. He assured Americans that the government now stood behind the banks. The next day, March 13, the nation's largest and strongest banks opened their doors; at the end of the day, customers had deposited more cash than they withdrew. The banking crisis was over.

"Capitalism was saved in eight days," boasted one of Roosevelt's advisers. Most surprising was the conservative nature of FDR's action. Instead of nationalizing the banks, he had simply thrown the government's resources behind them and preserved private ownership. Though some other New Deal measures would be more radical, Roosevelt set the tone in the banking crisis. He was out to reform and restore the American economy system, not change it drastically.

For the next three months, Congress responded to a series of presidential initiatives. During the Hundred Days, Roosevelt sent fifteen major requests to Congress and obtained fifteen pieces of legislation. One of these, the **Tennessee Valley Authority (TVA),** was one of the most ambitious of Roosevelt's New Deal measures. This innovative effort at regional planning resulted in the building of a series of dams in seven states along the Tennessee River to control floods, ease navigation, and produce electricity. Although critics lamented the cost of the project and its impact on the environment and certain local communities, it went far toward bringing one of the most underdeveloped parts of the country into the modern era.

Other New Deal agencies were temporary, designed to meet the specific economic problems of the depression. None was completely successful; the depression would continue for another six years. But psychologically, the nation turned the corner in the spring of 1933. Under FDR, the government seemed to be responding to the economic crisis, enabling people to look to the future with hope for the first time since 1929.

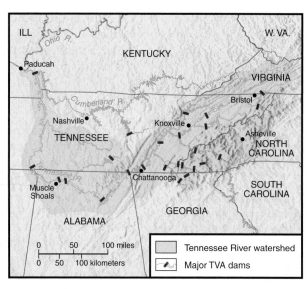

TENNESSEE VALLEY AUTHORITY   *The Tennessee Valley Authority (TVA) served a seven-state region in the Southeast. Developing such a vast project required federal funding and management, both of which were provided through a federally owned corporation. The TVA expanded the hydroelectric plants at Muscle Shoals, Alabama, and built dams, power plants, and transmission lines to service the surrounding area.* ■

Tennessee Valley Authority (TVA) A New Deal effort at regional planning created by Congress in 1933, this agency built dams and power plants on the Tennessee River. Its programs for flood control, soil conservation, and reforestation helped raise the standard of living of millions in the Tennessee River Valley.

National Recovery Administration (NRA) New Deal federal agency created in 1933 to promote economic recovery and revive industry during the Great Depression.

Roosevelt and Recovery

Two major New Deal programs launched during the Hundred Days were aimed at industrial and agricultural recovery. The first was the **National Recovery Administration (NRA),** FDR's attempt to achieve economic advance through planning and cooperation among government, business, and labor. Businessmen were intent on stabilizing production and raising prices for their goods. Spokesmen for labor were equally determined to spread gainful work by setting maximum hours and minimum wages.

The NRA hoped to achieve both goals by permitting companies in each major industry to cooperate in writing codes of fair competition that would set realistic limits on production, allocate percentages to individual producers, and set firm guidelines on prices. Section 7a of the enabling act mandated protection for labor in all the codes by establishing maximum hours, minimum wages, and the guarantee of collective bargaining by unions. No company could be compelled to join, but the New Deal sought complete participation by appealing to patriotism. Each firm that took part could display a blue eagle and stamp the symbol on its products. Led by Hugh Johnson, the NRA quickly enrolled the nation's leading companies and unions.

The NRA soon bogged down in a huge bureaucratic morass. The codes proved difficult to enforce and favored big business at the expense of smaller competitors. In addition, labor quickly became disenchanted with Section 7a. By 1934, more and more businessmen were complaining about the new agency. When the Supreme

Court finally invalidated the NRA in 1935 on constitutional grounds, few mourned its demise. The idea of trying to overcome the depression by relying on voluntary cooperation between competing businessmen and labor leaders had collapsed in the face of individual self-interest and greed.

The New Deal's attempt at farm recovery fared a little better. Henry A. Wallace, FDR's secretary of agriculture, came up with an answer to the farmer's old dilemma of overproduction. The government would act as a clearinghouse for producers of major crops, arranging for them to set production limits for wheat, cotton, corn, and other leading crops. Under the **Agricultural Adjustment Administration (AAA),** the government would allocate acreage among individual farmers, encouraging them to take land out of production by paying them subsidies.

After initial problems in 1933, the AAA program worked better in 1934 and 1935 as land removed from production led to smaller harvests and rising farm prices. Farm income rose for the first time since World War I. Most of the gain came from the subsidy payments themselves rather than from higher market prices.

On the whole, large farmers benefited most from the program. Possessing the capital to buy machinery and fertilizer, they were able to farm more efficiently than before on fewer acres of land. Small farmers, tenants, and sharecroppers did not fare as well, receiving little of the government payments and often being driven off the land as owners took acreage previously cultivated by tenants and sharecroppers out of production. In the long run, the New Deal reforms improved the efficiency of American agriculture, but at a real human cost.

The Supreme Court eventually found the AAA unconstitutional in 1936, but Congress reenacted it in modified form that year and again in 1938. The system of allotments became a standard feature of the farm economy. In another effort to assist the rural poor, the Farm Security Administration (FSA) loaned tenant farmers and sharecroppers money to buy their own land. But congressional appropriations were so modest that only about 2 percent obtained loans. The result of the New Deal for American farming was to hasten its transformation into a business in which only the efficient and well capitalized would thrive.

Roosevelt and Relief

The New Deal was far more successful in meeting the most immediate problem of the 1930s, relief for the millions of unemployed and destitute citizens. Roosevelt never shared Hoover's distaste for direct federal support; in May 1933, Congress authorized the Reconstruction Finance Corporation to distribute $500 million to the states to help individuals and families in need.

Roosevelt brought in former social worker Harry Hopkins to direct the relief program. By the end of 1933, Hopkins had cut through red tape to distribute money to nearly one-sixth of the American people. The relief payments were modest, but they enabled millions to avoid starvation and stay out of humiliating breadlines.

An imaginative early effort was the **Civilian Conservation Corps (CCC),** which enrolled young males from city families on relief and sent them to work on the nation's public lands, cutting trails, planting trees, building bridges, and paving roads. The program contributed both to their families' incomes and to the nation's welfare.

Hopkins realized the need to do more than just keep people alive, and he soon became an advocate of work relief. Hopkins argued that the government should put the jobless to work, not just to encourage self-respect but also to enable them to earn enough to purchase consumer goods and thus stimulate the entire economy. The Public Works Administration (PWA), headed by Secretary of the Interior Harold Ickes, had been authorized in 1933, but Ickes failed to put many people to work.

The final commitment to the idea of work relief came in 1935 when Roosevelt established the **Works Progress Administration (WPA)** to spend nearly $5 billion

---

Agricultural Adjustment Administration (AAA) Created by Congress in 1933 as part of the New Deal, this agency attempted to restrict agricultural production by paying farmers subsidies to take land out of production.

Civilian Conservation Corps (CCC) One of the most popular New Deal programs, the CCC was created by Congress to provide government jobs to young men between 18 and 25 in reforestation and other conservation projects.

Works Progress Administration (WPA) Congress created this New Deal agency in 1935 to provide work relief for the unemployed. Federal works projects included building roads, bridges, and schools, but the WPA also funded projects for artists, writers, and young people.

A Look at the Past

FSA Photos

"Migrant Mother" (left) is one of the best-known photographs commissioned by the Farm Security Administration (FSA) during the 1930s. The FSA used photographs to document rural problems and to build support for its resettlement program. Roy Stryker, the project's director, wanted the photographs to convince the public that rural Americans faced difficulties but with help were capable of overcoming those troubles. Rural Americans had to appear deserving. Photographers such as Dorothea Lange, who took these photographs, experimented with compositions in an effort to capture artistically pleasing images that provoked the reactions Stryker wanted. Compare Lange's famous image to the one she never intended to publish. ✳ Why would the photograph on the right fail to meet Stryker's demands? What emotions do the photograph on the left evoke? How does the image on the left meet Stryker's requirements?

authorized by Congress for emergency relief. The WPA put the unemployed on the federal payroll so that they could earn enough to meet their basic needs and help stimulate the stagnant economy. The WPA provided work for skilled and unskilled alike. It also tried to preserve the skills of American artists, actors, and writers by paying them to practice their craft.

The WPA helped ease the burden for the unemployed, but it failed to overcome the depression. Rather than spending too much, as his critics charged, Roosevelt's greatest failure was not spending enough to prime the American economy by increasing consumer purchasing power. By responding to basic human needs, Roosevelt had made the depression bearable, but the New Deal's failure to go beyond relief to achieve prosperity led to growing frustration and prompted more radical alternatives that challenged the conservative nature of the New Deal and forced FDR to shift to the left.

ROOSEVELT AND REFORM

In 1935, the focus of the New Deal shifted from relief and recovery to reform. During his first two years in office, FDR had concentrated on fighting the depression by shoring up the sagging American economy. He was developing a "broker state" concept of government, responding to pressures from organized elements such as corporations, labor unions, and farm groups while ignoring the needs and wants of the dispossessed who had no clear political voice.

The continuing depression and the high unemployment built pressures for more sweeping changes. Roosevelt faced the choice of either exploring more radical programs designed to end historical inequities in American life or deferring to others' solutions. Bolstered by an impressive Democratic victory in the 1934 congressional elections, FDR responded by embracing a reform program that marked the climax of the New Deal.

Challenges to FDR

The signs of discontent were visible everywhere by 1935. In the upper Midwest, progressives and agrarian radicals, led by Minnesota Governor Floyd Olsen, were demanding substantial changes to raise farmers' and workers' incomes. Textile plant strikes shut down mills in twenty states. The most serious challenge to Roosevelt's leadership, however, came from three demagogues who captured national attention in the mid-1930s.

The first was Father Charles Coughlin, a Roman Catholic priest from Detroit who had originally supported FDR. Speaking to a rapt nationwide radio audience, Coughlin appealed to the discontented with a strange mix of crank monetary schemes and anti-Semitism. He broke with the New Deal in late 1934, calling for monetary inflation and nationalization of the banking system.

A more benign but equally threatening figure appeared in California. Dr. Francis Townsend, a 67-year-old physician, came forward in 1934 with a scheme to assist the elderly, who were suffering greatly during the depression. The Townsend Plan proposed giving everyone over the age of 60 a monthly pension of $200 with the provision that it must be spent within thirty days. It would thus provide an old-age pension and stimulate the economy. Although impractical, more than ten million people signed petitions endorsing the Townsend Plan.

A third new voice of protest was that of Huey Long, a flamboyant senator from Louisiana. An early New Deal supporter, Long turned against FDR and by 1935 had become a major political threat to the president. In 1934, he announced a nationwide "Share the Wealth" movement. He spoke grandly of taking from the rich to make "Every Man a King," guaranteeing each American a home worth $5000 and an annual income of $2500. To finance the plan, Long advocated seizing all fortunes of more than $5 million and levying a tax of 100 percent on income over $1 million. Millions of Americans responded favorably to Long's plan. Threatening to run as a third-party candidate in 1936, Long generated fear among Democratic leaders that he might attract three or four million votes, possibly enough to swing the election to the Republicans. Although he was assassinated in 1935, his popularity showed the need for the New Deal to do more to help those still in distress.

Social Security

When the new Congress met in January 1935, Roosevelt was ready to support a series of reform measures designed to take the edge off national dissent. Many of the Democrats in Congress were to the left of Roosevelt, favoring increased spending and more sweeping federal programs. Congress was prepared to enact virtually any proposal that Roosevelt offered.

Past and Present

Challenging Social Security

Conservatives lost the fight over President Franklin Roosevelt's Social Security program in the 1930s, but they hardly abandoned their opposition to the program. For nearly two decades, Republicans pledged to repeal Social Security should they ever reclaim Congress and the White House. Many objected to the expense of the program, which started small but eventually—as contributors retired, and especially as life expectancies after retirement increased—became one of the largest of all federal programs. Other critics focused on what they considered to be the destructive erosion of personal responsibility as Americans looked to government rather than to themselves or their families for financial security in old age.

Not until 1953 did the Republicans win back Congress and the presidency. At that point, GOP conservatives sought to redeem their party's promise to undo the Democrats' handiwork. But President Dwight Eisenhower and other Republican moderates realized that repealing Social Security would upset the retirement plans millions of Americans had made during the previous eighteen years. Moreover, the Republican president judged that an attack on Social Security would be politically suicidal. "Should any political party attempt to abolish Social Security . . . " Eisenhower remarked, "you would not hear of that party again in our political history." Rather than repeal Social Security, the Eisenhower administration sponsored an increase in benefits and an extension of the system to 10 million persons previously uncovered.

Subsequent decades saw more of the same. As the number of recipients grew, so did their political influence, and Congress responded by repeatedly boosting benefits. In the early 1970s, congressional Democrats and the Republican administration of President Richard Nixon collaborated to link Social Security benefits to the cost of living, thereby ensuring that recipients not lose ground relative to inflation. (In fact, the formula applied probably enabled retirees to *gain* ground on the still-working citizens.) During much of this period, Social Security was called the "third rail" of American politics, in wry reference to the rail on subways that conducts electricity and kills anyone who approaches it too closely.

Even so, the criticism of Social Security never quite disappeared, and as the country turned more conservative during the 1980s and 1990s occasional calls were heard for revamping the system. The election of George W. Bush in 2000 and particularly his re-election in 2004 brought Social Security squarely into the political spotlight again. As projections of future deficits in the system mounted, Bush proposed privatizing part of the system—that is, allowing workers to invest some of their contributions in private retirement accounts. The president made his privatization plan a centerpiece of his legislative program in 2005 and campaigned around the country on its behalf.

But his efforts failed utterly. Critics charged that privatization would enrich Wall Street while rendering retirees subject to the whims of the stock market. More broadly, Americans had simply grown too comfortable with the Social Security status quo to be willing to risk a substantial revision. Bush backed off, and the system that Franklin Roosevelt had created seventy years earlier emerged unscathed.

The most significant reform enacted in 1935 was the **Social Security Act.** Unlike other modern industrial nations, the United States had never developed a welfare system to aid the aged, the disabled, and the unemployed. FDR's plan had three major parts. First, it provided for old-age pensions financed by a tax on employers and workers, with no government contributions. Second, it set up a system of unemployment compensation on a federal-state basis, with employers paying a payroll tax and each state setting the benefit levels and administering the program locally. Finally, it provided for direct federal grants to the states, on a matching basis, for welfare payments to the blind, handicapped, needy elderly, and dependent children. Despite some criticism from the right and the left, Congress overwhelmingly passed the Social Security Act.

Since its passage, critics have pointed out its shortcomings. The old-age pensions and grants to the handicapped and dependent children were paltry, and not everyone was covered. People who needed the most protection in their old age, such as farmers and domestic servants, were not included. The regressive feature of the act was even worse. All participants, regardless of income or economic status, paid in at the same rate, with no supplement from the general revenue. The trust fund also took out of circulation money that was desperately needed to stimulate the economy in the 1930s.

The conservative nature of the legislation reflected Roosevelt's own fiscal orthodoxy, but even more it was a product of his political realism. Despite the

Social Security Act This 1935 New Deal legislation established a system of old age, unemployment, and survivors' insurance funded by wage and payroll taxes. It did not include health insurance and did not originally cover many of the most needy groups and individuals.

Despite the Roosevelt administration's boosterism, many believed that Social Security could not fulfill its promises.

Wagner Act Formally known as the National Labor Relations Act, this New Deal legislation enacted in 1935 created the National Labor Relations Board to supervise union elections and designate winning unions as official bargaining agents. The board could also issue cease-and-desist orders to employers who dealt unfairly with their workers.

severity of the depression, he realized that establishing a system of federal welfare went against deeply rooted American convictions. He insisted on a tax on participants to give those involved in the pension plan a vested interest in Social Security. He wanted them to feel that they had earned their pensions and that in the future no one would dare take them away. Above all, FDR had succeeded in establishing the principle of governmental responsibility for the aged, the handicapped, and the unemployed. Whatever the defects of the legislation, Social Security stood as a landmark of the New Deal, creating a system to provide for the welfare of individuals in a complex industrial society.

Labor Legislation

The other major reform achievement in 1935 was passage of the National Labor Relations Act or the **Wagner Act,** as it became known. Senator Robert Wagner of New York introduced legislation in 1934 to outlaw company unions and other unfair labor practices in order to ensure collective bargaining for unions. Although initially opposed by Roosevelt, the bill gained support in Congress and was signed into law in July 1935.

The Wagner Act created the National Labor Relations Board to preside over labor-management relations and enable unions to engage in collective bargaining with federal support. The act outlawed a variety of union-busting tactics and in its key provision decreed that whenever the majority of a company's workers voted for a union to represent them, management would be compelled to negotiate with the union on all matters of wages, hours, and working conditions. With this unprecedented government sanction, labor unions could now proceed to recruit the large number of unorganized workers throughout the country. The Wagner Act, the most far-reaching of all New Deal measures, led to the revitalization of the American labor movement and a permanent change in labor-management relations.

Three years later, Congress passed a second law that had a lasting impact on American workers, the Fair Labor Standards Act. A long-sought goal of the New Deal, the measure aimed to establish both minimum wages and maximum hours of work per week. The act was aimed at unorganized workers and met with only grudging support from unions. Southern conservatives opposed it strongly, both on ideological grounds and because it threatened the very low wages in the South that had attracted northern industry since Reconstruction.

Roosevelt finally succeeded in winning passage of the Fair Labor Standards Act in 1938, but only at the cost of exempting many key industries from its coverage. Despite its loopholes, the legislation did lead to pay raises for the twelve million workers earning less than the newly set minimum wage of 40 cents an hour. More important, like Social Security, it set up a system on which Congress could build in the future to reach more generous and humane levels.

All in all, Roosevelt's record in reform was similar to that in relief and recovery—modest success but no sweeping victory. A cautious and pragmatic leader, FDR moved far enough to the left to overcome the challenges of Coughlin, Townsend, and Long without venturing too far from the mainstream. His reforms improved the quality of life in America significantly, but he made no effort to correct all the nation's social and economic wrongs.

IMPACT OF THE NEW DEAL

The New Deal had a broad influence on the quality of life in the United States in the 1930s. Government programs reached into areas hitherto untouched. Many of them brought about long overdue improvements, but others failed to make any significant dent in historic inequities. The most important advances came with the dramatic growth of labor unions; conditions for working women and minorities showed no comparable advance.

Rise of Organized Labor

Trade unions were weak at the onset of the Great Depression, with a membership of fewer than three million workers. Most were in the American Federation of Labor (AFL), a collection of craft unions that served the needs of skilled workers. The nation's basic industries, including steel and automobiles, were unorganized; the great mass of unskilled workers thus fared poorly in terms of wages and working conditions.

John L. Lewis, head of the United Mine Workers, took the lead in organizing unskilled workers in mass production industries by forming the Committee on Industrial Organization (CIO) in 1935. Dynamic and ruthless, Lewis first battled with the conservative leadership of the AFL, and then, after being expelled, he renamed his group the Congress of Industrial Organizations and announced in 1936 that he would use the Wagner Act to extend collective bargaining to the nation's auto and steel industries.

Within five years, Lewis had scored a remarkable series of victories. The big steel companies, led by U.S. Steel, surrendered without a fight in 1937; the smaller firms engaged in violent resistance, as did the automobile industry. When General Motors resisted, members of the newly created United Automobile Workers (UAW) simply sat down in the factory, refusing to leave until the company recognized their union and threatening to destroy the valuable tools and machines if they were removed forcibly. General Motors conceded defeat and signed a contract with the UAW. Chrysler quickly followed suit, and after a hard fight, so did Ford.

By the end of the 1930s, the CIO had some five million members, slightly more than the AFL. The successes were remarkable; organizers for the CIO and the AFL had been successful in the automaking, steel, textile, rubber, electrical, and metal industries. For the first time, unskilled as well as skilled workers were unionized. Because women and blacks made up a substantial proportion of the unskilled workforce, they too benefited from the creation of the CIO.

■ *In some cases, striking union members met with brute force. Philip Evergood's 1937 painting,* The American Tragedy, *recounts the violence of the Republic Steel strike.* ■

Yet despite the impressive gains, only 28 percent of all Americans (excluding farmworkers) belonged to unions in 1940. Employer resistance and traditional hostility to unions blocked further progress, as did the aloof attitude of President Roosevelt. The Wagner Act had helped open the way, but labor leaders deserved most of the credit for the gains that were achieved.

The New Deal Record on Help to Minorities

The Roosevelt administration's attempts to aid the downtrodden were least effective among African Americans and other racial minorities. The Great Depression had hit blacks with special force. The fall in the price of cotton had ruined many sharecroppers and tenant farmers, and by 1933, more than 50 percent of urban blacks were unemployed. To make matters worse, hard times exacerbated racial prejudice.

The New Deal helped blacks survive the depression, but it never tried to confront the racial injustice built into federal relief programs. Although the programs served blacks as well as whites, in the South, the weekly payments blacks received were much smaller. Neither the minimum wage nor Social Security covered the 65 percent of all black workers who worked as farmers or domestic servants. In almost every agency, including the TVA, the interests of blacks counted little, if at all.

Despite this bleak record, African Americans rallied behind Roosevelt's leadership, abandoning their historic ties to the Republican party. In part, this switch came in response to Roosevelt's appointment of a number of prominent blacks to high-ranking government positions. The president's wife, Eleanor Roosevelt, spoke out eloquently throughout the decade against racial discrimination. But perhaps the most influential factor in the blacks' political switch was the color-blind policy of Harry Hopkins. He had more than one million African Americans working for the WPA by 1939. Uneven as his record was, Roosevelt had still done more to aid this oppressed minority than any previous president since Lincoln.

The New Deal did far less for Mexican Americans. Engaged primarily in agricultural labor, these people found their wages in the California fields dropping steadily. The Roosevelt administration cut off any further influx from Mexico, and local authorities rounded up and shipped migrants back to Mexico to reduce the welfare rolls. Despite a few benefits from New Deal relief programs, the overall pattern was one of very great economic hardship and relatively little federal assistance for Mexican Americans.

Native Americans, after decades of neglect, fared slightly better under the New Deal. Roosevelt appointed John Collier, a social worker who championed Indian rights, to serve as commissioner of Indian affairs. In 1934, Congress passed the Indian Reorganization Act, a reform measure designed to stress tribal unity and autonomy instead of attempting (as previous policy had done) to transform Indians into self-sufficient farmers by granting them small plots of land. Modest gains also occurred in education, but more than 300,000 Native Americans remained the nation's most impoverished citizens.

Women at Work

The decade witnessed a continued decline in the status of American women. Since men were considered the major breadwinners, women were often fired first. A Gallup poll revealed that 82 percent of the people disapproved of working wives, with 75 percent of the women polled agreeing.

Many of the working women in the 1930s were either single or the sole support of an entire family. Yet their wages remained lower than those for men, and their unemployment rate ran higher than 20 percent throughout the decade. The New Deal offered little encouragement. NRA codes sanctioned lower wages for women. The minimum wage did help women employed in industry, but too many worked as maids and waitresses, jobs not covered by the law. The percentage of women in the workforce was no higher in 1940 than it had been in 1910, and the sexist inequities in the marketplace were as great as ever.

The one area of advance in the 1930s came in government. Eleanor Roosevelt set an example that encouraged millions of American women. She traveled continually around the country, always eager to uncover wrongs and bring them to the president's attention. Frances Perkins, the secretary of labor, became the first woman cabinet member; FDR appointed women as ambassadors and federal judges for the first time; and women were elected to the Senate and the House of Representatives. But overall, a decade that was grim for most Americans was especially hard on American women.

END OF THE NEW DEAL

The New Deal reached its high point in 1936, when Roosevelt was overwhelmingly re-elected and the Democratic party strengthened its hold on Congress. But this political triumph was deceptive. In the next two years, Roosevelt met with a series of defeats in Congress. Yet despite these setbacks, he remained a popular political leader who had restored American self-confidence as he attempted to meet the challenges of the Great Depression.

The Election of 1936

Roosevelt enjoyed his finest political hour in 1936. A man who loved the give-and-take of politics, FDR faced challenges from both the left and the right as he sought re-election. Father Coughlin and Gerald L. K. Smith organized the Union party, with North Dakota Progressive Congressman William Lemke heading the ticket. At the other extreme, a group of wealthy industrialists formed the Liberty League to fight what they saw as the New Deal's assault on property rights. In 1936, the Liberty League endorsed the Republican presidential candidate, Governor Alfred M. Landon of Kansas. A moderate, colorless figure, Landon disappointed his backers by refusing to campaign for repeal of the popular New Deal reforms.

Roosevelt ignored Lemke and the Union party, focusing attention instead on the assault from the right. Democratic spokesmen condemned the Liberty League as a "millionaires' union" and reminded the American people of how much Roosevelt had done for them in fighting unemployment and providing relief. In his speeches, FDR said he welcomed the hatred of the "economic royalists." This frank appeal to class sympathies proved enormously successful, and Roosevelt scored an easy victory at the polls.

Equally important, the election marked the stunning success of a new political coalition that would dominate American politics for the next three decades. FDR, building on the inroads into the Republican majority that Al Smith had begun in 1928, carried urban areas by impressive margins, held on to the traditional Democratic votes in the South and West, and added to them by appealing strongly to the diverse religious and ethnic groups in the northern cities. The strong support of labor and blacks indicated that the nation's new alignment followed economic as well as cultural lines. The poor and the oppressed became attached to the Democratic party, leaving the GOP in a minority position, limited to the well-to-do and to rural and small-town Americans of native stock.

The Supreme Court Fight

FDR proved far more adept at winning elections than at achieving his goals in Congress. In 1937, he attempted to use his recent success to overcome the one obstacle remaining in his path, the Supreme Court. During his first term, the Court

MAJOR NEW DEAL LEGISLATION AND AGENCIES

Year Created	Act or Agency	Provisions
1933	Agricultural Adjustment Administration (AAA)	Attempted to regulate agricultural production through farm subsidies; reworked after the Supreme Court ruled its key regulatory provisions unconstitutional in 1936; coordinated agricultural production during World War II, after which it was disbanded.
	Banking Act of 1933 (Glass-Steagall Act)	Prohibited commercial banks from selling stock or financing corporations; created FDIC.
	Civilian Conservation Corps (CCC)	Young men between the ages of 18 and 25 volunteered to be placed in camps to work on regional environmental projects, mainly west of the Mississippi; they received $30 a month, of which $25 was sent home; disbanded during World War II.
	Civil Works Administration (CWA)	Emergency work relief program put more than four million people to work during the extremely cold winter of 1933–1934, after which it was disbanded.
	Federal Deposit Insurance Corporation (FDIC)	A federal guarantee of savings bank deposits initially of up to $2500, raised to $5000 in 1934, and frequently thereafter; continues today with a limit of $100,000.
	Federal Emergency Relief Administration (FERA)	Combined cash relief to needy families with work relief; superseded in early 1935 by the extensive work relief projects of the WPA and unemployment insurance established by Social Security.
	National Recovery Administration (NRA)	Attempted to combat the Great Depression through national economic planning by establishing and administering a system of industrial codes to control production, prices, labor relations, and trade practices among leading business interests; ruled unconstitutional by the Supreme Court in 1935.
	Public Works Administration (PWA)	Financed more than 34,000 federal and nonfederal construction projects at a cost of more than $6 billion; initiated the first federal public housing program, made the federal government the nation's leading producer of power, and advanced conservation of the nation's natural resources; discontinued in 1939 due to its effectiveness at reducing unemployment and promoting private investment.
	Tennessee Valley Authority (TVA)	An attempt at regional planning. Included provisions for environment and recreational design; architectural, educational, and health projects; and controversial public power projects; continues today to meet the Tennessee Valley's energy and flood-control needs.

"Court-packing" scheme
Concerned that the conservative Supreme Court might declare all his New Deal programs unconstitutional, President Roosevelt asked Congress to allow him to appoint additional justices to the Court. Both Congress and the public rejected this "Court-packing" scheme, and it was defeated.

had declared several New Deal programs unconstitutional. The justices were elderly men who were generally hostile to New Deal measures; one, Willis Van Devanter, even postponed retirement to be able to express his strong opposition.

When Congress convened in 1937, the president offered a startling proposal to thwart the Court's threat to the New Deal. Declaring that the Court was falling behind schedule because of the age of its members, he asked Congress to appoint a new justice for each member of the Court over the age of 70, up to a maximum of six.

Although the **"Court-packing" scheme,** as critics quickly dubbed it, was perfectly legal, it outraged not only conservatives but liberals as well, who realized that it could set a dangerous precedent for the future. Republicans wisely kept silent, letting prominent Democrats lead the fight against Roosevelt's plan. Despite all-out pressure from the White House, resistance in the Senate blocked early action on the proposal.

The Court defended itself well, pointing out that it was not behind schedule. The Court then surprised observers with a series of rulings approving such controversial New Deal measures as the Wagner Act and Social Security. In the midst of the struggle, Justice Van Devanter resigned, enabling FDR to make his first appoint-

Year Created	Act or Agency	Provisions
1934	Federal Communications Commission (FCC)	Regulatory agency with wide discretionary powers established to oversee wired and wireless communication; reflected growing importance of radio in everyday lives of Americans during the Great Depression; continues to regulate television as well as radio.
	Federal Housing Administration (FHA)	Expanded private home ownership among moderate-income families through federal guarantees of private mortgages, the reduction of down payments from 30 to 10 percent, and the extension of repayment from 20 to 30 years; continues to function today.
	Securities and Exchange Commission (SEC)	Continues today to regulate trading practices in stocks and bonds according to federal laws.
1935	National Labor Relations Board (NLRB); established by Wagner Act	Greatly enhanced power of American labor by overseeing collective bargaining; continues to arbitrate labor-management disputes today.
	National Youth Administration (NYA)	Established by the WPA to reduce competition for jobs by supporting education and training of youth; paid grants to more than 2 million high school and college students in return for work performed in their schools; also trained another 2.6 million out-of-school youths as skilled labor to prepare them for later employment in the private sector; disbanded during World War II.
	Rural Electrification Administration (REA)	Transformed American rural life by making electricity available at low rates to American farm families in areas that private power companies refused to service; closed the cultural gap between rural and urban everyday life by making modern amenities, such as radio, available in rural areas.
	Social Security Act	Guaranteed retirement payments for enrolled workers beginning at age 65; set up federal-state system of unemployment insurance and care for dependent mothers and children, the handicapped, and public health; continues today.
	Works Progress Administration (WPA)	Massive work relief program funded projects ranging from construction to acting; disbanded by FDR during World War II.
1937	Farm Security Administration (FSA)	Granted loans to small farmers and tenants for rehabilitation and purchase of small-sized farms; Congress slashed its appropriations during World War II when many poor farmers entered the armed forces or migrated to urban areas.
1938	Fair Labor Standards Act	Established a minimum wage of 40 cents an hour and a maximum workweek of 40 hours for businesses engaged in interstate commerce.

ment to the Court since taking office in 1933. Feeling that he had proved his point, FDR allowed his Court-packing plan to die in the Senate.

Although Roosevelt made four more appointments during the next few years, the Court fight had weakened his relations with Congress and with members of his own party. Many senators and representatives, mostly Southerners, who had voted reluctantly for Roosevelt's measures during the depths of the depression now felt free to oppose any further New Deal reforms.

The New Deal in Decline

The legislative record during Roosevelt's second term was meager. Aside from the minimum wage and a maximum hour law passed in 1938, Congress did not extend the New Deal into any new areas. Disturbed by growing congressional resistance, Roosevelt set out in the spring of 1938 to defeat a number of conservative Democratic congressmen and senators. His efforts were unsuccessful, however, and the failure of this attempted purge further underscored Roosevelt's strained relations with Congress.

The worst blow came in the economic sector. The slow but steady improvement in the economy suddenly gave way to a sharp recession in the late summer of 1937. In the next ten months, industrial production fell by one-third, and nearly four million workers lost their jobs. Critics of the New Deal quickly labeled the downturn the "Roosevelt recession."

The criticism was overblown but not without basis. In an effort to reduce expanding budget deficits, Roosevelt had cut back sharply on WPA and other government programs after the election. This led to a reduction in consumer spending. Urged by economists, Roosevelt finally requested a $3.75 billion relief appropriation in April 1938, and the economy began to revive. But the president's premature attempt to balance the budget meant two more years of hard times and marred his reputation as the energetic warrior of the depression.

The political result of the attempted purge and the recession was a strong Republican upsurge in the 1938 elections. In addition, after 1938, anti–New Deal Southerners voted more and more often with Republican conservatives to block social and economic reform measures. Not only was the New Deal over by the end of 1938, but a new bipartisan conservative coalition that would prevail for a quarter century had formed in Congress.

CONCLUSION: EVALUATION OF THE NEW DEAL

The New Deal lasted a brief five years, and most of its measures came in two legislative bursts in the spring of 1933 and the summer of 1935. Yet its impact on American life was enduring. Nearly every aspect of economic, social, and political development in the decades that followed bore the imprint of Roosevelt's leadership.

The least impressive achievement of the New Deal came in the economic realm. Whatever credit Roosevelt is given for relieving human suffering in the depths of the Great Depression must be balanced against his failure to achieve recovery in the 1930s. His modest programs produced only slow and halting improvement. Although much of the advance came as a result of government spending, FDR never embraced the concept of planned deficits, striving instead for a balanced budget. As a result, the nation had barely reached the 1929 level of production a decade later, and nearly ten million men and women were still unemployed.

Equally important, Roosevelt refused to make sweeping changes in the American economic system. Aside from the TVA program of dam construction and electrification, he promoted no broad experiments in regional planning and no attempts to alter free enterprise beyond imposing limited forms of governmental reg-

Chronology

1932	Franklin D. Roosevelt is elected president (November)
1933	Emergency Banking Relief Act is passed in one day (March) ▪ Twenty-First Amendment repeals prohibition (December)
1934	Securities and Exchange Commission is authorized (June)
1935	Works Progress Administration (WPA) hires unemployed (April) ▪ Wagner Act grants workers collective bargaining (July) ▪ Congress passes Social Security Act (August)
1936	FDR wins second term as president (November)
1937	Auto workers' sit-down strike forces General Motors contract (February) ▪ FDR loses Court-packing battle (July) ▪ "Roosevelt recession" begins (August)
1938	Congress sets minimum wage at 40 cents an hour (June)

ulation. The New Deal did nothing to alter the basic distribution of wealth and power in the nation. The outcome was the preservation of the traditional capitalist system with a thin overlay of federal control.

More significant change occurred with the adoption of Social Security. The government acknowledged for the first time a responsibility to provide for the welfare of citizens unable to care for themselves in an industrial society. The Wagner Act helped stimulate the growth of labor unions to balance corporate power, and the minimum wage law provided a much needed floor for many workers. Yet the New Deal tended to help only the more vocal and organized groups, such as union members and commercial farmers. People without effective voices or political clout received scant help from the New Deal. Roosevelt did little more than Hoover in responding to the long-term needs of the dispossessed.

The most lasting impact of the Roosevelt leadership came in politics. FDR forged a new coalition. He united rural and urban Democrats and attracted new groups to the Democratic party, principally blacks and organized labor. His political success led to a major realignment that lasted long after he left the scene.

His political achievement also reveals the true nature of Roosevelt's success. He was a brilliant politician who recognized the essence of leadership in a democracy—appealing directly to the people and infusing them with a sense of purpose. Thus despite his limitations as a reformer, Roosevelt proved to be the man the American people needed in the 1930s, the leader who gave them the psychological lift that helped them endure and survive the Great Depression.

KEY TERMS

New Deal, p. 500

bonus army, p. 503

Tennessee Valley Authority (TVA), p. 505

National Recovery Administration (NRA), p. 505

Agricultural Adjustment Administration (AAA), p. 506

Civilian Conservation Corps (CCC), p. 506

Works Progress Administration (WPA), p. 506

Social Security Act, p. 509

Wagner Act, p. 510

"Court-packing" scheme, p. 514

RECOMMENDED READING

The best overall account of political developments in the 1930s is William Leuchtenburg, *Franklin D. Roosevelt and the New Deal* (1963). Leuchtenburg offers a balanced treatment but concludes by defending Roosevelt's record. For a more critical view, see James MacGregor Burns, *Roosevelt: The Lion and the Fox* (1956), which portrays FDR as an overly cautious political leader; and Robert A. McElvaine, *The Great Depression: America, 1929–1941* (1984), which laments the New Deal's failure to make more sweeping changes in American life. Gene Smiley, *Rethinking the Great Depression* (2002), succinctly challenges conventional wisdom on the subject. Alonzo Hamby, *For the Survival of Democracy* (2004), compares the American New Deal to reform in other countries.

David M. Kennedy provides a comprehensive portrait of American life during both the Great Depression and World War II in *Freedom from Fear* (1999). More succinct is Gerald D. Nash, *The Crucial Era: The Great Depression and World War II, 1929–1945* (1992). For a sympathetic examination of the New Deal through 1936, see Arthur M. Schlesinger, Jr., *The Age of Roosevelt*, 3 vols. (1957–1960);

Paul Conkin offers a brief but provocative critique of Roosevelt's policies in *The New Deal* (1967). George McJimsy, *The Presidency of Franklin Delano Roosevelt* (2000), is the most recent and best-balanced account.

John Kenneth Galbraith, *The Great Crash, 1929* (1961), has long been the standard treatment of that stomach-churning event, but Maury Klein, *Rainbow's End* (2001), may displace it. Alan Brinkley, *Voices of Protest* (1982), assesses the challenges to Roosevelt from the left and the right. Lizabeth Cohen, *Making a New Deal: Industrial Workers in Chicago, 1919–1939* (1990), examines the effects of the Great Depression and the New Deal on the working class. Blanche Wiesen Cook's continuing biography, *Eleanor Roosevelt*, 2 vols. to date (1992–), shows the transformation of the first lady into an advocate of the poor and dispossessed. Franklin Roosevelt's troubles with the Supreme Court are traced in William Leuchtenburg, *The Supreme Court Reborn* (1995); and Barry Cushman, *Rethinking the New Deal Court* (1998). The waning of the New Deal is the theme of Alan Brinkley, *The End of Reform* (1995).

SUGGESTED WEB SITES

Voices from the Dust Bowl: The Charles L. Todd and Robert Sonkin Migrant Worker Collection, 1940–1941
memory.loc.gov/ammem/afctshtml/tshome.html
Farm Security Administration (FSA) studies of migrant work camps in central California in 1940 and 1941 are the bulk of this site. The collection includes audio recordings, photographs, manuscript materials, and publications.

New Deal Network
newdeal.feri.org/
This database includes photographs, political cartoons, and texts—including speeches, letters, and other historic documents—from the New Deal period.

Franklin Delano Roosevelt
www.ipl.org/ref/potus/fdroosevelt.html
This site provides information about FDR, the only president to serve more than two terms.

A New Deal for the Arts
www.archives.gov/exhibits/new_deal_for_the_arts/index.html
Artwork, documents, and photographs recount the federal government's efforts to fund artists in the 1930s in this National Archives site.

America from the Great Depression to World War II: Photographs from the FSA and OWI, ca. 1935–1945
memory.loc.gov/ammem/fsowhome.html
These images in the Farm Security Administration–Office of War Information Collection show Americans from all over the nation experiencing everything from despair to triumph in the 1930s and 1940s.

Chapter 27

America and the World, 1921–1945

A Pact Without Power

On August 27, 1928, U.S. Secretary of State Frank B. Kellogg, French Foreign Minister Aristide Briand, and representatives of twelve other nations met in Paris to sign a pact outlawing war. Spectators watched and photographers recorded the historic ceremony. In the United States, a senator called the **Kellogg-Briand Pact** "the most telling action ever taken in human history to abolish war."

In reality, the Pact of Paris was the result of a determined American effort to avoid involvement in the European alliance system. In June 1927, Briand had sent a message to the American people inviting the United States to join with France in signing a pact to outlaw war between the two nations. The invitation struck a sympathetic response, but the State Department feared correctly that Briand's true intention was to establish a close tie between France and the United States. France believed that an antiwar pact with the United States would at least ensure American sympathy, if not involvement, in case of another European war. Kellogg outmaneuvered Briand by proposing that the pledge against war not be confined to just France and the United States, but instead be extended to all nations. An unhappy Briand had no choice but to agree, and so the diplomatic charade finally culminated in the elaborate signing ceremony in Paris.

Eventually, the signers of the Kellogg-Briand Pact included nearly every nation in the world, but the effect was negligible. All promised to renounce war as an instrument of national policy, except in matters of self-defense. The pact relied solely on the moral force of world opinion.

Unfortunately, the Kellogg-Briand Pact was symbolic of American foreign policy in the years immediately following World War I. Instead of asserting the role of world leadership its resources and power commanded, the United States retreated from involvement with other nations. America went its own way, extending trade and economic dominance but refusing to take the lead in maintaining world order. This retreat from responsibility seemed unimportant in the 1920s when the very exhaustion from World War I ensured relative peace and tranquillity. But in the 1930s, when threats to world order arose in Europe and Asia, the American people retreated even deeper, searching for an isolationist policy that would spare them the agony of another great war.

There was no place to hide in the modern world. The Nazi onslaught in Europe and the Japanese expansion in Asia finally convinced America to reverse its isolationist stance and become involved in World War II in late 1941, at a time when the chances for an Allied victory seemed most remote. With incredible swiftness, the nation mobilized its military and industrial strength. American armies were soon fighting on three

Kellogg-Briand Pact Also called the Pact of Paris, this 1928 agreement pledged its signatories, eventually including nearly all nations, to shun war as an instrument of policy. Derided as an "international kiss," it had little effect on the actual conduct of world affairs.

Outline

continents, the U.S. Navy controlled the world's oceans, and the nation's factories were sending a vast stream of war supplies to more than twenty Allied countries.

When Allied victory came in 1945, the United States was by far the most powerful nation in the world. But instead of the enduring peace that might have permitted a return to a less active foreign policy, the onset of the Cold War with the Soviet Union brought on a new era of tension and rivalry. This time the United States could not retreat from responsibility. World War II was a coming of age for American foreign policy.

RETREAT, REVERSAL, AND RIVALRY

Bitter disillusionment ran through every aspect of American foreign policy in the 1920s. Wilsonian idealism was gone. American diplomats made loans, negotiated treaties and agreements, and pledged the nation's good faith, but they were careful not to make any binding commitments on behalf of world order. The result was neither isolation nor involvement but rather a cautious middle course that managed to alienate friends and encourage foes.

Retreat in Europe

The United States emerged from World War I the richest nation on earth, displacing Britain from its prewar position of economic primacy. Each year of the 1920s saw the nation increase its economic lead as the balance of trade tipped heavily in America's favor. The war-ravaged countries of Europe borrowed enormous amounts from American bankers to rebuild their economies, and American exports and overseas investments far exceeded prewar levels.

The European nations could no longer compete on equal terms. The high American tariff, first imposed in 1922 and raised again in 1930, frustrated attempts by Britain, France, and a defeated Germany to earn the dollars necessary to meet their American financial obligations. Although the Allied partners in World War I asked Washington to cancel $10 billion in war debts, American leaders from Wilson to Hoover indignantly refused.

Only a continuing flow of private American capital to Germany allowed the payment of reparations to the Allies and the partial repayment of war debts in the 1920s. The financial crash of 1929 halted the flow of dollars across the Atlantic and led to subsequent default on the debt payments, with accompanying bitterness on both sides of the ocean.

Political relations fared little better. The United States never joined the League of Nations, nor did it take part in the attempts by Britain and France to negotiate European security treaties. The Republican administrations of the 1920s refused to compromise American freedom of action by embracing collective security, the principle on which the League was founded. And FDR made no effort to renew Wilson's futile quest. Remaining aloof from the European balance of power, the United States refused to stand behind the increasingly shaky Versailles settlement.

The United States ignored the Soviet Union throughout the 1920s. American businessmen, however, actively traded with the Soviets and pressed for diplomatic recognition of the Bolshevik regime. In 1933, Roosevelt finally signed an agreement opening up diplomatic relations between the two countries.

Cooperation in Latin America

United States policy in the Western Hemisphere was both more active and more enlightened than in Europe. The State Department sought new ways in the 1920s to pursue traditional goals of political dominance and economic advantage in Latin

America. Both Republican and Democratic administrations worked hard to limit American military involvement and to extend American trade and investment in the nations to the south. Under Harding, Coolidge, and Hoover, American marines were withdrawn from Haiti, the Dominican Republic, and Nicaragua. Renewed unrest in Nicaragua in 1925, however, led to a second intervention that lasted until the early 1930s.

Showing a new sensitivity, the State Department in 1930 released the Clark Memorandum, a policy statement repudiating the controversial Roosevelt Corollary to the Monroe Doctrine. The United States had no right to intervene in neighboring states under the Monroe Doctrine, declared Undersecretary of State J. Reuben Clark, although he asserted a traditional claim to protect American lives and property under international law.

When FDR took office in 1933, relations with Latin America were far better than they had been under Wilson, but American trade in the hemisphere had fallen drastically as the Great Depression worsened. Roosevelt moved quickly to solidify the improved relations and gain economic benefits. He proclaimed a **Good Neighbor Policy** and then proceeded to win goodwill by renouncing the imperialism of the past.

Starting in 1933, Roosevelt's secretary of state, Cordell Hull, moved toward a policy of nonintervention. A year later, the United States loosened its grip on Cuba (renouncing the Platt Amendment) and Panama. By 1936, American troops were no longer occupying any Latin American nation. But the United States had not changed its basic goal of political and economic dominance in the hemisphere. Rather, the new policy of benevolence reflected Roosevelt's belief that cooperation and friendship were more effective tactics than threats and armed intervention.

The Good Neighbor Policy opened up new trade opportunities. American commerce with Latin America increased fourfold in the 1930s, and investment rose substantially from its Great Depression low. Most important, FDR succeeded in forging a new policy of regional collective security between the nations of the Western Hemisphere and the United States.

Good Neighbor Policy
President Franklin D. Roosevelt's administration initiated a new approach to Western hemispheric relations with a policy declaring America's intention to use cooperation and friendship in place of threats and armed intervention in its dealings with Latin America.

Rivalry in Asia

In the years following World War I, the United States and Japan were on a collision course in the Pacific. The Japanese, lacking the raw materials to sustain their developing industrial economy, were determined to expand onto the Asian mainland. They had taken Korea by 1905 and during World War I had extended their control over the mines, harbors, and railroads of Manchuria, the industrial region of northeastern China. The American Open Door policy remained the primary obstacle to complete Japanese domination over China. The United States thus faced the clear-cut choice of either abandoning China or forcefully opposing Japan's expansion. American efforts to avoid making this painful decision postponed the eventual showdown but not the growing rivalry.

The first attempt at a solution came in 1921 when the United States convened the Washington Conference. The major objective was a political settlement of the tense Asian situation, but the most pressing issue was a dangerous naval race between Japan and the United States. Projected construction indicated that both countries would overtake the British navy by the end of the decade. Japan, spending nearly one-third of its budget on naval construction, was eager for an agreement; in the United States, too, growing congressional concern over appropriations suggested the need for slowing the naval buildup.

Secretary of State Charles Evans Hughes outlined a specific plan for naval disarmament. After three months of discussion, the delegates signed the Five Power Treaty limiting capital ships (battleships and aircraft carriers) in a ratio of 5:5:3 for the United States, Britain, and Japan, respectively, and 1.67:1.67 for France and

Italy. Japan agreed to the lower ratio only in return for an American pledge not to fortify Pacific bases such as the Philippines and Guam. The treaty cooled off the naval race even though it did not cover cruisers, destroyers, or submarines.

The Washington Conference also produced the Nine Power Treaty, which pledged the signatories to uphold the Open Door policy, and the Four Power Treaty, which created a new Pacific security pact. Neither document contained any enforcement provision beyond a promise to consult in case of violation. In essence, the Washington treaties formed a parchment peace, a pious set of pledges that attempted to freeze the status quo in the Pacific.

This compromise lasted less than a decade. In September 1931, Japanese forces overran Manchuria in a brutal act of aggression. The United States, paralyzed by the Great Depression, responded feebly. In January 1932, Secretary of State Henry L. Stimson vowed that the United States would not recognize the legality of the Japanese seizure of Manchuria. Despite ultimate concurrence by the League of Nations on nonrecognition, the Japanese ignored the American moral sanction and incorporated the former Chinese province into their expanding empire.

Aside from the Good Neighbor approach in the Western Hemisphere, American foreign policy faithfully reflected the prevailing disillusionment with world power that gripped the country after World War I. The United States avoided taking any constructive steps toward preserving world order, preferring instead the empty symbolism of the Washington treaties and the Kellogg-Briand Pact.

ISOLATIONISM

The retreat from an active world policy in the 1920s turned into a headlong flight back to isolationism in the 1930s. Two factors were responsible. First, the Great Depression made foreign policy seem remote and unimportant to most Americans. Second, the danger of war abroad, when it did finally penetrate the American consciousness, served only to strengthen the desire to escape involvement.

Three powerful and discontented nations were on the march in the 1930s—Germany, Italy, and Japan. In Germany, Adolf Hitler came to power in 1933 as the head of the National Socialist, or Nazi, movement. A shrewd and charismatic leader, Hitler capitalized on both domestic discontent and bitterness over Germany's defeat in World War I. Blaming the Jews and the Communists for all of Germany's ills and asserting the supremacy of the "Aryan" race of blond, blue-eyed Germans, he quickly imposed a totalitarian dictatorship in which the Nazi party ruled and the Führer (leader) was supreme. As he consolidated his power, his ultimate threat to world peace became clear. Hitler took Germany out of the League of Nations, reoccupied the Rhineland, and formally denounced the Treaty of Versailles.

In Italy, another dictator, Benito Mussolini, had come to power in 1922. Emboldened by Hitler's success, he embarked on an aggressive foreign policy in 1935. His invasion of Ethiopia led its emperor, Haile Selassie, to call on the League of Nations for support. The League's halfway measures utterly failed to halt Mussolini's conquest. Collective security had failed its most important test.

Japan formed the third element in the threat to world peace. Militarists began to dominate the government in Tokyo by the mid-1930s, using tactics of fear and even assassination against their liberal opponents. By 1936, Japan had left the League of Nations and had repudiated the Washington treaties. A year later, its armies began an invasion of China that signified the beginning of the Pacific phase of World War II.

The resurgence of militarism in Germany, Italy, and Japan undermined the Versailles settlement and threatened to destroy the existing balance of

■ Millions of Germans idolized Adolf Hitler, portrayed in this captured German painting as a white knight. After the painting came into American hands, a GI slashed Hitler's face to indicate his displeasure with the mystique of the Führer. ■

power. In 1937, the three totalitarian nations signed a pact creating a Berlin-Rome-Tokyo axis. The alliance of the **Axis Powers** ostensibly was aimed at the Soviet Union, but in fact it threatened the entire world. Only a determined American response could unite the other nations against the Axis threat. Unfortunately, the United States deliberately abstained from assuming this role of leadership until it was nearly too late.

The Lure of Pacifism and Neutrality

The growing danger of war abroad led to a rising American desire for noninvolvement. Memories of the horrors of World War I contributed heavily. Historians began to treat the Great War as a mistake, criticizing Wilson for failing to preserve American neutrality and claiming that the clever British had duped the United States into entering the war.

American youth made clear their determination not to repeat the mistakes of their elders. Pacifism swept college campuses. In April 1934, students and professors walked out of class to attend massive antiwar rallies, which became an annual rite of spring in the 1930s. Pacifist orators urged students to sign a pledge not to support their country "in any war it might conduct."

The pacifist movement found a scapegoat in the munitions industry. The publication of several books exposing the unsavory business tactics of the large arms dealers such as Krupps in Germany and Vickers in Britain led to the demand to curb these "merchants of death." Senator Gerald Nye of North Dakota headed a special Senate committee that spent two years investigating the dealings that brought enormous profits to munitions firms such as Du Pont. Nye went further, charging that bankers and munitions makers were responsible for American intervention in 1917. Although he offered no proof, the public—prepared to believe the worst of business during the Great Depression—accepted the merchants-of-death thesis.

The Nye Committee's revelations culminated in neutrality legislation aimed at avoiding involvement in European conflicts. In August 1935, Congress passed the first of three **neutrality acts.** The 1935 law banned the sale of arms to nations at war and warned American citizens not to sail on belligerent ships. In 1936, a second act added a ban on loans, and in 1937, a third neutrality act made these prohibitions permanent and required, on a two-year trial basis, that all trade other than munitions be conducted on a cash-and-carry basis.

President Roosevelt played a passive role in the adoption of the neutrality legislation. Privately, he expressed some reservations, but publicly he bowed to the prevailing isolationism. Yet FDR did take a few steps to try to limit the nation's retreat into isolationism. His failure to invoke the neutrality act after the Japanese invasion of China in 1937 enabled the hard-pressed Chinese to continue buying arms from the United States. In January 1938, he used his influence to block a proposal by Indiana Congressman Louis Ludlow to require a nationwide referendum before Congress could declare war. FDR's strongest public statement came earlier, in Chicago in October 1937, when he denounced "the epidemic of world lawlessness" and called for an international effort to "quarantine" this disease.

War in Europe

The neutrality legislation played directly into the hands of Adolf Hitler. Bent on the conquest of Europe, he could now proceed without worrying about American interference. In March 1938, he seized Austria in a bloodless coup. Six months later, he was demanding the Sudetenland, a province of Czechoslovakia with a large German population. When British and French leaders approved Hitler's move at their Munich conference, FDR gave his tacit consent.

Axis Powers During World War II, the alliance between Germany, Italy, and Japan was known as the Berlin-Rome-Tokyo axis, and the three members were called the Axis Powers. They fought against the Allied Powers, led by the United States, Britain, and the Soviet Union.

neutrality acts Reacting to their disillusionment with World War I and absorbed in the domestic crisis of the Great Depression, Americans backed Congress's three neutrality acts in the 1930s. The 1935 and 1936 acts forbade selling munitions or lending money to belligerents in a war. The 1937 act required that all remaining trade be conducted on a cash-and-carry basis.

■ *Hitler sent his armies into Poland with tremendous force and firepower, devastating the country. Here, German troops observe as the German Luftwaffe bombs Warsaw in September 1939, destroying the city and forcing its inhabitants to surrender.* ■

Within six months of the meeting at Munich, Hitler violated his promises by seizing nearly all of Czechoslovakia. In the United States, the State Department, with FDR's approval, pressed for neutrality revision, hoping to place *all* trade with belligerents, including munitions, on a cash-and-carry basis. The House, however, rejected the proposal, aware that it would favor Britain and France, who controlled the sea.

In July 1939, Roosevelt finally abandoned his aloof position and met with Senate leaders to plead for reconsideration. Even with the threat of war in Europe, strong isolationist sentiment prevailed. Congressional leaders refused to alter the neutrality acts.

On September 1, 1939, Hitler began World War II by invading Poland. Britain and France responded two days later by declaring war. The Soviets had played a key role by signing a nonaggression treaty with Hitler in late August. The Nazi-Soviet pact enabled Germany to avoid a two-front war; the Russians were rewarded with a generous slice of eastern Poland.

President Roosevelt reacted to the outbreak of war by proclaiming American neutrality, but the successful aggression by Nazi Germany brought into question the isolationist assumption that American well-being did not depend on the European balance of power. Strategic as well as ideological considerations began to undermine the earlier belief that the United States could safely pursue a policy of neutrality and noninvolvement. Americans came to realize that their own democracy and security were at stake in the European war.

THE ROAD TO WAR

For two years, the United States tried to remain at peace while war raged in Europe and Asia. In contrast to Wilson's attempt to be impartial during most of World War I, however, the American people displayed an overwhelming sympathy for the Allies and total distaste for Germany and Japan. Roosevelt made no secret of his preference for an Allied victory, but a fear of isolationist criticism compelled him to move slowly, and often deviously, in adopting a policy of aid for Britain and France short of actually entering the war.

From Neutrality to Undeclared War

Two weeks after the outbreak of war in Europe, Roosevelt called Congress into special session to revise the neutrality legislation. His aim was to repeal the arms embargo in order to supply weapons to Britain and France, but he refused to state this openly. Instead he asked Congress to replace the arms embargo with cash-and-carry regulations. Congress passed the revised neutrality policy by heavy margins in early November 1939.

A series of dramatic German victories had a profound impact on American opinion. In the spring of 1940, Germany seized Denmark and Norway and unleashed the *Blitzkrieg* ("lightning war") on the western front. Using tanks, armored columns, and dive bombers in close coordination, the German army drove the British off the continent in three weeks; three weeks later, France fell to Hitler's victorious armies.

Americans were stunned. Hitler had taken only six weeks to achieve what Germany had failed to do in four years of fighting in World War I. Suddenly they realized that they did have a stake in the outcome; if Britain fell, Hitler might well gain control of the British navy and the Atlantic, opening the New World to German penetration.

Roosevelt responded by invoking a policy of all-out aid to the Allies short of war. Denouncing Germany and Italy as representing "the gods of force and hate," he pledged American support for Britain and its allies. In early September, FDR announced the transfer of fifty old destroyers to Britain in exchange for rights to build air and naval bases on eight British possessions in the Western Hemisphere. Giving warships to a belligerent nation was clearly a breach of neutrality, but Roosevelt stressed the importance of the United States' guarding its Atlantic approaches.

Isolationists protested against this departure from neutrality. Roosevelt's opponents in the Midwest formed the America First Committee to oppose the drift toward war. Such diverse individuals as aviator-hero Charles Lindbergh, conservative Senator Robert A. Taft, and socialist leader Norman Thomas condemned FDR for involving the United States in a foreign conflict that they claimed in no way threatened America.

To support the administration's policies, moderate New Dealers, eastern seaboard Anglophiles, and liberal Republicans joined forces to organize the Committee to Defend America by Aiding the Allies. Kansas newspaper editor William Allen White served as chairman of this interventionist organization, which advocated unlimited assistance to the British short of war. Above all, the interventionists challenged the isolationist premise that events in Europe did not affect American security. As White declared, "The future of western civilization is being decided upon the battlefield of Europe."

In the ensuing debate, the American people gradually came to agree with the interventionists. Frightened by the events in Europe, Congress approved large sums for preparedness, increasing the defense budget from $2 billion to $10 billion during 1940. Roosevelt courageously asked for a peacetime draft, the first in American history, to build up the army, and Congress consented.

The sense of crisis affected domestic politics. Roosevelt ran for an unprecedented third term in 1940 because of the war; the Republicans nominated Wendell Willkie, who shared FDR's commitment to aid for Britain. Roosevelt's decisive victory made it clear that the nation supported his departure from neutrality.

After the election, FDR took his boldest step. Responding to British Prime Minister Winston Churchill's warning that his nation was running out of money, the president asked Congress to approve a new program to lend and lease goods and weapons to countries fighting against aggressors. Roosevelt's call for America to become "the great arsenal of democracy" seemed straightforward enough, but he acted somewhat deviously by naming the program **Lend-Lease** and by comparing it to loaning a garden hose to put out a fire.

Isolationists angrily denounced Lend-Lease as both unnecessary and untruthful. In March 1941, however, Congress voted by substantial margins to authorize the president to "sell, transfer title to, exchange, lease, lend, or otherwise dispose of" war supplies to "any country the president deems vital to the defense of the United States." The accompanying $7 billion appropriation ended the "cash" part of cash-and-carry and ensured full British access to American war supplies.

The "carry" problem still remained. German submarines were sinking more than 500,000 tons of shipping a month. Britain desperately needed the help of the American navy in escorting convoys across the U-boat-infested waters of the North Atlantic. Roosevelt responded with naval patrols as far east as Iceland. Hitler placed his submarine commanders under strict restraints to avoid drawing America into the European war. Nevertheless, incidents were bound to occur.

Undeclared naval war quickly followed. A German submarine damaged the U.S. destroyer *Kearney,* and another sank the *Reuben James.* FDR issued orders for the destroyers to shoot U-boats on sight. At Roosevelt's request, Congress repealed the "carry" section of the neutrality laws and permitted American ships to deliver

Lend-Lease Plan approved by Congress in 1941 that allowed the United States to sell, lend, lease, or transfer war materials to any country whose defense the president declared as vital to that of the United States.

supplies to Britain. Now American merchant ships as well as destroyers would become targets for German attacks. By December 1941, war with Germany seemed inevitable.

In leading the nation to the brink of war in Europe, Roosevelt opened himself to criticism from both sides in the domestic debate. Interventionists believed he was too cautious; isolationists claimed that he had misled the American people by professing peace while plotting for war. Roosevelt was certainly less than candid, relying on executive discretion to engage in highly provocative acts in the North Atlantic. Although he clearly saw the threat that Germany represented, he was also aware that most Americans wanted to stay out of another war. Realizing that leading a divided nation into war would be disastrous, FDR played for time, inching the country toward war while waiting for the Axis nations to make the ultimate move. Japan finally obliged at Pearl Harbor.

Showdown in the Pacific

Japan had taken advantage of the war in Europe to expand in Asia. The defeat of France and the Netherlands in 1940 left French and Dutch colonial possessions in the East Indies and Indochina vulnerable and defenseless. Japan now set out to incorporate these territories—rich in oil, tin, and rubber—into what was called the Greater East Asia Co-Prosperity Sphere.

The Roosevelt administration countered with economic pressure. Japan depended heavily on the United States for petroleum and scrap iron and steel. In July 1940, FDR signed an order setting up a licensing and quota system for the export of these crucial materials to Japan and banned the sale of aviation gasoline altogether. The United States was now employing economic sanctions to block Japanese expansion in Southeast Asia.

Tokyo appeared unimpressed. In early September 1940, Japanese troops occupied strategic bases in the northern part of French Indochina. Later in the month, Japan signed the Tripartite Pact with Germany and Italy, a defensive treaty that confronted the United States with a possible two-ocean war and a global totalitarian threat. Roosevelt and his advisers, however, saw Germany as the primary danger; thus they pursued a policy of all-out aid to Britain while hoping that economic measures alone would deter Japan.

The embargo on aviation gasoline, extended to include scrap iron and steel, was a burden Japan could bear, but a possible ban on all oil shipments was a different matter. Entirely dependent on oil imports from the United States and the Dutch East Indies, Japan tried to negotiate with the United States, but these talks broke down. Tokyo wanted nothing less than a free hand in China and an end to American sanctions, while the United States insisted on an eventual Japanese evacuation of all of China.

In July 1941, Japan invaded southern Indochina, beginning the chain of events that led to war. Washington knew of this aggression before it occurred. Naval intelligence experts had broken the Japanese diplomatic code and were intercepting and reading all messages between Tokyo and the Japanese embassy in Washington. FDR responded on July 25, 1941, with an order freezing all Japanese assets in the United States. Trade with Japan, including the vital oil shipments, came to a complete halt. When the Dutch government-in-exile took similar actions, Japan faced a dilemma: to have oil shipments resumed, Tokyo would have to end its aggression; the alternative would be to seize the needed petroleum supplies in the Dutch East Indies, an action that would mean war.

With General Hideki Tojo, an army militant, as the premier of Japan, the Tokyo government moved toward war. To mask its war preparations, Tokyo sent yet another envoy to Washington with new peace proposals, a mission both Japan and the United States knew was futile. Army and navy leaders urged FDR to seek a temporary settlement with Japan to give them time to prepare American defenses in the Pacific. Secretary of State Hull, however, refused to allow any concessions, sending a stiff ten-point reply to Tokyo that included a demand for Japanese withdrawal from China.

Two weeks later, on the evening of December 6, 1941, the first thirteen parts of the Japanese reply to Hull's note arrived in Washington. After reading the decoded text late that night, President Roosevelt said, "This means war."

The fourteenth part of Japan's reply arrived the next day, December 7, revealing Japan's complete rejection of the American position. Officials in Washington tried to warn American bases in the Pacific, but they were too late. Just before 1 P.M. Washington time, squadrons of Japanese carrier-based planes caught the American fleet at **Pearl Harbor,** Hawaii, totally by surprise. In a little more than an hour, the Japanese crippled the American Pacific fleet and destroyed its base at Pearl Harbor, sinking eight battleships and killing more than 2,400 American sailors.

Speaking before Congress the next day, President Roosevelt termed December 7 "a date which will live in infamy" and asked for a declaration of war against Japan. With only one dissenting vote, both chambers consented. On December 11, Germany and Italy declared war against the United States; the nation was now fully involved in World War II.

The whole country united behind Roosevelt's leadership to seek revenge for Pearl Harbor and to defeat the Axis threat to American security. After the war, however, critics charged that FDR had entered the conflict by a back door, claiming that the president had deliberately exposed the Pacific fleet to attack. Subsequent investigations uncovered negligence in both Hawaii and Washington but no evidence to support the conspiracy charge. Both military experts and FDR had badly underestimated the daring and skill of the Japanese, but there was no plot. Perhaps the most frightening aspect of the whole episode is that it took the shock of the Japanese sneak attack to make the American people aware of the full extent of the Axis threat to their well-being and persuade them out of the long fruitless effort to stay out of the war.

Pearl Harbor On December 7, 1941, Japanese warplanes attacked U.S. naval forces at Pearl Harbor, Hawaii, sinking several ships and killing more than 2400 American sailors. The event marked America's entrance into World War II.

■ *American ships were destroyed in the surprise attack on Pearl Harbor, December 7, 1941. Caught completely off guard, U.S. forces still managed to shoot down twenty-nine enemy planes.* ■

TURNING THE TIDE AGAINST THE AXIS

In the first few months after the United States entered the war, the outlook for victory was bleak. In Europe, Hitler's armies controlled virtually the entire continent, from Norway in the north to Greece in the south. Despite the nonaggression pact, German armies had penetrated deep into the Soviet Union after an initial invasion in June 1941. In North Africa, General Erwin Rommel's Afrika Korps had pushed the British back into Egypt and threatened the Suez Canal.

The situation was no better in Asia. The Pearl Harbor attack had enabled the Japanese to move unopposed across Southeast Asia. Within three months, they had conquered Malaya and the Dutch East Indies, with its valuable oil fields, and were pressing the British back in both Burma and New Guinea. American forces under General Douglas MacArthur had tried but failed to block the Japanese conquest of the Philippines. With the American navy still recovering from the devastation at Pearl Harbor, Japan controlled the western half of the Pacific.

It took the United States and its allies two years to halt the German and Japanese offensives. Then they faced the difficult process of driving back the enemy, freeing the vast conquered areas, and defeating the Axis powers on their home territory. It was a difficult and costly struggle requiring great sacrifice and heavy losses; World War II tested American will and resourcefulness to the hilt.

Wartime Partnerships

The greatest single advantage that the United States and its partners possessed was their willingness to form a genuine coalition to bring about the defeat of the Axis powers. In striking contrast was the behavior of Germany and Japan, each fighting a separate war without any attempt at cooperation.

The United States and Britain achieved a complete wartime partnership. Prewar military talks led to the formation of the Combined Chiefs of Staff, which directed Anglo-American military operations. The close cooperation between FDR and Prime Minister Churchill ensured a common strategy. The leaders decided at the outset that a German victory posed the greater danger and thus gave priority to the European theater in the conduct of the war.

Relations with the other members of the coalition in World War II were not quite so harmonious. The decision to defeat Germany first displeased the Chinese, who had been at war with Japan since 1937. Roosevelt tried to appease Chiang Kai-shek with a trickle of supplies. France posed a more delicate problem. FDR virtually ignored the Free French government in exile under General Charles de Gaulle. Roosevelt preferred to deal with the Vichy regime, despite its collaboration with Germany, because it still controlled the French fleet and retained France's overseas territories.

The greatest strain of all within the wartime coalition was with the Soviet Union. Although Roosevelt had ended the long period of nonrecognition in 1933, close ties had failed to develop. The great Russian purge trials and the temporary Nazi-Soviet alliance from 1939 to 1941, along with deep-seated cultural and ideological differences, made wartime cooperation difficult.

Ever the pragmatist, Roosevelt tried hard to break down the old hostility and establish a more cordial relationship with the Soviets during the war. He was quick to give Lend-Lease aid to the USSR, and in May 1942, he promised a visiting Russian diplomat that the United States would create a second front in Europe by the end of that year, a pledge he could not fulfill. In January 1943, Roosevelt and Churchill met in Casablanca, Morocco, to declare a policy of unconditional surrender, vowing that the Western Allies would fight on until the Axis nations were completely defeated.

Despite the promises, the Soviet Union bore the brunt of the battle against Hitler in the early years of the war. The United States and Britain, grateful for the respite to build up their forces, could do little more than offer promises of future help and send Lend-Lease supplies. The result was a rift that never fully healed—one that did not prevent the defeat of Germany but did ensure future tensions and uncertainties between the Soviet Union and the Western nations.

Halting the German Blitz

From the outset, the United States favored an invasion across the English Channel as the key to victory in Europe. Roosevelt and his leading military advisers were convinced that such a frontal assault would be the quickest way to win the war. Army Chief of Staff George C. Marshall placed his protégé, Dwight D. Eisenhower, in charge of drawing up and implementing the invasion.

But the British preferred a perimeter approach, with air and naval attacks around the edge of the continent, until Germany was softened up for the final invasion. Roosevelt temporarily consented to this plan, and in November 1942, American and British troops landed on the Atlantic and Mediterranean coasts of Morocco and Algeria.

The British launched an attack against Rommel at El Alamein in Egypt and soon forced the Afrika Korps to retreat across Libya to Tunisia. American forces then hit Rommel in Tunisia. After a humiliating defeat at the Kasserine Pass, General George Patton rallied the demoralized American soldiers, and by May 1943, Germany had been driven from Africa, leaving behind nearly 300,000 troops. During these same months, the Red Army broke the back of German military power after Hitler poured in division after division in what was ultimately a critical defeat at the battle of Stalingrad.

At Churchill's insistence, FDR agreed to follow up the North African victory with the invasion first of Sicily and then Italy in the summer of 1943. Italy dropped out of the war when Mussolini fled to Germany, but the Italian campaign proved to be a strategic dead end. Germany sent in enough divisions to establish a strong defensive line in the mountains south of Rome; American and British troops were forced to fight their way slowly up the peninsula, suffering heavy casualties.

More important, these Mediterranean operations delayed the second front, postponing it eventually to the spring of 1944. Meanwhile, the Soviets began to push the Germans out and looked forward to the liberation of Poland, Hungary, and Romania, where they could establish "friendly" Communist regimes. Having borne the brunt of the fighting against Nazi Germany, Stalin was ready to claim his reward—the postwar domination of eastern Europe.

Checking Japan in the Pacific

The decision to defeat Germany first and the vast expanses of the Pacific dictated the nature of the war against Japan—amphibious, island-hopping campaigns rather than any attempt to reconquer the Dutch East Indies, Southeast Asia, and China. There would be two separate American operations. One, led by Douglas MacArthur based in Australia, would move from New Guinea back to the Philippines, while the other, commanded by Admiral Chester Nimitz from Hawaii, was directed at key Japanese islands in the central Pacific. The original plan called for the two offensives to come together for the final invasion of the Japanese home islands.

Success in the Pacific depended above all on control of the sea. In the battle of the Coral Sea in May 1942, American naval forces blocked a Japanese thrust to outflank Australia. The turning point came one month later at Midway. In this

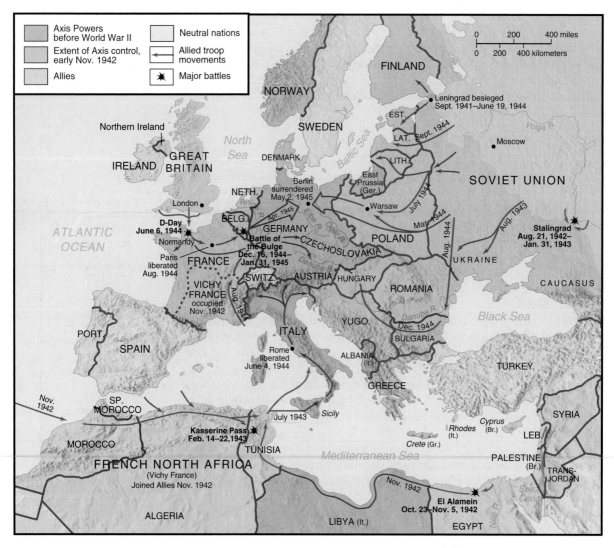

WORLD WAR II IN EUROPE AND NORTH AFRICA *The tide of battle shifted in this theater of war during the winter of 1942–1943. The massive German assault on the eastern front was turned back by the Russians at Stalingrad, and the Allied forces recaptured North Africa.* ■

important battle, superior American air power enabled Nimitz's forces to engage the enemy at long range. The battle of Midway ended with the loss of four Japanese aircraft carriers compared to just one American. It was the first defeat the modern Japanese navy had ever suffered, and it left the United States in control of the central Pacific.

Encouraged by the victory, American forces launched their first Pacific offensive in the Solomon Islands, east of New Guinea, in August 1942. Six months later, the last Japanese were driven from the key island of Guadalcanal. At the same time, MacArthur began the long, bloody job of driving the Japanese back along the north coast of New Guinea.

By early 1943, the defensive phase of the war with Japan was over. The enemy surge had been halted in both the central and the southwestern Pacific, and the United States was ready to move back toward the Philippines. Just as Soviet Russia had broken German power in Europe, the United States had halted the Japanese. And like the Soviet plans for eastern Europe, America expected to reap the rewards of victory by dominating the Pacific in the future.

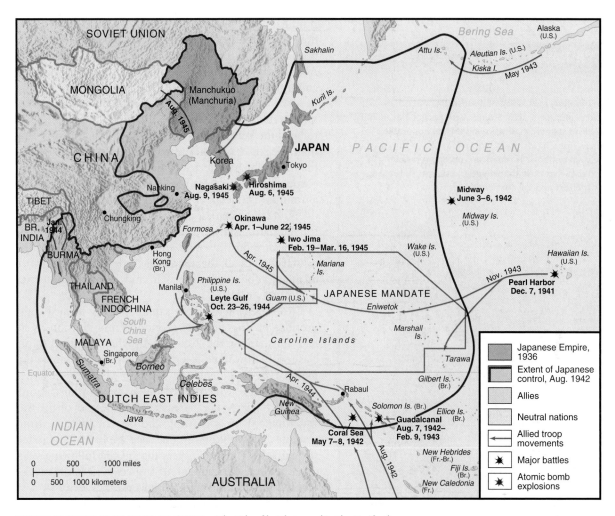

WORLD WAR II IN THE PACIFIC   *The tide of battle turned in the Pacific the same year as in Europe. The balance of sea power shifted back to the United States from Japan after the naval victories of 1942.* ∎

THE HOME FRONT

World War II had a greater impact than the Great Depression on American life. While American soldiers and sailors fought abroad, the nation underwent sweeping social and economic changes at home. American industry worked to capacity to meet the need for war materials. Increased production in both industry and agriculture benefited workers and farmers alike. The expansion of war-related industries encouraged many people to move to where new jobs had sprung up. Women moved out of the home into the paid workforce; rural dwellers relocated to urban areas, and northerners and easterners sought new opportunities and new homes in the South and West. Another beneficiary of the return to prosperity brought on by the war was FDR, who had seen the nation through the dark days of the depression. The nation's economic recovery helped him win re-election to the presidency for a fourth term in 1944.

The Arsenal of Democracy

American industry made the nation's single most important contribution to victory. The manufacturing plants that had run at half capacity through the 1930s now hummed with activity. In Detroit, automobile assembly lines were converted to

A Look at the Past

WWII Ration Stamps

Ration stamps became necessary during World War II when gasoline, tires, selected foodstuffs, and other products became scarce. Stamps with patriotic or military symbolism suggest that rationing was an honorable sacrifice, not a hardship. ✱ How effective was the tactic of using such symbols? If Americans accepted rationing as their duty, what does that suggest about attitudes toward the war effort and government?

produce tanks and airplanes with the same efficiency as they had once turned out cars. Shipmakers were just as productive. In part, America won the battle of the Atlantic by building ships faster than German U-boats could sink them.

The vast industrial expansion, however, created many problems. In 1942, FDR appointed Donald Nelson to head the War Production Board (WPB). An easygoing man, Nelson was soon outmaneuvered by the army and the navy, which preferred to negotiate directly with large corporations. Shortages of such critical materials as steel, aluminum, and copper led to an allocation system based on military priorities. However, through tax incentives for industrialists and rationing of import products, American industries were able to meet the needs of the military. All in all, the nation's factories turned out twice as many goods as the German and Japanese industries combined.

Roosevelt revealed the same tendency toward compromise in directing the economic mobilization as he had in shaping the New Deal. When administrators clashed, FDR worked toward a consensus and fair settlements. The president was also forced to compromise with Congress, which pared down the administration's requests for large tax increases. Half the cost of the war was financed by borrowing; the other half came from revenues. A $7 billion revenue increase in 1942 included so many first-time taxpayers that in the following year, the Treasury Department instituted a new practice—withholding income taxes from workers' wages.

The result of this wartime economic explosion was growing affluence. Despite the federal incentives to business, heavy excess-profit taxes and a 94 percent tax rate for the very rich kept the wealthy from benefiting unduly. The huge increase in federal spending, from $9 billion in 1940 to $98 billion in 1944, spread through American society. A government agreement with labor unions in 1943 held wage rates to a 15 percent increase, but the long hours of overtime doubled and sometimes tripled the weekly paychecks of factory workers. Farmers shared in the new prosperity as their incomes quadrupled between 1940 and 1945. Most important, this rising income ensured postwar prosperity. Workers and farmers saved their money, channeling much of it into government war bonds, waiting for the day when they could buy the cars and home appliances they could not have obtained during the long years of depression and war.

A Nation on the Move

The war led to a vast migration of the American population. Young men left their homes for training camps and then for service overseas. Defense workers and their families moved to the new booming shipyards, munitions factories, and aircraft plants. Rural areas lost population while coastal regions, especially along the Pacific and the Gulf of Mexico, drew millions of people. California had the greatest gains, adding nearly two million to its population in less than five years.

The movement of people caused severe social problems. Housing was in short supply. Migrating workers crowded into house trailers and boardinghouses, bringing unexpected windfalls to landlords. Family life suffered under these crowded living conditions; an increase in the number of marriages was offset by a rising divorce rate. In addition, schools and other social agencies were hard pressed to service the remarkable baby boom that began during the war.

The demand for workers led to a dramatic rise in female employment. Women entered industries once viewed as exclusively male; by the end of the war, they worked alongside men tending blast furnaces in steel mills and welding hulls in shipyards. The wartime experience helped undermine the concept that woman's only proper place was in the home.

African Americans shared in the wartime migration, but racial prejudice limited their social and economic gains. Nearly one million served in the armed forces, but few saw combat. The army placed blacks in segregated units and used them for service and construction tasks. The navy was even worse, relegating them to menial jobs until late in the war.

Black civilians fared a little better. In 1941, black labor leader A. Philip Randolph threatened a massive march on Washington to force Roosevelt to end racial discrimination in defense industries and government employment and to integrate the armed forces. FDR compromised, persuading Randolph to call off the march and drop his integration demand in return for an executive order creating the Fair Employment Practices Committee (FEPC) to ban racial discrimination in war industries. As a result, black employment by the federal government rose sharply; the FEPC proved less successful in the private sector. The nationwide shortage of labor was more influential than the FEPC in the rise in black employment during wartime. Blacks moved from the rural South to northern and western cities, finding occupations in the automobile, aircraft, and shipbuilding industries.

The movement of an estimated 700,000 people helped transform black-white relations from a regional issue into a national concern that could no longer be ignored. The limited housing and recreational facilities for both black and white war workers created tensions that led to urban race riots. The worst riot took place in Detroit in June 1943; twenty-three blacks and nine whites died in the fighting. These outbursts of racial violence fueled the resentments that would grow into the postwar civil rights movement. For most blacks, despite the economic gain, World War II was a reminder of the inequality of American life.

One-third of a million Mexican Americans served in the armed forces and shared some of the same experiences as blacks. At home, Spanish-speaking people left the rural areas of the Southwest for jobs in the cities. Despite low wages and union resistance, they managed to improve their economic position substantially. But they still faced discrimination based both on skin color and language, most notably in the Los Angeles "zoot suit" riots in 1943, when white servicemen attacked Mexican American youths dressed in their distinctive long jackets and pegged trousers. The racial prejudice heightened feelings of ethnic identity and led returning Mexican American veterans to form organizations to press for equal rights in the future.

A tragic counterpoint to the voluntary movement of American workers in search of jobs was the forced relocation of 120,000 Japanese Americans from the West Coast. Responding to racial fears in California after Pearl Harbor, FDR approved an army order in February 1942 to move both the Issei (Japanese Americans who had emigrated from Japan) and the Nisei (people of Japanese ancestry born in the United States and therefore U.S. citizens) to "detention centers" in the interior. Forced to dispose of their farms and businesses at distress prices, the Japanese Americans lost not only their liberty but also most of their worldly goods. Herded into detention centers, they lived as prisoners in tar-papered barracks behind barbed wire, guarded by armed troops.

A Look at the Past

Service Star

Households with members enlisted in the armed forces earned the privilege to display service stars in their windows. Each blue star represented one family member, whether male or female, active in the armed services. A gold star was displayed (sometimes covering a blue star) when the family member was killed in action or died in service. ✷ Why would the federal government issue service stars? How would displaying service stars aid the war effort? How might families with no family members eligible for serving in the military have felt about having no service stars?

Appeals to the Supreme Court proved fruitless; the justices upheld relocation on the grounds of national security in wartime. Beginning in 1943, individual Japanese Americans could win release by pledging their loyalty and finding a job away from the West Coast, but the detention centers were not closed down until March 1946. Although the Japanese Americans never experienced the torture and mass death of the German concentration camps, their treatment was a disgrace to a nation fighting for freedom and democracy.

Win-the-War Politics

Roosevelt used World War II to strengthen his leadership and maintain Democratic political dominance. As war brought about prosperity and removed the economic discontent that had sustained the New Deal, FDR announced that "Dr. New Deal" had given way to "Dr. Win-the-War." Congress, already controlled by a conservative coalition of southern Democrats and northern Republicans, had almost slipped into GOP hands in 1942. With very low voter turnout, the Republicans won forty-four new seats in the House and nine in the Senate.

In 1944, Roosevelt responded to the Democratic slippage by dropping Henry Wallace, his liberal vice president, for Harry Truman, a moderate and down-to-earth Missouri senator who was acceptable to all factions of the Democratic party. Equally important, FDR received increased political support from organized labor.

The Republicans nominated Thomas E. Dewey, a moderate from New York who made Roosevelt's age and health the primary issues, along with the charge that the Democrats were soft on communism. His foreign policy statements were far more internationalist than previous Republican policy. Indeed, Dewey pioneered a bipartisan approach to foreign policy. He accepted wartime planning for the future United Nations and kept the issue of an international organization out of the campaign.

FDR's vitality impressed the voters, however, and in November 1944, he swept back into office for a fourth term. But the war years had taken their toll. The president, suffering from high blood pressure and congestive heart failure, would lead the nation for only a few months more.

VICTORY

World War II ended with surprising swiftness. Once the Axis tide had been turned in Europe and Asia, it did not take long for the Soviet Union, the United States, and Britain to mount the offensives that drove Germany and Japan back across the vast areas they had conquered and set the stage for their final defeat.

The long-awaited second front finally came on June 6, 1944. For two years, the United States and Britain had concentrated on building up an invasion force of nearly three million troops and a vast armada of ships and landing craft to carry them across the English Channel. In hopes of catching Hitler by surprise, Eisenhower chose the Normandy peninsula, where the absence of good harbors had justified light German fortifications.

D-Day was originally set for June 5, but bad weather forced a delay. At dawn on June 6, the British and American troops fought their way ashore along a 40-mile stretch of beach, encountering stiff German resistance at several points. By the end of the day, however, Eisenhower had won his beachhead; a week later, more than 300,000 men were slowly pushing back the German forces through the hedgerows of Normandy. The breakthrough came on July 25 at Saint-Lô, opening a gap for General George Patton's Third Army. Soon American forces liberated Paris and reached the Rhine River, but a shortage of supplies, especially gasoline, forced a three-month halt.

D-Day The day Allied troops crossed the English Channel and opened a second front in western Europe, June 6, 1944. The "D" stands for "disembarkation": to leave a ship and go ashore.

Hitler took advantage of this breathing spell to deliver a daring counterattack. In mid-December, the remaining German armored divisions burst through a weak point in the Allied lines in the Ardennes Forest, planning to cut off nearly one-third of Eisenhower's forces. The gamble, however, failed. By committing nearly all his reserves to this effort, known as the Battle of the Bulge, Hitler had delayed Eisenhower's advance into Germany, but he had fatally weakened German resistance in the west.

The end came quickly. During the spring of 1945, Soviet and American troops moved separately toward Berlin. A massive Soviet offensive began in mid-January and swept across the Oder River. General Bradley's troops crossed the Rhine, and Allied forces captured the industrial Ruhr basin. In April, the two armies met at the Elbe River. With the Red Army already in the suburbs of Berlin, Adolf Hitler committed suicide on April 30. A week later, on May 7, 1945, Eisenhower accepted the unconditional surrender of all German forces. Just eleven months and a day after the landing in Normandy, the Allied forces had brought the war in Europe to a successful end.

■ *Two survivors at the Mittlebau Dora camp at Nordhausen, Germany, lie among hundreds of dead on the barrack floors. Photos of the death camps made the almost unimaginable atrocities of the Führer's regime real to Americans at home.* ■

Yalta Conference Yalta, a city in the Russian Crimea, hosted this wartime conference of the Allies in February 1945 in which the Allies agreed to final plans for the defeat of Germany and the terms of its occupation. The Soviets agreed to allow free elections in Poland, but the elections were never held.

After they entered Germany, American troops found horrifying evidence of the Holocaust—Hitler's eradication of 6 million European Jews. American soldiers were shocked at the conditions within the German concentration camps—lethal gas chambers, huge ovens for cremation, bodies stacked like cords of wood, and, most vivid of all, the emaciated, skeleton-like survivors with their blank stares. These awful discoveries removed any doubt in the minds of the American people about the evil nature of the Nazi regime they had just helped to destroy.

War Aims and Wartime Diplomacy

The American contribution to Hitler's defeat was relatively minor compared to the damage inflicted by the Soviet Union. As his armies overran Poland and the Balkan countries, Joseph Stalin was determined to retain control over this region, which had been the historic pathway for western invaders into Russia. Delay in opening the second front and an innate distrust of the West convinced the Soviets that they should maximize their territorial gains by imposing communist regimes on eastern Europe.

American postwar goals were quite different. Now believing that the failure to join the League of Nations in 1919 had laid the groundwork for World War II, the American people and their leaders vowed to put their faith in a new attempt at collective security. At Moscow in 1943, Secretary of State Hull won Soviet agreement to participate in a future world organization at the war's end. In the first wartime Big Three conference, held at Teheran, Iran, in late 1943, Stalin reaffirmed his commitment and also indicated to FDR that the USSR would enter the war against Japan once Germany was defeated.

By the time the Big Three met again in February 1945 at the **Yalta Conference,** the military situation favored the Soviets. Stalin drove a series of hard bargains. He refused to give up his plans for communist domination of Poland and the Balkans, although he did agree to hold free elections in eastern Europe. More important for the United States, Stalin promised to enter the Pacific war three months after Germany surrendered. In return, Roosevelt offered extensive concessions in Asia, including Soviet control over Manchuria. Although neither a sellout nor a betrayal, Yalta was, as some critics have charged, a diplomatic victory for the Soviets, reflecting their major contribution to victory in Europe.

For the president, the long journey to Yalta proved too much. In early April 1945, FDR left Washington for Warm Springs, Georgia, where he had always been able to relax. He was sitting for his portrait at midday on April 12, 1945, when he suddenly complained of a "terrific headache," then slumped forward and died. The nation mourned a man who had gallantly met the challenges of depression and global war but had not lived to see the final victory. Unfortunately, he had taken no steps to prepare his successor for the difficult problems that lay ahead.

The defeat of Nazi Germany dissolved the bond between the United States and the Soviet Union in World War II. With very different histories, cultures, and ideologies, the two nations had little in common beyond their enmity toward Hitler. It was now up to the inexperienced Harry Truman to deal with the growing rift that was destined to develop into the Cold War.

Triumph and Tragedy in the Pacific

The total defeat of Germany in May 1945 turned all eyes toward Japan. The American forces were moving swiftly; by the end of 1944, they had secured bases for further advances and were building airfields for American B-29s to begin a deadly bombardment of the Japanese home islands. In addition, by the end of the year, General MacArthur had retaken the Philippines. The Japanese navy, in a Pacific version of the Battle of the Bulge, launched a daring three-pronged attack on the American invasion fleet in Leyte Gulf. The U.S. Navy rallied to blunt all three Japanese thrusts, sinking four carriers and ending any further Japanese naval threat.

The defeat of Japan was now only a matter of time. The United States had three ways to proceed. Diplomats suggested a negotiated peace, urging that the United States modify the unconditional-surrender formula to permit Japan to retain the institution of the emperor. The military favored a full-scale invasion and estimated that it would suffer hundreds of thousands of casualties.

The third possibility involved the highly secret **Manhattan Project.** Since 1939, the United States had spent $2 billion to develop an atomic bomb based on the fission of radioactive uranium and plutonium. Scientists, many of them refugees from Europe, worked at the University of Chicago; at Oak Ridge, Tennessee; at Hanford, Washington; and at a remote laboratory in Los Alamos, New Mexico, to perfect this deadly new weapon. On July 16, 1945, they successfully tested the first atomic bomb in the New Mexico desert, creating a fireball brighter than several suns and a telltale mushroom cloud that rose 40,000 feet above an enormous crater in the desert floor.

When informed of the achievement, President Truman authorized the army air force to use the atomic bomb against Japan. He followed the recommendation of a committee headed by Secretary of War Henry L. Stimson to drop the bomb on a Japanese city without any prior warning. Both Truman and Stimson viewed the decision as a legitimate wartime measure, one designed to save the hundreds of thousands of American and Japanese lives that would be lost in a full-scale invasion.

Manhattan Project In early 1942, Franklin Roosevelt, alarmed by reports that German scientists were working on an atomic bomb, authorized a crash program to build the bomb first. The Manhattan Project, named for the Corps of Engineers district originally in charge, spent $2 billion and produced the weapons that devastated Hiroshima and Nagasaki in 1945.

Chronology

1922	Washington Naval Conference limits tonnage
1928	Kellogg-Briand Pact outlaws war ▪ Clark Memorandum repudiates Roosevelt Corollary (issued publicly in 1930)
1931	Japan occupies China's Manchuria province
1933	FDR extends diplomatic recognition to the USSR
1936	Hitler's troops reoccupy the Rhineland
1937	FDR signs permanent neutrality act ▪ FDR urges quarantine of aggressor nations
1938	Munich Conference appeases Hitler
1939	Germany invades Poland; World War II begins
1941	Japanese attack Pearl Harbor; United States enters World War II
1942	U.S. defeats Japanese at Midway ▪ Allies land in North Africa
1943	Soviets smash Nazis at Stalingrad
1944	Allies land on Normandy beachheads
1945	Big Three meet at Yalta ▪ FDR dies; Harry Truman becomes president ▪ Germany surrenders unconditionally ▪ United States drops atomic bombs on Hiroshima and Nagasaki; Japan surrenders

Weather conditions on the morning of August 6 dictated the choice of Hiroshima as the bomb's target. The explosion incinerated 4 square miles of the city and killed more than sixty thousand people instantly. Two days later, the Soviet Union entered the war against Japan, and the next day, August 9, the United States dropped a second bomb, this time on Nagasaki. No more atomic bombs were available, but no more were needed. Japan surrendered unconditionally on August 14, 1945. Three weeks later, Japan signed a formal capitulation agreement on the decks of the battleship *Missouri* in Tokyo Bay to bring World War II to its official close.

CONCLUSION: THE TRANSFORMING POWER OF WAR

The second great war of the twentieth century has had a lasting impact on American life. For the first time, the nation's military potential had been reached; in 1945, it was unquestionably the strongest country on the earth. In the future, the United States would be involved in all parts of the world. And despite its enormous strength in 1945, the nation's new world role would encompass failure and frustration as well as power and dominion.

The legacy of war was equally strong at home. Four years of fighting brought about industrial recovery and unparalleled prosperity. The old pattern of unregulated free enterprise was as much a victim of the war as of the New Deal; big government and huge deficits had now become the norm as economic control passed from New York and Wall Street to Washington and Pennsylvania Avenue. The war led to far-reaching changes in American society that would become apparent decades later. Such distinctive patterns of recent American life as the baby boom and the growth of the Sunbelt can be traced back to wartime origins. The war was a watershed in twentieth-century America, ushering in a new age of global concerns and domestic upheaval.

KEY TERMS

Kellogg-Briand Pact, p. 519

Good Neighbor Policy, p. 521

Axis Powers, p. 523

neutrality acts, p. 523

Lend-Lease, p. 525

Pearl Harbor, p. 527

D-Day, p. 535

Yalta Conference, p. 536

Manhattan Project, p. 537

RECOMMENDED READING

The best general account of American attitudes toward the world in the 1920s can be found in Warren I. Cohen, *Empire Without Tears* (1987). Robert Dallek provides a thorough account of FDR's diplomacy in *Franklin D. Roosevelt and American Foreign Policy, 1932–1945* (1979). For a more critical view, see Robert A. Divine, *Roosevelt and World War II* (1969). David M. Kennedy, *Freedom from Fear* (1999), sets Roosevelt's foreign and wartime policies against the background of domestic politics.

Two good books on the continuing controversy over Pearl Harbor are Roberta Wohlstetter, *Pearl Harbor: Warning and Decision* (1962), and Gordon W. Prange, *At Dawn We*

Slept (1981). Both authors deny the charge that Roosevelt deliberately exposed the naval base to attack.

In his brief overview of wartime diplomacy, *American Diplomacy During the Second World War*, 2nd ed. (1985), Gaddis Smith stresses the tensions within the victorious coalition. So does Mark Stoler in *Allies and Adversaries* (2000). Kenneth S. Davis, *FDR: The War President* (2000); Thomas Fleming, *The New Dealers' War* (2001); and Michael Beschloss, *The Conquerors* (2002), portray American leadership during the war. Williamson Murray and Allan R. Millett, *A War to Be Won* (2000), and Carlo D'Este, *Eisenhower: A Soldier's Life* (2002), focus on the fighting. Robert S. Norris,

Racing for the Bomb (2002), and Gregg Herken, *Brotherhood of the Bomb* (2002), describe the Manhattan Project and what it led to.

The best accounts of the home front are Kennedy, *Freedom from Fear;* Richard Polenberg, *War and Society* (1972); John M. Blum, *V Was for Victory* (1976); and Doris Kearns Goodwin, *No Ordinary Time* (1995). Daniel Kryder, *Divided Arsenal* (2000); Ronald Takaki, *Double Victory* (2000); and Greg Robinson, *By Order of the President* (2001), trace the war's effects on racial and ethnic minorities in the United States.

SUGGESTED WEB SITES

A People at War
www.archives.gov/exhibits/a_people_at_war/
This National Archives Exhibit takes a close look at the contributions millions of Americans made to the war effort.

Powers of Persuasion—Poster Art of World War II
www.archives.gov/exhibits/powers_of_persuasion/
These powerful posters at the National Archives were part of the battle for the hearts and minds of the American people.

America from the Great Depression to World War II: Photographs from the FSA and OWI, ca. 1935–1945
memory.loc.gov/ammem/fsowhome.html
These images in the Farm Security Administration–Office of War Information Collection show Americans from all over the nation experiencing everything from despair to triumph in the 1930s and 1940s.

A-Bomb WWW Museum
www.csi.ad.jp/ABOMB/
This site offers information about the impact of the first atomic bomb as well as the background and context of weapons of total destruction.

United States Holocaust Memorial Museum
www.ushmm.org/
This is the official site of the Holocaust Museum in Washington, D.C.

Tuskegee Airmen
www.wpafb.af.mil/museum/history/prewwii/ta.htm
The Air Force Museum at Wright-Patterson Air Force Base maintains this site about the African American pilots of World War II.

Abraham Lincoln Brigade Archives
www.alba-valb.org
This Brandeis University site has posters and photographs from the Spanish civil war and the unit of American volunteers who fought in it.

World War II Resources: Primary Source Materials on the Web
www.ibiblio.org/pha/index.html
This site has a large number of searchable primary texts from all aspects of World War II.

Chapter 28

The Onset of the Cold War

The Potsdam Summit

I am getting ready to go see Stalin and Churchill," President Truman wrote to his mother in July 1945, "and it is a chore." On board the cruiser *Augusta,* the new president continued to complain about the trip to Potsdam in his diary. Halfway around the world, Joseph Stalin left Moscow a day late because of a slight heart attack. Obsessed with security and hating to fly, he traveled to Potsdam, a suburb of Berlin, by rail. He was ready to claim the spoils of war.

The two men, one the veteran revolutionary who had been in power for two decades, the other an untested leader in office barely three months, symbolized the enormous differences that now separated the wartime allies. Stalin was above all a realist. Brutal in securing total control at home, he was more flexible in his foreign policy, bent on exploiting the Soviet Union's victory in World War II rather than aiming at world domination. Cunning and caution were the hallmarks of his diplomatic style. Truman, in contrast, personified traditional Wilsonian idealism. Lacking Roosevelt's guile, the new president placed his faith in international cooperation. Like many Americans, he believed implicitly in his country's innate goodness. Self-assured to the point of cockiness, he came to Potsdam clothed in the armor of self-righteousness.

Truman accepted Stalin at face value, believing that he could deal with the Soviet leader. Together with Winston Churchill and his replacement, Clement Attlee, whose Labour party had just triumphed in British elections, Truman and Stalin clashed over such difficult issues as reparations, the Polish border, and the fate of eastern Europe. Truman tried to move the agenda along briskly, and he was upset by the constant delays. In an indirect way, he informed Stalin of the existence of the atomic bomb, tested successfully in the New Mexico desert just before the conference began. Stalin's only comment was that he hoped the United States would make "good use of it against the Japanese."

Reparations proved to be the crucial issue at the **Potsdam Conference.** The Soviets wanted to rebuild their war-ravaged economy with German industry; the United States feared it would be saddled with the entire cost of caring for the defeated Germans. A compromise was finally reached. Each side would take reparations primarily from its own occupation zone, a solution that unwittingly set the stage for the future division of Germany. "Because they could not agree on 'how to govern Europe,'" wrote historian Daniel Yergin, Truman and Stalin "began to divide it."

The conference thus ended on an apparent note of harmony; beneath the surface, however, the bitter antagonism of the Cold War was already festering. The United States and the Union of Soviet Socialist Republics, each distrustful of the

other, were preparing for a long and bitter confrontation. A dozen
Truman reminisced to an old associate about Potsdam. He recalled h
and Stalin's duplicity. Then he added ruefully, "And I liked the little sor

Potsdam marked the end of the wartime alliance. America and Rus
trustful of the other, began to engage in a long and bitter confrontation.
decade, the two superpowers would vie for control of postwar Europ
clash over the spread of communism to Asia. By the time Truman's and
cessors met for the next summit conference, at Geneva in 1955, the Col
its height.

The Cold War Begins

The conflict between the United States and the Soviet Union began gradually. For two years, the nations tried to adjust their differences—over the division of Europe, postwar economic aid, and the atomic bomb—through discussion and negotiation. The Council of Foreign Ministers provided the forum. Beginning in London in the fall of 1945 and meeting with their Soviet counterparts in Paris, New York, and Moscow, American diplomats searched for a way to live in peace with a suspicious Soviet Union.

The Division of Europe

The fundamental disagreement was over who would control postwar Europe. In the east, the Red Army had swept over Poland and the Balkans, laying the basis for Soviet domination there. American and British forces had liberated western Europe, from Scandinavia to Italy. The Russians were intent on imposing communist governments loyal to Moscow in the Soviet sphere. The United States insisted on national self-determination. The Soviets regarded this demand for free elections as subversive. Suspecting American duplicity, Stalin brought down what Churchill characterized as an **Iron Curtain** from the Baltic to the Adriatic as he set up a series of satellite governments.

Iron Curtain British Prime Minister Winston Churchill coined the term "Iron Curtain" to refer to the boundary in Europe that divided Soviet-dominated eastern and central Europe from western Europe, which was free from Soviet control.

Germany was the key. The temporary zones of occupation gradually hardened into permanent lines of division. Ignoring the Potsdam Conference agreement that the country be treated as an economic unit, the United States and Great Britain by 1946 were refusing to permit the Soviets to take reparations from the industrial western zones. The United States and England merged their zones and championed the idea of the unification of all Germany. Russia, fearing a resurgence of German military power, responded by intensifying the communization of its zone, which included the jointly occupied city of Berlin. By 1947, Britain, France, and the United States were laying plans to transfer their authority to an independent West Germany.

The Soviet Union consolidated its grip on eastern Europe in 1946 and 1947. One by one, communist governments took power in Poland, Hungary, Romania, and Bulgaria, each ultimately controlled by Stalin. The climax came in March 1948 when a coup in Czechoslovakia overthrew a democratic government and gave the Soviets a strategic foothold in central Europe.

The division of Europe was an inevitable outgrowth of World War II. Both sides were intent on imposing their values—the Soviets stood in eastern Europe, and the United States and Britain were present in Germany, France, and Italy. A frank recognition of competing spheres of influence might have avoided further escalation of tension. But the Western nations, remembering Hitler's aggression in the 1930s, began to see Stalin as an equally dangerous threat to their well-being. Instead of accepting him as a cautious leader bent on protecting Russian security,

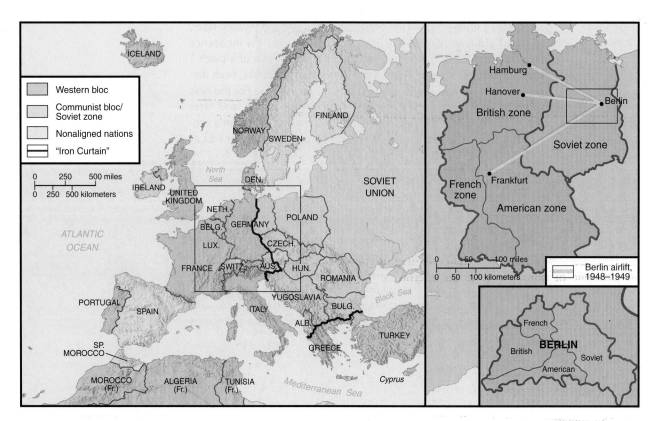

EUROPE AFTER WORLD WAR II   *The heavy red line splitting Germany shows in graphic form the division of Europe between the Western and Soviet spheres of influence. The two power blocs faced each other across an "Iron Curtain."* ■

they perceived him as an aggressive dictator leading a communist drive for world domination.

Withholding Economic Aid

The Second World War had inflicted enormous damage on the USSR in terms of lost lives, destroyed factories, and torn-up railroad track. The industrialization that Stalin had achieved at great sacrifice in the 1930s had been badly set back; even agricultural production had fallen by half during the war. Outside aid and assistance were vital for the reconstruction of the Soviet Union. American leaders knew of the Soviets' plight and hoped to use it to good advantage. Truman was convinced that economically "we held all the cards and the Russians had to come to us."

There were two possible forms of postwar assistance: loans and Lend-Lease. In January 1945, the Soviets requested a $6 million loan to finance postwar reconstruction. Despite initial American encouragement, FDR deferred action on this request; as relations cooled, the chances for action dimmed. By the war's end, the loan request, though never formally turned down, was dead.

Lend-Lease proved no more successful. On May 11, 1945, Truman terminated all Lend-Lease shipments to the Soviet Union, including those already at sea. The State Department saw the action as applying "leverage"; Stalin termed it "brutal." Heeding Soviet protests, Truman resumed Lend-Lease shipments, but only until the war was over in August. After that, all Lend-Lease ended.

Deprived of American assistance, the Soviets were forced to rebuild their economy through reparations, which they extracted from their zone of Germany, eastern Europe, and Manchuria. Slowly, the economy recovered from the war, but bitterness over the American refusal to extend aid convinced Stalin of Western hostility and deepened the growing antagonism.

The Atomic Dilemma

Overshadowing all else was the atomic bomb. The new weapon raised problems that would have been difficult for friendly nations to resolve. The effect was disastrous, given the uneasy state of Soviet-American relations.

The wartime policy followed by Roosevelt and Churchill ensured a postwar nuclear arms race. Instead of informing their major ally of the developing atomic bomb, they kept it a closely guarded secret. Stalin learned of the Manhattan Project through espionage and responded by starting a Soviet atomic program in 1943. By the time Truman told Stalin of the weapon's existence at Potsdam, the Russians were well on the way to making their own bomb.

After the war, the United States developed a disarmament plan based on turning first control of fissionable material, then the processing plants, and ultimately its stockpile of bombs over to an international agency. Later, Bernard Baruch, whom Truman chose to present the plan to the United Nations, added provisions aimed at imposing sanctions against violators and exempting the international agency from the UN veto. Ignoring scientists who pleaded for a more cooperative position, Baruch followed instead the advice of Army Chief of Staff Dwight D. Eisenhower, who cited the rapid demobilization of American armed forces to argue that "we cannot at this time limit our capability to produce or use this weapon." In effect, the **Baruch Plan,** with its multiple stages and emphasis on inspection, would preserve the American atomic monopoly for the indefinite future.

The Soviets responded predictably. They called for a total ban on the production and use of the new weapon as well as the destruction of all existing bombs. This proposal was founded on the same perception of national self-interest as the American plan. The Red Army was still relatively strong, and Soviet leaders wanted to maximize its conventional strength by outlawing the atomic bomb.

No agreement was possible. Neither the United States nor the Soviet Union could abandon its position without surrendering a vital national interest. America stressed the need for inspection and control; Russia advocated immediate disarmament. The two superpowers agreed to disagree. Trusting neither each other nor any form of international cooperation, each concentrated on taking maximum advantage of its wartime gains. Thus the Soviets exploited the territory they had conquered in Europe while the United States retained its economic and strategic advantages over the Soviet Union. The result was the Cold War.

Baruch Plan In 1946, Bernard Baruch presented an American plan to control and eventually outlaw nuclear weapons. The plan called for UN control of nuclear weapons in three stages before the United States gave up its stockpile. Soviet insistence on immediate nuclear disarmament without inspection doomed the Baruch Plan and led to a nuclear arms race between the United States and the Soviet Union.

CONTAINMENT

A major departure in American foreign policy occurred in January 1947 when General George C. Marshall became secretary of state. He had the capacity to think in broad, strategic terms. An extraordinarily good judge of ability, he relied on gifted subordinates to handle the day-to-day implementation of his policies. In the months after taking office, he came to rely on two exceptionally gifted men in particular.

Dean Acheson, an experienced Washington lawyer and bureaucrat, was appointed undersecretary of state and given free rein by Marshall to conduct American diplomacy. An ardent Anglophile, he wanted to see the United States take over a faltering Britain's role as the supreme arbiter of world affairs. Recalling the lesson taught by the Munich Conference of 1938, he opposed appeasement and advocated a policy of negotiating only from strength.

Marshall's other mainstay was George Kennan, the Soviet expert who headed the newly created Policy Planning Staff. A career foreign service officer, he had served in Moscow, where he developed a profound distrust for the Soviet regime.

He believed that only strong and sustained resistance could halt the outward flow of Soviet power. In the spring of 1947, a sense of crisis impelled Marshall, Acheson, and Kennan to set out on a new course in American diplomacy: "a long-term, patient but firm containment of Russian expansionist tendencies." The new **containment** policy both consolidated America's evolving postwar anticommunism and established guidelines that would shape the nation's role in the world for the next two decades.

containment First proposed by George Kennan in 1947, containment became the basic strategy of the United States throughout the Cold War. Kennan argued that firm American resistance to Soviet expansion would eventually compel Moscow to adopt more peaceful policies.

The Truman Doctrine

The initial step came in response to an urgent British request. On February 21, 1947, the British informed the United States that they could no longer afford to aid the anticommunist governments in Greece or Turkey. Believing that the Soviets were responsible for the strife in Greece (in fact they were not), Marshall, Acheson, and Kennan quickly decided that the United States would have to take over Britain's role in the eastern Mediterranean.

Attempting to secure congressional support for their policy, Acheson warned that if Greece went communist, it would threaten Iran, all the Mideast, Africa, Italy, and France. The bipartisan group of congressional leaders was deeply impressed. Finally, Republican Senator Arthur M. Vandenberg spoke up, saying he would support the president but adding that to ensure public backing, Truman would have to "scare hell" out of the American people.

The president followed Vandenberg's advice. On March 12, 1947, he asked Congress for $400 million for military and economic assistance to Greece and Turkey. He made clear that more was involved than just these two countries, that America must aid free peoples resisting subjugation. After a brief debate, both the House and the Senate approved the program.

The **Truman Doctrine** marked an informal declaration of "cold war" against the Soviet Union. Truman used the crisis in Greece to secure congressional approval and build a national consensus for the policy of containment. In less than two years, the civil war in Greece ended, but the American commitment to oppose communist expansion, whether by internal subversion or external aggression, placed the United States on a collision course with the Soviet Union around the globe.

Truman Doctrine In 1947, President Truman asked Congress for money to aid the Greek and Turkish governments that were then threatened by communist rebels. Arguing for the appropriations, Truman asserted his doctrine that the United States was committed to support free people everywhere who were resisting subjugation by communist attack or rebellion.

The Marshall Plan

By 1947, many Americans believed that western Europe, far more vital to U.S. interests than the eastern Mediterranean, was vulnerable to Soviet penetration. The problem was economic. World War II had taken a terrible toll on Britain, France, Italy, and other European countries. Food was scarce, industrial machinery was broken and obsolete, and workers were demoralized by years of depression and war. Resentment and discontent led to growing communist voting strength, especially in Italy and France. Unless the United States could do something to reverse the process, it seemed as though all Europe might drift into the communist orbit.

Acheson believed that it was time to extend American "economic power" in Europe both "to call an effective halt to the Soviet Union's expansionism" and "to create a basis for political stability and economic well-being." The experts drew up a plan for the massive infusion of American capital to finance the economic recovery of Europe. In a commencement speech at Harvard on June 5, 1947, Marshall proposed American aid to foster the "political and social conditions in which free institutions can exist."

The fate of the **Marshall Plan** depended on the reaction of the Soviet Union and the U.S. Congress. Marshall had taken a gamble by including the USSR in his

Marshall Plan In 1947, Secretary of State George Marshall proposed a massive economic aid program to rebuild the war-torn economies of western European nations. The plan was motivated by both humanitarian concern for the conditions of those nations' economies and fear that economic dislocation would promote communism in western Europe.

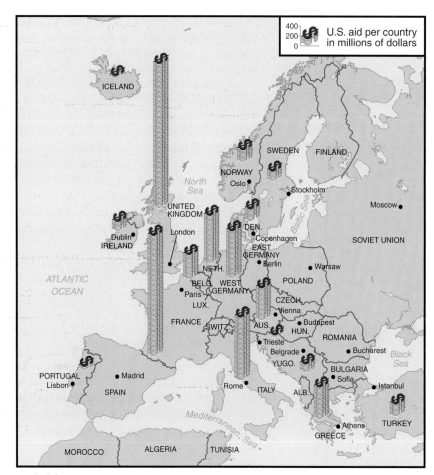

MARSHALL PLAN AID TO EUROPE, 1948–1952 *The Marshall Plan, also known as the European Recovery Program, provided aid totaling $13 billion to European countries following World War II. Most of the money went to former allies Great Britain and France, but former enemies Italy and West Germany also received substantial aid. To receive the grants, countries pledged to control inflation and lower tariffs.* ■

offer of aid. At a meeting of the European nations in Paris in July 1947, the Soviet foreign minister ended the suspense by abruptly withdrawing. Neither the USSR nor its satellites would take part, apparently because Moscow saw the Marshall Plan as an American attempt to weaken Soviet control over eastern Europe. The other European countries then made a formal request for $17 billion in assistance over the next four years.

Congress responded cautiously to this proposal. The administration lobbied vigorously, pointing out that the Marshall Plan would help the United States by stimulating trade with Europe as well as checking Soviet expansion. It was the latter argument, however, that proved decisive, especially after the Czech coup in March 1948. Congress approved the Marshall Plan by heavy majorities. The United States quickly put forth loans that generated a broad industrial revival in western Europe that became self-sustaining by the 1950s. The threat of communist domination faded, and Europe's return to prosperity proved to be a bonanza for American farmers, miners, and manufacturers.

The Western Military Alliance

The final phase of containment came in 1949 with the establishment of the **North Atlantic Treaty Organization (NATO).** NATO grew out of European fears of Soviet military aggression. Recalling Hitler's tactics in the 1930s, the people of western Europe wanted assurance that the United States would protect them from attack as they began to achieve economic recovery.

North Atlantic Treaty Organization (NATO) In 1949, the United States, Canada, and ten European nations formed this military mutual-defense pact. In 1955, the Soviet Union countered NATO with the formation of the Warsaw Pact, a military alliance among those nations within its own sphere of influence.

In January 1949, Truman called for a defense pact; ten European nations joined the United States and Canada in signing the North Atlantic Treaty. This historic departure from the traditional policy of isolation caused extensive debate, but the Senate ratified it in July 1949.

There were two main features of NATO. First, the United States committed itself to the defense of Europe in case of an attack. In effect, the United States was extending its atomic shield over Europe. The second feature was designed to reassure worried Europeans that the United States would honor this commitment. In late 1950, Truman appointed General Eisenhower to the post of NATO supreme commander and authorized the stationing of four American divisions in Europe to serve as the nucleus of the NATO army. Now any assault would automatically involve American troops, a fact that would deter the Soviet Union.

The Western military alliance escalated the developing Cold War. It represented an overreaction to the Soviet danger. Americans and Europeans alike were attempting to apply the lesson of Munich to the Cold War. But there was no evidence of any Soviet plan to invade western Europe, and in the face of the American atomic bomb, none was likely. All NATO did was intensify Russian fears of the West and thus increase the level of international tension. The USSR and its satellites responded to NATO with the Warsaw Pact, a defense community of their own.

The Berlin Blockade

The main Soviet response to containment came in 1948 at the West's most vulnerable point. American, British, French, and Soviet troops each occupied a sector of Berlin, but the city was located more than 100 miles inside the Soviet zone of Germany. Stalin decided to test his opponents' resolve by cutting off all rail and highway traffic to Berlin on June 20, 1948.

The timing was very awkward for Truman, who was locked in a tight presidential race. Immersed in election-year politics, he was caught unprepared by the Berlin blockade. The alternatives were not very appealing. The United States could withdraw its forces and lose not just the city but the confidence of all Europe; it could try to send in reinforcements and fight for Berlin; or it could sit tight and attempt to find a diplomatic solution. Truman decided to fight to save Berlin.

The administration adopted a two-phase policy. The first part was a massive airlift of food, fuel, and supplies for both the troops and civilians in Berlin. Then, to guard against Soviet interruption of the **Berlin airlift**, Truman transferred sixty American B-29s, planes capable of delivering atomic bombs, to bases in England. The president was bluffing; the B-29s were not equipped with atomic bombs, but at the time the threat was effective.

For a few weeks, the world teetered on the edge of war. Stalin did not attempt to disrupt the flights to Berlin, but he rejected all American diplomatic initiatives. At any time the Soviets could have halted the airlift by jamming radar or shooting down the defenseless cargo planes. For Truman, the tension was fierce. He feared that America was dreadfully close to war.

Slowly, the tension eased. The Russians did not shoot down any planes, and Truman was re-elected, in part because the Berlin crisis had rallied the nation behind his leadership. In early 1949, the Soviets gave in, ending the blockade in return for another meeting of the Council of Foreign Ministers on Germany—a conclave that proved as unproductive as all the earlier ones.

The Berlin crisis marked the end of the initial phase of the Cold War. The airlift had given the United States a striking political victory, showing the world the triumph of American ingenuity over Russian stubbornness. Yet it could not disguise the fact that the Cold War had cut Europe in two. A divided Europe—politically, economically, and now militarily—was a far cry from the wartime hopes for a peaceful world. Such was the bitter legacy of World War II.

Berlin airlift In 1948, in response to a Soviet land blockade of Berlin, the United States carried out a massive effort to supply the 2 million Berlin citizens with food, fuel, and other goods by air for more than six months, forcing the Soviets to end the blockade in 1949.

THE COLD WAR EXPANDS

The rivalry between the United States and the Soviet Union grew in the late 1940s and the early 1950s. Both sides began to rebuild their military forces with new methods and advanced weapons. Equally significant, the diplomatic competition spread from Europe to Asia as each of the superpowers sought to enhance its influence in the East. By the time Truman left office in early 1953, the Cold War had taken on global proportions.

The Military Dimension

After World War II, American leaders were intent on reforming the nation's military system in light of the wartime experience. Two goals were uppermost. First, nearly everyone agreed in the aftermath of Pearl Harbor that the armed services should be unified into an integrated military system. The developing Cold War reinforced this decision. Equally important, planners realized the need for new institutions to coordinate military and diplomatic strategy so that the nation could cope effectively with threats to its security.

In 1947, Congress passed the **National Security Act,** which established the Department of Defense. In addition, the act created the Central Intelligence Agency (CIA) to coordinate the intelligence-gathering activities of various government agencies. Finally, the act established the National Security Council (NSC) to advise the president on all matters regarding the nation's security.

Despite the appearance of equality among the services, the newly created air force quickly emerged as the dominant power in the atomic age. Both Truman and Congress allotted more money to the air force than to the army or the navy.

American military planners received a great boost in the fall of 1949 when the Soviet Union exploded its first atomic bomb. President Truman appointed a high-level committee to explore mounting an all-out effort to build a hydrogen bomb to maintain American nuclear supremacy.

Some scientists had technical objections to the H-bomb; others opposed the new weapon on moral grounds, claiming that its enormous destructive power (one thousand times greater than the atomic bomb) made it unthinkable. But Dean Acheson—who succeeded Marshall as secretary of state in early 1949—believed it was imperative that the United States develop the hydrogen bomb before the Soviet Union did. When Acheson presented the committee's favorable report to the president in January 1950, Truman took only seven minutes to decide to go ahead with the new bomb.

National Security Act
Congress passed the National Security Act in 1947 in response to perceived threats from the Soviet Union after World War II. It established the Department of Defense and created the Central Intelligence Agency and National Security Council.

The explosion of a U.S. test bomb over an uninhabited island in the Pacific on November 1, 1952, demonstrated to the world the fearsome power of the hydrogen bomb. This early H-bomb was capable of destroying a city the size of Washington, D.C. During the next decade, both the United States and the Soviet Union developed far more powerful bombs.

NSC-68 National Security Council planning paper No. 68 redefined America's national defense policy. Adopted in 1950, it committed the United States to a massive military buildup to meet the challenge believed to be posed by the Soviet Union.

At the same time, Acheson ordered the Policy Planning Staff to draw up a new statement of national defense policy. **NSC-68,** as the document eventually became known, was based on the premise that the Soviet Union sought "to impose its absolute authority over the rest of the world" and thus "mortally challenged" the United States. Paul Nitze, who headed the Policy Planning Staff, advocated a massive expansion of American military power so that the United States could halt and overcome the Soviet threat. NSC-68 stood as a symbol of the Truman administration's determination to win the Cold War regardless of cost.

The Cold War in Asia

The Soviet-American conflict developed more slowly in Asia. At Yalta, the two superpowers had agreed to a Far Eastern balance of power, with the USSR dominating northeastern Asia and the United States in control of the Pacific, including Japan and its former island empire.

The United States moved quickly to consolidate its sphere of influence. General Douglas MacArthur, in charge of Japanese occupation, denied the Soviet Union any role in the reconstruction of Japan. Instead, he supervised the transition of the Japanese government into a constitutional democracy in which communists were barred from all government posts. The Japanese willingly renounced war in their new constitution, relying instead on American forces to protect their security. In addition, the United States held full control over the Marshall, Mariana, and Caroline Islands.

As defined at Yalta, China lay between the Soviet and American spheres. When World War II ended, the country was torn between Chiang Kai-shek's Nationalists in the south and Mao Tse-tung's Communists in the north. Although Chiang received American political and economic backing, his regime was corrupt, and a raging inflation rate devastated the Chinese middle classes and thus eroded his base of power. Mao used tight discipline and patriotic appeals to strengthen his hold on the peasantry and extend his influence. When the Soviets abruptly vacated Manchuria in 1946, Mao inherited control of this rich northern province. Ignoring American advice, Chiang rushed north to occupy Manchurian cities, overextending his supply lines and exposing his forces to Communist counterattack.

American policy aimed at averting a Chinese civil war by encouraging Chiang and Mao to form a coalition government. The policy failed. By 1947, as China

■ *The Soviet view of the Cold War, as depicted in this Soviet cartoon, shows the United States stretching out long arms to take hold of Korea, Iran, Turkey, Taiwan, and Vietnam.* ■

plunged into full-scale civil war, the Truman administration had given up any serious effort to influence the outcome. Political mediation had failed, military intervention was out of the question, and a policy of continued American economic aid served only to appease domestic supporters of Chiang; 80 percent of the military supplies ended up in Communist hands.

The climax came at the end of the decade. Mao's forces drove the Nationalists out of Manchuria in late 1948 and advanced across the Yangtze River by mid-1949. Acheson released a lengthy report justifying American policy in China on the grounds that the civil war there "was beyond the control of the government of the United States." Republican senators, however, disagreed, blaming American diplomats for sabotaging the Nationalists. While the domestic debate raged over responsibility for the loss of China, Chiang's forces fled the mainland for sanctuary on Formosa (Taiwan) in December 1949. Two months later, Mao and Stalin signed a Sino-Soviet treaty of mutual assistance that clearly placed China in the Russian orbit.

The American response to the Communist triumph in China was twofold. First, the State Department refused to recognize the legitimacy of the new regime in Peking (Beijing), maintaining instead formal diplomatic relations with the Nationalists on Formosa. Then, to compensate for the loss of China, the United States focused on Japan as its main ally in Asia. The State Department encouraged the buildup of Japanese industry, and the Pentagon expanded American bases on the Japanese home islands and Okinawa. As it had done in Europe, the Cold War had now split east Asia in two.

The Korean War

The showdown between the United States and the Soviet Union in Asia came in Korea, which had been divided at the 38th parallel in 1945. The Soviets occupied the industrial North, installing a Communist government under the leadership of Kim Il-Sung. In the agrarian South, Syngman Rhee emerged as the American-sponsored ruler. The two superpowers pulled out most of their occupation forces by 1949. The Soviets, however, helped train a well-equipped army in the North, while the United States gave much more limited military assistance to South Korea.

On June 25, 1950, the North Korean army suddenly crossed the 38th parallel in great strength. We now know that Stalin had approved this act of aggression in advance. In January 1950, the Soviet leader had told Mao Tse-tung that he was ready to overthrow the Yalta settlement in the Far East. In April, when Kim Il-Sung came to Moscow to gain approval for the assault on South Korea, Stalin gave it willingly, apparently in the belief that the United States was ready to abandon Syngman Rhee. But the ever cautious Stalin warned Kim not to count on Soviet assistance, saying, "If you should get kicked in the teeth, I shall not lift a finger. You have to ask Mao for all the help." In May, despite expressing some reservations, Mao also approved the planned North Korean aggression.

Both Stalin and Mao had badly miscalculated the American response. President Truman saw the invasion

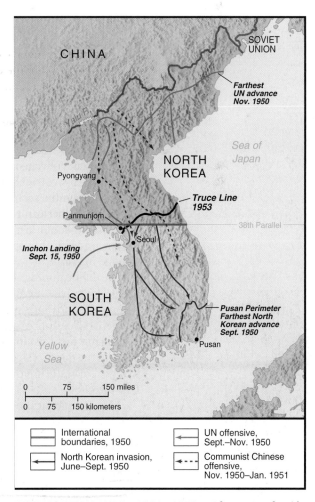

THE KOREAN WAR, 1950–1953 *After a year of rapid movement up and down the Korean peninsula, the fighting stalled just north of the 38th parallel. The resulting truce line has divided North and South Korea ever since the July 1953 armistice.* ■

Past and Present

War Strategy: Korea and Iraq

During the Korean War, President Truman's decision to take advantage of General MacArthur's stunning victory at Inchon and order American forces to cross the 38th parallel in October 1950 had fateful consequences. If the United States had halted at the 38th parallel, achieving its initial objective of defending South Korea after the invasion from the north, the Korean War might well have been over by the end of 1950. Instead, the attempt to unify Korea by armed force led to nearly three more years of fighting, heavy casualties after the intervention of China, the firing of General MacArthur, and growing discontent with the war at home. The final outcome, a truce line near the 38th parallel, hardly seemed worth the effort.

Just over four decades later, President George H.W. Bush faced a similar dilemma at the height of the Persian Gulf War, initiated in response to Iraqi dictator Saddam Hussein's invasion of Kuwait and threats to Saudi Arabia and the oil-rich Persian Gulf area. After five weeks of aerial bombardment of Iraq, American forces had moved swiftly to liberate Kuwait and send the vaunted Iraqi Republican Guard fleeing back across the Euphrates River. Eager army commanders wanted to pursue the defeated enemy and to march on an undefended Baghdad, but the members of the coalition Bush had assembled to free Kuwait refused to expand the war by invading Iraq. The president and his advisers, fearful of fighting alone to conquer Iraq and aware of the Korean precedent, ended the hostilities after only 100 hours of ground warfare.

George Bush had avoided the entanglement that ensnared Harry Truman after his decision to cross the 38th parallel, but the consequences were not all favorable. Saddam Hussein, despite losing the war, was able to suppress a Shi'ite insurgency and reestablish his brutal control of Iraq. Over a decade later, President George W. Bush, deciding to finish the job his father had started, launched a war to remove Saddam from power. Despite initial success, and the eventual capture of Saddam, the occupation of Iraq led to a Sunni insurgency that cost more American lives than the initial conquest. In retrospect, the elder Bush, aware of Truman's difficulty in Korea, had correctly calculated the difficulty of trying to use armed force to bring peace and democracy to the people of Iraq.

as a clear-cut case of Soviet aggression reminiscent of the 1930s. "Communism was acting in Korea just as Hitler, Mussolini, and the Japanese had acted ten, fifteen, and twenty years earlier," he commented in his memoirs. Following Acheson's advice, the president convened the UN Security Council and, taking advantage of a temporary Soviet boycott, secured a resolution condemning North Korea as an aggressor and calling on the member nations to engage in a collective security action. Within a few days, American troops from Japan were in combat in South Korea. The conflict, which would last for more than three years, was technically a police action fought under UN auspices; in reality, the United States was at war with a Soviet satellite in Asia.

In the beginning, the fighting went badly as the North Koreans continued to drive down the peninsula. But by August, American forces had halted the Communist advance near Pusan. In September, General MacArthur changed the whole complexion of the war by carrying out a brilliant amphibious assault at Inchon, on the waist of Korea, cutting off and destroying most of the North Korean army in the South. Encouraged by this victory, Truman began to shift from his original goal of restoring the 38th parallel to a new one: reunification of Korea by military force.

The administration ignored warnings from Peking, sent by way of India, against an American invasion of North Korea. Both Acheson and MacArthur advised Truman that the Chinese would not enter the conflict. Rarely has an American president received worse advice. The UN forces crossed the 38th parallel in October, advanced confidently to the Yalu River in November, and then were completely routed by a massive Chinese counterattack that drove them out of all North Korea by December. MacArthur finally stabilized the fighting near the 38th parallel, but when Truman decided to give up his attempt to unify Korea, the general protested to Congress, calling for a renewed offensive and proclaiming, "There is no substitute for victory."

Truman courageously relieved the popular hero of the Pacific of his command on April 11, 1951. The Korean War then settled into a stalemate near the 38th parallel as truce talks with the Communists bogged down for the rest of Truman's term in office. The president could take heart from the fact that he had achieved his primary goals, defense of South Korea and the principle of collective security. Yet by taking the gamble to reunify Korea by force, he had confused the American people and humiliated the United States in the eyes of the world.

In the last analysis, the most significant result of the Korean conflict was massive American rearmament. The war led to the implementation of NSC-68—the army expanded to 3.5 million troops, the defense budget increased to $50 billion a year by 1952, and the United States acquired military bases in distant quarters of the world. America was now committed to waging a global contest against the Soviet Union with arms as well as words.

THE COLD WAR AT HOME

The Cold War cast a long shadow over American life in the late 1940s and early 1950s. Truman tried to carry on the New Deal reform tradition he had inherited from FDR, but the American people were more concerned about events abroad. The Republican party used growing dissatisfaction with both postwar economic adjustment and fears of communist penetration of the United States to revive its sagging fortunes and regain control of the White House in 1952 for the first time in twenty years.

Truman's Troubles and Vindication

Matching his foreign policy successes with equal achievements at home was not easy for Truman. As a senator, he had faithfully supported Roosevelt's policies, and he had earned a reputation as a hardworking, reliable legislator. But when he assumed the presidency, he was relatively unknown to the public, and his background as a Missouri county judge associated with Kansas City machine politics did not inspire confidence in his leadership abilities. Surprisingly well read, Truman possessed sound judgment, the ability to reach decisions quickly, and a fierce and uncompromising sense of right and wrong.

Two weaknesses marred his performance in the White House. One was his fondness for old friends, which resulted in the appointment of many Missouri and Senate cronies to high office. These men brought little credit to his administration. Truman's other serious limitation was his lack of political vision. He tried to perpetuate FDR's New Deal, but he engaged in a running battle with Congress rather than pursuing a coherent legislative program.

The fact that the postwar mood was not conducive to a new outburst of reform, of course, handicapped Truman's performance. Not only were the American people enjoying material prosperity, but the Cold War also diverted attention from domestic problems. Congress did pass the Employment Act of 1946, which asserted the principle that the government was responsible for the state of the economy and created the Council of Economic Advisers to guide the president. But the original goal of mandatory federal planning to achieve full employment failed to survive the legislative process.

After the Republican victory in 1946, relations between the president and Congress became increasingly stormy. Truman successfully vetoed two GOP measures to give large tax cuts to the wealthy, but Congress overrode his veto of the **Taft-Hartley Act** in 1947. Designed to redress the imbalance in labor-management relations created by the Wagner Act, the Taft-Hartley Act outlawed specific union practices, and it permitted the president to invoke an eighty-day cooling-off period to delay strikes that might endanger national health or safety.

Taft-Hartley Act This 1947 anti-union legislation outlawed the closed shop and secondary boycotts. It also authorized the president to seek injunctions to prevent strikes that posed a threat to national security.

■ *A jubilant Harry Truman, on the morning after his 1948 election win, displays the headline blazoned on the front page of the* Chicago Daily Tribune—*a newspaper that believed the pollsters.* ■

Dixiecrats A group of southern Democrats who bolted from their party in 1948 and supported Governor Strom Thurmond of South Carolina as the presidential candidate of the States' Rights party.

Truman's political fortunes reached their lowest ebb in early 1948. Former Vice President Henry A. Wallace announced his third-party (Progressive) candidacy in the presidential contest that year. Although Truman was renominated by the Democratic party, his prospects for victory looked dim, especially after disgruntled Southerners, alarmed by Truman's civil rights advocacy, bolted the Democratic party to nominate Strom Thurmond, the governor of South Carolina, on the States' Rights party ticket.

The defection of the **Dixiecrats** in the South and Wallace's liberal followers in the North led political experts to predict an almost certain victory for the Republican candidate, Governor Thomas E. Dewey of New York. While Dewey waged a cautious, uninspired campaign, Truman barnstormed around the country denouncing the "do-nothing" Republican Eightieth Congress. To the amazement of the pollsters, Truman won a narrow victory in November. The old Roosevelt coalition—farmers, organized labor, urban ethnic groups, and blacks—had held together, enabling Truman to remain in the White House and the Democrats to gain control of Congress.

There was one more reason for Truman's win in 1948. During the election, held at the height of the Berlin crisis, the GOP failed to challenge Truman's conduct of the Cold War. Locked in a tense rivalry with the Soviet Union, the American people saw no reason to reject a president who had countered aggression overseas with the Truman Doctrine and the Marshall Plan. Until the Republicans found a way to challenge Truman's Cold War policies, they had little chance to regain the White House.

The Loyalty Issue

Despite Truman's surprise victory in 1948, there was one area on which the Democrats were vulnerable. The fear of communism abroad that had led to the bipartisan containment policy could be used against them at home by politicians who were more willing to exploit the public's deep-seated anxiety.

Fear of radicalism has been a recurrent feature of American life since the early days of the republic. The Cold War heightened the traditional belief that subversion from abroad endangered the nation. Bold rhetoric from members of the Truman administration, portraying the men in the Kremlin as inspired revolutionaries bent on world conquest, frightened the American people. They viewed the Soviet Union as a successor of Nazi Germany—a totalitarian police state that threatened the basic liberties of free people.

A series of revelations of communist espionage activities reinforced these fears, sparking a second "Red Scare." A Soviet spy ring was uncovered in Canada in 1946, and the **House Un-American Activities Committee (HUAC)** held hearings that indicated that communist agents had flourished in government departments in the 1930s. Although Truman tried to dismiss the loyalty issue as a red herring, he felt compelled to take protective measures, thus lending substance to the charges of subversion. In March 1947, he had initiated a loyalty program, ordering security checks on government employees to root out communists. Originally intended to remove subversives for whom "reasonable grounds exist for belief that the person involved is disloyal," within four years the Loyalty Review Board was dismissing workers as security risks if there was "reasonable doubt" of their loyalty. Thousands of government workers lost their jobs, charged with guilt by association with radicals or with membership in left-wing organizations.

The most famous disclosure came in August 1948 when Whittaker Chambers, a repentant communist, accused Alger Hiss, once a prominent State Department official, of having been a Soviet spy in the 1930s. When Hiss denied the charges, Chambers produced microfilms of confidential government documents that he claimed Hiss had given him in the late 1930s. Although the statute of limitations prevented a charge of treason against Hiss, he was convicted of perjury in January 1950 and sentenced to a five-year prison term.

Events abroad intensified the sense of danger. The Communist triumph in China in the fall of 1949 came as a shock; soon there were charges that "fellow travelers" in the State Department were responsible for "the loss of China." In September 1949, when the Truman administration announced that the USSR had detonated its first atomic bomb, the loss of America's nuclear monopoly was blamed on Soviet espionage. In early 1950, Klaus Fuchs, a British scientist who had worked on the wartime Manhattan Project, admitted giving the Soviets vital information about the A-bomb.

A few months later, the government charged American Communists Ethel and Julius Rosenberg with conspiracy to transmit atomic secrets to the Soviet Union. They were found guilty of treason in 1951 and, despite their claims of innocence and worldwide appeals for clemency on their behalf, were executed in 1953. Thus by the early 1950s, nearly all the ingredients were at hand for a new outburst of hysteria—fear of communism, evidence of espionage, belief in a vast conspiracy. The only element missing was a leader to focus this new wave of intolerance.

> **House Un-American Activities Committee (HUAC)** This congressional committee played a prominent role in attempting to uncover and punish those suspected of aiding the communist cause in the early years of the Cold War.

McCarthyism in Action

On February 12, 1950, Senator Joseph R. McCarthy of Wisconsin delivered a routine speech in Wheeling, West Virginia. A little known Republican, he suddenly attracted national attention when he declared, "I have here in my hand a list of 205—a list of names that were made known to the secretary of state as being members of the Communist party and who nevertheless are still working and shaping policy in the State Department." Although he never substantiated his charge, McCarthy's speech triggered a four-and-a-half-year crusade to hunt down alleged communists in government. The stridency and sensationalism of the senator's accusations soon won the name **McCarthyism.**

McCarthy's basic technique was the multiple untruth. He leveled a bevy of charges of treasonable activities in government. While officials were refuting his initial accusations, he brought forth a steady stream of new ones so that the corrections never caught up. He failed to unearth a single confirmed communist in government, but he kept the Truman administration in turmoil. He exploited the

> **McCarthyism** In 1950, Senator Joseph R. McCarthy began a sensational campaign against communists in government that led to more than four years of charges and countercharges, ending when the Senate censured him in 1954. McCarthyism became the contemporary name for the Red Scare of the 1950s.

press with great skill, combining current accusations with promises of future disclosures to guarantee headlines.

The secret of McCarthy's power was the fear he engendered among his Senate colleagues. They believed McCarthy's opposition would doom their chances for reelection. McCarthy delighted in making sweeping, startling charges of communist sympathies against prominent public figures. A favorite target was aristocratic Secretary of State Dean Acheson, but General George Marshall and even fellow Republicans were also named in his charges.

The attacks on the wealthy, famous, and privileged won McCarthy a devoted national following, although the public opinion polls indicated his approval rating never rose above 50 percent. He drew a disproportionate backing from working-class Catholics and ethnic groups who usually voted Democratic. He offered a simple solution to the complicated Cold War: defeat the enemy at home rather than continue to engage in costly foreign aid programs and entangling alliances abroad. Above all, McCarthy appealed to conservative Republicans in the Midwest who shared his right-wing views and felt cheated by Truman's upset victory in 1948. Even GOP leaders who viewed McCarthy's tactics with distaste quietly encouraged him to attack vulnerable Democrats.

The Republicans in Power

In 1952, the GOP capitalized on a growing sense of national frustration to capture the presidency. The stalemate in Korea and the second Red Scare at home created the desire for change; revelations of scandals by several individuals close to Truman intensified the feeling that someone needed to clean up "the mess in Washington." In Dwight D. Eisenhower, the Republican party found the perfect candidate to explore what one senator called K_1C_2—Korea, communism, and corruption.

A war hero with an amiable manner and a winning smile, Eisenhower seemed to have the gifts to unite a divided nation. While his running mate, Senator Richard M. Nixon of California, hammered away at the Democrats on communism and corruption, "Ike" promised that once elected, he would go to Korea if necessary to bring "an early and honorable end" to the war. In the November election, Eisenhower handily defeated Illinois governor Adlai Stevenson.

Once elected, Eisenhower moved quickly to fulfill his campaign pledge. He went to Korea, assessed the battlefield options, ruled out a new offensive, and turned his attention to a diplomatic settlement, even hinting to China that he might use nuclear weapons to break the stalemated peace talks. That threat, together with the death of Joseph Stalin in early March, finally led to the signing of an armistice on July 27, 1953, which ended the fighting but left Korea divided, as it had been before the war, near the 38th parallel.

Eisenhower was less effective in dealing with the problem raised by Senator McCarthy. McCarthy did not end his crusade with the Republican victory in 1952. Instead, he used his new position as chairman of the Senate Committee on Government Operations as a base for ferreting out suspected communists on the federal payroll. Eisenhower's advisers urged the president to use his own great prestige to stop McCarthy. But Ike refused such a confrontation, saying, "I will not get into a pissing contest with that skunk."

The Wisconsin senator finally overreached himself. In 1954, he uncovered an army dentist suspected of disloyalty and proceeded to attack the upper echelons of the U.S. Army. The controversy culminated in the televised Army-McCarthy hearings. For six weeks, the senator revealed his crude, bullying behavior to the American people. Viewers were repelled by his frequent outbursts and by his attempt to slur the reputation of a young lawyer associated with army counsel Joseph Welch. This last maneuver led Welch to condemn McCarthy for his "reckless cruelty" and ask rhetorically, as millions watched on television, "Have you no sense of decency, sir?"

Courageous Republicans, such as Margaret Chase Smith of Maine, joined with Democrats to bring about Senate censure of McCarthy in December 1954. The vote was 67 to 22. Rebuked, McCarthy fell quickly from prominence. He died three years later virtually unnoticed and unmourned.

Yet his influence was profound. Not only did he paralyze national life with shameful activities, but he also helped impose a political and cultural conformity that froze dissent for the rest of the 1950s. Long after McCarthy's passing, the nation tolerated loyalty oaths for teachers, the banning of left-wing books in public libraries, and the blacklisting of entertainers in radio, television, and films. Freedom of expression was inhibited, and the opportunity to try out new ideas and approaches was lost as the United States settled into a sterile Cold War consensus.

Although Eisenhower could claim that his policy of giving McCarthy enough rope to hang himself had worked, it is possible that a bolder and more forthright presidential attack on the senator might have spared the nation some of the excesses of the second Red Scare.

EISENHOWER WAGES THE COLD WAR

Dwight D. Eisenhower came to the presidency in 1952 unusually well prepared to lead the nation at the height of the Cold War. His long years of military service had exposed him to a wide variety of international issues and a broad array of world leaders. His gifts were political and diplomatic as well as military. He was blessed with a sharp, pragmatic mind and a genius for organization that enabled him to plan and carry out large enterprises. And he had serene confidence in his own ability.

Eisenhower chose John Foster Dulles as his secretary of state. The myth soon developed that Ike gave Dulles free rein to conduct American diplomacy. Such was not the case. Eisenhower let Dulles make the public speeches and appearances before congressional committees, but Dulles carefully consulted with the president before every appearance. Ike respected Dulles's opinions, but he made all the major decisions himself.

From the outset, Eisenhower was determined to bring the Cold War under control. Ideally, he wanted to end it, but as a realist, he would settle for a relaxation of tensions with the Soviet Union. In part, he was motivated by a deeply held budgetary concern; Ike was convinced that the nation was in danger of going bankrupt unless military spending was reduced. As president, he inaugurated a "new look" for American defense, cutting back on the army and navy and relying even more heavily than Truman had on the air force and its nuclear striking power. As a result, the defense budget dropped from $50 billion to $40 billion annually. In 1954, Dulles announced reliance on **massive retaliation**—actually a continuation of Truman's policy of deterrence. Rather than becoming involved in limited wars as in Korea, the United States would consider the possibility of using nuclear weapons to halt any communist aggression that threatened vital U.S. interests anywhere in the world.

massive retaliation The "new look" defense policy of the Eisenhower administration in the 1950s was to threaten massive retaliation with nuclear weapons in response to any act of aggression by a potential enemy.

While he permitted Dulles to make his veiled nuclear threats, Eisenhower's fondest dream was to end the arms race. Sobered by the development of the hydrogen bomb, the president began a new effort at disarmament with the Soviets. Yet before this initiative could take effect, Ike had to weather a series of crises around the world that tested his skill and patience to the utmost.

Entanglement in Indochina

The first crisis facing the new president came in Indochina. Since 1950, the United States had been giving France military and economic aid in a war in Indochina against communist guerrillas led by Ho Chi Minh. The Chinese increased their

Dien Bien Phu In 1954, Vietminh rebels besieged a French garrison at Dien Bien Phu, deep in the interior of northern Vietnam. In May, after the United States refused to intervene, Dien Bien Phu fell to the communists.

support to Ho's forces, known as the Vietminh, after the Korean War ended; by the spring of 1954, the French were on the brink of defeat. The Vietminh had surrounded nearly ten thousand French troops at **Dien Bien Phu** deep in the interior of northern Indochina; in desperation, France turned to the United States for help. Admiral Arthur Radford, chairman of the Joint Chiefs of Staff, proposed an American air strike to lift the siege. Although the other Joint Chiefs had strong objections to involving American forces in another Asian war so soon after Korea, hawkish Republican senators were clamoring for action.

Eisenhower decided against Radford's bold proposal, but he killed it in his typically indirect fashion. Fearful that an air attack would lead inevitably to the use of ground troops, Ike insisted that both Congress and American allies in Europe approve the strike in advance. Congressional leaders, recalling the recent Korean stalemate, were reluctant to agree; the British were appalled and ruled out any joint action. The president used these objections to reject intervention in Indochina in 1954.

Dien Bien Phu fell to the Vietminh in May 1954. At an international conference held in Geneva a few weeks later, Indochina was divided at the 17th parallel. Ho gained control of North Vietnam, while the French continued to rule in the South, with provision for a general election within two years to unify the country. The election was never held, largely because Eisenhower feared it would result in an overwhelming mandate for Ho. Instead, the United States gradually took over from the French in South Vietnam, sponsoring a new government in Saigon headed by Ngo Dinh Diem, a Vietnamese nationalist from a northern Catholic family. While Eisenhower can be given credit for refusing to engage American forces on behalf of French colonialism in Indochina, his determination to resist communist expansion had committed the United States to a long and eventually futile struggle to prevent Ho Chi Minh from achieving his long-sought goal of a unified, independent Vietnam.

■ *Cartoonist Herblock, a sharp critic of Dulles's hard line, depicts him in a Superman suit pushing Uncle Sam to the brink of nuclear war.* ■

Containing China

The Communist government in Peking posed a serious challenge to the Eisenhower administration. Senate Republicans blamed the Democrats for the "loss" of China. They viewed Mao as a puppet of the Soviet Union and insisted that the United States recognize the Nationalists on Formosa as the only legitimate government of China. While State Department experts realized that there were underlying tensions between China and the Soviet Union, Mao's intervention in the Korean War had convinced most Americans that the Chinese Communists were an integral part of a larger communist effort at world domination. Thus Truman and Acheson had abandoned any hope of trying to exploit differences between Mao and Stalin by wooing China away from the Soviet Union.

Eisenhower and Dulles chose to accentuate the potential conflict between China and the Soviet Union. They adopted a strong line, hoping to please congressional hawks and show China that the Soviet Union could not protect China's interests. Eisenhower and Dulles hoped that a policy of firmness would contain Communist Chinese expansion and drive a wedge between Moscow and Peking.

A crisis in the Formosa Straits provided the first test of the new policy. In the fall of 1954, the mainland government threatened to seize islands off the coast of China occupied by the Nationalists. Fearful that this would be the first step toward an invasion of Formosa, Eisenhower committed the United States to defend Formosa. Once he received congressional support for his action, he and Dulles started to hint that they were prepared to use nuclear weapons to protect Formosa. The Chinese leaders, unsure whether Eisenhower was bluffing, decided not to test American resolve.

The apparent refusal of the Soviet Union to come to China's aid in the crisis contributed to the growing rift between the two communist nations, but the Eisenhower administration failed to take full advantage of it.

Turmoil in the Middle East

The gravest crisis came in the Middle East when Egyptian leader Gamal Nasser seized the Suez Canal in July 1956. Britain and France were ready to use force immediately; their citizens owned the canal company, and their economies were dependent on the canal for the flow of oil from the Persian Gulf. Eisenhower, however, was staunchly opposed to intervention, preferring to seek a diplomatic solution with Nasser, who kept the canal running smoothly. The European allies nevertheless decided to take a desperate gamble—invade Egypt and seize the canal while relying on the United States to prevent any Soviet interference.

When Britain and France launched their attack in early November, Eisenhower was furious. Unhesitatingly, he instructed Dulles to sponsor a UN resolution calling for the two nations' withdrawal from Egypt. Yet when the USSR supported the proposal and went further, threatening rocket attacks on British and French cities and offering to send "volunteers" to fight in Egypt, Ike made it clear that he would not allow Soviet interference.

Just after noon on election day, November 6, 1956, British Prime Minister Anthony Eden called the president to inform him that Britain and France were ending their invasion. Eisenhower breathed a sigh of relief. American voters rallied behind Ike, electing him to a second term. As a result of the **Suez crisis,** the United States replaced Britain and France as the main Western influence in the Middle East. With the Soviets strongly backing Egypt and Syria, the Cold War had found yet another battleground.

Two years later, Eisenhower found it necessary to intervene in the strategic Middle Eastern country of Lebanon. Political power in this neutral nation was divided between Christian and Muslim elements. When the outgoing Christian president, Camille Chamoun, broke with tradition by seeking a second term, Muslim groups (aided by Egypt and Syria) threatened to launch a rebellion. After some hesitation, Ike decided to intervene to uphold the U.S. commitment to political stability in the Middle East.

American marines moved swiftly ashore on July 15, 1958, securing the Beirut airport and preparing the way for a force of some fourteen thousand troops. Lebanese political leaders quickly agreed on a successor to Chamoun, and American soldiers left the country before the end of October. This restrained use of force achieved Eisenhower's primary goal of quieting the explosive Middle East. It also served, as Dulles pointed out, "to reassure many small nations that they could call on us in a time of crisis."

Suez crisis Egyptian leader Gamal Nasser nationalized the Suez Canal in 1956 when the United States withdrew promised aid to build the Aswan Dam on the Nile. Britain and France, dependent on Middle East oil that was transported through the Suez Canal, launched an armed attack to regain control. President Eisenhower protested the use of force and persuaded Britain and France to withdraw their troops.

Covert Actions

Amid these dangerous crises, the Eisenhower administration worked behind the scenes in the 1950s to expand the nation's global influence. In 1953, the CIA was instrumental in overthrowing a popularly elected government in Iran and placing the

A Look at the Past

Fallout Shelter

Fallout shelters caught the interest and attention of both private citizens and entire communities during the early years of the Cold War. Directions for constructing and stocking the shelters appeared in official government documents as well as magazines such as *Popular Mechanics.* Whether specially constructed, elaborate shelters or merely a protected corner of the basement as shown here, fallout shelters revealed how seriously Americans viewed the threat of nuclear war. The shelters also indicated that people believed it possible to survive a nuclear war. Contrast those attitudes to ours. ✳ Do we consider nuclear war to be a real threat or survivable if it did occur? Examine the design and furnishings of this shelter. Was this designed only to meet standards for survival? Could this be used for other purposes? What do the supplies shown here suggest about how long people expected to remain in the shelter in the event of a nuclear attack?

Sputnik In October 1957, the Soviet Union surprised the world by launching this first artificial satellite to orbit the earth. The resulting outcry in the United States, especially fears that the Soviets were ahead in both space exploration and military missiles, forced the Eisenhower administration to accelerate America's space program and increase defense spending.

shah in full control of that country. American oil companies were rewarded with lucrative concessions, and Eisenhower believed that he had gained a valuable ally on the Soviet border. But these short-run gains created a deep-seated animosity among Iranians that would haunt the United States in the years to come.

Closer to home in Latin America, Ike once again relied on covert action. In 1954, the CIA masterminded the overthrow of a leftist regime in Guatemala. The immediate advantage was in denying the Soviets a possible foothold in the Western Hemisphere, but Latin Americans resented the thinly disguised interference of the United States in their internal affairs. More important, when Fidel Castro seized power in Cuba in 1959, the Eisenhower administration adopted a hard line that helped drive Cuba into the Soviet orbit and led in turn to covert action against Castro.

Eisenhower's record as a cold warrior was thus mixed. His successful ending of the Korean War and his peacekeeping efforts in Indochina and Formosa and in the Suez crisis are all to his credit. Yet his reliance on coups and subversion directed by the CIA in Iran and Guatemala reveal Ike's corrupting belief that the end justified the means. Nevertheless, he could boast, as he did in 1962, of his ability to keep the peace.

Waging Peace

Eisenhower hoped to ease Cold War tensions by ending the nuclear arms race. The development of the hydrogen bomb and long-range ballistic missiles raised the stakes considerably. By the mid-1950s, peace, as Winston Churchill noted, depended on a balance of terror.

Throughout the 1950s, Eisenhower sought a way out of the nuclear dilemma. In April 1953, shortly after Stalin's death, he called on the Soviets to join him in a new effort at disarmament. They ignored this appeal, but Eisenhower kept trying. He outlined an atoms-for-peace plan whereby both the United States and the Soviet Union would donate fissionable material to be used for peaceful purposes, and at the Geneva summit conference in 1955 he suggested an "open skies" program of mutual aerial surveillance. Unfortunately, the Soviets rebuffed both of Eisenhower's overtures.

After his re-election in 1956, the president renewed efforts toward nuclear arms control. Concern over atmospheric fallout from nuclear testing led both Eisenhower and Nikita Khrushchev, who had emerged as Stalin's successor, to seek a ban on such experiments. In October 1958, Eisenhower and Khrushchev each voluntarily suspended further weapons tests pending the outcome of a conference held at Geneva to work out a test ban treaty. Although the Geneva Conference failed to make progress, neither the United States nor the Soviet Union resumed testing for the remainder of Ike's term.

The suspension of testing halted the pollution of the world's atmosphere, but it did not lead to the improvement in Soviet-American relations that Eisenhower sought. In the late 1950s, Khrushchev took advantage of the Soviet feat in launching *Sputnik,* the first artificial satellite to orbit the earth, to intensify the Cold War. Playing on Western fears that the Soviets had made a breakthrough in missile tech-

Chronology

1945	Truman meets Stalin at Potsdam Conference (July) ▪ World War II ends with Japanese surrender (August)
1946	Winston Churchill gives "Iron Curtain" speech
1947	Truman Doctrine announced to Congress (March) ▪ George Marshall outlines Marshall Plan (June) ▪ Truman orders loyalty program for government employees (March)
1948	Soviets begin blockade of Berlin (June) ▪ Truman scores upset victory in presidential election
1949	NATO treaty signed in Washington (April) ▪ Soviet Union tests its first atomic bomb (August)
1950	Truman authorizes building of hydrogen bomb (January) ▪ Senator Joseph McCarthy claims communists in government (February) ▪ North Korea invades South Korea (June)
1951	Truman recalls MacArthur from Korea
1952	Dwight D. Eisenhower elected president
1953	Julius and Ethel Rosenberg executed for atomic-secrets spying (June) ▪ Korean War truce signed at Panmunjom (July)
1954	Fall of Dien Bien Phu to the Vietminh ends French control of Indochina
1956	England and France touch off Suez crisis
1957	Russia launches *Sputnik* satellite
1959	Fidel Castro takes power in Cuba
1960	American U-2 spy plane shot down over Russia

nology, the Russian leader began to issue threats, proclaiming, "We will bury capitalism." The most serious threat of all came in November 1958, when Khrushchev declared that within six months he would sign a separate peace treaty with East Germany, thereby ending American, British, and French occupation rights in Berlin. Eisenhower refused to abandon Berlin, however, and prudent diplomacy convinced Khrushchev not to act on his threat.

In 1959, Khrushchev visited the United States and agreed to attend a summit conference in Paris in May 1960. This much heralded meeting never took place. On May 1, the Soviets shot down an American U-2 plane piloted by Francis Gary Powers. The United States had been overflying the Soviet Union since 1956 in these high-altitude spy planes, gaining vital information about the Soviet missile program. When Eisenhower belatedly took full responsibility for the Powers overflight, Khrushchev responded with a scathing personal denunciation and a refusal to meet with Eisenhower.

CONCLUSION: THE CONTINUING COLD WAR

The breakup of the Paris summit marked the end of Eisenhower's attempt to moderate the Cold War. The disillusioned leader told an aide that the "stupid U-2 mess" had destroyed all his efforts for peace. Before he left office, however, Eisenhower made one final effort. He delivered a farewell address in which he gave a somber warning about the danger of massive military spending. "In the councils of government, we must guard against the acquisition of unwarranted influence, whether sought or unsought, by the military-industrial complex," he declared. "The potential for the disastrous rise of misplaced power exists and will persist."

Rarely has an American president been more prophetic. In the years that followed, the level of defense spending skyrocketed as the Cold War escalated. The **military-industrial complex** reached its acme of power in the 1960s when the United States realized the full implications of Truman's doctrine of containment. Eisenhower had succeeded in keeping the peace for eight years, but he had failed to halt the momentum of the Cold War he had inherited from Truman. Ike's efforts to ease tension with the Soviet Union were dashed by his own distrust of communism and by Khrushchev's belligerent rhetoric and behavior. Still, he had begun the process of relaxing tensions that would survive the troubled 1960s and, after a few false starts, would finally begin to erode the Cold War by the end of the 1980s.

military-industrial complex
In his farewell address in January 1961, President Eisenhower used this term to warn about the danger of massive defense spending and the close relationship between the armed forces and industrial corporations that supplied their weapons.

KEY TERMS

Potsdam Conference, p. 540

Iron Curtain, p. 541

Baruch Plan, p. 543

containment, p. 544

Truman Doctrine, p. 544

Marshall Plan, p. 544

North Atlantic Treaty Organization (NATO), p. 545

Berlin airlift, p. 546

National Security Act, p. 547

NSC-68, p. 548

Taft-Hartley Act, p. 551

Dixiecrats, p. 552

House Un-American Activities Committee (HUAC), p. 553

McCarthyism, p. 553

massive retaliation, p. 555

Dien Bien Phu, p. 556

Suez crisis, p. 557

Sputnik, p. 558

military-industrial complex, p. 560

RECOMMENDED READING

The Cold War spawned a vast array of books, some enduring in nature and many that are already outdated. The best general guide to American diplomacy since World War II is Walter LaFeber, *America, Russia and the Cold War, 1945–2000,* 9th ed. (2002). On the much-debated question of the origins of the Cold War, the most balanced account is Daniel Yergin, *Shattered Peace* (1977); for a dissenting view, see Thomas G. Paterson, *On Every Front* (1979). John Lewis Gaddis, *We Now Know* (1997), integrates new disclosures from Soviet and Chinese archives to provide the best rounded account of the Cold War through the early 1960s.

The classic account of containment is still the lucid recollection of its chief architect, George Kennan, *Memoirs, 1925–1950* (1967). John Lewis Gaddis uses Kennan's ideas as a point of departure for his account of the changing nature of American Cold War policy in *Strategies of Containment* (1982). Melvyn P. Leffler offers a full account of the development of containment in *A Preponderance of Power* (1992); Arnold A. Offner is more critical of Truman's policies in *Another Such Victory* (2002). Kai Bird and Martin J. Sherwin

probe Robert Oppenheimer's opposition to development of the hydrogen bomb in their biography, *American Prometheus* (2005). For developments in the Far East, consult the perceptive book by Akira Iriye, *The Cold War in Asia* (1974). On the Korean conflict, see Burton Kaufman, *The Korean War,* 2nd ed. (1997), and Bruce Cumings, *The Origins of the Korean War,* 2 vols. (1981 and 1991).

The best book on the Truman period is Alonzo L. Hamby, *Man of the People* (1995), which provides a balanced portrait of a controversial leader. Richard M. Fried offers a perceptive overview of the postwar anticommunist crusade in *Nightmare in Red: The McCarthy Era in Perspective* (1990); the best biography of McCarthy is David Oshinsky, *A Conspiracy So Immense* (1983).

Stephen A. Ambrose evaluates Dwight D. Eisenhower positively in the second volume of his biography, *Eisenhower: The President* (1985). For an equally favorable analysis, see Robert A. Divine, *Eisenhower and the Cold War* (1981). Richard H. Immerman provides a balanced portrait of Eisenhower's secretary of state in *John Foster Dulles* (1999).

SUGGESTED WEB SITES

Harry S Truman
www.ipl.org/div/potus/hstruman.html
This page contains basic factual data about his election and presidency, speeches, and on-line biographies.

Harry S Truman Library and Museum
www.trumanlibrary.org
This presidential library site has numerous photos and various important primary documents relating to Truman.

Cold War
cnn.com/SPECIALS/cold.war/
This is the companion site to the CNN *Perspectives* series on the Cold War. It contains information including interactive timelines and a quiz.

Korean War Project
www.koreanwar.org
This site has information about the Korean War and is a guide to resources on the struggle.

NATO at 50
www.cnn.com/SPECIALS/1999/nato/
This site from CNN has an excellent timeline and images telling the history of the North Atlantic Treaty Organization.

Senator Joe McCarthy—A Multimedia Celebration
webcorp.com/mccarthy/
This webcorp site includes audio and visual clips of McCarthy's speeches.

Chapter 29

Affluence and Anxiety

Levittown: The Flight to the Suburbs

On May 7, 1947, William Levitt announced plans to build two thousand houses in a former potato field on Long Island, 30 miles from midtown Manhattan. Using mass production techniques he had learned while erecting navy housing during the war, Levitt quickly built four thousand homes. In 1948, he began offering his houses for sale for a small amount down and a low monthly payment. Young couples, crowded in city apartments or still living with their parents, rushed out to buy Levitt's houses. By the time **Levittown** was completed in 1951, it contained more than seventeen thousand homes.

Levitt eventually built two more Levittowns, one in Pennsylvania and one in New Jersey. Each contained the same curving streets, neighborhood parks and playgrounds, and community swimming pools as the first development. Levitt's houses were ideal for young people just starting out in life. They were cheap, comfortable, and efficient, and each house came with a refrigerator, range, and washing machine. Despite the conformity of the houses, the three Levittowns were surprisingly diverse communities; residents had a wide variety of religious, ethnic, and occupational backgrounds. Blacks, however, were rigidly excluded. In time, as the more successful families moved on to larger homes in more exclusive neighborhoods, the Levittowns became enclaves for lower-middle-class families.

Levittown symbolized the most significant social trend of the postwar era in the United States—the flight to the suburbs. While central cities remained relatively stagnant during the decade, suburbs grew by 46 percent; by 1960, one-third of the nation lived in the suburbs. This massive shift in population from the central city was accompanied by a **baby boom** that started during World War II. Young married couples began to have three, four, even five children, and these larger families led to a 19 percent growth in the nation's population between 1950 and 1960, the greatest increase in growth rate since 1910.

The economy soared along with residential construction. A multitude of new consumer products—ranging from frozen foods to filtered cigarettes, from high-fidelity phonographs to cars equipped with automatic transmissions and tubeless tires—appeared in stores and showrooms. And in the suburbs, the supermarket replaced the corner grocer.

Although a new affluence for most Americans replaced the poverty and hunger of the Great Depression, the haunting memories of the 1930s remained vivid. The absorption of material goods took on an almost desperate quality, as if a profusion of houses, cars, and home appliances could guarantee that the nightmare of economic depression would never return. Critics were quick to condemn the conformity, charging the newly affluent with forsaking traditional American individualism to live in identical houses, drive look-alike cars, and accumulate the same material possessions.

Events abroad added to the feeling of anxiety in the postwar years. Nuclear war became a frighteningly real possibility. The rivalry with the Soviet Union had led to the second Red Scare, with charges of treason and disloyalty being leveled at loyal Americans. Many Americans joined Senator Joseph McCarthy in searching for the communist enemy at home rather than abroad. Loyalty oaths and book burning revealed how insecure Americans had become in the era of the Cold War. The 1950s also witnessed a growing demand by African Americans for equal opportunity in an age of abundance. The civil rights movement, along with strident criticism of the consumer culture, revealed that beneath the bland surface of suburban affluence forces for change were at work.

THE POSTWAR BOOM

For fifteen years following World War II, the nation witnessed a period of unparalleled economic growth. Pent-up demand for consumer goods fueled a steady industrial expansion, and heavy government spending during the Cold War added an extra stimulus to the economy, offsetting brief recessions in 1949 and 1953 and moderating a steeper one in 1957–1958. By the end of the 1950s, the majority of the population had achieved an affluence that finally dimmed lingering fears of the Great Depression.

Postwar Prosperity

The economy began to move forward as the result of two long-term factors. First, American consumers, after being held in check by depression and then by wartime scarcities, finally had a chance to indulge their suppressed appetites for material goods. Initially, American factories could not turn out enough automobiles and appliances to satisfy the hordes of buyers, whose personal savings at war's end stood at $37 billion. By 1950, however, production had finally caught up with demand.

The Cold War provided the extra stimulus the economy needed when postwar expansion slowed. The Marshall Plan and other foreign aid programs financed a heavy export trade. The Korean War helped overturn a brief recession and ensure continued prosperity as the government spent massive amounts on guns, planes, and munitions.

In the 1950s, the baby boom and the spectacular growth of suburbia served as great stimulants to the consumer goods industries. Manufacturers turned out an ever-increasing number of refrigerators, washing machines, and dishwashers to equip the kitchens in the houses that were being built across America. The automobile industry thrived with suburban expansion as two-car families became more and more common. The electronics industry took off. Customers were especially eager to acquire the latest marvel of home entertainment, the television set.

Yet the economic abundance of the 1950s was not without its problems. While some sections of the nation (notably the emerging Sunbelt areas of the South and West) benefited enormously from the growth of the aircraft and electronics industries, older manufacturing regions did not fare as well. The steel industry fell behind the rate of national growth, agriculture did not share in the general affluence, and unemployment persisted despite the boom. Moreover, the rate of economic growth slowed in the second half of the decade, causing concern about the continuing vitality of the American economy.

None of these flaws, however, could disguise the fact that the nation was prospering to an extent no one dreamed possible a decade or two earlier. The gross national product more than doubled its 1940 level. More important, workers now

A Look at the Past

Western-themed Toys

Following World War II, westerns enjoyed enormous popularity. TV and movie westerns provided inspiration to both children and manufacturers. Plastic cowboys and Indians, miniature frontier towns, ranches, and forts invited children to reenact western dramas. Western-themed toys, with heroes adults approved of, enabled children to extend screen fantasies into their lives. Westerns permitted adults to escape their worries and experience a world where good and evil were clearly defined and good always triumphed. ✳ Why do you think westerns and their associated goods appealed so strongly to Americans during the postwar period?

labored less than forty hours a week; they rarely worked on Saturdays, and nearly all enjoyed a two-week paid vacation each year. By the mid-1950s, the average American family had twice as much real income to spend as its counterpart had possessed in the boom years of the 1920s. The American people, in one generation, had moved from poverty and depression to the highest standard of living the world had ever known.

Life in the Suburbs

Rather than forming a homogeneous social group, the suburbs contained a surprising variety of people from all social classes. Doctors and lawyers, shoe salesmen and master plumbers often lived in the same developments. The traditional distinctions of ancestry, education, and size of residence no longer differentiated people so easily.

Yet suburbs could vary widely, from working-class communities clustered near factories built in the countryside to old, elitist areas such as Scarsdale, New York, and Shaker Heights, Ohio. Most were almost exclusively white and Christian; a few enabled Jews and blacks to join in the flight from the inner city.

Life in these suburban communities depended on the automobile. Highways and expressways allowed husbands to commute to jobs in the cities. Wives drove to the shopping centers that spread across the countryside by the mid-1950s. Children rode buses to school, then were driven to piano lessons and Little League ball games.

The home became the focus for activities and aspirations. Men and women who moved to the suburbs prized the new kitchens, extra bedrooms, large garages, and small, neat lawns. *Togetherness* became the byword of the 1950s. Families did things together—gathering around the TV sets that dominated living rooms, attending community activities, or going on vacations or outings in the huge station wagons of the era.

Emphasis on family life did little to encourage the advancement of feminism. The end of the war saw many women who had entered the workforce return to the home, where the role of wife and mother continued to be viewed as the ideal one for women in the 1950s. Trends toward getting married earlier and having larger families reinforced the tendency of women to devote all their efforts to housework and child rearing rather than acquiring professional skills and pursuing careers outside the home. Dr. Benjamin Spock's 1946 best-seller *Baby and Child Care* became a fixture in millions of homes, and the traditional women's magazines such as *McCall's* and *Good Housekeeping* thrived by featuring articles and inspirational pieces such as "Homemaking Is My Vocation."

Nevertheless, the number of working wives doubled between 1940 and 1960. The heavy expenses involved in rearing and educating children led wives and mothers to seek ways to augment the family income, unintentionally preparing the way for a new demand for equality in the 1960s.

THE GOOD LIFE?

Consumerism was the dominant social theme of the 1950s. Yet even with an abundance of creature comforts and added hours of leisure time, the quality of life left many Americans anxious and dissatisfied.

Areas of Greatest Growth

Organized religion flourished in the climate of the 1950s. Church and synagogue attendance rose, but some observers condemned the bland, secular nature of suburban churches, which seemed to be part of the consumer society. Yet the emergence of neo-orthodoxy in Protestant seminaries and the rapid spread of radical forms of fundamentalism (such as the Assemblies of God) indicated that millions of Americans were searching for inner faith.

The growth of the new suburban communities caused major problems for schools. The unprecedented increase in the number of school-age children overwhelmed the resources of many local districts, leading to demands for federal aid. Except for programs set up in reaction to Soviet scientific advances in space during the late 1950s, Congress and the Eisenhower administration provided only limited assistance to schools.

An important controversy arose over the nature of education in the 1950s. Critics of "progressive" education called for sweeping educational reforms and a new stress on traditional academic subjects. This issue often split suburban communities. The one thing all seemed to agree on was the desirability of a college education, and the number of young people attending college more than doubled between 1940 and 1960.

The largest growth area was the exciting new mass medium of television. From a shaky start just after the war, TV blossomed in the 1950s. By 1957, three national networks controlled the airways, reaching forty million sets over nearly five hundred stations. Advertisers soon took charge of the new medium, using many of the techniques first pioneered in radio, including taped commercials, quiz shows, and soap operas.

At first, the insatiable demand for programs encouraged a burst of creativity. Playwrights such as Reginald Rose, Rod Serling, and Paddy Chayefsky wrote notable dramas for *Playhouse 90, Studio One,* and the *Goodyear Television Playhouse.* Broadcast live from cramped studios, these productions thrived on tight dramatic structures, movable scenery, and frequent close-ups of the actors.

Advertisers, however, quickly became disillusioned with the live anthology programs, which usually dealt with controversial subjects or focused on ordinary people and events. Sponsors wanted shows that stressed excitement, glamour, and success. Westerns and situation comedies soon prevailed; a fling with quiz shows ended in scandal. Despite its early promise of innovation, television soon became a technologically sophisticated but unadventurous conveyor of the consumer culture.

Critics of the Consumer Society

One striking feature of the 1950s was the abundance of self-criticism. A number of widely read books explored the flaws in the new suburbia, criticizing the movement toward conformity and the obsession with material goods. The most sweeping indictment came in William H. Whyte's book *The Organization Man* (1956), delineating the change from the old Protestant ethic, with its emphasis on hard work and personal responsibility, to a new social ethic, where everything centered on "the team" and the ultimate goal was "belongingness." The result was a stifling conformity and a loss of personal identity.

Harvard sociologist David Riesman was the most influential social critic of the 1950s. His book, *The Lonely Crowd,* appeared in 1950 and set the tone for intellectual commentary about suburbia for the rest of the decade. Riesman described the shift from the "inner-directed" American of the past, who had relied on such traditional values as self-denial and frugality, to the "other-directed" American of the consumer society, who constantly adapted his behavior to conform to social pressures. The consequence—a decline in individualism and a tendency for people to become acutely sensitive to the expectations of others—produced a bland and tolerant society of consumers short on creativity and daring. More caustically, in *White Collar* (1951) and *The Power Elite* (1956), C. Wright Mills attacked the modern corporation for depriving workers of their own identities and imposing an impersonal discipline through manipulation and propaganda.

beats In the late 1950s, young poets and novelists such as Jack Kerouac became known as the beats or "beatniks" for their innovative writing and bizarre behavior. Calling themselves members of "the beat generation," they challenged the prevailing materialism of the consumer culture.

The disenchantment with the consumer culture was expressed most eloquently by the **beats,** literary groups that rebelled against the materialism of the 1950s. The name came from the quest for beatitude, a state of inner grace that is sought in Zen Buddhism. Jack Kerouac's novel *On the Road* (1957) set the tone for the fledgling movement. Flouting the respectability of suburbia, the "beatniks," as middle-class America termed them and their followers, were easily identified by their long hair, bizarre clothing, and penchant for sexual promiscuity and drug experimentation. They were conspicuous dropouts from a society they found senseless. Yet as highly visible nonconformists in an era of stifling conformity, the beats demonstrated a style of social protest that would flower into the counterculture of the 1960s.

The Reaction to *Sputnik*

The profound insecurity that underlay American life throughout the 1950s surfaced in October 1957, when the Soviets sent the satellite *Sputnik* into orbit around the earth. The American public's reaction to this impressive scientific feat was panic. Declining economic growth, the recession of 1957–1958, the growing concern that American schools were lagging behind their Russian counterparts—all contributed to a conviction that the nation had somehow lost its previously unquestioned primacy in the world.

After *Sputnik,* the president and Congress moved to restore national confidence. In 1958, Congress created the National Aeronautics and Space Administration (NASA), appropriating vast sums to allow the agency to compete with the Russians in the space race. Soon a new group of heroes, the astronauts, began the training that led to suborbital flights and eventually to John Glenn's five-hour flight around the globe in 1962. Congress also sought to match Soviet educational advances by passing the **National Defense Education Act (NDEA).** This legislation authorized federal financing of scientific and foreign language programs in the nation's schools and colleges.

National Defense Education Act (NDEA) Passed in response to *Sputnik,* this 1958 legislation provided an opportunity and stimulus for college education for many Americans. It allocated funds for upgrading studies in the sciences, foreign languages, guidance services, and teaching innovation.

The belief persisted, however, that the faults lay deeper, that in the midst of affluence and abundance Americans had lost their competitive edge. Economists

■ Sputnik I *on its support stand before launching. The first news of* Sputnik *was not carried in Soviet newspapers until two days after the launch.* ■

pointed to the higher rate of Soviet economic growth, and social critics bemoaned a supermarket culture that stressed consumption over production, comfort over hard work. It would take time for the American people to recover their traditional optimism and sense of national purpose after the shock of *Sputnik.*

FAREWELL TO REFORM

It is not surprising that the spirit of reform underlying the New Deal failed to flourish in the postwar years. Growing affluence took away the sense of grievance and the cry for change that was so strong in the 1930s. Eager to enjoy the new prosperity after years of want and sacrifice, the American people lost their enthusiasm for federal regulation and welfare programs.

Truman and the Fair Deal

After his 1948 victory, a triumphant Harry Truman announced his legislative program on January 5, 1949. He called for a **Fair Deal,** a reform package that comprised a new program of national medical insurance, federal aid to education, the Fair Employment Practices Commission (FEPC) to prevent economic discrimination against blacks, and an overhaul of the farm subsidy program.

The Fair Deal was never enacted. Except for raising the minimum wage and broadening Social Security, Congress refused to pass any of Truman's health, education, or civil rights measures. In part, Truman was to blame for trying to secure too much too soon. More important, however, was the fact that Congress remained under the control of a bipartisan conservative coalition of northern Republicans and southern Democrats.

Although his legislative failure became certain in 1950 when war once again subordinated domestic issues to foreign policy, Truman deserves credit for maintaining and consolidating the New Deal. His spirited leadership prevented any

Fair Deal A series of reform measures proposed by President Truman in 1949, including federal aid to education, civil rights measures, and national medical insurance. A bipartisan conservative coalition in Congress blocked this effort to move beyond the New Deal reforms of the 1930s.

Republican effort to repeal the gains of the 1930s. Moreover, even though he failed to get any new measures enacted, he broadened the reform agenda and laid the groundwork for future advances in health care, aid to education, and civil rights.

Eisenhower's Modern Republicanism

Moderation was the keynote of the Eisenhower presidency. His major goal from the outset was to restore calm and tranquillity to a badly divided nation. Unlike FDR and Truman, he had no commitment to social change or economic reform, yet he had no plans to dismantle the social programs of the New Deal. He sought instead to work toward balancing the budget, to keep military spending in check, to encourage as much private initiative as possible, and to reduce federal activities to the bare minimum. Defining his position as **modern Republicanism,** he claimed that he was "conservative when it comes to money and liberal when it comes to human beings."

modern Republicanism
President Eisenhower characterized his views as "modern Republicanism." Claiming he was liberal toward people but conservative about spending public money, he helped balance the federal budget and lower taxes without destroying existing social programs.

On domestic issues, Eisenhower preferred to delegate authority and to play a passive role. He concentrated his own efforts on the Cold War abroad. The men he chose to run the nation reflected his preference for successful corporation executives. Eisenhower was equally reluctant to play an active role in dealing with Congress. A fervent believer in the separation of powers, Ike did not want to engage in intensive lobbying. Such skillful aides as Sherman Adams, the White House chief of staff, insulated Eisenhower from many of the nation's pressing domestic problems.

Republican losses in the midterm election of 1954 weakened Eisenhower's relations with Congress. The Democrats regained control of both houses and kept it throughout the 1950s. The president had to rely on two Texas Democrats, Senate Majority Leader Lyndon B. Johnson and House Speaker Sam Rayburn, for legislative action; at best, it was an awkward and uneasy relationship.

The result was a very modest legislative record. Eisenhower extended Social Security benefits and raised the minimum wage. He consolidated the administration of welfare programs by creating the Department of Health, Education, and Welfare in 1953. But Ike steadfastly opposed Democratic plans for compulsory health insurance and comprehensive federal aid to education. The lack of presidential support and the continuing grip of the conservative coalition in Congress blocked any further reform in the 1950s.

Highway Act of 1956 A significant legislative achievement of Eisenhower's presidency that created the interstate highway system. The system, built over twenty years, provided jobs in construction, shortened travel times, and increased dependence on the automobile while weakening the railroads.

The one significant legislative achievement of the Eisenhower years came with the passage of the **Highway Act of 1956.** After a twelve-year delay, Congress appropriated funds for a 41,000-mile interstate system of multilane divided expressways that would connect all the nation's major cities. Although the act hurt railroad interests, it pleased a variety of road users: the trucking industry, automobile clubs, organized labor (eager for construction jobs), farmers, and state highway officials. Built over the next twenty years, the interstate system had a profound influence on American life. It stimulated the economy and shortened travel time dramatically while intensifying the nation's dependence on the automobile and distorting metropolitan growth patterns into long strips paralleling the new expressways.

Overall, the Eisenhower years marked an era of political moderation. The American people, enjoying the abundance of the 1950s, seemed quite content with legislative inaction. He was sensitive to the nation's economic health; when recessions developed in 1953 and 1957, he quickly abandoned his goal of a balanced budget in favor of a policy advocating government spending to restore prosperity. Thus Eisenhower maintained the New Deal legacy of federal responsibility for social welfare and the state of the economy while successfully resisting demands for more extensive government involvement in American life.

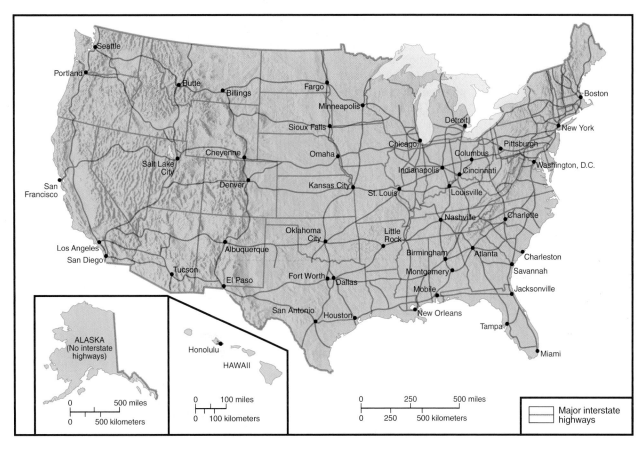

THE INTERSTATE HIGHWAY SYSTEM   *The 1956 plan to create an interstate highway system drastically changed America's landscape and culture. Today, the system covers about 45,000 miles, only a few thousand more miles than called for in the original plan.* ■

THE STRUGGLE OVER CIVIL RIGHTS

Although the Cold War gave birth to the ugly loyalty issue, it had a more positive effect on another social problem, the denial of civil rights to African Americans. The contradiction between the denunciation of the Soviet Union for its human rights violations and the second-class status of African Americans began to arouse the national conscience. Fighting for freedom against communist tyranny abroad, Americans had to face the reality of the continued denial of freedom to a submerged minority at home.

Blacks had benefited economically from World War II, but they were still a seriously disadvantaged group. Those who moved for better opportunities to northern and western cities were concentrated in blighted and segregated neighborhoods, working at low-paying jobs, suffering economic and social discrimination, and failing to share fully in the postwar prosperity.

In the South, conditions were much worse. State laws forced blacks to live almost totally apart from white society. Blacks attended separate schools and were rigidly excluded from all public facilities. They were forced to use separate waiting rooms in train stations, separate seats on all forms of transportation, and separate rest rooms and drinking fountains. Segregation was enforced at all places of public entertainment and in hospitals, prisons, mental institutions, and nursing homes.

Civil Rights as a Political Issue

Truman was the first president to attempt to alter the historic pattern of racial discrimination in the United States. But southern resistance blocked any action by Congress, and the inclusion of a strong civil rights plank in the 1948 Democratic platform led to the walkout of some southern delegations and a separate States' Rights (Dixiecrat) ticket in several states of the South that fall.

Black voters in the North overwhelmingly backed Truman over Dewey in the 1948 election. In key states—California, Ohio, and Illinois—it was the black voters in Los Angeles, Cleveland, and Chicago that ensured the Democratic victory. Truman responded by including civil rights legislation in his Fair Deal program in 1949. Once again, however, determined southern opposition blocked congressional action on a permanent fair employment commission and an antilynching measure.

Even though Truman was unable to secure any significant legislation, he did succeed in adding civil rights to the liberal, Democratic agenda and used his executive power to assist blacks seeking redress of grievances in school and housing issues. He strengthened the civil rights division of the Justice Department, which aided black groups in these issues. Most important, in 1948, Truman issued an order calling for the desegregation of the armed forces. By the end of the 1950s, the military had become far more integrated than American society at large.

Desegregating the Schools

The nation's schools soon became the primary target of civil rights advocates. The NAACP concentrated first on the universities, successfully waging an intensive legal battle to win admission for qualified blacks to graduate and professional schools. Led by Thurgood Marshall, NAACP lawyers then took on the broader issue of segregation in the country's public schools. Challenging the 1896 Supreme Court decision in *Plessy* v. *Ferguson* that upheld the constitutionality of "separate but equal" public facilities, Marshall argued that even substantially equal but separate schools did profound psychological damage to black children and thus violated the Fourteenth Amendment.

Brown v. *Board of Education of Topeka* In 1954, the Supreme Court reversed the *Plessy* v. *Ferguson* decision (1896) that established the "separate but equal" doctrine. The *Brown* decision found segregation in schools inherently unequal and initiated a long and difficult effort to integrate the nation's public schools.

A unanimous Supreme Court agreed in its 1954 decision in the case of ***Brown*** v. ***Board of Education of Topeka.*** Chief Justice Earl Warren wrote the landmark opinion, which flatly declared that "separate educational facilities are inherently unequal." Recognizing that it would be difficult to change historic patterns of segregation quickly, the Court ruled in 1955 that desegregation should proceed "with all deliberate speed" and left the details to the lower federal courts.

"All deliberate speed" proved agonizingly slow. Southern states responded with a policy of massive resistance. Encouraged by a "southern manifesto" signed by 101 congressmen and senators, which denounced the *Brown* decision as "a clear abuse of judicial power," school boards found ways to evade the Court's ruling. By the end of the decade, fewer than 1 percent of the black children in the Deep South attended school with whites.

A conspicuous lack of presidential support further weakened the desegregation effort. Eisenhower was not a racist, but he believed that people's attitudes could not be changed by "cold lawmaking," only "by appealing to reason, by prayer, and by constantly working at it through our own efforts." Quietly and unobtrusively, he worked to achieve desegregation in federal facilities. Yet he refrained from endorsing the *Brown* decision.

Southern leaders mistook Ike's silence for tacit support of segregation. In 1957, however, Eisenhower corrected this misunderstanding. Backing the federal courts, he used federal troops to ensure the integration of Little Rock's Central High

School. The troops remained there for the rest of the school year. Little Rock authorities then closed Central High School for two years; when it reopened, there were only three blacks in attendance.

Despite the snail's pace of school desegregation, the *Brown* decision led to other advances. In 1957, Eisenhower proposed and Congress passed a bill creating a permanent Commission for Civil Rights, one of Truman's original goals. It also provided for federal efforts aimed at "securing and protecting the right to vote." A second civil rights act in 1960 slightly strengthened the voting rights section.

Like the desegregation effort, the attempt to ensure black voting rights in the South was still largely symbolic. Southern registrars used a variety of devices, ranging from intimidation to unfair tests, to deny blacks the suffrage. Yet the actions of Congress and the Supreme Court marked a vital turning point in national policy toward racial justice.

The Beginnings of Black Activism

The most dynamic force for change came from blacks themselves. The shift from legal struggles in the courts to black protest in the streets began with an incident in Montgomery, Alabama. On December 1, 1955, Rosa Parks, a black seamstress who had been active in the local NAACP chapter, violated a city ordinance by refusing to give up her seat to a white person on a local bus. After her arrest, blacks gathered to protest and found a young, eloquent leader in Martin Luther King, Jr. He agreed to lead a massive boycott of the city's bus system, which depended heavily on black patronage.

■ *Angry whites taunt Elizabeth Eckford, one of nine African American students who enrolled at Little Rock's Central High School in 1957. The Arkansas National Guard, acting on orders from the state's governor Orval Faubus, refused the students entry into the school. The students were finally able to enter the school under the escort of paratroopers from the 101st Airborne Division.* ■

The **Montgomery bus boycott**'s goal was at first modest. King simply asked that seats be taken on a first-come, first-served basis, with blacks being seated from the back and whites from the front of each bus. The boycotters became more assertive as they endured both legal harassment and sporadic acts of violence. An effective system of car pools enabled the protesters to avoid the city buses. Soon they were insisting on a total end to segregated seating.

The boycott ended in victory a year later when the Supreme Court ruled the Alabama segregated-seating law unconstitutional. The protest movement had won far more than this limited dent in the wall of segregation, however. King had provided blacks with a new weapon to fight racial oppression: a policy of passive resistance that stressed nonviolence and goodwill.

A year after the successful bus boycott, King founded the **Southern Christian Leadership Conference (SCLC)** to direct the crusade against segregation. Then in February 1960, another spontaneous event sparked a further advance for passive resistance. Four black students from North Carolina Agricultural and Technical College sat down at a dime-store lunch counter in Greensboro, North Carolina. After being denied service, they refused to move. Other students, both whites and blacks, joined in similar "sit-ins" across the South. By the end of the year, some fifty thousand young people had succeeded in desegregating public facilities in more than a hundred southern cities. Several thousand of the demonstrators were arrested and put in jail, but the movement

Montgomery bus boycott In late 1955, African Americans led by Martin Luther King, Jr., boycotted the buses in Montgomery, Alabama, after seamstress Rosa Parks was arrested for refusing to move to the back of a bus. The boycott, which ended when the Supreme Court ruled in favor of the protesters, marked the beginning of a new, activist phase of the civil rights movement.

Southern Christian Leadership Conference (SCLC) An organization founded by Martin Luther King, Jr., to direct the crusade against segregation. Its weapon was passive resistance that stressed nonviolence and love, and its tactic direct, though peaceful, confrontation.

■ *In February 1960, black students from North Carolina A&T College staged a sit-in at a "whites only" Woolworth's lunch counter in Greensboro, North Carolina. Their act of nonviolent protest spurred similar demonstrations in public spaces across the South in an effort to draw national attention to racial injustice, to demand desegregation of public facilities, and to prompt the federal government to take a more active role to end segregation. At right, civil rights activists from Tougaloo College in Mississippi bear the verbal and physical abuse of white hecklers at a sit-in demonstration at a Woolworth's lunch counter on May 28, 1963.* ■

Student Nonviolent Coordinating Committee (SNCC) A radical group advocating black power, the SNCC's leaders, scornful of integration and interracial cooperation, broke with Martin Luther King, Jr., to advocate greater militancy and acts of violence.

gained strength, leading to the formation of the **Student Nonviolent Coordinating Committee (SNCC)** in April 1960. From this time on, SCLC and SNCC, with their tactics of direct peaceful confrontation, would replace the NAACP, with its reliance on court action, in the forefront of the civil rights movement. The change would eventually lead to dramatic success, but it also ushered in a period of heightened tension and social turmoil in the 1960s.

CONCLUSION: RESTORING NATIONAL CONFIDENCE

In 1959, disturbed by the criticism of American society sparked by *Sputnik*, President Eisenhower appointed a Commission on National Goals "to develop a broad outline of national objectives for the next decade and longer." The commission eventually issued a report that called for increased military spending abroad, greater economic growth at home, broader educational opportunities, and more government support for both scientific research and the advancement of the arts. The consensus seemed to be that rather than a change of direction, all the United States needed was a renewed commitment to the pursuit of excellence.

The 1950s ended with the national mood less troubled than when the decade began amid the turmoil of the second Red Scare and the Korean War, yet hardly as tranquil or confident as Eisenhower had hoped it would be. The American people felt reassured about the state of the economy, no longer fearing a return to the grim years of the Great Depression. At the same time, however, they were aware that abundance alone did not guarantee the quality of everyday life and realized that there was still a huge gap between American ideals and the reality of race relations, in the North as well as the South.

Chronology

1946	Republicans win control of both houses of Congress in November elections
1947	William Levitt announces first Levittown
1948	Truman orders end to segregation in armed forces
1949	Minimum wage raised from 40 to 75 cents an hour
1950	Gwendolyn Brooks becomes first African American woman to be awarded Pulitzer Prize
1951	Remington Rand unveils UNIVAC, the first electronic digital computer to be marketed commercially
1952	Edward R. Murrow inaugurates television news show *See It Now*
1953	McDonald's chooses golden arches design for its hamburger shops
1954	Supreme Court orders schools desegregated in *Brown* v. *Board of Education of Topeka*
1955	Dr. Jonas Salk reports success of antipolio vaccine (April) ■ African Americans begin boycott of Montgomery, Alabama, bus company (December)
1956	Eisenhower signs legislation creating the interstate highway system
1957	Congress passes first Civil Rights Act since Reconstruction
1958	Charles Van Doren confesses to cheating on television quiz show *Twenty-one*
1960	African American college students stage sit-in in Greensboro, North Carolina

KEY TERMS

Levittown, p. 562

baby boom, p. 562

beats, p. 566

National Defense Education Act (NDEA), p. 566

Fair Deal, p. 567

modern Republicanism, p. 568

Highway Act of 1956, p. 568

Brown v. *Board of Education of Topeka*, p. 570

Montgomery bus boycott, p. 571

Southern Christian Leadership Conference (SCLC), p. 571

Student Nonviolent Coordinating Committee (SNCC), p. 572

RECOMMENDED READING

Two excellent books survey the social, cultural, and political trends in the United States during the postwar period. In *One Nation Divisible* (1980), Richard Polenberg analyzes class, ethnic, and racial changes; James T. Patterson offers a perceptive overview of American life from the end of World War II through the mid-1970s in *Grand Expectations* (1996).

Richard Pells provides a sweeping survey of the American intellectual community's response to the Cold War in *The Liberal Mind in a Conservative Age* (1985). The broadest account of American life during the decade is David Halberstam, *The Fifties* (1993). Other important books on social and cultural trends include Elaine Tyler May, *Homeward Bound: American Families in the Cold War Era* (1988); Kenneth A. Jackson, *Crabgrass Frontier* (1986);

Lisabeth Cohen, *A Consumer's Republic* (2003); and Serge Guilbaut, *How New York Stole the Idea of Modern Art* (1983).

Charles Alexander provides a balanced view of the Eisenhower years in *Holding the Line* (1975), portraying the Republican president as an able chief executive who was well suited to the times. Fred Greenstein, *The Hidden Hand Presidency* (1982), explores Eisenhower's fondness for indirect leadership. For the impact of *Sputnik* and the space program, see Walter A. MacDougall, *The Heavens and the Earth* (1985) and Robert A. Divine, *The* Sputnik *Challenge* (1993).

Taylor Branch gives a comprehensive account of the genesis of the civil rights movement in *Parting the Waters: America in the King Years, 1954–1963* (1988). Three fine biographies—David L. Lewis's *King* (1970), Stephen B. Oates's

Let the Trumpet Sound (1982), and David Garrow's *Bearing the Cross* (1986)—present perceptive portraits of Martin Luther King, Jr., the movement's most influential leader. On civil rights, see also Adam Fairclough, *To Redeem the Soul of America* (1987), Joanne Grant, *Ella Baker* (1999);

and James T. Patterson, *Brown* v. *Board of Education* (2001). The fullest account of the passage of the 1957 civil rights act is the third volume of Robert Caro's biography of Lyndon Johnson, *Master of the Senate* (2002).

SUGGESTED WEB SITES

Fifties Web Site Home Page

www.fiftiesweb.com/

This entertaining site tells about and samples music and television from the 1950s. It also includes a related links page.

1950s America

www.english.upenn.edu/~afilreis/50/home.html

This site by Professor Al Filreis of the University of Pennsylvania contains a large array of 1950s literature and images in an alphabetical index.

Levittown: Documents of an Ideal American Suburb

www.uic.edu/~pbhales/Levittown/

The postwar boom in housing made suburban living the cultural norm in America and shaped a generation. The story of

the classic suburb, Levittown, is told on this site in pictures and text.

Dwight David Eisenhower

www.ipl.org/div/potus/ddeisenhower.html

This site contains basic factual data about Eisenhower's election and presidency, including speeches and other materials.

The Dwight D. Eisenhower Library and Museum

www.eisenhower.utexas.edu/

This site contains mainly photos of the president.

Chapter 30

The Turbulent Sixties

Kennedy versus Nixon:
The First Televised Presidential Candidate Debate

On Monday evening, September 26, 1960, Senator John F. Kennedy and Vice President Richard M. Nixon faced each other in the nation's first televised debate between two presidential candidates. Kennedy, the relatively unknown Democratic challenger, had proposed the debates; Nixon, confident of his mastery of television, had accepted even though as the early front-runner in the election he had more to lose and less to gain.

Nixon arrived an hour early, looking tired and ill at ease. He was still recuperating from a knee injury that had slowed his campaign and left him pale and weak as he pursued a hectic catch-up schedule. Makeup experts offered to hide Nixon's heavy beard and soften his prominent jowls, but the GOP candidate declined. Kennedy, tanned from open-air campaigning in California and rested by a day spent nearly free of distracting activity, wore very light makeup and changed from a gray to a dark blue suit better adapted to the intense lighting on the set.

Before an audience estimated at 77 million, Kennedy led off, echoing Abraham Lincoln by saying that the nation faced the question of "whether the world will exist half-slave and half-free." Although the ground rules limited the first debate to domestic issues, Kennedy argued that foreign and domestic policy were inseparable. He accused the Republicans of letting the country drift at home and abroad. Nixon, caught off guard, seemed to agree with Kennedy's assessment of the nation's problems, but he contended that he had better solutions.

For the rest of the hour, the two candidates answered questions from a panel of journalists. Radiating confidence and self-assurance, Kennedy used a flow of statistics and details to create the image of a man deeply knowledgeable about all aspects of government. Nixon seemed nervous and unsure of himself.

Polls taken over the next few weeks revealed a sharp swing to Kennedy. Nixon suffered more from his less attractive physical image than from what he said; those who heard the debate on radio thought that the Republican candidate more than held his own. Nixon improved his appearance and strategy in the three additional debates, but the damage had been done. A postelection poll revealed that of four million voters who were influenced by the debates, three million voted for Kennedy.

The television debates were only one of many factors influencing the outcome of the 1960 election. During the fall campaign, Kennedy exploited the national mood of frustration that had followed *Sputnik*. At home, he promised to stimulate the lagging economy and implement long-overdue reforms in education, health care, and civil rights. Abroad, he pledged a renewed commitment to the Cold War, vowing that he would lead the nation to victory over the Soviet Union.

The Democratic victory of 1960 was paper-thin. Kennedy's edge in the popular vote was only two-tenths of 1 percent. Yet even though he had no mandate, Kennedy's triumph did mark a sharp political shift. In contrast to the aging Eisenhower, Kennedy symbolized youth, energy, and ambition. His mastery of the new medium of television reflected his sensitivity to the changes taking place in American life. He came to office promising reform at home and advance abroad. Over the next eight years, he and his vice president, Lyndon Johnson, achieved many of their goals only to find the nation caught up in new and even greater dilemmas.

KENNEDY INTENSIFIES THE COLD WAR

John F. Kennedy was determined to succeed where he believed Eisenhower had failed. Critical of his predecessor for holding down defense spending and apparently allowing the Soviet Union to open up a dangerous lead in intercontinental ballistic missiles (ICBMs), Kennedy sought to warn the nation of its peril and lead it to victory in the Cold War. In his inaugural address, he ignored domestic issues and warned the world that "we shall pay any price, bear any burden, meet any hardship, support any friend, oppose any foe, to assure the survival and success of liberty."

From the day he took office, Kennedy gave foreign policy top priority. In part, this decision reflected the perilous world situation, the immediate dangers ranging from the unresolved Berlin crisis to the emergence of Fidel Castro as a Soviet ally in Cuba. But it also corresponded to Kennedy's personal priorities. As a congressman and senator, he had been an intense cold warrior, supporting containment after World War II, lamenting the loss of China, and accusing the Eisenhower administration of allowing the USSR to open up a dangerous missile gap.

Kennedy's appointments reflected his determination to win the Cold War. His choice of Dean Rusk, an experienced but unassertive diplomat, to head the State Department indicated that Kennedy planned to be his own secretary of state. He surrounded himself with young, pragmatic advisers who prided themselves on toughness: McGeorge Bundy, dean of Harvard College, became national security adviser; Walt W. Rostow, an MIT economist, was Bundy's deputy; and Robert McNamara, the youthful president of the Ford Motor Company, took over as secretary of defense. These New Frontiersmen all shared a hard-line view of the Soviet Union and the belief that American security depended on superior force and the willingness to use it.

Flexible Response

The first goal of the Kennedy administration was to build up the nation's armed forces. During the 1960 campaign, Kennedy had claimed that the Soviets were opening a missile gap. In fact, the United States had a significant lead in nuclear striking power by early 1961. Paying little heed to Eisenhower's somber farewell warning about the danger of massive military spending, the new administration, intent on putting the Soviets on the defensive, authorized the construction of an awesome nuclear arsenal that included one thousand Minuteman ICBMs. The United States thus opened a missile gap in reverse, creating the possibility of a successful American first strike.

At the same time, the Kennedy administration reinforced its conventional military strength. Secretary of Defense McNamara developed plans to add five combat-ready army divisions, three tactical air wings, and a ten-division strategic reserve. The president took a personal interest in counterinsurgency. He expanded the

Special Forces unit at Fort Bragg, North Carolina, and insisted, over army objections, that it adopt a distinctive green beret as a symbol of its elite status.

The purpose of this buildup was to create an alternative to Eisenhower's policy of massive retaliation. Instead of responding to communist moves with nuclear threats, the United States could now call on a wide spectrum of force, ranging from ICBMs to Green Berets. The danger of this new strategy of **flexible response,** however, was that the existence of such a powerful arsenal would tempt the new administration to test its strength against the Soviet Union.

Crisis over Berlin

The first test came in Germany. Since 1958, Soviet Premier Khrushchev had been threatening to sign a peace treaty that would put access to the isolated western zones of Berlin under the control of East Germany. The steady flight of skilled workers to the West through the Berlin escape route weakened the East German regime dangerously, and the Soviets believed they had to resolve this issue quickly.

At a summit meeting in Vienna in June 1961, Kennedy and Khrushchev focused on Berlin as the key issue. In a series of meetings, the two leaders failed to find a solution. During their last session, the failure to reach agreement took on an ominous tone. "I want peace," Khrushchev declared, "but if you want war, that is your problem." "It is you, not I," the young president replied, "who wants to force a change." When the Soviet leader said he would sign a German peace treaty by December, Kennedy added, "It will be a cold winter."

The climax came sooner than either man expected. On July 25, Kennedy delivered an impassioned televised address to the American people in which he called the defense of Berlin "essential" to "the entire Free World." He took the unprecedented step of calling more than 150,000 reservists and National Guardsmen to active duty. Above all, he sought to convince Khrushchev of his determination and resolve.

Aware of superior American nuclear striking power, Khrushchev settled for a stalemate. On August 13, the Soviets sealed off their zone of the city. They began the construction of the **Berlin Wall** to stop the flow of brains and talent to the West. For a brief time, Russian and American tanks maneuvered within sight of each other at Checkpoint Charlie, but the tension gradually eased. The Soviets signed the separate peace treaty; Berlin—like Germany and, indeed, all Europe—remained divided between the East and the West. Neither side could claim a victory, but Kennedy believed that at least he had proved America's willingness to honor its commitments.

Containment in Southeast Asia

Two weeks before Kennedy's inaugural, Khrushchev gave a speech in Moscow in which he declared Soviet support for "wars of national liberation." His words were actually aimed more at China than the United States, but Kennedy concluded that the United States and the Soviet Union were now locked in a struggle for the hearts and minds of the uncommitted in Asia, Africa, and Latin America.

Calling for a new policy of nation building, Kennedy advocated financial and technical assistance designed to help Third World nations achieve economic modernization and stable, pro-Western governments. Measures ranging from the formation of the idealistic Peace Corps to the creation of the ambitious Alliance for Progress—a massive economic aid program for Latin America—were part of this effort. Unfortunately, Kennedy relied even more on counterinsurgency and the Green Berets to beat back the communist challenge.

Southeast Asia offered the gravest test. The American decision to back Ngo Dinh Diem had prevented the holding of elections throughout Vietnam in 1956, as called for in the Geneva accords. Instead, Diem sought to establish a separate government in the South with large-scale American economic and military aid. By the time Kennedy

flexible response The Kennedy administration rejected the Eisenhower strategy of massive retaliation in favor of flexible response, which emphasized the use of conventional as well as nuclear weapons in meeting threats to American security.

Berlin Wall In 1961, the Soviet Union built a high barrier to seal off its sector of Berlin in order to stop the flow of refugees out of the Soviet zone of Germany.

Flames engulf a Buddhist monk, the Reverend Quang Duc, who set himself afire at an intersection in Saigon, Vietnam, to protest persecution of Buddhists by Vietnam President Ngo Dinh Diem and his government. Other monks placed themselves in front of the wheels of nearby fire trucks to prevent them from reaching Duc.

entered the White House, however, the Communist government in North Vietnam, led by Ho Chi Minh, was directing the efforts of Viet Cong rebels in the South.

As the guerrilla war intensified in the fall of 1961, Kennedy sent two trusted advisers, Walt Rostow and General Maxwell Taylor, to South Vietnam. They returned favoring the dispatch of eight thousand American combat troops. General Taylor described the risks of "backing into" a major Asian war by way of South Vietnam as "present but not impressive."

Kennedy decided against sending in combat troops in 1961, but he authorized substantial increases not only in economic aid to Diem but also in the size of the military mission in Saigon. The number of American advisers grew from fewer than a thousand in 1961 to more than sixteen thousand by late 1963. American aid slowed the Communists' momentum, but by 1963, the situation had again become critical. Diem had failed to win the support of his own people; Buddhist monks set themselves aflame in public protests, and even Diem's own generals plotted his overthrow.

President Kennedy was in a quandary. He realized that the fate of South Vietnam would be determined not by Americans but by the Vietnamese. But at the same time, he was not prepared to accept the possible loss of all Southeast Asia. Although aides later claimed he planned to pull out after the 1964 election, Kennedy raised the stakes by tacitly approving a coup that led to Diem's overthrow and death on November 1, 1963. The resulting power vacuum in Saigon made further American involvement in Vietnam almost certain.

Containing Castro: The Bay of Pigs Fiasco

Kennedy's determination to check global communist expansion reached a peak of intensity in Cuba. In the 1960 presidential campaign, pointing to the growing ties between the Soviet Union and Fidel Castro's regime, he had accused the Republicans of permitting a "Communist satellite" to arise on "our very doorstep." Kennedy had even issued a statement backing "anti-Castro forces in exile."

In reality, the Eisenhower administration had been training a group of Cuban exiles in Guatemala since March 1960 as part of a CIA plan to topple the Castro regime. Many of Kennedy's advisers had tactical and moral doubts about the proposed invasion, but the president, committed by his own campaign rhetoric and assured of success by the military, decided to go ahead.

Bay of Pigs In April 1961, a group of Cuban exiles organized and supported by the CIA landed on the southern coast of Cuba in an effort to overthrow Fidel Castro. When the invasion ended in disaster, President Kennedy took full responsibility for the failure.

On April 17, 1961, fourteen hundred Cuban exiles moved ashore at the **Bay of Pigs** on the southern coast of Cuba. Even though the United States had masterminded the entire operation, Kennedy insisted on covert action, even canceling at the last minute a planned American air strike on the beachhead. With air superiority, Castro's well-trained forces had no difficulty quashing the invasion.

Aghast at the swiftness of the defeat, Kennedy took personal responsibility for the failure. In his address to the American people, however, he showed no remorse for arranging the violation of a neighboring country's sovereignty, only regret at the outcome. Above all, he expressed renewed defiance, asserting that the United States would resist "Communist penetration" in the Western Hemisphere. For the remainder of his presidency, Kennedy continued to harass the Castro regime.

Containing Castro: The Cuban Missile Crisis

The climax of Kennedy's crusade came in October 1962 with the **Cuban missile crisis.** Throughout the summer and early fall, the Soviets engaged in a massive arms buildup in Cuba, ostensibly to protect Castro from an American invasion. Although Kennedy had warned the Soviets against the introduction of any offensive weapons, Khrushchev secretly took a daring gamble and started to build missile sites in Cuba. Later he claimed that his purpose was purely defensive, but most likely he was responding to the pressures from his own military to close the enormous strategic gap in nuclear striking power that Kennedy had opened.

On October 14, 1962, American U-2 planes finally discovered the missile sites, which were nearing completion. As soon as he learned what Khrushchev had done, Kennedy decided to seek a showdown. Insisting on absolute secrecy, he convinced a special group of advisers to come up with a response.

Weighing his alternatives, Kennedy decided on a two-step procedure. He would proclaim a quarantine of Cuba to prevent the arrival of new missiles and threaten a nuclear strike to force the removal of those already there. If the Soviets did not cooperate, the United States would invade Cuba and dismantle the missiles by force.

On the evening of October 22, Kennedy informed the nation of the existence of the Soviet missiles and his plans to remove them. He spared no words in blaming Khrushchev, and he made it clear that any missile attack from Cuba would lead to "a full retaliatory response upon the Soviet Union."

For the next six days, the world hovered on the brink of nuclear catastrophe. Khrushchev replied defiantly, and some sixteen Soviet ships continued on course toward Cuba. While the U.S. Navy deployed to intercept those ships 500 miles from the island, American troops assembled in Florida in preparation for an invasion.

The first break came at midweek when the Soviet ships suddenly halted to avert a confrontation at sea. Kennedy felt better on Friday when Khrushchev sent him a long, rambling letter offering a face-saving way out: the Soviets would remove the missiles in return for an American promise never to invade Cuba. Kennedy was ready to accept when a second Russian message raised the stakes by insisting that American missiles be withdrawn from Turkey. Attorney General Robert Kennedy—the president's brother and most trusted adviser—suggested that he ignore the second Russian message and accept the original offer.

On Saturday night, October 27, Robert Kennedy met with the Soviet ambassador, Anatoly Dobrynin, to make it clear that this was the last chance to avert nuclear conflict. The next morning, Khrushchev agreed to remove the missiles in return for Kennedy's promise not to invade Cuba. The crisis was over.

On the surface, Kennedy appeared to have won a stunning personal and political victory. His party successfully overcame the Republican challenge in the November elections, and his own popularity reached new heights in the polls. The American people, on the defensive since *Sputnik,* suddenly felt that they had proved their superiority over the Soviets.

The Cuban missile crisis had more substantial results as well. Shaken by their close call, Kennedy and Khrushchev agreed to install a "hot line" to speed direct communication between Washington and Moscow in an emergency. Long-stalled negotiations over the reduction of nuclear testing suddenly resumed, leading to the limited test ban treaty of 1963, which outlawed tests in the atmosphere while still permitting them underground. Above all, Kennedy displayed a new maturity as a result of the crisis. He shifted from the rhetoric of confrontation to that of conciliation.

Despite these hopeful signs, the missile crisis also had an unfortunate consequence. Policymakers who believed that the Soviets understood only the language of force were confirmed in their penchant for a hard line. Hawks who had backed Kennedy's military buildup felt that events had justified a policy of nuclear superiority. The Soviet leaders drew similar conclusions. "Never will we be caught like this

Cuban missile crisis In October 1962, the United States and the Soviet Union came close to nuclear war when President Kennedy insisted that Nikita Khrushchev remove the forty-two missiles he had secretly deployed in Cuba. The Soviets eventually did so, nuclear war was averted, and the crisis ended.

again," vowed one Russian official. After 1962, the Soviets embarked on a crash program to build up their navy and to overtake the American lead in nuclear missiles. Kennedy's moment of triumph thus ensured the escalation of the arms race. His legacy was one of short-term success and long-term anxiety.

THE NEW FRONTIER AT HOME

The election of John F. Kennedy marked the arrival of a new generation of leadership. For the first time, people born in the twentieth century who had entered political life after World War II were in charge of national affairs. Kennedy himself had been elected to Congress in 1946 at the age of twenty-nine and had won a Senate seat in 1952. Although he had not sponsored any significant legislation as a senator, he championed the traditional Democratic reforms during his presidential campaign, under the banner of the **New Frontier.** More important was his criticism of the Republicans for allowing sluggish economic growth and failing to deal with such pressing social problems as health care and education. His call to get the nation moving again was particularly attractive to young people, who had shunned political involvement during the Eisenhower years.

New Frontier The campaign program advocated by John F. Kennedy in the 1960 election. He promised to revitalize the stagnant economy and enact reform legislation in education, health care, and civil rights.

The new administration reflected Kennedy's aura of youth and energy. The most controversial cabinet choice was Robert F. Kennedy, the president's brother, as attorney general. Critics scoffed at his lack of legal experience, but the president prized his brother's loyalty and shrewd political advice. As important as his cabinet appointments were his White House staff appointments. Like their counterparts in foreign policy, these New Frontiersmen prided themselves on being tough-minded and pragmatic. In contrast to Eisenhower, Kennedy relied heavily on academics and intellectuals to help him infuse the nation with energy and a new sense of direction.

Kennedy's greatest asset was his personality. A cool, handsome, and intelligent man, he possessed a sense of style that endeared him to the American public. He seemed to be a new Lancelot, bent on calling forth the best in national life; admirers likened his inner circle to King Arthur's court at Camelot. Reporters loved him, both for his fact-filled and candid press conferences and for his witty comments.

The Congressional Obstacle and Economic Advance

Neither Kennedy's wit nor his charm proved strong enough to break the logjam in Congress. Since the late 1940s, a series of reform bills ranging from health care to federal aid to education had been stalled on Capitol Hill. Although Kennedy embraced these Democratic measures, he was hurt by the loss of twenty seats in the House and two in the Senate. The conservative coalition of northern Republicans and southern Democrats opposed all efforts at reform.

The situation was especially critical in the House, where 101 southern representatives held the balance of power between 160 northern Democrats and 174 Republicans. Aided by Speaker Sam Rayburn, Kennedy was able to enlarge the Rules Committee and overcome a conservative roadblock, but the narrow vote, 217 to 212, revealed how difficult it would be to enact his education and health care proposals. Thus the composition of Congress, coupled with Kennedy's distaste for legislative infighting, caused the New Frontier to languish.

Kennedy gave a higher priority to the sluggish American economy. He was determined to recover quickly from the recession he had inherited and to stimulate the economy to achieve a much higher rate of long-term growth. In part, he wanted to redeem his campaign pledge to get the nation moving again; he also believed that the United States had to surpass the Soviet Union in economic vitality.

Rejecting the idea of massive spending on public works, Kennedy sided with the experts who claimed that the problem was essentially technological and urged training and redevelopment programs to modernize American industry. The actual stimulation of the economy, however, came not from such social programs but from greatly increased appropriations for defense and space. By 1962, more than half the federal budget was devoted to space and defense; aircraft and computer companies in the South and West benefited, but unemployment remained uncomfortably high in the older industrial areas of the Northeast and Midwest.

The administration's desire to keep the inflation rate low led to a serious confrontation with the business community. Kennedy relied on informal wage and price guidelines to hold down the cost of living. But in April 1962, just after the president had persuaded the steelworker's union to accept a new contract with no wage increases, U.S. Steel head Roger Blough informed Kennedy that his company was raising steel prices by $6 a ton. Outraged, Kennedy publicly criticized the action. Privately, he confided to aides, "My father always told me that all businessmen were sons-of-bitches, but I never believed it till now."

Threatened with a cutoff in Pentagon steel orders and an antitrust suit, Blough reconsidered. When several smaller steel companies refused to raise their prices in the hope of expanding their share of the market, U.S. Steel capitulated and rolled back its prices. But the business community deeply resented the president's action.

Troubled by his strained relations with business and by the continued lag in economic growth, Kennedy decided to adopt a more unorthodox approach in 1963. Walter Heller, chairman of the Council of Economic Advisers, had long urged a major cut in taxes to stimulate consumer spending and give the economy the jolt it needed. The idea of a tax cut and resulting deficits during a period of prosperity went against economic orthodoxy, but Kennedy finally gave his approval. When enacted by Congress in 1964, the massive tax cut ($13.5 billion) led to one of the longest sustained economic advances in American history.

Kennedy's economic policy was far more successful than his legislative efforts. Although the rate of economic growth doubled to 4.5 percent by the end of 1963 and unemployment was reduced substantially, the cost of living rose only 1.3 percent a year. Personal income went up 13 percent in the early 1960s, but the greatest gains came in corporate profits, up 67 percent in this period. Critics pointed out that the Kennedy administration failed to close the glaring loopholes in the tax law that benefited the rich and that it made no effort to help those at the bottom by forcing a redistribution of national wealth. And in spite of the overall economic growth, the public sector remained neglected. Ecological and social problems continued to grow at an alarming rate.

Moving Slowly on Civil Rights

Kennedy faced a genuine dilemma over the issue of civil rights. During the 1960 campaign, he had promised to launch an attack on segregation in the Deep South, but fear of alienating the large bloc of southern Democrats, however, forced him to play down civil rights legislation.

The president's solution was to defer congressional action in favor of executive leadership in this area. He directed his brother, Attorney General Robert Kennedy, to continue and expand the Eisenhower administration's efforts to achieve voting rights for southern blacks. Working with the civil rights movement, the Justice Department labored to register previously disfranchised blacks. But the attorney general could not force the FBI to provide protection for the civil rights volunteers who risked their lives by encouraging blacks to register. Kennedy's other efforts to improve the conditions for blacks in America had limited results.

The civil rights movement refused to accept the administration's indirect approach. In May 1961, the Congress of Racial Equality (CORE) sponsored a **freedom ride** in which a biracial group attempted to test a 1960 Supreme Court decision

freedom ride A freedom ride, sponsored by the Congress of Racial Equality (CORE), was a bus trip taken by both black and white civil rights advocates in the 1960s. They rode buses through the South to test the enforcement of federal regulations that prohibited segregation in interstate public transportation.

outlawing segregation in all bus and train stations used in interstate commerce. When they arrived in Birmingham, Alabama, the freedom riders were attacked by a mob of angry whites. The attorney general quickly dispatched several hundred federal marshals to protect the freedom riders, but the president was more upset at the distraction the protesters created. Deeply involved in the Berlin crisis, Kennedy directed an aide to get in touch with CORE leaders. "Tell them to call it off," he demanded. "Stop them."

In September, after the attorney general finally convinced the Interstate Commerce Commission to issue an order banning segregation in interstate terminals and buses, the freedom rides ended. The Kennedy administration then sought to prevent further confrontations by involving civil rights activists in its voting drive.

A pattern of belated reaction to southern racism marked the basic approach of the Kennedys. When James Meredith courageously sought admission to the all-white University of Mississippi in 1962, the president and the attorney general worked closely with Mississippi Governor Ross Barnett to avoid violence. But despite Barnett's later promise of cooperation, the night before Meredith enrolled at the University of Mississippi, a mob attacked the federal marshals and National Guard troops sent to protect him. The violence left two dead and 375 injured, but Meredith attended the university and eventually graduated.

"I Have a Dream"

Martin Luther King, Jr., finally forced President Kennedy to abandon his cautious tactics and come out openly in behalf of racial justice. In the spring of 1963, King began a massive protest in Birmingham, one of the South's most segregated cities. Public marches and demonstrations aimed at integrating public facilities and opening up jobs for blacks quickly led to police harassment and many arrests, including that of King himself. Police Commissioner Eugene "Bull" Connor was determined to crush the civil rights movement; King was equally determined to prevail.

Connor played directly into King's hands. On May 3, as six thousand children marched in place of the jailed protesters, authorities broke up a demonstration with clubs, snarling police dogs, and high-pressure hoses. With a horrified nation watching scene after scene of this brutality on television, the Kennedy administration quickly intervened to arrange a settlement with the Birmingham civil leaders that ended the violence and granted most of the blacks' demands.

More important, Kennedy finally ended his long hesitation and sounded the call for action. Calling the problem a "moral issue," he sponsored civil rights legislation providing equal access to all public accommodations as well as an extension of voting rights for blacks.

Despite pleas from the government for an end to demonstrations and protests, the movement's leaders decided to keep pressure on the administration. On August 28, 1963, more than 200,000 marchers gathered in the nation's capital for a daylong rally in front of the Lincoln

■ *The Reverend Martin Luther King, Jr., addresses the crowd at the March on Washington in August 1963. The largest single demonstration of the early 1960s, the march reflected the spirit and determination of many devoted to the cause of equality for African Americans. In his speech, King recounted the difficulties of blacks' struggle for freedom, then stirred the crowd with the description of his dream for America: "I have a dream that one day this nation will rise up and live out the true meaning of its creed—we hold these truths to be self-evident, that all men are created equal."* ■

Memorial, where they listened to hymns, speeches, and prayers for racial justice. The climax of the **March on Washington** was King's eloquent description of his dream for a united America.

By the time of Kennedy's death in November 1963, his civil rights legislation was well on its way to passage in Congress. Yet even this achievement did not fully satisfy his critics. They pointed to his failure to issue an executive order to end housing discrimination and to make good on his other campaign promises. For many, Kennedy had raised hopes for racial equality that he never fulfilled.

But unlike Eisenhower, he had provided presidential leadership for the civil rights movement. His emphasis on executive action gradually paid off, especially in extending voting rights. By early 1964, some 40 percent of southern blacks had the franchise. Moreover, Kennedy's sense of caution and restraint, painful and frustrating as it was to black activists, had proved well founded. Avoiding an early, and possibly fatal, defeat in Congress, he had waited until a national consensus emerged and then had carefully channeled it behind effective legislation. Behaving very much the way Franklin Roosevelt did in guiding the nation into World War II, Kennedy chose to be a fox rather than a lion on civil rights.

The Supreme Court and Reform

The most active impulse for social change in the early 1960s came from a surprising source: the usually staid and conservative Supreme Court. Under the leadership of Earl Warren, the Court ventured into new areas. A group of liberal judges—especially William O. Douglas, Hugo Black, and William J. Brennan, Jr.—argued for social reform, while advocates of judicial restraint (such as Felix Frankfurter) fought stubbornly against the new activism.

In addition to ruling against segregation, the Warren Court in the Eisenhower years had angered conservatives by protecting the constitutional rights of victims of McCarthyism. In *Yates* v. *United States* (1956), the judges reversed the conviction of fourteen communist leaders, claiming that government prosecutors had failed to prove that the accused had actually organized a plot to overthrow the government. Mere advocacy of revolution, the Court said, did not justify conviction.

The resignation of Felix Frankfurter in 1962 enabled Kennedy to appoint Arthur Goldberg, a committed liberal, to the Supreme Court. With a clear majority now favoring judicial intervention, the Warren Court issued a series of landmark decisions designed to extend to state and local jurisdictions the traditional rights afforded the accused in federal courts. The Court in *Gideon* v. *Wainwright* (1963), *Escobedo* v. *Illinois* (1964), and *Miranda* v. *Arizona* (1966) decreed that defendants had to be provided lawyers, had to be informed of their constitutional rights, and could not be interrogated or induced to confess to a crime without defense counsel present. In effect, the Court extended to the poor and the ignorant constitutional guarantees that had always been available to the rich and the knowledgeable.

The most far-reaching Warren Court decisions came in the area of legislative reapportionment. In *Baker* v. *Carr* (1962), the Court required Tennessee to redistrict its legislative seats to redress rural overrepresentation in its state government. The Court proclaimed that places in all legislative bodies be allocated on the basis of "people, not land or trees or pastures." The principle of "one man, one vote" greatly increased the political power of cities at the expense of rural areas.

The activism of the Supreme Court stirred up a storm of criticism. The rulings that extended protection to criminals and subversives led some Americans to charge that the Court was encouraging crime and weakening national security. Decisions banning school prayers and permitting pornography incensed many conservative Americans who saw the Court as undermining moral values. Legal scholars worried more about the weakening of the Court's prestige as it became

March on Washington In August 1963, civil rights leaders organized a massive rally in Washington to urge passage of President Kennedy's civil rights bill. The high point came when Martin Luther King, Jr., gave his "I Have a Dream" speech to more than two hundred thousand marchers in front of the Lincoln Memorial.

more directly involved in the political process. On balance, however, the Warren Court helped achieve greater social justice by protecting the rights of the underprivileged and by permitting dissent and free expression to flourish.

"LET US CONTINUE"

The New Frontier came to a sudden and violent end on November 22, 1963, when Lee Harvey Oswald assassinated John F. Kennedy as the president rode in a motorcade in downtown Dallas. The shock of losing the young leader, who had become a symbol of hope and promise for a whole generation, stunned the world. The American people were bewildered by the rapid sequence of events: the brutal killing of their beloved president; the slaying of Oswald by Jack Ruby, captured on TV; and the hurried Warren Commission report, which identified Oswald as the lone assassin.

President Lyndon B. Johnson moved quickly to fill the vacuum left by Kennedy's death. He soon met with a stream of world leaders to reassure them of American political stability. Five days after the tragedy in Dallas, Johnson spoke eloquently to a special joint session of Congress. Asking Congress to enact Kennedy's tax and civil rights bills as a tribute to the fallen leader, LBJ concluded, "Let us here highly resolve that John Fitzgerald Kennedy did not live or die in vain."

Johnson in Action

Johnson suffered in the inevitable comparison with his younger and more stylish predecessor. LBJ was acutely aware of his own lack of polish, but his assets—an intimate knowledge of Congress and incredible energy and determination to succeed—more than compensated. His ego was legendary. When a young marine officer tried to direct him to the proper helicopter, saying, "This one is yours," Johnson responded, "Son, they are all my helicopters."

LBJ's height and intensity gave him a powerful presence; he dominated any room he entered. Yet he found it impossible to project his intelligence and vitality to large audiences. Unlike Kennedy, he wilted before the camera, turning his televised speeches into stilted and awkward performances. Johnson, trying to belie his reputation as a riverboat gambler, came across like a foxy grandpa, clever and calculating and not to be trusted.

Whatever his shortcomings in style, however, Johnson possessed far greater ability than Kennedy in dealing with Congress. He entered the White House with more than thirty years' experience in Washington as a legislative aide, congressman, and senator. His encyclopedic knowledge of the legislative process and his shrewd manipulation of individual senators had enabled him to become the most influential Senate majority leader in history.

Above all, Johnson sought consensus. Indifferent to ideology, he had moved easily from New Deal liberalism to oil-and-gas conservatism as his career advanced. He could work comfortably with southern conservatives or liberals. Suddenly thrust into power, Johnson used his gifts wisely. Citing his favorite scriptural passage from Isaiah, "Come now, and let us reason together, saith the Lord," he concentrated on securing passage of Kennedy's tax and civil rights bills in 1964.

The tax cut came first. In February, after skillful maneuvering by Johnson, Congress reduced personal income taxes by more than $10 billion, touching off a sustained economic boom. Consumer spending increased by an impressive $43 billion in the next eighteen months, and new jobs opened up at the rate of one million a year.

Johnson was even more influential in passing the Kennedy civil rights measure. Staying in the background, he encouraged liberal amendments that strengthened the bill in the House. With Hubert Humphrey leading the floor fight in the Senate, Johnson refused all efforts at compromise, counting on growing public pressure to force northern Republicans to abandon their traditional alliance with southern Democrats. After a fifty-five-day filibuster failed, Johnson won the fight.

The 1964 Civil Rights Act, signed on June 2, outlawed the segregation of blacks in public facilities, established the Fair Employment Practices Committee to lessen racial discrimination in employment, and protected the voting rights of blacks. An amendment sponsored by segregationists in an effort to weaken the bill added gender to the prohibition of discrimination in Title VII of the act; in the future, women's groups would use this clause to secure government support for greater equality in employment and education.

The Election of 1964

Passage of two key Kennedy measures within six months did not satisfy Johnson. Having established the theme of continuity, he now set out to win the presidency in his own right. Acutely aware of Kennedy's narrow victory in 1960, he hoped to win by a great landslide.

Searching for a cause of his own, LBJ found one in the issue of poverty. Beginning in the late 1950s, economists had warned that the prevailing affluence masked a persistent and deep-seated problem of poverty. In 1962, Michael Harrington's book *The Other America* attracted national attention. Writing with passion and eloquence, Harrington claimed that nearly one-fifth of the nation lived in poverty.

Three groups predominated among the poor: blacks, the aged, and households headed by women. The problem, Harrington contended, was that the poor were invisible, living in slums or depressed areas such as Appalachia and cut off from the educational facilities, medical care, and employment opportunities afforded more affluent Americans. Moreover, poverty was a vicious circle. The children of the poor were trapped in the same culture of poverty as their parents.

Johnson quickly took over proposals that Kennedy had been developing and made them his own. In his State of the Union address in January 1964, LBJ announced, "This administration, today, here and now, declares unconditional war on poverty in America." Over the next eight months, Johnson fashioned a comprehensive poverty program.

The new Office of Economic Opportunity (OEO) set up a wide variety of programs, ranging from Head Start for preschoolers to the Job Corps for high school dropouts in need of vocational training. The emphasis was on self-help, with the government providing money and know-how, but the level of funding was never high enough to meet the OEO's ambitious goals. Nevertheless, the **War on Poverty,** along with the economic growth provided by the tax cut, helped reduce the ranks of the poor by nearly ten million between 1964 and 1967.

For Johnson, the new program established his reputation as a reformer in an election year. The man he faced in the election had a different sort of reputation. Senator Barry Goldwater, the Republican candidate, was an outspoken conservative from Arizona. A dignified and articulate man, Goldwater openly advocated a rejection of the welfare state and a return to unregulated free enterprise. He spoke out boldly against the Tennessee Valley Authority, denounced Social Security, and advocated a hawkish foreign policy.

Johnson stuck carefully to the middle of the road, embracing the liberal reform program—which he now called the **Great Society**—while stressing his concern for balanced budgets and fiscal orthodoxy. On election day, LBJ did even better than FDR had in 1936, receiving 61.1 percent of the popular vote and sweeping the electoral college 486 to 52. The Democrats also achieved huge gains in Congress. Kennedy's legacy and Goldwater's candor had enabled Johnson to break the conservative grip on Congress for the first time in a quarter of a century.

War on Poverty President Johnson declared war on poverty in his 1964 State of the Union address. A new Office of Economic Opportunity (OEO) oversaw a variety of programs to help the poor, including the Job Corps and Head Start.

Great Society President Johnson called his version of the Democratic reform program the Great Society. In 1965, Congress passed many Great Society measures, including Medicare, civil rights legislation, and federal aid to education.

The Triumph of Reform

Medicare The 1965 Medicare Act provided Social Security funding for hospitalization insurance for people over 65 and a voluntary plan to cover doctor bills paid in part by the federal government.

LBJ moved quickly to secure his legislative goals. He gave two traditional Democratic reforms, health care and education, top priority. Aware of strong opposition to a comprehensive medical program, LBJ settled for **Medicare,** which mandated health insurance under the Social Security program for Americans over age 65, with a supplementary Medicaid program for the indigent.

On education, LBJ overcame the religious hurdle by supporting a child benefit approach, allocating federal money to advance the education of students in parochial as well as public schools. The Elementary and Secondary Education Act of 1965 provided more than $1 billion in federal aid. During his administration, federal aid to education increased sharply.

Civil rights proved to be the most difficult test of Johnson's leadership. Martin Luther King, Jr., concerned that three million southern blacks were still denied the right to vote, in early 1965 chose Selma, Alabama, as a test case. The white authorities in Selma, led by Sheriff James Clark, used cattle prods and bullwhips to break up the demonstrations and jailed more than two thousand blacks. Johnson intervened in March, ordering the Alabama National Guard to federal duty to protect the demonstrators. He also had the Justice Department draw up a new voting rights bill and personally addressed Congress on civil rights.

Voting Rights Act of 1965 This law effectively banned literacy tests for voting rights and provided for federal registrars to ensure the franchise to minority voters. Within a few years, a majority of African Americans had become registered voters in the southern states.

Five months later, Congress passed the **Voting Rights Act of 1965.** The act banned literacy tests in states and counties in which less than half the population had voted in 1964 and provided for federal registrars in these areas to ensure blacks the franchise. The results were dramatic. For the first time since Reconstruction, blacks were playing an active and effective role in southern politics.

Before the eighty-ninth Congress ended its first session in the fall of 1965, it had passed eighty-nine bills. These measures ranged from ensuring clean air and water to improving education and housing. In nine months, Johnson had enacted the entire Democratic reform agenda, moving the nation beyond the New Deal by mandating federal concern for health, education, and the quality of life in both city and countryside.

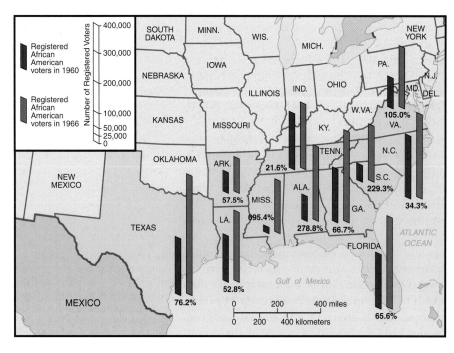

AFRICAN AMERICAN VOTER REGISTRATION BEFORE AND AFTER THE VOTING RIGHTS ACT OF 1965   *The percentages shown on the map indicate the increase in African American voter registration between 1960 and 1966.* ■

The man responsible for this great leap forward, however, had failed to win the public adulation he so deeply desired. The people did not respond to Johnson's leadership with the warmth and praise they had showered on Kennedy, and reporters continued to portray him as a crude wheeler-dealer. No one was more aware of this lack of affection than LBJ himself. When foreign policy problems soon eroded his popularity, few remembered his remarkable legislative achievement at home. Yet in one brief outburst of reform, he had accomplished more than any president since FDR.

Johnson's Great Society had a lasting impact on American life. Federal aid to education, the enactment of Medicare and Medicaid, and the civil rights acts of 1964 and 1965 changed the nation irrevocably. The aged and the poor now were guaranteed access to medical care, communities saw an infusion of federal funds to improve local education, and African Americans could now attend integrated schools, enjoy public facilities, and gain political power by exercising the right to vote. But even at this moment of triumph for liberal reform, new currents of dissent and rebellion were brewing.

JOHNSON ESCALATES THE VIETNAM WAR

Lyndon Johnson stressed continuity in foreign policy just as he had in enacting Kennedy's domestic reforms. Not only had he inherited the policy of containment from Kennedy, but he also had the same Cold War beliefs and convictions. Feeling less confident about dealing with international issues, he tended to rely on Kennedy's advisers—notably Secretary of State Rusk, Secretary of Defense McNamara, and McGeorge Bundy, the national security adviser until he was replaced in 1966 by the even more hawkish Walt Rostow.

Although Johnson had had broad exposure to national security affairs, he fully accepted the common assumptions of Americans influenced by the "lessons" of World War II. Like many people of his generation, he believed that weakness, not strength, led to war. And he had also seen the devastating political impact of the communist triumph in China on the Democratic party in the 1940s. "I am not going to lose Vietnam," he told the American ambassador to Saigon just after taking office in 1963. "I am not going to be the president who saw Southeast Asia go the way China went."

Aware of the problem Castro had caused John Kennedy, LBJ moved firmly to contain communism in the Western Hemisphere. When a military junta overthrew a leftist regime in Brazil, Johnson offered covert aid and open encouragement. In 1965, to block the possible emergence of a Castro-type government, LBJ sent twenty thousand American troops to the Dominican Republic. His flimsy justification served only to alienate liberal critics in the United States. The intervention ended in 1966 with the election of a conservative government. But the cost of Johnson's victories was substantial. Such liberals as Senate Foreign Relations Committee Chairman William Fulbright deserted LBJ. The more Johnson struggled to uphold the traditional Cold War policies he had inherited from Kennedy, the more he found himself under attack from Congress, the media, and the universities.

The Vietnam Dilemma

It was Vietnam rather than Latin America that became Lyndon Johnson's obsession and led ultimately to his political downfall. He inherited the civil war in South Vietnam and the American commitment to Diem's regime in Saigon from Eisenhower and Kennedy.

The situation in Vietnam plagued Johnson from the outset. He took office only three weeks after the coup that had removed Diem and left a vacuum of power. In 1964, seven different governments ruled South Vietnam, and the mood in Saigon was tense and restless. Resisting pressure from the Joint Chiefs of Staff for direct American military involvement, LBJ simply continued Kennedy's policy of economic and technical assistance. He insisted it was still up to the Vietnamese themselves to win the war. At the same time, he expanded American support for covert operations, including amphibious raids on the North.

The undercover activities led directly to the Gulf of Tonkin affair. On August 2, 1964, North Vietnamese torpedo boats attacked the *Maddox*, an American destroyer engaged in electronic intelligence gathering in the Gulf of Tonkin, in the belief that the American ship had been involved in a South Vietnamese raid nearby. The *Maddox* escaped unscathed, but to show American resolve, the navy sent in another destroyer, the *C. Turner Joy*. On the evening of August 4, the two destroyers, responding to sonar and radar contacts, opened fire on North Vietnamese gunboats in the area. Later investigation suggested that the North Vietnamese gunboats had not attacked the American ships, but Johnson ordered retaliatory air strikes on North Vietnamese naval bases.

The next day, the president asked Congress to pass a resolution authorizing him to take "all necessary measures to repel any armed attack against the forces of the United States and to prevent further aggression." Later, critics charged that LBJ wanted a blank check from Congress to carry out the future escalation of the Vietnam War, but such a motive is unlikely. In part, he wanted the **Gulf of Tonkin Resolution** to demonstrate to North Vietnam the American determination to defend South Vietnam at any cost. He also wanted to preempt the Vietnam issue from his Republican opponent, Barry Goldwater, who had been advocating a tougher policy. By taking a firm stand on the Gulf of Tonkin incident, Johnson could both impress the North Vietnamese and outmaneuver a political rival at home. Later, after the incident had served its purpose, Johnson dismissed the attack with, "Hell, I think we may have fired at a whale."

Congress responded with alacrity. The House acted unanimously, and only two senators, both Democrats, voted against the Gulf of Tonkin Resolution. Johnson appeared to have won a spectacular victory, and his approval rating in the polls shot up from 42 to 72 percent.

In the long run, however, the easy victory proved costly. Once having used force against North Vietnam, LBJ was more likely to do so in the future, and the congressional resolution was phrased broadly enough to enable him to use whatever level of force he wanted—including unlimited military intervention. Above all, when he did wage war in Vietnam, he left himself open to the charge of deliberately misleading Congress. Presidential credibility proved to be Johnson's Achilles heel; in that sense, his political downfall began with the Gulf of Tonkin Resolution.

Gulf of Tonkin Resolution

After a North Vietnamese attack on an American destroyer in the Gulf of Tonkin in 1964, President Johnson persuaded Congress to pass a resolution giving him the authority to use armed force in Vietnam.

Escalation

The full-scale American involvement in Vietnam began in 1965 in a series of steps designed primarily to prevent a North Vietnamese victory. With the political situation in Saigon growing more hopeless every day, the president's advisers urged the bombing of the North as the only conceivable solution. American air attacks would serve several purposes: they would block North Vietnamese infiltration routes, make Hanoi pay a heavy price for its role, and lift the sagging morale of the South Vietnamese. Most important, they would save South Vietnam from utter defeat. Johnson responded in February 1965 by ordering a long-planned aerial bombardment of selected North Vietnamese targets.

The air strikes proved ineffective. In April, Johnson authorized the use of American ground forces in South Vietnam, but he restricted them to defensive operations intended to protect American air bases. Rejecting the clear-cut alternatives of withdrawal or the massive use of force, LBJ settled for a steady military escalation designed to compel Hanoi to accept a diplomatic solution. In July, the president permitted a gradual increase in the bombing of North Vietnam and allowed American ground commanders to conduct combat operations in the South. Most ominously, he approved the immediate dispatch of fifty thousand troops to Vietnam and the future commitment of fifty thousand more.

The July decisions formed "an open-ended commitment to employ American military forces as the situation demanded," wrote historian George Herring. Convinced that withdrawal would destroy American credibility before the world and that an invasion of the North would lead to World War III, Johnson opted for large-scale but limited military intervention. Moreover, LBJ feared the domestic consequences of either extreme. A pullout could cause a massive political backlash at home as conservatives condemned him for betraying South Vietnam to communism. All-out war, however, would mean the end of his social programs. So he settled for a limited war, committing a half million American troops to battle in Southeast Asia, all the while pretending it was a minor engagement and refusing to ask the American people for the support and sacrifice required for victory.

Johnson was not solely responsible for the Vietnam War. He inherited a policy that assumed that Vietnam was vital to the national interest and a deteriorating situation that demanded a more active American role. Truman, Eisenhower, and Kennedy had taken the United States deep into the Vietnam maze; it was Johnson's fate to have to find a way out. But LBJ assumed full responsibility for the way he tried to resolve his dilemma. Failing to acknowledge the stark choices involved, insisting on secrecy and deceit, refusing to acknowledge that he had committed the nation to a dangerous military involvement—these were Johnson's sins in Vietnam.

Stalemate

For the next three years, Americans waged an intensive war in Vietnam and succeeded only in preventing a Communist victory. Bombing of North Vietnam proved ineffective, failing either to damage its essentially agrarian economy or to block the flow of supplies southward through Laos and Cambodia. In fact, the American air attacks, with their resultant civilian casualties, supplied North Vietnam with a powerful propaganda weapon, which it effectively used to sway world opinion against the United States.

The war in the South went no better. Despite the steady increase in American ground forces, from 184,000 in late 1965 to more than 500,000 in early 1968, the Viet Cong still controlled much of the countryside. The search-and-destroy tactics employed by the Americans proved ill suited. The Viet Cong waged a war of insurgency, avoiding fixed positions and striking from ambush. In a vain effort to destroy the enemy, General William Westmoreland used superior American firepower

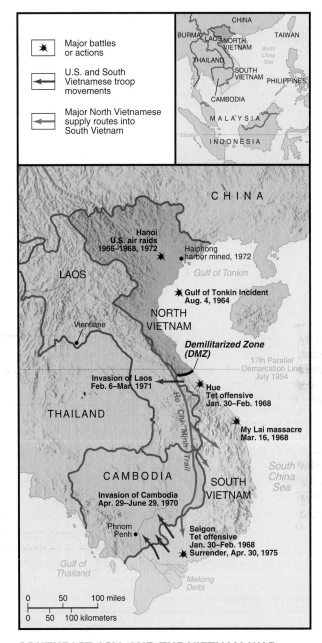

SOUTHEAST ASIA AND THE VIETNAM WAR
American combat forces in South Vietnam rose from 16,000 in 1963 to 500,000 in 1968, but a successful conclusion to the conflict was no closer. ■

U.S. TROOP LEVELS IN VIETNAM (DECEMBER 31 OF EACH YEAR)

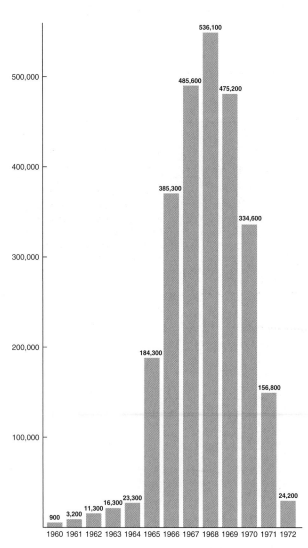

Source: U.S. Department of Defense

wantonly, devastating the countryside, causing civilian casualties, and driving the peasantry into the arms of the guerrillas.

The main premise of Westmoreland's strategy was to wage a war of attrition that would finally reach a "crossover point" when communist losses each month would be greater than the number of new troops they could recruit. He hoped to lure the Viet Cong and the North Vietnamese regulars into pitched battles in which American firepower would inflict heavy casualties. But soon it was the communists who were deciding where and when the fighting would take place, provoking American attacks in remote areas of South Vietnam that favored the defenders and made Westmoreland pay heavily in American lives for the communist losses. By the end of 1967, the nearly half million American troops Johnson had sent to Vietnam had failed to defeat the enemy. At best, LBJ had only achieved a bloody stalemate that gradually turned the American people against a war they had once eagerly embraced.

YEARS OF TURMOIL

The Vietnam War became the focal point for a growing movement of youthful protest that made the 1960s the most turbulent decade of the twentieth century. Disenchantment with conventional middle-class values, a rapid increase in college enrollments as a result of the post–World War II baby boom, a reaction against the crass materialism of the affluent society—with its endless suburbs and shopping malls—all led American youth to embrace an alternative lifestyle based on the belief that people are "sensitive, searching, poetic, and capable of love." They were ready to create a counterculture.

The agitation of the 1960s was at its height from 1965 to 1968, the years that marked the escalation of the Vietnam War. Disturbances that began on college campuses quickly spread to infect the entire society, from the ghettos of the cities to the lettuce fields of the Southwest. All who felt disadvantaged and dissatisfied—students, blacks, browns, women, hippies—took to the streets to give vent to their feelings.

The Student Revolt

The first sign of student rebellion came in the fall of 1964 at the prestigious University of California at Berkeley. A small group of radical students resisted university efforts to deny them a place to solicit volunteers and funds for off-campus causes. Forming the Free Speech Movement, they struck back by occupying administration buildings and blocking the arrest of a nonstudent protester. For the next two months, the campus was in turmoil.

In the end, the protesters won the rights of free speech and association that they championed, and youth everywhere had a new model for effective direction. The hero was Mario Savio, a student who had eloquently summed up the cause by likening the university to a great machine and telling others "You've got to put your bodies upon the gears, and upon the wheels, upon the levers, upon all the apparatus, and you've got to make it stop."

The Free Speech Movement at Berkeley offered many insights into the causes of campus unrest. It was fueled in part by student suspicion of the older Great Depression–born generation that viewed affluence as the answer to all problems. Unable to exert much influence on the power structure that directed the consumer society, the students turned on the university, which they viewed as the faithful servant of the corporate and political elite as it trained hordes of technicians to operate the new computers, harbored the research laboratories that perfected dreadful military weapons, and regimented its students with IBM punch cards.

Student protest found its full expression in the explosive growth of the **Students for a Democratic Society (SDS).** Founded in Port Huron, Michigan, in 1962, the radical organization wanted to rid American society of poverty, racism, and violence. Although the SDS embraced many traditional liberal reforms, such as expanded public housing and comprehensive health insurance, its founders advocated a new approach called participatory democracy. In contrast to both liberalism and old-style socialism, the SDS sought salvation through the individual rather than the group. Personal control of one's life and destiny, not the creation of new bureaucracies, was the hallmark of the New Left.

In the next few years, the SDS grew phenomenally. Spurred on by the Vietnam War and massive campus unrest, the SDS could count more than a hundred thousand followers and was responsible for disruptions at nearly a thousand colleges in 1968. Yet its very emphasis on the individual and its fear of bureaucracy left it leaderless and subject to division and disunity. By 1970, a split between factions, some of which were given to violence, led to its complete demise.

The meteoric career of the SDS symbolized the turbulence of the 1960s. For a brief time, it seemed as though the nation's youth had gone berserk, indulging in a wave of experimentation with drugs, sex, and rock music. Older Americans believed that all the nation's traditional values, from the Puritan work ethic to the family, were under attack. Not all American youth joined in the cultural insurgency; the rebellion was generally limited to children of the upper middle class. But like the flappers of the 1920s, the protesters set the tone for an entire era and left a lasting impression on American society.

Protesting the Vietnam War

The most dramatic aspect of the youthful rebellion came in opposing the Vietnam War. The first student "teach-ins" began at the University of Michigan in March 1965; soon they spread to campuses across the nation.

One of the great ironies of the Vietnam War was the system of student draft deferments, which enabled students enrolled in college to avoid military service. As a result, the children of the well-to-do, who were more likely to attend college, were able to escape the draft. Those too poor to attend college served in Vietnam in much larger numbers. One survey revealed that men from disadvantaged families, including a disproportionately large number of blacks and Hispanics, were twice as likely to be drafted and sent into combat in Vietnam as those from more privileged backgrounds. Consequently, a sense of guilt led many college activists, safe from Vietnam because of their student status, to take the lead in denouncing an unjust war.

As the fighting in Southeast Asia intensified in 1966 and 1967, the protests grew larger and the slogans more extreme. "Hey, hey, LBJ, how many kids have you killed today?" chanted students. At the Pentagon in October 1967, more than 100,000 demonstrators confronted a cordon of military policemen guarding the heart of the nation's war machine. From the windows above, Secretary of Defense McNamara and his generals looked down on the angry protesters.

Students for a Democratic Society (SDS) Founded in 1962, SDS was a popular college student organization that protested shortcomings in American life, notably racial injustice and the Vietnam War. It led thousands of campus protests before it split apart at the end of the 1960s.

A Look at the Past

Army Fatigue Jacket

Gray flannel suits with conservative ties and dresses with tightly fitted bodices represented the standard uniform during the years of 1950s conformity. By the late 1960s, American youth had cast aside those conservative clothes and instead wore tie-dyed shirts, jeans, and clothes made from Indian print fabrics. Many young people, especially antiwar protesters, also wore military surplus clothing such as this army fatigue jacket. ✳ Why do you think civilians protesting the Vietnam War chose to adopt military attire? Can you think of other examples of clothing used for political or social protest?

The climax came in the spring of 1968. Driven both by opposition to the war and concern for social justice, the SDS and black radicals at Columbia University joined forces in April. They seized five buildings, effectively paralyzing one of the country's leading colleges. After eight days of tension, the New York City police regained control. The brutal repression quickened the pace of protest elsewhere. Sit-ins, violent marches, and arrests became common.

The students failed to stop the war, but they did succeed in gaining a voice in their education. University administrations allowed undergraduates to sit on faculty committees to plan the curriculum and gave up their once rigid control of dormitory and social life. But the students' greatest impact lay outside politics and the campus. They spawned a cultural uprising that transformed the manners and mores of America.

The Cultural Revolution

In contrast to the political revolt of the elitist SDS, the cultural rebellion by youth in the 1960s was pervasive. Led by college students, young people challenged the prevailing adult values, in clothing, hairstyles, sexual conduct, work habits, and music. Blue jeans and love beads took the place of business suits and pearl necklaces, and family life gave way to communes for the "flower children" of the 1960s.

Music became the touchstone of the new departure. Folksingers such as Joan Baez and Bob Dylan, popular for their songs of social protest in the mid-1960s, gave way to rock groups such as the Beatles, whose lyrics were often suggestive of drug use, and finally to "acid rock" as symbolized by the Grateful Dead. The climactic event of the decade came at an outdoor concert near Woodstock, New York, when 400,000 young people indulged in a three-day orgy of rock music, drug experimentation, and sexual activity.

The cultural revolution was heavily influenced by the drug scene. Former Harvard psychology professor Timothy Leary invited youth to "tune in, turn on, drop out," literally, as they experimented with marijuana, LSD, and other drugs.

Its ultimate expression of insurgency was the Yippie movement, led by such men as Jerry Rubin and Abbie Hoffman. The Yippies mocked the consumer culture and delighted in capitalizing on the mood of social protest to win attention. They succeeded in revealing the hypocrisy in American society, but in the process they fragmented the protest movement; serious radicals dismissed them as parasites.

"Black Power"

The civil rights movement, which had conceived the mood of protest in the 1960s, fell on hard times. The legislative triumphs of 1964 and 1965 were relatively easy victories over southern bigotry. Now the movement faced the far more complex problem of achieving economic equality in the cities of the North. Mired in poverty, crowded into ghettos, blacks had actually fallen further behind whites in disposable income since the beginning of the integration effort. The civil rights movement had raised the expectations of urban African Americans; frustration mounted as they failed to experience any significant economic gain.

The first sign of trouble came in the summer of 1964, when black teenagers in Harlem and Rochester, New York, rioted. The next summer, a massive outburst of rage and destruction swept the Watts neighborhood of Los Angeles as the inhabitants burned buildings and looted stores. In 1967, the worst riots yet took place in Newark and Detroit, where forty-three people were killed and hundreds injured.

The civil rights coalition fell apart, a victim of both its legislative success and its economic failure. Black militants took over the leadership of the Student Nonviolent Coordinating Committee (SNCC); they disdained white help and even reversed Martin Luther King's insistence on nonviolence. SNCC's new leader, Stokely Carmichael, told blacks that they should seize power in those parts of the South where they outnumbered whites. "I am not going to beg the white man for anything I deserve," he said, "I'm going to take it." Soon his calls for "black power" became a rallying cry for more militant African Americans who advocated the need for blacks to form their "own institutions, credit unions, co-ops, [and] political parties" and even write their "own history."

Others went further than calls for ethnic separation. H. Rap Brown, who replaced Carmichael as the leader of SNCC in 1967, told a black crowd in Cambridge, Maryland, to "get your guns" and "burn this town down," while Huey Newton, one of the founders of the militant Black Panther party, proclaimed that "political power comes through the barrel of a gun."

A Look at the Past

Woodstock Brochure

The dove and guitar on this brochure for the 1969 Woodstock Music Festival graphically present Woodstock's purpose: peaceful, joyful coexistence. More than 400,000 revelers ignored bad weather and poor conditions to listen to folk and rock music. The age of Aquarius, when peace and harmony would triumph, had seemingly arrived. ✳ How do you explain the contradiction between the call for peace and harmony and the growing violence of the 1960s?

King suffered most from this extremism. His denunciation of the Vietnam War cost him the support of the Johnson administration and the more conservative civil rights groups such as the NAACP and the Urban League. Radical blacks rejected his nonviolent approach to change. King finally seized on poverty as the proper enemy for attack, but before he could lead his Poor People's March on Washington in 1968, he was assassinated in Memphis in early April.

Both blacks and whites realized that the nation had lost its most eloquent spokesman for racial harmony. His tragic death elevated King to the status of a martyr, but it also led to one last outbreak of widespread urban violence. Blacks exploded in angry riots in 125 cities across the nation; in Chicago and Baltimore, army units were needed to restore order in the ghettos. The worst rioting took place in Washington, D.C., where buildings were set on fire within a few blocks of the White House.

Yet there was a positive side to the emotions engendered by black nationalism. Spokespersons began to urge blacks to take pride in their ethnic heritage, to embrace their blackness as a positive value. Blacks began to wear bushy "Afro" hairstyles and take interest in their African roots. The word *Negro*—identified with white supremacy of the past—virtually disappeared from usage overnight, replaced by *Afro-American* or *black*. Singer James Brown best expressed the sense of racial identity: "Say It Loud—I'm Black and I'm Proud."

Ethnic Nationalism

Other groups quickly emulated the black phenomenon. Native Americans decried the callous use of their identity as football mascots; Puerto Ricans demanded that their history be included in school and college texts; and Polish, Italian, and Czech groups insisted on respect for their nationalities. Congress acknowledged these demands with passage of the Ethnic Heritage Studies Act of 1972, which recognized ethnicity as a positive force in American society and appropriated money to subsidize ethnic studies courses.

Mexican Americans were in the forefront of the ethnic groups that became active in the 1970s. The primary impulse came from the efforts of César Chávez to organize the poorly paid grape pickers and lettuce workers in California into the National Farm Workers Association (NFWA). Chávez appealed to ethnic nationalism in mobilizing Mexican American field hands to strike against grape growers in the San Joaquin Valley in 1965. Once Chávez had won the attention of the media, a national boycott of grapes by Mexican Americans and their sympathizers among the young people of the country led to a series of hard-fought victories over the growers. The five-year struggle brought union victory in 1970, but at an enormous cost—95 percent of the farmworkers had lost their homes and their cars. Undaunted, Chávez turned next to the lettuce fields, and although he met with strong resistance, he succeeded in raising the hourly wage of farmworkers in California to $3.53 by 1977 (it had been $1.20 in 1965).

Chávez's efforts helped spark an outburst of ethnic consciousness among Mexican Americans that swept through the urban barrios of the Southwest. Aware that a majority of their compatriots were functionally illiterate as a result of language difficulties and inferior schools, Mexican American leaders campaigned for bilingual programs and improved educational opportunities. Young activists began to call themselves Chicanos, which had previously been a derogatory term, and to take pride in their cultural heritage; in 1968, they succeeded in estab-

■ *In March 1966, César Chávez, shown here talking with workers, led striking grape pickers on a 250-mile march from Delano, California, to the state capital at Sacramento to dramatize the plight of the migrant farmworkers. With the slogan, "God is beside you on the picket line," the march took on the character of a religious pilgrimage.* ■

lishing the first Mexican American studies program at California State College at Los Angeles. In addition, student protests in several leading southwestern cities led to significant reforms, such as the introduction of bilingual programs in grade schools and the hiring of more Chicano teachers at all levels.

Women's Liberation

Active as they were in the civil rights and antiwar movements, women soon learned that the male leaders of protest causes were little different from corporate executives—they expected women to fix the food and type the communiqués while the men made the decisions. Women soon realized that they could achieve respect and equality only by mounting their own protest.

In some ways, the position of women in American society was worse in the 1960s than it had been in the 1920s. After forty years, there was a lower percentage of women enrolled in the nation's colleges and professional schools, and women with college degrees earned only half as much as similarly trained men. Women were still relegated to stereotypical occupations such as nursing and teaching. And gender roles, as portrayed in the media, continued to call for the husband to be the breadwinner and the wife to be the homemaker.

Betty Friedan poses with a copy of her groundbreaking book, The Feminine Mystique. *In the work, Friedan castigated advertisers, educators, and others for promoting what she labeled the feminine mystique—the idea that women could find fulfillment only in their roles as wives and mothers. Friedan helped spark the modern feminist movement, which had its roots in the nineteenth-century women's rights movement and built on the efforts of earlier activists such as Susan B. Anthony, Lucretia Mott, and Elizabeth Cady Stanton.*

Betty Friedan was the first to put into words the sense of grievance and discrimination that developed among women in the 1960s in her 1963 book *The Feminine Mystique.* Calling the American home "a comfortable concentration camp," she attacked the prevailing view that women were completely contented with their housekeeping and child-rearing tasks, claiming that housewives had no self-esteem and no sense of identity.

The 1964 Civil Rights Act helped women attack economic inequality head-on by making it illegal to discriminate in employment on the basis of gender. Women filed suit for equal wages, demanded (with little success) that companies provide day care for their infants and preschool children, and entered politics to lobby against laws that were unfair to women. As the women's liberation movement grew, its advocates began to attack laws banning abortion and waged a campaign to toughen the enforcement of rape laws.

The women's movement met with many of the same obstacles as other protest groups in the 1960s. The moderate leadership of the **National Organization for Women (NOW),** founded by Friedan in 1966, was soon challenged by members with more extreme views. The harsh rhetoric and militancy of the extremists repelled many women who expressed satisfaction with their lives. But despite these disagreements, most women—and a great many men—supported the effort to achieve equal status, and in 1972, Congress responded by approving the Equal Rights Amendment to the Constitution. This measure, first introduced in Congress in 1923, now faced a vote in the state legislatures, the final step toward ratification.

National Organization for Women (NOW) Founded in 1966, this organization called for equal employment opportunity and equal pay for women. NOW also championed the legalization of abortion and passage of the Equal Rights Amendment to the Constitution.

THE RETURN OF RICHARD NIXON

The turmoil of the 1960s reached a crescendo in 1968 as the American people responded to the two dominant events of the decade—the war in Vietnam and the cultural insurgency at home. In an election marked by a series of bizarre events, including riots and an assassination, Richard Nixon staged a remarkable comeback to win the post denied him in 1960.

Vietnam Undermines Lyndon Johnson

The climax of the war in Vietnam came in late January 1968 when the Viet Cong, aided by North Vietnamese regulars, launched an offensive during Tet, the lunar New Year, recklessly attacking the South Vietnamese cities and provincial capitals. American and government troops quickly beat back the **Tet offensive,** but at home, television viewers were shocked by scenes of Viet Cong fighting within the walls of the American embassy compound in Saigon. The outcome was a tactical defeat for the Communists but a decided political setback for the United States. President Johnson had been hammering away at the idea that the war was almost over; suddenly it appeared to be nearly lost.

Johnson reluctantly came to the conclusion that the war would end in a stalemate. In mid-March, he decided to limit the bombing of North Vietnam in an effort to open up peace negotiations with Hanoi. In a speech to the nation on Sunday evening, March 31, 1968, Johnson outlined his plans for a new effort at ending the war peacefully and concluded by saying, as proof of his sincerity, "I shall not seek, and I will not accept, the nomination of my party for another term as your president." Thus a stunned nation learned that LBJ had become the first major political casualty of the Vietnam War.

In the fourteen years since the siege of Dien Bien Phu, American policy had gone full circle in Vietnam. Even though Eisenhower had decided against using force to rescue the French, his commitment to the Diem regime in Saigon had led eventually to American military involvement on a massive scale. Three years of inconclusive fighting and a steadily mounting loss of American lives had disillusioned the American people and finally cost Lyndon Johnson the presidency. And the full price the nation would have to pay for its folly in Southeast Asia was still unknown—the Vietnam experience would continue to cast a shadow over American life for years to come.

The failure in Vietnam reflected the difficulty the United States faced in pursuing containment on a global scale. Policies that had worked well in Europe in the 1940s had little relevance to the very different situation in Southeast Asia. Intent on halting the spread of communism, American leaders never grasped the political realities in Vietnam. The United States ended up backing a series of corrupt regimes in Saigon while the Viet Cong won the struggle for the hearts and minds of the Vietnamese people. More than anything else, the Vietnam War revealed the need for a thorough reexamination of the basic premises of American foreign policy in the Cold War.

Democrats Divided

Lyndon Johnson's withdrawal from the presidential race after the Tet offensive set the tone for the 1968 election. LBJ's decision had come in response to political as well as military realities. By 1966, the antiwar movement had spread from the college campuses to Capitol Hill. Former supporters such as Senator William Fulbright began to question the conflict. Housewives and middle-class professionals were attending the antiwar rallies. Johnson felt like a prisoner in the White House, since in his infrequent public appearances he was hounded by larger and larger gatherings of antiwar demonstrators.

Tet offensive In February 1968, the Viet Cong launched a major offensive in the cities of South Vietnam. Although caught by surprise, American and South Vietnamese forces successfully quashed this attack, yet the Tet offensive was a blow to American public opinion and led President Johnson to end the escalation of the war and seek a negotiated peace.

The essentially leaderless protest against the war had taken on a new quality on January 3, 1968, when Senator Eugene McCarthy, a Democrat from Minnesota, announced that he would challenge LBJ for the party's presidential nomination. Cool and aloof, McCarthy was an intellectual motivated primarily by a belief that Kennedy and Johnson had abused the power of the presidency. McCarthy's idealism proclaimed, "Whatever is morally necessary must be made politically possible." His stance against the war attracted the support of American youth. In the New Hampshire primary in early March, the nation's earliest political test, McCarthy shocked the political experts by coming within a few thousand votes of defeating Johnson.

McCarthy's strong showing in New Hampshire led Robert Kennedy to enter the presidential race. Despite the obvious charge of opportunism he faced, Kennedy had a much better chance than McCarthy to defeat LBJ and win in the fall. Unlike McCarthy, whose appeal was largely limited to upper-middle-class whites and college students, Kennedy attracted strong support among blue-collar workers, blacks, Chicanos, and other minorities who formed the nucleus of the continuing New Deal coalition.

LBJ's dramatic withdrawal caused an uproar in the Democratic party. With Johnson's tacit backing and strong support from party regulars and organized labor, Vice President Hubert H. Humphrey, a classic Cold War liberal who had worked equally hard for social reform at home and American expansion abroad, declared his candidacy. The antiwar movement, however, considered him totally unacceptable. Accordingly, he decided to avoid the primaries and work for nomination within the framework of the party.

■ President Johnson, in the Cabinet room, rests his head on his hand as he listens to a tape from his son-in-law Marine Captain Charles Robb recounting his combat experiences in Vietnam. Johnson stunned the nation with his announcement on March 31, 1968, that he would not seek re-election. Poor results in the March primaries and public opinion polls indicated that support for LBJ was eroding. ■

Kennedy and McCarthy, the two antiwar candidates, were thus left to contest the spring primaries, causing agonizing choices among voters who sought change. Kennedy won everywhere except in Oregon, but his narrow victory in California ended in tragedy when a Palestinian immigrant, Sirhan Sirhan, assassinated him in a Los Angeles hotel.

With his strongest opponent struck down, Humphrey had little difficulty turning back the challenges from McCarthy and from George McGovern at the Chicago convention. Backed by party leaders, including Chicago's political boss, Mayor Richard J. Daley, Humphrey supporters defeated an antiwar resolution and won the nomination on the first ballot.

Humphrey's triumph was marred by violence outside the heavily guarded convention hall. Radical groups had urged their members to come to Chicago to agitate; the turnout was relatively small but included many who were ready to provoke the authorities in their despair over the convention's outcome. Epithets and cries of "pigs" brought about a savage response from Daley's police, who shared their mayor's contempt for the protesters.

The bitter fumes of tear gas hung in the streets for days afterward; the battered heads and bodies of demonstrators and innocent bystanders alike flooded the city's hospital emergency rooms. What an official investigation later termed a "police riot" marred Humphrey's nomination and made a sad mockery of his call for "the politics of joy." The Democratic party itself had become a victim of the Vietnam War.

The Republican Resurgence

The primary beneficiary of the Democratic debacle was Richard Nixon. Written off as politically dead after his unsuccessful race for governor of California in 1962, Nixon had slowly rebuilt his place within the party. Positioning himself squarely in the middle, he quickly became the front-runner for the Republican nomination. At the GOP convention in Miami Beach, Nixon won an easy first-ballot nomination and chose Maryland Governor Spiro Agnew as his running mate.

In the fall campaign, Nixon opened up a wide lead by avoiding controversy and reaping the benefit of discontent with the Vietnam War. He played the peace issue shrewdly, appearing to advocate an end to the conflict without ever taking a definite stand. Above all, he chose the role of reconciler for a nation torn by emotion, a leader who promised to bring a divided country together again.

Humphrey, in contrast, found himself hounded by antiwar demonstrators who heckled him constantly. He walked a tightrope, desperate for the continued support of Johnson but handicapped by LBJ's stubborn refusal to end all bombing of North Vietnam. His campaign gradually gained momentum, however, as he picked up support from union leaders and from blacks who remembered his strong stand on civil rights. When he broke with Johnson in late September by announcing that if elected, he would "stop the bombing of North Vietnam as an acceptable risk for peace," he began to close in on Nixon.

Unfortunately for Humphrey, a third-party candidate cut deeply into the usual Democratic majority. George Wallace had first gained attention as the racist governor of Alabama whose motto was "Segregation now, segregation tomorrow, segregation forever." His appeal was to blue-collar workers and white ethnics who believed that many of the gains made by blacks during the 1960s had come at their expense.

Running on the ticket of the American Independent party, Wallace was a close third in the September polls, but as the election neared, his following declined. Humphrey continued to gain, especially after Johnson agreed in late October to end all bombing of North Vietnam. By the first week in November, the outcome was too close for the experts to call.

Nixon won the election by just 500,000 votes—and with the smallest share of the popular vote of any winning candidate since 1916—but scored a clear-cut victory in the electoral college, sweeping a broad band of states from Virginia and the Carolinas through the Midwest to the Pacific. As expected, Humphrey did well in the urban Northeast, and Wallace made a strong showing in the Deep South.

CONCLUSION: THE END OF AN ERA

The election marked a repudiation of the politics of protest and the cultural insurgency of the mid-1960s. The combined popular vote for Nixon and Wallace, 56.5 percent of the electorate, signified that there was a "silent majority" that was fed up with violence and confrontation. A growing concern over psychedelic drugs, rock music, lack of decorum in dress and behavior, and sexual permissiveness offset the

Chronology

1961	JFK establishes Peace Corps (March) ▪ U.S.-backed Bay of Pigs invasion crushed by Cubans (April)
1962	Astronaut John H. Glenn, Jr., becomes first American to orbit the earth (February) ▪ President Kennedy forces U.S. Steel to roll back price hike (April) ▪ Cuban missile crisis takes world to brink of nuclear war (October)
1963	United States, Great Britain, and USSR sign Limited Nuclear Test Ban Treaty (August) ▪ JFK assassinated; Lyndon B. Johnson sworn in as president (November)
1964	President Johnson declares war on poverty (January) ▪ Congress overwhelmingly passes Gulf of Tonkin Resolution (August) ▪ Johnson wins presidency in landslide (November)
1965	LBJ commits fifty thousand American troops to combat in Vietnam (July) ▪ Congress enacts Medicare and Medicaid (July)
1966	National Organization for Women (NOW) formed
1967	Israel wins Six Day War in Middle East (June) ▪ Riots in Detroit kill forty-three, injure two thousand, leave five thousand homeless (July)
1968	Viet Cong launch Tet offensive (January) ▪ Johnson announces he will not seek re-election (March) ▪ Martin Luther King, Jr., assassinated in Memphis (April) ▪ Robert Kennedy assassinated in Los Angeles (June)

usual Democratic advantage on economic issues and led to the election of a Republican president. By voting for Nixon and Wallace, the American people were sending out a message: they wanted a return to traditional values and an end to the war in Vietnam.

At the election of Richard Nixon, an era came to an end with the passing of two concepts that had guided American life since the 1930s. First, the liberal reform impulse, which reached its zenith with the Great Society legislation in 1965, had clearly run its course. Civil rights, Medicare, and federal aid to education would continue in place, but Nixon's triumph signaled a strong reaction against the growth of federal power. At the same time, the Vietnam fiasco spelled the end of activist foreign policy that had begun with American entry into World War II. Containment, so successful in protecting western Europe against the Soviet threat, had proved a disastrous failure when applied on a global scale. The last three decades of the twentieth century would witness a struggle to replace outmoded liberal internationalism with new policies at home and abroad.

KEY TERMS

flexible response, p. 577

Berlin Wall, p. 577

Bay of Pigs, p. 578

Cuban missile crisis, p. 579

New Frontier, p. 580

freedom ride, p. 581

March on Washington, p. 583

War on Poverty, p. 585

Great Society, p. 585

Medicare, p. 586

Voting Rights Act of 1965, p. 586

Gulf of Tonkin Resolution, p. 588

Students for a Democratic Society (SDS), p. 591

National Organization for Women (NOW), p. 595

Tet offensive, p. 596

RECOMMENDED READING

The best general account of the 1960s is Jim F. Heath, *Decade of Disillusionment* (1975), which stresses the continuity in policy between the Kennedy and Johnson administrations. Arthur M. Schlesinger, Jr., *A Thousand Days* (1965) is the classic history of the Kennedy administration; for a more balanced view, see Richard Reeves, *President Kennedy* (1993). The best study of Kennedy's foreign policy is Michael R. Beschloss, *The Crisis Years: Kennedy and Khrushchev, 1960–1963* (1991); for the Cuban missile crisis, consult Graham Allison and Philip Zelikow, *Essence of Decision*, 2nd ed. (1999) and Sheldon Stern, *The Week the World Stood Still* (2005).

Victor S. Navasky offers a critical view of Robert Kennedy as attorney general in *Kennedy Justice* (1971). The best overview of civil rights developments in the 1960s is Hugh Davis Graham, *The Civil Rights Era, 1960–1972* (1990). Nick Kotz explores the difficult relationship between Lyndon Johnson and Martin Luther King, Jr., in *Judgment Days* (2005), while Taylor Branch places that relationship in a broader setting in *At Canaan's Edge* (2006), the third and final volume of his monumental series, "America in the King Years."

Robert Dallek offers a balanced view of Johnson's presidential years in *Flawed Giant* (1998). The best one-volume biography of Lyndon Johnson is Irwin Unger and Debi Unger, *LBJ* (1999); John A. Andrew III provides a concise account of LBJ's domestic program in *Lyndon Johnson and the Great Society* (1998). For the impact of the 1965 immigration legislation, see Hugh Davis Graham, *Collision Course* (2002). For LBJ's foreign policy, see H. W. Brands, *The Wages of Globalism* (1995). The best introduction to the Vietnam War is the balanced survey by George Herring, *America's Longest War*, 4th ed. (2002). For differing views of Johnson's responsibility for the Vietnam conflict, see Fredrik Logevall, *Choosing War* (1999), highly critical, Lloyd Gardner, *Pay Any Price* (1995), more understanding, and Gareth Porter, *Perils of Dominance* (2005).

The most comprehensive account of the student protests is Terry Anderson, *The Movement and the Sixties* (1995), but see also Todd Gitlin, *The Sixties* (1987), more sympathetic to the youthful protesters; W. J. Rorabaugh, *Berkeley at War* (1989); and Rhodri Jeffrey-Jones, *Peace Now!* (1999).

Garry Wills provides the most revealing portrait of Richard Nixon's character and prepresidential career in *Nixon Agonistes* (1970). The best account of the 1968 election is Lewis L. Gould, *1968: The Election That Changed America* (1993).

SUGGESTED WEB SITES

The Avalon Project: The Cuban Missile Crisis
www.yale.edu/lawweb/avalon/diplomacy/forrel/cuba/cubamenu.htm

Part of the foreign relations series of the Avalon Project at Yale Law School, this site includes a collection of on-line documents pertaining to the Cuban Missile Crisis and its aftermath.

John Fitzgerald Kennedy
www.ipl.org/div/potus/jfkennedy.html

This site contains basic factual data about Kennedy's election and presidency, speeches, and on-line biographies.

The Kennedy Assassination
mcadams.posc.mu.edu/home.htm

This well-organized site has images, essays, and photos on the assassination.

Lyndon B. Johnson
www.ipl.org/div/potus/lbjohnson.html

This page contains basic factual data about his election and presidency, speeches, and on-line biographies.

Lyndon B. Johnson Library and Museum
www.lbjlib.utexas.edu/

This presidential library contains images and on-line exhibits.

National Aeronautics and Space Administration
www.hq.nasa.gov/office/pao/History/histsub.htm

NASA's Office of Policy and Plans History Office maintains this site about NASA and its history.

Investigating the Vietnam War
www.spartacus.schoolnet.co.uk/vietintro.htm

This site from Spartacus Educational Publishing, U.K., has an excellent list of annotated links to the best Vietnam-related sites.

Vietnam On-line
www.pbs.org/wgbh/pages/amex/vietnam/index.html

From PBS and the American Experience, this site contains a detailed, interactive timeline of the war, interpretive essays, and autobiographical reflections.

My Lai Courts Martial (1970)
www.law.umkc.edu/faculty/projects/ftrials/mylai/mylai.htm

This site contains images, chronology, and court and official documents maintained by Dr. Doug Linder at University of Missouri–Kansas City Law School.

Martin Luther King, Jr., Papers Project
www.stanford.edu/group/King/

This site at Stanford University has links and selected digital documents by and concerning Martin Luther King, Jr.

National Civil Rights Museum

www.mecca.org/~crights/nc2.html

This site provides a virtual tour of the museum with its interpretive exhibits.

The Digger Archives

www.diggers.org/

This site provides information about The San Francisco Diggers who became one of the legendary groups in the Haight-Ashbury district during the years 1966 to 1968.

Free Speech Movement: Student Protest— U.C. Berkeley, 1964–65

www.lib.berkeley.edu/BANC/FSM/

The Bancroft Library at U.C.–Berkeley houses this exhibit with oral histories, a chronology, and documents.

Voices of the Civil Rights Era

www.webcorp.com/civilrights/index.htm

Webcorp provides audio clips from prominent figures of the Civil Rights era including Martin Luther King, Jr., and Malcolm X.

Martin Luther King, Jr.

www.seattletimes.com/mlk/

This site from the *Seattle Times* has several articles about King and the civil rights movement.

The Sixties Project

lists.village.virginia.edu/sixties/

This University of Virginia site has extensive exhibits, documents, and personal narratives from the 1960s.

Civil Rights Oral History Bibliography

www-dept.usm.edu/~mcrohb/

This University of Southern Mississippi site includes complete transcripts of the selected oral resources.

1969 Woodstock Festival and Concert

www.woodstock69.com/index.htm

This site provides pictures and lists of songs from the famous rock festival.

United States v. *Cecil Price et al.* (The "Mississippi Burning" Trial) 1967

www.law.umkc.edu/faculty/projects/ftrials/price&bowers/price&bowers.htm

This site contains images, chronology, and court and official documents maintained by Dr. Doug Linder at University of Missouri–Kansas City Law School.

Unintended Consequences
The Second Great Migration

"This is not a revolutionary bill," President Lyndon Johnson declared when he signed the Immigration Act of 1965 into law. Rarely has a president been so wrong. The changes Congress made in American immigration policy led a second great migration, larger and even more diverse than the first, which took place in the thirty years before World War I. By the end of the century, the second great wave of immigration had profoundly altered the ethnic composition of the United States.

The political leaders responsible for changing immigration policy in the 1960s had very different intentions. Focused on removing long-standing inequities in the law, they sought to replace the national origins system, adopted in the 1920s, which favored people from western Europe, with a new set of criteria designed to bring in newcomers with economic skills the United States needed and to reunite broken families. Above all, the architects of change wanted to end the unfair race-based quotas for people of Asian extraction and the evident discrimination against applicants from eastern and southern Europe. Attorney General Robert Kennedy called the national origins quotas "a standing affront to many Americans and to many countries." At the height of the Cold War, realism seemed to join with idealism in the effort to end a discriminatory immigration policy that smacked of racism.

The legislative process, however, often works in mysterious ways. The bill passed by Congress did end the national origins system, as its framers desired, but reversed the new priorities, giving highest preference to family reunification and less emphasis to job skills and asylum for refugees. As en-

THE SECOND GREAT MIGRATION: A THEORETICAL EXAMPLE

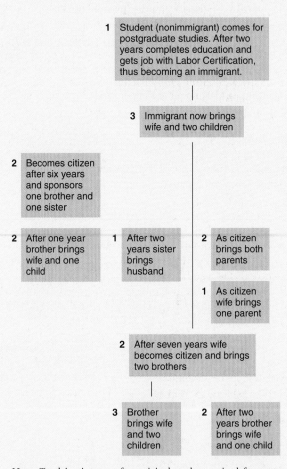

1 Student (nonimmigrant) comes for postgraduate studies. After two years completes education and gets job with Labor Certification, thus becoming an immigrant.

3 Immigrant now brings wife and two children

2 Becomes citizen after six years and sponsors one brother and one sister

2 After one year brother brings wife and one child

1 After two years sister brings husband

2 As citizen brings both parents

1 As citizen wife brings one parent

2 After seven years wife becomes citizen and brings two brothers

3 Brother brings wife and two children

2 After two years brother brings wife and one child

Note: Total is nineteen after original student arrived for post-graduate education ten years earlier. Adapted from David M. Reimer, *Still the Golden Door,* 2d ed. (New York: Columbia University Press, 1992), p. 95.

acted and later amended, the 1965 Immigration Act set an annual limit of 170,000 for immigrants from Europe, Asia, and Africa, and 120,000 for those from Western Hemisphere countries, with a ceiling of 20,000 for immigrants from any one country. The total of 290,000, would be only slightly higher than the number admitted under the old system.

By the end of the 1970s, it was clear that the family preferences, which made up nearly 70 percent of the allotted visas, were allowing recent immigrants to bring in large numbers of relatives, instead of reuniting immigrants who had been in the United States for years with their families. The figure, "The Second Great Migration: A Theoretical Example," shows how one postgraduate student with a nonimmigrant visa, by adroit use of the available family preferences, could easily gain the admission of eighteen relatives in just a decade. Moreover, once resident aliens became citizens, they could bring in "immediate relatives"—spouses, children under 21, and parents—without regard to visa limits.

Two significant developments flowed directly from the Great Society's immigration policy. First, annual immigration increased steadily from an average of 250,000 in the 1950s to at least 1 million by the end of the century. In 1990, in an effort to place "immediate relatives" under an effective limit, Congress approved an overall ceiling of just under 700,000 immigrants a year, except for refugees. But other legislation allowing undocumented workers to gain legal status, as

well as an estimated 300,000 illegal immigrants a year, swelled the actual total to more than 1 million. In effect, the 1965 legislation had led to a quadrupling of newcomers entering the United States every year.

The other unintended consequence of the 1965 Immigration Act was a rapid shift in the source of the new immigrants. Europe, the traditional place of origin for immigrants, fell from providing 70 percent of newcomers in the 1950s, to just 16 percent by the mid-1990s. Latin American immigrants rose from 25 to 49 percent of the total, while Asia supplied 32 percent by the end of the century, up from just 6 percent in the 1950s. This change in the countries of origin was as striking as the similar shift from western to eastern Europe in the first great migration. Where once Germany, Great Britain, and Ireland had furnished the majority of newcomers, by 1989 it was Mexico, the Philippines, and Vietnam that led the list, with no European country among the top ten.

The result was a growing diversity that promised to make the United

States a truly multiethnic society in the twenty-first century. By the 1990s, the number of foreign-born Americans had more than doubled to 10 percent of the population. Hispanic Americans were the most rapidly growing segment, replacing African Americans as the nation's largest minority in 2001. Asian Americans, although much smaller in number, grew at a fast pace and had greater success economically than any other ethnic group.

By the end of the century it was clear that the Immigration Act of 1965 had led to a major shift in the racial and ethnic composition of the United States. The effort to erase past discriminatory and race-based quotas resulted in an unexpected flow of people from Asia and Latin America that ensured the end of traditional European dominance. By 2050, according to Census Bureau projections, the country is expected to be almost evenly divided between non-Hispanic whites and minorities. Social harmony in the twenty-first century will depend on whether the melting pot continues to melt, blending ethnic groups into mainstream America, or whether these groups, as their numbers grow, will shape the society into one that political leaders of the 1960s such as Lyndon Johnson and Robert Kennedy could never have foreseen.

Questions for Discussion

* Do you think the immigration policy adopted in 1965 was a great improvement on the old policy? Why or why not?
* How does the Immigration Act of 1965 relate to the contemporary debate over immigration policy?

REGION OF BIRTH OF FOREIGN BORN, 2000

Region	Number
Latin America	16,086,974
Asia	8,226,254
Europe	4,915,557
Africa	881,300
North America	829,442
Australia, New Zealand, and Pacific Islands	168,046

Source: Associated Press, June 9, 2002.

Chapter 31

To a New Conservatism, 1969–1988

Reagan and America's Shift to the Right

In October 1964, the Republican National Committee sponsored a televised address by Hollywood actor Ronald Reagan on behalf of Barry Goldwater's presidential candidacy. In contrast to Goldwater's strident rhetoric, Reagan used relaxed, confident, and persuasive terms to put forth the case for a return to individual freedom. Instead of the usual choice between increased government activity and less government involvement, Reagan presented the options of either going up or down—"up to the maximum of human freedom consistent with law and order, or down to the ant heap of totalitarianism."

Although the speech did not rescue Goldwater's unpopular candidacy, it marked the beginning of Ronald Reagan's remarkable political career. A popular actor whose movie career had begun to fade in the 1950s, Reagan had become an effective television performer as host of *The General Electric Theater.* His political views, once liberal, moved steadily to the right as he became a spokesperson for a major American corporation. In 1965, a group of wealthy friends persuaded him to run for the California governorship.

Reagan proved to be an attractive candidate. He won handily by appealing effectively to rising middle-class suburban resentment over high taxes, expanding welfare programs, and bureaucratic regulation. In two terms as governor, Reagan displayed natural ability as a political leader. Instead of insisting on implementing all of his conservative beliefs, he proved surprisingly flexible. Faced with a Democratic legislature, he yielded on raising taxes and increasing state spending while managing to trim the welfare rolls.

By the time Reagan left the governor's office in 1974, many signs pointed to a growing conservative mood across the nation. Religious leaders were especially outraged over the 1962 Supreme Court ruling in *Engel* v. *Vitale* outlawing school prayer. In the South, where daily prayers were the customary way of beginning the school day, the reaction was intense.

Concern over school prayer, along with rising abortion and divorce rates, impelled religious groups to engage in political activity to defend what they viewed as traditional family values. Jerry Falwell, a successful Virginia radio and television evangelist, founded the **Moral Majority,** a fundamentalist group dedicated to preserving the "American way of life."

The population shift of the 1970s, especially the rapid growth of the Sunbelt region in the South and West (see p. 636), added momentum to the conservative upsurge. Those moving to the Sunbelt tended to be white, middle- and upper-class suburbanites—mainly skilled workers, young professionals, and business executives who were attracted both by economic opportunity and by a political climate stressing low taxes, less government regulation, and more reliance on the marketplace.

The political impact of population shifts from East to West and North to South was reflected in the congressional seats gained by Sunbelt and Far West states.

Conservatives also succeeded in making their cause intellectually respectable. Scholars and academics on the right flourished. Writer William Buckley and economist Milton Friedman proved to be effective advocates of conservative causes in print and on television. **Neoconservatism,** led by Norman Podhoretz's magazine *Commentary,* became fashionable among many intellectuals who were former liberal stalwarts. They denounced liberals for being too soft on the communist threat abroad and too willing to compromise high standards at home in the face of demands for equality from African Americans, women, and the disadvantaged. Neoconservatives called for a reaffirmation of capitalism and a new emphasis on what was right about America rather than an obsessive concern with social ills.

neoconservatism Former liberals who advocated a strong stand against communism abroad and free market capitalism at home became known as neoconservatives. These intellectuals stressed the positive values of American society in contrast to liberals who emphasized social ills.

By the end of the 1970s, a decade marked by military defeat in Vietnam, political scandal that destroyed the administration of Richard Nixon, economic ills that vexed the country under Gerald Ford and Jimmy Carter, and unprecedented social strains on families and traditional institutions, millions of Americans had come to believe that Cold War liberalism had run its course. Ronald Reagan, as the acknowledged leader of the conservative resurgence, was ideally placed to capitalize on this discontent. His personal charm and his conviction that America could regain its traditional self-confidence by reaffirming basic ideals had a broad appeal to a nation facing new challenges at home and abroad. Competing against George H. W. Bush, he won the Republican nomination for President in 1980.

In his acceptance speech at the Republican convention in Detroit, Reagan set forth the themes that endeared him to conservatives: less government, a balanced budget, family values, and peace through greater military spending. He offered reassurance and hope for the future. In Ronald Reagan, the Republicans had found the perfect figure to lead Americans into a new conservative era.

THE TEMPTING OF RICHARD NIXON

Following the divisive campaign of 1968, Richard Nixon's presidency proved to be one of the most controversial in American history. Nixon's domestic policies had limited success, and though his diplomacy broke new ground in relations with China and the Soviet Union and ended American fighting in Vietnam, he was forced to resign the presidency under the dark cloud of the Watergate scandal.

Pragmatic Liberalism

Nixon began his first term on a hopeful note, promising the nation peace and respite from the chaos of the 1960s. Rejecting the divisions that had driven Americans apart, he pledged in his inaugural address to bring the country together.

Nixon's moderate language appeared to herald a return to the politics of accommodation that had characterized the Eisenhower era. Faced with a Democratic Congress, Nixon, like Ike, reconciled himself to the broad outlines of the welfare state. Instead of trying to overthrow the Great Society, he focused on making the federal bureaucracy function more efficiently. In some areas he actually expanded federal programs and responsibilities.

On civil rights, for example, Nixon was the first president to adopt **affirmative action** as an explicit policy. He also expanded it to include women. The goal, a Nixon executive order explained, was for the federal government to achieve "the prompt and full utilization of minorities and women at all levels in all segments of its work force."

affirmative action The use of laws or regulations to achieve racial, ethnic, gender, or other diversity, as in hiring or school admissions. Such efforts are often aimed at improving employment or educational opportunities for women and minorities.

Environmental Protection Agency (EPA) Congress created this agency in 1970 as part of a broader effort to protect the environment and curb the pollution of the nation's air and water.

Nixon broke new ground in other areas associated with liberalism. He approved the creation of the Occupational Safety and Health Administration, which assumed responsibility for reducing workplace injuries. He oversaw the establishment of the **Environmental Protection Agency (EPA),** the federal watchdog on environmental affairs. He signed the Clean Air Act, which provided the basis for tackling smog and other air pollutants. He supported automatic cost-of-living increases to Social Security, ensuring that the elderly did not lose ground to the inflation that increasingly vexed the American economy. Nixon's liberalism was pragmatic, even opportunistic, rather than principled. Planning big changes in American foreign policy, he chose not to buck the liberal tide that was still flowing from the 1960s.

Nixon did try to shape that tide. Under the label of the "new federalism," he shifted responsibility for many social programs from Washington to state and local authorities. He developed the concept of revenue sharing, by which federal funds were dispersed to state, county, and city agencies to meet local needs. An accompanying ceiling of $2.5 billion a year on federal welfare payments meant that much of the revenue sharing payments had to be allocated by cities and states to programs previously paid for by the federal government.

Nixon's civil rights policy was similarly calculating. Action by Congress and the Johnson administration had ensured that massive desegregation of southern schools would begin just as Nixon took office. Nixon and his attorney general, John Mitchell, decided to shift the responsibility for this process to the courts. In the summer of 1969, the Justice Department asked a federal judge to delay the integration of thirty-three school districts in Mississippi. The Supreme Court quickly ruled against the Justice Department. Thus, in the minds of southern white voters, it was the hated Supreme Court, not Richard Nixon, who had forced them to integrate their schools.

The upshot of Nixon's domestic policies was to extend the welfare state in some areas, reshape it in others, and leave liberals and conservatives alike wondering just where Nixon stood.

Détente

Foreign policy was Nixon's pride and joy. He was determined to improve the state of the world. To assist him in this endeavor, he appointed Henry Kissinger as national security adviser. A refugee from Nazi Germany, Kissinger had become a professor of government at Harvard, the author of several influential books, and an acknowledged authority on international affairs. Nixon and Kissinger approached foreign policy from a realistic perspective. They saw the Cold War as a traditional great-power rivalry to be managed and controlled rather than won.

Realizing that recent events, especially the Vietnam War and the rapid Soviet arms buildup of the 1960s, had eroded America's position of primacy in the world, Nixon and Kissinger planned a strategic retreat. Russia now had great military strength, but its economy was weak and it had a dangerous rival in China. Nixon planned to use American trade to induce Soviet cooperation while improving U.S. relations with China as well.

▧ *Kissinger's search for détente began with a calculated decision to improve relations with China. In a highly publicized state visit, Nixon and Chinese leaders were photographed sharing banquets and touring the Great Wall of China.* ▧

Nixon and Kissinger shrewdly played the China card as their first step toward achieving **détente**—a relaxation of tension—with the Soviet Union. In February 1972, accompanied by a planeload of reporters and television camera crews, Nixon visited China, meeting with the communist leaders and ending more than two decades of Sino-American hostility.

The Soviets responded by agreeing to an arms control pact with the United States. The **Strategic Arms Limitation Talks (SALT)** had been under way since 1969. During a visit to Moscow in May 1972, Nixon signed two vital documents with Soviet leader Leonid Brezhnev. The first limited the two superpowers to two hundred antiballistic missiles (ABMs) apiece. The second froze the number of offensive ballistic missiles for a five-year period. The SALT I agreements recognized the existing Soviet lead in missiles, but the American deployment of multiple independently targeted reentry vehicles (MIRVs) ensured a continuing strategic advantage for the United States.

The SALT I agreements were most important as a symbolic first step toward control of the nuclear arms race. They signified that the United States and the Soviet Union were trying to achieve a settlement of their differences by peaceful means.

détente President Nixon and Henry Kissinger pursued a policy of détente, a French word meaning a relaxation of tension, with the Soviet Union as a way to lessen the possibility of nuclear war in the 1970s.

Strategic Arms Limitation Talks (SALT) In 1972, the United States and the Soviet Union culminated four years of Strategic Arms Limitation Talks by signing a treaty limiting the deployment of antiballistic missiles (ABMs) and an agreement to freeze the number of offensive missiles for five years.

Ending the Vietnam War

Vietnam remained the one foreign policy challenge that Nixon could not overcome. He had a three-part plan to end the conflict: gradual withdrawal of American troops, accompanied by training of South Vietnamese forces to take over the combat role; renewed bombing; and a hard line in negotiations with Hanoi.

Renewed bombing proved the most controversial part of the plan. In April 1970, Nixon ordered air and ground strikes into Cambodia, causing a massive outburst of antiwar protests on college campuses. Tragedy struck at Kent State University in Ohio in early May when National Guardsmen opened fire on rioters, killing four students and wounding eleven more. The victims had been innocent bystanders. A week later, two African American student demonstrators were killed

The renewed bombing of North Vietnam and invasion of Cambodia ordered by Nixon in hopes of ending the conflict precipitated student protests at many campuses. At Kent State University in Ohio, demonstrators and bystanders were shot by national guardsmen. ■

at Jackson State College in Mississippi. Riots and protests soon raged on more than four hundred campuses across the country.

Nixon had little sympathy for the demonstrators, calling the students "bums" who were intent on "blowing up the campuses." One poll showed that most Americans blamed the students, not the National Guard, for the deaths at Kent State. Nixon's Cambodian invasion did little to shorten the Vietnam War, but the public reaction reinforced the president's resolve not to surrender.

The third tactic, negotiation with Hanoi, finally proved successful. Beginning in the summer of 1969, Kissinger held a series of secret meetings with North Vietnam's foreign minister, Le Duc Tho. In the summer and fall of 1972, the two sides neared agreement until South Vietnamese objections blocked a settlement. When the North Vietnamese tried to make last-minute changes, Nixon ordered a series of heavy B-52 raids on Hanoi that finally led to the signing of a truce on January 27, 1973. In return for the release of all American prisoners of war, the United States agreed to remove its troops from South Vietnam within sixty days. The political clauses allowed the North Vietnamese to keep their troops in the South, thus virtually guaranteeing future control of all Vietnam by the communists.

For two years after the accords the communists waited, weighing, among other things, the willingness of Americans to continue to support South Vietnam. As Nixon became enmeshed in the Watergate scandal (see below), his grip on foreign policy weakened. By the time he was forced from office in August 1974 most Americans simply wanted to forget Vietnam. The following spring the communists mounted a major offensive and in just weeks completed their takeover of Vietnam. Ten years after the American escalation of the war, and after the loss of sixty thousand American lives, the American effort to preserve South Vietnam from communism had proved a tragic failure.

The Watergate Scandal

Nixon's Vietnam problems and especially his formulation of détente made him sensitive to the unauthorized release of information about American foreign policy. The White House established an informal office of covert surveillance—the "plumbers," its operatives were called—which began investigating national security breaches but, during the presidential campaign of 1972, branched out into spying on Nixon's Democratic opponents and engaging in political dirty tricks.

Five of the "plumbers" were arrested in June 1972 during a break-in at the headquarters of the Democratic National Committee at the Watergate office complex in Washington. The Nixon White House took pains to conceal its connection to the incident. Nixon personally ordered the cover-up.

The cover-up succeeded long enough to ensure Nixon's landslide re-election victory. In the months after the election, though, it began to unravel. By April 1973, Nixon was compelled to fire aide John Dean, who had directed the cover-up but who now refused to become a scapegoat. Two other aides were also forced to resign.

The Senate then appointed a special committee to investigate the unfolding **Watergate scandal.** In a week of dramatic testimony, Dean revealed the president's personal involvement in the affair. Still, it was basically a matter of whose word was to be believed, and Nixon hoped to weather the storm.

The committee's discovery of the existence of tape recordings of conversations in the Oval Office, made regularly since 1970, proved the beginning of the end for Nixon. At first, the president tried to invoke executive privilege to withhold the tapes. When Archibald Cox, appointed as Watergate special prosecutor, demanded the release of the tapes, Nixon fired him. In June 1974, the Supreme Court ruled unanimously that the tapes had to be turned over for examination.

By this time, the House Judiciary Committee had voted three articles of impeachment, charging Nixon with obstruction of justice, abuse of power, and con-

Watergate scandal A break-in at the Democratic National Committee offices in the Watergate complex in Washington was carried out under the direction of White House employees. Disclosure of the White House involvement in the break-in and subsequent cover-up forced President Nixon to resign in 1974 to avoid impeachment.

tempt of Congress. Faced with the release of tapes that directly implicated him in the cover-up, the president chose to resign on August 9, 1974.

Nixon's resignation represented the culmination of the Watergate scandal. The entire episode revealed both the weaknesses and strengths of the American political system. Most regrettable was the abuse of presidential authority—a reflection of the growing power of the modern presidency and of the fatal flaws in Richard Nixon's character. Realizing he had reached the White House almost by accident, Nixon did everything possible to retain his hold on his office.

Watergate also demonstrated the vitality of a democratic society. The press showed how investigative reporting could unlock even the most closely guarded executive secrets. Judge Sirica proved that an independent judiciary was still the best bulwark for individual freedom. And Congress carried out a successful investigation of executive misconduct and followed it with a scrupulous impeachment process.

The nation survived the shock of Watergate with its institutions intact. Congress, in decline since Lyndon Johnson's exercise of executive dominance, was rejuvenated.

THE ECONOMY OF STAGFLATION

In the midst of Watergate, the outbreak of war in the Middle East threatened a vital national interest: the unimpeded and inexpensive flow of oil to the United States. The resulting energy crisis helped spark a raging price inflation that had a profound impact on the national economy and on American society at large.

War and Oil

On October 6, 1973, Egypt and Syria launched a surprise attack on Israel. Catching Israel off guard, they won early battles but eventually lost the initiative and were forced to give up the ground they had recovered. The Israelis would have delivered another devastating defeat to the Arabs if not for the diplomatic intervention of Nixon and Kissinger, who, despite America's previous strong support for Israel, believed a decisive Israeli victory would destabilize the Middle East even more.

The American diplomatic triumph, however, was offset by an unforeseen consequence of the October War (also called the Yom Kippur War, as it started on the Jewish holy day). On October 17, the Arab members of the **Organization of Petroleum Exporting Countries (OPEC)** announced a 5 percent cut in oil production, and vowed additional cuts of 5 percent each month until Israel surrendered the lands it had taken in the Six Day's War of 1967. Three days later, following Nixon's announcement of an emergency aid package for Israel, Saudi Arabia cut off oil shipments to the United States.

The Arab oil embargo had a disastrous impact on the American economy. With Arab producers cutting production by 25 percent from the September 1973 level, world supplies fell by 10 percent. For the United States, this meant a loss of nearly 2 million barrels a day. Long lines formed at gas stations as motorists feared running out of fuel.

A dramatic increase in oil prices proved to be a far more significant result of the embargo. After the Arab embargo began, OPEC raised crude oil prices fourfold. In the United States, gasoline prices at the pumps nearly doubled in a few weeks' time, while the cost of home heating fuel rose even more.

Nixon responded with a series of temporary measures, including pleas to Americans to turn down their thermostats in homes and offices and avoid driving simply for pleasure. When the Arab oil embargo ended in March, after Kissinger negotiated an Israeli pullback in the Sinai, the American public relaxed. Gasoline once again became plentiful, thermostats were raised, and people resumed their love affair with the automobile.

Organization of Petroleum Exporting Countries (OPEC)
A cartel of oil-exporting nations. In late 1973, OPEC took advantage of the October War and an oil embargo by its Arab members to quadruple the price of oil. This huge increase had a devastating impact on the American economy.

The Arab action marked the beginning of a new era in American history, however. The United States had been responsible for nearly 40 percent of the world's energy consumption. In 1970, domestic oil production began to decline. The embargo served only to highlight the fact that the nation was now dependent on other countries, notably those in the Persian Gulf, for its economic well-being. A nation that based its way of life on abundance and expansion suddenly was faced with the reality of limited resources and economic stagnation.

The Great Inflation

The price spike from the October War was merely the first of the oil shocks of the 1970s. Cheap energy had been a primary contributor to the relentless growth of the American economy after World War II. Large cars, sprawling suburbs, detached houses heated by fuel oil and natural gas and cooled by central air-conditioning produced a dependence on inexpensive energy that Americans took for granted.

The quadrupling of oil prices in 1973–1974 suddenly put all this at risk. Because oil or its equivalent in energy was required for most services and the production and transportation of manufactured goods, rising oil prices caused the prices of nearly everything else to increase as well.

Other factors added to that trend. The Vietnam War had created massive federal budget deficits. A worldwide shortage of food triggered a 20 percent rise in American food prices in 1973 alone. But the primary source of the great inflation of the 1970s remained the sixfold increase in petroleum prices.

The impact on consumers was staggering. The price of an automobile jumped 72 percent between 1973 and 1978. During the decade, the price of a hamburger doubled, milk went from 28 to 59 cents a quart, and a loaf of bread rose from 24 to 89 cents. Corresponding wage increases failed to keep pace with inflation.

Often inflation signals economic exuberance, and rising prices indicate a rapid rate of growth. The inflation of the 1970s reflected economic weakness, however. American GNP dropped by 6 percent in 1974, and unemployment rose to more than 9 percent, the highest level since the Great Depression of the 1930s.

President Gerald R. Ford, who followed Richard Nixon into the White House (see p. 618), responded belatedly to the recession by proposing a tax cut to stimulate

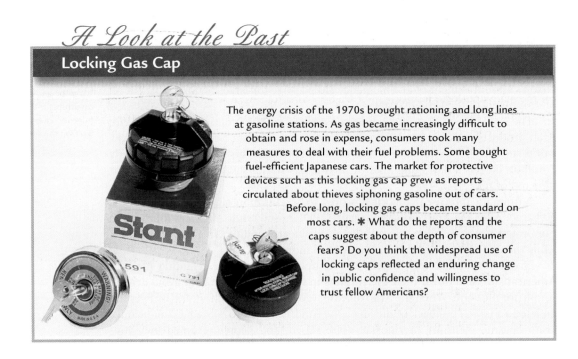

A Look at the Past

Locking Gas Cap

The energy crisis of the 1970s brought rationing and long lines at gasoline stations. As gas became increasingly difficult to obtain and rose in expense, consumers took many measures to deal with their fuel problems. Some bought fuel-efficient Japanese cars. The market for protective devices such as this locking gas cap grew as reports circulated about thieves siphoning gasoline out of cars. Before long, locking gas caps became standard on most cars. ✱ What do the reports and the caps suggest about the depth of consumer fears? Do you think the widespread use of locking caps reflected an enduring change in public confidence and willingness to trust fellow Americans?

consumer spending. Congress passed a $23 billion reduction in taxes in early 1975, which led to a gradual recovery by 1976. But the resulting budget deficits helped keep inflation high and prevented a return to full economic health.

Jimmy Carter, who succeeded Ford (see p. 618), had little more success in reviving the economy. Continued federal deficits and relatively high interest rates kept the economy sluggish throughout 1977 and 1978. Then the outbreak of the Iranian Revolution and the overthrow of the shah in 1979 touched off another oil shock. The members of the OPEC cartel took advantage of the situation to double prices over the next eighteen months.

Finally, in late 1979, the Federal Reserve Board began a sustained effort to halt inflation by mandating increased bank reserves to curtail the supply of money in circulation. The new tight-money policy served only to heighten inflation in the short run by driving interest rates up to record levels.

The Shifting American Economy

Inflation and the oil shocks helped bring about significant changes in American business and industry in the 1970s. The most obvious result was the slowing rate of economic growth, with the GNP advancing only 3.2 percent for the decade, compared to 3.7 percent in the 1960s. In 1959, U.S. firms had been world leaders in eleven of thirteen major industrial sectors, ranging from manufacturing to banking. By 1976, American companies led in only seven areas, and in all but one category—aerospace—U.S. corporations had declined in relation to Japanese and western European competitors.

The most serious losses came in the heavy industries. New companies in western Europe, Japan, and the Third World began producing steel far more efficiently than their American counterparts. By the end of the 1970s, firms were closing down their obsolete mills in the East and Midwest, putting thousands out of work.

Foreign competition did even more damage in the automobile industry. The oil shocks led to a consumer demand for small, efficient cars. By 1977, imported cars had captured nearly a fifth of the American market, with Germany and Japan leading the way. In response, Detroit spent $70 billion retooling to produce a new fleet of smaller, lighter front-wheel-drive cars. American manufacturers barely survived the foreign invasion.

The decline in manufacturing led to significant shifts in the labor movement. The industrial unions such as the United Automobile Workers (UAW) lost members steadily in the 1960s and 1970s. At the same time, public employee unions enjoyed rapid growth and acceptance. The Great Society legislation, the baby boom with the resulting need for many more teachers, and the growth of social agencies on the state and local levels opened up new jobs for social workers, teachers, and government employees. The rise of public employee unions also opened the way for greater participation by African Americans and women than in the older trade and industrial unions.

Just as public employee unions prospered from the shifts in the American economy in the 1970s, so too did many American corporations. Multinationals that had emerged in the boom years of the 1960s continued to thrive. The growth of conglomerates—huge corporations that combined many dissimilar industrial concerns—accelerated. The growth of high-technology industries proved to be the most profitable new trend of the 1970s. Computer companies and electronics firms grew at a rapid rate, especially after the development of the silicon chip, a small, wafer-thin microprocessor capable of performing complex calculations almost instantly.

The result was a geographic shift of American industry from the East and Midwest to the Sunbelt. Electronics manufacturers flourished in California, Texas, and North Carolina, where they grew up around major universities. The absence of entrenched labor unions, the availability of skilled labor, and the warm and attractive climate of the southern and western states lured many new concerns to the Sunbelt. The decline of the steel and auto industries continued to result in massive unemployment and economic stagnation in the northern industrial heartland.

The overall pattern was one of an economy in transition. The oil shocks had caused serious problems of inflation, slower economic growth, and rising unemployment rates. But American business still displayed the enterprise and the ability to develop new technologies that gave promise of renewed economic vitality.

A New Environmentalism

The oil shocks had another effect: They injected new life into the environmental movement. The high price of gasoline made pocketbook conservationists of millions of Americans who had not before thought twice about their country's heavy dependence on foreign oil. It also spurred Congress to press automakers to improve the fuel efficiency of their cars. The 1975 Energy Policy and Conservation Act set standards for gas mileage. Manufacturers who failed to achieve the mandated averages faced stiff fines and other sanctions.

Environmentalists and consumers, meanwhile, began searching for alternative sources of energy. Solar power appealed to some as clean and endlessly renewable. But it was also expensive (solar panels and related technologies remained underdeveloped) and intermittent (clouds cut off the power). Hydropower—electricity generated by falling water—was better proven and more reliable, but most of the suitable dam sites had already been built upon. Wind power worked in some areas (where the wind blew frequently and without obstruction), but those were precisely the areas where few people lived. Coal power was reliable, proven, and cheap, but it was also dirty (the gases emitted by coal plants fouled the air) and dangerous (to the men and women who mined the coal).

Nuclear power had its advocates. It had been in use in America since the 1950s, and its characteristics were well known. Its fuel—uranium—was essentially inexhaustible, and nuclear reactors, in normal operations, produced no noxious gases. Nor did they produce any greenhouse gases—carbon dioxide and other heat-trapping gases—that contributed to **global warming,** a rise in average temperatures that was just beginning to worry some earth scientists.

global warming A general rise in temperatures, believed by most scientists to be caused by human activities such as burning fossil fuels, which expels into the earth's atmosphere excess carbon dioxide and other gases that prevent solar heat from escaping, a phenomenon known as the "greenhouse effect."

But nuclear power made many environmentalists nervous. The waste products of the reactors were radioactive, and would remain so for thousands of years. Guaranteeing that wastes not contaminate water supplies for fifty generations into the future was a daunting challenge. And occasionally nuclear reactors malfunctioned in terrifying ways. An accident at Chernobyl, in the Soviet Ukraine, in 1986, which released large amounts of radiation into the atmosphere and caused many deaths, reinforced fears.

The debate over alternative energy sources was part of a larger discussion concerning the environment. Earth Day, first celebrated in April 1970, became an annual event at which participants considered the effects of human actions on their natural surroundings. Groups such as the Sierra Club and Friends of the Earth lobbied to reinforce antipollution laws, to clean up toxic wastes, and to increase gas mileage standards further. Furthermore, Congress strengthened the Clean Air Act and created the federal Superfund in 1980 for toxic cleanups. But with rising oil imports, environmental concerns only increased.

PRIVATE LIVES, PUBLIC ISSUES

Sweeping changes in the private lives of the American people began in the 1970s and continued for the rest of the century. The traditional American family gave way to more diverse living arrangements. The number of working women, including wives and mothers, increased sharply. The wage gap between the sexes narrowed, although women still lagged noticeably behind men. An active gay rights movement emerged after 1970 as more and more gay, lesbian, and bisexual Americans began to disclose their sexual identities and demand an end to discrimination.

The Changing American Family

Family life underwent a number of significant shifts at this time. A decline in the number of families with two parents and one or more children under 18 was most noticeable. By the end of the 1980s, in only one two-parent family out of five was the mother solely engaged in child rearing. A few fathers stayed at home with the children, but in the great majority of these families, both parents worked outside the home.

The traditional nuclear family of the 1950s no longer prevailed in America by the end of the twentieth century. The number of married couple households with children dropped from 30 percent in the 1970s to 23 percent by 2000. The number of unmarried couples doubled in the 1990s, while adults living alone surpassed the number of married couples with children for the first time in American history.

The divorce rate, which doubled between the mid-1960s and the late 1970s, leveled off for the rest of the century. Nevertheless, half of all first marriages still ended in divorce. After a sharp fall in the 1970s, the birthrate climbed again as the baby boom generation began to mature. There was a marked increase in the number of births to women over age 30, as well as a very high proportion of children born to single mothers, who composed 7 percent of all households by 2000, a 25 percent increase since 1990. Conservatives, alarmed by the decline of the nuclear family, began to call for change.

For better or worse, the American family structure changed significantly in the last three decades of the twentieth century, with a large number of people either never marrying or postponing marriage until late in the childbearing period. The traditional family unit rapidly declined. Most mothers worked outside the home, and many were the sole support for their children. The proportion of children living with only one parent doubled in twenty years. Women without partners headed more than one-third of all impoverished families, and children made up 40 percent of the nation's poor. Although politicians referred to family values during campaigns, the fact remains that the American family underwent great stress due to social changes in the last third of the twentieth century. Children suffered disproportionately.

Gains and Setbacks for Women

American women experienced significant changes in the last quarter of the twentieth century. The prevailing theme concerned the increasing percentage of working women. There was a rapid movement of women into the labor force in the 1970s. Combined incomes of husband and wife became increasingly necessary to keep up with inflation. The trend continued through the 1980s, as 61 percent of the nearly nineteen million new jobs created during the decade were filled by women.

Women scored some impressive breakthroughs. They began to enter corporation boardrooms, became presidents of major universities, and were admitted to the nation's military academies. Women entered blue-collar, professional, and small-business fields traditionally dominated by men. Ronald Reagan's appointment of Sandra Day O'Connor to the Supreme Court in 1981 marked a historic first; Bill Clinton doubled the number of women on the Court with his selection of Ruth Bader Ginsburg.

Yet at the same time, women encountered a great deal of resistance. Most women continued to work in female-dominated fields—as nurses, secretaries,

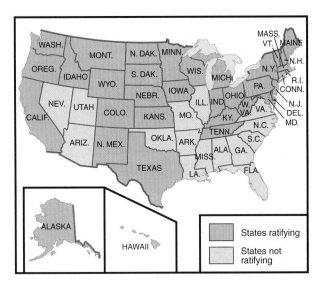

VOTING ON THE EQUAL RIGHTS AMENDMENT
By the end of 1974, thirty-four states had ratified the ERA; Indiana finally approved the amendment in 1977, but the remaining fifteen states held out, leaving ratification three states short of the required three-fourths majority. ■

teachers, and waitresses. In 1990, only 4.3 percent of corporate officers were women. Most women in business worked at the middle and lower rungs of management with staff jobs in personnel and public relations, not key operational positions in sales and marketing that would lead to the boardroom. The economic boom of the 1990s, however, led to a steady increase in the number of women executives.

Even with these gains, by 2002 women's wages still averaged only 77.5 percent of men's earnings. A woman with a college degree made only $600 a year more on the average than a man with a high school diploma. Younger women did best. Older women, who often had no other source of support, fared poorly.

The most encouraging development for women came in business ownership. Often blocked by the "glass ceiling" and seeking flexible schedules, more and more women went into business for themselves. The number of female business owners increased 40 percent between 1987 and 1992, twice the national rate of business growth. A women's trade group estimated that in 1996 women owned almost eight million businesses, employing more than eighteen million workers—one out of four American workers.

Beyond economic opportunity, the women's movement had two goals. The first was ratification of the **Equal Rights Amendment (ERA)**. Approved by Congress in 1972, the ERA stated simply, "Equality of rights under the law shall not be denied or abridged by the United States or any state on account of sex." Within a year, twenty-two states had approved the amendment, but the efforts gradually faltered just three states short of ratification. Opposition came in part from working-class women who feared loss of protection from state laws that regulated wages and hours of work for women. Right-wing activist Phyllis Schlafly led an organized effort to defeat the ERA, claiming the amendment would lead to unisex toilets, homosexual marriages, and the drafting of women. The deadline for ratification finally passed on June 30, 1982, with the ERA forces still three states short.

The women's movement focused even more of its energies in protecting a major victory concerning abortion rights that it had won in *Roe* v. *Wade* in 1973. Prolife groups fought back. Congress passed the Hyde amendment in 1978, which denied the use of federal funds to pay for abortions for poor women. Nevertheless, prochoice groups organized privately funded family planning agencies and abortion clinics to give more women a chance to exercise their constitutional right to abortion.

As Republican presidents appointed more conservative judges to the Court, however, prochoice groups began to fear the future overturn of *Roe* v. *Wade.* The Court avoided a direct challenge, upholding the rights of states to regulate abortion

Equal Rights Amendment (ERA) In 1972, Congress approved this constitutional amendment, a measure designed to guarantee women equal treatment under the law. Despite a three-year extension in the time allowed for ratification by the states, ERA supporters fell three states short of winning adoption.

Roe* v. *Wade In 1973, the Supreme Court ruled in *Roe* v. *Wade* that women had a constitutional right to abortion during the early stages of pregnancy. The decision provoked a vigorous right-to-life movement that opposed abortion.

clinics, impose a 24-hour waiting period, and require the approval of one parent or a judge before a minor could have an abortion. Bill Clinton's election and appointment of Ruth Bader Ginsburg to the Court appeared to end the danger to *Roe* v. *Wade,* but in 2000 the Court margin in rejecting a Nebraska law forbidding certain late-term abortions fell to a bare majority, 5–4. And even the exercise of the right to abortion proved difficult and sometimes dangerous in view of the often violent protests of prolife groups outside abortion clinics. For many women, abortion was a hard-won right they still had to struggle to protect.

The Gay Liberation Movement

On the evening of June 27, 1969, a squad of New York policemen raided the Stonewall Inn, a Greenwich Village bar frequented by "drag queens" and lesbians. As the patrons were being herded into vans, a crowd of gay onlookers began to jeer and taunt the police. A riot quickly broke out. The next night, more than four hundred police officers battled two thousand gay demonstrators through the streets of Greenwich Village. The two-day Stonewall Riots marked the beginning of the modern **gay liberation movement.** Refusing to play the role of victims any longer, gays and lesbians decided to affirm their sexual orientation and demand an end to discrimination.

Within a few days, two new organizations were formed in New York, the Gay Liberation Front and the Gay Activist Alliance, with branches and offshoots quickly appearing in cities across the country. The basic theme of gay liberation was to urge all homosexuals to "come out of the closet" and affirm with pride their sexual identity; instead of shame, they would find freedom and self-respect in the very act of coming out.

In the course of the 1970s, gays and lesbians formed more than a thousand local clubs and organizations and won a series of notable victories. In 1974, the American Psychiatric Association stopped classifying homosexuality as a mental disorder. By the end of the decade, half the states had repealed their sodomy statutes. Gays fought hard in cities and states for laws forbidding discrimination in housing and employment. In 1980, they finally succeeded in getting a gay rights plank in the Democratic National Platform.

In the 1980s, the onset of the AIDS epidemic (see pp. 616–617) forced the gay liberation movement onto the defensive. Stung by the accusation that AIDS was a "gay disease," male homosexuals faced new public condemnation at a time when they were trying desperately to care for the growing number of victims of the disease within their ranks. The gay organizations formed in the 1970s to win new rights now were channeling their energies into caring for the ill, promoting safe sex practices, and fighting for more public funding to help conquer AIDS. In 1986, ACT UP (AIDS Coalition to Unleash Power) began a series of violent demonstrations in an effort to shock the nation into doing more about AIDS.

The movement also continued to stimulate gay consciousness in the 1980s. In 1987, an estimated 600,000 gays and lesbians took part in a march on Washington on behalf of gay rights. Every year afterward, gay groups held a National Coming Out Day in October to encourage homosexuals to proclaim proudly their sexual identity. Gay leaders claimed there were more than twenty million gays and lesbians in the nation, basing this estimate on a Kinsey report which had stated in the late 1940s that one in ten American males had engaged in homosexual behavior. A sociological survey released in the spring of 1993 contradicted those numbers, finding only 1.1 percent of American males exclusively homosexual. Whatever the actual number, it was clear by the 1990s that gays and lesbians formed a significant minority that had succeeded in forcing the nation, however grudgingly, to respect its rights.

There was one battle, however, in which victory eluded the gay liberation movement. In the 1992 election, gays and lesbians strongly backed Democratic

gay liberation movement In the 1970s, homosexuals began an effort to win social and legal acceptance and to encourage all gays and lesbians to affirm their sexual identity.

candidate Bill Clinton, who promised, if elected, to end the ban on homosexuals in the military. In his first days in office, however, President Clinton stirred up great resistance in the Pentagon and Congress when he tried to issue an executive order forbidding such discrimination. The Joint Chiefs of Staff and many Democrats warned that acceptance of gays and lesbians would destroy morale and seriously weaken the armed forces. Clinton finally settled for the Pentagon's compromise "Don't ask, don't tell" policy that would permit homosexuals to continue serving in the military as long as they did not reveal their sexual preference and refrained from homosexual conduct.

Public attitudes toward gays and lesbians seemed to be changing in the 1990s, but growing tolerance was limited. In a 1996 poll, 85 percent of those questioned believed that gays should be treated equally in the workplace. Violence against gays, however, continued, spurring calls for hate-crime legislation.

The issue of same-sex marriage came to a head at the end of the century. In 1996, President Clinton signed the Defense of Marriage Act, which decreed that states did not have to recognize same-sex marriages performed elsewhere. But in 2000, following a state supreme court ruling, the Vermont legislature legalized civil unions between individuals of the same sex. Whether sanctioned by law or not, the number of gay and lesbian households steadily increased; the 2000 census revealed that there were nearly 600,000 homes in America headed by same-sex couples.

The AIDS Epidemic

AIDS Acquired immune deficiency syndrome (AIDS) is a disease of the immune system transmitted through blood especially by sexual contact or contaminated needles. AIDS reached epidemic proportions in the United States in the 1980s before it was gradually contained in the 1990s.

The outbreak of **AIDS** (acquired immune deficiency syndrome) in the early 1980s took most Americans by surprise. Even health experts had difficulty grasping the nature and extent of the new public health threat. The Centers for Disease Control noted the phenomenon in a June 1981 bulletin, but it was several years before researchers finally identified it as a hitherto unknown human immunodeficiency virus (HIV). HIV apparently originated in Central Africa and spread to the United States, where it found its first victims primarily among gay men.

Initially, AIDS was perceived as a threat only to gay men. With a growing sense of urgency as the death toll mounted, gay men began to practice safer sex, using condoms and confining themselves to trusted partners. AIDS soon began to appear among intravenous (IV) drug users who shared the same needles and eventually among hemophiliacs and others receiving frequent blood transfusions. The threat of the spread of AIDS to heterosexuals through the nation's blood supply terrified middle-class America.

Scientists tried to reassure the public by explaining that the virus could be spread only by the exchange of blood and semen and not by casual contact. The death of Hollywood movie star Rock Hudson from AIDS in the summer of 1985, however, intensified the sense of national panic. Controversy soon developed over proposals for mandatory blood tests for suspected HIV carriers and for the quarantine of AIDS victims. The integrity of hospital blood supplies caused the most realistic concern. In 1985, a new test finally gave reassurance that transfusions could be performed safely.

The Reagan administration proved slow and halting in its approach to the AIDS epidemic. The lack of sympathy for gays and a need to reduce the deficit worked against any large increase in health spending to educate the public. The only real leadership came from Surgeon General C. Everett Koop, who surprised his conservative backers in 1986 by coming out boldly with proposals for sex education, the use of condoms to ensure "safer sex," and confidential blood testing to help contain the disease.

While the administration dallied, the grim toll mounted. Because the average time between the initial HIV infection and the first symptoms of AIDS was five years and the delay could be as long as fourteen years, efforts at prevention had little immediate impact. In November 1983, there were 2803 known cases and 1416 deaths; by the time Rock Hudson died from complications of HIV/AIDS in mid-1985, more than 12,000 cases and more than 6000 deaths had been reported.

Growing public concern finally led to action. In 1987, Reagan appointed a special presidential commission headed by Admiral James Watkins, a former chief of naval operations, to study the AIDS epidemic. The Watkins report in 1988 criticized the administration's AIDS efforts as "inconsistent" and recommended a new effort that included antidiscrimination legislation and explicit prevention education.

Despite new efforts, the epidemic continued to grow. In 1987, there were 50,000 cases. By mid-1989, the count had reached 100,000. The U.S. Centers for Disease Control in Atlanta reported more than 200,000 cases at the end of 1991. The total had increased to more than 500,000 by mid-1996. By then, 345,000 AIDS victims had died, making it the leading cause of death for Americans aged 25 to 44.

The number of those infected with HIV appeared to be stabilizing by the mid-1990s. Yet what was once known as the "gay disease" had spread far beyond that one group in society by the end of the century. Minorities and the young were at greatest risk. African American youths made up two-thirds of the new HIV cases among people under 25.

The most encouraging development was a fall-off in the death rate from AIDS that began in the mid-1990s. Health officials attributed the decline to heavier spending on treatment and prevention and, above all, to powerful new drug combinations. By 2001, however, the drop in new cases and deaths from AIDS began to level off. There was a particularly alarming increase in the number of new cases among young gay men who apparently believed that the new treatment had made the disease manageable. Unfortunately, the so-called AIDS cocktail was very expensive, and did not work for everyone. The growing realization that AIDS was threatening to decimate the population of Third World countries, especially sub-Sahara Africa, was even more disturbing.

A Look at the Past

AIDS Brochure

In response to the rapid spread of AIDS in the 1980s and the growing public concern about the new and deadly disease, Surgeon General C. Everett Koop wrote an eight-page brochure titled *Understanding AIDS* that was mailed out by the Public Health Service in 1988 to all 107 million U.S. households. It was the largest public health mailing ever done. Shown here is the first page of the booklet with a message from the surgeon general. Note the availability of a Spanish version of the publication. ✱ Why do you think the government sponsored a mass mailing on AIDS? According to this brochure, what is one chief weapon in stopping the AIDS epidemic? Why do you suppose that many people found the mailing controversial? Do you think it would still be considered controversial if it were mailed today?

POLITICS AND DIPLOMACY AFTER WATERGATE

The economic and social disruptions of the era contributed to problems of governance left over from Watergate. Even as many Americans worried about shrinking paychecks and disintegrating families, Congress increasingly challenged the prerogatives of the presidency. This made life in the White House difficult for Richard Nixon's immediate successors—and it made solving America's pressing problems nearly impossible.

The Ford Administration

Gerald R. Ford had the distinction of being the first president who had not been elected to national office. Ford, an amiable and unpretentious Michigan congressman who had risen to the post of House minority leader, seemed ready to restore public confidence in the presidency when he replaced Nixon in August 1974.

Ford's honeymoon lasted only a month. On September 8, 1974, he shocked the nation by announcing he had granted Richard Nixon a full and unconditional pardon for all federal crimes he may have committed. Ford apparently acted in an effort to end the bitterness over Watergate, but his attempt backfired, eroding public confidence in his leadership and linking him indelibly with the scandal.

Ford soon found himself fighting an equally difficult battle on behalf of the beleaguered CIA. The Watergate scandal and the Vietnam fiasco had challenged citizens' faith in their government and lent credibility to a startling series of disclosures about past covert actions. The president allowed the CIA to confirm some of the charges. He then made things worse by blurting out to the press the juiciest item of all: The CIA had been involved in plots to assassinate foreign leaders.

Senate and House select committees appointed to investigate the CIA now focused on the assassination issue, eventually charging that the agency had been involved in no less than eight separate attempts to kill Fidel Castro. Some worried that the revelations would damage the reputations of Democratic Presidents Kennedy and Johnson and so tried to put all the blame on the CIA.

In late 1975, President Ford finally moved to limit the damage to the CIA. He appointed George H. W. Bush, then a respected former Republican congressman, as the agency's new director and gave him the authority both to reform the CIA and to strengthen its role in shaping national security policy. Most notably, Ford issued an executive order outlawing assassination as an instrument of American foreign policy. To prevent future abuses, Congress created permanent House and Senate intelligence committees to exercise general oversight for covert CIA operations.

Ford proved less successful in his dealings with Congress on other issues. Although he prided himself on his good relations with members of both houses, he opposed Democratic measures such as federal aid to education and control over strip mining. In a little more than a year, he vetoed thirty-nine separate bills. Ford proved far more conservative than Nixon in the White House.

Carter and American Malaise

Ford's lackluster record and the legacy of Watergate made the Democratic nomination a prize worth fighting for in 1976. A large field of candidates entered the contest, but a virtual unknown, former Georgia governor James Earl Carter, quickly became the front-runner. Aware of the voters' disgust with politicians of both parties, Jimmy Carter ran as an outsider, portraying himself as a Southerner who had no experience in Washington and one who could thus give the nation fresh and untainted leadership.

Voters took Carter at his word, and elected him over Ford in a close contest. Unfortunately, Carter's outsider status, while attractive in a campaign, made governing as president difficult. He had no discernible political philosophy, no clear sense of direction. He called himself a populist, but that label meant little more than an appeal to the common man, a somewhat ironic appeal, given Carter's personal wealth.

Lacking both a clear set of priorities and a coherent political philosophy, the Carter administration had little chance to succeed. The president strove hard for a balanced budget but was forced to accept mounting deficits. Federal agencies fought to save the environment and help consumers but served only to anger industry.

In the crucial area of social services, Joseph Califano, secretary of Health, Education, and Welfare (HEW), failed repeatedly in efforts to carry out long-overdue reforms. His attempts to overhaul the nation's welfare program, which had become a $30 billion annual operation serving some thirty million Americans, won little support from the White House. Carter's unwillingness to take the political risks involved in revamping the overburdened Social Security system by reducing benefits and raising the retirement age blocked Califano's efforts. The HEW secretary finally gave up his attempt to draw up a workable national health insurance plan.

Informed by his pollsters in 1979 that he was losing the nation's confidence, Carter sought desperately to redeem himself. After a series of meetings at Camp David with a wide variety of advisers, he gave a speech in which he seemed to blame his failure on the American people. Then he requested the resignation of Califano and the secretary of the treasury. But neither the attempt to pin responsibility on the American people nor the firing of cabinet members could hide the fact that Carter, despite his good intentions and hard work, had failed to provide the bold leadership the nation needed.

Troubles Abroad

In the aftermath of the Vietnam War, most Americans wanted to have little to do with the world. Military intervention had failed in Southeast Asia. With the American economy in trouble, the country's economic leverage appeared minimal. Moreover, the point of détente was to diminish the need for American intervention abroad by directing the superpower contest with the Soviet Union into political channels.

Yet various groups in the Third World had not gotten the message of détente. Central America, for example, witnessed numerous uprisings against entrenched authoritarian regimes. In mid-1979, dictator Anastasio Somoza capitulated to the Sandinista forces in Nicaragua. Despite American attempts to moderate the Sandinista revolution, the new regime moved steadily to the left, developing close ties with Castro's Cuba. Unable to find a workable alternative between the extremes of reactionary dictatorship and radical revolution in Central America, Carter tried to use American economic aid to encourage democratic reforms. But after guerrillas in El Salvador launched a major offensive in January 1981, he authorized large-scale military assistance to the government for its war against the insurgents, setting a precedent for the future.

Carter initially had better luck in the Middle East. In 1978, he invited Egyptian president Anwar Sadat and Israeli prime minister Menachem Begin to negotiate a peace treaty under his guidance at Camp David, eventually called the **Camp David accords.** As a framework for negotiations, the Camp David accords paved the way for a 1979 treaty between these principal antagonists in the Arab-Israeli conflict. The treaty provided for the gradual return of the Sinai to Egypt but left the fate of the Palestinians, the Arab inhabitants of the West Bank and the Gaza Strip, unsettled.

Any sense of progress in the Middle East was quickly offset in 1979 with the outbreak of the Iranian Revolution. Under Nixon and Kissinger, the United States had come to depend heavily on the Iranian shah

Camp David Accords In 1978, President Carter mediated a peace agreement between the leaders of Egypt and Israel at Camp David, a presidential retreat near Washington, D.C. The next year, Israel and Egypt signed a peace treaty based on the Camp David Accords.

■ *A highlight of Carter's presidency was his role in helping negotiate the Camp David accords between Egyptian President Anwar Sadat (left) and Israeli Prime Minister Menachem Begin (right). The agreements set the stage for a peace treaty between Israel and Egypt.* ■

for defense of the vital Persian Gulf. By 1978, Iran was in chaos as the exiled Ayatollah Ruholla Khomeini led a fundamentalist Muslim revolt against the shah, who was forced to flee the country.

In October 1979, Carter permitted the shah to enter the United States for medical treatment. Irate mobs in Iran denounced the United States. On November 4, militants seized the U.S. embassy in Teheran and took fifty-three Americans prisoner. The prolonged **Iranian hostage crisis** revealed the extent to which American power had declined in the 1970s. Carter relied first on diplomacy and economic reprisals in a vain attempt to free the hostages. In April 1980, the president authorized a desperate rescue mission that ended in failure when several helicopters broke down in the Iranian desert and an accident cost the lives of eight crewmen. The hostage crisis dragged on and proved to be a powerful political handicap to Carter in the election.

Iranian hostage crisis In 1979, Iranian fundamentalists seized the American embassy in Teheran and held fifty-three American diplomats hostages for over a year. The Iranian hostage crisis weakened the Carter presidency; the hostages were finally released on January 20, 1981, the day Ronald Reagan became president.

The Collapse of Détente

The policy of détente was already in trouble when Carter took office in 1977. Congressional refusal to relax trade restrictions on the Soviet Union had doomed Kissinger's attempts to win political concessions from the Soviets through economic incentives. The Kremlin's repression of the growing dissident movement and its harsh policy restricting the emigration of Soviet Jews had caused many Americans to doubt the wisdom of seeking accommodation with the Soviet Union.

President Carter's emphasis on human rights appeared to the Russians a direct repudiation of détente. Carter withheld aid from authoritarian governments in Chile and Argentina, but equally repressive regimes in South Korea and the Philippines continued to receive generous American support. The Soviets, however, found even an inconsistent human rights policy threatening, particularly after Carter received Soviet exiles in the White House.

Secretary of State Cyrus Vance concentrated on continuing the main pillar of détente, the Strategic Arms Limitation Talks (SALT). In 1974, President Ford and Brezhnev reached tentative agreement on the outline of SALT II. The chief provision was for a ceiling of 2400 nuclear launchers by each side. In March 1977, Vance went to Moscow to propose a drastic reduction in this level. The Soviets, already angry over human rights, rejected the American proposal as an attempt to overcome the Soviet lead in land-based ICBMs.

Zbigniew Brzezinski, Carter's national security adviser, worked from the outset to reverse the policy of détente. He favored confrontation with the Kremlin. Although Carter signed a SALT II treaty with Russia in 1979, growing opposition in the Senate played directly into Brzezinski's hands. He prevailed on the president to advocate adoption of a new MX missile to replace the existing Minuteman ICBMs. This new weapons system ensured that, regardless of SALT, the nuclear arms race would be speeded up in the 1980s.

Brzezinski also was successful in persuading the president to use China to outmaneuver the Soviets. On January 1, 1979, the United States and China exchanged ambassadors, thereby completing the reconciliation that Nixon had begun in 1971. The new relationship between Beijing and Washington presented the Soviet Union with the problem of a link between its two most powerful enemies.

The Cold War, in abeyance for nearly a decade, resumed with full fury in December 1979 when the Soviet Union invaded Afghanistan. Although this move was designed to ensure a regime friendly to the Soviet Union, it appeared to many the beginning of a Soviet thrust toward the Indian Ocean and the Persian Gulf. Carter responded to this aggression by declaring a Carter doctrine that threatened armed opposition to any further Soviet advance toward the Gulf. The president banned the sale of high technology to Russia, embargoed the export of grain, resumed draft registration, and even boycotted the 1980 Moscow Olympics.

The Soviet action and the American reaction doomed détente. Aware that he could not get a two-thirds vote in the Senate, Carter withdrew the SALT II treaty. The hopeful phrases of détente gave way to belligerent rhetoric as groups such as the Committee on the Present Danger called for an all-out effort against the Soviet Union. Jimmy Carter, who had come into office hoping to advance human rights and control the nuclear arms race, now found himself a victim of a renewed Cold War.

THE REAGAN REVOLUTION

After the turmoil of the 1960s, the economic and political troubles of the 1970s made Americans' turn to conservatism almost inevitable. The Watergate scandal won the Democrats a brief reprieve, but when the Republicans discovered an attractive candidate in Ronald Reagan, a decisive Republican victory was essentially assured.

The Election of 1980

In 1980, Jimmy Carter found himself in serious trouble. Inflation, touched off by the second oil shock of the 1970s, reached double-digit figures. The Federal Reserve Board's effort to tighten the money supply had led to a recession, with unemployment climbing to nearly 8 percent. The combined rate of inflation and unemployment hit 28 percent early in 1980 and stayed above 20 percent throughout the year.

Foreign policy proved almost as damaging to Carter. The Soviet invasion of Afghanistan had exploded hopes for continued détente and made Carter appear naive. The continuing hostage crisis in Iran underlined the administration's helplessness.

Ronald Reagan and his running mate, George H. W. Bush, hammered away at the state of the economy and the world. Reagan scored heavily among traditionally Democratic blue-collar groups by blaming Carter for inflation. He also accused Carter of allowing the Soviets to outstrip the United States militarily and promised a massive buildup of American forces if he was elected.

The president fought back by claiming that Reagan was too reckless to conduct American foreign policy in the nuclear age. Reagan deflected the charge and summarized the case against the administration by putting a simple question to voters: "Are you better off now than you were four years ago?"

Voters answered with a resounding "no." Reagan carried forty-four states and gained 51 percent of the popular vote. Carter won only six states and 41 percent of the popular vote. Reagan clearly benefited from the growing political power of the Sunbelt; he carried every state west of the Mississippi except Minnesota, the home state of Carter's running mate, Walter Mondale. In the South, Reagan lost only Georgia, Carter's home state. Even more impressive were Reagan's inroads into the old New Deal coalition. He received 50.5 percent of the blue-collar vote and 46 percent of the Jewish vote, the best showing by a Republican since 1928. Only one group remained loyal to Carter: African American voters gave him 85 percent of their ballots.

Republican gains in Congress were even more surprising. For the first time since 1954, the GOP gained control of the Senate. The party also picked up seats in the House to narrow the Democratic margin. Though the full implications of the 1980 election remained to be seen, the outcome suggested that the Democratic coalition that had dominated American politics since the days of Franklin Roosevelt was falling apart.

Cutting Taxes and Spending

When Ronald Reagan took office in January 1981, the ravages of inflation had devastated the economy. The new president blamed federal spending and excessive

supply-side economics
Advocates of supply-side economics claimed that tax cuts would stimulate the economy by giving individuals a greater incentive to earn more money, which would lead to greater investment and eventually larger tax revenues at a lower rate. Critics replied that supply-side economics would only burden the economy with larger government deficits.

taxation for the mess. "Government is not the solution to our problems," Reagan announced in his inaugural address. "Government is the problem."

The president embraced the concept of **supply-side economics** as the remedy for the nation's economic ills. Supply-side economists believed that the private sector, if encouraged by tax cuts, would shift its resources from tax shelters to productive investment, leading to an economic boom that would provide enough new income to offset the lost revenue. Although many economists worried that the 30 percent cut in income taxes that Reagan favored would lead to large deficits, the president was confident that his program would both stimulate the economy and reduce the role of government.

The president made federal spending his first target. Quickly deciding not to attack such popular middle-class entitlement programs as Social Security and Medicare, Republicans concentrated on slashing $41 billion from the budget by cutting heavily into other social services such as food stamps and by reducing public service jobs, student loans, and support for urban mass transit. Reagan used his charm and powers of persuasion to woo conservative Democrats. Appearing before a joint session of Congress only weeks after an attempt on his life, Reagan won a commanding victory for his budget.

The president proved equally successful in trimming taxes. Reagan's proposal, amended to satisfy Democrats, was to cut taxes by 5 percent for the first year with full 10 percent reductions for the second and third years. In July, both houses passed the tax cut by impressive margins.

In securing reductions in spending and lowering taxes, Reagan demonstrated beyond doubt his ability to wield presidential power effectively.

Unleashing the Private Sector

deregulation Process of cutting back on the scope of federal agencies and relying instead on the free market to keep prices of consumer goods and services low and quality high. Ronald Reagan continued the deregulation process begun by Jimmy Carter.

Reagan met with only mixed success in his other efforts to restrict government activity and reduce federal regulation of the economy. To achieve his goal of **deregulation** he appointed men and women who shared his belief in relying on the marketplace rather than the bureaucracy to direct the nation's economy. To the outrage of environmentalists, Secretary of the Interior James Watt opened up federal land to coal and timber production, halted the growth of national parkland, and made more than a billion acres available for offshore oil drilling. The administration continued its policy of reducing government intervention in business long after Watt was forced to resign.

Transportation Secretary Drew Lewis proved to be the most effective cabinet member in the administration's first two years. He helped relieve the troubled American automobile industry of many of the regulations adopted in the 1970s to reduce air pollution and increase passenger safety. He also played a key role in negotiations with Japan to restrict its automobile exports to the United States through 1984. This action enabled the Reagan administration to help Detroit's carmakers without openly violating its free market position.

Lewis gained notoriety in opposing a strike by the air traffic controllers' union (PATCO) in the summer of 1981. The president fired the striking workers, decertified the union, and ordered Lewis to hire and train thousands of new air traffic controllers. For the Reagan administration, it was worth paying to prove that no group of government employees had the right to defy the public interest.

The Reagan administration was less successful in trying to cut back on the entitlement programs that it viewed as the primary cause of growing budget deficits. Social Security was the greatest offender. A 500 percent increase in Social Security benefits in the 1970s threatened to bankrupt the system's trust fund by the end of the century. Reagan met a sharp rebuff when he tried to make substantial cuts in future benefits. He then appointed a bipartisan commission to recommend ways to protect the system. In March 1983, Congress approved a series of changes that guaranteed the solvency of Social Security by gradually raising the retirement age, delaying cost-of-living increases for six months, and taxing pensions paid to the well-to-do elderly.

The administration's record in dealing with women's concerns and civil rights proved clumsy and divisive. Although feminist groups were disappointed by the administration's strong rhetorical attacks on legalized abortion, the appointment of Sandra Day O'Connor to the Supreme Court pleased them. By this one shrewd move, Reagan was able both to fulfill a campaign pledge and to make a symbolic gesture to women. His appointments to the lower federal courts were a better indication of his administration's relatively low regard for women and African Americans.

Aware of how few African Americans had supported the GOP in 1980, Reagan made no effort to reward this group with government jobs or favors. Instead, the Justice Department actively opposed busing to achieve school integration and affirmative action measures that resulted in minority hiring quotas.

■ *Chief Justice Warren Burger swears in Sandra Day O'Connor, the first woman to serve on the U.S. Supreme Court, in September 1981. In 2005, she retired after 24 years on the bench.* ■

REAGAN AND THE WORLD

Reagan believed that under Carter, American prestige and standing in the world had dropped to an all-time low. Intent on restoring traditional American pride and influence, Reagan devoted himself to strengthening America's defenses and recapturing world supremacy from the Soviet Union.

Challenging the "Evil Empire"

The president scored his first foreign policy victory on the day he took office, thanks to diplomatic efforts begun under Carter. On January 20, 1981, Iran released the fifty-three Americans held hostage and thus enabled Reagan to begin his presidency on a positive note.

He built upon this accomplishment by embarking on a major military expansion. Here again he continued efforts begun by Carter, who after the Soviet invasion of Afghanistan had persuaded Congress to fund a 5 percent increase in defense spending. The Reagan expansion went far beyond Carter's, proposing to double defense spending. The emphasis was on new weapons, ranging from the B-1 bomber and the controversial MX nuclear missile to the expansion of the navy. Despite some opposition in Congress, Reagan's staff got most of what they wanted, and by 1985 the defense budget grew to more than $300 billion.

The justification for all the new weapons was Reagan's belief that the Soviet Union was a deadly enemy that threatened the well-being and security of the United States. Reagan saw the Russians as bent on world revolution. Citing what he called a "record of tyranny," Reagan denounced the Russians before the UN in 1982.

Given this view of the USSR as "the focus of evil in the modern world," it is not surprising that the new president continued Carter's hard line. Despite strong protests from the Soviet Union, as well as growing uneasiness in Europe and an increasingly vocal nuclear freeze movement at home, the United States began putting new missiles in bases in Great Britain and Germany in November 1983. The Soviets responded by breaking off disarmament negotiations in Geneva.

The nuclear arms race had now reached a more dangerous level than ever before. The United States stepped up research and development of the **Strategic Defense Initiative (SDI),** an antimissile system based on the use of lasers and

Strategic Defense Initiative (SDI) Popularly known as "Star Wars," President Reagan's Strategic Defense Initiative (SDI) proposed the construction of an elaborate computer-controlled, antimissile defense system capable of destroying enemy missiles in outer space. Critics claimed SDI could never be perfected.

particle beams to destroy incoming missiles in outer space. SDI was quickly dubbed "Star Wars" by the media. Critics believed that SDI, if perfected, would merely escalate the arms race. The Reagan administration, however, defended SDI as a legitimate attempt to free the United States from the deadly trap of deterrence. Meanwhile, the Soviet Union kept deploying larger and more accurate land-based ICBMs. Although both sides continued to observe the unratified SALT II agreements, the fact remained that between them the two superpowers had nearly fifty thousand warheads in their nuclear arsenals.

Confrontation in Central America

Reagan perceived the Soviet challenge as extending across the globe. In Central America, with a small landowning elite and masses of peasants mired in poverty, the United States had traditionally looked for moderate middle-class regimes to support. But these were hard to find, and Washington often ended up backing repressive right-wing dictatorships rather than the leftist groups that raised the radical issues of land reform and redistribution of wealth. Yet it was often oppression by U.S.-supported regimes that drove those seeking political change to embrace revolutionary tactics.

This was precisely what happened in Nicaragua, where the leftist Sandinista coalition finally succeeded in overthrowing the authoritarian Somoza regime in 1979. The Reagan administration quickly reversed Carter's policy of economic aid to the Sandinista government. Secretary of State Alexander Haig cut off aid to Nicaragua in the spring of 1981, accusing the Sandinistas of driving out the moderates, welcoming Cuban advisers and Soviet military assistance, and serving as a supply base for leftist guerrillas in nearby El Salvador. The criticism became a self-fulfilling prophecy as Nicaragua became even more dependent on Cuba and the Soviet Union.

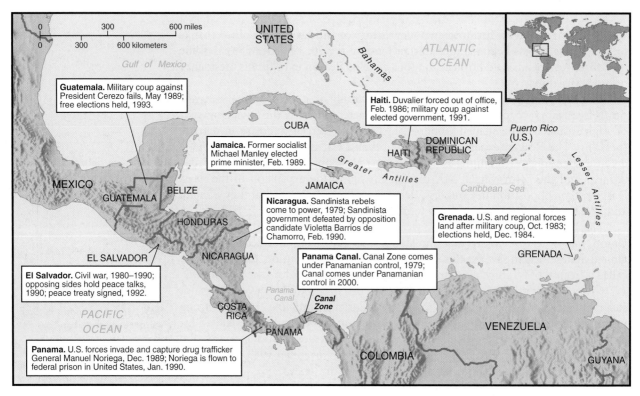

TROUBLE SPOTS IN CENTRAL AMERICA AND THE CARIBBEAN *U.S. involvement in Central American trouble spots intensified in the 1980s and early 1990s.* ∎

The United States and Nicaragua were soon on a collision course. In April 1983, Reagan asked Congress for the money and authority to oust the Sandinistas. When Congress refused, Reagan opted for covert action. The CIA began supplying the Contras, exiles fighting against the Sandinistas from bases in Honduras and Costa Rica. The U.S.-backed rebels tried to disrupt the Nicaraguan economy, raiding villages, blowing up oil tanks, and even mining harbors. Then, in 1984, Congress passed the Boland Amendment prohibiting any U.S. agency from spending money in Central America. This left the Contras in a precarious position.

More Trouble in the Middle East

Reagan tried to continue Carter's basic policy in the turbulent Middle East. In April 1982, the Israelis honored a Camp David pledge by making their final withdrawal from the Sinai. Reagan hoped to achieve the other Camp David objective of providing a homeland for the Palestinian Arabs on the West Bank, but Israel instead continued to extend Jewish settlements into the disputed area. The threat of raids by the Palestine Liberation Organization (PLO) seemed the major obstacle to progress.

On June 6, 1982, with tacit American encouragement, Israel invaded southern Lebanon in order to secure its northern border and destroy the PLO. The Reagan administration made no effort to halt the offensive but did join with France and Italy in sending a multinational force to permit the PLO to evacuate to Tunisia. Unfortunately, the United States soon became enmeshed in the Lebanese civil war, which had been raging since 1975. American marines, sent to Lebanon as part of the multinational force to restore order, were caught up in the renewed hostilities between Muslim and Christian militia. The Muslims perceived the marines as aiding the Christian-dominated government of Lebanon instead of acting as neutral peacekeepers, and they began firing on the vulnerable American troops.

In the face of growing congressional demands for the withdrawal of the marines, Reagan declared they were there to protect Lebanon from the designs of Soviet-backed Syria. But finally, after terrorists drove a truck loaded with explosives into the American barracks, killing 241 marines, the president saw no choice but to pull out. Despite his good intentions, Reagan had experienced a humiliation similar

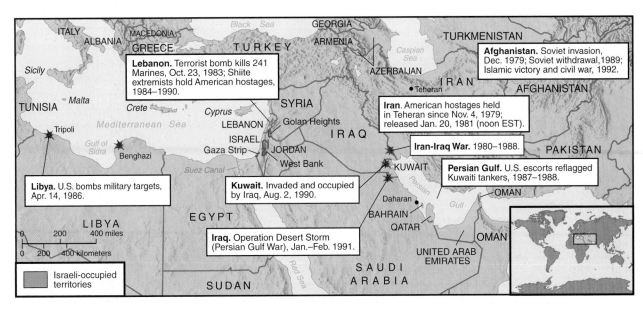

TROUBLE SPOTS IN THE MIDDLE EAST   *Armed conflict and territorial attacks in this region intensified in the 1980s and early 1990s.* ■

to Carter's in Iran—one that left Lebanon in shambles and the Arab-Israeli situation worse than ever.

Trading Arms for Hostages

Reagan's Middle Eastern troubles didn't prevent his easy re-election in 1984. Voters gave him credit for curbing inflation, reviving the economy, and challenging communism; compared to these major achievements, the miscue in Lebanon appeared minor. Democratic candidate Walter Mondale, formerly Jimmy Carter's vice president, provided a jolt to the campaign by choosing Representative Geraldine Ferraro of New York as his running mate. But even the presence of the first woman on the national ticket of a major American party couldn't deny Reagan's enormous popularity. He swept to victory with 59 percent of the popular vote and carried every state except Mondale's home, Minnesota.

Yet the troubles abroad persisted. Not long after Reagan's second inauguration, his administration's policies in the Middle East and Central America reached a tragic convergence in the **Iran-Contra affair.** In mid-1985, Robert McFarlane, who had become national security adviser a year earlier, began a new initiative designed to restore American influence in the troubled Middle East. Concerned over the fate of six Americans held hostage in Lebanon by groups thought to be loyal to Iran's Ayatollah Khomeini, McFarlane proposed trading American antitank missiles to Iran in return for the hostages' release. The Iranians, desperate for weapons in the war they had been waging against Iraq since 1980, seemed willing to comply.

McFarlane soon found himself in over his head. He relied heavily on a young marine lieutenant colonel assigned to the National Security Council (NSC), Oliver North. North in turn sought the assistance of CIA director William Casey, who interpreted the Iran initiative as an opportunity to use the NSC to mount the kind of covert operation denied the CIA under the post-1975 congressional oversight policy. By early 1986, Casey was able to persuade the president to go ahead with weapons shipments to Iran.

The arms deal with Iran was bad policy, but what came next was criminal. Ever since the Boland Amendment in late 1984 had cut off congressional funding, the Reagan administration had been searching for ways to supply the Contras in Nicaragua. Oliver North was put in charge of soliciting donations from wealthy right-wing Americans. In early 1986, he began using profits from the sale of weapons to Iran to finance the Contras. North's ploy was both illegal and unconstitutional, since it meant usurping the congressional power of the purse.

Ultimately the secret got out. Administration officials tried to shield Reagan from blame, and even after a congressional investigation it was unclear whether the president had approved the Contra diversion. Reagan's reputation survived the scandal, albeit tarnished. Several of his subordinates, including North, were prosecuted.

Reagan the Peacemaker

Americans' tolerance of Reagan's mistakes in the Iran-Contra affair resulted in part from the progress he was making on the larger issue of U.S.-Soviet relations. Elected as an anticommunist hardliner, Reagan softened during his second term to become an advocate of cooperation with Moscow.

A momentous change in leadership in the Soviet Union had much to do with the change in Reagan's approach. The illness and death of Leonid Brezhnev in 1982, followed in rapid succession by the deaths of his aged successors, Yuri Andropov and Konstantin Chernenko, led finally to the selection of Mikhail Gorbachev, a

Iran-Contra affair The Iran-Contra affair involved officials high in the Reagan administration secretly selling arms to Iran and using the proceeds to finance the Contra rebels in Nicaragua. This illegal transaction usurped the congressional power of the purse.

Chronology

1969	Stonewall riots in New York's Greenwich Village spark gay rights movement (June) ■ American astronauts land on the moon (July)
1970	U.S. forces invade Cambodia (April) ■ Ohio National Guardsmen kill four students at Kent State University (May)
1971	States ratify Twenty-sixth Amendment to the Constitution, giving 18-year-olds the right to vote (July) ■ President Nixon freezes wages and prices for ninety days (August)
1972	President Nixon visits China (February) ■ U.S. and USSR sign SALT I accords in Moscow (May) ■ White House "plumbers" unit breaks into Democratic headquarters in Watergate complex (June) ■ Richard Nixon wins re-election in landslide victory over George McGovern (November)
1973	United States and North Vietnam sign truce (January) ■ Arab oil embargo creates energy crisis in the United States (October)
1974	Supreme Court orders Nixon to surrender White House tapes (June) ■ Richard M. Nixon resigns presidency (August)
1975	Last evacuation helicopter leaves roof of U.S. embassy in Saigon, South Vietnam (April)
1976	Nation celebrates bicentennial with fireworks, patriotic music, and parade of sailing ships (July) ■ Jimmy Carter defeats Gerald Ford in presidential election (November)
1977	President Carter signs Panama Canal treaties restoring sovereignty to Panama (September) ■ Sales of imported cars, mainly from Japan, surpass two million a year for first time
1978	President Carter signs law raising mandatory retirement age from 65 to 70 (April) ■ Over nine hundred followers of Reverend Jim Jones die in a mass suicide in Guyana (November)
1979	Iranian militants take fifty-three Americans hostage in U.S. embassy in Teheran (November) ■ Soviet invasion of Afghanistan leads to U.S. withdrawal from 1980 Moscow Olympics (December) ■ Congress approves loan of $1.5 billion to rescue the ailing Chrysler Corporation (December)
1980	Ronald Reagan wins presidency in landslide
1981	American hostages in Iran released after 444 days in captivity (January) ■ Sandra Day O'Connor becomes first woman U.S. Supreme Court justice (September)
1982	Equal Rights Amendment fails state ratification (June) ■ Unemployment reaches postwar record high of 10.4 percent (October)
1983	Soviets shoot down Korean airliner (September) ■ U.S. invades Grenada (October)
1984	Russia boycotts summer Olympics in Los Angeles (July) ■ Ronald Reagan re-elected president (November)
1985	Mikhail Gorbachev becomes leader of the Soviet Union (March)
1986	Space shuttle *Challenger* explodes, killing seven astronauts (January) ■ Iran-Contra affair made public (November)
1987	Reagan and Gorbachev sign INF treaty at Washington summit
1988	George H. W. Bush defeats Michael Dukakis decisively in presidential election

■ *Reagan and Gorbachev in Red Square. During the summits between the two leaders, the American public grew to admire the Soviet premier for his policies of* perestroika *(restructuring) and* glasnost *(openness).* ■

Intermediate Nuclear Forces agreement Signed by President Reagan and Soviet President Gorbachev in Washington in late 1987, this agreement provided for the destruction of all intermediate-range nuclear missiles and permitted on-site inspection for the first time during the Cold War.

younger and more dynamic Soviet leader. Gorbachev was intent on improving relations with the United States as part of his new policy of *perestroika* (restructuring the Soviet economy) and *glasnost* (political openness). Soviet economic performance had been deteriorating steadily, and the war in Afghanistan had become a major liability. Gorbachev needed a breathing spell in the arms race and a reduction in Cold War tensions in order to carry out his sweeping changes at home.

A series of summit meetings between Reagan and Gorbachev broke the chill in superpower relations and led in December 1987 to an **Intermediate Nuclear Forces Treaty,** by which Reagan and Gorbachev agreed to remove and destroy all intermediate-range missiles in Europe. The most important arms control agreement since SALT I of 1972, the INF treaty raised hopes that an end to the Cold War was finally in sight.

During the president's last year in office, the Soviets cooperated with the United States in pressuring Iran and Iraq to end their long war. Most significant of all, Gorbachev moved to end the war in Afghanistan. By the time Reagan left office in January 1989, he had scored a series of foreign policy triumphs that offset the Iran-Contra fiasco and thus helped redeem his presidency.

CONCLUSION: CHALLENGING THE NEW DEAL

Though trouble dogged the final years of his presidency, the overall effect of Reagan's two terms was to reshape the landscape of American politics. The Democratic coalition forged by Franklin Roosevelt during the New Deal finally broke down as the Republicans captured the South and made deep inroads into organized labor.

More significantly, Reagan challenged the liberal premises of the New Deal by asserting that the private sector, rather than the federal government, ought to be the source of remedies to most of America's ills. Reagan prudently left intact the centerpieces of the welfare state—Social Security and Medicare—but he trimmed other programs and made any comparable expansion of federal authority nearly impossible. By the time he left office, small-government conservatism seemed the undeniable wave of the American future.

KEY TERMS

RECOMMENDED READING

The most comprehensive account of Nixon's political career and presidency is the three-volume biography by Stephen E. Ambrose, *Nixon* (1987–1992). Melvin Small offers a balanced assessment of Nixon's White House years in *The Presidency of Richard Nixon* (1999); for a more detailed view, see Richard Reeves, *President Nixon* (2001). Stanley Kutler provides a thorough account of the scandal that drove Nixon from office in *The Wars of Watergate* (1990).

H. W. Brands surveys American foreign policy from the mid-1970s through the mid-1990s in *Since Vietnam* (1995). For foreign policy under Nixon, see William P. Bundy, *A Tangled Web* (1998), and Jeffrey Kimball, *Nixon's Vietnam War* (1998). Raymond L. Garthoff, *Détente and Confrontation* (1985) covers relations with the Soviet Union in the 1970s. The best study of Henry Kissinger's diplomacy is Jussi Hanhimaki, *The Flawed Architect* (2004). James Bamford, *Body of Secrets* (2001), deals with the highly secretive National Security Agency.

In *The Prize* (1991), Daniel Yergin puts the energy crisis of the 1970s in historical perspective. Richard Barnet gives a thorough description of the impact of the energy crisis and foreign competition on the American economy in the 1970s in *The Lean Years* (1980). For economic policy under Carter, see W. Carl Biven, *Jimmy Carter's Economy* (2002).

Two books survey popular culture in the 1970s: David Frum, *How We Got Here: The 70's* (2000) and Bruce J. Schulman, *The Seventies* (2001).

For the Ford and Carter administrations, see John R. Greene, *The Presidency of Gerald R. Ford* (1995), and Burton I. Kaufman, *The Presidency of Jimmy Carter* (1993). Gaddis Smith surveys Carter's foreign policy in *Morality, Reason, and Power* (1985). For the crisis with Iran, see Barry Rubin, *Paved with Good Intentions* (1980).

On the rise of Ronald Reagan, see Lou Cannon, *Governor Reagan* (2003). The most insightful account of the Reagan presidency is Richard Reeves, *President Reagan* (2005).

SUGGESTED WEB SITES

May 4 Collection Home Page

speccoll.library.kent.edu/4may70/

This site commemorates the May 4, 1970, shootings at Kent State University with a detailed chronology and other historical information.

Documents from the Women's Liberation Movement

scriptorium.lib.duke.edu/wlm/

Primary documents on-line from the Special Collections Library at Duke University provide firsthand information about the women's liberation movement.

Stonewall and Beyond: Lesbian and Gay Culture

www.columbia.edu/cu/lweb/eresources/exhibitions/sw25/

On-line edition of a Columbia University Library exhibition commemorating the twenty-fifth anniversary of the Stonewall riots.

Constitutional Issues: Watergate and the Constitution

www.archives.gov/education/lessons/Watergate-constitution/

From the National Archives' teaching materials, this site has a good chronology of Watergate and a 1974 memorandum from the Watergate Special Prosecution Force weighing the pros and cons of seeking an indictment against former President Richard Nixon.

CNN 1970s Interactive Timeline

cnn.com/SPECIALS/1999/century/episodes/08/

CNN has a series of interactive timelines with several interesting sites. This one covers the years from 1970 to 1979.

Revisiting Watergate

www.washingtonpost.com/wp-srv/national/longterm/watergate/front.htm

This site features a chronology, images, searchable articles, and a good deal of background information about the burglary and its consequences, as well as an update on the revelation of Deep Throat's identity in 2005.

Richard Milhous Nixon

www.ipl.org/div/potus/rmnixon.html

This site contains basic factual data about Nixon's election and presidency, speeches, and on-line biographies.

Gerald Rudolph Ford

www.ipl.org/div/potus/grford.html

This site contains basic information about Ford's election and presidency, speeches, and on-line biographies.

James Earl Carter, Jr.

www.ipl.org/div/potus/jecarter.html

Basic factual data about Carter's election and presidency, speeches, and on-line biographies.

Ronald Reagan
www.ipl.org/div/potus/rwreagan.html
Basic factual data about Reagan's election and presidency, speeches, and on-line biographies.

One Giant Leap
cnn.com/TECH/specials/apollo/
This CNN site commemorates the thirtieth anniversary of the 1969 moonwalk and tells the story of NASA and the ongoing space program.

The American Experience: Meltdown at Three Mile Island
www.pbs.org/wgbh/amex/three/
Companion to the PBS documentary, this site includes a chronology and description of the 1979 nuclear accident.

U.S. Environmental Protection Agency
www.epa.gov/history
This history of the EPA includes a timeline, topical information, publications, and a document collection.

The 80s Server
www.80s.com
Contains information on life in the 1980s.

In Their Own Words
aidshistory.nih.gov
National Institutes of Health researchers recall the early years of HIV/AIDS.

Chapter 32

To the Twenty-first Century, 1989–2006

"This Will Not Stand": Foreign Policy in the Post-Cold War Era

On the evening of August 1, 1990, George H. W. Bush sat in a T-shirt in the medical office in the basement of the White House. Bush was an avid golfer, but his duties as president kept him from playing as much as he would have liked, and when he did find time to squeeze in a round or some practice, he tended to overdo things. This summer day he had strained a shoulder muscle hitting practice balls, and now he rested on the exam table while a therapist applied deep heat. He planned a quiet evening and hoped the soreness would be gone by morning.

Two unexpected visitors altered his plans. Brent Scowcroft, Bush's national security adviser, and Richard Haass, the Middle East expert of the National Security Council, appeared at the door of the exam room. Bush had known Scowcroft for years, and the look on his face told him something was seriously amiss.

For months, the Bush administration had been monitoring a territorial and financial dispute between Iraq and Kuwait. Iraqi dictator Saddam Hussein was rattling the saber against the much smaller Kuwait, but Saddam had rattled sabers before without actually using them. The previous week, Saddam had spoken with the American ambassador in Iraq, April Glaspie, who came away from the meeting with the belief that his bellicose talk was chiefly for political effect. The United States had indicated its displeasure with Saddam's threats, and Glaspie judged that he had gotten the message.

For this reason Saddam's decision to invade Kuwait at the beginning of August caught the Bush administration by surprise. American intelligence agencies detected Iraq's mobilization; this was what brought Scowcroft and Haass to the White House on the evening of August 1. Haass suggested that the president call Saddam and warn him not to go through with the attack. But even as Bush considered this suggestion, Scowcroft received a message from the State Department that the American embassy in Kuwait had reported shooting in downtown Kuwait City. Within hours, the Iraqi forces crushed all resistance in Kuwait.

Bush, Scrowcroft, and other American officials recognized that the Iraqi takeover of Kuwait constituted the first crisis of the post–Cold War era. During the Cold War, a de facto division of labor had developed, with the United States and the Soviet Union each generally keeping its clients and allies in line, typically by threatening to withhold weapons or other assistance. Had the Soviet Union still been a superpower, Saddam, a longtime recipient of Soviet aid, likely would have heeded Moscow's warnings to settle his dispute with Kuwait peacefully. But in 1990 the Soviet system was disintegrating, and the Kremlin's clients were on their own.

It was this belief that shaped the Bush administration's response to the crisis. As the sole remaining superpower, the United States had the opportunity to employ its military and economic resources more freely than at any time in history. But with that freedom came unprecedented responsibility. During the Cold War, the United States could cite the threat of Soviet retaliation as reason to avoid intervening in the affairs of other countries; with that threat gone, American leaders would have to weigh each prospective intervention on its own merits. If one country attacked another, should the United States defend the victim? If the government of a country oppressed its own people, should the United States move to stop the oppression? These questions—and the answers American presidents gave to them—would define American foreign policy in the era after the Cold War.

Bush sensed the importance of the United States' responses, and he convened his principal deputies to discuss the particular stakes with Iraq and in the surrounding Persian Gulf. Saddam's seizure of Kuwait gave Iraq control of a large part of the world's oil supply, but the real prize was Saudi Arabia. "Saudi Arabia and others will cut and run if we are weak," Defense Secretary Dick Cheney predicted.

Bush consulted America's oldest allies. Britain's Margaret Thatcher urged the president to oppose Saddam most vigorously. "If Iraq wins, no small state is safe," the prime minister declared. "We must win this. . . . We cannot give in to dictators."

Bush asked his generals for his military options. He was told that American air power could punish Saddam and perhaps soften him up, but ground forces—in large numbers—would be required to guarantee victory.

By August 5 Bush had made up his mind. As he exited the helicopter that brought him back from another high-level meeting at Camp David to the White House, reporters crowded the South Lawn. One unscripted remark by the president summarized the policy that soon began to unfold: "This will not stand, this aggression against Kuwait."

THE FIRST PRESIDENT BUSH

Elected on the strength of his association with Ronald Reagan, George H. W. Bush appeared poised to confirm the ascendancy of the conservative values Reagan forced to the center stage of American life. But events abroad distracted Bush, whose principal contribution proved to be in the area of foreign affairs. Bush brought the Cold War to a peaceful and triumphant conclusion, and he launched America toward the new opportunities and new challenges of the twenty-first century.

Republicans at Home

Democrats approached the 1988 presidential election with high hopes, having regained control of the Senate in 1986 and not having to face the popular Reagan. But Vice President George H. W. Bush proved a stronger candidate than almost anyone had expected, and in a contest that confirmed the Republicans' hold on the Sunbelt, he defeated Massachusetts governor Michael Dukakis.

Many people expected the policies of the Bush administration to reflect the reputation of the new president—bland and cautious, lacking in vision but safely predictable. At home, he lived up (or down) to his reputation, sponsoring few initiatives in education, health care, or environmental protection while continuing the Reagan theme of limiting federal interference in the everyday lives of American citizens. He vetoed family leave legislation, declined to endorse meaningful health care reform, and watered down civil rights proposals in Congress. The one exception was the **Americans with Disabilities Act (ADA),** passed by Congress in 1991, which prohibited discrimination against the disabled in hiring, transportation, and public accommodations. Beginning in July 1992, ADA called for all public buildings, restaurants, and stores to be made accessible to those with physical

Americans with Disabilities Act (ADA) Passed by Congress in 1991, the ADA banned discrimination against the disabled in employment and mandated easy access to all public and commercial buildings.

handicaps and required that businesses with twenty-five or more workers hire new employees without regard to disability.

Bush's time on domestic affairs was taken up with two pressing issues: the possible meltdown of the savings and loan industry and the soaring federal budget deficit. The thrift industry, based on U.S. government–insured deposits, had fallen into deep trouble as a result of lax regulation and unwise, and in some cases fraudulent, loan policies. Bush sought to stanch the bleeding by merging the weakest of the remaining thrifts with the stronger, and by regulating the survivors more carefully. Congress consented, and in August 1989 passed a bill to close or merge more than seven hundred ailing savings and loans and to restructure the federal regulatory system. A new agency, the Resolution Trust Corporation, took over properties on which developers had secured loans many times their actual value, and it gradually sold them off at discount prices. By the time the Resolution Trust Corporation expired in 1992, the cost to the government had passed $150 billion; the eventual bill for the savings and loan cleanup, including interest, was estimated at between $500 and $700 billion.

The federal budget deficit posed an even greater challenge. The deficits Bush inherited from Reagan topped $150 million per year, and conventional financial wisdom dictated that something be done to bring them down. In campaigning for president, Bush had promised "no new taxes," but in the fall of 1990 he broke the pledge. In a package deal negotiated with the leaders of Congress, he agreed to a budget that included new taxes along with substantial spending cuts, especially on the military.

Unfortunately for the president, the budget deal coincided with the beginning of a slow but painful recession that ended the Republican prosperity of the 1980s. Not only did Bush face recriminations from voters for breaking a campaign pledge not to raise taxes, but the economic decline led to greatly reduced government revenues. As a result, the deficit continued to soar, rising from $150 billion in fiscal year 1989 to just under $300 billion in 1992. Despite the 1990 budget agreement, the national debt increased by more than $1 trillion during Bush's presidency.

Ending the Cold War

Bush might have accomplished more in domestic affairs had not the international developments begun during the Reagan years not accelerated dramatically. Bush had been in office only months when, in country after country, the communist system of the Cold War began giving way to democracy more quickly than anyone had expected.

An early attempt at anticommunist liberation proved tragically abortive. In May 1989, students in China began a month-long demonstration for democracy in Beijing's Tiananmen Square. Watching television coverage of Gorbachev's visit to China in mid-May, Americans were fascinated to see the Chinese students call for democracy with a hunger strike and a handcrafted replica of the Statue of Liberty. But on the evening of June 4, the Chinese leaders sent tanks and troops to Tiananmen Square to crush the student demonstration. By the next day, full-scale repression swept over China; several hundred protesters were killed and thousands were injured. Chinese leaders imposed martial law to quell the dissent and shatter American hopes for a democratic China.

Bush wanted to preserve American influence with the Chinese government. Despite official statements denouncing the crackdown, he sent National Security Adviser Brent Scowcroft on a secret mission to Beijing to maintain a working relationship with the Chinese leaders.

A far more promising trend toward freedom began in Europe in mid-1989. In June, Lech Walesa and his Solidarity movement came to power in free elections in Poland. A new regime in Hungary opened its borders to the West in September, allowing thousands of East German tourists in Hungary to flee to freedom. One by

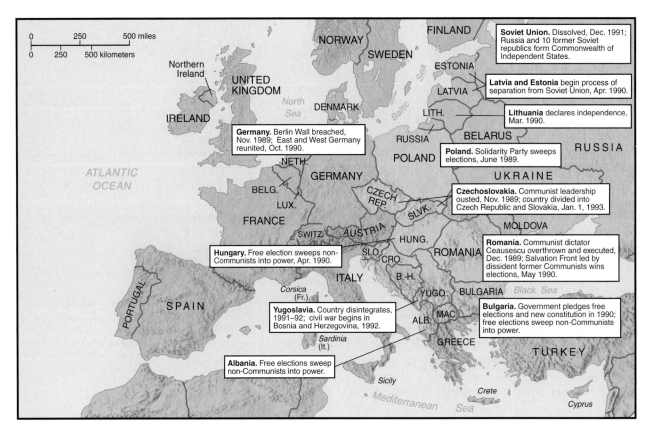

THE END OF THE COLD WAR   *Free elections in Poland in June 1989 triggered the domino effect in the fall of communism in eastern Europe and the former Soviet Union. Changes in policy came quickly, but the restructuring of social and economic institutions continues to take time.* ▪

one, the repressive governments of East Germany, Czechoslovakia, Bulgaria, and Romania fell. The most heartening scene of all took place in East Germany in early November when the new communist leaders suddenly announced the opening of the Berlin Wall. Workers quickly and joyously demolished a large section of the despised physical symbol of the Cold War.

Most people realized it was Mikhail Gorbachev who was responsible for the liberation of eastern Europe. It was his refusal to use armed force to keep repressive regimes in power that permitted the long-delayed liberation of the captive peoples of central and eastern Europe.

By the end of 1991, both Gorbachev and the Soviet Union had become victims of the demise of communism. On August 19, 1991, right-wing plotters placed Gorbachev under arrest. Boris Yeltsin, the newly elected president of the Russian Republic, broke up the coup by mounting a tank in Moscow and demanding Gorbachev's release. The coup failed and Gorbachev was released, only to resign in December 1991 after the fifteen republics dissolved the Soviet Union. Russia, by far the largest and most powerful of the former Soviet republics, took the lead in joining with ten others to form a loose alignment called the Commonwealth of Independent States (CIS). Yeltsin then disbanded the Communist party and continued the reforms begun by Gorbachev to establish democracy and a free market system in Russia.

The Bush administration, although criticized for its cautious approach, welcomed the demise of communism. Bush facilitated the reunification of Germany and offered economic assistance to Russia and the other members of the new CIS. He also negotiated significant nuclear arms reductions treaties with Russian leaders.

The Gulf War

Amid the disintegration of the Soviet system, Iraq in August 1990 invaded Kuwait. Although Bush quickly concluded that Saddam Hussein's aggression must be reversed, actually removing Iraq from Kuwait took time and great effort. The president started by persuading Saudi Arabia to accept a huge American troop buildup, dubbed Desert Shield. This American presence would prevent Saddam from advancing beyond Kuwait into Saudi Arabia; it would also allow the United States to launch a ground attack against Iraqi forces if and when the president determined such an attack was necessary.

While the American buildup took place, Bush arranged an international coalition to condemn the Iraqi invasion and endorse economic sanctions against Iraq. Not every member of the coalition subscribed to the "new world order" that Bush said the liberation of Kuwait would help establish, but all concurred in the general principle of deterring international aggression.

Congress required somewhat more convincing. Many Democrats supported economic sanctions against Iraq but opposed the use of force. As the troop buildup in the Persian Gulf proceeded—as Operation Desert Shield evolved into what would be called **Operation Desert Storm**—and as the sanctions failed to dislodge Iraq from Kuwait, some of the skeptics gradually came around. After securing UN support for military action, Bush barely persuaded Congress to approve the use of force to liberate Kuwait.

On January 17, 1991, the president unleashed a devastating aerial assault on Iraq. After knocking out the Iraqi air defense network in a few hours, F-117A stealth fighters and Tomahawk cruise missiles hit key targets in Baghdad. The air attack, virtually unchallenged by the Iraqis, wiped out command and control centers and enabled the bombers of the United States and its coalition partners (chiefly Britain) to demoralize the beleaguered enemy troops.

After five weeks of this, Bush gave the order for the ground assault. Led by General Norman Schwarzkopf, American and allied armored units swept across the desert in a great flanking operation while a combined force of U.S. marines and Saudi troops drove directly into Kuwait City. In just one hundred hours, the American-led offensive liberated Kuwait and sent Saddam Hussein's vaunted Republican Guard fleeing back into Iraq.

Operation Desert Storm
Desert Storm was the code name used by the United States and its coalition partners in waging war against Iraq in early 1991 to liberate Kuwait.

■ *Anti-aircraft fire lights up the sky over Baghdad, Iraq, during the 1991 Persian Gulf War. A month of strikes on Iraqi targets was followed by a ground offensive that lasted only one hundred hours before Iraqi troops began to surrender and President Bush ordered a cease-fire. Critics of Bush's decision argued that stopping the advance allowed an unvanquished Saddam Hussein to remain in power in Iraq. ■*

In a controversial decision, President Bush, acting on the advice of General Colin Powell, chairman of the Joint Chiefs, halted the advance and agreed to an armistice with Iraq. Critics claimed that with just a few more days of fighting, perhaps even just a few more hours, American forces could have encircled the Republican Guard and ended Saddam's cruel regime. But the president, fearful of disrupting the allied coalition and of having American troops mired down in a guerrilla war, stopped when he had achieved his announced goal of liberating Kuwait. He hoped that a chastened Saddam would help balance the threat of Iran in the volatile Persian Gulf region.

Desert Storm brought mixed blessings. It was a great personal victory for George Bush, who saw his approval rating climb to an unprecedented 90 percent. American military leaders believed they had finally atoned for Vietnam, a sentiment widely shared by an euphoric public. The United States had deployed more than 500,000 troops, as many as were in Vietnam in 1968, and had lost just 146 lives in inflicting a stinging defeat on a dangerous bully. Moreover, the price of oil, which had climbed to nearly $40 a barrel in October, fell back to less than $20, allowing Americans to fill the gas tanks of their cars for just over $1 a gallon.

At the same time, however, Saddam Hussein continued to rule in Baghdad, persecuting Kurds in northern Iraq and Shi'ite Muslims in the south. He survived several attempts on his life and tightened his grip on Iraq, frustrating U.S. efforts to uncover and destroy his suspected chemical, biological, and nuclear weapons facilities. During the next dozen years, many Americans would conclude that if Bush had completed the ouster of Saddam in 1991, he would have spared the United States and the world a great deal of trouble.

THE CHANGING FACES OF AMERICA

From the *Mayflower* to the covered wagon, movement has always characterized the American people. The final years of the twentieth century and the early years of the twenty-first witnessed two significant shifts in the American population: continued movement internally to the Sunbelt region of the South and West, and a remarkable influx of immigrants from developing nations. These changes led to increased urbanization, greater ethnic diversity, and growing social unrest.

A People on the Move

Sunbelt This region consists of a broad band of states running across the South from Florida to Texas, extending west and north to include California and the Pacific Northwest. Beginning in the 1970s, this area experienced rapid economic growth and major gains in population.

By the 1990s, a majority of Americans lived in the **Sunbelt** of the South and West. Best defined as a broad band running across the country below the 37th parallel from the Carolinas to Southern California, the Sunbelt had begun to flourish with the buildup of military bases and defense plants during World War II. Rapid population growth continued with the stimulus of heavy Cold War defense spending and accelerated in the 1970s when both new high-technology firms and more established industries were attracted by lower labor costs and the favorable climate of the Sunbelt states. Florida, Texas, and California led the way, each gaining more than two million new residents in the 1970s.

The flow continued at a slightly lower rate over the next two decades. The Northeast and the Middle West continued losing people to the South and West. In 1994, Texas surpassed New York as the nation's second most populous state. The 2000 census revealed that while all regions had gained population in the 1990s, the South and West had expanded by nearly 20 percent, compared to around 6 percent for the Northeast and Middle West. Phoenix was typical of the phenomenal growth of Sunbelt cities, adding a million residents in the 1990s to grow at a 45 percent rate.

The increasing urbanization of America had positive and negative aspects. People living in the large metropolitan areas were both more affluent and better educated than their rural counterparts. Yet these advantages were offset by higher urban crime rates, longer commuting time in heavy traffic, and higher living costs. Nevertheless, the big cities and their suburbs continued to thrive, accounting for 80 percent of all Americans by 2000.

Another striking population trend was the nationwide rise in the number of the elderly. At the beginning of the twentieth century, only 4.1 percent of the population was aged 65 or older; by 2000, those over 65 made up more than 12 percent of the population, with the nearly four million over 85 the fastest growing group of all. Census Bureau projections suggested that by the year 2030, one out of every five Americans would be over age 65.

Six of every ten older Americans were women, and they tended to have a higher rate of chronic disease and to be worse off economically than men the same age. Many of the oldest old, those over 85, lived in nursing homes and accounted for one-third of all Medicaid payments. Yet only 10 percent of the elderly lived below the poverty line and three-fourths owned their own homes. The annual cost-of-living increases in Social Security payments spared them the worst ravages of inflation. With more than 30 million members, the AARP (formerly known as the American Association of Retired People) proved very effective in Washington in representing the interests of the elderly, particularly in regard to Medicare.

The Revival of Immigration

The flow of immigrants into the United States reached record proportions in the 1990s as a result of the new policies adopted in 1965. (See the "We Americans" essay after Chapter 30, "Unintended Consequences: The Second Great Migration," pp. 602–603.) The number of arrivals continued to grow during the first decade of the new century, with nearly 8 million immigrants reaching America between the beginning of 2000 and early 2005. By 2005, a record high of 35 million foreign-born persons lived in the United States, constituting 12 percent of the total population.

The new wave of immigrants came mainly from Latin America and Asia. These immigrants tended to settle in urban areas in California, Texas, New York, Florida, Illinois, and New Jersey. In California, the influx of immigrants from Asia and Mexico created growing pressure on public services, especially during recessions.

The arrival of so many immigrants was bound to lead to controversy over whether immigrants were a benefit or a liability to American society. A study by the National Academy of Sciences in 1997 reported that while government services used by immigrants—schools, welfare, health clinics—cost more initially than was collected from them in taxes, in the long run, immigrants and their families more than paid their way. In regard to employment,

■ *Newly sworn in citizens of the United States wave U.S. flags during a naturalization ceremony in Miami on April 28, 2006. Days later, more than one million immigrants participated in a nationwide boycott called "A Day Without Immigrants" to protest the proposed tightening of U.S. immigration laws.* ■

immigrants tended to help consumers and employers by working for relatively low wages in restaurants, the textile industry, and farming, but they hurt low-skilled U.S. workers, notably high school dropouts and many African Americans, by keeping wages low. Economists claimed that the new immigrants, lacking necessary education and job skills, were likely to remain a permanent underclass.

Emerging Hispanics

People of Hispanic origin became the nation's largest ethnic group in 2002, surpassing African Americans for the first time. The rapidly growing Hispanic population climbed to over 41 million by 2005, accounting for 14 percent of the nation's population.

The Census Bureau identified four major Hispanic groups: Mexican Americans, Puerto Ricans, Cuban Americans, and other Hispanics, including many from Central America. Even though most of the Hispanic population was concentrated in cities such as New York, Los Angeles, San Antonio, and Miami, the 2000 census showed a surprising geographical spread. Hispanics made up 20 percent of the population in individual counties in states such as Georgia, Iowa, and Minnesota.

The Hispanic groups had several features in common. All were relatively youthful, with a median age of 22 and a high fertility rate. They tended to be relatively poor, with one-fourth falling below the poverty line, and to be employed in low-paying positions as manual laborers, domestic servants, and migrant workers. Although the economic position of Hispanics had improved considerably in the boom years of the 1980s and 1990s, their poverty rate was twice the national average. Family median income in 2005 was $34,000, or roughly two-thirds the level for whites.

Lack of education was a key factor in preventing economic progress for Hispanics. Fewer Hispanics graduated from high school than other minorities and their school dropout rate was the nation's highest at more than 50 percent. Hispanic leaders warned that these figures boded ill not just for their own group, but for society as a whole.

undocumented aliens Once derisively called "wetbacks," undocumented aliens are illegal immigrants, mainly from Mexico and Central America.

The entry of several million illegal immigrants from Mexico, now known as **undocumented aliens,** created a substantial social problem for the nation and especially for the Southwest. Critics argued that the aliens took jobs from U.S. citizens, kept wages artificially low, and received extensive welfare and medical benefits that strained budgets in states such as Texas and California.

Defenders of undocumented aliens contended that the nation gained from the abundant supply of workers who were willing to work in fields and factories at backbreaking jobs shunned by most Americans. Moreover, defenders stated, illegal entrants usually paid sales and withholding taxes but rarely used government services for fear of being deported. Whichever view was correct, an exploited class of illegal aliens was living on the edge of poverty.

Concern over economic competition from Mexican "illegals" had led Congress to pass legislation in 1986 that penalized employers who hired undocumented workers. Congress permitted those aliens who could show that they were living in the United States before 1982 to become legal residents; nearly three million accepted this offer of amnesty to become legal residents. The reform effort, however, failed to stem the continued flow of undocumented workers northward from Mexico in the 1990s and early 2000s. The Congressional Research Service estimated that more than 9 million foreigners were living illegally in the United States in 2002.

Despite stepped-up border enforcement efforts after the September 11, 2001, terrorist attacks, illegal immigrants continued to move northward from Mexico and Central America. The trip could be dangerous, even lethal. Mexican experts estimated that more than 3000 migrants lost their lives attempting to enter the United States illegally between 1997 and 2006. Nineteen Mexican and Central American workers died from suffocation in south Texas in May 2003—nearly one hundred illegal aliens had been jammed into a truck trailer without access to water or fresh air. Yet the movement continued.

Advance and Retreat for African Americans

African Americans formed the second largest of the nation's ethnic minorities. In 2004, there were just over 39 million blacks in the United States, 13.4 percent of the population. Although the heaviest concentration of African Americans was in northern cities, notably New York and Chicago, there was a significant movement back to the South. This shift, which began in the 1970s and accelerated during the 1990s, meant that by 2000 nearly 54 percent of those identifying themselves as black for the census lived in the sixteen states of the Sunbelt. Family ties and a search for ancestral roots explained much of this movement, but it also reflected the same economic incentives that drew so many Americans to the Sunbelt in the last three decades of the twentieth century.

African Americans made substantial gains in certain areas of life. In 2004, some 81 percent of blacks aged 25 and older had earned a high school diploma, and 18 percent of African Americans possessed a college degree, 5 percent more than a decade earlier. The number of black-owned businesses topped 1.2 million, up more than 45 percent since 1997.

Yet in other respects African Americans did less well. The black poverty rate was nearly 25 percent, and the median income for black families was less than two-thirds of that for whites. Blacks remained clustered in entry-level jobs, where they faced increasing competition from immigrants. The African American incarceration rate was much higher than the national average. Blacks were also more likely to be victims of crime, especially violent crime. Homicide was the leading cause of death among black males between the ages of 15 and 34.

Two events summarized much of the frustration African Americans felt. In March 1991 a bystander videotaped four Los Angeles policemen brutally beating Rodney King, an African American who had been stopped for a traffic violation. The pictures of the rain of blows on King shocked the nation. Nearly a year later, when an all-white jury acquitted the four officers of charges of police brutality, rioting erupted in South Central Los Angeles that for a time threatened the entire city when the police failed to respond promptly. In the aftermath of the riot, which took fifty-three lives and did more than $1 billion in damage, government and state agencies promised new efforts to help inner-city dwellers. But the efforts produced little effect, and life for many urban blacks remained difficult and dangerous.

A tragedy of a different sort occurred fourteen years later. In August 2005, Hurricane Katrina ravaged the Gulf Coast and broke levees in New Orleans. The high winds and water killed more than a thousand persons, destroyed hundreds of thousands of homes, and forced the evacuation of millions of men, women, and children. Television cameras captured the plight of the several thousand who took refuge in the New Orleans Superdome, only to be

■ *In August 2005, the catastrophic Hurricane Katrina devastated much of the Louisiana and Mississippi Gulf Coast. In the wake of the storm, the levee system of New Orleans failed and flooded nearly 80 percent of the city. Particularly hard hit were low-lying areas such as the Lower Ninth Ward, where police rescue boats are shown here rescuing residents. All levels of government were criticized for halting, inadequate responses to the disaster.* ■

stranded when state and federal relief efforts failed. Most conspicuous in the footage was the fact that the vast majority of those suffering the worst in New Orleans were black. Their neighborhoods were the lowest-lying in the city, and hence the worst flooded. Many lacked the cars necessary to flee the city in advance of the hurricane; others lacked the means to pay for hotels or apartments had they been able to get out. Though the relief efforts were largely color-blind (despite early allegations to the contrary), the entire experience demonstrated that poverty in America most certainly was not.

Americans from Asia and the Middle East

Asian Americans were the fasting-growing minority group at the beginning of the twenty-first century. According to the 2000 census, there were more than 12 million Americans of Asian or Pacific Island descent. Although they represented only 4 percent of the total population, they were increasing at seven times the national rate, and future projections indicated that by 2050 one in ten Americans would be of Asian ancestry.

The Chinese formed the largest single group of Asian Americans, followed by Filipinos, Japanese, Indians, Koreans, and Vietnamese. Immigration was the primary reason for the rapid growth of all these groups except the Japanese. During the 1980s, Asia had provided nearly half of all immigrants to the United States. Though the influx subsequently slowed, the children of the immigrants added to the Asian numbers.

Compared to other minorities, Asian Americans were well educated and affluent. Three out of four Asian youths graduated from high school. Asian Americans also had the highest percentage of college graduates and recipients of doctoral degrees of any minority group; they were better represented in colleges and universities than the white majority. Many Asians entered professional fields, and in part as a result, the median income for Asian American families in 2004 was nearly 20 percent higher than the national average.

Not all Asian Americans fared so well, however. Refugees from Southeast Asia experienced both economic hardship and persecution. The median family income for Vietnamese Americans fell substantially below the national average. Nearly half the Laotian refugees living in Minnesota were unemployed because they had great difficulty learning to read and write English. Vietnamese fishermen who settled on the Gulf Coast of Texas and Louisiana experienced repeated attacks on their livelihood and their homes. In the Los Angeles riots in 1992, Korean stores and shops became a main target for looting and firebombing.

But the overall experience of Asian Americans was a positive one. They came to America seeking economic opportunity. Many appeared to be finding it.

The number of Americans from the Middle East grew almost as fast as the number of those from Asia in the 1990s. The 2000 census counted 1.5 million Americans of Middle Eastern ancestry, up from 200,000 thirty years earlier. Most came from Arab countries, as well as Israel and Iran. Concentrated in California, New York, and Michigan, Middle Eastern Americans were well-educated, with nearly half having college degrees. Many Arab Americans felt nervous after the terrorist attacks of September 11, 2001, that were committed by Arab extremists; some experienced actual violence at the hands of persons who wanted to blame anyone of Arab descent for the shocking mass murders. Most Arab Americans carried on as before, however, pursuing their interpretation of the American dream.

Assimilation or Diversity?

The influx of people from all around the world, not just from Europe, had profound implications for American culture. Traditionally, the favorite American self-image was the melting pot, the title of Israel Zangwill's play written in 1908, at the height of European immigration into the nation. "America is God's crucible, the great Melting-Pot where all the races of Europe are melting and reforming," one of his characters proclaimed.

The melting pot image carried with it the concept of stripping newcomers of their culture and national traits. Dubious for European immigration in view of the way each ethnic group retained its separate identity, this analogy seemed increasingly irrelevant to the Latin America, Asian, and Middle Eastern migration to America. Instead of recasting immigrants into an American type, immigration could better be seen as broadening the diversity that had always characterized the United States.

The new awareness of ethnic diversity manifested itself in many ways. In public education, blacks led a crusade against Eurocentric curriculum and demanded a new emphasis on the influence of African culture. On college campuses, the call for multicultural courses and separate departments for African American, Asian American, and Hispanic studies created controversy. Citing the forecasts of a declining Anglo dominance and the rise of minority groups in the twenty-first century, ethnic leaders advocated cultural pluralism.

Many Americans found themselves perplexed and uncertain of their cultural identity. A Census Bureau survey, asking people to state their ancestry, revealed that fully one-fourth of Americans listed Germany first, with Ireland and England a distant second and third. Some Hispanics found the census racial classifications—black, Asian–Pacific Islander, white, or American Indian—meaningless. People of Arab descent felt equally confused.

In the 1990s, people of mixed racial parentage demanded that the census for 2000 include a box labeled "multiracial" rather than just the meaningless "other." A group called Project RACE (Reclassify All Children Equally) argued that the four million children of more than a million interracial marriages deserved their own census category. The professional golf champion Tiger Woods—whose ancestry is part black, part Thai, part Chinese, part Native American, and part Caucasian—agreed, saying that as a child he called himself "Cablinasian." Civil rights groups, however, objected, fearing cuts in government benefits to minorities based on the census figures. The Census Bureau compromised in 2000 by adding four new dual race categories: American Indian-white, American Indian-black, Asian-white, and black-white. In addition, individuals of mixed ancestry could mark several racial categories, not just one as in the past. The results were startling. Nearly seven million Americans claimed to be multiracial, with most choosing either black-white or Asian-white.

Perhaps Horace Kallen, one of the early critics of Zangwill's melting pot analogy, offered the most appealing image of the nation's diverse heritage. He likened the United States to a symphony orchestra, in which each nationality and ethnic group contributed its "own specific timbre and tonality" to create "a multiplicity in a unity, an orchestration of mankind."

THE NEW DEMOCRATS

The Democrats, victims of the runaway inflation of the 1970s, became the beneficiaries of the lingering recession of the early 1990s. Moving away from its traditional reliance on big government, the party regained strength by choosing moderate candidates and tailoring its programs to appeal to the hard-pressed middle class. These tactics enabled the Democrats to regain the White House in 1992 and retain it in 1996, despite a Republican sweep of Congress in 1994. The key figure in this political shift was Bill Clinton, who overcame some early setbacks to reap the rewards of a sustained economic boom.

The Election of 1992

The persistence of the recession that had begun two years earlier became a major political issue in 1992. Although mild by postwar standards, the economic downturn that began in July 1990 proved unusually stubborn, especially in states such as California that relied heavily on the defense industry, which was hurt by the end of the Cold War. The recovery, which started just after the end of the Persian Gulf War in the spring of 1991, proved slow and uneven. Three million Americans joined the ranks of the unemployed, many white-collar employees. Although the economy began to advance more briskly in 1992, unemployment persisted.

As Bush's popularity plummeted, two men sought to capitalize on the dismal state of the U.S. economy. First, Arkansas governor Bill Clinton defeated a field of five other challengers for the Democratic nomination by becoming the champion of economic renewal. Forgoing traditional liberal appeals to interest groups, Clinton stressed the need for investment in the nation's future—rebuilding roads and bridges, training workers for high-tech jobs, and solving the growing national health care crisis.

Despite his victories in the Democratic primaries, however, Clinton faced a new rival in H. Ross Perot. An eccentric Texas billionaire, Perot singled out the deficit as the nation's gravest problem and agreed to run as an independent candidate in response to a grassroots movement (which he financed) to place his name on the November ballot.

When Clinton and his running mate, Senator Albert Gore, Jr., of Tennessee, succeeded in unifying the Democratic party and gaining agreement on a moderate platform promising economic change, Perot stunned his supporters by suddenly dropping out of the race in July. Clinton immediately became the front-runner.

A relentless Democratic attack on the administration's lackluster economic performance overcame all the president's efforts to remind the nation of Reagan prosperity and Bush triumphs abroad. Even GOP assaults on Clinton's character, notably his evasion of the draft during the Vietnam War, failed to halt the Democratic momentum. Clinton wound up with 43 percent of the popular vote but with a commanding lead in the electoral college, 370 to 168 for Bush. Perot, who had reentered the race, won 19 percent of the popular vote but failed to carry a single state.

Clinton and Congress

In the White House, Bill Clinton proved to be the most adept politician since Franklin Roosevelt. Born in Hope, Arkansas, in 1946, Clinton weathered a difficult childhood with an alcoholic stepfather using personal charm to achieve his goals. Intelligent and ambitious, he completed his undergraduate work at Georgetown University, studied law at Yale, and spent two years as a Rhodes scholar at Oxford University in England. Entering politics, he won election first as Arkansas attorney general and then as governor in 1978. Defeated after his first term, Clinton regained the governor's office in 1982 and would be elected three more times.

In keeping with the theme of his campaign, Clinton concentrated at first on the economy. The federal budget he proposed to Congress in February 1993 called for tax increases and spending cuts to achieve a balanced budget. Clinton cajoled, shamed, and threatened sufficient members to win approval of $241 billion in new taxes and $255 billion in spending cuts, for a total deficit reduction of $496 billion over four years. This major achievement earned Clinton the confidence of financial markets and helped fuel the economic boom of the 1990s.

Clinton scored another victory when Congress approved the **North American Free Trade Agreement (NAFTA)** in the fall of 1993. NAFTA, initiated and nearly completed by Bush, was a free trade plan that united the United States, Mexico, and

North American Free Trade Agreement (NAFTA) A free trade plan initiated in the first Bush administration and enacted by a narrow vote in Congress in the early months of the Clinton administration. It established a common market without tariff barriers between the United States, Canada, and Mexico.

Canada into a common market without tariff barriers. Clinton endorsed the treaty as a way of securing American prosperity and spreading American values. Critics complained that free trade would cost American workers their jobs as American companies moved production overseas. But Clinton carried the day, winning a bruising fight in the House and an easier contest in the Senate.

Although Clinton's NAFTA coalition included many congressional Republicans, on other issues the GOP staunchly opposed the president. Republicans hated his tax increases and scuttled his attempt to revamp the nation's health care system. Leading the opposition was a young congressman, Newton Leroy "Newt" Gingrich, who asked all GOP candidates in the 1994 congressional races to sign a ten-point **Contract with America.** The contract consisted of familiar conservative goals, including a balanced budget amendment to the Constitution, term limits for members of Congress, a line-item veto for the president, and a middle-class tax cut. For the first time in recent political history, a party sought to win Congress on ideological issues rather than relying on individual personalities.

A series of embarrassing disclosures involving Bill Clinton's character made this tactic particularly effective in 1994. During the 1992 campaign, the *New York Times* had raised questions about a bankrupt Arkansas land development called Whitewater in which the Clintons had lost a modest investment. Additional scandals began to surface. Travelgate was the name given to the firing, apparently at the urging of First Lady Hillary Clinton, of several White House employees who arranged travel for the press covering the president. Then in early 1994, Paula Jones, a former Arkansas state employee, filed a sexual harassment suit against Clinton.

The Republican Congressional gains in 1994 stunned political observers. Newt Gingrich, who had worked so hard to ensure the change in leadership in the Congress, became speaker of the House. The GOP also captured 32 governorships, including those of New York, California, and Texas, where George W. Bush, the son of the man Clinton beat in 1992, won handily.

The Republicans claimed a mandate to resume the Reagan Revolution: to cut taxes, diminish the scope of government, and empower the private sector. Clinton and the Democrats managed to keep the Republicans in check on matters of substance, but the Republicans in turn contrived to hobble Clinton. The administration and the Republicans collaborated on welfare reform and a modest increase in the minimum wage, but deadlock descended on Washington otherwise.

Clinton turned the deadlock to his benefit in 1996 after the Republicans, having failed to force him to accept cuts in Medicare, college loans, and other social services, refused to pass a budget bill, and thereby shut down the federal government. Clinton proved more deft at finger-pointing than Gingrich and the Republicans did, and he succeeded in persuading voters that the Republicans were to blame. He carried this theme into his 1996 re-election campaign. The Republican nominee, Robert Dole of Kansas, lacked Clinton's charisma and failed to shake the impression that the Republicans were flint-hearts who wanted to cut the pet programs of the American people. Clinton won decisively, holding the presidency for the Democrats even while the Republicans continued to control Congress.

Contract with America In the 1994 congressional election, Congressman Newt Gingrich had Republican candidates sign a "contract" in which they pledged their support for such things as a balanced budget amendment, term limits for members of Congress, and a middle-class tax cut.

Scandal in the White House

Despite Clinton's re-election, rumors of wrongdoing still clung to his presidency. The special prosecutor appointed to probe the Whitewater transactions, Kenneth Starr, turned over stone after stone in search of evidence of malfeasance, until he came across rumors that Clinton had conducted a clandestine affair with a White House intern, Monica Lewinsky.

Clinton initially denied the affair. But Starr subpoenaed Lewinsky, who eventually gave a detailed account of her sexual encounters with the president and provided crucial physical evidence implicating Clinton.

■ *Members of the House Judiciary Committee listen to Clinton's testimony during the hearings on the president's impeachment in December 1998. The Committee sent four articles of impeachment to the full House, and the House adopted two— one count of perjury and one of obstruction of justice. The Senate could not muster the two-thirds majority required for conviction, and so Clinton was acquitted of both articles.* ■

Realizing that he could no longer deny the affair, on August 17, 1998, Clinton appeared before Starr's grand jury and admitted to having "inappropriate intimate contact" with Lewinsky. That evening he spoke briefly to the nation. For the first time, he admitted to a relationship with Lewinsky that was "not appropriate" and "wrong." He said he regretted misleading the people and especially his wife, but he refused to apologize for his behavior or his false denials.

Clinton's fate hung in the balance. Even members of his own party criticized him. But just when Clinton seemed most vulnerable, the special prosecutor inadvertently rescued him. In early September, Starr sent a 452-page report to Congress outlining eleven possible impeachment charges against Clinton. The key one was perjury, and Starr provided painstakingly graphic detail on all of the sexual encounters between Clinton and Lewinsky to prove that the president had lied when he denied engaging in sexual relations with the intern.

Many Americans responded by condemning Starr rather than the president. Shocked by the sordid details, they blamed the prosecutor for exposing families to distasteful sexual practices on the evening news. When Hillary Clinton stood staunchly by her husband, a majority of the public seemed to conclude that however bad the president's conduct, it was a private matter.

Republican leaders ignored the public sentiment and pressed ahead with impeachment proceedings. In December, the House (where the 1998 midterm elections had narrowed the GOP advantage to six) voted on four articles of impeachment, rejecting two, but approving two others—perjury and obstruction of justice—by small margins in nearly straight party-line votes.

The final showdown in the Senate was anticlimatic. With a two-thirds vote required to find the president guilty and remove him from office, there was no chance of conviction in the highly charged partisan mood that prevailed. On February 12, 1999, the GOP was unable to muster even a majority on the perjury charge, with 45 in favor and 55 opposed. After a second, closer vote, 50 to 50, on obstruction of justice, the presiding officer, Chief Justice William Rehnquist, declared, "Acquitted of the charges."

Clinton had survived the Monica Lewinsky affair, but he emerged from the ordeal with his presidency badly damaged. His final two years in office would be devoted to a concerted effort to restore his damaged reputation. Desperate for a legacy to mark his White House years, Clinton failed to realize that he had already created an enduring one—he would always be remembered as the president who dishonored his office by his affair with a young intern.

CLINTON AND THE WORLD

Neither Clinton's scandals nor his struggle with Congress allowed Americans to forget about the rest of the world. The Cold War had ended, but the post–Cold War world was plenty threatening. While the United States was the only superpower still standing, America's power preserved Americans from having to make difficult decisions about how to use that power.

Old Rivals in New Light

Inheriting the chaos left by the breakup of the Soviet Union, Clinton concentrated on two issues in dealing with Russia and its neighbors. First, as Bush had done, he strongly supported Russian President Boris Yeltsin. In 1993, Clinton persuaded Congress to provide a $2.5 billion aid package to help Yeltsin carry out his free market reforms of the devastated Russian economy. Although the expansion of NATO to include Poland, Hungary, and the Czech Republic and plans for a missile defense system created some tension, the Clinton administration succeeded in maintaining good relations with Russia.

Clinton was even more successful on the second big issue left over from the Cold War against the Soviets: preventing the proliferation of nuclear weapons among the former republics of the Soviet Union. With patient diplomacy, Secretary of State Warren Christopher won agreements from Belarus and Kazakhstan to scrap their deadly ICBMs. Ukraine proved more difficult, but in 1994, Clinton persuaded the president of Ukraine to surrender his country's entire nuclear stockpile. Clinton's effort on behalf of nuclear nonproliferation in the former Soviet Union was perhaps his most important, if least heralded, achievement.

The president's policy toward China was more questionable. Clinton ignored China's dismal human rights record and continued Bush's policy of annually extending most favored nation status to Beijing. The growing importance of trade with China, whose economic output in 1993 exceeded Britain's, led Clinton to overlook the memory of the Tiananmen Square massacre and the continued persecution of dissidents in China. As trade with China began to rival that with Japan, the president announced a policy of "constructive engagement." It was better, he contended, to keep talking, and trading, with China than to harden Chinese resentment against the West by harping on moral issues. In 2000, Clinton won a notable victory for free trade when the House voted to give China permanent most favored nation status.

The Chinese, however, proved to be less than fully cooperative. China ignored U.S. protests of its export of missiles to Iran and nuclear technology to Pakistan, and it continued to stifle dissent at home. China conducted provocative missile tests near Taiwan, which Beijing still claimed for China. When the Clinton administration sent aircraft carriers to patrol the waters off Taiwan, a Chinese official talked casually about raining nuclear bombs upon Los Angeles. Constructive engagement clearly had its limits.

To Intervene or Not

The most difficult foreign policy decisions for the Clinton administration came over the use of American troops abroad. The absence of the Cold War threat made it much more difficult for the president and his advisers to decide when the national interest required sending American servicemen and servicewomen into harm's way. Between 1993 and 1999, Clinton opted for foreign intervention in four areas—Somalia, Haiti, Bosnia, and Kosovo—with decidedly mixed results.

Clinton inherited the Somalian venture from Bush, who in December 1992 had sent 25,000 American troops to that starving country on a humanitarian mission. Under Clinton, however, the original aim of using troops to protect the flow of food supplies and relief workers gradually shifted to supporting a UN effort at nation building. Tragedy struck in October 1993 when eighteen American soldiers died in a botched attempt to capture a local warlord in Mogadishu. After television cameras recorded the naked corpse of a U.S. helicopter pilot being dragged through the streets of Somalia's capital, an angry Congress demanded a quick end to the intervention. American forces left Somalia by the end of March 1994 in what was unquestionably the low point of Clinton's foreign policy.

The lack of clear criteria governing intervention that had brought on the disaster in Somalia almost led to another fiasco in Haiti. Seeking to halt the flow into Florida of thousands of Haitians fleeing both poverty and tyranny, Clinton worked to compel the military rulers of Haiti to abdicate in favor of the man they had overthrown in 1991, Jean-Bertrand Aristide. After nearly a year of trade sanctions and increasing diplomatic pressure, the president prepared to use force to remove the military regime. At the last minute, a three-member peace mission led by former President Jimmy Carter worked out a compromise that allowed U.S. troops to land unopposed in late September 1994. Aristide returned to Haiti, but he could do little either to restore democracy or achieve economic progress in view of his country's bankrupt treasury, ruined economy, and deep political divisions. By the time Aristide turned over the presidency to his elected successor in 1996, Haiti remained mired in hopeless poverty.

The Balkan Wars

Two other U.S. interventions, in Bosnia and Kosovo in the Balkan Peninsula, were more difficult but more successful. The breakup of Yugoslavia in 1991 led the Muslim president of Bosnia to ask the European community to recognize the independence of Bosnia-Herzegovina. But Bosnia's ethnic and religious makeup—44 percent Muslim, 31 percent Serb, and 17 percent Croat—contributed to a civil war in which the Bosnian Serbs used the weapons of the former Yugoslavian army to seize more than 70 percent of Bosnian territory. The Muslim and Croatian forces were unable to prevent the Serb bombardment of the capital, Sarajevo, or the Serb policy of "ethnic cleansing"—driving Muslims and Croats from their ancestral homes.

Clinton initially backed a plan to divide Bosnia into ten ethnic provinces. When the Serbs rejected the proposal in the spring of 1993, the president fell back on using American air power to patrol no-fly zones over Bosnia designed to protect UN peacekeeping efforts. Meanwhile, Serb artillery continued to pour a withering fire on the civilian population of Sarajevo, and journalists reported a series of brutal atrocities in which Serb troops slaughtered thousands of Muslim men and raped thousands of Muslim women.

These reports forced Clinton's hand. In the summer of 1995, American planes under NATO auspices began a series of air strikes on the Serb forces. The air campaign along with a major counteroffensive by better equipped Croatian and Muslim forces, led to a cease-fire in October 1995. After three weeks of talks in Dayton, Ohio, between the three warring factions, U.S. mediator Richard Holbrooke secured agreement to create a weak central government for all Bosnia at Sarajevo and to divide the rest of the country into two parts. The Dayton plan called for free elections, the return of refugees to their former homes, and a NATO force to oversee the peace process.

The U.S. intervention in Kosovo was similarly rooted in the breakup of Yugoslavia. Serbian leader Slobodan Milosevic had ended Kosovo's autonomy within Yugoslavia and imposed Serbian rule, even though 90 percent of the province's population was ethnic Albanian. When these Kosovars launched a guerrilla war against the Serbian police, Milosevic responded with a campaign of repression that outraged world opinion. Diplomatic efforts failed to achieve a ceasefire, prompting Clinton and the heads of government of other NATO countries in March 1999 to order an aerial assault on Serbia.

At first it appeared that Clinton had miscalculated. The initial air attacks, directed at empty barracks and remote military bases, led Milosevic to step up the ethnic cleansing in Kosovo. Clinton and the NATO governments shifted the focus of the air assault to Serbia's infrastructure, targeting bridges, oil refineries, and, most important of all, power stations. Domestic pressure on Milosevic began to mount, and he finally agreed to halt his attempts to purge Kosovo of its Albanian inhabitants. An agreement signed on June 10, 1999, called for the withdrawal of all Serb forces and placed Kosovo under UN supervision, with NATO troops acting as peacekeepers.

The conflict over Kosovo revealed both the strengths and weaknesses of the United States in the turbulent post–Cold War world. American military power, while great, was limited by a strong desire to avoid risking American lives. Clinton could boast of an amazing result—NATO had waged a 12-week air campaign without the loss of a single pilot. Yet the United States had been unable to prevent Milosevic from uprooting and terrorizing nearly one million Kosovars. When the fighting ended, the Kosovars returned to their devastated homeland and soon NATO troops had the thankless task of preventing the Albanians from seeking revenge against the Serbian minority in Kosovo.

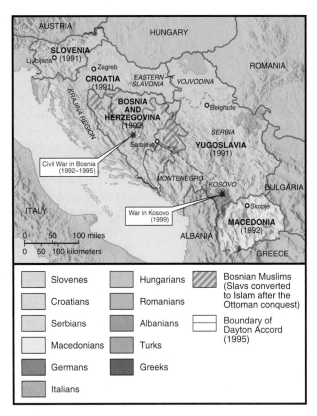

THE BREAKUP OF YUGOSLAVIA/CIVIL WAR IN BOSNIA   *With the end of the communist regime in Yugoslavia in the early 1990s, the country broke apart into ethnically distinct regions. In Bosnia, Muslims, Croatians, and Serbians fought a bloody civil war rife with atrocities on all sides over the issue of ethnic cleansing.* ■

REPUBLICANS TRIUMPHANT

Clinton's eight years in the White House gave Democrats hope that the conservative gains of the 1980s had been only temporary. They pointed to the booming economy of the 1990s and the absence of any serious threat to American security as reasons for voters to leave the presidency in Democratic hands. The election of 2000 proved a bitter disappointment—and all the more so by the way in which it made Republican George W. Bush president.

The Disputed Election of 2000

If history had been the guide, the prosperity of the 1990s should have guaranteed victory to Clinton's protégé, Vice President Al Gore. The state of the economy generally determines the outcome of presidential elections, and entering 2000 the American economy had never appeared stronger. The stock market had soared, spreading wealth among tens of millions of Americans. The federal deficit of the Reagan years had given way to large and growing surpluses.

But Clinton's personal problems muddled the issue. Clinton had survived his impeachment trial, yet the experience tainted his record and left many voters unwilling to reward the Democrats by promoting his vice president.

Certain other domestic problems unnerved voters, as well. The 1995 bombing of a federal building in Oklahoma City by two domestic terrorists killed 168 people and suggested that irrational violence threatened the daily lives of ordinary Americans. This feeling was reinforced by a 1999 shooting rampage at Columbine High School near Denver, Colorado, which left twelve students and one teacher dead, besides the two shooters, who killed themselves. The apparent conflict between material abundance and moral values resulted in the closest election in more than a century.

The two candidates, Vice President Gore of Tennessee and Governor Bush of Texas, had little in common beyond being the sons of successful political fathers. Gore had spent eighteen years in Washington as a congressman, senator, and vice president. He had mastered the intricacies of all the major policy issues and had the experience and knowledge to lead the nation. Bush, by contrast, had pursued a business career before winning the governorship of Texas in 1994. Personable and outgoing, Bush had the temperament for leadership but lacked not only experience but a full grasp of national issues. Journalists were quick to seize on the weaknesses of both men, accusing Gore of frequent and misleading exaggeration and Bush of mangling words and speaking only in generalities.

The candidacy of consumer advocate Ralph Nader, who ran on the Green Party ticket, complicated the political reckoning. Nader never seemed likely to win more than a small percentage of the votes, but in a close election a few points could make all the difference. His presence pushed Gore to the left, leaving room for Bush among independent-minded swing voters.

The race appeared close until election day, and even closer on election night. Gore seemed the likely winner when the major television networks predicted a Democratic victory in Florida. They reconsidered as Bush swept the South, including the Clinton and Gore home states of Arkansas and Tennessee. After midnight, the networks again called Florida, but this time for Bush, and the vice president telephoned the governor to concede, only to recant an hour later when it became clear that the Bush margin in Florida was paper thin.

There things stuck, and for the next month all eyes were on Florida. Gore had 200,000 more popular votes nationwide than Bush, and 267 electoral votes to Bush's 246. Yet with Florida's 25 electoral votes, Bush could win the presidency. Both sides sent teams of lawyers to Florida. Bush's team, working with Florida's Republican secretary of state, sought to certify the results that showed the GOP candidate with a lead of 930 votes out of nearly 6 million cast. Citing many voting problems disclosed by the media, Gore asked for a recount in three heavily Democratic counties in south Florida. All three used antiquated punch card machines that resulted in some ballots not being clearly marked for any presidential candidate when the chads, the bits of paper removed when a card is punched, were not completely detached from the cards.

The decision finally came in the courts. Democrats appealed the initial attempt to certify Bush as the victor to the Florida Supreme Court. The Florida court twice ordered recounts, the second time for all counties in the state, but Bush's lawyers appealed to the United States Supreme Court. On December 12, five weeks after the election, the Court overruled the state court's call for a recount, in a 5 to 4 decision that reflected a long-standing ideological divide among the nine justices. The next day, Gore gracefully conceded, and Bush finally became president-elect.

Bush's narrow victory revealed deep divisions in American life at the beginning of the twenty-first century. The rural west and south went for Bush, along with a few key Midwest and border states, while Gore won the urban states along both coasts. There was an equally strong divide along economic lines, with the poor voting for Gore, the rich for Bush, and the middle class dividing evenly between the two candidates. Gore benefited from the gender gap, winning 54 percent of the women's vote, and he won an even larger share of the black vote, 90 percent, than Clinton in 1996. Bush did manage to narrow the Democratic margin among Hispanic voters, taking 35 percent, compared to only 28 percent for Dole four years earlier. The two candidates split the suburban vote evenly, while Bush reclaimed the Catholic vote for Republicans.

George W. Bush at Home

Bush's first order of business was a large tax cut, which required intense lobbying from the White House. The president had to win over enough conservative southern Democrats to compensate for losing Republican moderates who insisted on reducing the federal debt before cutting taxes. Bush managed the feat. In June 2005, Congress passed legislation that slashed taxes by a staggering $1.35 trillion over a ten-year period. While critics saw this measure as a betrayal of the long effort to balance the budget, Bush contended that future budget surpluses would more than offset the loss of tax revenue.

A slowdown in the American economy, which soon turned the projected budget surplus into annual deficits, failed to halt the Bush administration's tax cut momentum. In 2003, arguing that a further reduction in taxes would stimulate the stalled economy, Bush prevailed upon Congress to adopt another $350 billion in cuts. Like the 2001 cuts, the new reductions were temporary in order to preserve the possibility of a balanced budget by 2010. Opponents charged that if a future Congress made these tax cuts permanent, as seemed likely, the total cost would rise to nearly $1 trillion.

Although it took a bit longer, the president also succeeded in persuading Congress to enact a program of education reform. Borrowing the label "No Child Left Behind" from liberal Democrats, the administration pushed hard for a new policy requiring states to give annual performance tests to all elementary school students. Democrats countered with demands for increased federal funding of public education to assist states and local school boards in raising their standards. Bush shrewdly cultivated the support of liberal Democrats to forge a bipartisan consensus. The final measure increased federal aid to education and mandated state tests in reading and math.

By this time the economic slowdown had become a full-blown recession, the first in ten years. A glut of unsold goods forced manufacturers to curtail production and lay off workers. Unemployment rose, eventually to 6 percent, despite the efforts to cut interest rates. Tax rebates boosted the economy slightly during the summer of 2001, but then the September 11 terrorist attacks on New York and the Pentagon led to a further decline. In 2002, the economy once again began

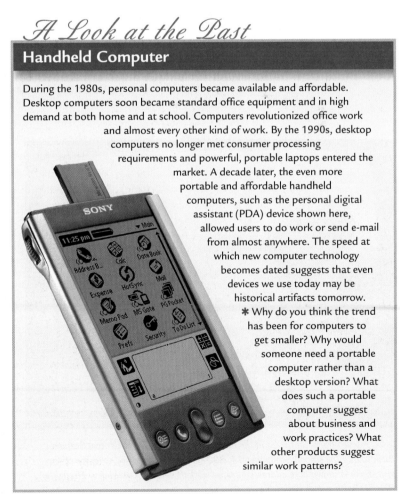

A Look at the Past

Handheld Computer

During the 1980s, personal computers became available and affordable. Desktop computers soon became standard office equipment and in high demand at both home and at school. Computers revolutionized office work and almost every other kind of work. By the 1990s, desktop computers no longer met consumer processing requirements and powerful, portable laptops entered the market. A decade later, the even more portable and affordable handheld computers, such as the personal digital assistant (PDA) device shown here, allowed users to do work or send e-mail from almost anywhere. The speed at which new computer technology becomes dated suggests that even devices we use today may be historical artifacts tomorrow.

✳ Why do you think the trend has been for computers to get smaller? Why would someone need a portable computer rather than a desktop version? What does such a portable computer suggest about business and work practices? What other products suggest similar work patterns?

to recover, only to relapse late in the year amid concern over the threat of war with Iraq.

One of the most troubling aspects of the economic downturn was the implosion of several major corporations and the subsequent revelation of shocking financial practices. WorldCom, Inc., a major telecommunications company, became the largest corporation in American history to declare bankruptcy, while a New York grand jury charged executives of Tyco International, a large electronics company, with stealing more than $600 million from shareholders through stock fraud, false expense reports, and unauthorized bonuses.

These scandals, however, paled before the misdeeds of Enron, a Houston energy company that failed in late 2001 as the result of corrupt business practices, including fraudulent accounting and private partnerships designed to inflate profits and hide losses. When investors began to sell their overvalued Enron stock, shares that were once worth nearly $100 fell to less than $1. Enron declared bankruptcy and the remaining shareholders lost over $50 billion, while rank-and-file employees lost not only their jobs but much of their retirement savings.

The War on Terror

On the morning of September 11, 2001, nineteen Islamic militant terrorists hijacked four U.S. airliners and turned them to attack targets in New York City and Washington, D.C. The hijackers took over two planes flying out of Boston's Logan Airport en route to California, and flew them into the World Trade Center (WTC) in New York. One plane slammed into the north tower just before 9 A.M. and the second hit the south tower only 20 minutes later. Within two hours, both towers had collapsed, taking the lives of nearly 3000 victims trapped in the buildings or crushed by the debris and more than 300 firefighters and other rescue workers who had attempted to save them.

In Washington, an American Airlines flight that left Dulles Airport bound for Los Angeles met a similar fate. Taken over by terrorists, the Boeing 757 plowed into the Pentagon, destroying one wing of the building and killing 189 military personnel and civilian workers. The terrorists had seized a fourth plane, United Airlines flight 93, scheduled to fly from Newark, New Jersey, to San Francisco. Over Pennsylvania, as the hijackers attempted to turn the plane toward the nation's capital, the passengers fought to regain control of the plane. They failed to do so, but prevented the plane from hitting another target in Washington—perhaps the White House or the Capitol building. Flight 93 crashed in southern Pennsylvania, killing all forty-four passengers and crew as well as the hijackers.

Bush vowed to find and punish those responsible for the attacks, as well as any who assisted them. He didn't have to look long to discover the mastermind behind the September 11 attacks. Osama bin Laden, a wealthy Saudi, released videotapes claiming responsibility on behalf of his terrorist organization, al Qaeda ("the Base" in Arabic). Once an ally, bin Laden

■ As rescue efforts continued in the rubble of the World Trade Center, President Bush toured the site on September 14, 2001. In CNN's televised coverage of the visit, Bush is shown here addressing rescue workers through a bullhorn. Firefighter Bob Beckwith stands beside him. ■

had turned against the United States at the time of the 1991 Persian Gulf War, outraged by the presence of large numbers of American troops in his native Saudi Arabia. Evidence linked bin Laden and al Qaeda to the bombing of two American embassies in East Africa in 1998 and an attack on the American destroyer USS *Cole* in Yemen in 2000.

The United States had been trying to neutralize al Qaeda for a decade without success. Ordered out of Saudi Arabia in 1991, bin Laden had sought refuge in the Sudan and later in Afghanistan after the Taliban, another extremist Muslim group, took over that country. In Afghanistan, bin Laden set up camps to train hundreds of would-be terrorists, mainly from Arab countries but including recruits from the Philippines, Indonesia, and Central Asia. After the 1998 embassy bombings, President Clinton ordered cruise missile attacks on several of these camps in the hope of killing bin Laden. The al Qaeda leader survived, though, leaving one of the targets only a few hours before the strike.

Bush's determination to go after those harboring terrorists made Afghanistan the prime target for the American counterattack. The president ordered the Pentagon and the CIA, which already had agents on the scene, to launch an invasion of Afghanistan to destroy the Taliban, wipe out al Qaeda, and capture or kill Osama bin Laden.

In early October 2001, the CIA and Army Special Forces began the operation, relying on the Northern Alliance, an Afghan political coalition resisting the Taliban. Using a variety of methods, ranging from bribes of local warlords to air strikes, American forces quickly routed the Taliban and by December had installed a U.S.-friendly regime in Kabul. Most of Afghanistan remained in chaos, and bin Laden again avoided capture.

While waging the **war on terror** abroad, the Bush administration also focused on the problem of securing the United States from any further terrorist assaults. At the president's urging, Congress approved a new Department of Homeland Security, combining the Customs Bureau, the Coast Guard, the Immigration and Naturalization Service (INS), and other government bureaus.

A primary focus of homeland security was on ensuring the safety of airline travel in the wake of the September 11 hijackings. In November 2001, Bush signed legislation replacing private companies with government employees at all airport screening stations. The airlines were required to replace cockpit doors with secure barriers and to permit armed air marshals to ride among the passengers. The understandable public fear of flying after September 11 nevertheless had a devastating effect on the airline industry, forcing the cancellation of many flights and the laying off of thousands of pilots and other workers. Despite a $15 billion government bailout approved in late September 2001, the airlines continued to experience heavy losses, and several filed for bankruptcy.

The war on terror raised an even more fundamental question than economic stagnation. Attorney General John Ashcroft, using new powers granted by Congress under the Patriot Act, conducted a broad crackdown on possible terrorists, detaining many Muslim Americans on flimsy evidence and insisting that concern for national security outweighed traditional civil liberties. Opponents quickly challenged Ashcroft, arguing that the terrorists would win their greatest victory if the United States violated its own historic principles of individual freedom in the name of fighting terrorism.

war on terror Initiated by President George W. Bush after the attacks of September 11, 2001, the broadly defined war on terror aimed to weed out terrorist operatives and their supporters throughout the world.

A New American Empire?

The terrorist attacks on the United States were the catalyst for a major change in direction for American foreign policy. Not only did the Bush administration wage an intensive effort to avenge the September 11 attacks and prevent further assaults; it initiated a new global policy of American preeminence. For the first time since the

A Look at the Past

Patriotic Symbols

Throughout U.S. history, Americans have used to patriotic symbols to express feelings of national unity and pride. Images of Uncle Sam, the Liberty Bell, and the Statue of Liberty are a few such emblems, but the most popular and enduring insignia have been the American flag and its red, white, and blue colors. In the aftermath of the terrorist attacks of September 11, 2001, many Americans decorated their homes, clothing, and cars with flags and other patriotic symbols. Storekeepers could not keep flags on the shelves and there were even reports of flags being stolen from businesses and homes. This September 2002 photograph shows a van in New York City decorated with flags and references to September 11 to commemorate the first anniversary of the attacks. ✳ Why do you think people responded to the tragic events of September 11 with such public displays of patriotic symbols? From your study of U.S. history, can you recall other times in which Americans responded to events with similar public displays? Do you notice any differences in the ways in which Americans express patriotism today as compared with the past? How do the ways we use patriotic symbols reflect contemporary culture?

end of the Cold War, the United States had a clear, if controversial, blueprint for international affairs.

The new administration rejected established forms of international cooperation. President Bush withdrew U.S. participation in the Kyoto Protocol to control global warming and announced plans to terminate the 1972 Antiballistic Missile (ABM) treaty with Russia. And he was outspoken in refusing to expose American servicepeople to the jurisdiction of the International Criminal Court for possible crimes committed in worldwide peacekeeping efforts.

The new direction of American foreign policy became clear on January 29, 2002, when Bush delivered his second State of the Union address to Congress and the nation. He repeated his vow to punish all nations sponsoring terrorism, and he specified three countries in particular. Iraq, Iran, and North Korea, he declared in a memorable phrase, constituted an "axis of evil." Nine months later, in September 2002, the Bush administration released a fully developed statement of its new world policy, "National Security Strategy (NSS) of the United States."

There were two main components of the new strategy, which critics quickly called **unilateralism.** The first was to accept fully the role the nation had been playing since the end of the Cold War: global policeman. The United States would not shrink from defending freedom anywhere in the world—with allies if possible, by itself if necessary. To implement this policy, NSS asserted that the Bush administration would maintain "military strength beyond challenge."

unilateralism A nation's policy of acting alone without regard for the support or opposition of other nations.

In playing the role of world cop, Bush and his advisers asserted the right to the preventive use of force. Learning from September 11, the NSS continued, "We cannot let our enemies strike first." Although promising to seek the support of the international community before using force, the NSS stated, "we will not hesitate to act alone, if necessary, to exercise our right of self-defense." In other words, the Bush administration, aware that the United States was far stronger militarily and economically than any other nation, accepted its new role as final arbiter of all international disputes.

Iraq quickly became the test case for this new shift in American foreign policy. After his "axis of evil" speech in January, President Bush focused on what he and his Pentagon advisers called **weapons of mass destruction (WMD)** that they claimed Saddam Hussein had been secretly amassing in large quantities. The United States demanded that Iraq permit UN inspectors (forced out of the country in 1998) to search for such weapons. Meanwhile, the Bush administration perfected plans for a unilateral American military solution to the Iraq question.

weapons of mass destruction (WMD) Biological, chemical, and nuclear weapons capable of widespread destruction.

Slowly, but inevitably, the United States moved toward war with Iraq in late 2002 and early 2003. Congress approved a resolution in October authorizing the president to use force against Saddam Hussein's regime. A month later, the UN Security Council voted unanimously to send its team of inspectors back into Iraq, warning Saddam of "severe consequences" if he failed to comply. Despite the failure of the international inspectors to find any evidence of chemical, biological, or nuclear weapons in Iraq, the Bush administration kept pressing for a Security Council resolution authorizing the use of force to compel Saddam to disarm. When France and Russia vowed to veto any such measure, Bush and his advisers decided to ignore the world body and proceed on their own.

The ensuing war with Iraq surprised both the backers and the critics of unilateralism. In March 2003, three columns of American troops, a total of 65,000, began to execute a two-pronged invasion of Iraq from bases in Kuwait. Britain helped by besieging the city of Basra and taking control of southern Iraq. Within two weeks, the U.S. army had captured the Baghdad international airport, and on April 8, just three weeks after the fighting had begun, marines marched virtually unopposed into the heart of the city. The American people watched the televised scene of joyous Iraqis toppling a statue of Saddam in Fardos Square.

The rapid success of the anti-Saddam offensive seemed to confirm the wisdom of Bush's decision for war. But the subsequent failure to find any weapons of mass destruction led critics to question the validity of the war. In response, the president's defenders stressed the importance of deposing Saddam by pointing to his brutal prisons and to the killing fields south of Baghdad where thousands of Shi'ite rebels had been slaughtered in 1991.

The problems of restoring order and rebuilding the shattered Iraqi economy quickly overshadowed the debate over the war's legitimacy. Daily attacks on American troops in the Sunni triangle north of Baghdad began in the summer of 2003 and increased in intensity during the fall, killing an average of three American soldiers each week. By October, more troops had died from these attacks than had been killed during the combat phase in March and April. Widespread looting, sabotage of oil pipelines, and difficulties in repairing and operating outdated power plants and oil facilities made economic recovery very slow and halting. U.S. efforts to involve occupation forces from other UN members yielded only a few troops.

The December 2003 arrest of the elusive Saddam revived American optimism. Yet the overall situation remained troubling. Despite slow but steady progress in restoring public services such as electric power and the gradual recovery of the Iraq oil industry, the armed insurrection against U.S. and Iraqi forces continued. Equally disturbing, conflicts of interest between Shi'ite and Sunni Muslims, as well as the Kurdish demand for autonomy, threatened the American goal of creating a stable Iraqi government.

■ *In a memorable image from the war in Iraq, Iraqi civilians and U.S. soldiers pull down a statue of Saddam Hussein in Baghdad on April 9, 2003. Eight months later, U.S. soldiers captured the former Iraqi president near Tikrit.* ■

Bush Re-elected

Not surprisingly, the war in Iraq became the central issue in the 2004 presidential race. Bush and his supporters contended that it would be reckless to change commanders in mid-conflict. Democrats initially favored former Vermont governor Howard Dean, who had opposed the invasion of Iraq and still strongly criticized Bush's conduct of the war. But the nomination ultimately went to Senator John Kerry of Massachusetts, a decorated Vietnam War veteran who voted for the war but later contended that the war in Iraq, rather than contributing to the war on terror, actually distracted from it.

The campaign was the most vitriolic in years. Democrats accused Bush of having stolen the election of 2000 (with the help of the Supreme Court) and of lying about Saddam's weapons. Republicans called Kerry's belated opposition to the war in Vietnam an insult to those Americans who had died there, and they cited certain of his votes in the Senate as evidence of a fatal inconsistency. Both sides employed the Internet to rally the faithful, raise money, and spread rumors.

The strong emotions produced a record turnout: 12 million more than in 2000. Bush won the popular vote by 2.5 percent, becoming the first victor since his father in 1988 to gain an absolute popular majority. The electoral race was comparably close, with 286 for Bush and 252 for Kerry. Taken together with the congressional elections, which increased the Republican majorities in both the Senate and the House of Representatives, the 2004 race confirmed a "red state/blue state" split in America, with the Republicans dominating the South, the Plains, and the Rockies, while the Democrats carried the Northeast, the Great Lakes, and the West Coast.

Despite his modest margin of victory, Bush claimed a mandate. He proposed to privatize part of the Social Security system and promised to stay the course in Iraq. His Social Security plan went nowhere, but the situation in Iraq briefly seemed to improve. Elections in January 2005 took place more calmly than many observers expected and appeared to place Iraq on the road to self-government.

Yet an escalation of the insurgency during 2005 and early 2006 pushed American deaths in Iraq beyond 2000. As the country verged on civil war, the American public grew more disillusioned than ever.

CHALLENGES OF THE NEW CENTURY

The war in Iraq was merely one example of the challenges facing Americans in the new century. Americans remained as divided as ever over cultural issues. A revival of the American economy after its recession masked a growing inequality between rich and poor and increasing insecurity even among those comparatively well off. The nation's health care and retirement systems sagged under the increasing demands placed upon them. Environmental worries rose along with rising global temperatures.

The Culture Wars Continue

The war in Iraq and the broader concerns about terrorism sometimes overshadowed but didn't erase the divisions among Americans on social and cultural issues. The race question remained alive and contentious, as affirmative action policies came under increasing scrutiny. The *Bakke* v. *Regents of the University of California* decision of 1978 had allowed the use of race as one factor in determining admission to colleges and universities, so long as rigid racial quotas weren't employed. This dissatisfied many conservatives, who during the 1980s and 1990s attacked affirmative action. In 1992, Cheryl Hopwood, an unsuccessful white applicant to the University of Texas Law School, contended that the school had admitted less-qualified African American applicants. In 1996, the Fifth Circuit Court of Appeals decided in her favor, which raised the hopes of anti-affirmative action groups that the Supreme Court would overturn *Bakke.* But in a 2003 case involving the University of Michigan, the Supreme Court ruled that "student body diversity is a compelling state interest that can justify the use of race in university admissions." Affirmative action in higher education could continue in spite of much controversy.

The abortion issue had also roiled American politics for years, but it did so particularly after the death of Chief Justice William Rehnquist in September 2005 and the concurrent retirement of Associate Justice Sandra Day O'Connor allowed George W. Bush to nominate their replacements. Rehnquist had been a reliable conservative, but O'Connor was a swing vote. Liberals feared that a more conservative successor would tip the balance against abortion rights. Yet John Roberts, Bush's nominee for chief justice, and Samuel Alito, the nominee for associate justice, dodged Democrats' questions in hearings, and both nominations succeeded. Almost immediately, South Dakota passed a law essentially banning abortion, and it appeared bound for the newly reconfigured court.

Gay rights provoked fresh controversy as gay advocates pushed for equal marital rights. After the Massachusetts supreme court in 2004 struck down a state law barring same-sex marriages, gay advocates celebrated, but conservatives in dozens of states pressed for laws and constitutional amendments reaffirming traditional views on marriage. Nearly all the efforts were successful, suggesting that, on this front at least, the advances gay men and women had achieved since the 1960s had hit a wall.

Science and religion continued to battle in America's classrooms. Opponents of evolution revised their challenge to Darwin, replacing creationism with "intelligent design" and demanding that this version of their beliefs be aired in biology classes. Ohio embraced intelligent

■ *Marriage ceremony of Hillary, left, and Julie Goodridge in Boston on May 17, 2004, the first day of state-sanctioned same-sex marriage in the United States. The couple were the lead plaintiffs in the landmark lawsuit in which the Massachusetts supreme court struck down a state law barring same-sex marriages. In the first year, more than 6,000 gay and lesbian couples wed in the state.* ■

design only to reject it following an adverse 2005 court decision. Given that public opinion polls consistently showed a majority of Americans rejecting evolution in favor of divine creation—the margin was 3 to 1 in a CBS News poll in early 2006—the fight was sure to continue.

Prosperity—for Whom?

After the recession of George W. Bush's first term, the economy gradually recovered. The economy as a whole grew steadily, and the jobless rate fell to less than 5 percent, not far from the level of the booming 1990s. Corporate profits soared, registering double-digit increases for three years running.

But the good news disguised some unsettling trends. Median family income declined slightly. Although corporate executives commanded seven- and eight-digit pay packages, ordinary workers watched their compensation diminish. Wages were flat, while medical and retirement benefits fell. The poverty rate increased; in 2004, some 37 million Americans lived below the poverty line. Nearly 46 million Americans lacked health insurance.

The globalization of the economy placed continued pressure on American jobs. The automobile industry suffered grievously. General Motors lost billions and was forced to slash tens of thousands of jobs. In early 2006, Ford announced the closing of fourteen plants in the United States and Canada. Even workers in industries formerly thought exempt from the export of jobs found themselves facing direct foreign competition. Telephone call centers moved from the American Midwest to Ireland; computer and other high-tech companies relocated research facilities to India and China.

Rising oil prices—triggered by the turmoil in the Middle East but also by rising demand from China—threatened the status quo in other ways. The rise this time took place more gradually than during the 1970s—the price required a year, rather than weeks, to double—yet it did contribute to higher prices for a wide array of other goods and rekindled fears of inflation. At the gas pump, prices leaped to more than $3 a gallon. In the long term, the higher prices would prompt the purchase of more efficient cars; in the meantime, drivers simply had to grin and bear $40 fill-ups as best they could.

Doubting the Future

During most of American history, every generation had been better off materially than the generation before. Events of the early twenty-first century called this implicit guarantee into question. To an unprecedented extent, the American economy was at the mercy of developments beyond American shores. The pressure on American jobs would continue and probably intensify. Also, foreign investors held huge quantities of America's public debt. Should they decide to divest themselves of their dollar holdings, interest rates in the United States would probably balloon. Some of the foreign investors were already diversifying from Treasury bonds into ownership of American capital assets, making the American economy—and even American physical safety—further subject to foreign influence.

■ *Employees at a busy call center in Bangalore, India, provide service support to international customers. India is the leading market to which developed nations such as the United States outsource high-technology jobs.* ■

Chronology

1989	*Exxon Valdez* oil spill pollutes more than 500 square miles of Alaskan waters (March) ■ San Francisco rocked by massive earthquake (October) ■ Berlin Wall crumbles (November)
1990	Saddam Hussein invades Kuwait (August) ■ Bush breaks "no new taxes" campaign pledge, supports $500 billion budget deal (November)
1991	Operation Desert Storm frees Kuwait and crushes Iraqi invasion force (January–February) ■ Soviet Union dissolved, replaced by Commonwealth of Independent States (December)
1992	Riots devastate South Central Los Angeles after verdict in Rodney King case (May) ■ Bill Clinton elected president (November)
1993	General Motors announces loss of $23.4 billion, the largest one-year loss in U.S. corporate history
1994	Former football star O. J. Simpson charged with killing ex-wife Nicole Brown Simpson and her friend Ronald Goldman (June) ■ Republicans gain control of both houses of Congress (November)
1995	U.S. troops arrive in Bosnia as part of international peacekeeping force (December)
1996	FBI arrests Theodore Kaczynzki, suspected Unabomber, in Montana (April) ■ Clinton signs major welfare reform measure (August)
1997	Federal jury gives Timothy McVeigh death sentence for Oklahoma City bombing
1998	Terrorists bomb American embassies in Kenya and Tanzania
1999	Senate acquits Clinton of impeachment charges (February) ■ Dow Jones Industrial Average goes over 10,000 for first time (March)
2000	Y2K furor proves unfounded ■ George W. Bush wins contested presidential election
2001	American economy goes into recession, ending the longest period of expansion in U.S. history (March) ■ Terrorist attacks on World Trade Center and the Pentagon (September 11) ■ Anthrax spores found in mail (October) ■ United States military action against the Taliban regime in Afghanistan (October–December)
2002	Department of Homeland Security created (November)
2003	U.S. troops invade Iraq and overthrow Saddam Hussein's regime (March–April) ■ Saddam Hussein captured (December)
2004	Insurgency in Iraq escalates ■ Global warming gains international attention ■ George W. Bush re-elected (November)
2005	Bush's plan for Social Security reform fails ■ Hurricane Katrina (August) devastates Gulf Coast and forces evacuation of New Orleans
2006	Proposed constitutional amendment to ban same-sex marriage fails to achieve required two-thirds majority in the Senate

Internal problems appeared hardly more tractable. As the baby boom generation neared retirement, the load on the Social Security system increased. Everyone realized something would have to be done to keep the pension program afloat, but after the rejection of George W. Bush's privatization scheme, no one could figure out how to make the necessary changes politically palatable. Middle-aged Americans faced the prospect of delayed retirement, smaller pensions, or both. Still, younger Americans resisted the tax increases that could have spared the elders from facing rising health care costs.

Immigration became more controversial than at any time since the 1920s. The number of persons entering the country illegally soared, but efforts to rectify the situation foundered on the opposition of immigrant advocates, of businesses, and of assorted other groups.

Environmental problems demanded attention, which they got, and solutions, which they didn't. A consensus emerged among the scientific community that global warming had to be addressed, but the proposed solutions—higher mileage standards for automobiles, a "carbon tax" on emissions of greenhouse gases, greater reliance on nuclear energy, among others—were costly, intrusive, unproven, or environmentally problematic in their own ways.

CONCLUSION: THE PARADOX OF POWER

Events of the early twenty-first century highlighted a paradox of contemporary American life. Never in their history had Americans been more powerful relative to the rest of the world, yet rarely in their history had they felt more at risk. Their superpower status couldn't preserve them from the terrorist attacks of September 11, 2001, nor could it guarantee victory over the insurgents in Iraq. Had the United States been less powerful, it might not have become the target of al Qaeda's hijackers; had it been less powerful, it probably wouldn't have been tempted to invade Iraq. Power excited envy; it invited hubris. America might be the only remaining superpower, but it wasn't omnipotent, and it wasn't invulnerable.

Nor were Americans invulnerable to the challenges that crowded domestic life as the new century took shape. The American economy was still far and away the most powerful and dynamic in the world, but it was increasingly subject to unsettling foreign influences, and it failed distressingly often to deliver on the promise of equality to the most vulnerable in society. Conservatives and liberals fought over the values that ought to guide the country; different racial and ethnic groups proposed competing models of American pluralism.

The fundamental challenge for Americans of the twenty-first century was to balance their power against their vulnerabilities. This wasn't new; it has been the challenge for Americans of every generation. At times they have met the challenge brilliantly; at other times they've done less well. How they would fare this time was for the present generation to determine—guided, ideally, by the lessons of the past.

KEY TERMS

Americans with Disabilities Act (ADA), p. 632

Operation Desert Storm, p. 635

Sunbelt, p. 636

undocumented aliens, p. 638

North American Free Trade Agreement (NAFTA), p. 642

Contract with America, p. 643

war on terror, p. 651

unilateralism, p. 652

weapons of mass destruction (WMD), p. 653

RECOMMENDED READING

John Robert Greene provides a balanced view of the Bush administration in *The Presidency of George Bush* (2000). The best biography of the president is Herbert Parmet, *George Bush* (1997). For foreign policy, see George Bush and Brent Scowcroft, *A World Transformed* (1998). Bob Woodward traces the decisions leading to the Gulf War in *The Commanders* (1991). The best overview of the military oper-

ations is Michael R. Gordon and Bernard F. Trainor, *The Generals' War* (1995).

Bill Clinton's, *My Life* (2004), is wordy, like the author, but one of the most revealing of presidential memoirs. Sidney Blumenthal, *The Clinton Wars* (2003), settles accounts with some former colleagues from the Clinton administration even as he reveals how the administration operated. Joe

Klein, *The Natural* (2002), is sympathetic to Clinton; Rich Lowry, *Legacy* (2003), most definitely is not. Richard A. Posner, *An Affair of State* (1999), and Michael Isikoff, *Uncovering Clinton* (2000), dissect the Monica Lewinsky scandal and the ensuing impeachment proceedings.

Haynes Johnson, *The Best of Times* (2001), provides a journalistic account of the 1990s. John Cassidy, *dot.com* (2002) treats the Internet boom. The best survey of foreign policy in the Clinton years is David Halberstam, *War in a Time of Peace* (2001). On Bosnia, see Richard Holbrooke, *To End a War* (2001). David Fromkin covers the other Balkan crisis in *Kosovo Crossing* (1999).

The most balanced account of the disputed 2000 election is Howard Gillman, *The Votes that Counted* (2001). Contrasting views of George W. Bush can be found in Frank Bruni, *Ambling into History* (2002); David Frum, *The Right Man* (2003); and Maureen Dowd, *Bushworld* (2004). On the terrorist attacks of September 11, 2001, see Richard Bernstein et al., *Out of the Blue* (2002). Bob Woodward, *Plan of Attack* (2004), provides the most detailed account of the decision for war against Iraq (the second time around). George Packer, *The Assassin's Gate* (2005), offers a ground-level view of Iraq after the overthrow of Saddam Hussein.

Terry H. Anderson, *The Pursuit of Fairness* (2004), provides a history of affirmative action. Kevin Phillips, *Wealth and Democracy* (2002), traces the rise of economic inequality in America. Thomas L. Friedman, *The World is Flat* (2005), assesses the impact of globalization. Reasonable voices on the culture wars are hard to hear; one is Alan Wolfe, *One Nation after All* (1999).

SUGGESTED WEB SITES

George Herbert Walker Bush

www.ipl.org/div/potus/ghwbush.html

This site contains basic factual data about Bush's election and presidency, speeches, and on-line biographies.

The Gulf War

www.pbs.org/pages/frontline/gulf/index.html

This Frontline and PBS site combines personal accounts with a chronology and general information about the war.

Bill Clinton

www.ipl.org/div/potus/wjclinton.html

On Clinton's presidency.

Census 2000

www.census.gov/main/www/cen2000.html

U.S. Census Bureau gateway to its snapshot of the American people at the beginning of the new millennium.

George W. Bush

www.ipl.org/div/potus/gwbush.html

On the second Bush presidency.

9–11 Commission Report

www.9-11commission.gov/

The findings of the commission that investigated the terrorist attacks.

The National Security Archive at George Washington University

www.gmu.edu/~nsarchiv/

This site includes recent declassified documents and government records on topics of national security, foreign, intelligence, and economic policies of the United States.

War in Iraq

www.cnn.com/SPECIALS/2003/iraq/

A CNN special report on the war, including maps and video.

History of the Internet

www.isoc.org/internet/history/brief.shtml

The technology that wired the world.

Appendix

The Declaration of Independence

The Articles of Confederation

The Constitution of the United States of America

Amendments to the Constitution

Presidential Elections

Presidents and Vice Presidents

For additional reference material, go to
www.ablongman.com/americanhistory
The on-line appendix includes the following:

THE DECLARATION OF INDEPENDENCE

In Congress, July 4, 1776

The Unanimous Declaration of the Thirteen United States of America,

When, in the course of human events, it becomes necessary for one people to dissolve the political bonds which have connected them with another, and to assume, among the powers of the earth, the separate and equal station to which the laws of nature and of nature's God entitle them, a decent respect to the opinions of mankind requires that they should declare the causes which impel them to the separation.

We hold these truths to be self-evident: That all men are created equal; that they are endowed by their Creator with certain unalienable rights; that among these are life, liberty, and the pursuit of happiness; that, to secure these rights, governments are instituted among men, deriving their just powers from the consent of the governed; that whenever any form of government becomes destructive of these ends, it is the right of the people to alter or to abolish it, and to institute new government, laying its foundation on such principles, and organizing its powers in such form, as to them shall seem most likely to effect their safety and happiness. Prudence, indeed, will dictate that governments long established should not be changed for light and transient causes; and accordingly all experience hath shown that mankind are more disposed to suffer, while evils are sufferable, than to right themselves by abolishing the forms to which they are accustomed. But when a long train of abuses and usurpations, pursuing invariably the same object, evinces a design to reduce them under absolute despotism, it is their right, it is their duty, to throw off such government, and to provide new guards for their future security. Such has been the patient sufferance of these colonies; and such is now the necessity which constrains them to alter their former systems of government. The history of the present King of Great Britain is a history of repeated injuries and usurpations, all having in direct object the establishment of an absolute tyranny over these states. To prove this, let facts be submitted to a candid world.

He has refused his assent to laws, the most wholesome and necessary for the public good.

He has forbidden his governors to pass laws of immediate and pressing importance, unless suspended in their operation till his assent should be obtained; and, when so suspended, he has utterly neglected to attend to them.

He has refused to pass other laws for the accommodation of large districts of people, unless those people would relinquish the right of representation in the legislature, a right inestimable to them, and formidable to tyrants only.

He has called together legislative bodies at places unusual, uncomfortable, and distant from the depository of their public records, for the sole purpose of fatiguing them into compliance with his measures.

He has dissolved representative houses repeatedly, for opposing, with manly firmness, his invasions on the rights of the people.

He has refused for a long time, after such dissolutions, to cause others to be elected; whereby the legislative powers, incapable of annihilation, have returned to the people at large for their exercise; the state remaining, in the mean time, exposed to all the dangers of invasions from without and convulsions within.

He has endeavored to prevent the population of these states; for that purpose obstructing the laws for naturalization of foreigners; refusing to pass others to encourage their migration hither, and raising the conditions of new appropriations of lands.

He has obstructed the administration of justice, by refusing his assent to laws for establishing judiciary powers.

He has made judges dependent on his will alone, for the tenure of their offices, and the amount and payment of their salaries.

He has erected a multitude of new offices, and sent hither swarms of officers to harass our people and eat out their substance.

He has kept among us, in times of peace, standing armies, without the consent of our legislatures.

He has affected to render the military independent of, and superior to, the civil power.

He has combined with others to subject us to a jurisdiction foreign to our constitution, and unacknowledged by our laws, giving his assent to their acts of pretended legislation:

For quartering large bodies of armed troops among us;

For protecting them, by a mock trial, from punishment for any murder which they should commit on the inhabitants of these states;

For cutting off our trade with all parts of the world;

For imposing taxes on us without our consent;

For depriving us, in many cases, of the benefits of trial by jury;

For transporting us beyond seas, to be tried for pretended offenses;

For abolishing the free system of English laws in a neighboring province, establishing therein an arbitrary government, and enlarging its boundaries, so as to render it at once an example and fit instrument for introducing the same absolute rule into these colonies;

For taking away our charters, abolishing our most valuable laws, and altering fundamentally the forms of our governments;

For suspending our own legislatures, and declaring themselves invested with power to legislate for us in all cases whatsoever.

He has abdicated government here, by declaring us out of his protection and waging war against us.

He has plundered our seas, ravaged our coasts, burned our towns, and destroyed the lives of our people.

He is at this time transporting large armies of foreign mercenaries to complete the works of death, desolation, and tyranny already begun with circumstances of cruelty and perfidy scarcely paralleled in the most barbarous ages, and totally unworthy the head of a civilized nation.

He has constrained our fellow-citizens, taken captive on the high seas, to bear arms against their country, to become the executioners of their friends and brethren, or to fall themselves by their hands.

He has excited domestic insurrection among us, and has endeavored to bring on the inhabitants of our frontiers the merciless Indian savages, whose known rule of warfare is an undistinguished destruction of all ages, sexes, and conditions.

In every stage of these oppressions we have petitioned for redress in the most humble terms; our repeated petitions have been answered only by repeated injury. A prince, whose character is thus marked by every act which may define a tyrant, is unfit to be the ruler of a free people.

Nor have we been wanting in our attentions to our British brethren. We have warned them, from time to time, of attempts by their legislature to extend an unwarrantable jurisdiction over us. We have reminded them of the circumstances of our emigration and settlement here. We have appealed to their native justice and magnanimity; and we have conjured them, by the ties of our common kindred, to disavow these usurpations, which would inevitably interrupt our connections and correspondence. They, too, have been deaf to the voice of justice and of consanguinity. We must, therefore, acquiesce in the necessity which denounces our separation, and hold them, as we hold the rest of mankind, enemies in war, in peace friends.

We, therefore, the representatives of the United States of America, in General Congress assembled, appealing to the Supreme Judge of the world for the rectitude of our intentions, do, in the name and by the authority of the good people of these colonies, solemnly publish and declare, that these United Colonies are, and of right ought to be, FREE AND INDEPENDENT STATES; that they are absolved from all allegiance to the British crown, and that all political connection between them and the state of Great Britain is, and ought to be, totally dissolved; and that, as free and independent states, they have full power to levy war, conclude peace, contract alliances, establish commerce, and do all other acts and things which independent states may of right do. And for the support of this declaration, with a firm reliance on the protection of Divine Providence, we mutually pledge to each other our lives, our fortunes, and our sacred honor.

John Hancock

Button Gwinnett
Lyman Hall
Geo. Walton
Wm. Hooper
Joseph Hewes
John Penn
Edward Rutledge
Thos. Heyward, Junr.
Thomas Lynch, Junr.
Arthur Middleton
Samuel Chase
Wm. Paca
Thos. Stone
Charles Carroll of Carrollton
George Wythe
Richard Henry Lee
Th. Jefferson
Benj. Harrison
Thos. Nelson, Jr.

Francis Lightfoot Lee
Carter Braxton
Robt. Morris
Benjamin Rush
Benja. Franklin
John Morton
Geo. Clymer
Jas. Smith
Geo. Taylor
James Wilson
Geo. Ross
Caesar Rodney
Geo. Read
Tho. M'kean
Wm. Floyd
Phil. Livingston
Frans. Lewis
Lewis Morris
Richd. Stockton

Jno. Witherspoon
Fras. Hopkinson
John Hart
Abra. Clark
Josiah Bartlett
Wm. Whipple
Saml. Adams
John Adams
Robt. Treat Paine
Elbridge Gerry
Step. Hopkins
William Ellery
Roger Sherman
Sam'el Huntington
Wm. Williams
Oliver Wolcott
Matthew Thornton

THE ARTICLES OF CONFEDERATION

Between the States of New Hampshire, Massachusetts Bay, Rhode Island and Providence Plantations, Connecticut, New York, New Jersey, Pennsylvania, Delaware, Maryland, Virginia, North Carolina, South Carolina, Georgia

ARTICLE 1

The stile of this confederacy shall be "The United States of America."

ARTICLE 2

Each State retains its sovereignty, freedom and independence, and every power, jurisdiction, and right, which is not by this confederation expressly delegated to the United States, in Congress assembled.

ARTICLE 3

The said states hereby severally enter into a firm league of friendship with each other for their common defence, the security of their liberties and their mutual and general welfare; binding themselves to assist each other against all force offered to, or attacks made upon them, or any of them, on account of religion, sovereignty, trade, or any other pretence whatever.

ARTICLE 4

The better to secure and perpetuate mutual friendship and intercourse among the people of the different states in this union, the free inhabitants of each of these states, paupers, vagabonds, and fugitives from justice excepted, shall be entitled to all privileges and immunities of free citizens in the several states; and the people of each State shall have free ingress and regress to and from any other State, and shall enjoy therein all the privileges of trade and commerce, subject to the same duties, impositions, and restrictions, as the inhabitants thereof respectively; provided, that such restrictions shall not extend so far as to prevent the removal of property, imported into any State, to any other State of which the owner is an inhabitant; provided also, that no imposition, duties, or restriction, shall be laid by any State on the property of the United States, or either of them.

If any person guilty of, or charged with treason, felony, or other high misdemeanor in any State, shall flee from justice and be found in any of the United States, he shall, upon demand of the governor or executive power of the State from which he fled, be delivered up and removed to the State having jurisdiction of his offence.

Full faith and credit shall be given in each of these states to the records, acts, and judicial proceedings of the courts and magistrates of every other State.

ARTICLE 5

For the more convenient management of the general interests of the United States, delegates shall be annually appointed, in such manner as the legislature of each State shall direct, to meet in Congress, on the 1st Monday in November in every year, with a power reserved to each State to recall its delegates, or any of them, at any time within the year, and to send others in their stead for the remainder of the year.

No State shall be represented in Congress by less than two, nor by more than seven members; and no person shall be capable of being a delegate for more than three years in any term of six years; nor shall any person, being a delegate, be capable of holding any office under the United States, for which he, or any other for his benefit, receives any salary, fees, or emolument of any kind.

Each State shall maintain its own delegates in a meeting of the states, and while they act as members of the committee of the states.

In determining questions in the United States, in Congress assembled, each State shall have one vote.

Freedom of speech and debate in Congress shall not be impeached or questioned in any court or place out of Congress: and the members of Congress shall be protected in their persons from arrests and imprisonments, during the time of their going to and from, and attendance on Congress, except for treason, felony, or breach of the peace.

ARTICLE 6

No State, without the consent of the United States, in Congress assembled, shall send any embassy to, or receive any embassy from, or enter into any conference, agreement, alliance, or treaty with any king, prince, or state; nor shall any person, holding any office of profit or trust under the United States, or any of them, accept of any present, emolument, office or title, of any kind whatever, from any king, prince, or foreign state; nor shall the United States, in Congress assembled, or any of them, grant any title of nobility.

No two or more states shall enter into any treaty, confederation, or alliance, whatever, between them, without the consent of the United States, in Congress assembled, specifying accurately the purposes for which the same is to be entered into, and how long it shall continue.

No State shall lay any imposts or duties which may interfere with any stipulations in treaties entered into by the United States, in Congress assembled, with any king, prince, or state, in pursuance of any treaties already proposed by Congress to the courts of France and Spain.

No vessels of war shall be kept up in time of peace by any State, except such number only as shall be deemed necessary by the United States, in Congress assembled, for the defence of such State or its trade; nor shall any body of forces be kept up by any State, in time of peace, except such number only as, in the judgment of the United States, in Congress assembled, shall be deemed requisite to garrison the forts necessary for the defence of such State; but every State shall always keep up a well regulated and disciplined militia, sufficiently armed and accoutred, and shall provide, and constantly have ready for use, in public stores, a due number of field pieces and tents, and a proper quantity of arms, ammunition and camp equipage.

No State shall engage in any war without the consent of the United States, in Congress assembled, unless such State be actually invaded by enemies, or shall have received certain advice of a resolution being formed by some nation of Indians to invade such State, and the danger is so imminent as not to admit of a delay till the United States, in Congress assembled, can be consulted; nor shall any State grant commissions to any ships or vessels of war, nor letters of marque or reprisal, except it be after a declaration of war by the United States, in Congress assembled, and then only against the kingdom or state, and the subjects thereof, against which war has been so declared, and under such regulations as shall be established by the United States, in Congress assembled, unless such States be infested by pirates, in which case vessels of war may be fitted out for that occasion, and kept so long as the danger shall continue, or until the United States, in Congress assembled, shall determine otherwise.

ARTICLE 7

When land forces are raised by any State for the common defence, all officers of or under the rank of colonel, shall be appointed by the legislature of each State respectively, by whom such forces shall be raised, or in such manner as such State shall direct; and all vacancies shall be filled up by the State which first made the appointment.

ARTICLE 8

All charges of war and all other expences, that shall be incurred for the common defence or general welfare, and allowed by the United States, in Congress assembled, shall be defrayed out of a common treasury, which shall be supplied by the several states, in proportion to the value of all land within each State, granted to or surveyed for any person, as such land and the buildings and improvements thereon shall be estimated according to such mode as the United States, in Congress assembled, shall, from time to time, direct and appoint.

The taxes for paying that proportion shall be laid and levied by the authority and direction of the legislatures of the several states, within the time agreed upon by the United States, in Congress assembled.

ARTICLE 9

The United States, in Congress assembled, shall have the sole and exclusive right and power of determining on peace and war, except in the cases mentioned in the 6th article; of sending and receiving ambassadors; entering into treaties and alliances, provided that no treaty of commerce shall be made, whereby the legislative power of the respective states shall be restrained from imposing such imposts and duties on foreigners as their own people are subjected to, or from prohibiting the exportation or importation of any species of goods or commodities whatsoever; of establishing rules for deciding, in all cases, what captures on land or water shall be legal, and in what manner prizes, taken by land or naval forces in the service of the United States, shall be divided or appropriated; of granting letters of marque and reprisal in times of peace; appointing courts for the trial of piracies and felonies committed on the high seas, and establishing courts for receiving and determining, finally, appeals in all cases of captures; provided, that no member of Congress shall be appointed a judge of any of the said courts.

The United States, in Congress assembled, shall also be the last resort on appeal in all disputes and differences now subsisting, or that hereafter may arise between two or more states concerning boundary, jurisdiction or any other cause whatever; which authority shall always be exercised in the manner following: whenever the legislative or executive authority, or lawful agent of any State, in controversy with another, shall present a petition to Congress, stating the matter in question, and praying for a hearing, notice thereof shall be given, by order of Congress, to the legislative or executive authority of the other State in controversy, and a day assigned for the appearance of the parties by their lawful agents, who shall then be directed to appoint, by joint consent, commissioners or judges to constitute a court for hearing and determining the matter in question; but, if they cannot agree, Congress shall name three persons out of each of the United States, and from the list of such persons each party shall alternately strike out one, in the petitioners beginning, until the number shall be reduced to thirteen; and from that number not less than seven, nor more than nine names, as Congress shall direct, shall, in the presence of Congress, be drawn out by lot; and the persons whose names shall be drawn, or any five of them, shall be commissioners or judges to hear and finally determine the controversy, so always as a major part of the judges who shall hear the cause shall agree in the determination; and if either party shall neglect to attend at the day appointed, without shewing reasons which Congress shall judge sufficient, or, being present, shall refuse to strike, the Congress shall proceed to nominate three persons out of each State, and the secretary of Congress shall strike in behalf of such party absent or refusing; and the judgment and sentence of the court to be appointed, in the manner before prescribed, shall be final and conclusive; and if any of the parties shall refuse to submit to the authority of such court, or to appear or defend their claim or cause, the court shall nevertheless proceed to pronounce sentence or judgment, which shall, in like manner, be final and decisive, the judgment or sentence and other proceedings being, in either case, transmitted to Congress, and lodged among the acts of Congress for the security of the parties concerned: provided, that every commissioner, before he sits in judgment, shall take an oath, to be administered by one of the judges of the supreme or superior court of the State where the cause shall be tried, "well and truly to hear and determine the matter in question, according to the best of his judgment, without favour, affection, or hope of reward": provided, also, that no State shall be deprived of territory for the benefit of the United States.

All controversies concerning the private right of soil, claimed under different grants of two or more states, whose jurisdictions, as they may respect such lands and the states which passed such grants, are adjusted, the said grants, or either of them, being at the same time claimed to have originated antecedent to such settlement of jurisdiction, shall, on the petition of either party to the Congress of the United States, be finally determined, as near as may be, in the same manner as is before prescribed for deciding disputes respecting territorial jurisdiction between different states.

The United States, in Congress assembled, shall also have the sole and exclusive right and power of regulating the alloy and value of coin struck by their own authority, or by that of the respective states; fixing the standard of weights and measures throughout the United States; regulating the trade and managing all affairs with the Indians not members of any of the states; provided that the legislative right of any State within its own limits be not infringed or violated; establishing and regulating post offices from one State to another throughout all the United States, and exacting such postage on the papers passing through the same as may be requisite to defray the expences of the said office; appointing all officers of the land forces in the service of the United States, excepting regimental officers; appointing all the officers of the naval forces, and commissioning all officers whatever in the service of the United States; making rules for the government and regulation of the said land and naval forces, and directing their operations.

The United States, in Congress assembled, shall have authority to appoint a committee to sit in the recess of Congress, to be denominated "a Committee of the States," and to consist of one delegate from each State, and to appoint such other committees and civil officers as may be necessary for managing the general affairs of the United States, under their direction; to appoint one of their number to preside; provided that no person be allowed to serve in the office of president more than one year in any term of three years; to ascertain the necessary sums of money to be raised for the service of the United States, and to appropriate and apply the same for defraying the public expences; to borrow money or emit bills on the credit of the United States, transmitting, every half year, to the respective states, an account of the sums of money so borrowed or emitted; to build and equip a navy; to agree upon the number of land forces, and to make requisitions from each State for its quota, in proportion to the number of white inhabitants in such State; which requisitions shall be binding; and, thereupon, the legislature of each State shall appoint the regimental officers, raise the men, and cloathe, arm, and equip them in a soldier-like manner, at the expence of the United States; and the officers and men so cloathed, armed, and equipped, shall march to the place appointed and within the time agreed on by the United States, in Congress assembled; but if the United States, in Congress assembled, shall, on consideration of circumstances, judge proper that any State should not raise men, or should raise a smaller number than its quota, and that any other State should raise a greater number of men than the quota thereof, such extra number shall be raised, officered, cloathed, armed, and equipped in the same manner as the quota of such State, unless the legislature of such State shall judge that such extra number cannot be safely spared out of the same, in which case they shall raise, officer, cloathe, arm, and equip as many of such extra number as they judge can be safely spared. And the officers and men so cloathed, armed, and equipped, shall march to the place appointed and within the time agreed on by the United States, in Congress assembled.

The United States, in Congress assembled, shall never engage in a war, nor grant letters of marque and reprisal in time of peace, nor enter into any treaties or alliances, nor coin money, nor regulate the value thereof, nor ascertain the sums and expences necessary for the defence and welfare of the United States, or any of them: nor emit bills, nor borrow money on the credit of the United States, nor appropriate money, nor agree upon the number of vessels of war to be built or purchased, or the number of land or sea forces to be raised, nor appoint a commander in chief of the army or navy, unless nine states assent to the same; nor shall a question on any other point, except for adjourning from day to day, be determined, unless by the votes of a majority of the United States, in Congress assembled.

The Congress of the United States shall have power to adjourn to any time within the year, and to any place within the United States, so that no period of adjournment be for a longer duration than the space of six months, and shall publish the journal of their proceedings monthly, except such parts thereof, relating to treaties, alliances or military operations, as, in their judgment, require secrecy; and the yeas and nays of the delegates of each State on any question shall be entered on the journal, when it is desired by any delegate; and the delegates of a State, or any of them, at his, or their request, shall be furnished with a transcript of the said journal, except such parts as are above excepted, to lay before the legislatures of the several states.

ARTICLE 10

The committee of the states, or any nine of them, shall be authorized to execute, in the recess of Congress, such of the powers of Congress as the United States, in Congress assembled, by the consent of nine states, shall, from time to time, think expedient to vest them with; provided, that no power be delegated to the said committee for the exercise of which, by the articles of confederation, the voice of nine states, in the Congress of the United States assembled, is requisite.

ARTICLE 11

Canada acceding to this confederation, and joining in the measures of the United States, shall be admitted into and entitled to all the advantages of this union; but no other colony shall be admitted into the same, unless such admission be agreed to by nine states.

ARTICLE 12

All bills of credit emitted, monies borrowed and debts contracted by, or under the authority of Congress before the assembling of the United States, in pursuance of the present confederation, shall be deemed and considered as a charge against the United States, for payment and satisfaction whereof the said United States and the public faith are hereby solemnly pledged.

ARTICLE 13

Every State shall abide by the determinations of the United States, in Congress assembled, on all questions which, by this confederation, are submitted to them. And the articles of this confederation shall be inviolably observed by every State, and the union shall be perpetual; nor shall any alteration at any time hereafter be made in any of them, unless such alteration be agreed to in a Congress of the United States, and be afterwards confirmed by the legislatures of every State.

These articles shall be proposed to the legislatures of all the United States, to be considered, and if approved of by them, they are advised to authorize their delegates to ratify the same in the Congress of the United States; which being done, the same shall become conclusive.

THE CONSTITUTION OF THE UNITED STATES OF AMERICA

PREAMBLE

We the People of the United States, in Order to form a more perfect Union, establish Justice, insure domestic Tranquility, provide for the common defence, promote the general Welfare, and secure the Blessings of Liberty to ourselves and our Posterity, do ordain and establish this Constitution for the United States of America.

ARTICLE I

Section 1

All legislative Powers herein granted shall be vested in a Congress of the United States, which shall consist of a Senate and House of Representatives.

Section 2

The House of Representatives shall be composed of Members chosen every second Year by the People of the several States, and the Electors in each State shall have the Qualifications requisite for Electors of the most numerous Branch of the State Legislature.

No Person shall be a Representative who shall not have attained to the Age of twenty five Years, and been seven Years a Citizen of the United States, and who shall not, when elected, be an inhabitant of that State in which he shall be chosen.

Representatives and direct Taxes shall be apportioned among the several States which may be included within this Union, according to their respective Numbers, *which shall be determined by adding to the whole Number of free Persons, including those bound to Service for a Term of Years, and excluding Indians not taxed, three fifths of all other Persons.* * The actual Enumeration shall be made within three Years after the first Meeting of the Congress of the United States, and within every subsequent Term of ten Years, in such Manner as they shall by Law direct. The Number of Representatives shall not exceed one for every thirty Thousand, but each State shall have at Least one Representative; *and until such enumeration shall be made, the State of New Hampshire shall be entitled to chuse three, Massachusetts eight, Rhode-Island and Providence Plantations one, Connecticut five, New York six, New Jersey four, Pennsylvania eight, Delaware one, Maryland six, Virginia ten, North Carolina five, South Carolina five, and Georgia three.*

When vacancies happen in the Representation from any State, the Executive Authority thereof shall issue Writs of Election to fill such Vacancies.

The House of Representatives shall chuse their Speaker and other Officers; and shall have the sole Power of Impeachment.

Section 3

The Senate of the United States shall be composed of two Senators from each State, *chosen by the Legislature thereof,* for six Years; and each Senator shall have one Vote.

Immediately after they shall be assembled in Consequence of the first Election, they shall be divided as equally as may be into three Classes. The Seats of the Senators of the first Class shall be vacated at the Expiration of the second Year, of the second Class at the Expiration of the fourth Year, and of the third Class at the Expiration of the sixth Year so that one third may be chosen every second Year; and if Vacancies happen by Resignation, or otherwise, during the Recess of the Legislature of any state, the Executive thereof may make temporary Appointments until the next Meeting of the Legislature, which shall then fill such Vacancies.

No Person shall be a Senator who shall not have attained to the Age of thirty Years, and been nine Years a Citizen of the United States, and who shall not, when elected, be an Inhabitant of that State for which he shall be chosen.

The Vice President of the United States shall be President of the Senate, but shall have no Vote, unless they be equally divided.

The Senate shall chuse their other Officers, and also a President *pro tempore,* in the Absence of the Vice President, or when he shall exercise the Office of President of the United States.

The Senate shall have the sole Power to try all Impeachments. When sitting for that Purpose, they shall be on Oath or Affirmation. When the President of the United States is tried the Chief Justice shall preside: And no Person shall be convicted without the Concurrence of two thirds of the Members present.

Judgment in Cases of Impeachment shall not extend further than to removal from Office, and disqualification to hold and enjoy any Office of honor, Trust or Profit under the United States: but the Party convicted shall nevertheless be liable and subject to Indictment, Trial, Judgment and Punishment, according to Law.

Section 4

The Times, Places and Manner of holding Elections for Senators and Representatives, shall be prescribed in each State by the Legislature thereof; but the Congress may at any time by Law make or alter such Regulations, except as to the Places of chusing Senators.

The Congress shall assemble at least once in every Year, *and such Meeting shall be on the first Monday in December, unless they shall by Law appoint a different Day.*

---

*Passages no longer in effect are printed in italic type.

Section 5

Each House shall be the Judge of the Elections, Returns and Qualifications of its own Members, and a Majority of each shall constitute a Quorum to do Business; but a smaller Number may adjourn from day to day, and may be authorized to compel the Attendance of absent Members, in such Manner, and under such Penalties as each House may provide.

Each House may determine the Rules of its Proceedings, punish its Members for disorderly Behaviour, and, with the Concurrence of two thirds, expel a Member.

Each House shall keep a Journal of its Proceedings, and from time to time publish the same, excepting such Parts as may in their Judgment require Secrecy; and the Yeas and Nays of the Members of either House on any question shall, at the Desire of one fifth of those Present, be entered on the Journal.

Neither House, during the Session of Congress, shall, without the Consent of the other, adjourn for more than three days, nor to any other Place than that in which the two Houses shall be sitting.

Section 6

The Senators and Representatives shall receive a Compensation for their Services, to be ascertained by Law, and paid out of the Treasury of the United States. They shall in all Cases, except Treason, Felony and Breach of the Peace, be privileged from Arrest during their Attendance at the Session of their respective Houses, and in going to and returning from the same; and for any Speech or Debate in either House, they shall not be questioned in any other Place.

No Senator or Representative shall, during the Time for which he was elected, be appointed to any civil Office under the Authority of the United States, which shall have been created, or the Emoluments whereof shall have been encreased during such time, and no Person holding any Office under the United States, shall be a Member of either House during his Continuance in Office.

Section 7

All Bills for raising Revenue shall originate in the House of Representatives; but the Senate may propose or concur with Amendments as on other Bills.

Every Bill which shall have passed the House of Representatives and the Senate, shall, before it become a Law, be presented to the President of the United States; If he approve he shall sign it, but if not he shall return it, with his Objections to the House in which it shall have originated, who shall enter the Objections at large on their Journal, and proceed to reconsider it. If after such Reconsideration two thirds of that House shall agree to pass the Bill, it shall be sent, together with the Objections, to the other House, by which it shall likewise be reconsidered, and if approved by two thirds of that House, it shall become a Law. But in all such Cases the Votes of both Houses shall be determined by yeas and Nays, and the Names of the Persons voting for and against the Bill shall be entered on the Journal of each House respectively. If any Bill shall not be returned by the President within ten Days (Sundays excepted) after it shall have been presented to him, the Same shall be a Law, in like Manner as if he had signed it, unless the Congress by their Adjournment prevent its Return, in which Case it shall not be a Law.

Every Order, Resolution, or Vote to which the Concurrence of the Senate and House of Representatives may be necessary (except on a question of Adjournment) shall be presented to the President of the United States; and before the Same shall take Effect, shall be approved by him, or being disapproved by him, shall be repassed by two thirds of the Senate and House of Representatives, according to the Rules and Limitations prescribed in the Case of a Bill.

Section 8

The Congress shall have Power To lay and collect Taxes, Duties, Imposts and Excises, to pay the Debts and provide for the common Defence and general Welfare of the United States; but all Duties, Imposts and Excises shall be uniform throughout the United States;

To borrow Money on the credit of the United States;

To regulate Commerce with foreign Nations, and among the several States, and with the Indian Tribes;

To establish an uniform Rule of Naturalization, and uniform Laws on the subject of Bankruptcies throughout the United States;

To coin Money, regulate the Value thereof, and of foreign Coin, and fix the Standard of Weights and Measures;

To provide for the Punishment of counterfeiting the Securities and current Coin of the United States;

To establish Post Offices and post Roads;

To promote the Progress of Science and useful Arts, by securing for limited Times to Authors and Inventors the exclusive Right to their respective Writings and Discoveries;

To constitute Tribunals inferior to the supreme Court;

To define and punish Piracies and Felonies committed on the high Seas, and Offences against the Law of Nations;

To declare War, grant Letters of Marque and Reprisal, and make Rules concerning Captures on Land and Water;

To raise and support Armies, but no Appropriation of Money to that Use shall be for a longer Term than two Years;

To provide and maintain a Navy;

To make Rules for the Government and Regulation of the land and naval Forces;

To provide for calling forth the Militia to execute the Laws of the Union, suppress Insurrections and repel Invasions;

To provide for organizing, arming, and disciplining, the Militia, and for governing such Part of them as may be employed in the Service of the United States, reserving to the States respectively, the Appointment of the Officers, and the Authority of training the Militia according to the discipline prescribed by Congress;

To exercise exclusive Legislation in all Cases whatsoever, over such District (not exceeding ten Miles square) as may, by Cession of particular States, and the Acceptance of Congress, become the Seat of the Government of the United States, and to exercise like Authority over all Places purchased by the Consent of the Legislature of the State in which the Same shall be, for the Erection of Forts, Magazines, Arsenals, dock-Yards, and other needful Buildings;—And

To make all Laws which shall be necessary and proper for carrying into Execution the foregoing Powers, and all other Powers vested by this Constitution in the Government of the United States, or in any Department of Officer thereof.

Section 9

The Migration or Importation of such Persons as any of the States now existing shall think proper to admit, shall not be prohibited by the Congress prior to the Year one thousand eight hundred and eight, but a Tax or duty may be imposed on such Importation, not exceeding ten dollars for each Person.

The Privilege of the Writ of Habeas Corpus shall not be suspended, unless when in Cases of Rebellion or Invasion the public Safety may require it.

No Bill of Attainder or ex post facto Law shall be passed.

No Capitation, or other direct, Tax shall be laid, unless in Proportion to the Census or Enumeration herein before directed to be taken.

No Tax or Duty shall be laid on Articles exported from any State.

No Preference shall be given by any Regulation of Commerce or Revenue to the Ports of one State over those of another: nor shall Vessels bound to, or from, one State, be obliged to enter, clear, or pay Duties in another.

No Money shall be drawn from the Treasury, but in Consequence of Appropriations made by Law; and a regular Statement and Account of the Receipts and Expenditures of all public Money shall be published from time to time.

No Title of Nobility shall be granted by the United States: And no Person holding any Office of Profit or Trust under them, shall, without the Consent of the Congress, accept of any present, Emolument, Office, or Title, of any kind whatever, from any King, Prince, or foreign State.

Section 10

No State shall enter into any Treaty, Alliance, or Confederation; grant Letters of Marque and Reprisal; coin Money; emit Bills of Credit; make any Thing but gold and silver Coin a Tender in Payment of Debts; pass any Bill of Attainder, ex post facto Law, or Law impairing the obligation of Contracts, or grant any Title of Nobility.

No State shall, without the Consent of the Congress, lay any Imposts or Duties on Imports or Exports, except what may be absolutely necessary for executing its inspection Laws: and the net Produce of all Duties and Imposts, laid by any State on Imports or Exports, shall be for the Use of the Treasury of the United States; and all such Laws shall be subject to the Revision and Controul of the Congress.

No State shall, without the Consent of Congress, lay any Duty of Tonnage, keep Troops, or Ships of War in time of Peace, enter into any Agreement or Compact with another State, or with a foreign Power, or engage in War, unless actually invaded, or in such imminent Danger as will not admit of delay.

ARTICLE II

Section 1

The executive Power shall be vested in a President of the United States of America. He shall hold his Office during the Term of four Years, and, together with the Vice President, chosen for the same Term, be elected, as follows:

Each State shall appoint, in such Manner as the Legislature thereof may direct, a Number of Electors, equal to the whole Number of Senators and Representatives to which the State may be entitled in the Congress: but no Senator or Representative, or Person holding an Office of Trust or Profit under the United States, shall be appointed an Elector.

The Electors shall meet in their respective States, and vote by Ballot for two Persons, of whom one at least shall not be an Inhabitant of the same State with themselves. And they shall make a List of all the Persons voted for, and of the Number of Votes for each; which List they shall sign and certify, and transmit sealed to the Seat of the Government of the United States, directed to the President of the Senate. The President of the Senate shall, in the Presence of the Senate and House of Representatives, open all the Certificates, and the Votes shall then be counted. The Person having the greatest Number of Votes shall be the President, if such Number be a Majority of the whole number of Electors appointed; and if there be more than one who have such Majority, and have an equal Number of Votes, then the House of Representatives shall immediately chuse by Ballot one of them for President; and if no Person have a Majority, then from the five highest on the List the said House shall in like Manner chuse the President. But in chusing the President, the Votes shall be taken by States, the Representation from each State having one Vote; A quorum for this Purpose shall consist of a Member or Members from two thirds of the States, and a Majority of all the States shall be necessary to a Choice. In every Case, after the Choice of the President, the Person having the greatest Number of Votes of the Electors shall be the Vice President. But if there should remain two or more who have equal Votes, the Senate shall chuse from them by Ballot the Vice President.

The Congress may determine the time of chusing the Electors, and the Day on which they shall give their Votes; which Day shall be the same throughout the United States.

No person except a natural born Citizen, *or a Citizen of the United States, at the time of the Adoption of this Constitution*, shall be eligible to the Office of President; neither shall any Person be eligible to that Office who shall not have attained to the Age of thirty five Years, and been fourteen Years a Resident within the United States.

In Case of the Removal of the President from Office, or of his Death, Resignation, or Inability to discharge the Powers and Duties of the said Office, the Same shall devolve on the Vice President, and the Congress may by Law provide for the Case of Removal, Death, Resignation or Inability, both of the President and Vice President, declaring what Officer shall then act as President, and such Officer shall act accordingly, until the Disability be removed, or a President shall be elected.

The President shall, at stated Times, receive for his Services, a Compensation, which shall neither be encreased nor diminished during the Period for which he shall have been elected, and he shall not receive within that period any other Emolument from the United States, or any of them.

Before he enter on the Execution of his Office, he shall take the following Oath or Affirmation:—"I do solemnly swear (or affirm) that I will faithfully execute the Office of

President of the United States, and will to the best of my Ability, preserve, protect and defend the Constitution of the United States."

Section 2

The President shall be Commander in Chief of the Army and Navy of the United States, and of the Militia of the several States, when called into the actual Service of the United States; he may require the Opinion, in writing, of the principal Officer in each of the executive Departments, upon any Subject relating to the Duties of their respective Offices, and he shall have Power to grant Reprieves and Pardons for Offences against the United States, except in Cases of Impeachment.

He shall have Power, by and with the Advice and Consent of the Senate, to make Treaties, provided two thirds of the Senators present concur; and he shall nominate, and by and with the Advice and Consent of the Senate, shall appoint Ambassadors, other public Ministers and Consuls, Judges of the supreme Court, and all other Officers of the United States, whose Appointments are not herein otherwise provided for, and which shall be established by Law: but the Congress may by Law vest the Appointment of such inferior Officers, as they think proper in the President alone, in the Courts of Law, or in the Heads of Departments.

The President shall have Power to fill up all Vacancies that may happen during the Recess of the Senate, by granting Commissions which shall expire at the End of their next Session.

Section 3

He shall from time to time give to the Congress Information of the State of the Union, and recommend to their Consideration such Measures as he shall judge necessary and expedient; he may, on extraordinary Occasions, convene both Houses, or either of them, and in Case of disagreement between them, with Respect to the Time of Adjournment, he may adjourn them to such Time as he shall think proper; he shall receive Ambassadors and other public Ministers; he shall take Care that the Laws be faithfully executed, and shall Commission all the officers of the United States.

Section 4

The President, Vice President and all civil Officers of the United States, shall be removed from Office on Impeachment for, and Conviction of, Treason, Bribery or other high Crimes and Misdemeanors.

ARTICLE III

Section 1

The judicial Power of the United States, shall be vested in one supreme Court, and in such inferior Courts as the Congress may from time to time ordain and establish. The Judges, both of the supreme and inferior Courts, shall hold their offices during good Behaviour, and shall, at stated Times, receive for their Services, a Compensation, which shall not be diminished during their Continuance in Office.

Section 2

The judicial Power shall extend to all Cases, in Law and Equity, arising under this Constitution, the Laws of the United States, and Treaties made, or which shall be made, under their Authority;—to all Cases affecting Ambassadors, other public Ministers and Consuls;—to all Cases of admiralty and maritime Jurisdiction;—to Controversies to which the United States shall be a Party;—to Controversies between two or more States;—*between a State and Citizens of another State;*—between Citizens of different States;—between Citizens of the same State claiming Lands under Grants of different States, and between a State, or the Citizens thereof, and foreign States, Citizens or Subjects.

In all Cases affecting Ambassadors, other public Ministers and Consuls, and those in which a State shall be Party, the supreme Court shall have original Jurisdiction. In all the other Cases before mentioned, the supreme Court shall have appellate Jurisdiction, both as to Law and Fact, with such Exceptions, and under such Regulations as the Congress shall make.

The Trial of all Crimes, except in Cases of Impeachment, shall be by Jury; and such Trial shall be held in the State where the said Crimes shall have been committed, but when not committed within any State, the Trial shall be at such Place or Places as the Congress may by Law have directed.

Section 3

Treason against the United States, shall consist only in levying War against them, or in adhering to their Enemies, giving them Aid and Comfort. No person shall be convicted of Treason unless on the Testimony of two Witnesses to the same overt Act, or on Confession in open Court.

The Congress shall have Power to declare the Punishment of Treason, but no Attainder of Treason shall work Corruption of Blood, or Forfeiture except during the Life of the Person attainted.

ARTICLE IV

Section 1

Full Faith and Credit shall be given in each State to the public Acts, Records, and judicial Proceedings of every other State. And the Congress may by general Laws prescribe the Manner in which such Acts, Records and Proceedings shall be proved, and the Effect thereof.

Section 2

The Citizens of each State shall be entitled to all Privileges and Immunities of Citizens in the several States.

A Person charged in any State with Treason, Felony, or other Crime, who shall flee from Justice, and be found in another State, shall on Demand of the executive Authority of the State from which he fled, be delivered up, to be removed to the State having Jurisdiction of the Crime.

No Person held to Service or Labour in one State, under the Laws thereof, escaping into another, shall, in Consequence of any Law or Regulation therein, be discharged from such Service or Labour, but shall be delivered up on Claim of the Party to whom such Service or Labour may be due.

Section 3

New States may be admitted by the Congress into this Union; but no new State shall be formed or erected within the Jurisdiction of any other State; nor any State be formed by the Junction of two or more States, or Parts of States, without the Consent of the Legislatures of the States concerned as well as of the Congress.

The Congress shall have Power to dispose of and make all needful Rules and Regulations respecting the Territory or other Property belonging to the United States; and nothing in this Constitution shall be so construed as to Prejudice any Claims of the United States, or of any particular States.

Section 4

The United States shall guarantee to every State in this Union a Republican Form of Government, and shall protect each of them against Invasion; and on Application of the Legislature, or of the Executive (when the Legislature cannot be convened) against domestic violence.

ARTICLE V

The Congress, whenever two thirds of both Houses shall deem it necessary, shall propose Amendments to this Constitution, or, on the Application of the Legislatures of two thirds of the several States, shall call a Convention for proposing Amendments, which, in either Case, shall be valid to all Intents and Purposes, as Part of this Constitution, when ratified by the Legislatures of three fourths of the several States, or by Conventions in three fourths thereof, as the one or the other Mode of Ratification may be proposed by the Congress; Provided *that no Amendment which may be made prior to the Year One thousand eight hundred and eight shall in any Manner affect the first and fourth Clauses in the Ninth Section of the first Article;* and that no State, without its Consent, shall be deprived of its equal Suffrage in the Senate.

ARTICLE VI

All Debts contracted and Engagements entered into, before the Adoption of this Constitution, shall be as valid against the United States under this Constitution, as under the Confederation.

This Constitution, and Laws of the United States which shall be made in Pursuance thereof; and all Treaties made, or which shall be made, under the Authority of the United States, shall be the supreme Law of the Land; and the Judges in every State shall be bound thereby, any Thing in the Constitution or Laws of any State to the Contrary notwithstanding.

The Senators and Representatives before mentioned, and the Members of the several State Legislatures, and all executive and Judicial Officers, both of the United States and of the several States, shall be bound by Oath or Affirmation, to support this Constitution; but no religious Test shall ever be required as a Qualification to any Office of public Trust under the United States.

ARTICLE VII

The Ratification of the Conventions of nine States, shall be sufficient for the Establishment of this Constitution between the States so ratifying the Same.

Done in Convention by the Unanimous Consent of the States present the Seventeenth Day of September in the Year of our Lord one thousand seven hundred and Eighty seven and of the Independence of the United States of America the Twelfth* IN WITNESS whereof We have hereunto subscribed our Names,

George Washington
President and Deputy from Virginia

Delaware
George Read
Gunning Bedford, Jr.
John Dickinson
Richard Bassett
Jacob Broom

Maryland
James McHenry
Daniel of St. Thomas Jenifer
Daniel Carroll

Virginia
John Blair
James Madison, Jr.

North Carolina
William Blount
Richard Dobbs Spraight
Hugh Williamson

South Carolina
John Rutledge
Charles Cotesworth Pinckney
Charles Pinckney
Pierce Butler

Georgia
William Few
Abraham Baldwin

New Hampshire
John Langdon
Nicholas Gilman

Massachusetts
Nathaniel Gorham
Rufus King

Connecticut
William Samuel Johnson
Roger Sherman

New York
Alexander Hamilton

New Jersey
William Livingston
David Brearley
William Paterson
Jonathan Dayton

Pennsylvania
Benjamin Franklin
Thomas Mifflin
Robert Morris
George Clymer
Thomas FitzSimons
Jared Ingersoll
James Wilson
Gouverneur Morris

---

*The Constitution was submitted on September 17, 1787, by the Constitutional Convention, was ratified by the Convention of several states at various dates up to May 29, 1790, and became effective on March 4, 1789.

AMENDMENTS TO THE CONSTITUTION

AMENDMENT I

Congress shall make no law respecting an establishment of religion, or prohibiting the free exercise thereof; or abridging the freedom of speech, or of the press; or the right of the people peaceably to assemble, and to petition the Government for a redress of grievances.

AMENDMENT II

A well regulated Militia being necessary to the security of a free State, the right of the people to keep and bear Arms, shall not be infringed.

AMENDMENT III

No Soldier shall, in time of peace be quartered in any house, without the consent of the Owner, nor in time of war, but in a manner to be prescribed by law.

AMENDMENT IV

The right of the people to be secure in their persons, houses, papers, and effects, against unreasonable searches and seizures, shall not be violated, and no Warrants shall issue, but upon probable cause, supported by Oath or affirmation, and particularly describing the place to be searched, and the persons or things to be seized.

AMENDMENT V

No person shall be held to answer for a capital, or otherwise infamous crime, unless on a presentment or indictment of a Grand Jury, except in cases arising in the land or naval forces, or in the Militia, when in actual service in time of War or public danger; nor shall any person be subject for the same offense to be twice put in jeopardy of life or limb; nor shall be compelled in any criminal case to be a witness against himself, nor be deprived of life, liberty, or property, without due process of law; nor shall private property be taken for public use, without just compensation.

AMENDMENT VI

In all criminal prosecutions, the accused shall enjoy the right to a speedy and public trial, by an impartial jury of the State and district wherein the crime shall have been committed, which district shall have been previously ascertained by law, and to be informed of the nature and cause of the accusation; to be confronted with the witnesses against him; to have compulsory process for obtaining witnesses in his favor, and to have the Assistance of Counsel for his defence.

AMENDMENT VII

In Suits at common law, where the value in controversy shall exceed twenty dollars, the right of trial by jury shall be preserved, and no fact tried by a jury, shall be otherwise reexamined in any Court of the United States, than according to the rules of the common law.

AMENDMENT VIII

Excessive bail shall not be required, nor excessive fines imposed, nor cruel and unusual punishments inflicted.

AMENDMENT IX

The enumeration in the Constitution, of certain rights, shall not be construed to deny or disparage others retained by the people.

AMENDMENT X*

The powers not delegated to the United States by the Constitution, nor prohibited by it to the States, are reserved to the States respectively, or to the people.

AMENDMENT XI
[ADOPTED 1798]

The Judicial power of the United States shall not be construed to extend to any suit in law or equity, commenced or prosecuted against one of the United States by Citizens of another State, or by Citizens or Subjects of any Foreign State.

AMENDMENT XII
[ADOPTED 1804]

The Electors shall meet in their respective states, and vote by ballot for President and Vice President, one of whom, at least, shall not be an inhabitant of the same state with themselves; they shall name in their ballots the person voted for as President, and in distinct ballots the person voted for as Vice President, and they shall make distinct lists of all persons voted for as President, and of all persons voted for as Vice President, and of the number of votes for each, which lists they shall sign and certify, and transmit sealed to the seat of the government of the United States, directed to the President of the Senate;—The President of the Senate shall, in the presence of the Senate and House of Representatives, open all the certificates and the votes shall then be counted;—The person having the greatest number of votes for President, shall be the President, if such number be a majority of the whole number of Electors appointed; and if no person have such majority, then from the persons having the highest numbers not exceeding three on the list of those voted for as President, the House of Representatives shall choose immediately, by ballot, the President. But in choosing the President, the votes shall be taken by states, the representation from each state having one vote; a quorum for this purpose shall consist of a member or members from two-thirds of the states, and a majority of all the states shall be necessary to a choice. And if the House of

---

*The first ten amendments (the Bill of Rights) were ratified and their adoption was certified on December 15, 1791.

Representatives shall not choose a President whenever the right of choice shall devolve upon them, before *the fourth day of March* next following, then the Vice President shall act as President, as in the case of the death or other constitutional disability of the President.—The person having the greatest number of votes as Vice President, shall be the Vice President, if such number be a majority of the whole number of Electors appointed, and if no person have a majority, then from the two highest numbers on the list, the Senate shall choose the Vice President; a quorum for the purpose shall consist of two-thirds of the whole number of Senators, and a majority of the whole number shall be necessary to a choice. But no person constitutionally ineligible to the office of President shall be eligible to that of Vice President of the United States.

AMENDMENT XIII
[ADOPTED 1865]
Section 1
Neither slavery nor involuntary servitude, except as a punishment for crime whereof the party shall have been duly convicted, shall exist within the United States, or any place subject to their jurisdiction.

Section 2
Congress shall have power to enforce this article by appropriate legislation.

AMENDMENT XIV
[ADOPTED 1868]
Section 1
All persons born or naturalized in the United States, and subject to the jurisdiction thereof, are citizens of the United States and of the State wherein they reside. No State shall make or enforce any law which shall abridge the privileges or immunities of citizens of the United States; nor shall any State deprive any person of life, liberty, or property, without due process of law; nor deny to any person within its jurisdiction the equal protection of the laws.

Section 2
Representatives shall be apportioned among the several States according to their respective numbers, counting the whole number of persons in each State, excluding Indians not taxed. But when the right to vote at any election for the choice of electors for President and Vice President of the United States, Representatives in Congress, the Executive and Judicial officers of a State, or the members of the Legislature thereof, is denied to any of the male inhabitants of such State, being twenty-one years of age, and citizens of the United States, or in any way abridged, except for participation in rebellion, or other crime, the basis of representation therein shall be reduced in the proportion which the number of such male citizens shall bear to the whole number of male citizens twenty-one years of age in such State.

Section 3
No person shall be a Senator or Representative in Congress, or elector of President and Vice President, or hold any office, civil or military, under the United States, or under any State, who, having previously taken an oath, as a member of Congress, or as an officer of the United States, or as a member of any State legislature, or as an executive or judicial officer of any State, to support the Constitution of the United States, shall have engaged in insurrection or rebellion against the same, or given aid or comfort to the enemies thereof. But Congress may by a vote of two-thirds of each House, remove such disability.

Section 4
The validity of the public debt of the United States, authorized by law, including debts incurred for payment of pensions and bounties for services in suppressing insurrection or rebellion, shall not be questioned. But neither the United States nor any State shall assume or pay any debt or obligation incurred in aid of insurrection or rebellion against the United States, or any claim for the loss or emancipation of any slave; but all such debts, obligations and claims shall be held illegal and void.

Section 5
The Congress shall have power to enforce, by appropriate legislation, the provisions of this article.

AMENDMENT XV
[ADOPTED 1870]
Section 1
The right of citizens of the United States to vote shall not be denied or abridged by the United States or by any State on account of race, color, or previous condition of servitude.

Section 2
The Congress shall have power to enforce this article by appropriate legislation.

AMENDMENT XVI
[ADOPTED 1913]
The Congress shall have power to lay and collect taxes on incomes, from whatever source derived, without apportionment among the several States, and without regard to any census or enumeration.

AMENDMENT XVII
[ADOPTED 1913]
The Senate of the United States shall be composed of two Senators from each State, elected by the people thereof, for six years; and each Senator shall have one vote. The electors in each State shall have the qualifications requisite for electors of the most numerous branch of the State legislatures.

When vacancies happen in the representation of any State in the Senate, the executive authority of such State shall issue writs of election to fill such vacancies: *Provided,* That the legislature of any State may empower the executive thereof to make temporary appointments until the people fill the vacancies by election as the legislature may direct.

This amendment shall not be so construed as to affect the election or term of any Senator chosen before it becomes valid as part of the Constitution.

AMENDMENT XVIII

[ADOPTED 1919, REPEALED 1933]

Section 1

After one year from the ratification of this article the manufacture, sale, or transportation of intoxicating liquors within, the importation thereof into, or the exportation thereof from the United States and all territory subject to the jurisdiction thereof for beverage purposes is hereby prohibited.

Section 2

The Congress and the several States shall have concurrent power to enforce this article by appropriate legislation.

Section 3

This article shall be inoperative unless it shall have been ratified as an amendment to the Constitution by the legislatures of the several States, as provided in the Constitution, within seven years from the date of the submission hereof to the States by the Congress.

AMENDMENT XIX

[ADOPTED 1920]

The right of citizens of the United States to vote shall not be denied or abridged by the United States or by any State on account of sex.

Congress shall have power to enforce this article by appropriate legislation.

AMENDMENT XX

[ADOPTED 1933]

Section 1

The terms of the President and Vice President shall end at noon on the 20th day of January, and the terms of Senators and Representatives at noon on the 3d day of January, of the years in which such terms would have ended if this article had not been ratified and the terms of their successors shall then begin.

Section 2

The Congress shall assemble at least once in every year, and such meeting shall begin at noon on the 3d day of January, unless they shall by law appoint a different day.

Section 3

If, at the time fixed for the beginning of the term of the President, the President elect shall have died, the Vice President elect shall become President. If a President shall not have been chosen before the time fixed for the beginning of his term, or if the President elect shall have failed to qualify, then the Vice President elect shall act as President until a President shall have qualified; and the Congress may by law provide for the case wherein neither a President elect nor a Vice President elect shall have qualified, declaring

who shall then act as President, or the manner in which one who is to act shall be selected, and such person shall act accordingly until a President or Vice President shall have qualified.

Section 4

The Congress may by law provide for the case of the death of any of the persons from whom the House of Representatives may choose a President whenever the right of choice shall have devolved upon them, and for the case of the death of any of the persons from whom the Senate may choose a Vice President whenever the right of choice shall have devolved upon them.

Section 5

Sections 1 and 2 shall take effect on the 15th day of October following the ratification of this article.

Section 6

This article shall be inoperative unless it shall have been ratified as an amendment to the Constitution by the legislatures of three fourths of the several States within seven years from the date of its submission.

AMENDMENT XXI

[ADOPTED 1933]

Section 1

The eighteenth article of amendment to the Constitution of the United States is hereby repealed.

Section 2

The transportation or importation into any State, Territory, or possession of the United States for delivery or use therein of intoxicating liquors in violation of the laws thereof, is hereby prohibited.

Section 3

This article shall be inoperative unless it shall have been ratified as an amendment to the Constitution by conventions in the several States, as provided in the Constitution, within seven years from the date of the submission hereof to the States by the Congress.

AMENDMENT XXII

[ADOPTED 1951]

Section 1

No person shall be elected to the office of the President more than twice, and no person who has held the office of President, or acted as President, for more than two years of a term to which some other person was elected President shall be elected to the office of the President more than once. But this Article shall not apply to any person holding the office of President when this Article was proposed by the Congress, and shall not prevent any person who may be holding the office of President, or acting as President, during the term within which this Article becomes operative from holding the office of President or acting as President during the remainder of such term.

Section 2

This article shall be inoperative unless it shall have been ratified as an amendment to the Constitution by the legislatures of three-fourths of the several States within seven years from the date of its submission to the States by the Congress.

AMENDMENT XXIII

[ADOPTED 1961]

Section 1

The District constituting the seat of Government of the United States shall appoint in such manner as the Congress shall direct:

A number of electors of President and Vice President equal to the whole number of Senators and Representatives in Congress to which the District would be entitled if it were a State, but in no event more than the least populous State; they shall be in addition to those appointed by the States, but they shall be considered, for the purposes of the election of President and Vice President, to be electors appointed by a State; and they shall meet in the District and perform such duties as provided by the twelfth article of amendment.

Section 2

The Congress shall have power to enforce this article by appropriate legislation.

AMENDMENT XXIV

[ADOPTED 1964]

Section 1

The right of citizens of the United States to vote in any primary or other election for President or Vice President, for electors for President or Vice President, or for Senator or Representative in Congress, shall not be denied or abridged by the United States or any state by reason of failure to pay any poll tax or other tax.

Section 2

The Congress shall have the power to enforce this article by appropriate legislation.

AMENDMENT XXV

[ADOPTED 1967]

Section 1

In case of the removal of the President from office or his death or resignation, the Vice President shall become President.

Section 2

Whenever there is a vacancy in the office of the Vice President, the President shall nominate a Vice President who shall take the office upon confirmation by a majority vote of both houses of Congress.

Section 3

Whenever the President transmits to the President pro tempore of the Senate and the Speaker of the House of Representatives his written declaration that he is unable to discharge the powers and duties of his office, and until he transmits to them a written declaration to the contrary, such powers and duties shall be discharged by the Vice President as Acting President.

Section 4

Whenever the Vice President and a majority of either the principal officers of the executive departments or of such other body as Congress may by law provide, transmit to the President pro tempore of the Senate and the Speaker of the House of Representatives their written declaration that the President is unable to discharge the powers and duties of his office, the Vice President shall immediately assume the powers and duties of the office as Acting President.

Thereafter, when the President transmits to the President pro tempore of the Senate and the Speaker of the House of Representatives his written declaration that no inability exists, he shall resume the powers and duties of his office unless the Vice President and a majority of either the principal officers of the executive department or of such other body as Congress may by law provide, transmit within four days to the President pro tempore of the Senate and the Speaker of the House of Representatives their written declaration that the President is unable to discharge the powers and duties of his office. Thereupon Congress shall decide the issue, assembling within 48 hours for that purpose if not in session. If the Congress, within 21 days after receipt of the latter written declaration, or, if Congress is not in session, within 21 days after Congress is required to assemble, determines by two-thirds vote of both houses that the President is unable to discharge the powers and duties of his office, the Vice President shall continue to discharge the same as Acting President; otherwise, the President shall resume the powers and duties of his office.

AMENDMENT XXVI

[ADOPTED 1971]

Section 1

The right of citizens of the United States, who are 18 years of age or older, to vote shall not be denied or abridged by the United States or any state on account of age.

Section 2

The Congress shall have the power to enforce this article by appropriate legislation.

AMENDMENT XXVII

[ADOPTED 1992]

No law, varying the compensation for the services of the Senators and Representatives shall take effect, until an election of Representatives shall have intervened.

PRESIDENTIAL ELECTIONS

Year	Candidates	Parties	Popular Vote	Electoral Vote	Voter Participation
1789	**George Washington**		*	69	
	John Adams			34	
	Others			35	
1792	**George Washington**		*	132	
	John Adams			77	
	George Clinton			50	
	Others			5	
1796	**John Adams**	Federalist	*	71	
	Thomas Jefferson	Democratic-Republican		68	
	Thomas Pinckney	Federalist		59	
	Aaron Burr	Dem.-Rep.		30	
	Others			48	
1800	**Thomas Jefferson**	Dem.-Rep.	*	73	
	Aaron Burr	Dem.-Rep.		73	
	John Adams	Federalist		65	
	C. C. Pinckney	Federalist		64	
	John Jay	Federalist		1	
1804	**Thomas Jefferson**	Dem.-Rep.	*	162	
	C. C. Pinckney	Federalist		14	
1808	**James Madison**	Dem.-Rep.	*	122	
	C. C. Pinckney	Federalist		47	
	George Clinton	Dem.-Rep.		6	
1812	**James Madison**	Dem.-Rep.	*	128	
	De Witt Clinton	Federalist		89	
1816	**James Monroe**	Dem.-Rep.	*	183	
	Rufus King	Federalist		34	
1820	**James Monroe**	Dem.-Rep.	*	231	
	John Quincy Adams	Dem.-Rep.		1	
1824	**John Quincy Adams**	Dem.-Rep.	108,740 (30.5%)	84	26.9%
	Andrew Jackson	Dem.-Rep.	153,544 (43.1%)	99	
	William H. Crawford	Dem.-Rep.	46,618 (13.1%)	41	
	Henry Clay	Dem.-Rep.	47,136 (13.2%)	37	
1828	**Andrew Jackson**	Democratic	647,286 (56.0%)	178	57.6%
	John Quincy Adams	National Republican	508,064 (44.0%)	83	

*Electors selected by state legislatures.

Year	Candidates	Parties	Popular Vote	Electoral Vote	Voter Participation
1832	**Andrew Jackson**	Democratic	**688,242 (54.2%)**	219	55.4%
	Henry Clay	National Republican	473,462 (37.4%)	49	
	John Floyd	Independent		11	
	William Wirt	Anti-Mason	101,051 (7.8%)	7	
1836	**Martin Van Buren**	Democratic	**762,198 (50.8%)**	170	57.8%
	William Henry Harrison	Whig	549,508 (36.6%)	73	
	Hugh L. White	Whig	145,342 (9.7%)	26	
	Daniel Webster	Whig	41,287 (2.7%)	14	
	W. P. Magnum	Independent		11	
1840	**William Henry Harrison**	**Whig**	**1,274,624 (53.1%)**	234	80.2%
	Martin Van Buren	Democratic	1,127,781 (46.9%)	60	
	J. G. Birney	Liberty	7069	—	
1844	**James K. Polk**	Democratic	**1,338,464 (49.6%)**	170	78.9%
	Henry Clay	Whig	1,300,097 (48.1%)	105	
	J. G. Birney	Liberty	62,300 (2.3%)	—	
1848	**Zachary Taylor**	**Whig**	**1,360,967 (47.4%)**	163	72.7%
	Lewis Cass	Democratic	1,222,342 (42.5%)	127	
	Martin Van Buren	Free-Soil	291,263 (10.1%)	—	
1852	**Franklin Pierce**	Democratic	**1,601,117 (50.9%)**	254	69.6%
	Winfield Scott	Whig	1,385,453 (44.1%)	42	
	John P. Hale	Free-Soil	155,825 (5.0%)	—	
1856	**James Buchanan**	Democratic	**1,832,955 (45.3%)**	174	78.9%
	John C. Frémont	Republican	1,339,932 (33.1%)	114	
	Millard Fillmore	American	871,731 (21.6%)	8	
1860	**Abraham Lincoln**	**Republican**	**1,865,593 (39.8%)**	180	81.2%
	Stephen A. Douglas	Democratic	1,382,713 (29.5%)	12	
	John C. Breckinridge	Democratic	848,356 (18.1%)	72	
	John Bell	Union	592,906 (12.6%)	39	
1864	**Abraham Lincoln**	**Republican**	**2,213,655 (55.0%)**	212*	73.8%
	George B. McClellan	Democratic	1,805,237 (45.0%)	21	
1868	**Ulysses S. Grant**	**Republican**	**3,012,833 (52.7%)**	214	78.1%
	Horatio Seymour	Democratic	2,703,249 (47.3%)	80	
1872	**Ulysses S. Grant**	**Republican**	**3,597,132 (55.6%)**	286	71.3%
	Horace Greeley	Dem.; Liberal Republican	2,834,125 (43.9%)	66†	
1876	**Rutherford B. Hayes‡**	**Republican**	**4,036,298 (48.0%)**	185	81.8%
	Samuel J. Tilden	Democratic	4,300,590 (51.0%)	184	
1880	**James A. Garfield**	**Republican**	**4,454,416 (48.5%)**	214	79.4%
	Winfield S. Hancock	Democratic	4,444,952 (48.1%)	155	

*Eleven secessionist states did not participate.
†Greeley died before the electoral college met. His electoral votes were divided among the four minor candidates.
‡Contested result settled by special election.

Year	Candidates	Parties	Popular Vote	Electoral Vote	Voter Participation
1884	**Grover Cleveland**	Democratic	4,874,986 (48.5%)	219	77.5%
	James G. Blaine	Republican	4,851,981 (48.2%)	182	
1888	**Benjamin Harrison**	Republican	5,439,853 (47.9%)	233	79.3%
	Grover Cleveland	Democratic	5,540,309 (48.6%)	168	
1892	**Grover Cleveland**	Democratic	5,556,918 (46.1%)	277	74.7%
	Benjamin Harrison	Republican	5,176,108 (43.0%)	145	
	James B. Weaver	People's	1,029,329 (8.5%)	22	
1896	**William McKinley**	Republican	7,104,779 (51.1%)	271	79.3%
	William Jennings Bryan	Democratic People's	6,502,925 (47.7%)	176	
1900	**William McKinley**	Republican	7,207,923 (51.7%)	292	73.2%
	William Jennings Bryan	Dem.-Populist	6,358,133 (45.5%)	155	
1904	**Theodore Roosevelt**	Republican	7,623,486 (57.9%)	336	65.2%
	Alton B. Parker	Democratic	5,077,911 (37.6%)	140	
	Eugene V. Debs	Socialist	402,400 (3.0%)	—	
1908	**William H. Taft**	Republican	7,678,908 (51.6%)	321	65.4%
	William Jennings Bryan	Democratic	6,409,104 (43.1%)	162	
	Eugene V. Debs	Socialist	402,820 (2.8%)	—	
1912	**Woodrow Wilson**	Democratic	6,293,454 (41.9%)	435	58.8%
	Theodore Roosevelt	Progressive	4,119,538 (27.4%)	88	
	William H. Taft	Republican	3,484,980 (23.2%)	8	
	Eugene V. Debs	Socialist	900,672 (6.0%)	—	
1916	**Woodrow Wilson**	Democratic	9,129,606 (49.4%)	277	61.6%
	Charles E. Hughes	Republican	8,538,221 (46.2%)	254	
	A. L. Benson	Socialist	585,113 (3.2%)	—	
1920	**Warren G. Harding**	Republican	16,152,200 (60.4%)	404	49.2%
	James M. Cox	Democratic	9,147,353 (34.2%)	127	
	Eugene V. Debs	Socialist	917,799 (3.4%)	—	
1924	**Calvin Coolidge**	Republican	15,725,016 (54.0%)	382	48.9%
	John W. Davis	Democratic	8,386,503 (28.8%)	136	
	Robert M. La Follette	Progressive	4,822,856 (16.6%)	13	
1928	**Herbert Hoover**	Republican	21,391,381 (58.2%)	444	56.9%
	Alfred E. Smith	Democratic	15,016,443 (40.9%)	87	
	Norman Thomas	Socialist	267,835 (0.7%)	—	
1932	**Franklin D. Roosevelt**	Democratic	22,821,857 (57.4%)	472	56.9%
	Herbert Hoover	Republican	15,761,841 (39.7%)	59	
	Norman Thomas	Socialist	884,781 (2.2%)	—	
1936	**Franklin D. Roosevelt**	Democratic	27,751,597 (60.8%)	523	61.0%
	Alfred M. Landon	Republican	16,679,583 (36.5%)	8	
	William Lemke	Union	882,479 (1.9%)	—	
1940	**Franklin D. Roosevelt**	Democratic	27,244,160 (54.8%)	449	62.5%
	Wendell L. Willkie	Republican	22,305,198 (44.8%)	82	
1944	**Franklin D. Roosevelt**	Democratic	25,602,504 (53.5%)	432	55.9%
	Thomas E. Dewey	Republican	22,006,285 (46.0%)	99	

Year	Candidates	Parties	Popular Vote	Electoral Vote	Voter Participation
1948	Harry S Truman	Democratic	24,105,695 (49.5%)	304	53.0%
	Thomas E. Dewey	Republican	21,969,170 (45.1%)	189	
	J. Strom Thurmond	State-Rights Democratic	1,169,021 (2.4%)	38	
	Henry A. Wallace	Progressive	1,157,326 (2.4%)	—	
1952	Dwight D. Eisenhower	Republican	33,778,963 (55.1%)	442	63.3%
	Adlai E. Stevenson	Democratic	27,314,992 (44.4%)	89	
1956	Dwight D. Eisenhower	Republican	35,575,420 (57.6%)	457	60.6%
	Adlai E. Stevenson	Democratic	26,033,066 (42.1%)	73	
	Other	—	—	1	
1960	John F. Kennedy	Democratic	34,227,096 (49.9%)	303	62.8%
	Richard M. Nixon	Republican	34,108,546 (49.6%)	219	
	Other	—	—	15	
1964	Lyndon B. Johnson	Democratic	43,126,506 (61.1%)	486	61.7%
	Barry M. Goldwater	Republican	27,176,799 (38.5%)	52	
1968	Richard M. Nixon	Republican	31,770,237 (43.4%)	301	60.6%
	Hubert H. Humphrey	Democratic	31,270,533 (42.7%)	191	
	George Wallace	American Indep.	9,906,141 (13.5%)	46	
1972	Richard M. Nixon	Republican	46,740,323 (60.7%)	520	55.2%
	George S. McGovern	Democratic	28,901,598 (37.5%)	17	
	Other	—	—	1	
1976	Jimmy Carter	Democratic	40,828,587 (50.0%)	297	53.5%
	Gerald R. Ford	Republican	39,147,613 (47.9%)	241	
	Other	—	1,575,459 (2.1%)	—	
1980	Ronald Reagan	Republican	43,901,812 (50.7%)	489	52.6%
	Jimmy Carter	Democratic	35,483,820 (41.0%)	49	
	John B. Anderson	Independent	5,719,437 (6.6%)	—	
	Ed Clark	Libertarian	921,188 (1.1%)	—	
1984	Ronald Reagan	Republican	54,455,075 (59.0%)	525	53.3%
	Walter Mondale	Democratic	37,577,185 (41.0%)	13	
1988	George H. W. Bush	Republican	48,886,097 (53.4%)	426	57.4%
	Michael S. Dukakis	Democratic	41,809,074 (45.6%)	111	
1992	William J. Clinton	Democratic	44,908,254 (43%)	370	55.0%
	George H. W. Bush	Republican	39,102,343 (37.5%)	168	
	H. Ross Perot	Independent	19,741,065 (18.9%)	—	
1996	William J. Clinton	Democratic	45,590,703 (50%)	379	48.8%
	Robert Dole	Republican	37,816,307 (41%)	159	
	Ross Perot	Reform	7,866,284	—	
2000	George W. Bush	Republican	50,456,167 (47.88%)	271	51.2%
	Al Gore	Democratic	50,996,064 (48.39%)	266*	
	Ralph Nader	Green	2,864,810 (2.72%)	—	
	Other		834,774 (less than 1%)	—	
2004	George W. Bush	Republican	60,934,251 (51.0%)	286	50.0%
	John F. Kerry	Democratic	57,765,291 (48.0%)	252	
	Ralph Nader	Independent	405,933 (less than 1%)	—	

*One District of Columbia Gore elector abstained.

PRESIDENTS AND VICE PRESIDENTS

	President	Vice President	Term
1.	George Washington	John Adams	1789–1793
	George Washington	John Adams	1793–1797
2.	John Adams	Thomas Jefferson	1797–1801
3.	Thomas Jefferson	Aaron Burr	1801–1805
	Thomas Jefferson	George Clinton	1805–1809
4.	James Madison	George Clinton (d. 1812)	1809–1813
	James Madison	Elbridge Gerry (d. 1814)	1813–1817
5.	James Monroe	Daniel Tompkins	1817–1821
	James Monroe	Daniel Tompkins	1821–1825
6.	John Quincy Adams	John C. Calhoun	1825–1829
7.	Andrew Jackson	John C. Calhoun	1829–1833
	Andrew Jackson	Martin Van Buren	1833–1837
8.	Martin Van Buren	Richard M. Johnson	1837–1841
9.	William H. Harrison (d. 1841)	John Tyler	1841
10.	John Tyler	—	1841–1845
11.	James K. Polk	George M. Dallas	1845–1849
12.	Zachary Taylor (d. 1850)	Millard Fillmore	1849–1850
13.	Millard Fillmore	—	1850–1853
14.	Franklin Pierce	William R. King (d. 1853)	1853–1857
15.	James Buchanan	John C. Breckinridge	1857–1861
16.	Abraham Lincoln	Hannibal Hamlin	1861–1865
	Abraham Lincoln (d. 1865)	Andrew Johnson	1865
17.	Andrew Johnson	—	1865–1869
18.	Ulysses S. Grant	Schuyler Colfax	1869–1873
	Ulysses S. Grant	Henry Wilson (d. 1875)	1873–1877
19.	Rutherford B. Hayes	William A. Wheeler	1877–1881
20.	James A. Garfield (d. 1881)	Chester A. Arthur	1881
21.	Chester A. Arthur	—	1881–1885
22.	Grover Cleveland	Thomas A. Hendricks (d. 1885)	1885–1889
23.	Benjamin Harrison	Levi P. Morton	1889–1893
24.	Grover Cleveland	Adlai E. Stevenson	1893–1897
25.	William McKinley	Garret A. Hobart (d. 1899)	1897–1901
	William McKinley (d. 1901)	Theodore Roosevelt	1901
26.	Theodore Roosevelt	—	1901–1905
	Theodore Roosevelt	Charles Fairbanks	1905–1909
27.	William H. Taft	James S. Sherman (d. 1912)	1909–1913
28.	Woodrow Wilson	Thomas R. Marshall	1913–1917
	Woodrow Wilson	Thomas R. Marshall	1917–1921
29.	Warren G. Harding (d. 1923)	Calvin Coolidge	1921–1923

	President	Vice President	Term
30.	Calvin Coolidge	—	1923–1925
	Calvin Coolidge	Charles G. Dawes	1925–1929
31.	Herbert Hoover	Charles Curtis	1929–1933
32.	Franklin D. Roosevelt	John N. Garner	1933–1937
	Franklin D. Roosevelt	John N. Garner	1937–1941
	Franklin D. Roosevelt	Henry A. Wallace	1941–1945
	Franklin D. Roosevelt (d. 1945)	Harry S Truman	1945
33.	Harry S Truman	—	1945–1949
	Harry S Truman	Alben W. Barkley	1949–1953
34.	Dwight D. Eisenhower	Richard M. Nixon	1953–1957
	Dwight D. Eisenhower	Richard M. Nixon	1957–1961
35.	John F. Kennedy (d. 1963)	Lyndon B. Johnson	1961–1963
36.	Lyndon B. Johnson	—	1963–1965
	Lyndon B. Johnson	Hubert H. Humphrey	1965–1969
37.	Richard M. Nixon	Spiro T. Agnew	1969–1973
	Richard M. Nixon (resigned 1974)	Gerald R. Ford	1973–1974
38.	Gerald R. Ford	Nelson A. Rockefeller	1974–1977
39.	Jimmy Carter	Walter F. Mondale	1977–1981
40.	Ronald Reagan	George H.W. Bush	1981–1985
	Ronald Reagan	George H.W. Bush	1985–1989
41.	George H.W. Bush	J. Danforth Quayle	1989–1993
42.	William J. Clinton	Albert Gore, Jr.	1993–1997
	William J. Clinton	Albert Gore, Jr.	1997–2001
43.	George W. Bush	Richard Cheney	2001–2005
	George W. Bush	Richard Cheney	2005–

Credits

Unless otherwise credited, all photographs are the property of Pearson Education, Inc. Page abbreviations are as follows: **T** *top,* **C** *center,* **B** *bottom,* **L** *left,* **R** *right.*

CHAPTER 16
313 The Library of Congress; **318** Collection of the New-York Historical Society; **320** © Bettmann/Corbis; **323** Fair Street Pictures; **326** © Corbis

CHAPTER 17
335 From A Pictographic History of the Oglala Sioux by Amos Bad Heart Bull, text by Helen Blish, University of Nebraska Press; **337** Corbis; **342** California Vaquero Trousers, Wool, Cotton, Silver, 1834. Autry Museum of Western Heritage, Los Angeles. Acquisition made possible by the Ramona Chapter, Native Sons of the Golden West; **345** Jose H. Bailey © National Geographic Society; **351** Montana Historical Society, Helena

CHAPTER 18
353 *Treasures of Art, Industry, and Manufacture Represented in the American Centennial Exhibition in Philadelphia*, 1876. Plate 35 The Corliss Engine. Publisher Cosack & Co., Buffalo, New York, 1877. The Thomas J. Watson Library, The Metropolitan Museum of Art. Photograph © 1981 The Metropolitan Museum of Art; **355** Culver Pictures; **358** The Granger Collection, New York; **365** The Granger Collection, New York

CHAPTER 19
372 New York Public Library, Astor, Lenox and Tilden Foundations; **374** Collection of David J. and Janice L. Frent; **377** The Advertising Archive; **380** University of Michigan Medical School records, Bently Historical Library, University of Michigan. J. Jefferson Gibson, Photographer; **382** © The Museum of the City of New York, The Byron Collection; **387** Hulton Archive/Getty Images

CHAPTER 20
389 National Museum of American History, Smithsonian Institution; **393** The Kansas State Historical Society, Topeka, Kansas; **396** The Granger Collection, New York; **398** © Bettmann/Corbis; **400** Culver Pictures

CHAPTER 21
407 The State Historical Society of Wisconsin; **412** The Granger Collection, New York; **413** Courtesy of USMA Archives, West Point, N.Y.; **417** New York Public Library, Astor, Lenox and Tilden Foundations; **420** Culver Pictures

CHAPTER 22
424 The Granger Collection, New York; **425** New York Public Library, Astor, Lenox and Tilden Foundations; **431** Walter P. Reuther Library, Wayne State University; **433** The Granger Collection, New York; **435** *Cliff Dwellers* by George Wesley Bellows (United States 1882–1925), 1913. Los Angeles County Museum of Art, Los Angeles County Fund. Photograph © 2005 Museum Associates/LACMA

CHAPTER 23
445 Culver Pictures; **449** The Granger Collection, New York; **451** Smithsonian Institution; **455** Museum of American Political Life, University of Hartford; **458T** National Archives; **458B** Walter P. Reuther Library, Wayne State University

CHAPTER 24
467 © Bettmann/Corbis; **473** *The Victorious Retreat Back to the Rhine* by Frank Earle Schoonover (1877–1972). 1918, (oil on canvas). Delaware Art Museum, Wilmington, USA/Bridgeman Art Library, Gift of the Bank of Delaware; **474** Image Courtesy Smithsonian Institution; **475** Courtesy of the American Legion; **480** The Granger Collection, New York

CHAPTER 25
485 Picture History; **486** Gaslight Advertising Archives; **488** The Granger Collection, New York; **493** © Bettmann/Corbis; **496** The Library of Congress

CHAPTER 26
507L The Library of Congress; **507R** The Library of Congress; **510** The Library of Congress; **511** Mrs. Phillip Evergood/ACA Galleries

CHAPTER 27
522 U. S. Army Center of Photo History; **524** Bildarchiv Preussuscher Kulturbesitz; **527** Official U. S. Navy Photograph; **534L** Courtesy of Military Antiques, Petaluma, Ca.; **534R** Courtesy of Military Antiques, Petaluma, Ca.; **536** US Army Photo

CHAPTER 28
547 National Archives; **548** The Fotomas Index; **552** UPI/Corbis/Bettmann; **556B** 828B from Herb Block's Special for Today (Simon & Schuster, 1958). Originally appeared in the Washington Post.; **558** The National Archives

CHAPTER 29
564 © Christie's Images; **567L** Sovfoto; **567R** Copyright © 1957 by the New York Times Co. Reprinted by permission; **571** © Bettmann/Corbis; **572L** © Bettmann/Corbis; **572R** AP/Wide World Photos;

CHAPTER 30
578 AP/Wide World Photos; **582** AP/Wide World Photos; **592** Courtesy of Vintage Trends.com; **593** Archive Photos/Blank Archive/Getty Images; **594** Getty Images; **595** Nancy Ellison/Corbis; **597** Lyndon Baines Johnson Library

CHAPTER 31

606 AP/Wide World Photos; **607** Kent State University; **610** Courtesy of Stant Manufacturing Inc.; **617** Department of Health & Human Services; **619** Bill Fitz-Patrick/The White House; **623** Michael Evans/The White House; **628** MPI/Getty Images

CHAPTER 32

635 © Sygma/Corbis; **637** Roberto Schmidt/Getty Images; **639** Kyle Niemi/US Coast Guard via Getty Images/Getty Images; **644** © Trippett/Sipa Press; **649** AP/Wide World Photos/Sony Corporation; **650** Jeff Greenberg/PhotoEdit; **652** Eli Reed/Magnum Photos; **654** Jarome Delay/AP/Wide World Photos; **655** AP/Wide World Photos; **656** Sherwin Crasto/Reuters/Landov

Index

429–430; industrial, 352; manufacturing decline and, 611; National Recovery Administration and, 505; New Deal and, 510–511; in 1920s, 486; in postwar South, 316–317; regulation of, 444; scientific management and, 426; Taft-Hartley Act and, 551; in 2000s, 656; women and, 362–363; World War I and, 475–477. *See also* Child labor; Workers

Labor agents: immigrants and, 429; Mexican laborers and, 430

Labor Department, 457

Labor productivity: decline in, 430

Labor unions, 364–365, 611; American Federation of Labor, 430; blacks and, 428; Clayton Antitrust Act and, 431 (illus.), 456; in Great Depression, 511–512; Industrial Workers of the World, 431; Kennedy and, 581; membership growth in, 430; in 1920s, 486; Taft-Hartley Act and, 551; Wagner Act and, 510, 517; Wilson and, 457; women in, 430–431, 431 (illus.); Women's Trade Union League, 431; World War I and, 475–476; in World War II, 532

Labor violence. *See* Strikes

Ladies' Home Journal (magazine), 362, 377 (illus.), 423

La Follette, Robert M., 470; election of 1924 and, 496–497; tariff and, 453; Wisconsin Idea of, 448

Laissez-faire: in economic policy, 324; in New South, 326

Lake Shore and Michigan Southern Railway, 355 (illus.)

Land: as basis of wealth, 381; for blacks, 310; Dawes Act and, 335; Indian, 331, 332; legislation concerning, 338; in postwar South, 316–317; Reconstruction redistribution of, 315

Land-grant colleges: women in, 379, 380 (illus.)

Land grants: to railroads, 338, 354

Landon, Alfred M., 513

Land ownership: for individual Indians, 334–335; tribal, 335

Lange, Dorothea, 507 (illus.)

Lansing, Robert, 468, 469, 479

Laos: refugees from, 640; in Vietnam War, 589

Laramie, Fort, 337

Las Guasimas, battle at, 414

Lathrop, Julia, 431

Latin America: aid to, 577; covert actions in, 558; foreign policy toward, 520–522; Garfield and, 391; Good Neighbor policy and, 464; immigrants from, 637; interventions in, 465; Monroe Doctrine and, 408; nontransfer principle and, 408; Roosevelt Corollary and, 463–464; U.S. expansionism and, 408; Wilson and, 465. *See also* specific countries

Law(s): professionalization in, 441; sociological jurisprudence and, 444–445; workers' compensation, 447. *See also* specific acts

Lawrence, Massachusetts: strike in, 431

Lazarus, Emma, 386

Leadville, Colorado, 340

League for the Protection of the Family, 398

League of Nations, 478, 479; German withdrawal from, 522; Italian invasion of Ethiopia and, 522; Japan and, 522; United States and, 520

Lean Bear (Cheyenne chief), 330

Leary, Timothy, 593

Lease, Mary E., 393, 393 (illus.), 427

Lebanon: Eisenhower and, 557; Israeli invasion of, 625

Lee, Alice (Alice Roosevelt), 375

Lee, Ivy L., 432

Legislation: civil rights, 582, 583; interest groups and, 446; of New Deal, 514–515 (illus.). *See also* specific acts

Legislatures: "one man, one vote" principle in, 583. *See also* Congress (U.S.)

Leisure, 374, 376; in 1920s, 488–489; in Progressive Era, 433–434

Lemke, William, 513

Lend-Lease program, **525**; for Soviet Union, 528, 542

Lenin, V. I., 475

Lesbians: gay liberation movement and, 615–616. *See also* Gays

Levitt, William, 562

Levittown, 562

Lewinsky, Monica, 643–644

Lewis, David, 490

Lewis, Drew, 622

Lewis, John L., 511

Lewis, Sinclair, 489

Leyte Gulf, battle of, 537

Liberal Republicans, 324

Liberals and liberalism: Nixon and, 605–606; Supreme Court and, 583

Liberty(ies). *See* Freedom; Rights

Liberty League, 513

Libya, 529

Lichtman, Allan J., 497

Life expectancy: by 1900, 375; rise in, 432

Lifestyle: of blacks, 639; in cultural revolution of 1960s, 592–593; during Great Depression, 500, 502–503; in 1970s, 612–617; of Plains Indians, 332; in postwar period, 564–567; of Spanish-American War soldiers, 413; unmarried couples and, 613

Light bulb: carbon filament for, 361

Liliuokalani (Hawaii), 409

Limited government: Democrats and, 389

Limited test ban treaty (1963), 579

Lincoln, Abraham, 330; Reconstruction plan of, 311

Lindbergh, Charles, 488; as isolationist, 525

Lindsay, Vachel, 435

Literacy tests: ban on, 586; for immigrants, 387, 430, 492; for voting, 322, 327, 389

Literature: beats and, 566; black, 490; during depression of 1890s, 398–399; naturalism in, 398, 399; in 1920s, 489–490; popular, 434; realism in, 398–399; sexual themes in, 489; after World War I, 480

Little, Frank, 474

Little Bighorn: battle of, 334, 335 (illus.), 336

Little Rock, Ark.: school desegregation in, 571, 571 (illus.)

Lloyd George, David, 478

Loans: neutrality acts and, 523; to Soviet Union, 542; during World War I, 468

Lodge, Henry Cabot: Versailles Treaty and, 479, 480; Wilson and, 478

London, Jack, 399

Lonely Crowd, The (Riesman), 566

Long, Huey, 508, 510

Looking Backward (Bellamy), 381

Los Angeles: urban zoning ordinances in, 433

Louisiana, 390; black voting rights in, 389; Unionist government in, 311

"Love Song of J. Alfred Prufrock" (Eliot), 435

Lowell, Amy, 435

Loyalty issue: Truman and, 552–553

Loyalty oaths: in Cold War, 555; for former Confederates, 311

Loyalty Review Board, 553

Ludlow, Colorado: coal strike at, 457, 458 (illus.)

Ludlow, Louis, 523

Luftwaffe (German airforce), 524

Lunch counter sit-ins, 571–572, 572 (illus.)

Lusitania (ship), 461, 462, 468

Lynchings: of blacks, 326 (illus.), 327; of radicals, 491; of striking cotton pickers, 393; in World War I, 474

M

MacArthur, Douglas, 503; firing of, 550, 551; Japanese occupation and, 548; in Korean War, 550–551; in World War II, 528, 529, 530, 537

Machines: at Centennial Exposition, 352; farm, 344, 345; workers and, 426

Machines (political), 309, 373–374; Redeemers in New South and, 326

Mackay, John W., 340

Macune, Charles W., 393

Macy, R. H., 362

Maddox (ship), 588

Madero, Francisco I., 465–466

Madison Square Garden: labor pageant in, 431

Magazines: for women, 565

Mahan, Alfred Thayer, 410, 413

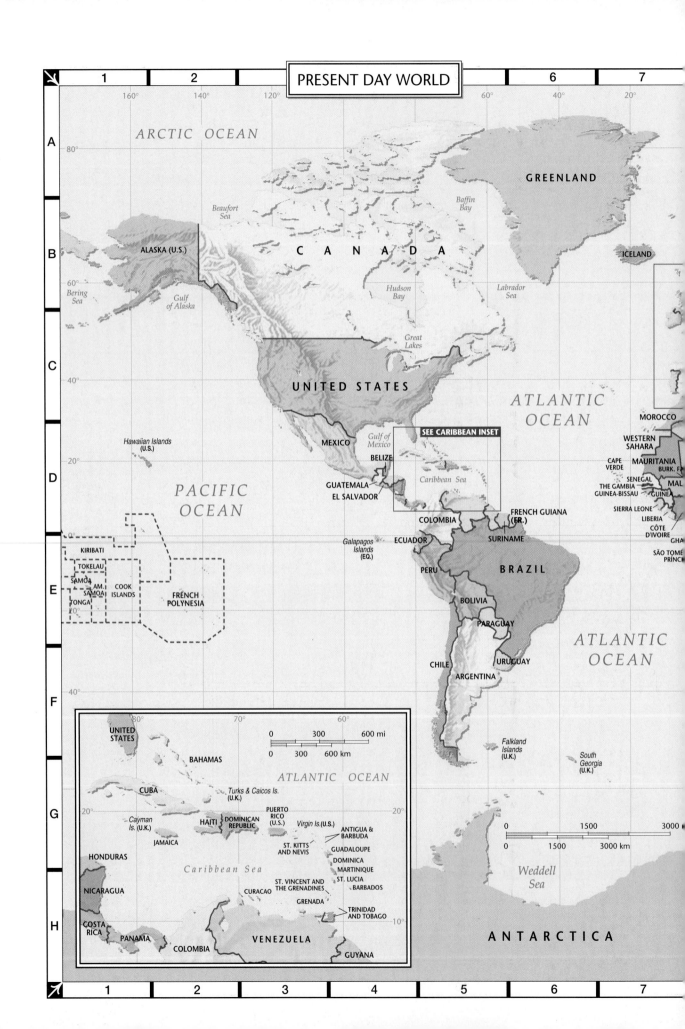

PRESENT DAY WORLD

ARCTIC OCEAN

GREENLAND

Beaufort Sea

ALASKA (U.S.)

C A N A D A

Baffin Bay

ICELAND

Bering Sea

Gulf of Alaska

Hudson Bay

Labrador Sea

Great Lakes

UNITED STATES

ATLANTIC OCEAN

MOROCCO

WESTERN SAHARA

Hawaiian Islands (U.S.)

MEXICO

Gulf of Mexico

SEE CARIBBEAN INSET

CAPE VERDE

MAURITANIA

BELIZE

Caribbean Sea

SENEGAL

THE GAMBIA

GUINEA-BISSAU

MALI

BURK. F.

PACIFIC OCEAN

GUATEMALA

EL SALVADOR

GUINEA

SIERRA LEONE

LIBERIA

CÔTE D'IVOIRE

GHA

COLOMBIA

FRENCH GUIANA (FR.)

Galapagos Islands (EQ.)

ECUADOR

SURINAME

SÃO TOMÉ PRÍNC

KIRIBATI

PERU

BRAZIL

TOKELAU

SAMOA

AM. SAMOA

COOK ISLANDS

FRENCH POLYNESIA

BOLIVIA

TONGA

PARAGUAY

ATLANTIC OCEAN

CHILE

URUGUAY

ARGENTINA

Falkland Islands (U.K.)

South Georgia (U.K.)

Weddell Sea

A N T A R C T I C A

Caribbean Inset

UNITED STATES

BAHAMAS

0   300   600 mi

0   300   600 km

ATLANTIC OCEAN

CUBA

Turks & Caicos Is. (U.K.)

Cayman Is. (U.K.)

HAITI

DOMINICAN REPUBLIC

PUERTO RICO (U.S.)

Virgin Is.(U.S.)

ANTIGUA & BARBUDA

JAMAICA

ST. KITTS AND NEVIS

GUADALOUPE

HONDURAS

Caribbean Sea

DOMINICA

MARTINIQUE

ST. LUCIA

ST. VINCENT AND THE GRENADINES

BARBADOS

NICARAGUA

CURACAO

GRENADA

TRINIDAD AND TOBAGO

COSTA RICA

PANAMA

COLOMBIA

VENEZUELA

GUYANA

0   1500   3000

0   1500   3000 km

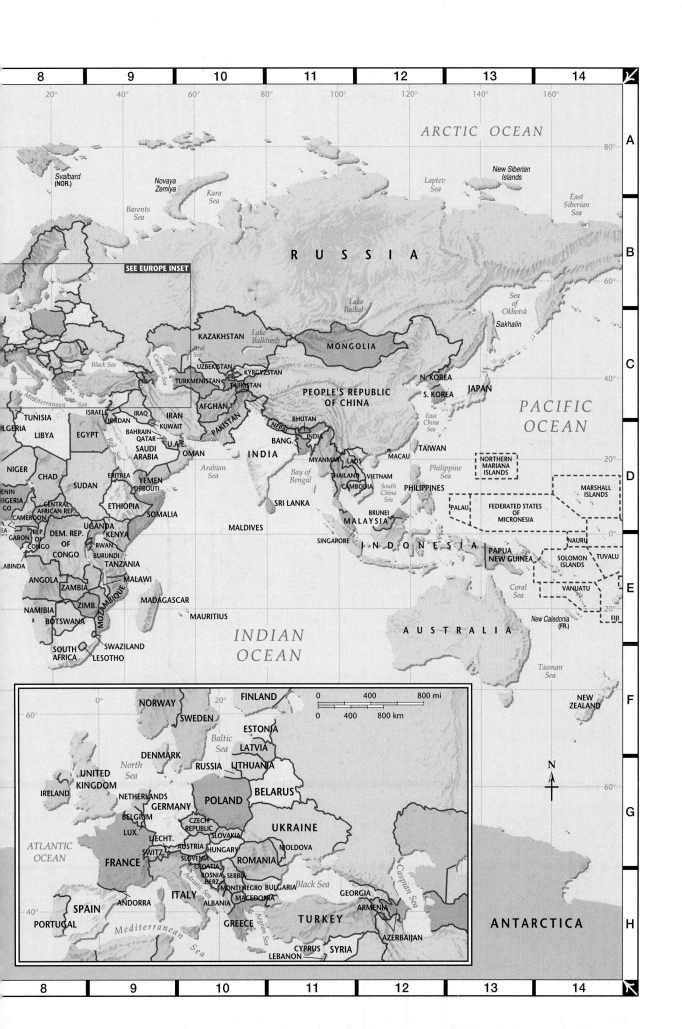